SUPERMAN ADVENTURES VOLUME 4

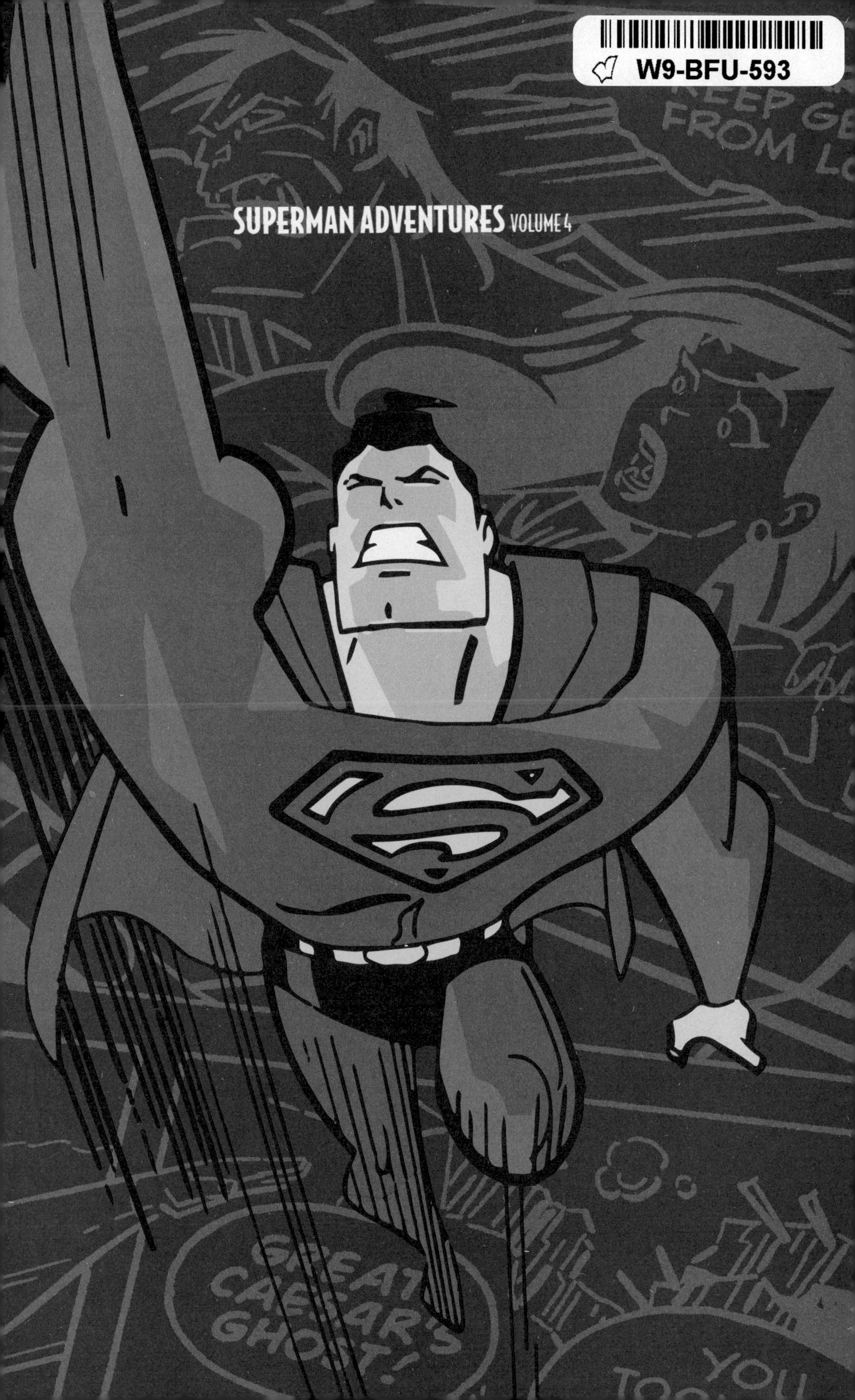
GREAT CAESAR'S GHOST!

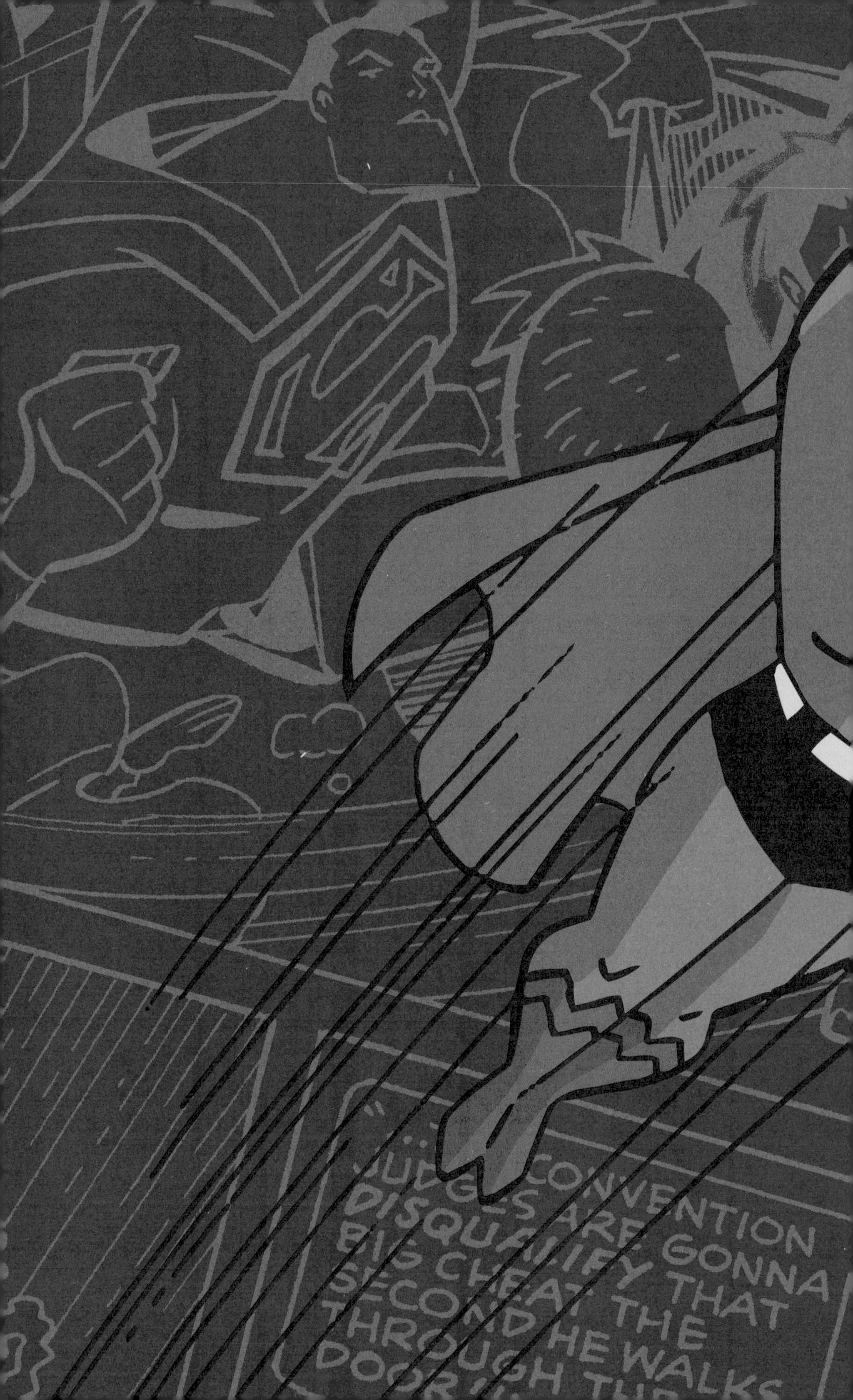
"...CONVENTION JUDGES ARE GONNA DISQUALIFY THAT BIG CHEAT THE SECOND HE WALKS THROUGH THE DOOR!

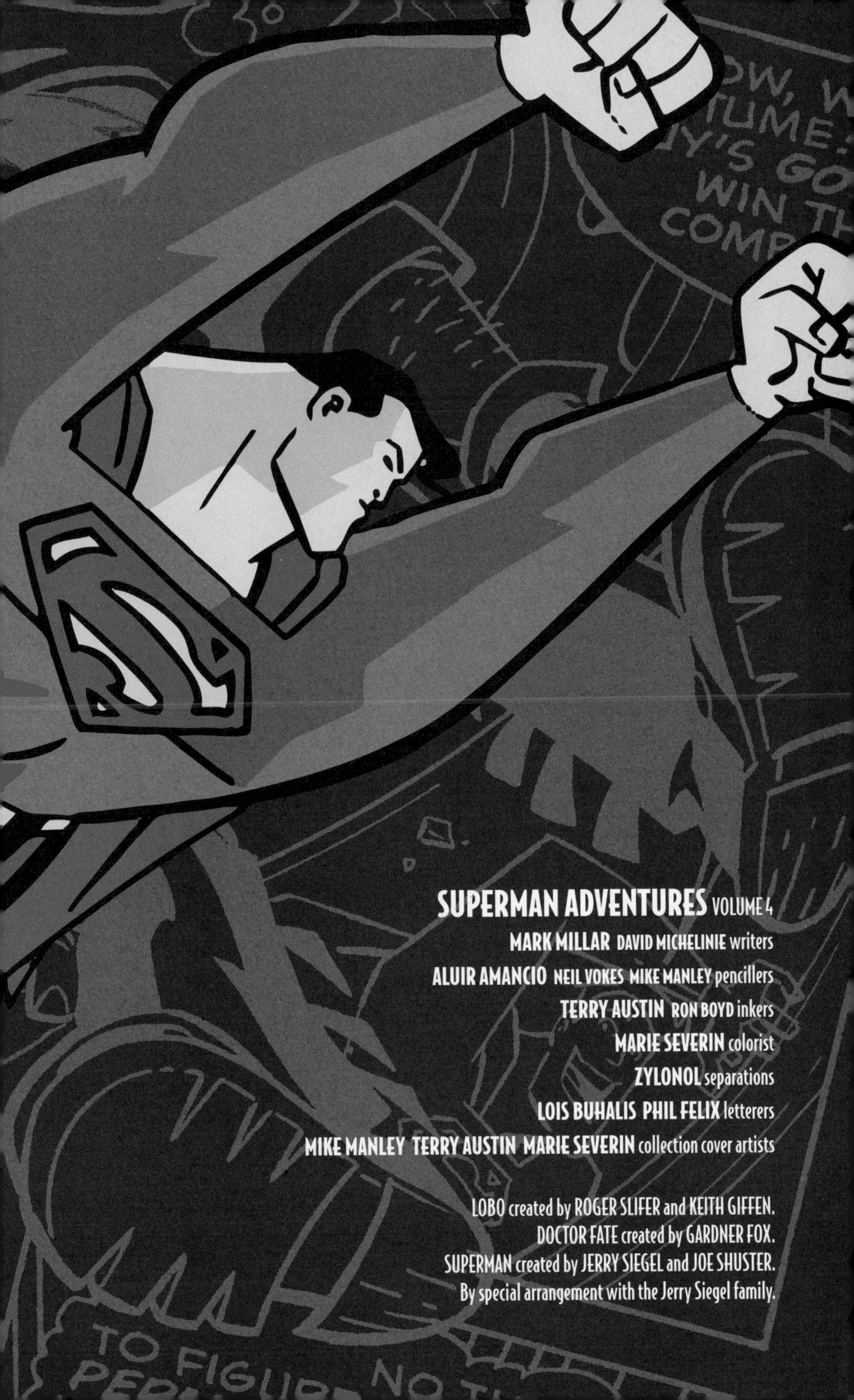

SUPERMAN ADVENTURES VOLUME 4

MARK MILLAR **DAVID MICHELINIE** writers

ALUIR AMANCIO **NEIL VOKES** **MIKE MANLEY** pencillers

TERRY AUSTIN **RON BOYD** inkers

MARIE SEVERIN colorist

ZYLONOL separations

LOIS BUHALIS **PHIL FELIX** letterers

MIKE MANLEY **TERRY AUSTIN** **MARIE SEVERIN** collection cover artists

LOBO created by ROGER SLIFER and KEITH GIFFEN.
DOCTOR FATE created by GARDNER FOX.
SUPERMAN created by JERRY SIEGEL and JOE SHUSTER.
By special arrangement with the Jerry Siegel family.

Mike McAvennie Editor – Original Series
Frank Berrios Assistant Editor – Original Series
Jeb Woodard Group Editor – Collected Editions
Erika Rothberg Editor – Collected Edition
Steve Cook Design Director – Books
Louis Prandi Publication Design

Bob Harras Senior VP – Editor-in-Chief, DC Comics
Pat McCallum Executive Editor, DC Comics

Diane Nelson President
Dan DiDio Publisher
Jim Lee Publisher
Geoff Johns President & Chief Creative Officer
Amit Desai Executive VP – Business & Marketing Strategy, Direct to Consumer & Global Franchise Management
Sam Ades Senior VP & General Manager, Digital Services
Bobbie Chase VP & Executive Editor, Young Reader & Talent Development
Mark Chiarello Senior VP – Art, Design & Collected Editions
John Cunningham Senior VP – Sales & Trade Marketing
Anne DePies Senior VP – Business Strategy, Finance & Administration
Don Falletti VP – Manufacturing Operations
Lawrence Ganem VP – Editorial Administration & Talent Relations
Alison Gill Senior VP – Manufacturing & Operations
Hank Kanalz Senior VP – Editorial Strategy & Administration
Jay Kogan VP – Legal Affairs
Jack Mahan VP – Business Affairs
Nick J. Napolitano VP – Manufacturing Administration
Eddie Scannell VP – Consumer Marketing
Courtney Simmons Senior VP – Publicity & Communications
Jim (Ski) Sokolowski VP – Comic Book Specialty Sales & Trade Marketing
Nancy Spears VP – Mass, Book, Digital Sales & Trade Marketing
Michele R. Wells VP – Content Strategy

SUPERMAN ADVENTURES VOLUME 4

Published by DC Comics. Compilation and all new material Copyright © 2017 DC Comics. All Rights Reserved. Originally published in single magazine form in SUPERMAN ADVENTURES 26-35. Copyright © 1998, 1999 DC Comics. All Rights Reserved. All characters, their distinctive likenesses and related elements featured in this publication are trademarks of DC Comics. The stories, characters and incidents featured in this publication are entirely fictional. DC Comics does not read or accept unsolicited submissions of ideas, stories or artwork.

DC Comics, 2900 West Alameda Ave., Burbank, CA 91505
Printed by LSC Communications, Owensville, MO, USA. 11/24/17. First Printing.
ISBN: 978-1-4012-7511-2

Library of Congress Cataloging-in-Publication Data is available.

PEFC Certified

Printed on paper from sustainably managed forests, controlled sources

PEFC/29-31-337   www.pefc.org

SUPERMAN ADVENTURES #26 cover by RICK BURCHETT, TERRY AUSTIN and RICHARD TAYLOR

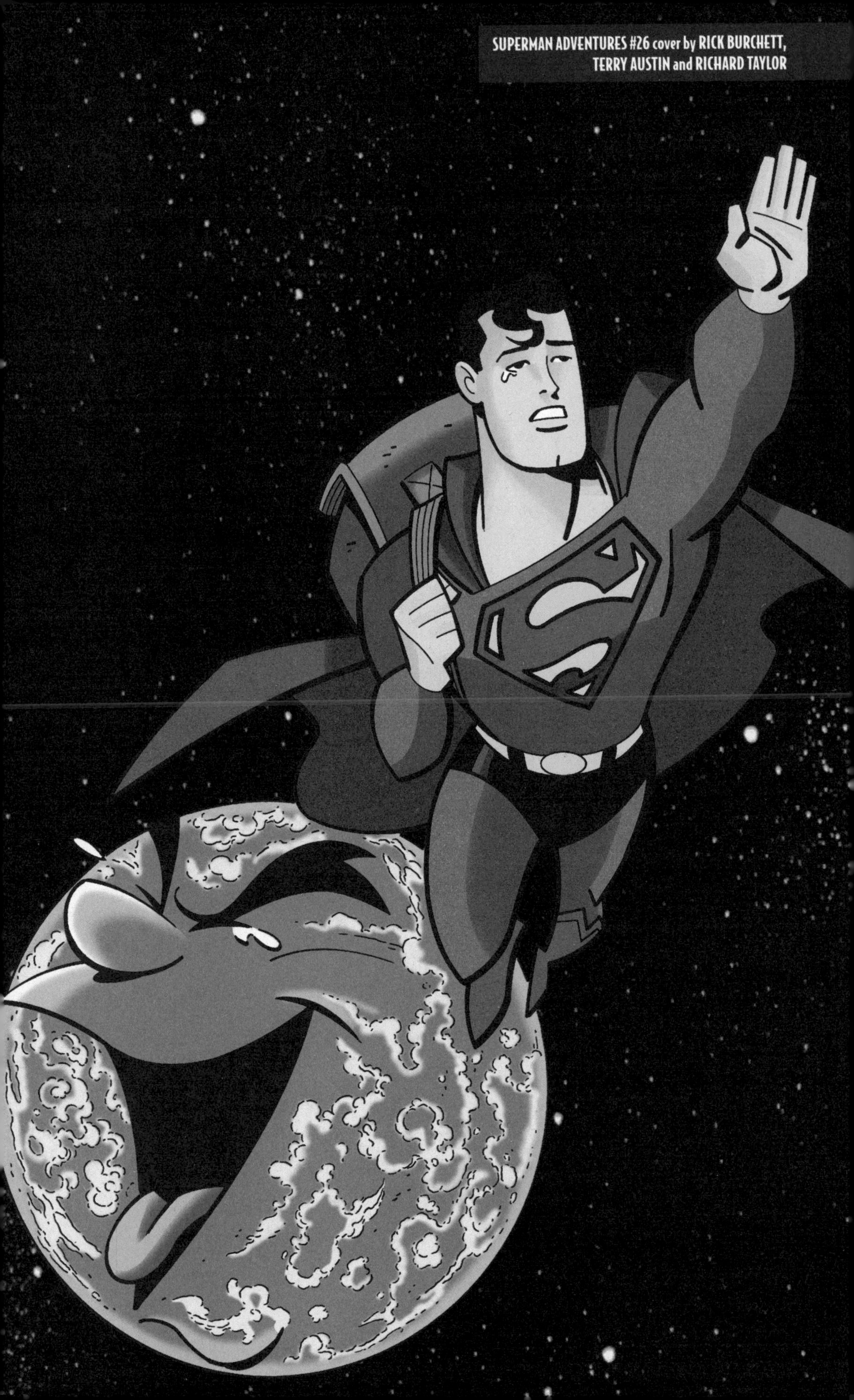

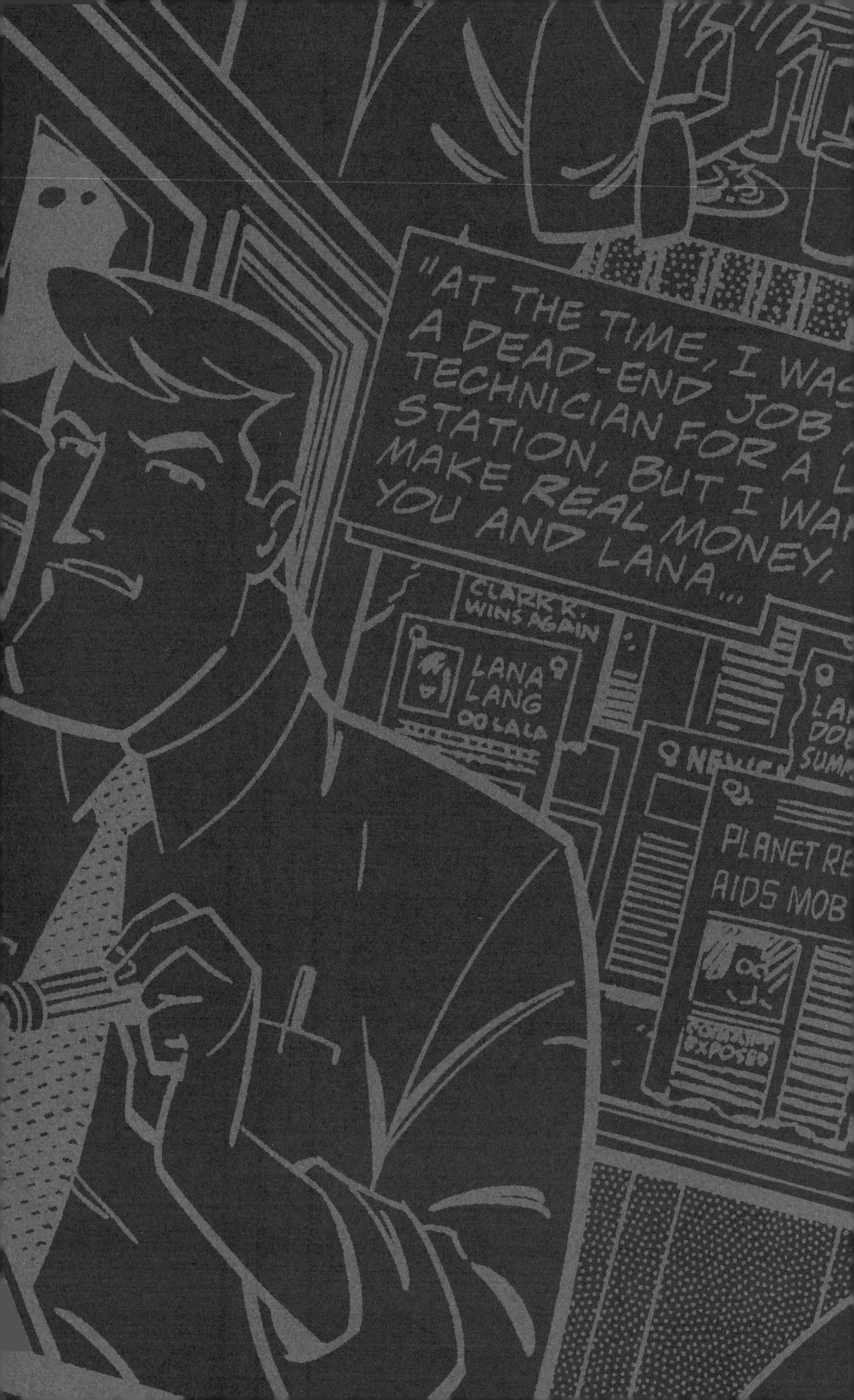
"AT THE TIME, I WAS
A DEAD-END JOB
TECHNICIAN FOR A
STATION, BUT I WA
MAKE REAL MONEY,
YOU AND LANA...
CLARK K. WINS AGAIN
LANA LANG OOLALA
AIDS MOB

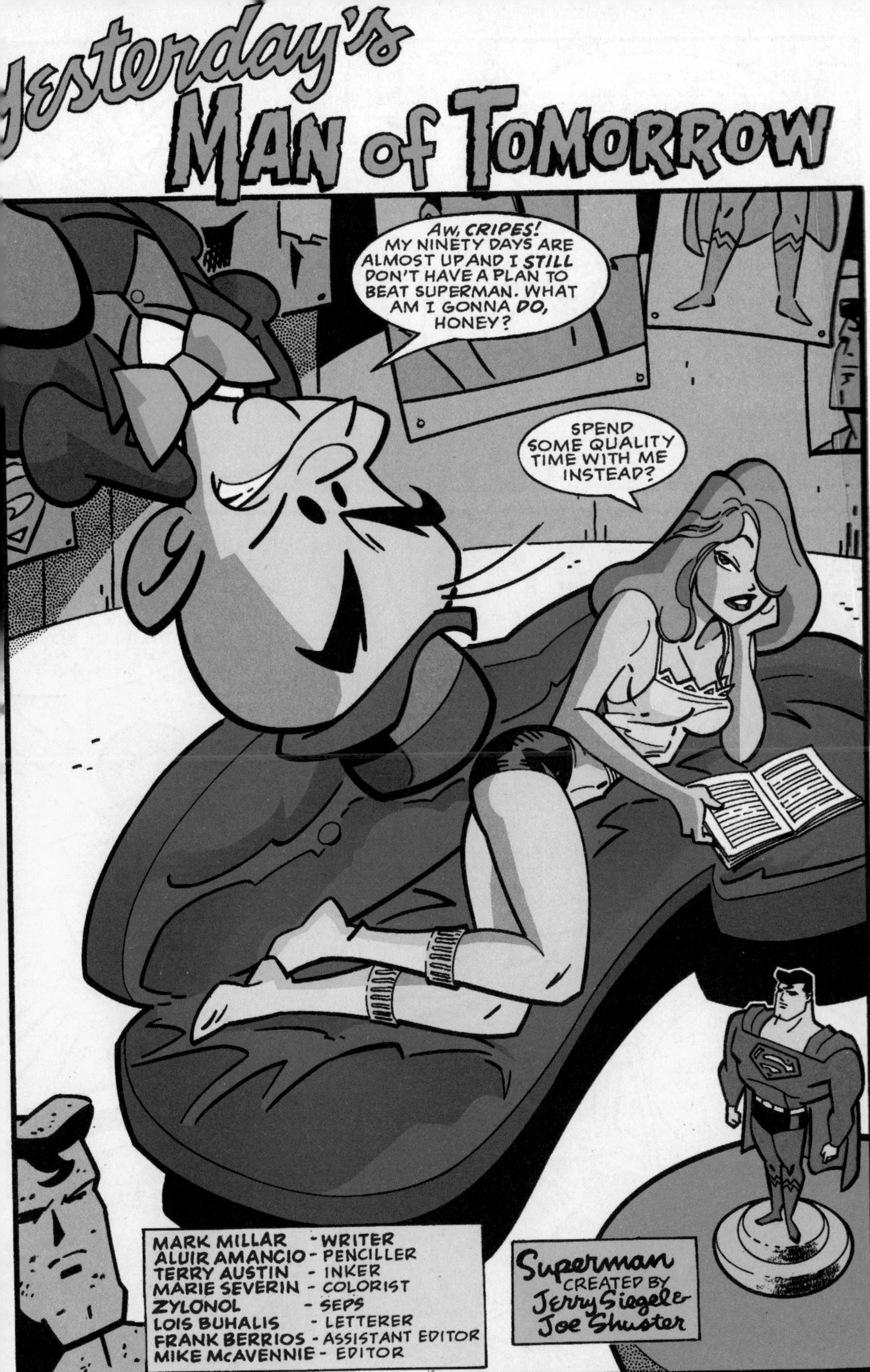
Yesterday's MAN of TOMORROW
AW, CRIPES! MY NINETY DAYS ARE ALMOST UP AND I STILL DON'T HAVE A PLAN TO BEAT SUPERMAN. WHAT AM I GONNA DO, HONEY?
SPEND SOME QUALITY TIME WITH ME INSTEAD?
MARK MILLAR - WRITER
ALUIR AMANCIO - PENCILLER
TERRY AUSTIN - INKER
MARIE SEVERIN - COLORIST
ZYLONOL - SEPS
LOIS BUHALIS - LETTERER
FRANK BERRIOS - ASSISTANT EDITOR
MIKE McAVENNIE - EDITOR
Superman CREATED BY Jerry Siegel & Joe Shuster

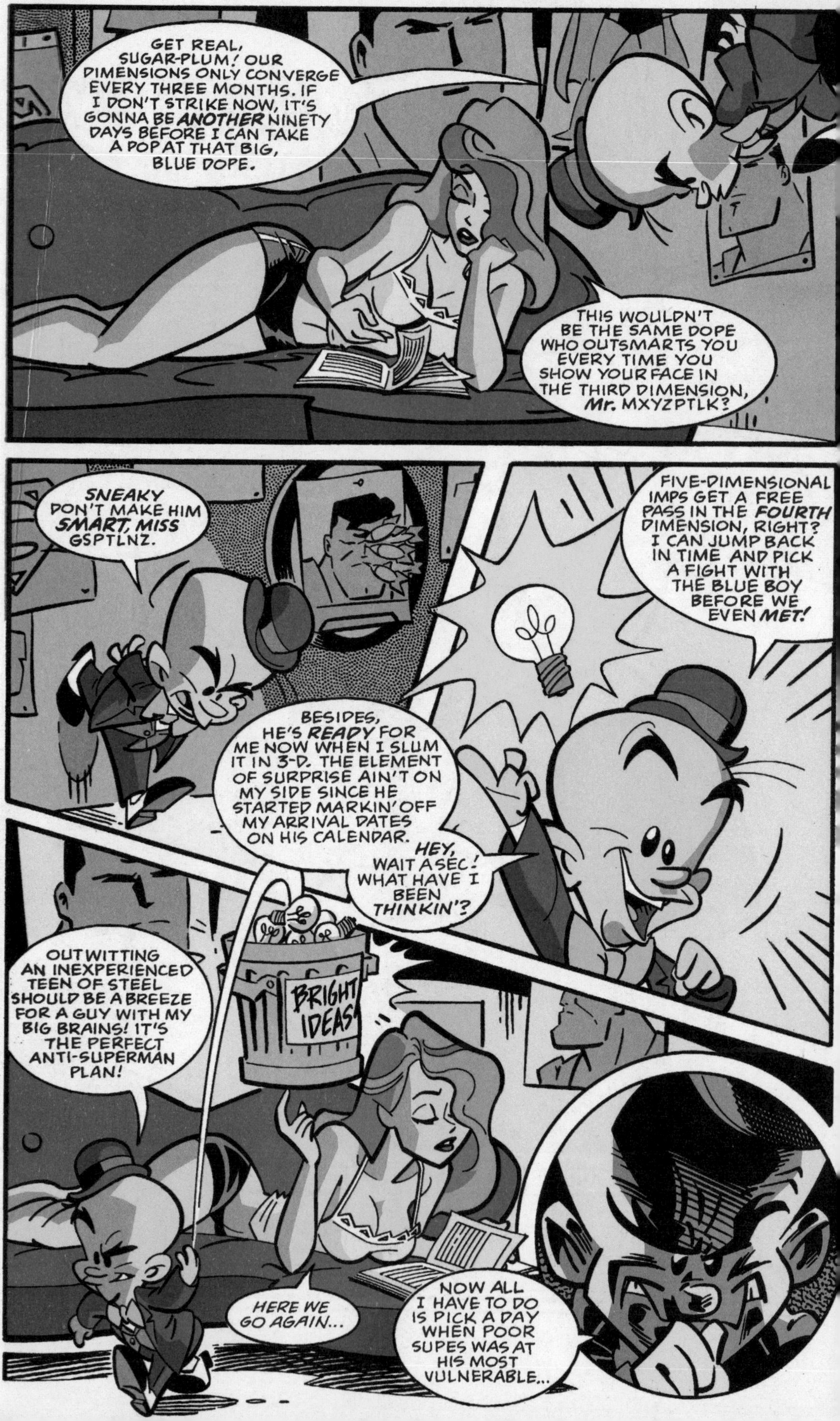
GET REAL, SUGAR-PLUM! OUR DIMENSIONS ONLY CONVERGE EVERY THREE MONTHS. IF I DON'T STRIKE NOW, IT'S GONNA BE ANOTHER NINETY DAYS BEFORE I CAN TAKE A POP AT THAT BIG, BLUE DOPE.
THIS WOULDN'T BE THE SAME DOPE WHO OUTSMARTS YOU EVERY TIME YOU SHOW YOUR FACE IN THE THIRD DIMENSION, MR. MXYZPTLK?
SNEAKY DON'T MAKE HIM SMART, MISS GSPTLNZ.
BESIDES, HE'S READY FOR ME NOW WHEN I SLUM IT IN 3-D. THE ELEMENT OF SURPRISE AIN'T ON MY SIDE SINCE HE STARTED MARKIN' OFF MY ARRIVAL DATES ON HIS CALENDAR.
FIVE-DIMENSIONAL IMPS GET A FREE PASS IN THE FOURTH DIMENSION, RIGHT? I CAN JUMP BACK IN TIME AND PICK A FIGHT WITH THE BLUE BOY BEFORE WE EVEN MET!
HEY, WAIT A SEC! WHAT HAVE I BEEN THINKIN'?
BRIGHT IDEAS
OUTWITTING AN INEXPERIENCED TEEN OF STEEL SHOULD BE A BREEZE FOR A GUY WITH MY BIG BRAINS! IT'S THE PERFECT ANTI-SUPERMAN PLAN!
HERE WE GO AGAIN...
NOW ALL I HAVE TO DO IS PICK A DAY WHEN POOR SUPES WAS AT HIS MOST VULNERABLE...

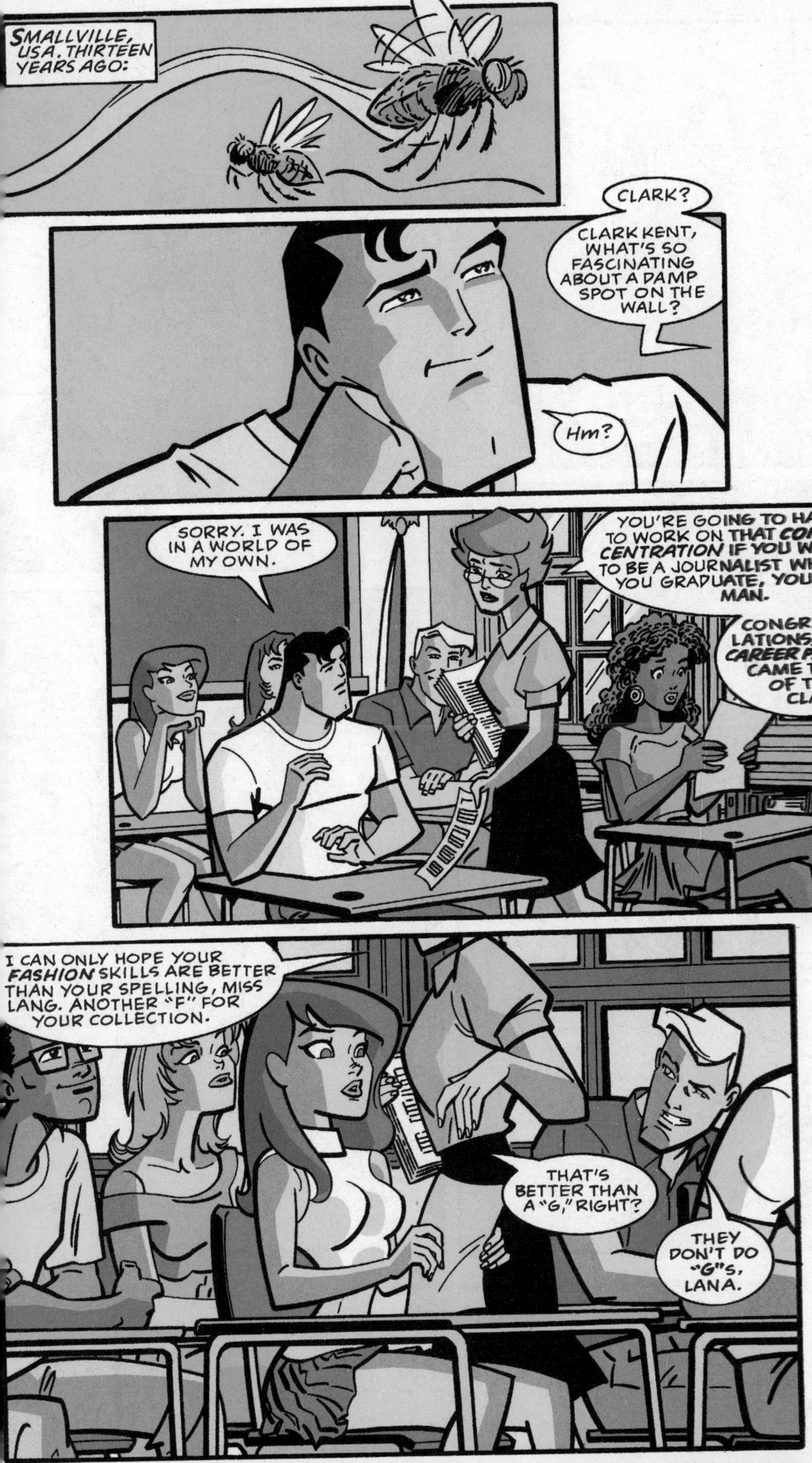
SMALLVILLE, USA. THIRTEEN YEARS AGO:
CLARK?
CLARK KENT, WHAT'S SO FASCINATING ABOUT A DAMP SPOT ON THE WALL?
Hm?
SORRY. I WAS IN A WORLD OF MY OWN.
YOU'RE GOING TO HAVE TO WORK ON THAT CONCENTRATION IF YOU WANT TO BE A JOURNALIST WHEN YOU GRADUATE, YOUNG MAN.
CONGRATULATIONS. YOUR CAREER PAPER CAME TOP OF THE CLASS.
I CAN ONLY HOPE YOUR FASHION SKILLS ARE BETTER THAN YOUR SPELLING, MISS LANG. ANOTHER "F" FOR YOUR COLLECTION.
THAT'S BETTER THAN A "G," RIGHT?
THEY DON'T DO "G"S, LANA.

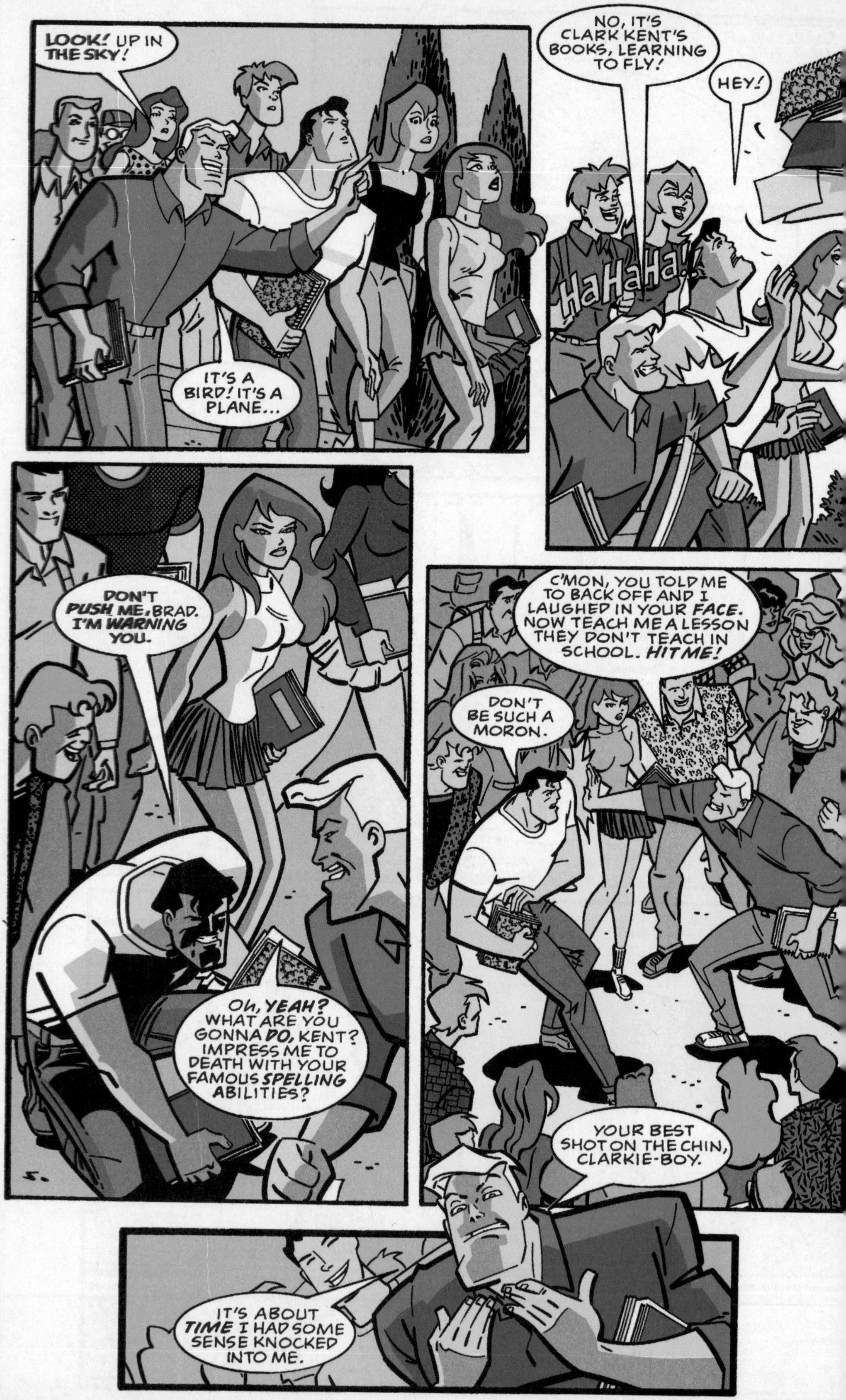
LOOK! UP IN THE SKY!
IT'S A BIRD! IT'S A PLANE...
NO, IT'S CLARK KENT'S BOOKS, LEARNING TO FLY!
HEY!
HaHaHa!
DON'T PUSH ME, BRAD. I'M WARNING YOU.
Oh, YEAH? WHAT ARE YOU GONNA DO, KENT? IMPRESS ME TO DEATH WITH YOUR FAMOUS SPELLING ABILITIES?
C'MON, YOU TOLD ME TO BACK OFF AND I LAUGHED IN YOUR FACE. NOW TEACH ME A LESSON THEY DON'T TEACH IN SCHOOL. HIT ME!
DON'T BE SUCH A MORON.
YOUR BEST SHOT ON THE CHIN, CLARKIE-BOY.
IT'S ABOUT TIME I HAD SOME SENSE KNOCKED INTO ME.

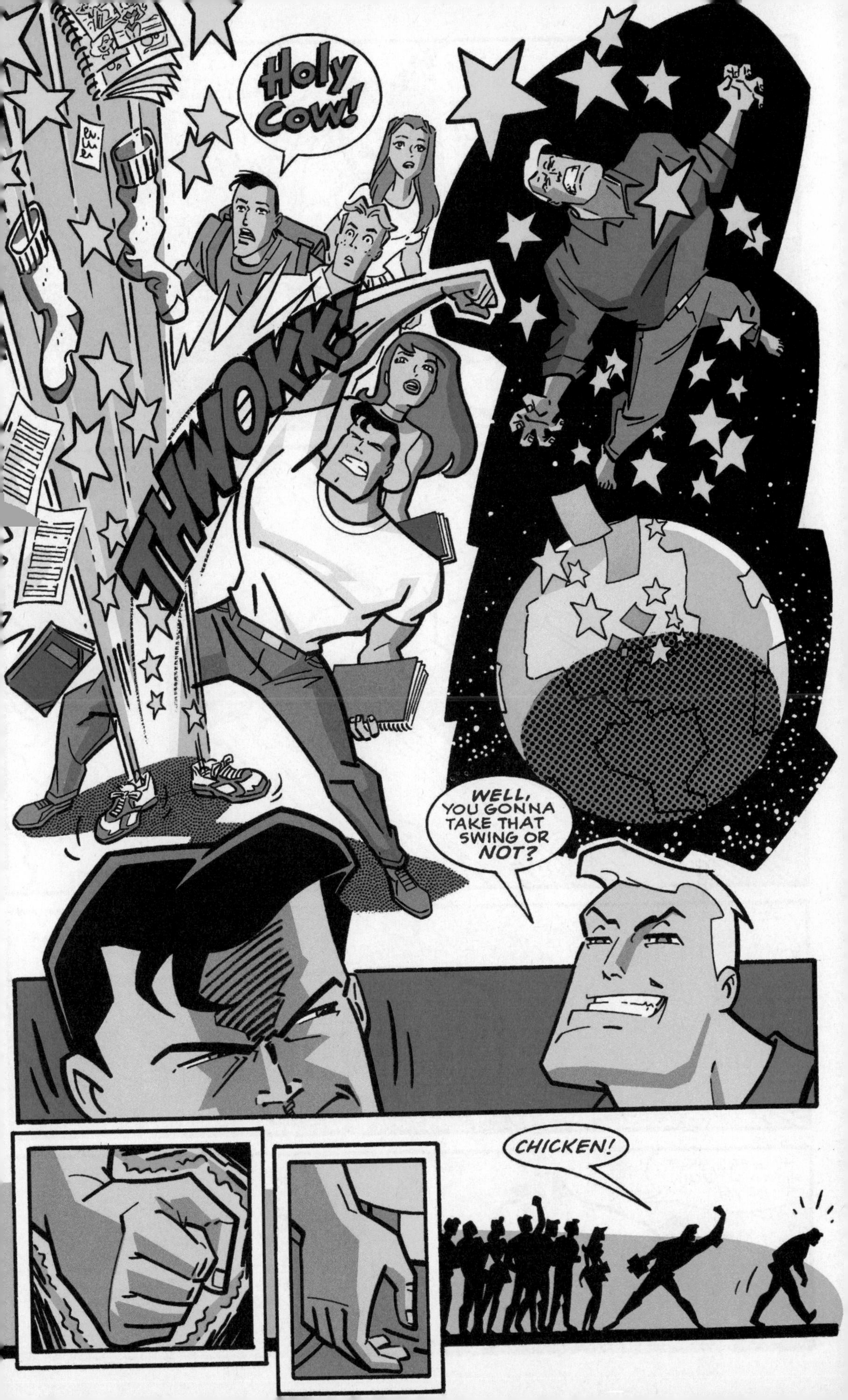
Holy Cow!
THWOKK!
WELL, YOU GONNA TAKE THAT SWING OR NOT?
CHICKEN!

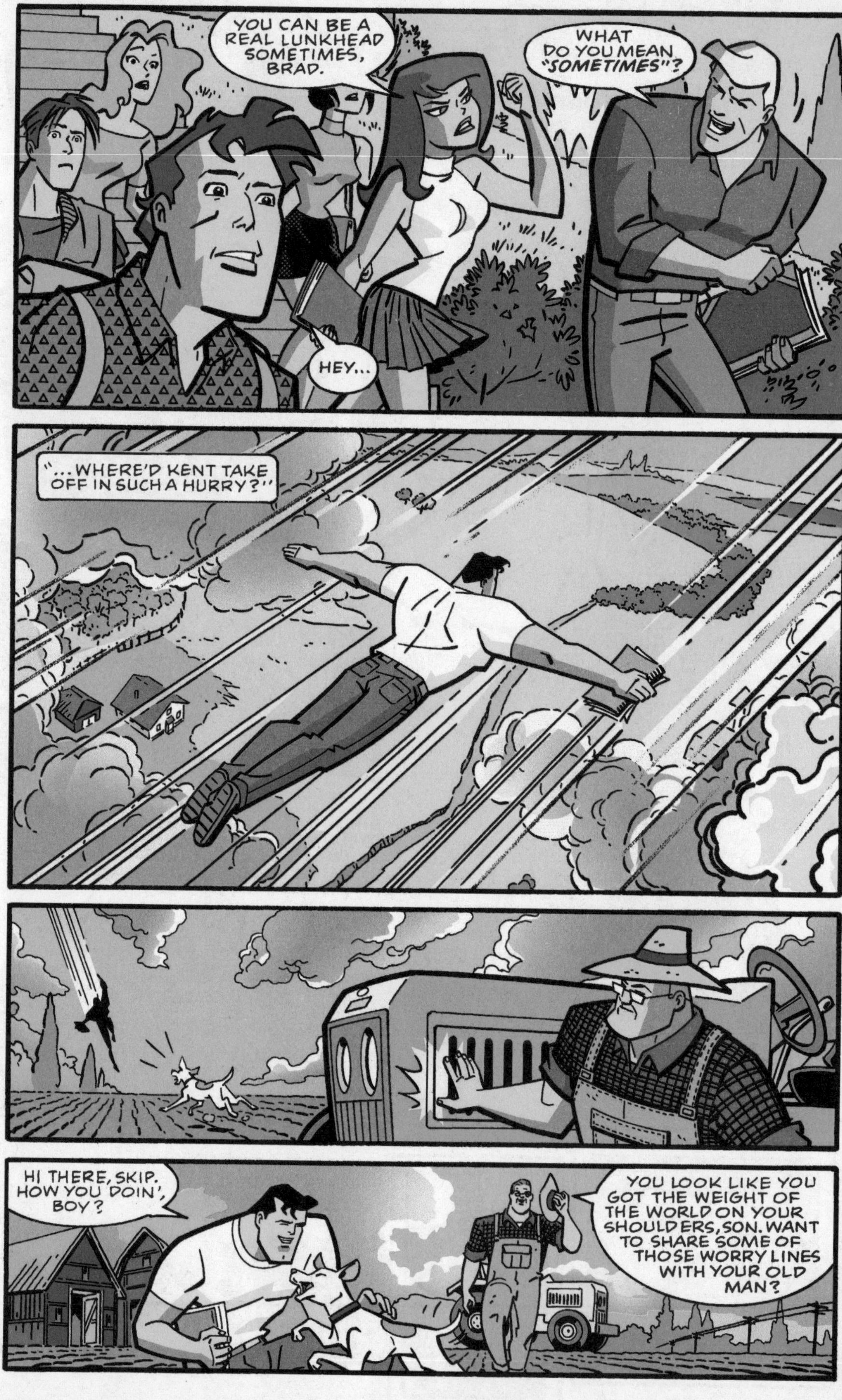
YOU CAN BE A REAL LUNKHEAD SOMETIMES, BRAD.
WHAT DO YOU MEAN "SOMETIMES"?
HEY...
"...WHERE'D KENT TAKE OFF IN SUCH A HURRY?"
HI THERE, SKIP. HOW YOU DOIN', BOY?
YOU LOOK LIKE YOU GOT THE WEIGHT OF THE WORLD ON YOUR SHOULDERS, SON. WANT TO SHARE SOME OF THOSE WORRY LINES WITH YOUR OLD MAN?

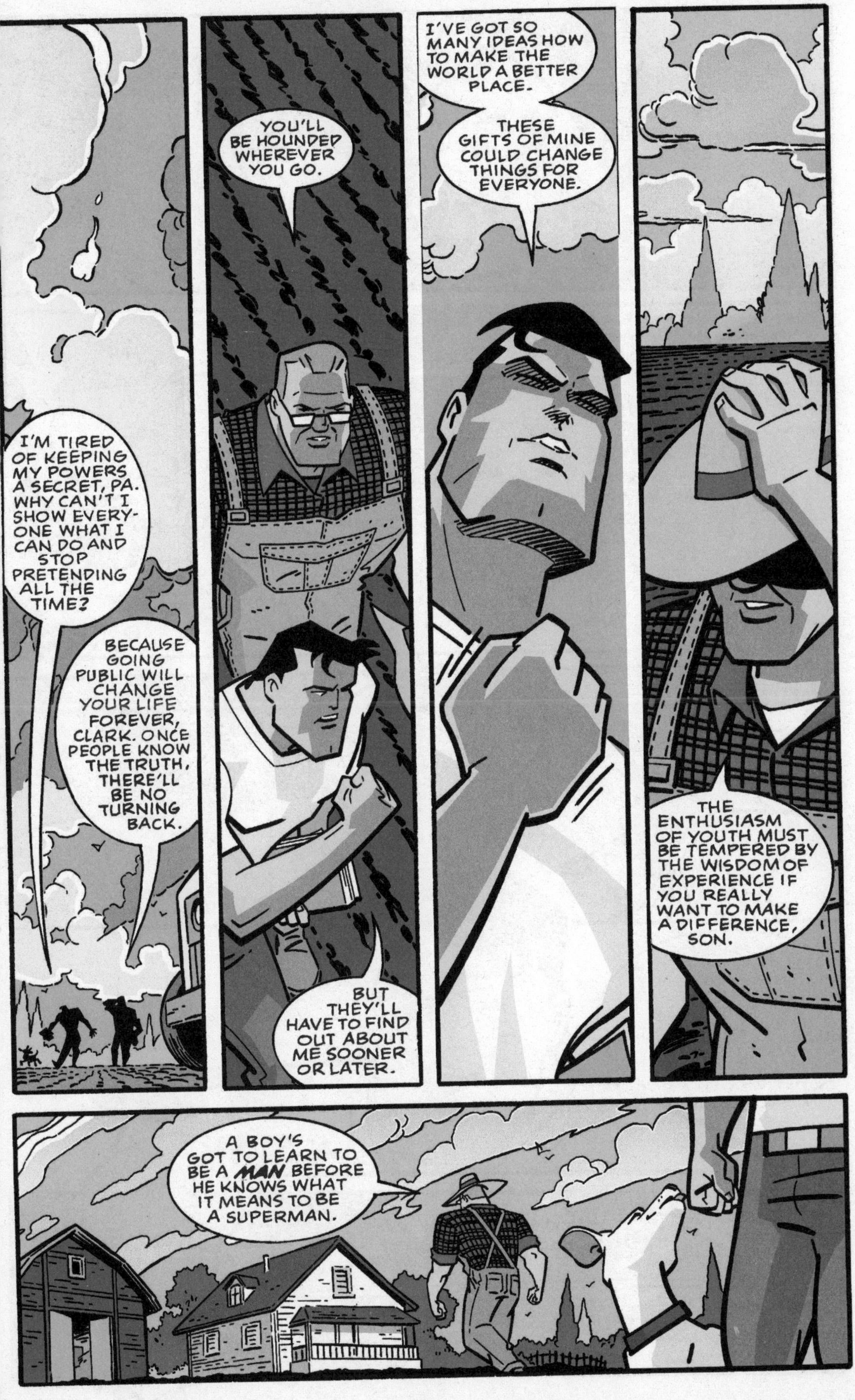
I'M TIRED OF KEEPING MY POWERS A SECRET, PA. WHY CAN'T I SHOW EVERY-ONE WHAT I CAN DO AND STOP PRETENDING ALL THE TIME?
BECAUSE GOING PUBLIC WILL CHANGE YOUR LIFE FOREVER, CLARK. ONCE PEOPLE KNOW THE TRUTH, THERE'LL BE NO TURNING BACK.
YOU'LL BE HOUNDED WHEREVER YOU GO.
BUT THEY'LL HAVE TO FIND OUT ABOUT ME SOONER OR LATER.
I'VE GOT SO MANY IDEAS HOW TO MAKE THE WORLD A BETTER PLACE.
THESE GIFTS OF MINE COULD CHANGE THINGS FOR EVERYONE.
THE ENTHUSIASM OF YOUTH MUST BE TEMPERED BY THE WISDOM OF EXPERIENCE IF YOU REALLY WANT TO MAKE A DIFFERENCE, SON.
A BOY'S GOT TO LEARN TO BE A ***MAN*** BEFORE HE KNOWS WHAT IT MEANS TO BE A SUPERMAN.

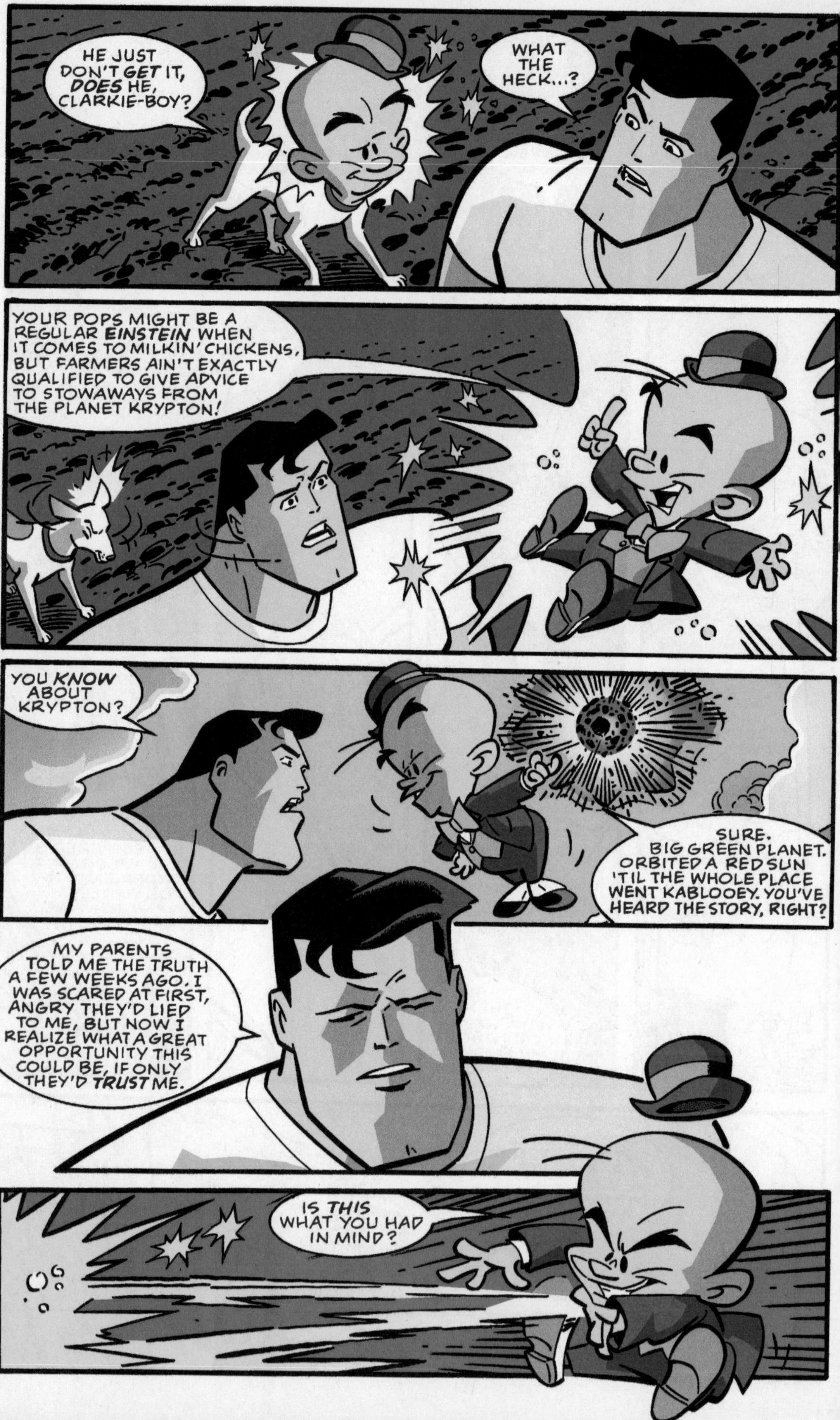
HE JUST DON'T GET IT, DOES HE, CLARKIE-BOY?
WHAT THE HECK...?
YOUR POPS MIGHT BE A REGULAR EINSTEIN WHEN IT COMES TO MILKIN' CHICKENS, BUT FARMERS AIN'T EXACTLY QUALIFIED TO GIVE ADVICE TO STOWAWAYS FROM THE PLANET KRYPTON!
YOU KNOW ABOUT KRYPTON?
SURE. BIG GREEN PLANET. ORBITED A RED SUN 'TIL THE WHOLE PLACE WENT KABLOOEY. YOU'VE HEARD THE STORY, RIGHT?
MY PARENTS TOLD ME THE TRUTH A FEW WEEKS AGO. I WAS SCARED AT FIRST, ANGRY THEY'D LIED TO ME, BUT NOW I REALIZE WHAT A GREAT OPPORTUNITY THIS COULD BE, IF ONLY THEY'D TRUST ME.
IS THIS WHAT YOU HAD IN MIND?

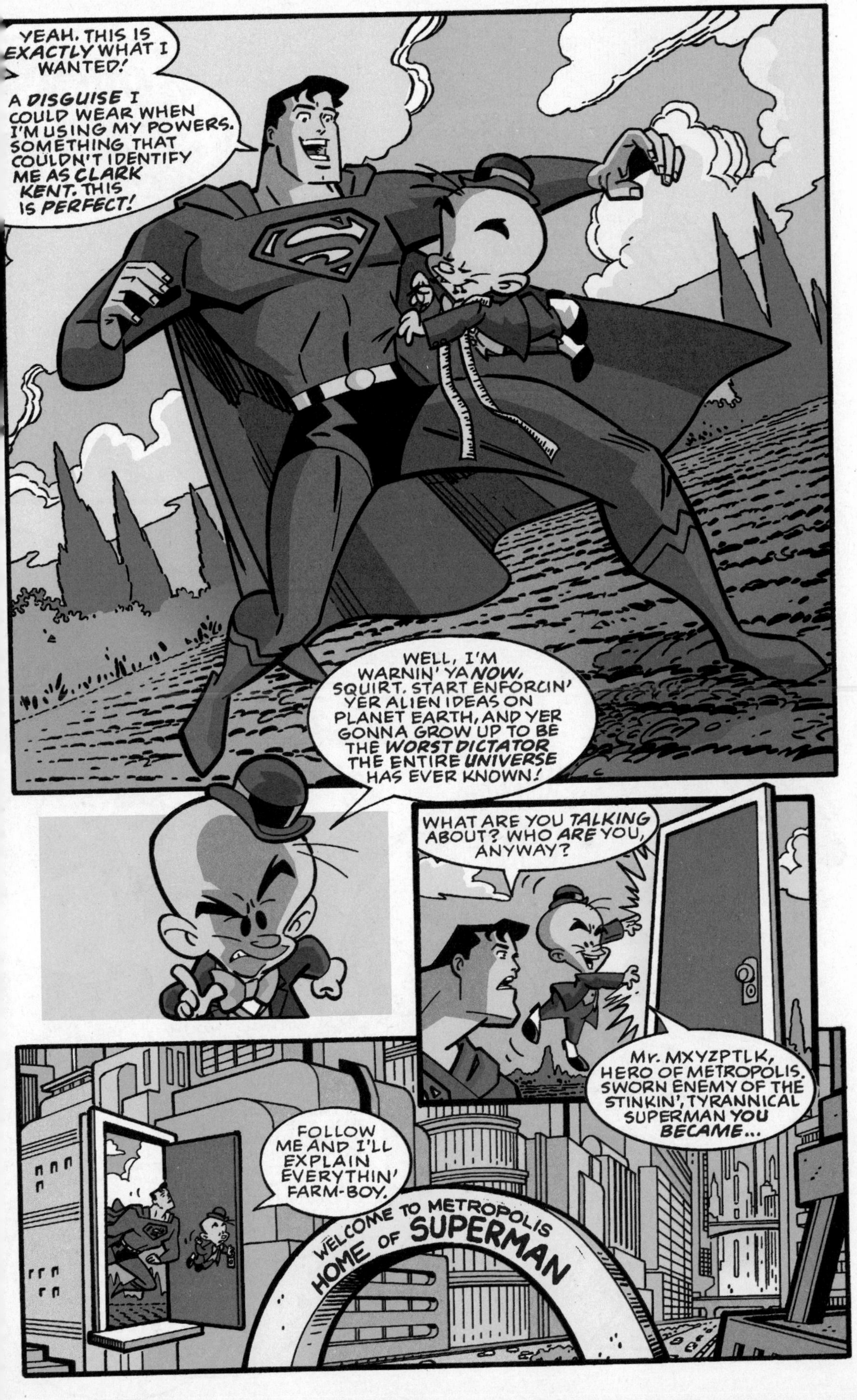
YEAH. THIS IS EXACTLY WHAT I WANTED!
A DISGUISE I COULD WEAR WHEN I'M USING MY POWERS. SOMETHING THAT COULDN'T IDENTIFY ME AS CLARK KENT. THIS IS PERFECT!
WELL, I'M WARNIN' YA NOW, SQUIRT. START ENFORCIN' YER ALIEN IDEAS ON PLANET EARTH, AND YER GONNA GROW UP TO BE THE WORST DICTATOR THE ENTIRE UNIVERSE HAS EVER KNOWN!
WHAT ARE YOU TALKING ABOUT? WHO ARE YOU, ANYWAY?
Mr. MXYZPTLK, HERO OF METROPOLIS. SWORN ENEMY OF THE STINKIN', TYRANNICAL SUPERMAN YOU BECAME...
FOLLOW ME AND I'LL EXPLAIN EVERYTHIN' FARM-BOY.
WELCOME TO METROPOLIS
HOME OF SUPERMAN

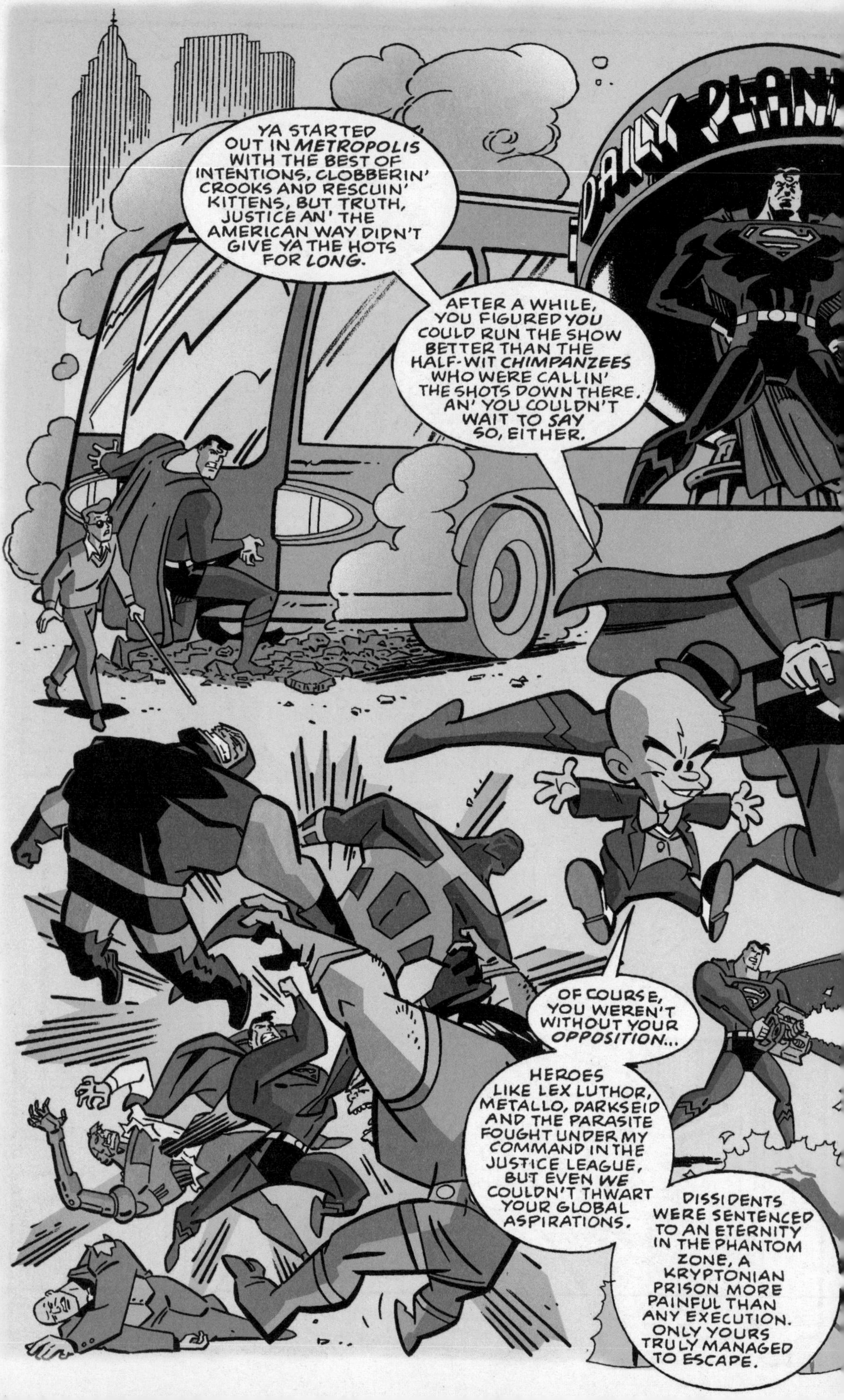

DAILY PLAN
YA STARTED OUT IN METROPOLIS WITH THE BEST OF INTENTIONS, CLOBBERIN' CROOKS AND RESCUIN' KITTENS, BUT TRUTH, JUSTICE AN' THE AMERICAN WAY DIDN'T GIVE YA THE HOTS FOR LONG.
AFTER A WHILE, YOU FIGURED YOU COULD RUN THE SHOW BETTER THAN THE HALF-WIT CHIMPANZEES WHO WERE CALLIN' THE SHOTS DOWN THERE. AN' YOU COULDN'T WAIT TO SAY SO, EITHER.
OF COURSE, YOU WEREN'T WITHOUT YOUR OPPOSITION...
HEROES LIKE LEX LUTHOR, METALLO, DARKSEID AND THE PARASITE FOUGHT UNDER MY COMMAND IN THE JUSTICE LEAGUE, BUT EVEN WE COULDN'T THWART YOUR GLOBAL ASPIRATIONS.
DISSIDENTS WERE SENTENCED TO AN ETERNITY IN THE PHANTOM ZONE, A KRYPTONIAN PRISON MORE PAINFUL THAN ANY EXECUTION. ONLY YOURS TRULY MANAGED TO ESCAPE.

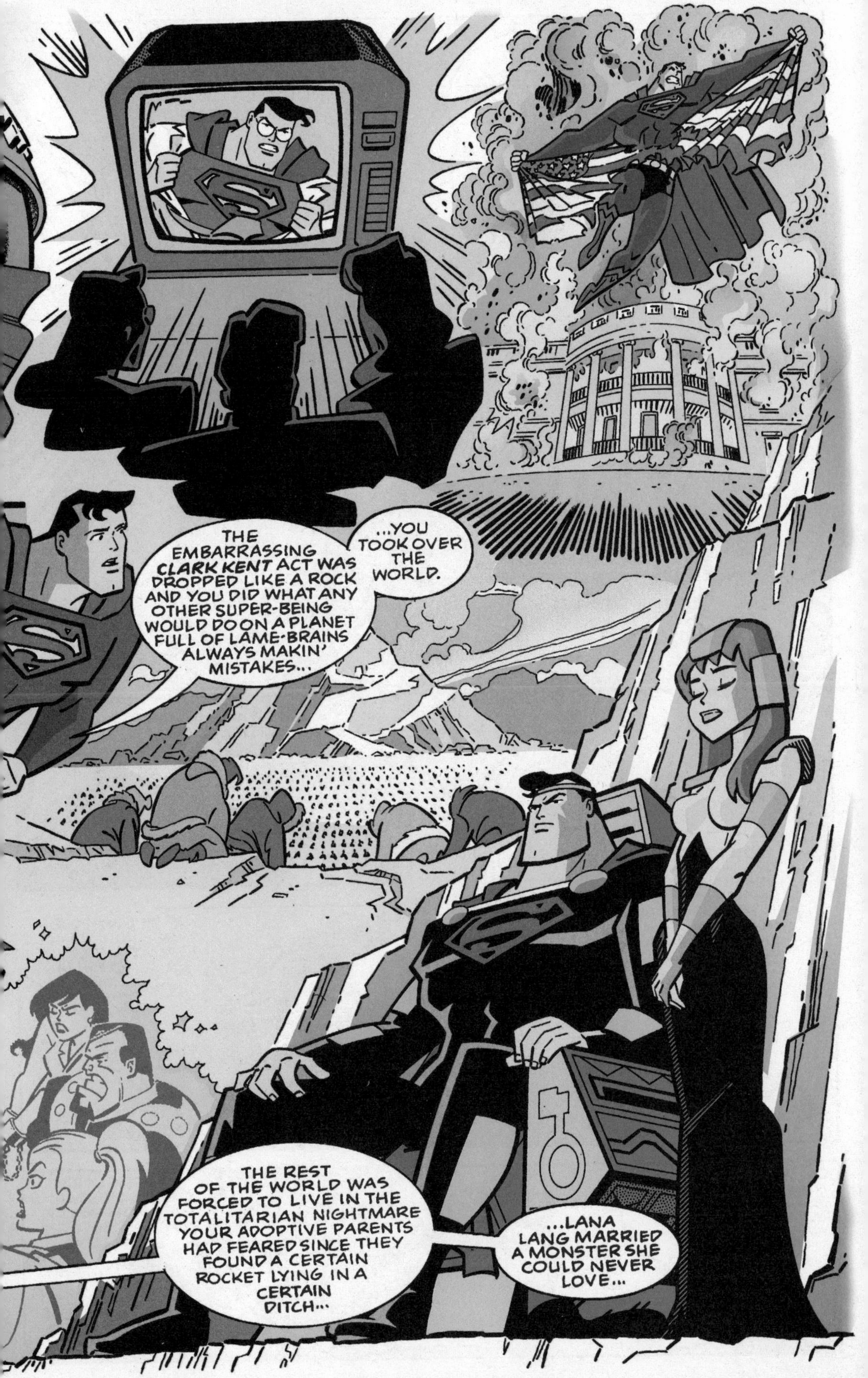
THE EMBARRASSING CLARK KENT ACT WAS DROPPED LIKE A ROCK AND YOU DID WHAT ANY OTHER SUPER-BEING WOULD DO ON A PLANET FULL OF LAME-BRAINS ALWAYS MAKIN' MISTAKES...
...YOU TOOK OVER THE WORLD.
THE REST OF THE WORLD WAS FORCED TO LIVE IN THE TOTALITARIAN NIGHTMARE YOUR ADOPTIVE PARENTS HAD FEARED SINCE THEY FOUND A CERTAIN ROCKET LYING IN A CERTAIN DITCH...
...LANA LANG MARRIED A MONSTER SHE COULD NEVER LOVE...

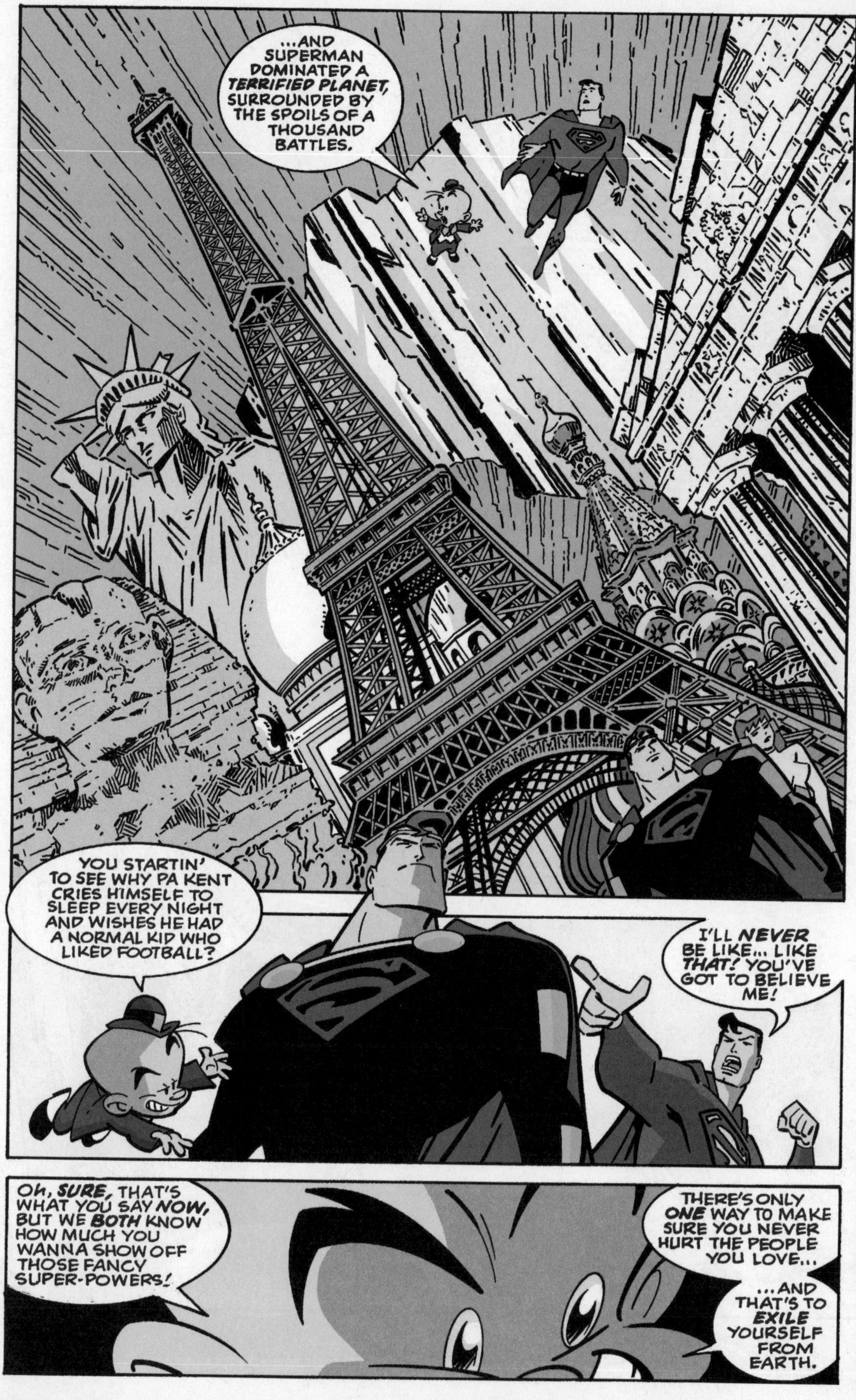
...AND SUPERMAN DOMINATED A TERRIFIED PLANET, SURROUNDED BY THE SPOILS OF A THOUSAND BATTLES.
YOU STARTIN' TO SEE WHY PA KENT CRIES HIMSELF TO SLEEP EVERY NIGHT AND WISHES HE HAD A NORMAL KID WHO LIKED FOOTBALL?
I'LL NEVER BE LIKE... LIKE THAT! YOU'VE GOT TO BELIEVE ME!
Oh, SURE, THAT'S WHAT YOU SAY NOW, BUT WE BOTH KNOW HOW MUCH YOU WANNA SHOW OFF THOSE FANCY SUPER-POWERS!
THERE'S ONLY ONE WAY TO MAKE SURE YOU NEVER HURT THE PEOPLE YOU LOVE...
...AND THAT'S TO EXILE YOURSELF FROM EARTH.

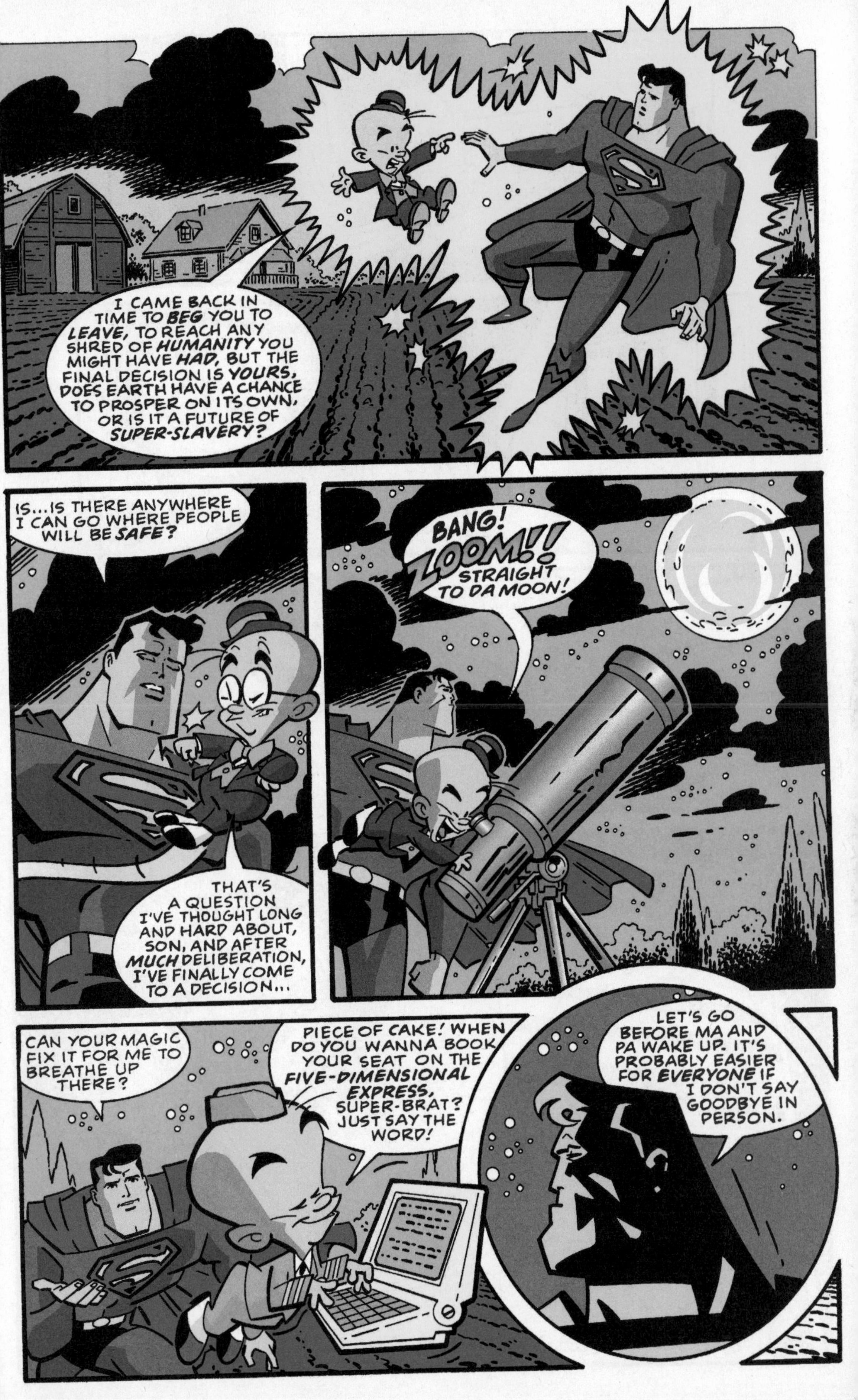
I CAME BACK IN TIME TO BEG YOU TO LEAVE, TO REACH ANY SHRED OF HUMANITY YOU MIGHT HAVE HAD, BUT THE FINAL DECISION IS YOURS. DOES EARTH HAVE A CHANCE TO PROSPER ON ITS OWN, OR IS IT A FUTURE OF SUPER-SLAVERY?
IS...IS THERE ANYWHERE I CAN GO WHERE PEOPLE WILL BE SAFE?
THAT'S A QUESTION I'VE THOUGHT LONG AND HARD ABOUT, SON, AND AFTER MUCH DELIBERATION, I'VE FINALLY COME TO A DECISION...
BANG! ZOOM!! STRAIGHT TO DA MOON!
CAN YOUR MAGIC FIX IT FOR ME TO BREATHE UP THERE?
PIECE OF CAKE! WHEN DO YOU WANNA BOOK YOUR SEAT ON THE FIVE-DIMENSIONAL EXPRESS, SUPER-BRAT? JUST SAY THE WORD!
LET'S GO BEFORE MA AND PA WAKE UP. IT'S PROBABLY EASIER FOR EVERYONE IF I DON'T SAY GOODBYE IN PERSON.

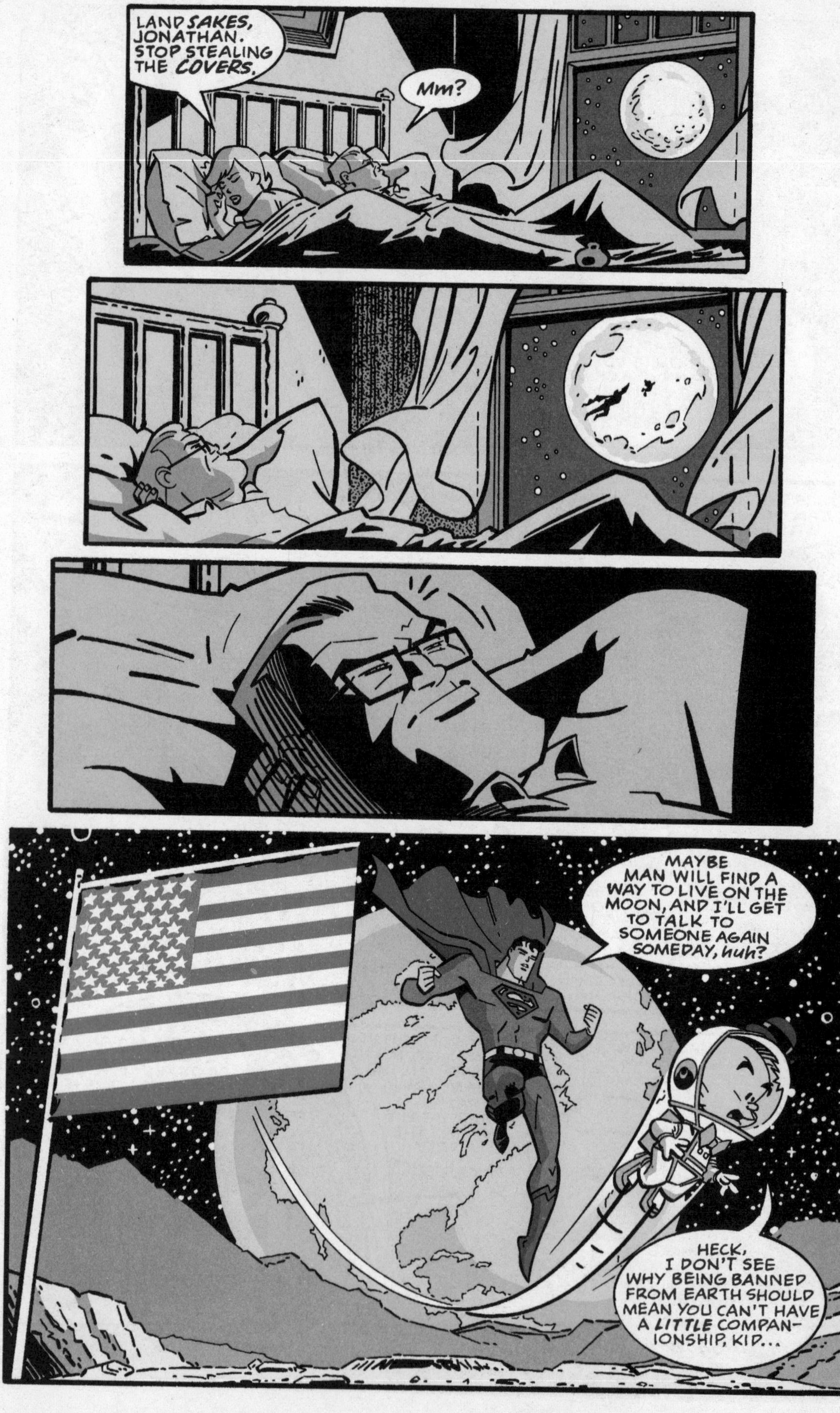
LAND SAKES, JONATHAN. STOP STEALING THE COVERS.
Mm?
MAYBE MAN WILL FIND A WAY TO LIVE ON THE MOON, AND I'LL GET TO TALK TO SOMEONE AGAIN SOMEDAY, huh?
HECK, I DON'T SEE WHY BEING BANNED FROM EARTH SHOULD MEAN YOU CAN'T HAVE A LITTLE COMPANIONSHIP, KID...

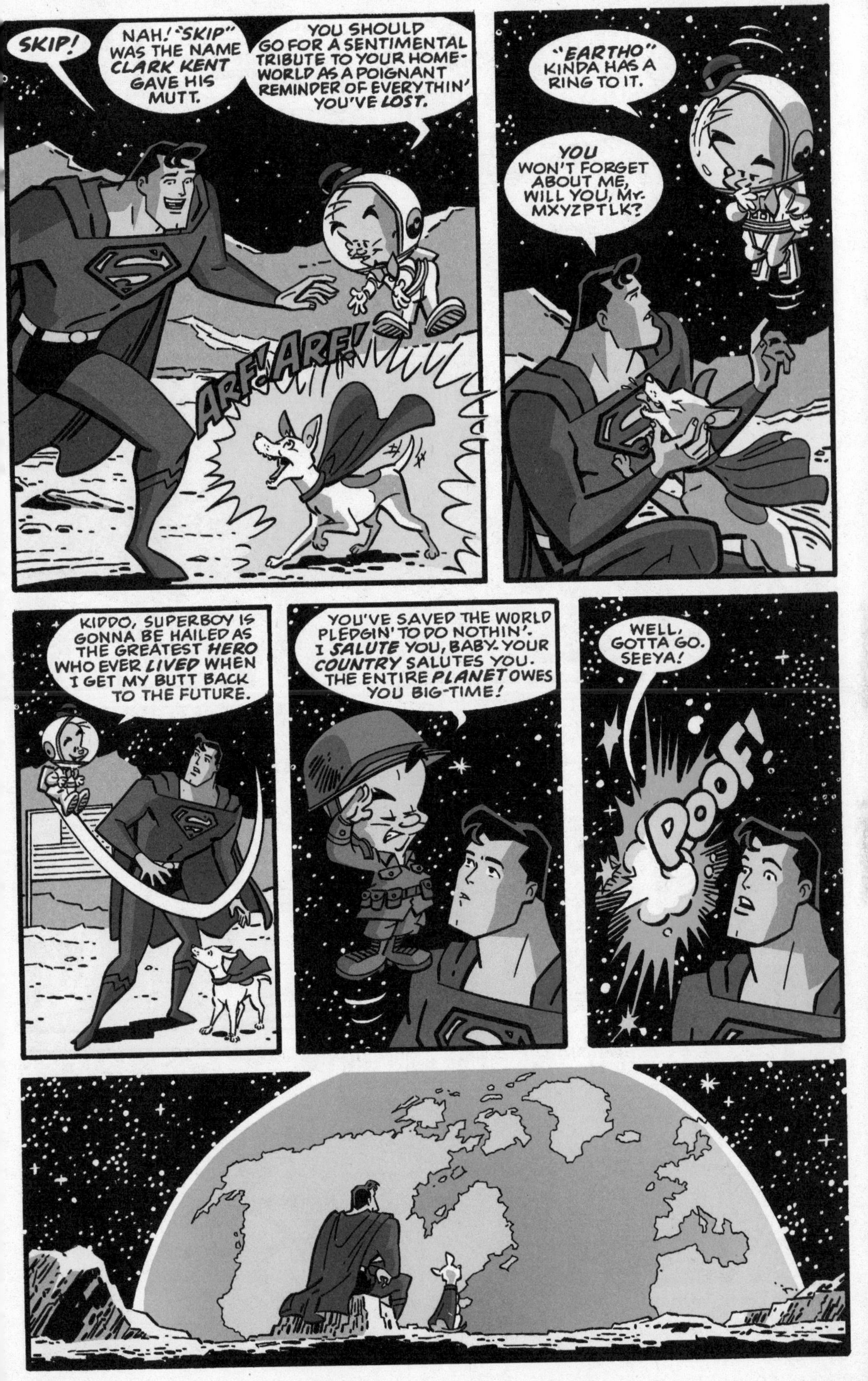
SKIP!
NAH! "SKIP" WAS THE NAME CLARK KENT GAVE HIS MUTT.
YOU SHOULD GO FOR A SENTIMENTAL TRIBUTE TO YOUR HOME-WORLD AS A POIGNANT REMINDER OF EVERYTHIN' YOU'VE LOST.
ARF! ARF!
"EARTHO" KINDA HAS A RING TO IT.
YOU WON'T FORGET ABOUT ME, WILL YOU, MR. MXYZPTLK?
KIDDO, SUPERBOY IS GONNA BE HAILED AS THE GREATEST HERO WHO EVER LIVED WHEN I GET MY BUTT BACK TO THE FUTURE.
YOU'VE SAVED THE WORLD PLEDGIN' TO DO NOTHIN'. I SALUTE YOU, BABY. YOUR COUNTRY SALUTES YOU. THE ENTIRE PLANET OWES YOU BIG-TIME!
WELL, GOTTA GO. SEEYA!
POOF!

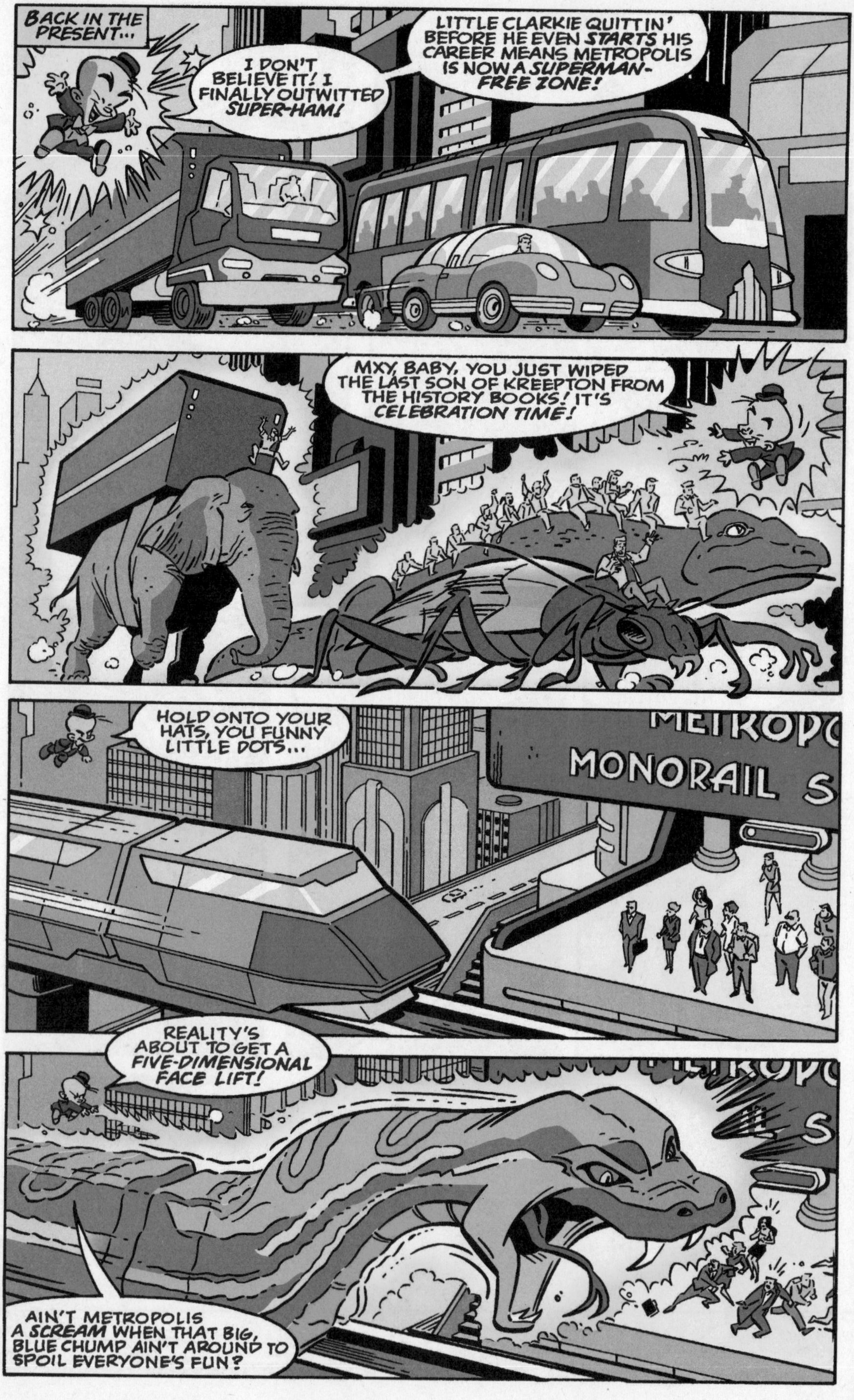
BACK IN THE PRESENT...
I DON'T BELIEVE IT! I FINALLY OUTWITTED SUPER-HAM!
LITTLE CLARKIE QUITTIN' BEFORE HE EVEN STARTS HIS CAREER MEANS METROPOLIS IS NOW A SUPERMAN-FREE ZONE!
MXY, BABY, YOU JUST WIPED THE LAST SON OF KREEPTON FROM THE HISTORY BOOKS! IT'S CELEBRATION TIME!
HOLD ONTO YOUR HATS, YOU FUNNY LITTLE DOTS...
MONORAIL
REALITY'S ABOUT TO GET A FIVE-DIMENSIONAL FACE LIFT!
AIN'T METROPOLIS A SCREAM WHEN THAT BIG, BLUE CHUMP AIN'T AROUND TO SPOIL EVERYONE'S FUN?

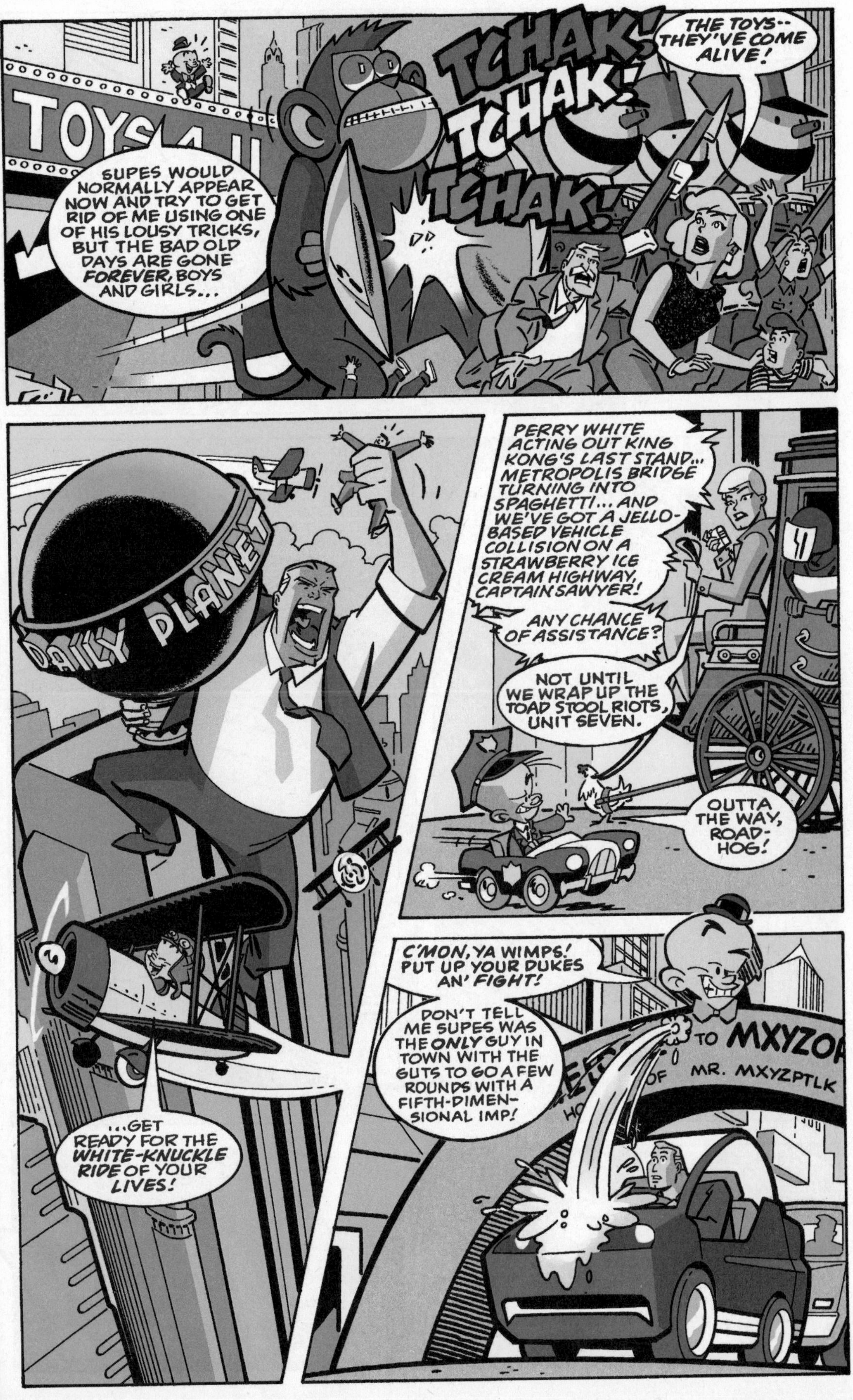
TOYS 4 U
SUPES WOULD NORMALLY APPEAR NOW AND TRY TO GET RID OF ME USING ONE OF HIS LOUSY TRICKS, BUT THE BAD OLD DAYS ARE GONE FOREVER, BOYS AND GIRLS...
TCHAK! TCHAK! TCHAK!
THE TOYS-- THEY'VE COME ALIVE!
DAILY PLANET
...GET READY FOR THE WHITE-KNUCKLE RIDE OF YOUR LIVES!
PERRY WHITE ACTING OUT KING KONG'S LAST STAND... METROPOLIS BRIDGE TURNING INTO SPAGHETTI... AND WE'VE GOT A JELLO-BASED VEHICLE COLLISION ON A STRAWBERRY ICE CREAM HIGHWAY, CAPTAIN SAWYER!
ANY CHANCE OF ASSISTANCE?
NOT UNTIL WE WRAP UP THE TOAD STOOL RIOTS, UNIT SEVEN.
OUTTA THE WAY, ROAD-HOG!
C'MON, YA WIMPS! PUT UP YOUR DUKES AN' FIGHT!
DON'T TELL ME SUPES WAS THE ONLY GUY IN TOWN WITH THE GUTS TO GO A FEW ROUNDS WITH A FIFTH-DIMENSIONAL IMP!
TO MXYZOP
OF MR. MXYZPTLK

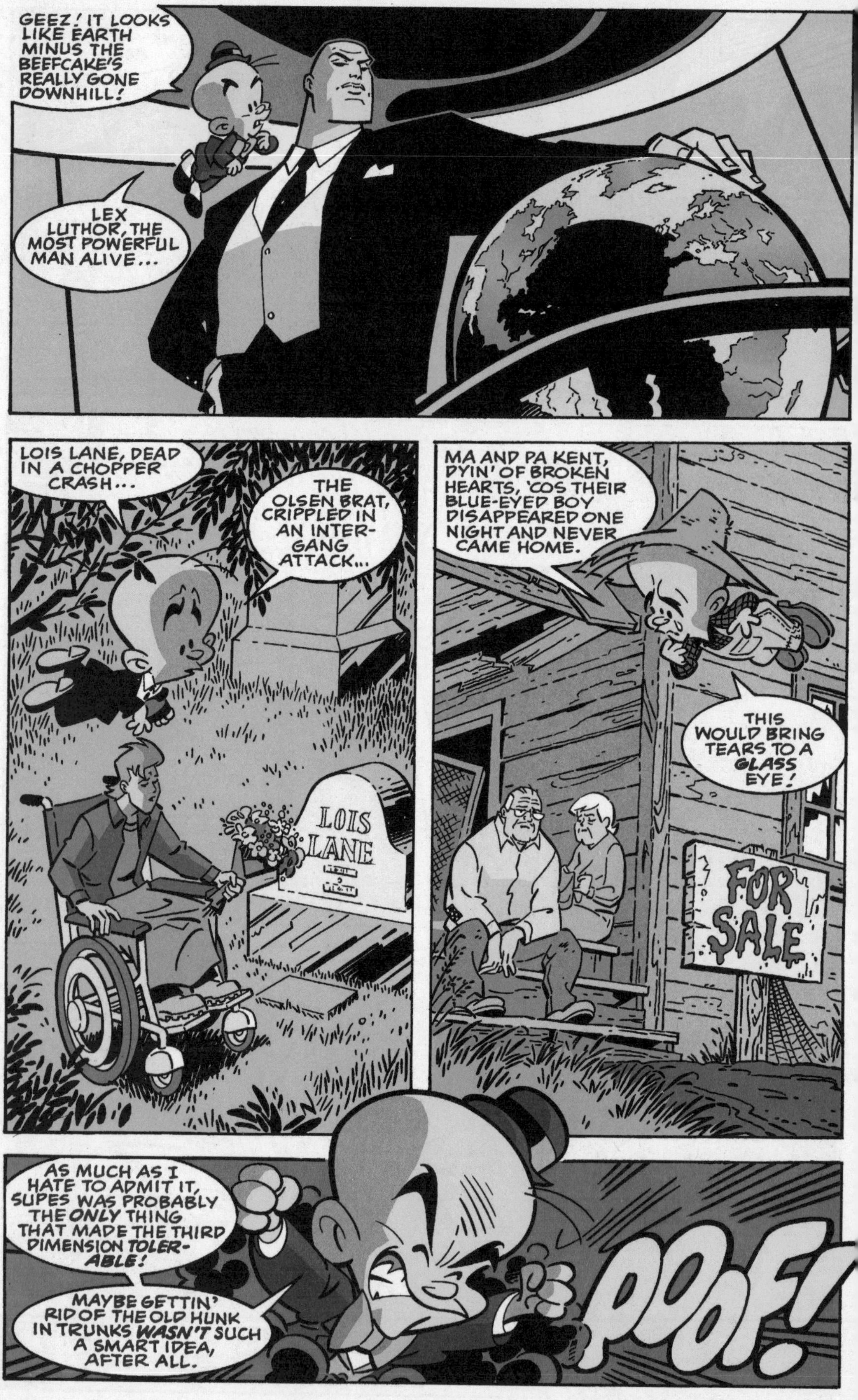

GEEZ! IT LOOKS LIKE EARTH MINUS THE BEEFCAKE'S REALLY GONE DOWNHILL!
LEX LUTHOR, THE MOST POWERFUL MAN ALIVE...
LOIS LANE, DEAD IN A CHOPPER CRASH...
THE OLSEN BRAT, CRIPPLED IN AN INTER-GANG ATTACK...
LOIS LANE
MA AND PA KENT, DYIN' OF BROKEN HEARTS, 'COS THEIR BLUE-EYED BOY DISAPPEARED ONE NIGHT AND NEVER CAME HOME.
THIS WOULD BRING TEARS TO A GLASS EYE!
FOR SALE
AS MUCH AS I HATE TO ADMIT IT, SUPES WAS PROBABLY THE ONLY THING THAT MADE THE THIRD DIMENSION TOLER-ABLE!
MAYBE GETTIN' RID OF THE OLD HUNK IN TRUNKS WASN'T SUCH A SMART IDEA, AFTER ALL.
POOF!

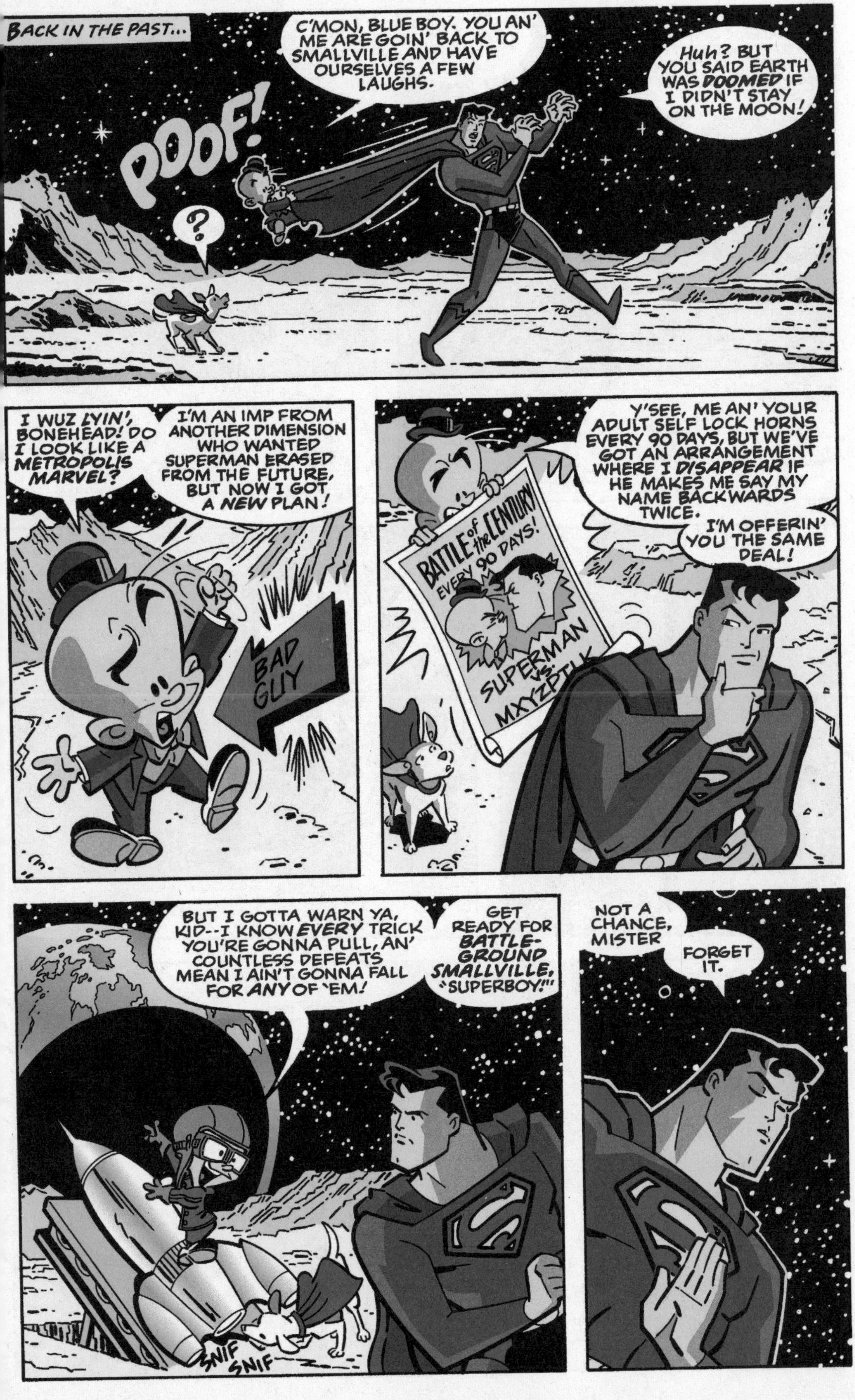
BACK IN THE PAST...
C'MON, BLUE BOY. YOU AN' ME ARE GOIN' BACK TO SMALLVILLE AND HAVE OURSELVES A FEW LAUGHS.
POOF!
?
Huh? BUT YOU SAID EARTH WAS DOOMED IF I DIDN'T STAY ON THE MOON!
I WUZ LYIN', BONEHEAD! DO I LOOK LIKE A METROPOLIS MARVEL?
I'M AN IMP FROM ANOTHER DIMENSION WHO WANTED SUPERMAN ERASED FROM THE FUTURE, BUT NOW I GOT A NEW PLAN!
BAD GUY
Y'SEE, ME AN' YOUR ADULT SELF LOCK HORNS EVERY 90 DAYS, BUT WE'VE GOT AN ARRANGEMENT WHERE I DISAPPEAR IF HE MAKES ME SAY MY NAME BACKWARDS TWICE.
I'M OFFERIN' YOU THE SAME DEAL!
BATTLE of the CENTURY EVERY 90 DAYS!
SUPERMAN VS. MXYZPTLK
BUT I GOTTA WARN YA, KID--I KNOW EVERY TRICK YOU'RE GONNA PULL, AN' COUNTLESS DEFEATS MEAN I AIN'T GONNA FALL FOR ANY OF 'EM!
GET READY FOR BATTLE-GROUND SMALLVILLE, "SUPERBOY!"
SNIF SNIF
NOT A CHANCE, MISTER
FORGET IT.

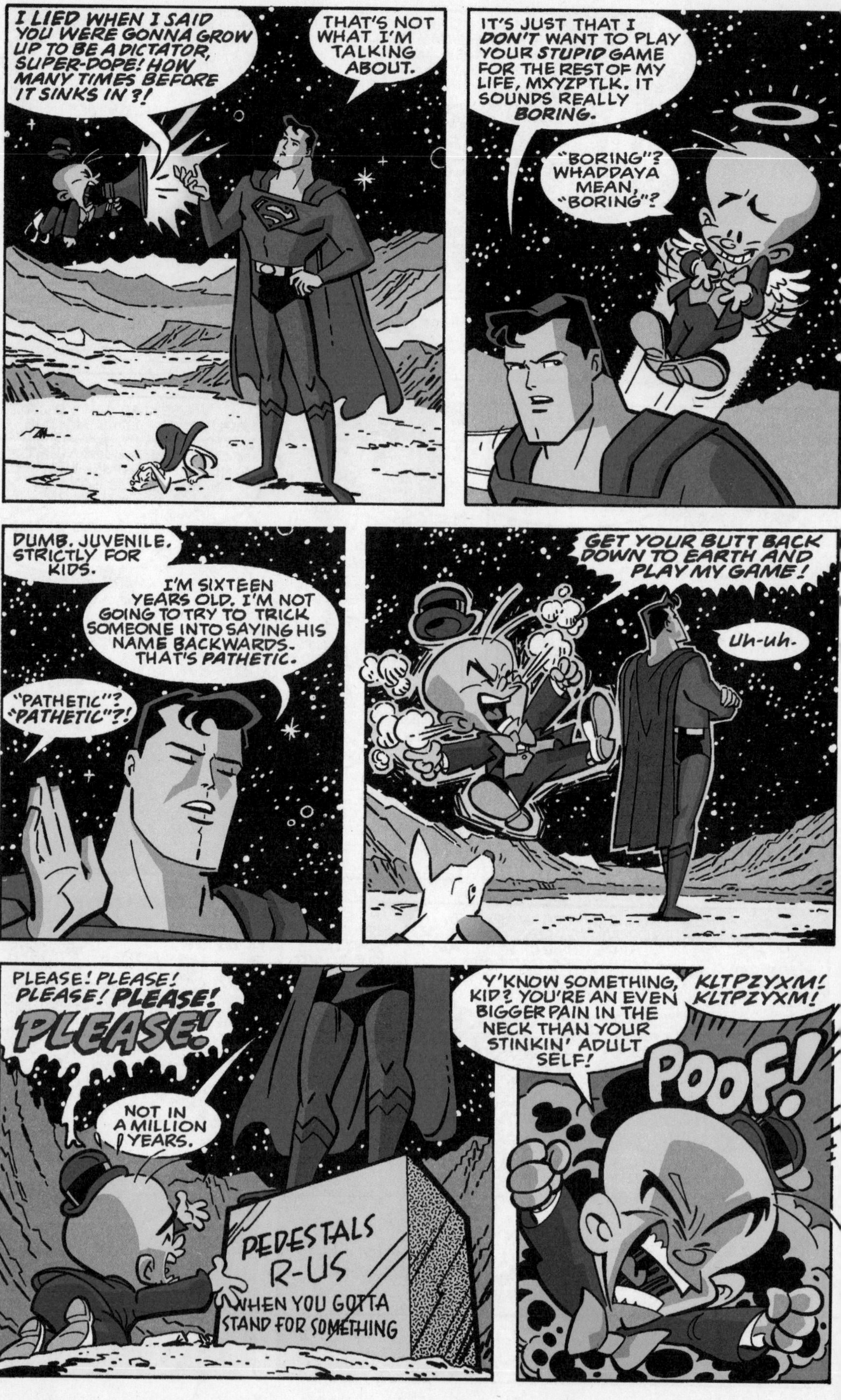
I LIED WHEN I SAID YOU WERE GONNA GROW UP TO BE A DICTATOR, SUPER-DOPE! HOW MANY TIMES BEFORE IT SINKS IN?!
THAT'S NOT WHAT I'M TALKING ABOUT.
IT'S JUST THAT I DON'T WANT TO PLAY YOUR STUPID GAME FOR THE REST OF MY LIFE, MXYZPTLK. IT SOUNDS REALLY BORING.
"BORING"? WHADDAYA MEAN, "BORING"?
DUMB. JUVENILE. STRICTLY FOR KIDS.
I'M SIXTEEN YEARS OLD. I'M NOT GOING TO TRY TO TRICK SOMEONE INTO SAYING HIS NAME BACKWARDS. THAT'S PATHETIC.
"PATHETIC"? "PATHETIC"?!
GET YOUR BUTT BACK DOWN TO EARTH AND PLAY MY GAME!
Uh-uh.
PLEASE! PLEASE! PLEASE! PLEASE! PLEASE!
NOT IN A MILLION YEARS.
PEDESTALS R-US
WHEN YOU GOTTA STAND FOR SOMETHING
Y'KNOW SOMETHING, KID? YOU'RE AN EVEN BIGGER PAIN IN THE NECK THAN YOUR STINKIN' ADULT SELF!
KLTPZYXM! KLTPZYXM!
POOF!

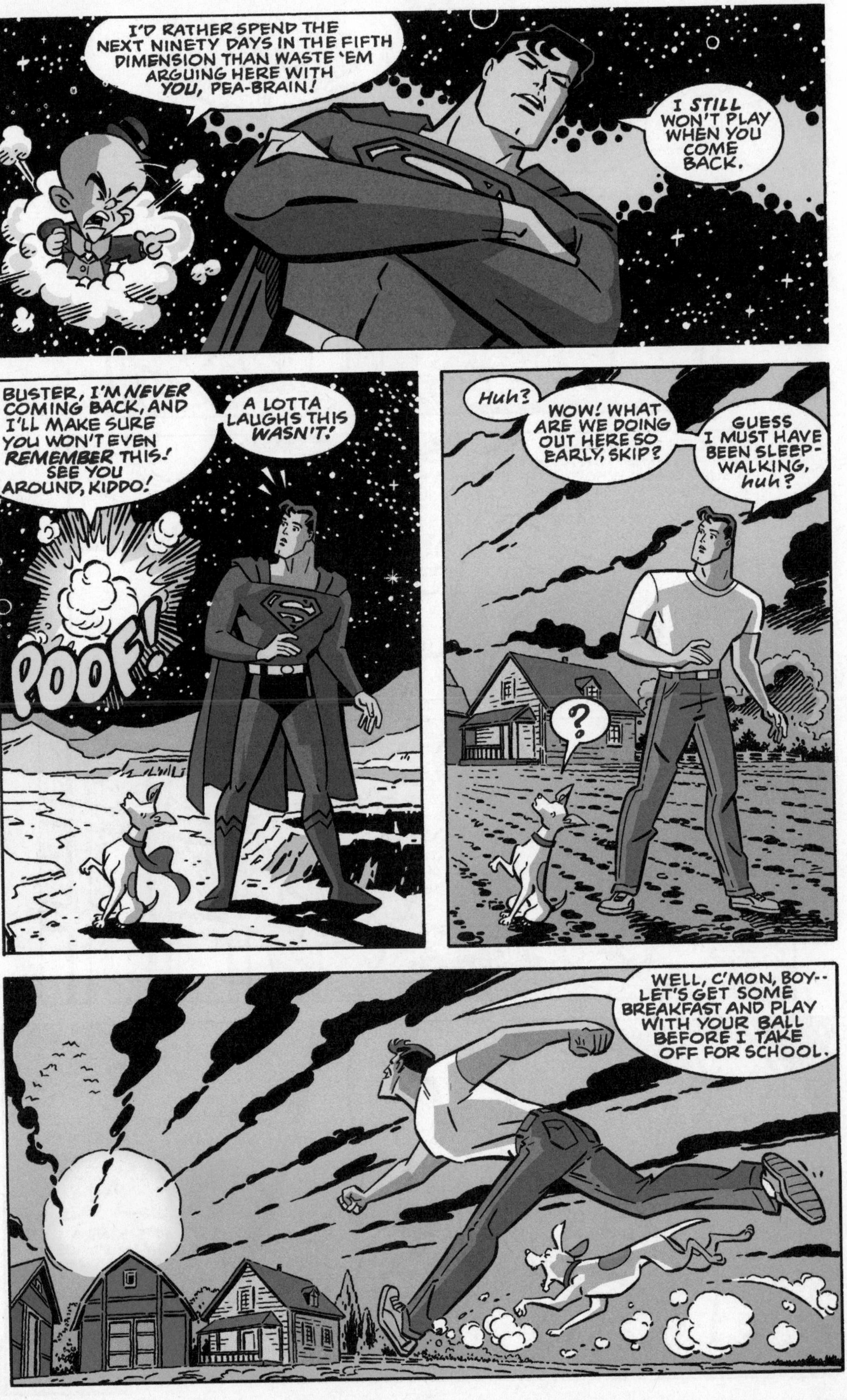
I'D RATHER SPEND THE NEXT NINETY DAYS IN THE FIFTH DIMENSION THAN WASTE 'EM ARGUING HERE WITH YOU, PEA-BRAIN!
I STILL WON'T PLAY WHEN YOU COME BACK.
BUSTER, I'M NEVER COMING BACK, AND I'LL MAKE SURE YOU WON'T EVEN REMEMBER THIS! SEE YOU AROUND, KIDDO!
A LOTTA LAUGHS THIS WASN'T!
POOF!
Huh?
WOW! WHAT ARE WE DOING OUT HERE SO EARLY, SKIP?
GUESS I MUST HAVE BEEN SLEEP-WALKING, huh?
?
WELL, C'MON, BOY-- LET'S GET SOME BREAKFAST AND PLAY WITH YOUR BALL BEFORE I TAKE OFF FOR SCHOOL.

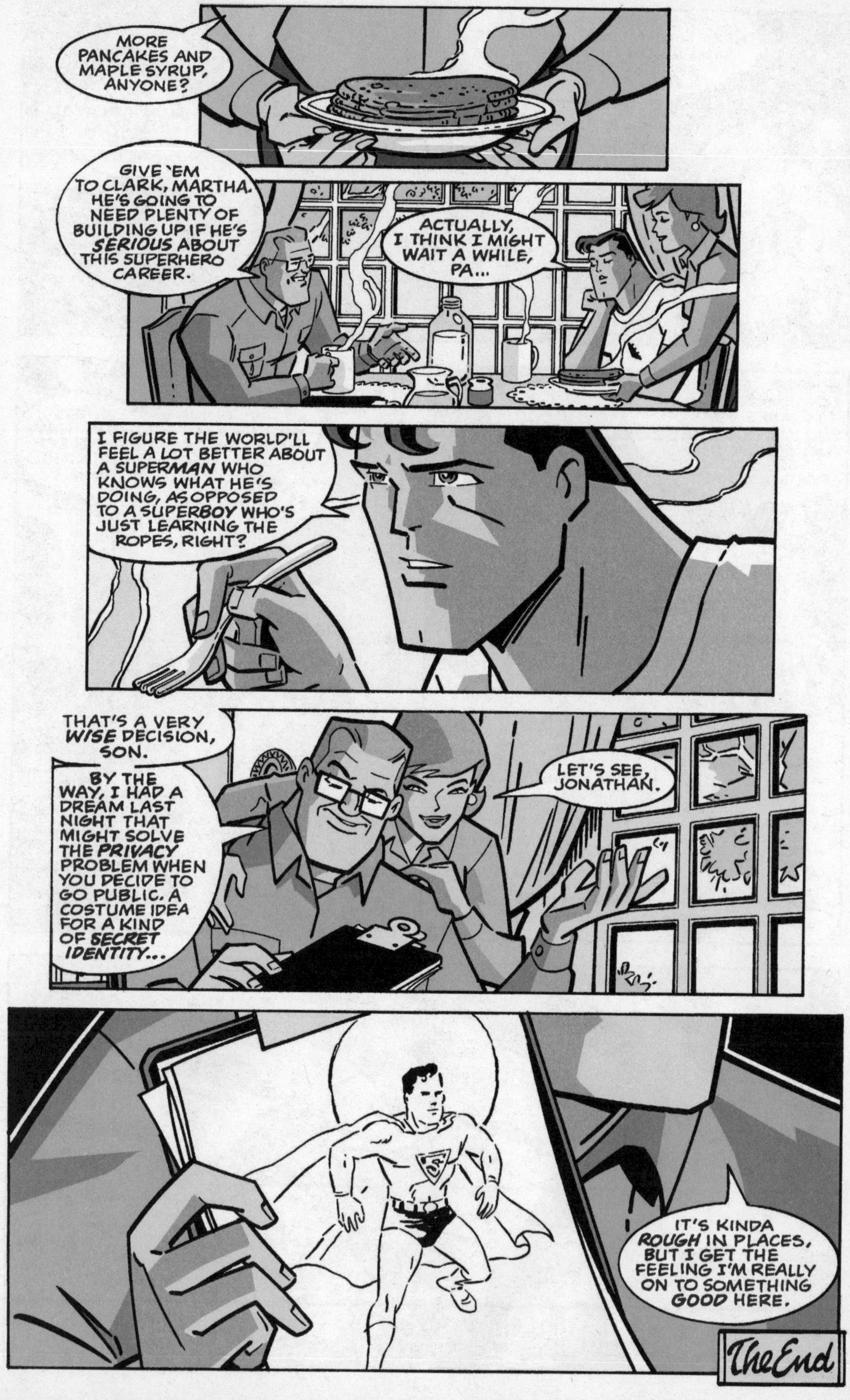
MORE PANCAKES AND MAPLE SYRUP, ANYONE?
GIVE 'EM TO CLARK, MARTHA. HE'S GOING TO NEED PLENTY OF BUILDING UP IF HE'S SERIOUS ABOUT THIS SUPERHERO CAREER.
ACTUALLY, I THINK I MIGHT WAIT A WHILE, PA...
I FIGURE THE WORLD'LL FEEL A LOT BETTER ABOUT A SUPERMAN WHO KNOWS WHAT HE'S DOING, AS OPPOSED TO A SUPERBOY WHO'S JUST LEARNING THE ROPES, RIGHT?
THAT'S A VERY WISE DECISION, SON.
BY THE WAY, I HAD A DREAM LAST NIGHT THAT MIGHT SOLVE THE PRIVACY PROBLEM WHEN YOU DECIDE TO GO PUBLIC. A COSTUME IDEA FOR A KIND OF SECRET IDENTITY...
LET'S SEE, JONATHAN.
IT'S KINDA ROUGH IN PLACES, BUT I GET THE FEELING I'M REALLY ON TO SOMETHING GOOD HERE.
The End

SUPERMAN ADVENTURES #27 cover by RICK BURCHETT, TERRY AUSTIN and MARIE SEVERIN

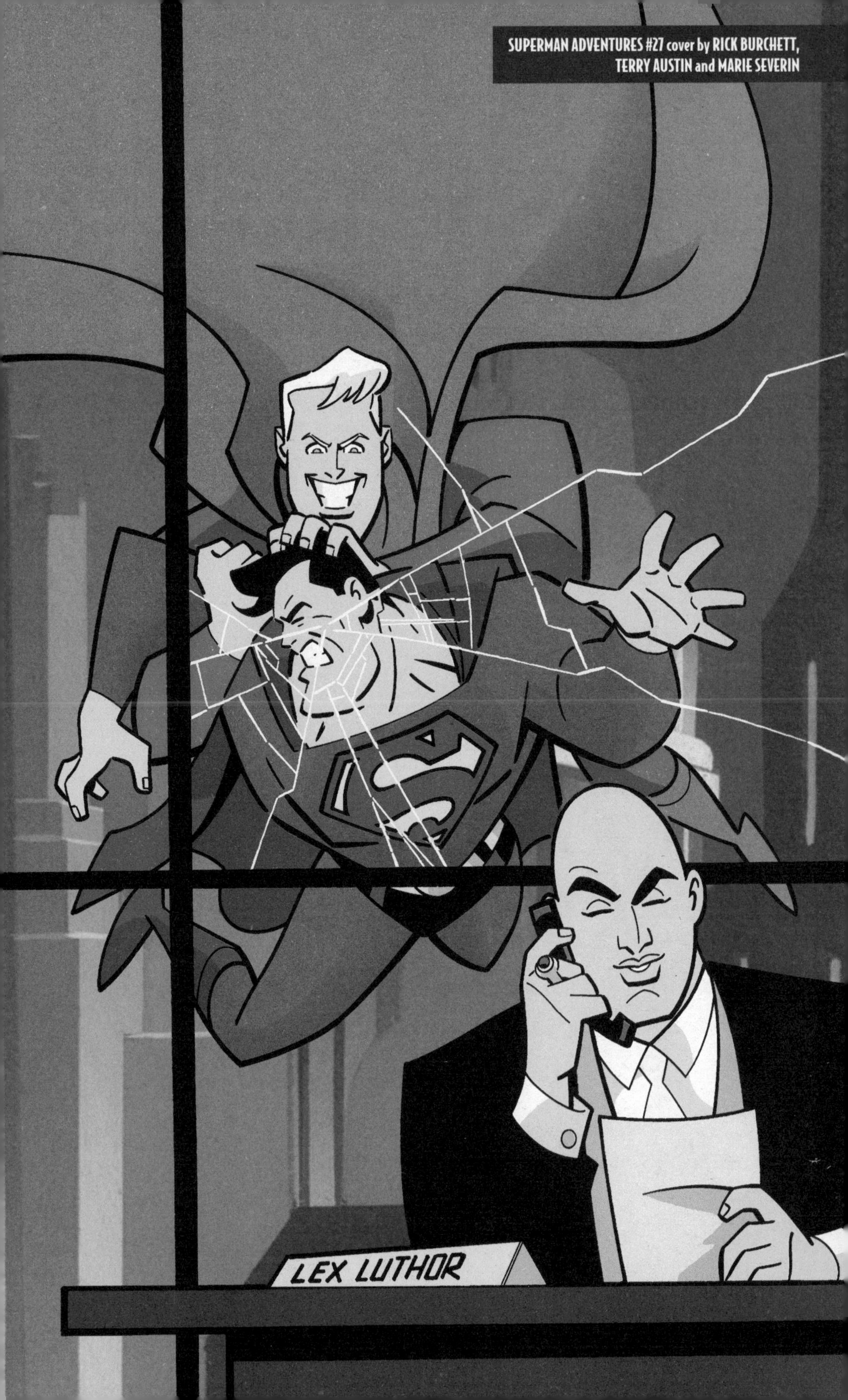
LEX LUTHOR

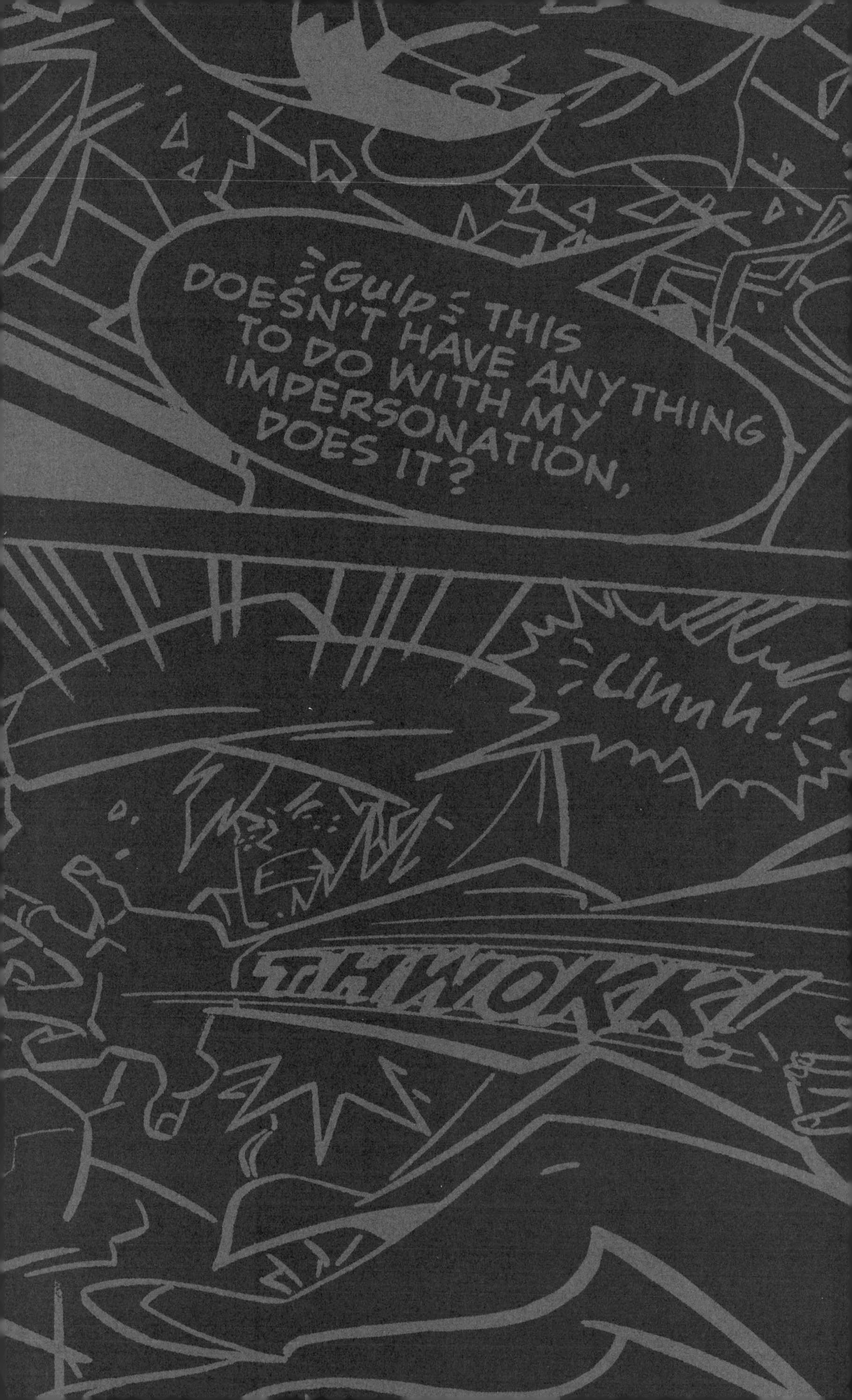
Gulp THIS DOESN'T HAVE ANYTHING TO DO WITH MY IMPERSONATION, DOES IT?
Uunh!
THWOKK!

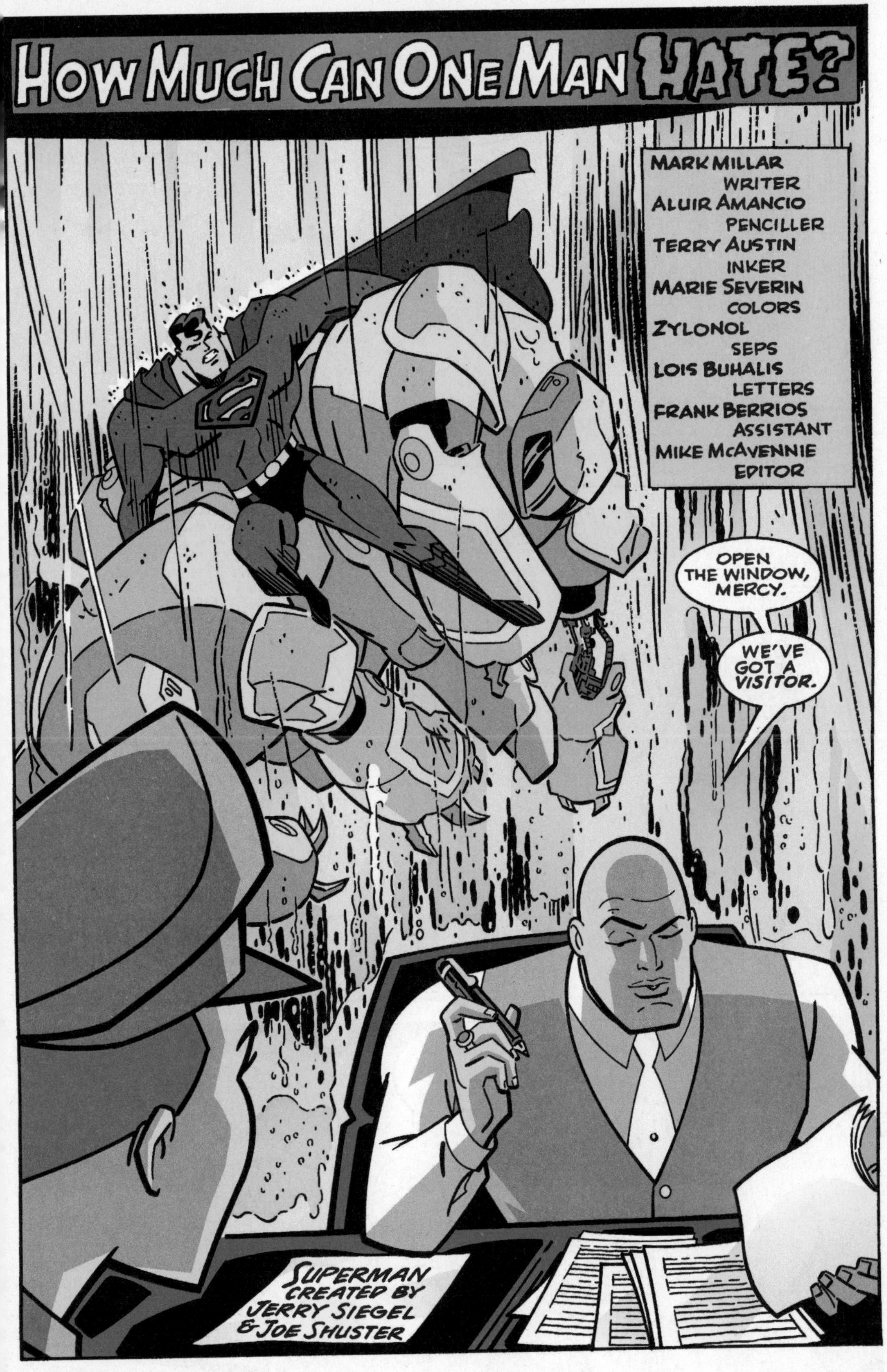
HOW MUCH CAN ONE MAN HATE?
MARK MILLAR WRITER
ALUIR AMANCIO PENCILLER
TERRY AUSTIN INKER
MARIE SEVERIN COLORS
ZYLONOL SEPS
LOIS BUHALIS LETTERS
FRANK BERRIOS ASSISTANT
MIKE McAVENNIE EDITOR
OPEN THE WINDOW, MERCY.
WE'VE GOT A VISITOR.
SUPERMAN CREATED BY JERRY SIEGEL & JOE SHUSTER

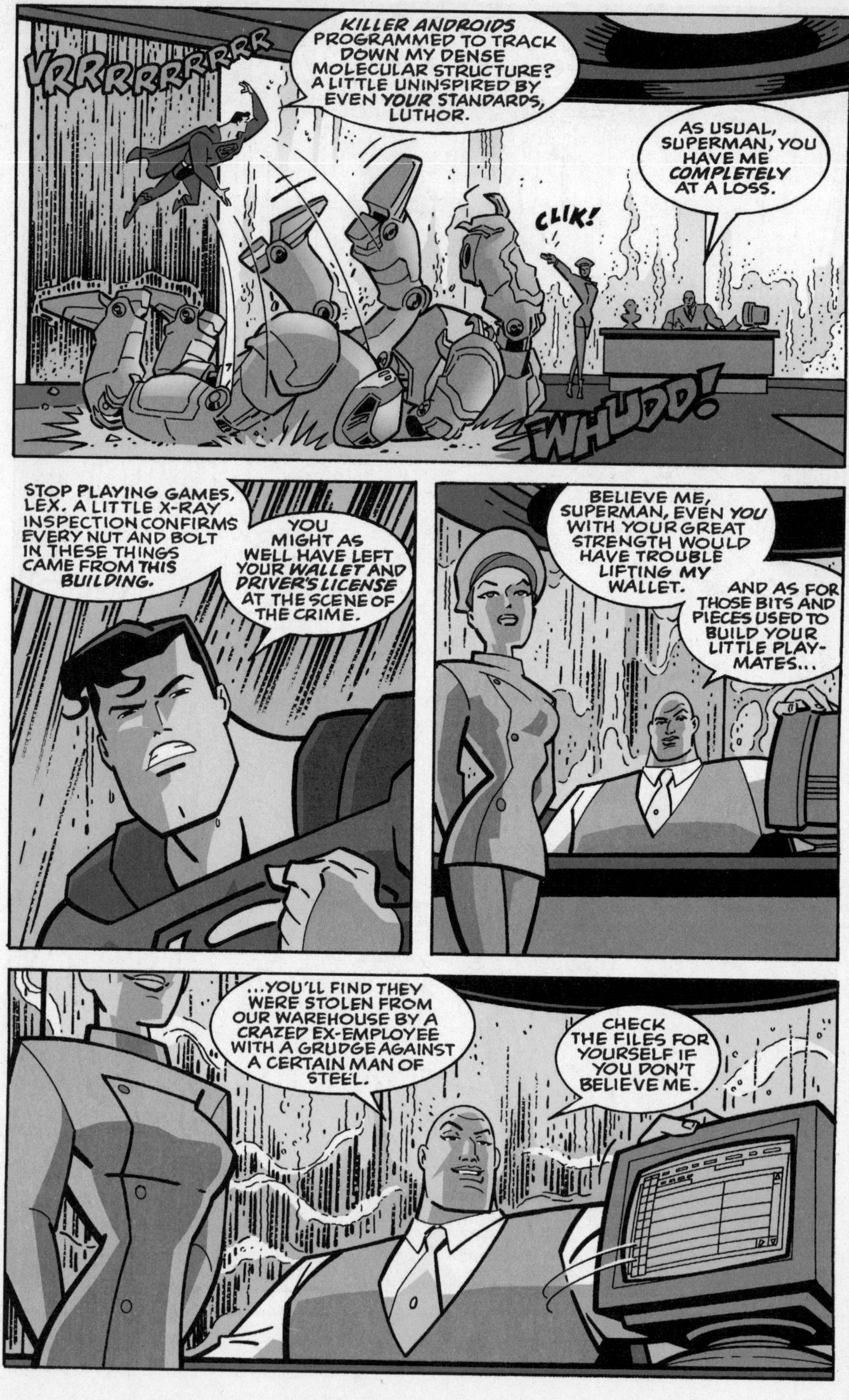
VRRRRRRRRR
KILLER ANDROIDS PROGRAMMED TO TRACK DOWN MY DENSE MOLECULAR STRUCTURE? A LITTLE UNINSPIRED BY EVEN YOUR STANDARDS, LUTHOR.
CLIK!
AS USUAL, SUPERMAN, YOU HAVE ME COMPLETELY AT A LOSS.
WHUDD!
STOP PLAYING GAMES, LEX. A LITTLE X-RAY INSPECTION CONFIRMS EVERY NUT AND BOLT IN THESE THINGS CAME FROM THIS BUILDING.
YOU MIGHT AS WELL HAVE LEFT YOUR WALLET AND DRIVER'S LICENSE AT THE SCENE OF THE CRIME.
BELIEVE ME, SUPERMAN, EVEN YOU WITH YOUR GREAT STRENGTH WOULD HAVE TROUBLE LIFTING MY WALLET.
AND AS FOR THOSE BITS AND PIECES USED TO BUILD YOUR LITTLE PLAYMATES...
...YOU'LL FIND THEY WERE STOLEN FROM OUR WAREHOUSE BY A CRAZED EX-EMPLOYEE WITH A GRUDGE AGAINST A CERTAIN MAN OF STEEL.
CHECK THE FILES FOR YOURSELF IF YOU DON'T BELIEVE ME.

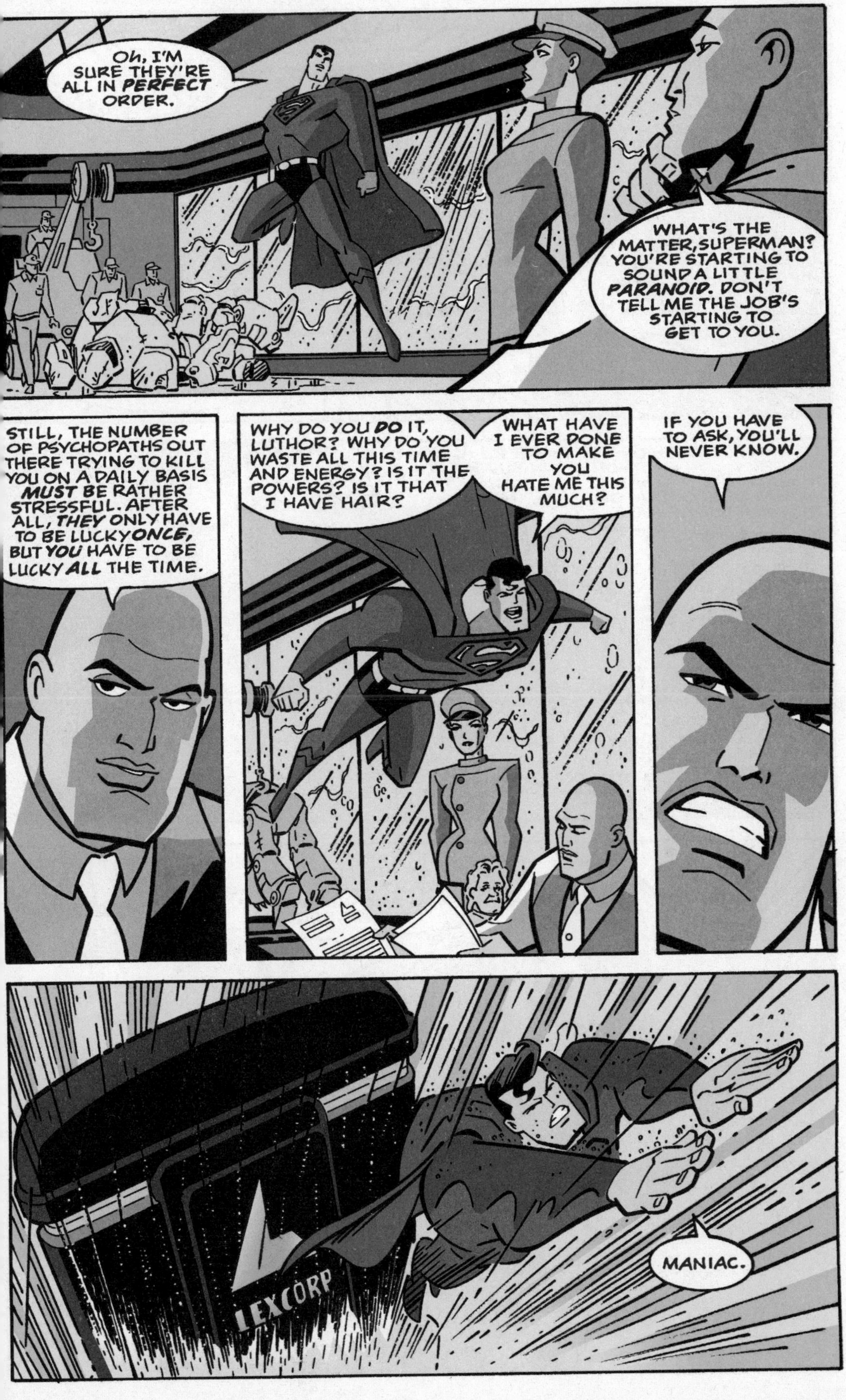

Oh, I'M SURE THEY'RE ALL IN PERFECT ORDER.
WHAT'S THE MATTER, SUPERMAN? YOU'RE STARTING TO SOUND A LITTLE PARANOID. DON'T TELL ME THE JOB'S STARTING TO GET TO YOU.
STILL, THE NUMBER OF PSYCHOPATHS OUT THERE TRYING TO KILL YOU ON A DAILY BASIS MUST BE RATHER STRESSFUL. AFTER ALL, THEY ONLY HAVE TO BE LUCKY ONCE, BUT YOU HAVE TO BE LUCKY ALL THE TIME.
WHY DO YOU DO IT, LUTHOR? WHY DO YOU WASTE ALL THIS TIME AND ENERGY? IS IT THE POWERS? IS IT THAT I HAVE HAIR?
WHAT HAVE I EVER DONE TO MAKE YOU HATE ME THIS MUCH?
IF YOU HAVE TO ASK, YOU'LL NEVER KNOW.
MANIAC.
LEXCORP

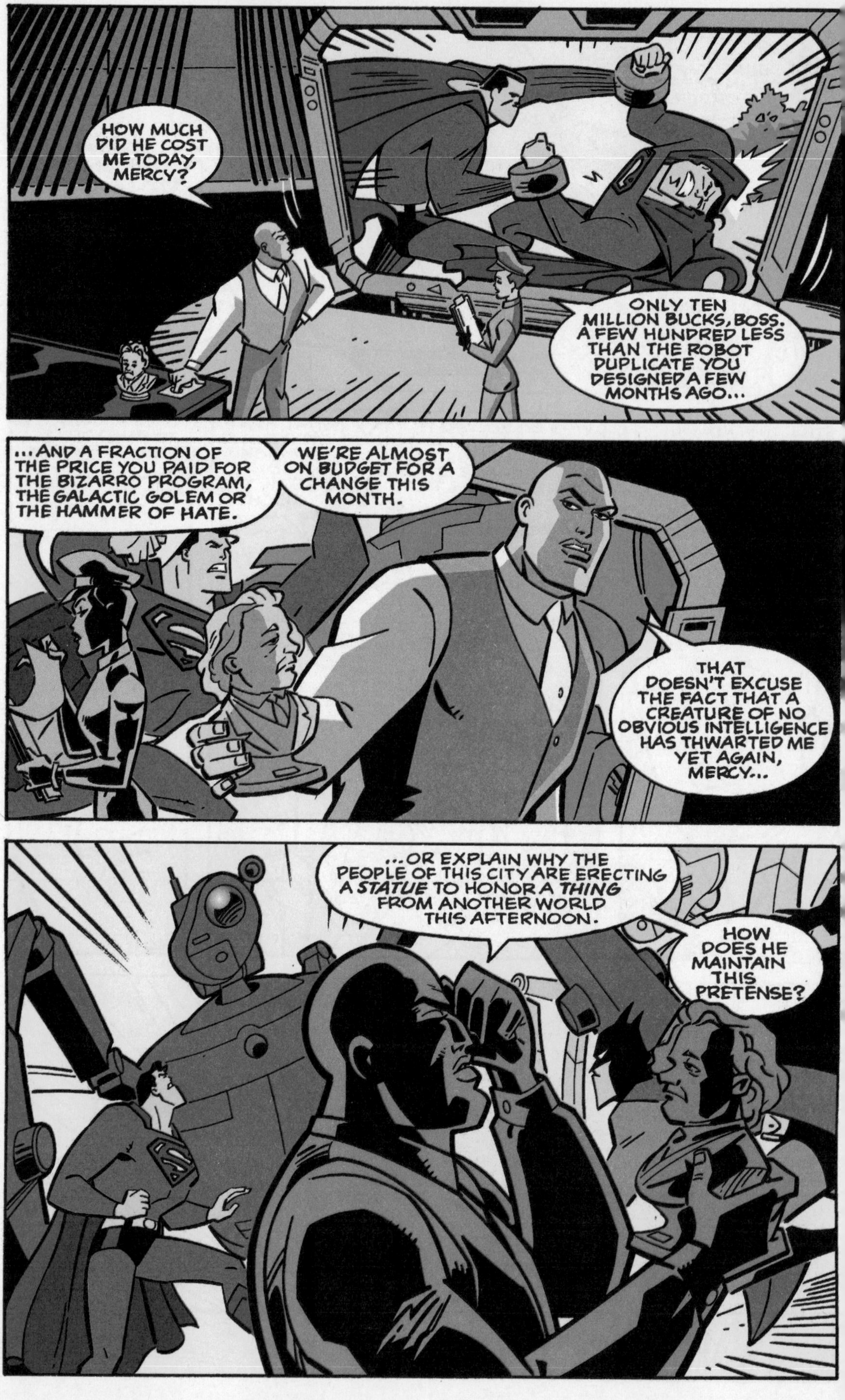
HOW MUCH DID HE COST ME TODAY, MERCY?
ONLY TEN MILLION BUCKS, BOSS. A FEW HUNDRED LESS THAN THE ROBOT DUPLICATE YOU DESIGNED A FEW MONTHS AGO...
...AND A FRACTION OF THE PRICE YOU PAID FOR THE BIZARRO PROGRAM, THE GALACTIC GOLEM OR THE HAMMER OF HATE.
WE'RE ALMOST ON BUDGET FOR A CHANGE THIS MONTH.
THAT DOESN'T EXCUSE THE FACT THAT A CREATURE OF NO OBVIOUS INTELLIGENCE HAS THWARTED ME YET AGAIN, MERCY...
...OR EXPLAIN WHY THE PEOPLE OF THIS CITY ARE ERECTING A *STATUE* TO HONOR A *THING* FROM ANOTHER WORLD THIS AFTERNOON.
HOW DOES HE MAINTAIN THIS PRETENSE?

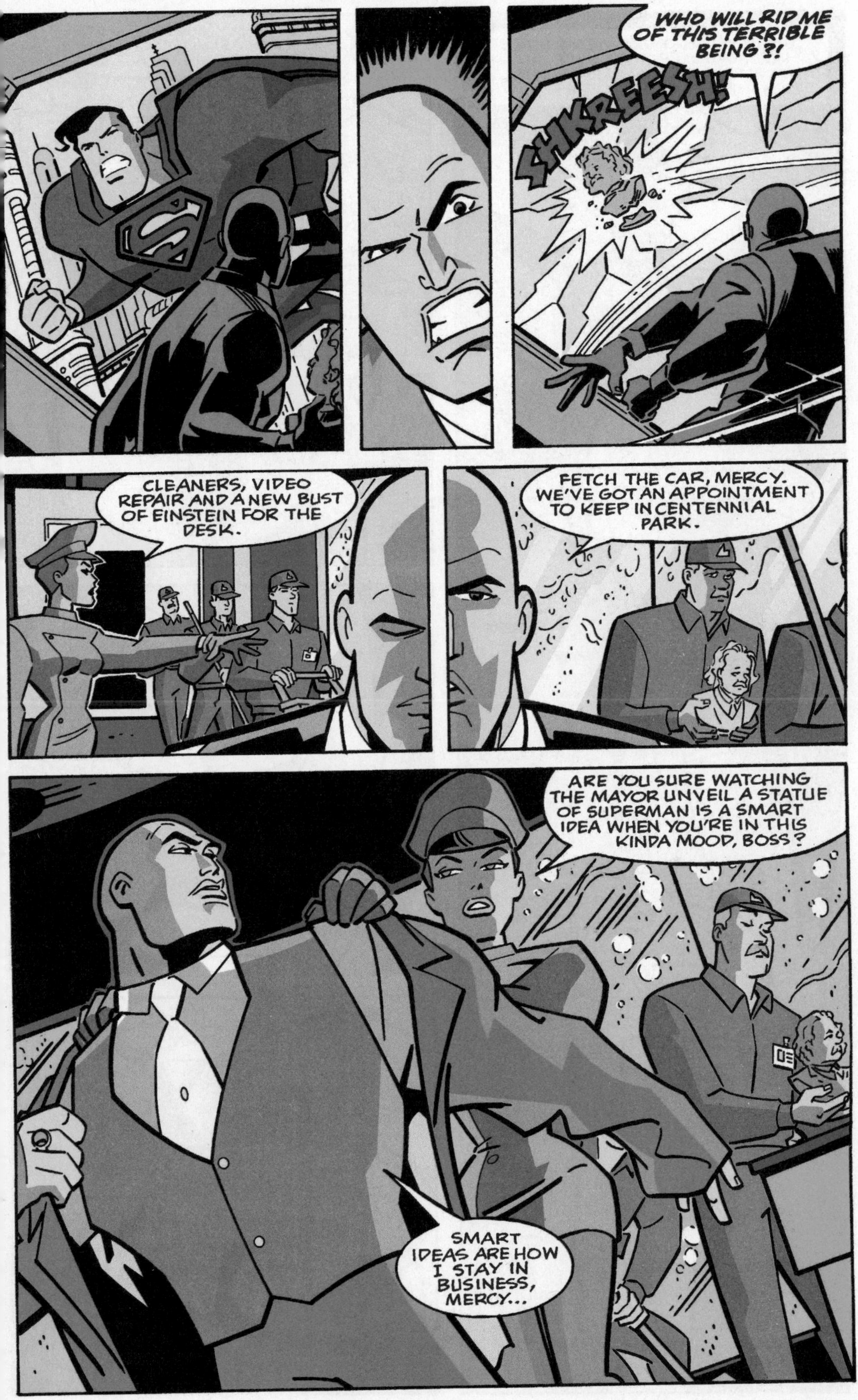
WHO WILL RID ME OF THIS TERRIBLE BEING ?!
SHKREESH!
CLEANERS, VIDEO REPAIR AND A NEW BUST OF EINSTEIN FOR THE DESK.
FETCH THE CAR, MERCY. WE'VE GOT AN APPOINTMENT TO KEEP IN CENTENNIAL PARK.
ARE YOU SURE WATCHING THE MAYOR UNVEIL A STATUE OF SUPERMAN IS A SMART IDEA WHEN YOU'RE IN THIS KINDA MOOD, BOSS?
SMART IDEAS ARE HOW I STAY IN BUSINESS, MERCY...

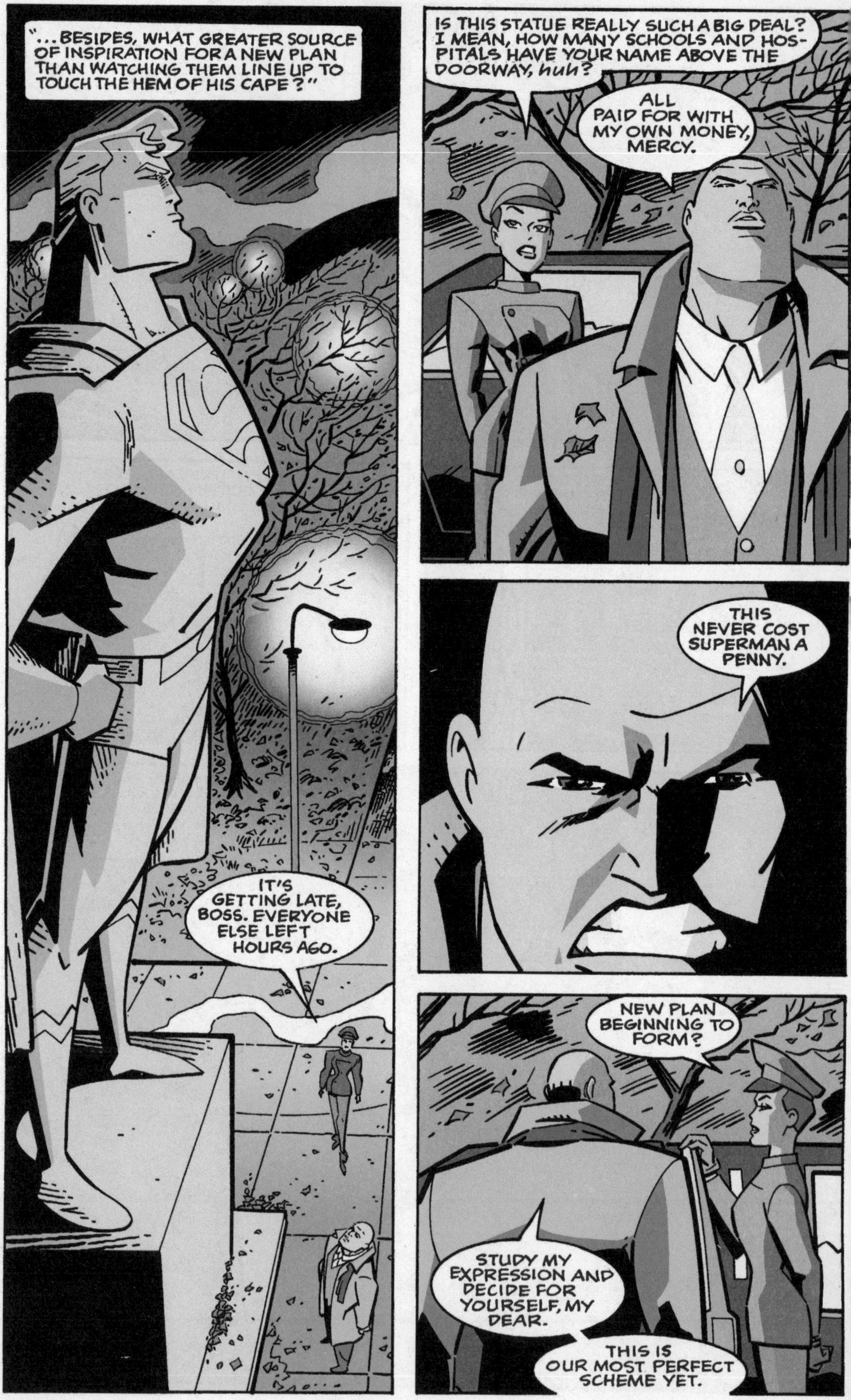
"...BESIDES, WHAT GREATER SOURCE OF INSPIRATION FOR A NEW PLAN THAN WATCHING THEM LINE UP TO TOUCH THE HEM OF HIS CAPE?"
IT'S GETTING LATE, BOSS. EVERYONE ELSE LEFT HOURS AGO.
IS THIS STATUE REALLY SUCH A BIG DEAL? I MEAN, HOW MANY SCHOOLS AND HOSPITALS HAVE YOUR NAME ABOVE THE DOORWAY, huh?
ALL PAID FOR WITH MY OWN MONEY, MERCY.
THIS NEVER COST SUPERMAN A PENNY.
NEW PLAN BEGINNING TO FORM?
STUDY MY EXPRESSION AND DECIDE FOR YOURSELF, MY DEAR.
THIS IS OUR MOST PERFECT SCHEME YET.

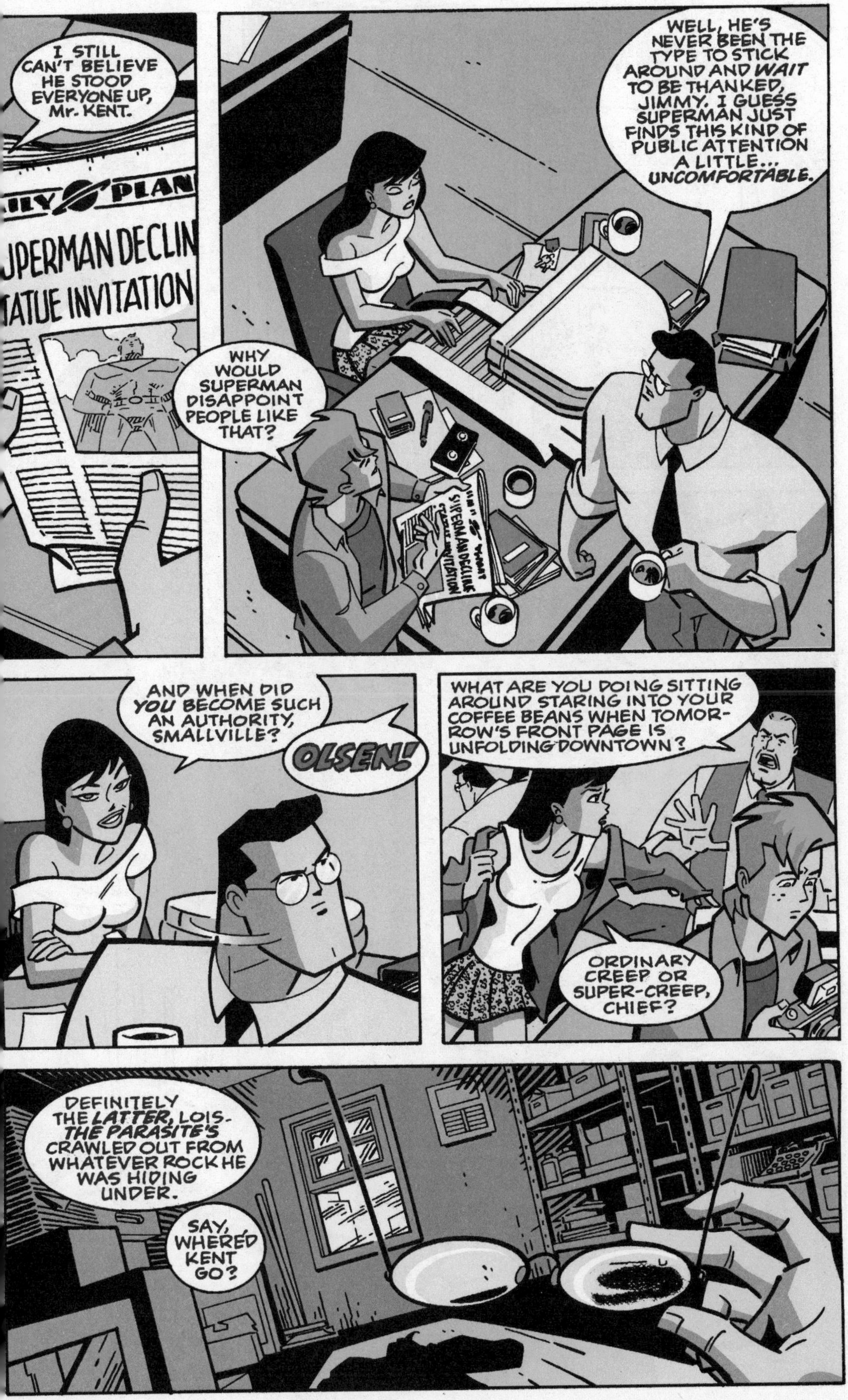
I STILL CAN'T BELIEVE HE STOOD EVERYONE UP, Mr. KENT.
WELL, HE'S NEVER BEEN THE TYPE TO STICK AROUND AND *WAIT* TO BE THANKED, JIMMY. I GUESS SUPERMAN JUST FINDS THIS KIND OF PUBLIC ATTENTION A LITTLE... *UNCOMFORTABLE.*
WHY WOULD SUPERMAN DISAPPOINT PEOPLE LIKE THAT?
AND WHEN DID *YOU* BECOME SUCH AN AUTHORITY, SMALLVILLE?
OLSEN!
WHAT ARE YOU DOING SITTING AROUND STARING INTO YOUR COFFEE BEANS WHEN TOMORROW'S FRONT PAGE IS UNFOLDING DOWNTOWN?
ORDINARY CREEP OR SUPER-CREEP, CHIEF?
DEFINITELY THE *LATTER*, LOIS. *THE PARASITE'S* CRAWLED OUT FROM WHATEVER ROCK HE WAS HIDING UNDER.
SAY, WHERE'D KENT GO?

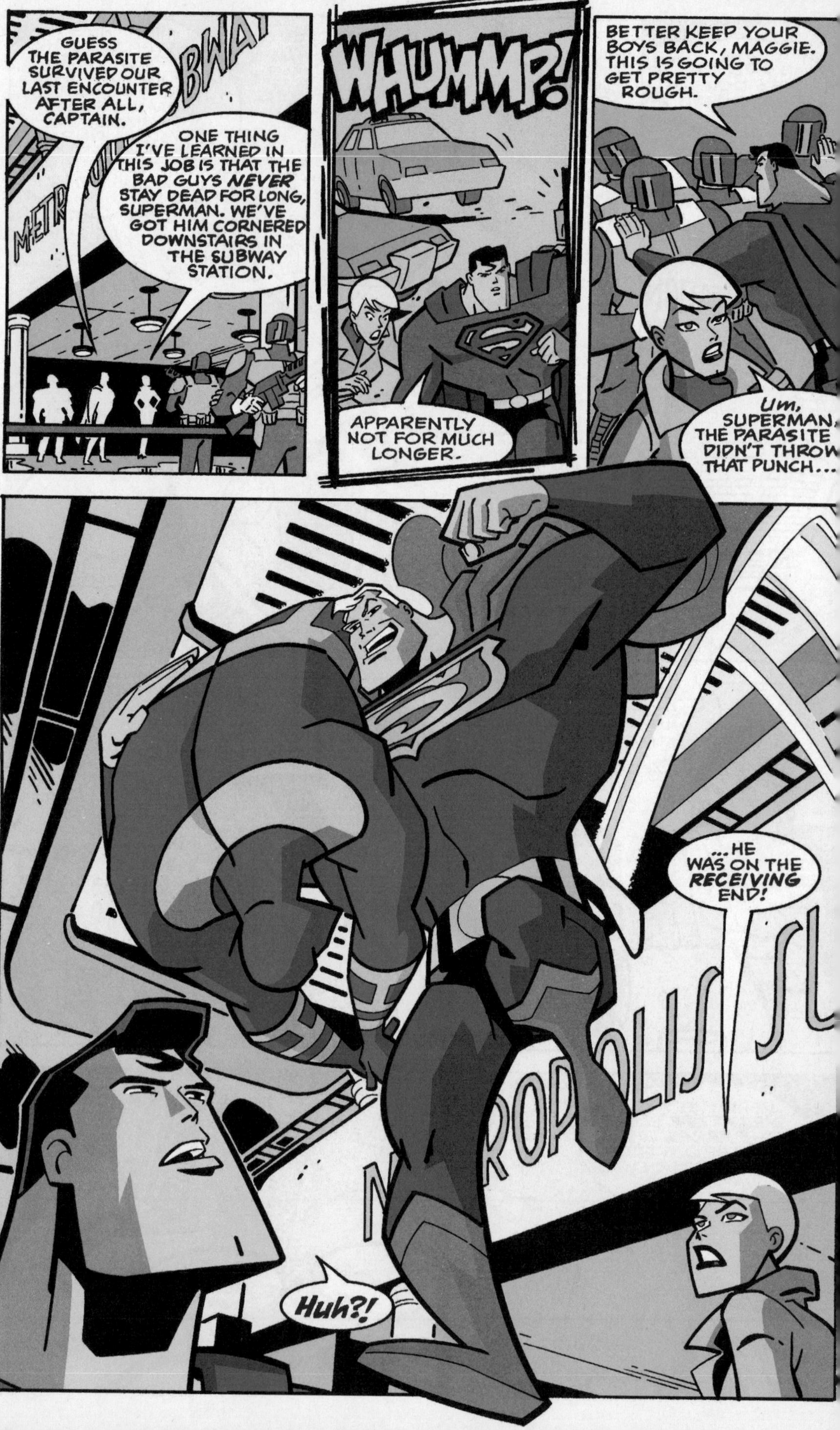

GUESS THE PARASITE SURVIVED OUR LAST ENCOUNTER AFTER ALL, CAPTAIN.
ONE THING I'VE LEARNED IN THIS JOB IS THAT THE BAD GUYS NEVER STAY DEAD FOR LONG, SUPERMAN. WE'VE GOT HIM CORNERED DOWNSTAIRS IN THE SUBWAY STATION.
WHUMMP!
APPARENTLY NOT FOR MUCH LONGER.
BETTER KEEP YOUR BOYS BACK, MAGGIE. THIS IS GOING TO GET PRETTY ROUGH.
Um, SUPERMAN, THE PARASITE DIDN'T THROW THAT PUNCH...
...HE WAS ON THE RECEIVING END!
Huh?!

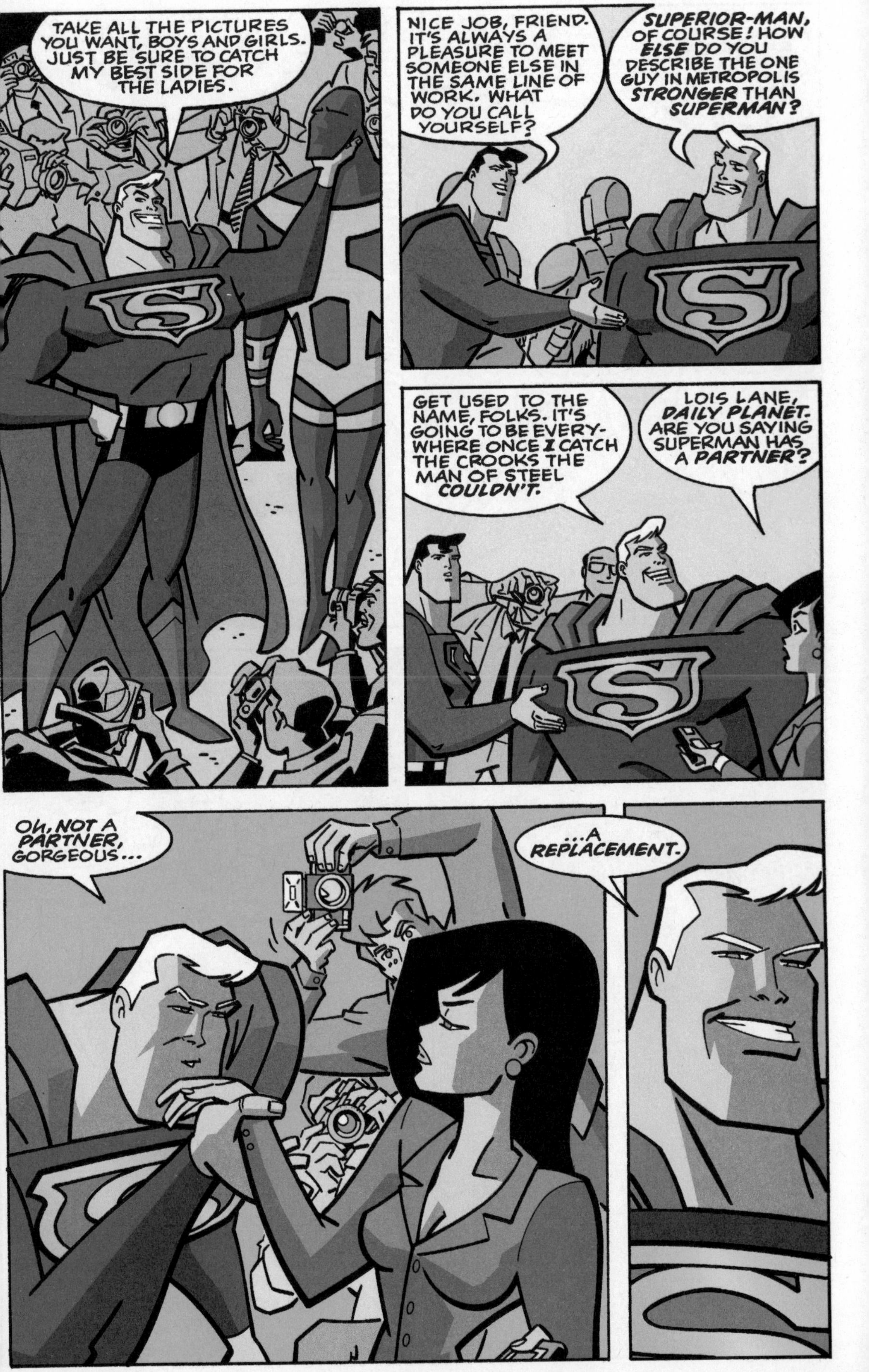
TAKE ALL THE PICTURES YOU WANT, BOYS AND GIRLS. JUST BE SURE TO CATCH MY BEST SIDE FOR THE LADIES.
NICE JOB, FRIEND. IT'S ALWAYS A PLEASURE TO MEET SOMEONE ELSE IN THE SAME LINE OF WORK. WHAT DO YOU CALL YOURSELF?
SUPERIOR-MAN, OF COURSE! HOW ELSE DO YOU DESCRIBE THE ONE GUY IN METROPOLIS STRONGER THAN SUPERMAN?
GET USED TO THE NAME, FOLKS. IT'S GOING TO BE EVERYWHERE ONCE I CATCH THE CROOKS THE MAN OF STEEL COULDN'T.
LOIS LANE, DAILY PLANET. ARE YOU SAYING SUPERMAN HAS A PARTNER?
OH, NOT A PARTNER, GORGEOUS...
...A REPLACEMENT.

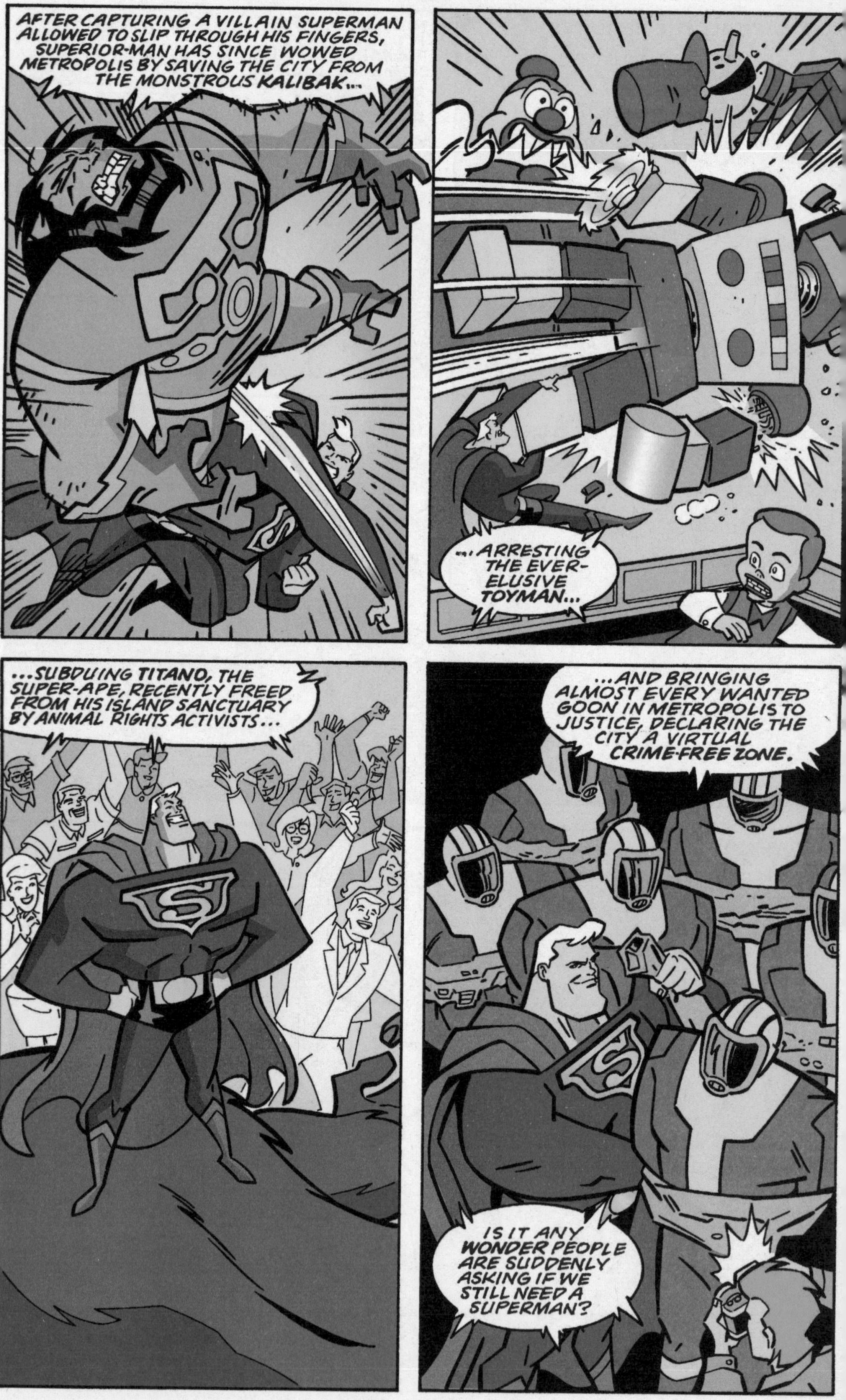
AFTER CAPTURING A VILLAIN SUPERMAN ALLOWED TO SLIP THROUGH HIS FINGERS, SUPERIOR-MAN HAS SINCE WOWED METROPOLIS BY SAVING THE CITY FROM THE MONSTROUS KALIBAK...
...ARRESTING THE EVER-ELUSIVE TOYMAN...
...SUBDUING TITANO, THE SUPER-APE, RECENTLY FREED FROM HIS ISLAND SANCTUARY BY ANIMAL RIGHTS ACTIVISTS...
...AND BRINGING ALMOST EVERY WANTED GOON IN METROPOLIS TO JUSTICE, DECLARING THE CITY A VIRTUAL CRIME-FREE ZONE.
IS IT ANY WONDER PEOPLE ARE SUDDENLY ASKING IF WE STILL NEED A SUPERMAN?

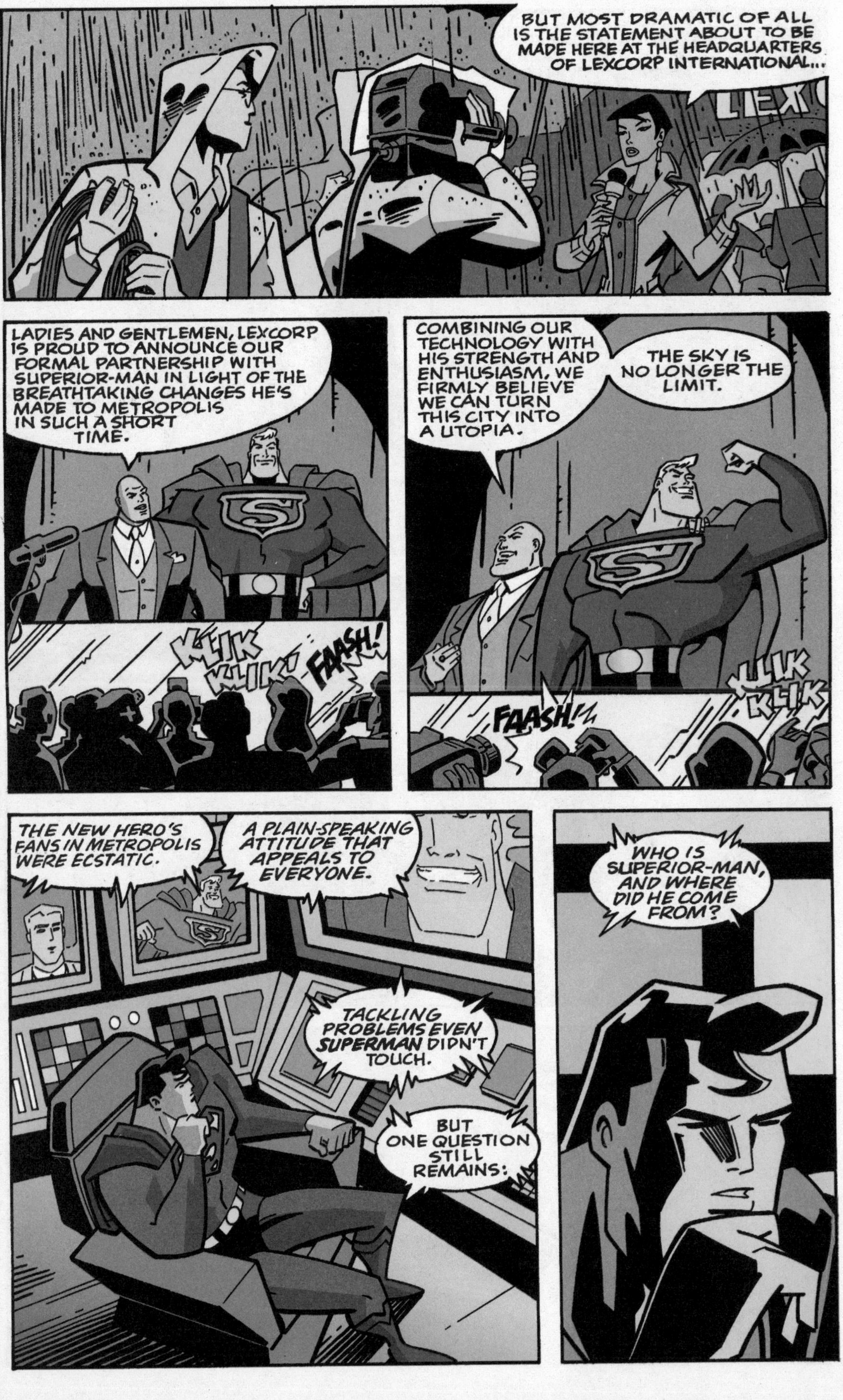
BUT MOST DRAMATIC OF ALL IS THE STATEMENT ABOUT TO BE MADE HERE AT THE HEADQUARTERS OF LEXCORP INTERNATIONAL...
LADIES AND GENTLEMEN, LEXCORP IS PROUD TO ANNOUNCE OUR FORMAL PARTNERSHIP WITH SUPERIOR-MAN IN LIGHT OF THE BREATHTAKING CHANGES HE'S MADE TO METROPOLIS IN SUCH A SHORT TIME.
KLIK KLIK!
FAASH!
COMBINING OUR TECHNOLOGY WITH HIS STRENGTH AND ENTHUSIASM, WE FIRMLY BELIEVE WE CAN TURN THIS CITY INTO A UTOPIA.
THE SKY IS NO LONGER THE LIMIT.
FAASH!
KLIK KLIK
THE NEW HERO'S FANS IN METROPOLIS WERE ECSTATIC.
A PLAIN-SPEAKING ATTITUDE THAT APPEALS TO EVERYONE.
TACKLING PROBLEMS EVEN SUPERMAN DIDN'T TOUCH.
BUT ONE QUESTION STILL REMAINS:
WHO IS SUPERIOR-MAN, AND WHERE DID HE COME FROM?

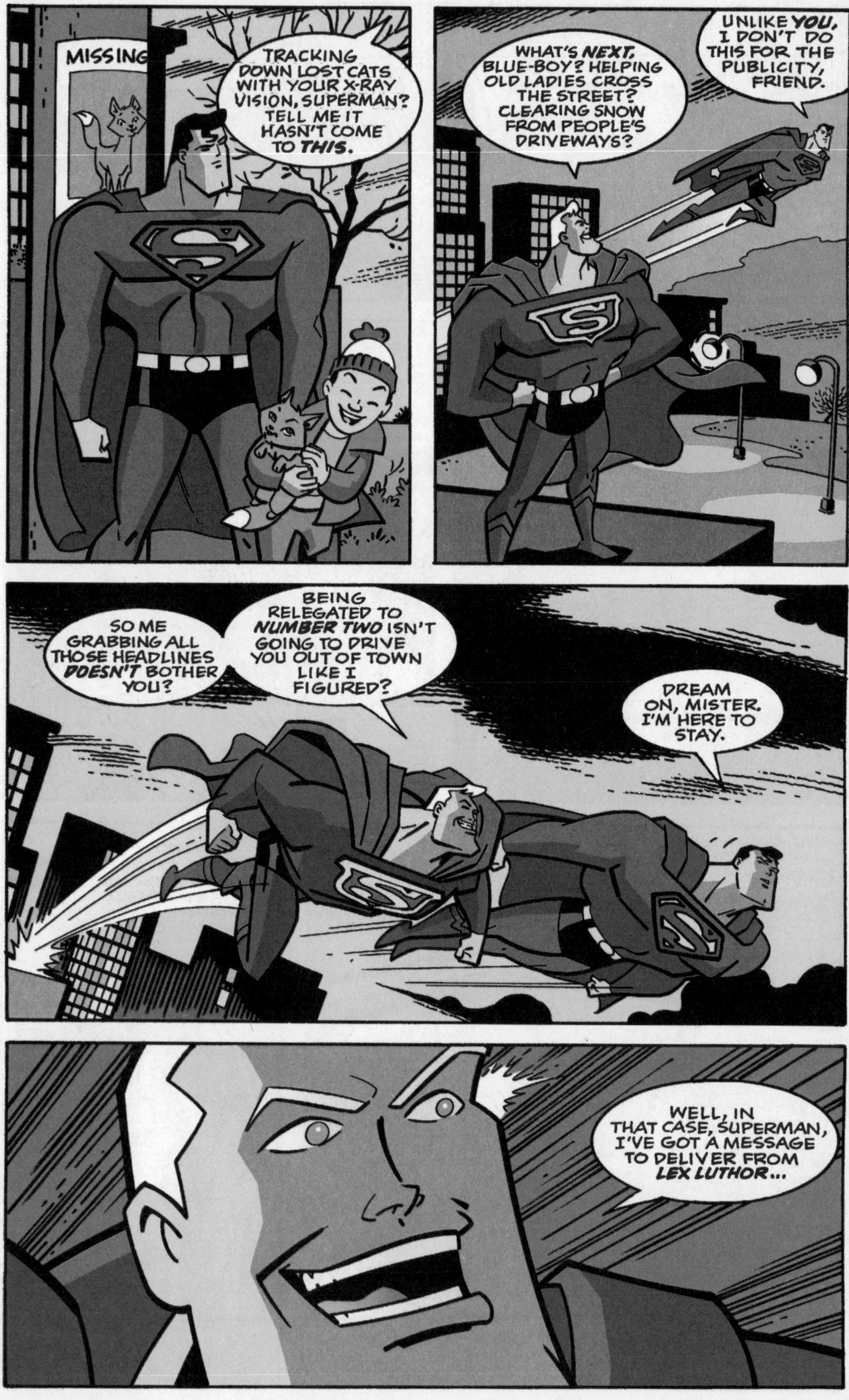
MISSING
TRACKING DOWN LOST CATS WITH YOUR X-RAY VISION, SUPERMAN? TELL ME IT HASN'T COME TO THIS.
WHAT'S NEXT, BLUE-BOY? HELPING OLD LADIES CROSS THE STREET? CLEARING SNOW FROM PEOPLE'S DRIVEWAYS?
UNLIKE YOU, I DON'T DO THIS FOR THE PUBLICITY, FRIEND.
SO ME GRABBING ALL THOSE HEADLINES DOESN'T BOTHER YOU?
BEING RELEGATED TO NUMBER TWO ISN'T GOING TO DRIVE YOU OUT OF TOWN LIKE I FIGURED?
DREAM ON, MISTER. I'M HERE TO STAY.
WELL, IN THAT CASE, SUPERMAN, I'VE GOT A MESSAGE TO DELIVER FROM LEX LUTHOR...

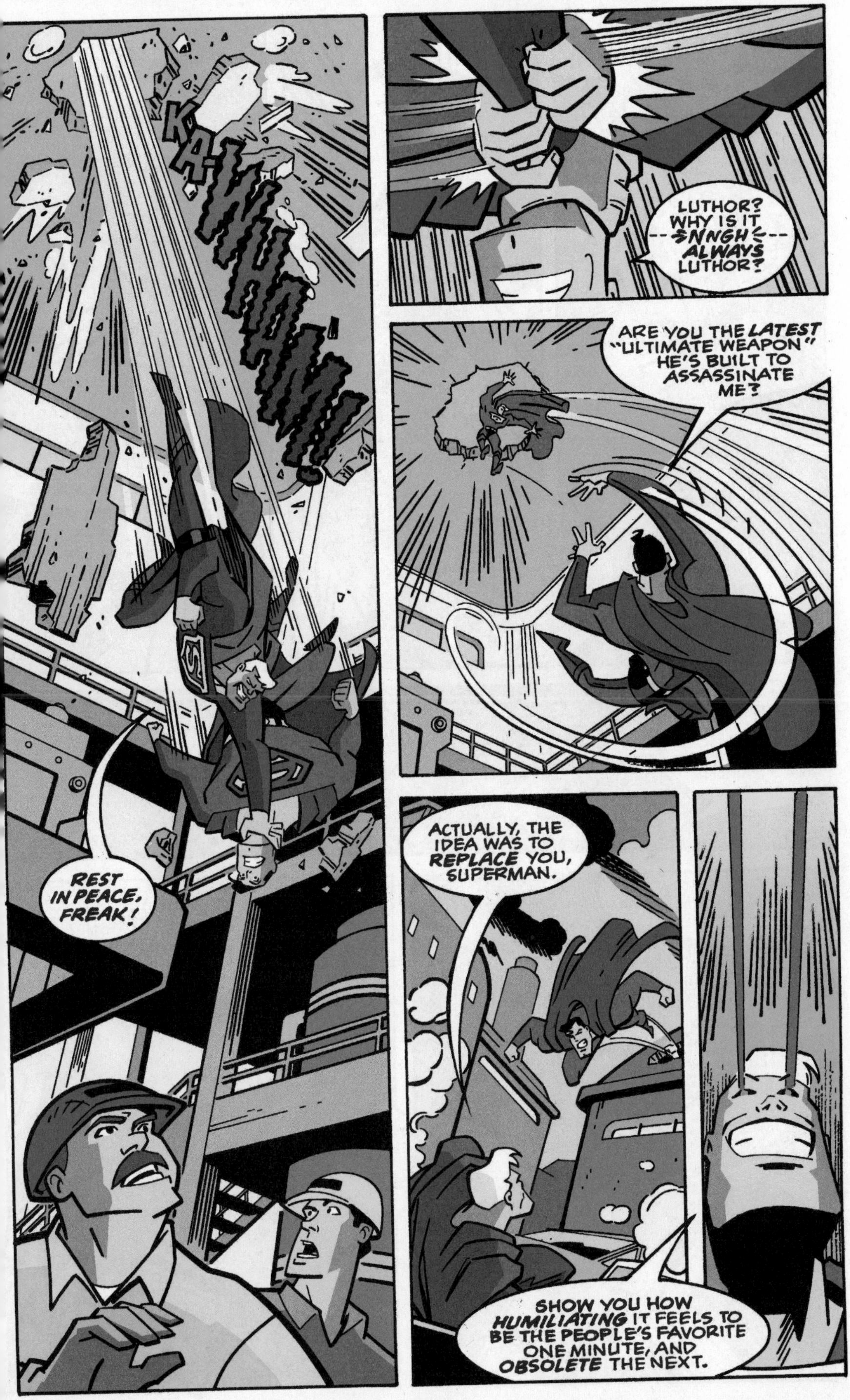
KA-WHOM!!
REST IN PEACE, FREAK!
LUTHOR? WHY IS IT --NNGH-- ALWAYS LUTHOR?
ARE YOU THE LATEST "ULTIMATE WEAPON" HE'S BUILT TO ASSASSINATE ME?
ACTUALLY, THE IDEA WAS TO REPLACE YOU, SUPERMAN.
SHOW YOU HOW HUMILIATING IT FEELS TO BE THE PEOPLE'S FAVORITE ONE MINUTE, AND OBSOLETE THE NEXT.

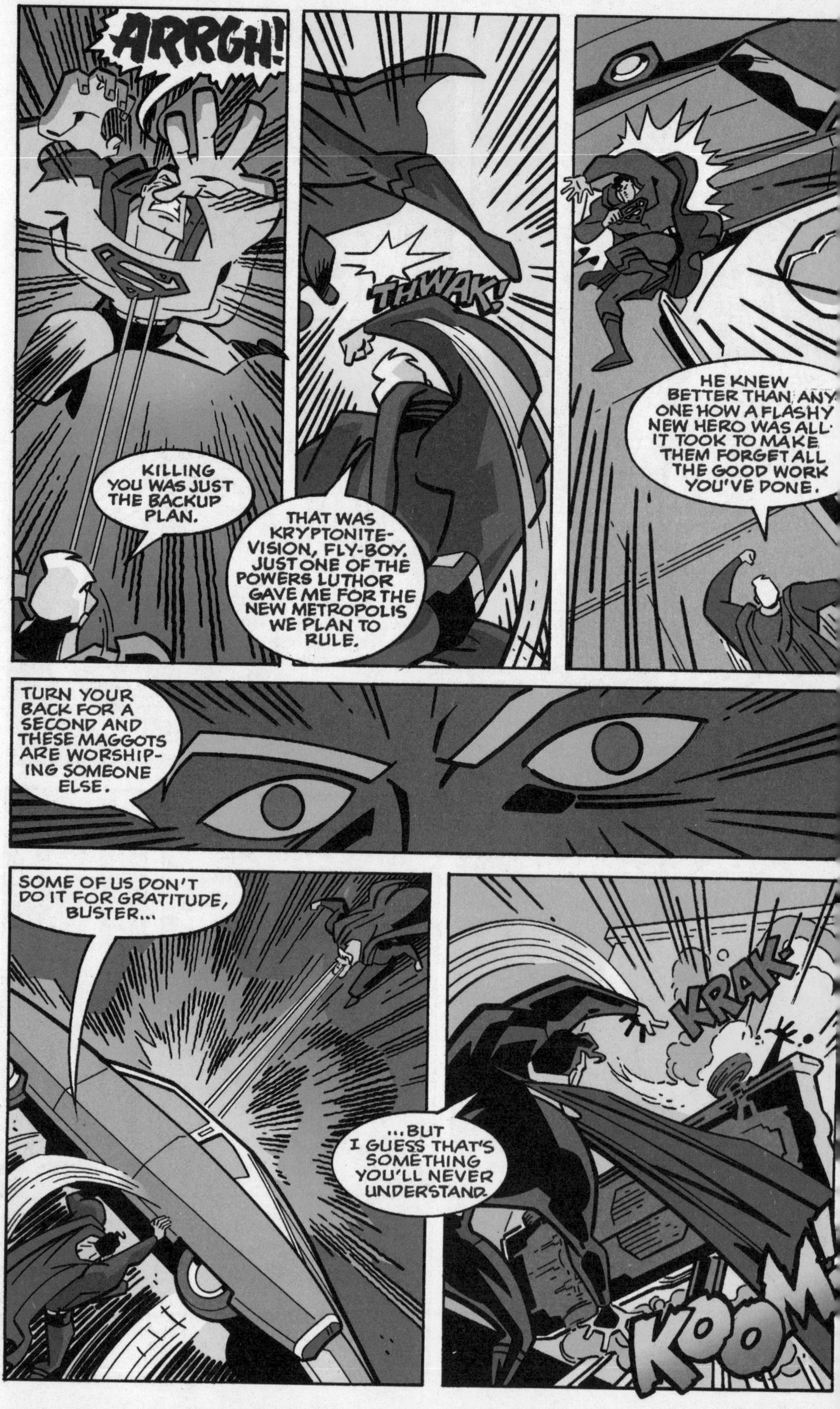
ARRGH!
KILLING YOU WAS JUST THE BACKUP PLAN.
THWAK!
THAT WAS KRYPTONITE-VISION, FLY-BOY. JUST ONE OF THE POWERS LUTHOR GAVE ME FOR THE NEW METROPOLIS WE PLAN TO RULE.
HE KNEW BETTER THAN ANY ONE HOW A FLASHY NEW HERO WAS ALL IT TOOK TO MAKE THEM FORGET ALL THE GOOD WORK YOU'VE DONE.
TURN YOUR BACK FOR A SECOND AND THESE MAGGOTS ARE WORSHIP-ING SOMEONE ELSE.
SOME OF US DON'T DO IT FOR GRATITUDE, BUSTER...
KRAK!
...BUT I GUESS THAT'S SOMETHING YOU'LL NEVER UNDERSTAND.
KOOM

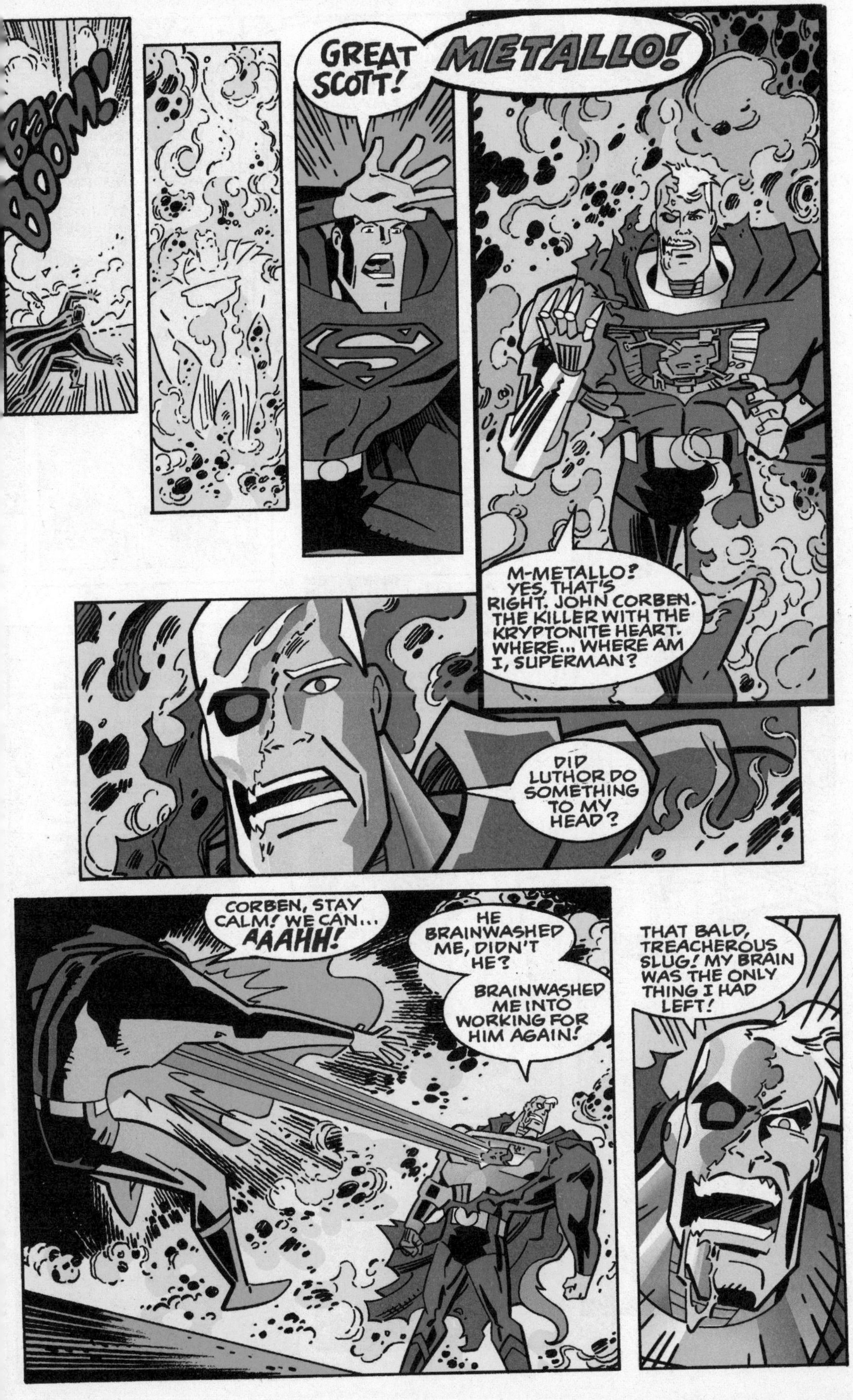
BA-BOOM!
GREAT SCOTT!
METALLO!
M-METALLO? YES, THAT'S RIGHT. JOHN CORBEN. THE KILLER WITH THE KRYPTONITE HEART. WHERE... WHERE AM I, SUPERMAN?
DID LUTHOR DO SOMETHING TO MY HEAD?
CORBEN, STAY CALM! WE CAN... AAAHH!
HE BRAINWASHED ME, DIDN'T HE?
BRAINWASHED ME INTO WORKING FOR HIM AGAIN!
THAT BALD, TREACHEROUS SLUG! MY BRAIN WAS THE ONLY THING I HAD LEFT!

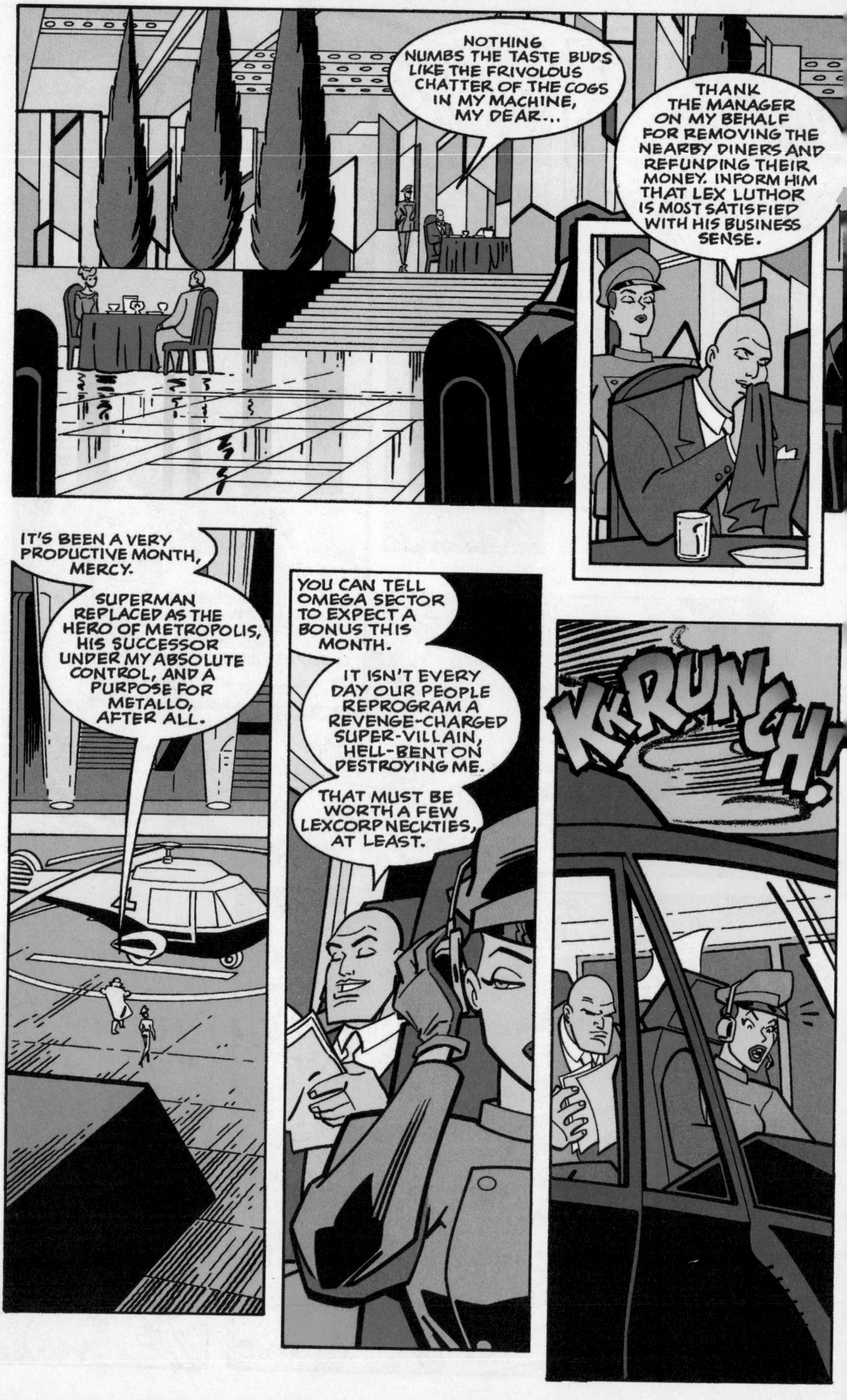
NOTHING NUMBS THE TASTE BUDS LIKE THE FRIVOLOUS CHATTER OF THE COGS IN MY MACHINE, MY DEAR...
THANK THE MANAGER ON MY BEHALF FOR REMOVING THE NEARBY DINERS AND REFUNDING THEIR MONEY. INFORM HIM THAT LEX LUTHOR IS MOST SATISFIED WITH HIS BUSINESS SENSE.
IT'S BEEN A VERY PRODUCTIVE MONTH, MERCY.
SUPERMAN REPLACED AS THE HERO OF METROPOLIS, HIS SUCCESSOR UNDER MY ABSOLUTE CONTROL, AND A PURPOSE FOR METALLO, AFTER ALL.
YOU CAN TELL OMEGA SECTOR TO EXPECT A BONUS THIS MONTH.
IT ISN'T EVERY DAY OUR PEOPLE REPROGRAM A REVENGE-CHARGED SUPER-VILLAIN, HELL-BENT ON DESTROYING ME.
THAT MUST BE WORTH A FEW LEXCORP NECKTIES, AT LEAST.
K-RUNCH!

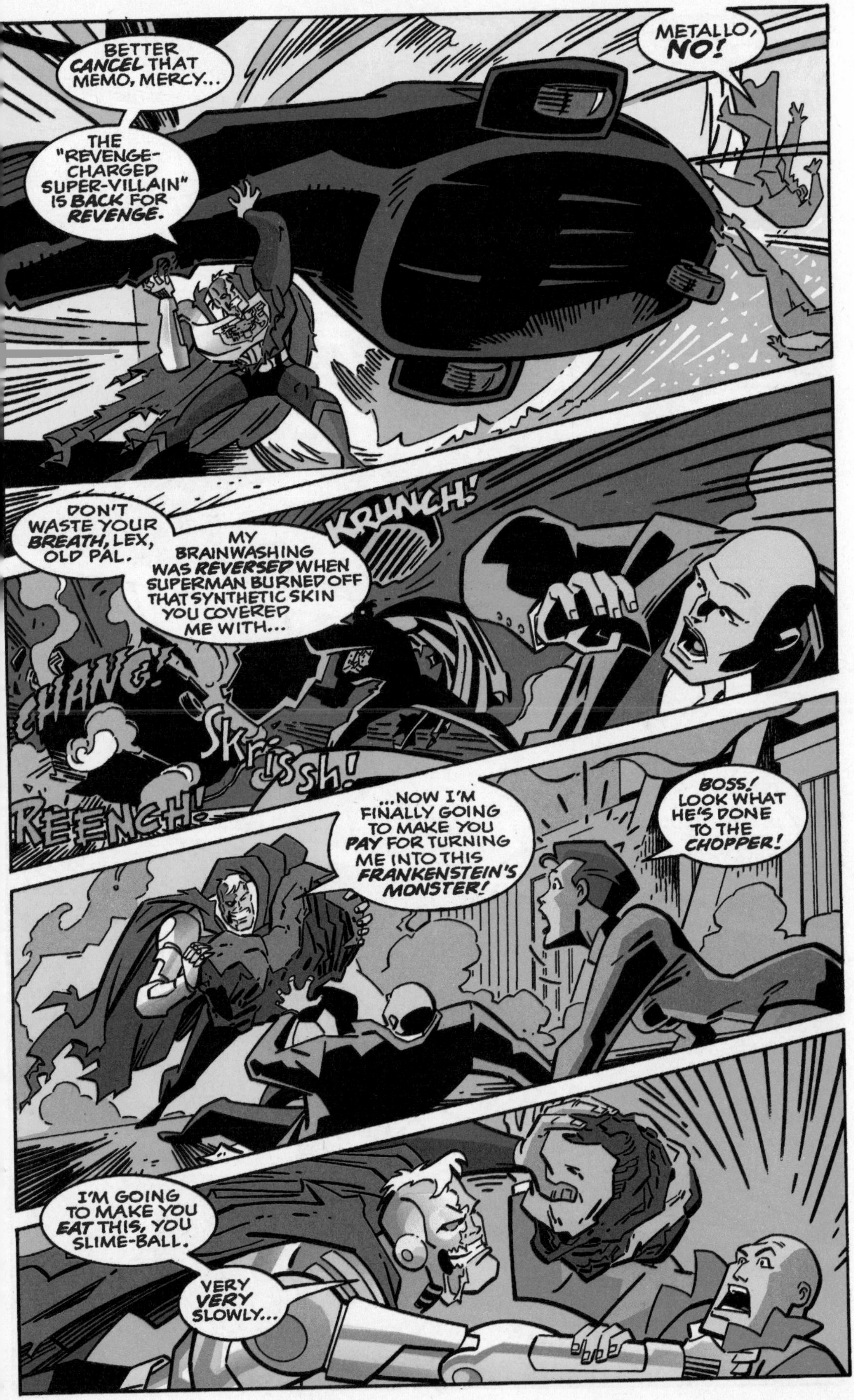
BETTER CANCEL THAT MEMO, MERCY...
THE "REVENGE-CHARGED SUPER-VILLAIN" IS BACK FOR REVENGE.
METALLO, NO!
DON'T WASTE YOUR BREATH, LEX, OLD PAL.
MY BRAINWASHING WAS REVERSED WHEN SUPERMAN BURNED OFF THAT SYNTHETIC SKIN YOU COVERED ME WITH...
KRUNCH!
CHANG!
SKRISSSH!
REENCH!
...NOW I'M FINALLY GOING TO MAKE YOU PAY FOR TURNING ME INTO THIS FRANKENSTEIN'S MONSTER!
BOSS! LOOK WHAT HE'S DONE TO THE CHOPPER!
I'M GOING TO MAKE YOU EAT THIS, YOU SLIME-BALL.
VERY VERY SLOWLY...

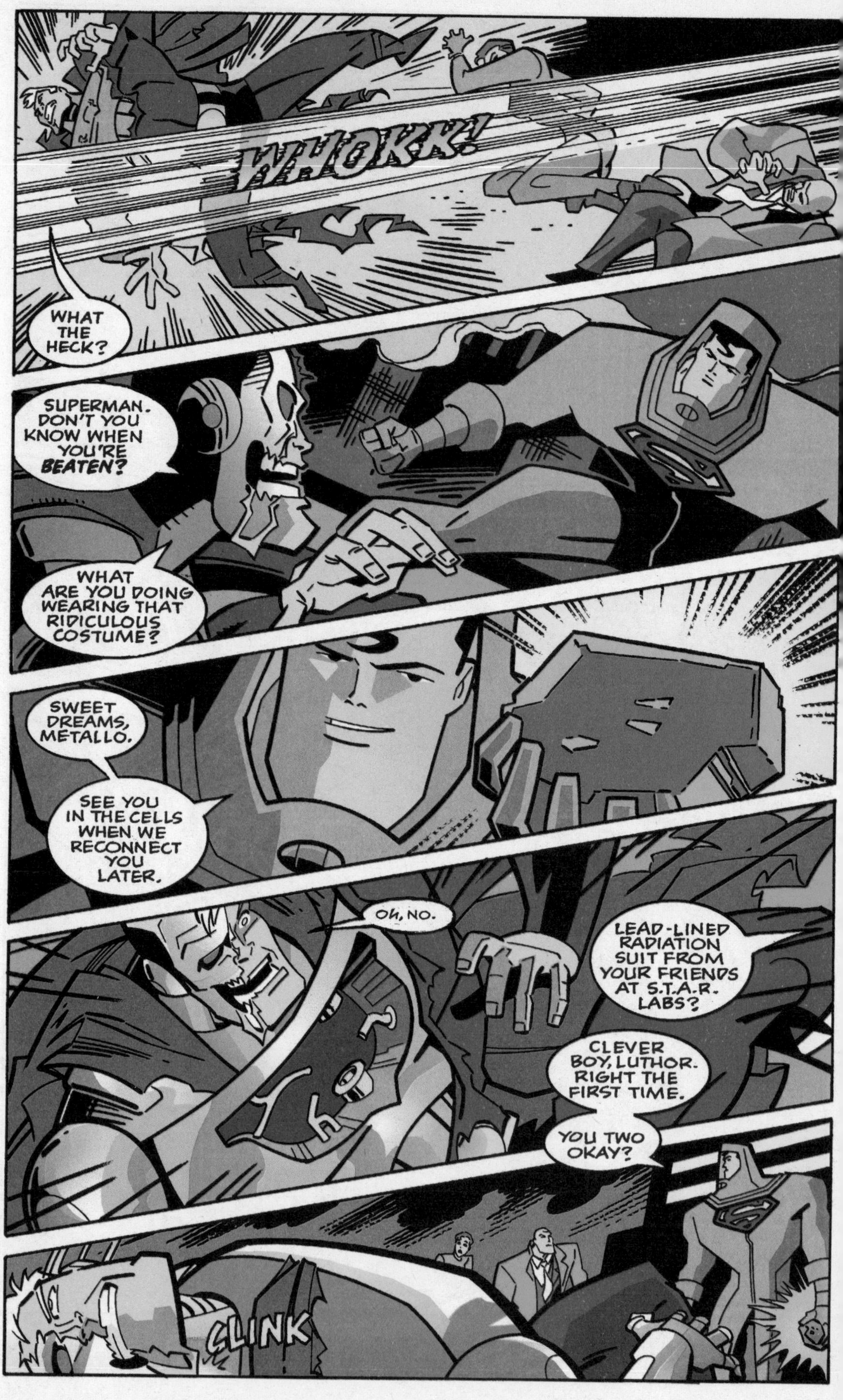
WHOKK!
WHAT THE HECK?
SUPERMAN. DON'T YOU KNOW WHEN YOU'RE BEATEN?
WHAT ARE YOU DOING WEARING THAT RIDICULOUS COSTUME?
SWEET DREAMS, METALLO.
SEE YOU IN THE CELLS WHEN WE RECONNECT YOU LATER.
OH, NO.
LEAD-LINED RADIATION SUIT FROM YOUR FRIENDS AT S.T.A.R. LABS?
CLEVER BOY, LUTHOR. RIGHT THE FIRST TIME.
YOU TWO OKAY?
CLINK

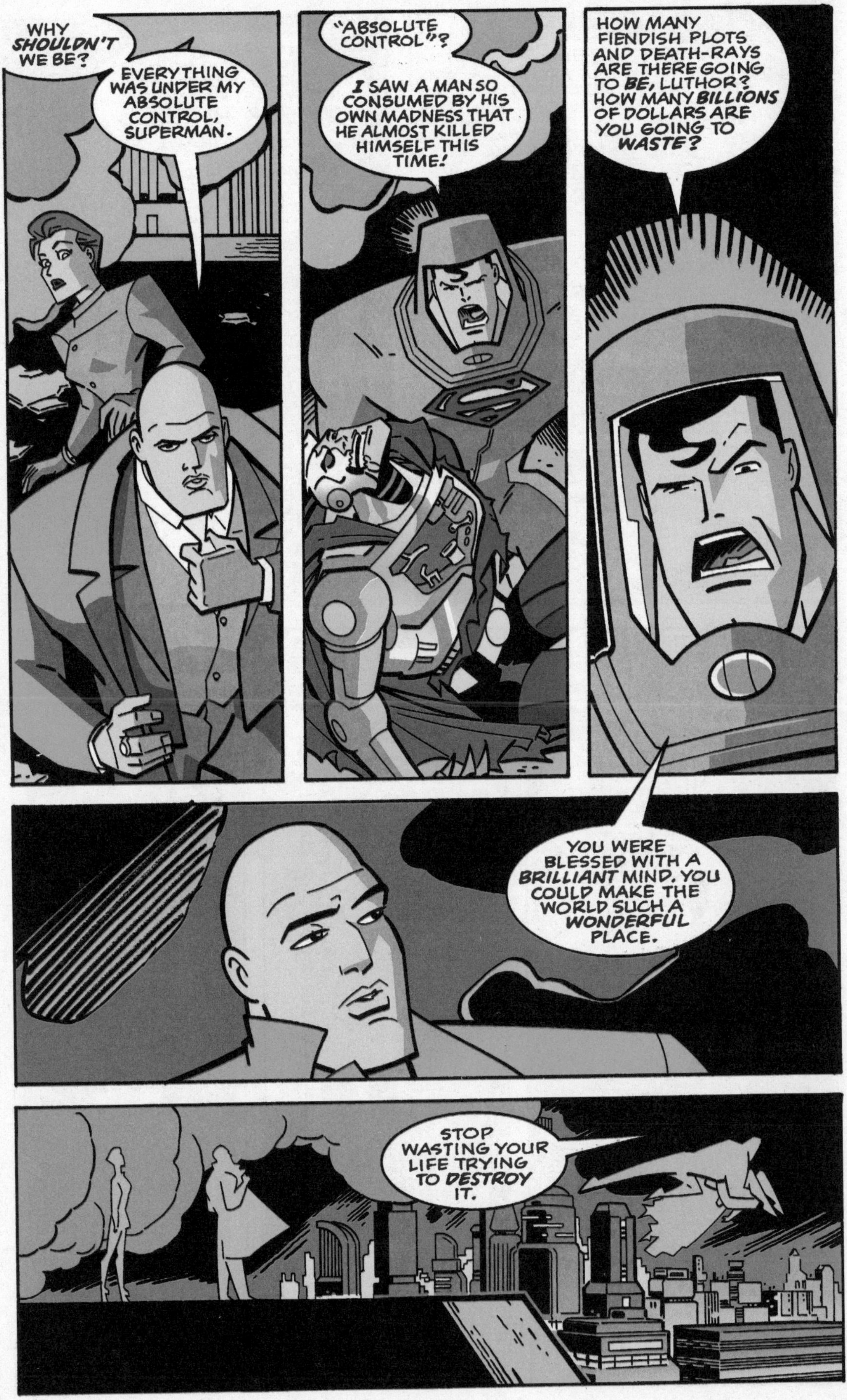
WHY *SHOULDN'T* WE BE?
EVERYTHING WAS UNDER MY ABSOLUTE CONTROL, SUPERMAN.
"ABSOLUTE CONTROL"?
I SAW A MAN SO CONSUMED BY HIS OWN MADNESS THAT HE ALMOST KILLED HIMSELF THIS TIME!
HOW MANY FIENDISH PLOTS AND DEATH-RAYS ARE THERE GOING TO *BE*, LUTHOR? HOW MANY *BILLIONS* OF DOLLARS ARE YOU GOING TO *WASTE*?
YOU WERE BLESSED WITH A *BRILLIANT* MIND. YOU COULD MAKE THE WORLD SUCH A *WONDERFUL* PLACE.
STOP WASTING YOUR LIFE TRYING TO *DESTROY* IT.

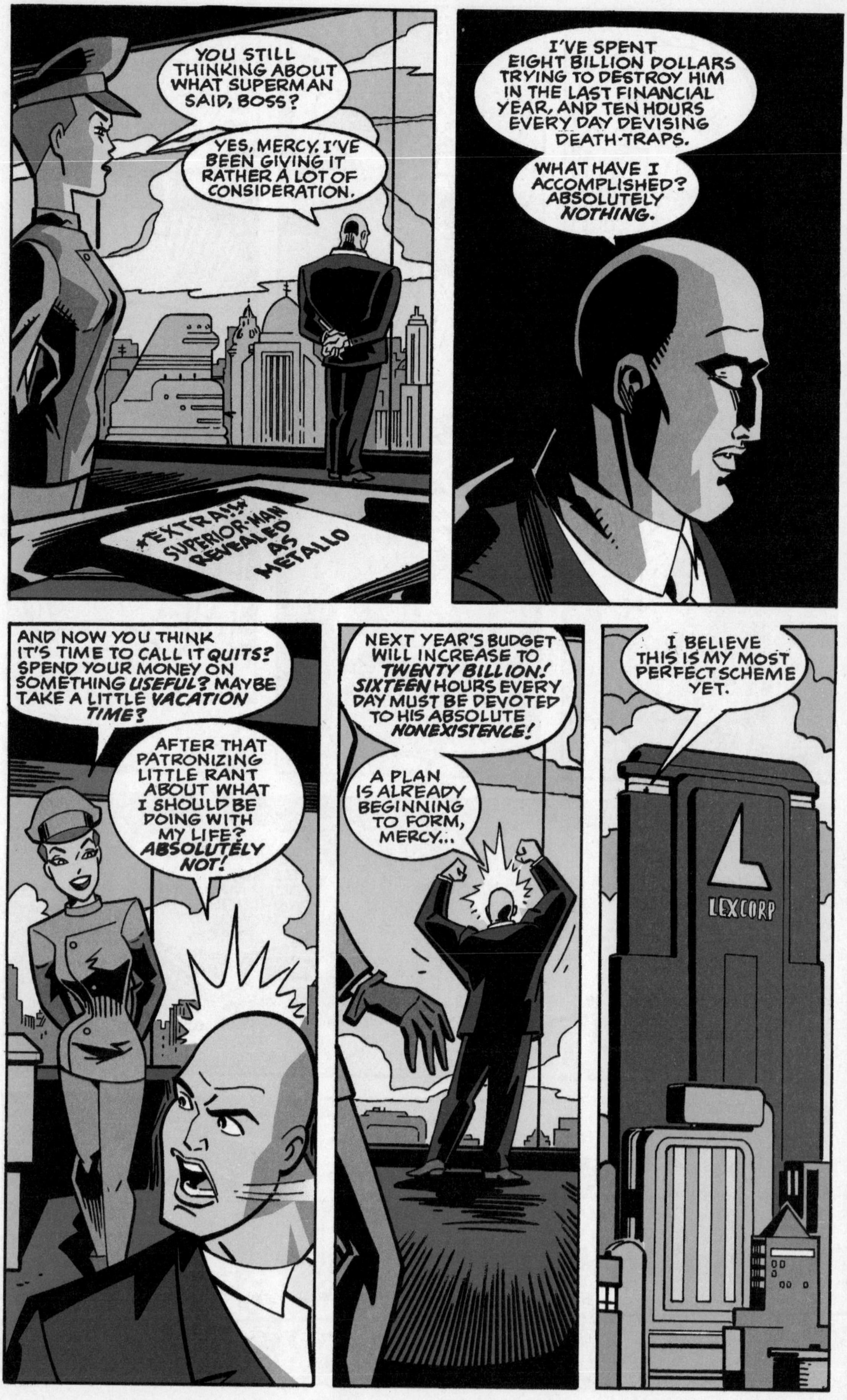
YOU STILL THINKING ABOUT WHAT SUPERMAN SAID, BOSS?
YES, MERCY. I'VE BEEN GIVING IT RATHER A LOT OF CONSIDERATION.
EXTRA!! SUPERIOR-MAN REVEALED AS METALLO
I'VE SPENT EIGHT BILLION DOLLARS TRYING TO DESTROY HIM IN THE LAST FINANCIAL YEAR, AND TEN HOURS EVERY DAY DEVISING DEATH-TRAPS.
WHAT HAVE I ACCOMPLISHED? ABSOLUTELY *NOTHING.*
AND NOW YOU THINK IT'S TIME TO CALL IT *QUITS?* SPEND YOUR MONEY ON SOMETHING *USEFUL?* MAYBE TAKE A LITTLE *VACATION TIME?*
AFTER THAT PATRONIZING LITTLE RANT ABOUT WHAT I SHOULD BE DOING WITH MY LIFE? *ABSOLUTELY NOT!*
NEXT YEAR'S BUDGET WILL INCREASE TO *TWENTY BILLION! SIXTEEN* HOURS EVERY DAY MUST BE DEVOTED TO HIS ABSOLUTE *NONEXISTENCE!*
A PLAN IS ALREADY BEGINNING TO FORM, MERCY...
I BELIEVE THIS IS MY MOST PERFECT SCHEME YET.
LEXCORP

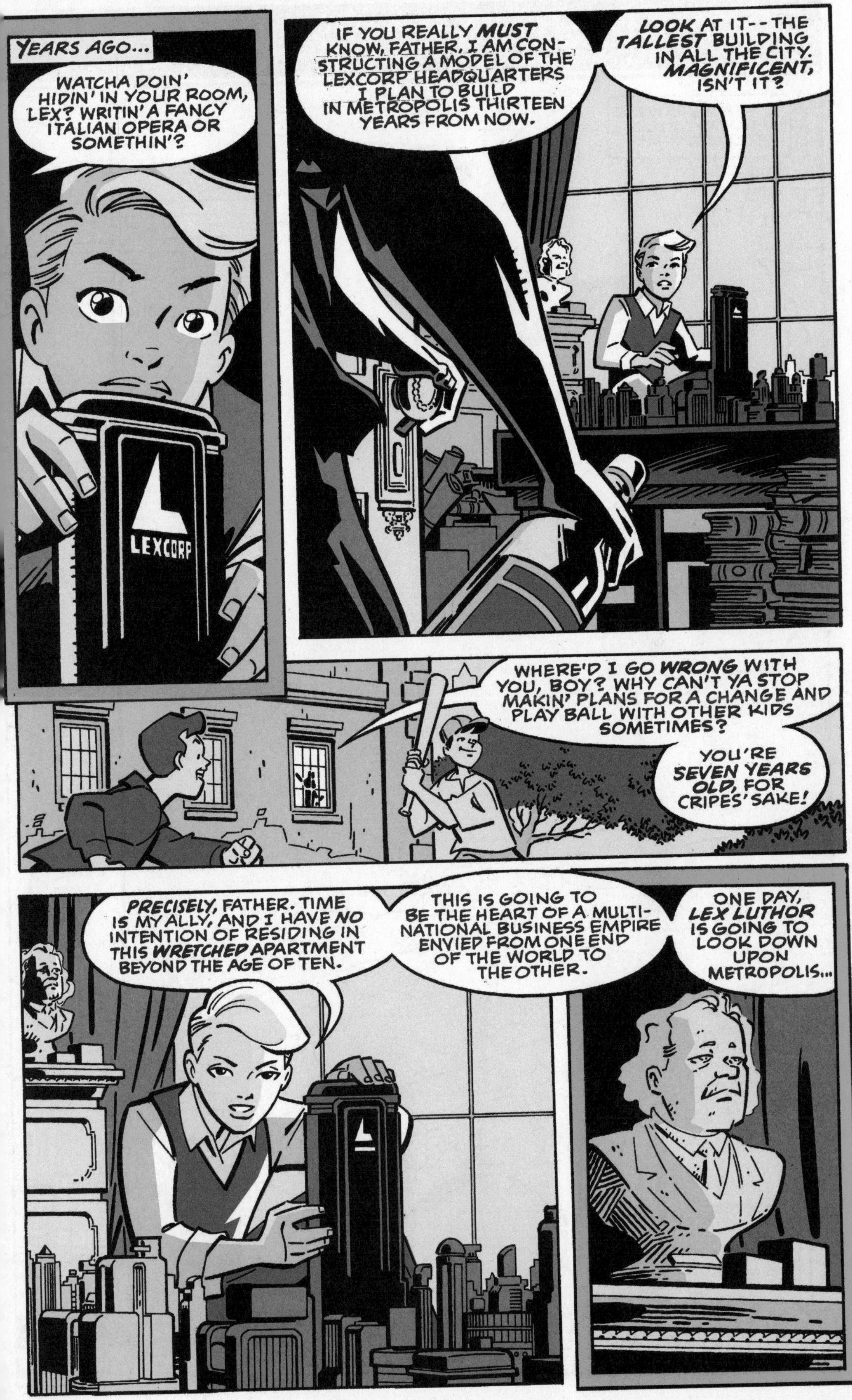
YEARS AGO...
WATCHA DOIN' HIDIN' IN YOUR ROOM, LEX? WRITIN' A FANCY ITALIAN OPERA OR SOMETHIN'?
LEXCORP
IF YOU REALLY MUST KNOW, FATHER, I AM CONSTRUCTING A MODEL OF THE LEXCORP HEADQUARTERS I PLAN TO BUILD IN METROPOLIS THIRTEEN YEARS FROM NOW.
LOOK AT IT--THE TALLEST BUILDING IN ALL THE CITY. MAGNIFICENT, ISN'T IT?
WHERE'D I GO WRONG WITH YOU, BOY? WHY CAN'T YA STOP MAKIN' PLANS FOR A CHANGE AND PLAY BALL WITH OTHER KIDS SOMETIMES?
YOU'RE SEVEN YEARS OLD, FOR CRIPES' SAKE!
PRECISELY, FATHER. TIME IS MY ALLY, AND I HAVE NO INTENTION OF RESIDING IN THIS WRETCHED APARTMENT BEYOND THE AGE OF TEN.
THIS IS GOING TO BE THE HEART OF A MULTI-NATIONAL BUSINESS EMPIRE ENVIED FROM ONE END OF THE WORLD TO THE OTHER.
ONE DAY, LEX LUTHOR IS GOING TO LOOK DOWN UPON METROPOLIS...

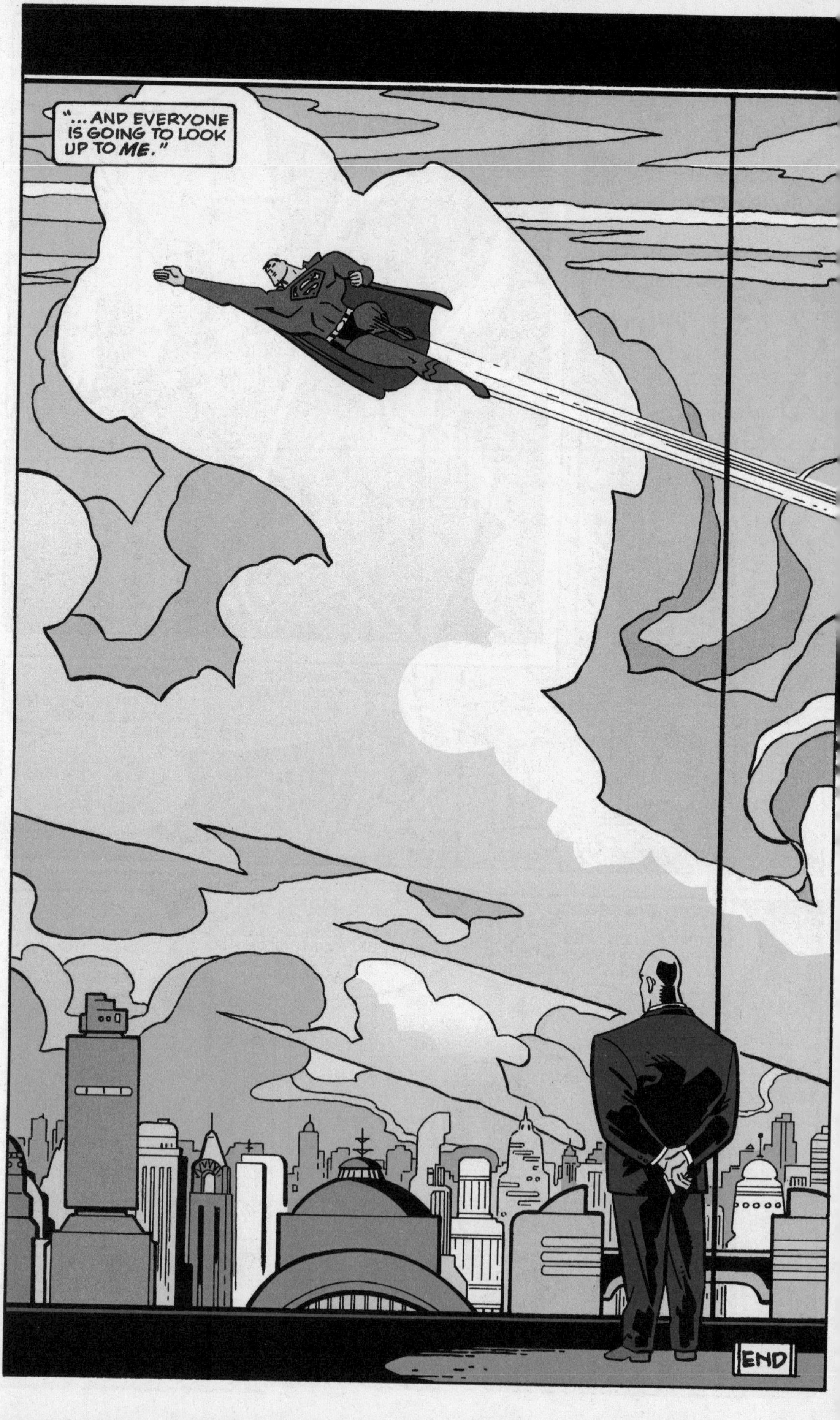
"...AND EVERYONE IS GOING TO LOOK UP TO ME."
END

SUPERMAN ADVENTURES #28 cover by RICK BURCHETT, TERRY AUSTIN and MARIE SEVERIN

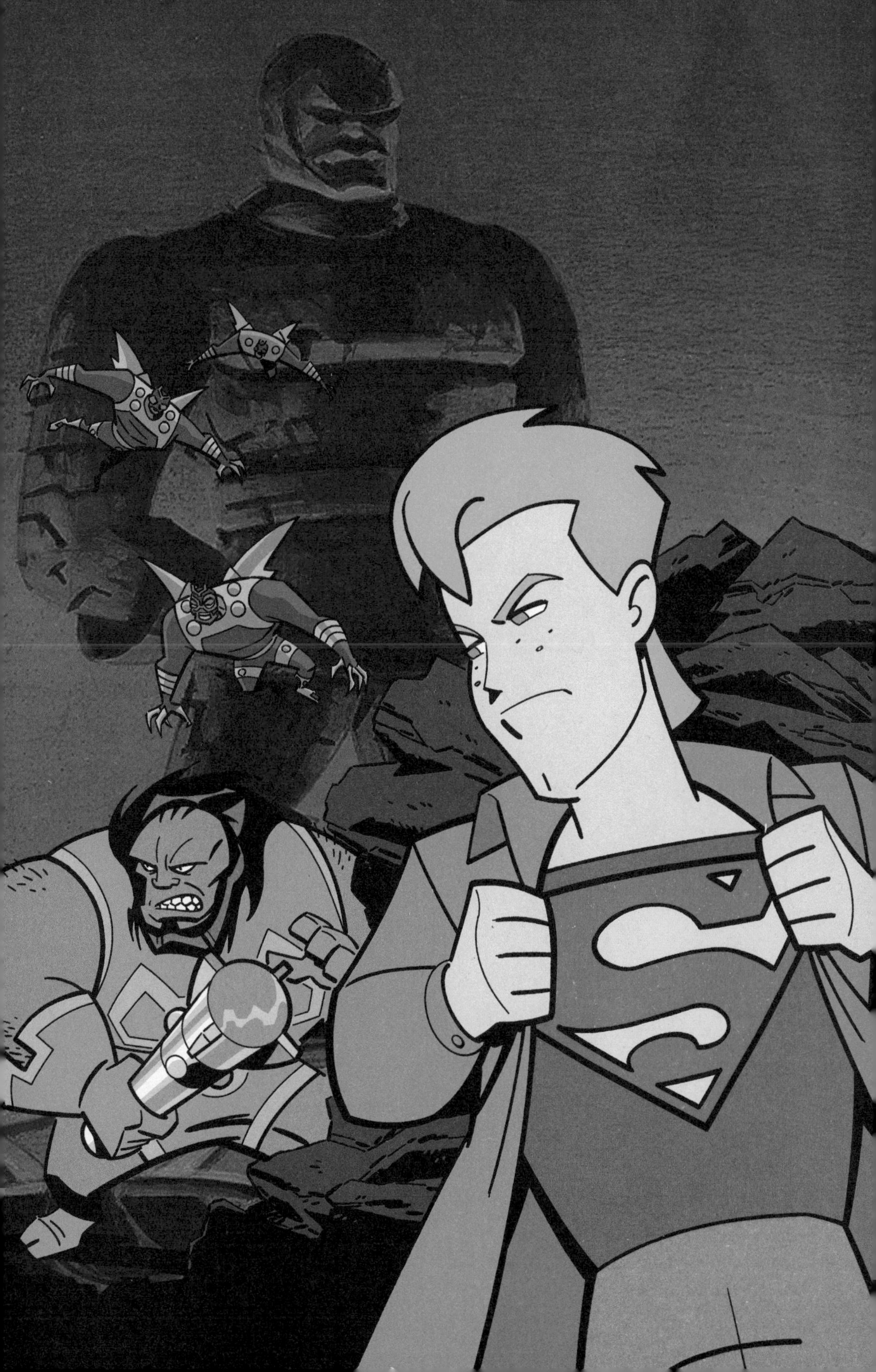

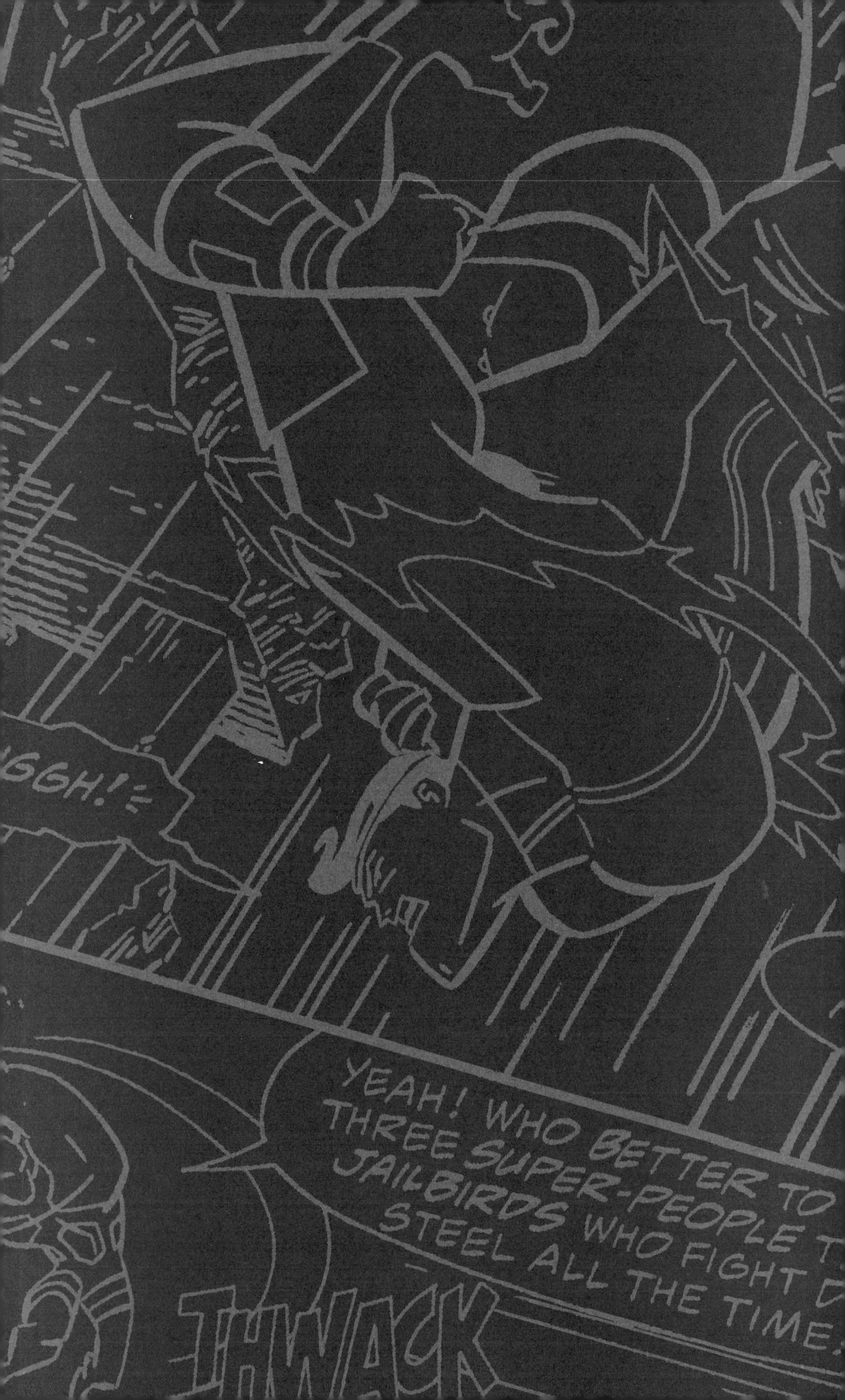
GGH!
YEAH! WHO BETTER TO
THREE SUPER-PEOPLE T
JAILBIRDS WHO FIGHT
STEEL ALL THE TIME.
THWACK

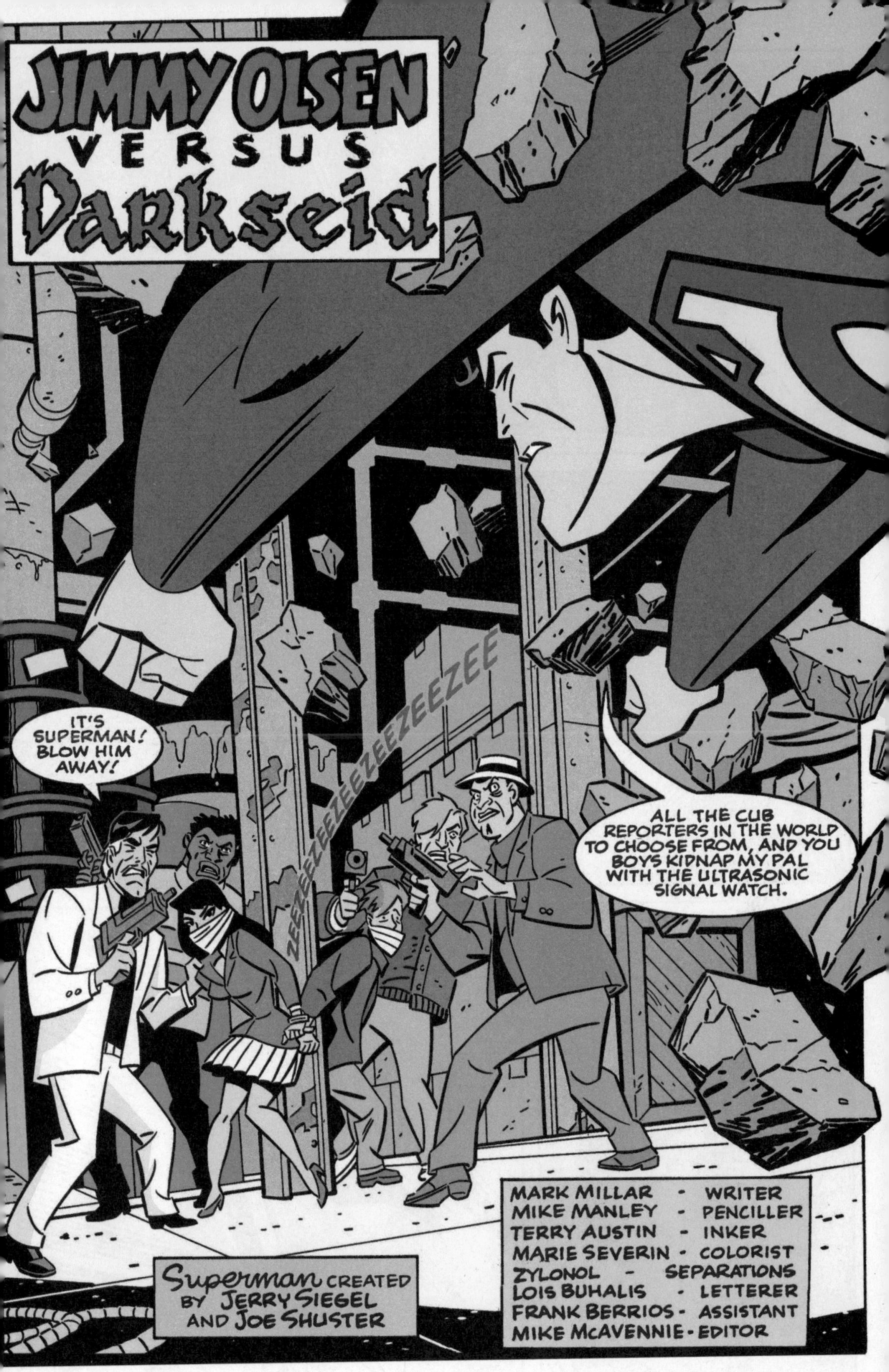
JIMMY OLSEN VERSUS Darkseid
IT'S SUPERMAN! BLOW HIM AWAY!
ZEEZEEZEEZEEZEEZEEZEE
ALL THE CUB REPORTERS IN THE WORLD TO CHOOSE FROM, AND YOU BOYS KIDNAP MY PAL WITH THE ULTRASONIC SIGNAL WATCH.
Superman CREATED BY JERRY SIEGEL AND JOE SHUSTER
MARK MILLAR - WRITER
MIKE MANLEY - PENCILLER
TERRY AUSTIN - INKER
MARIE SEVERIN - COLORIST
ZYLONOL - SEPARATIONS
LOIS BUHALIS - LETTERER
FRANK BERRIOS - ASSISTANT
MIKE McAVENNIE - EDITOR

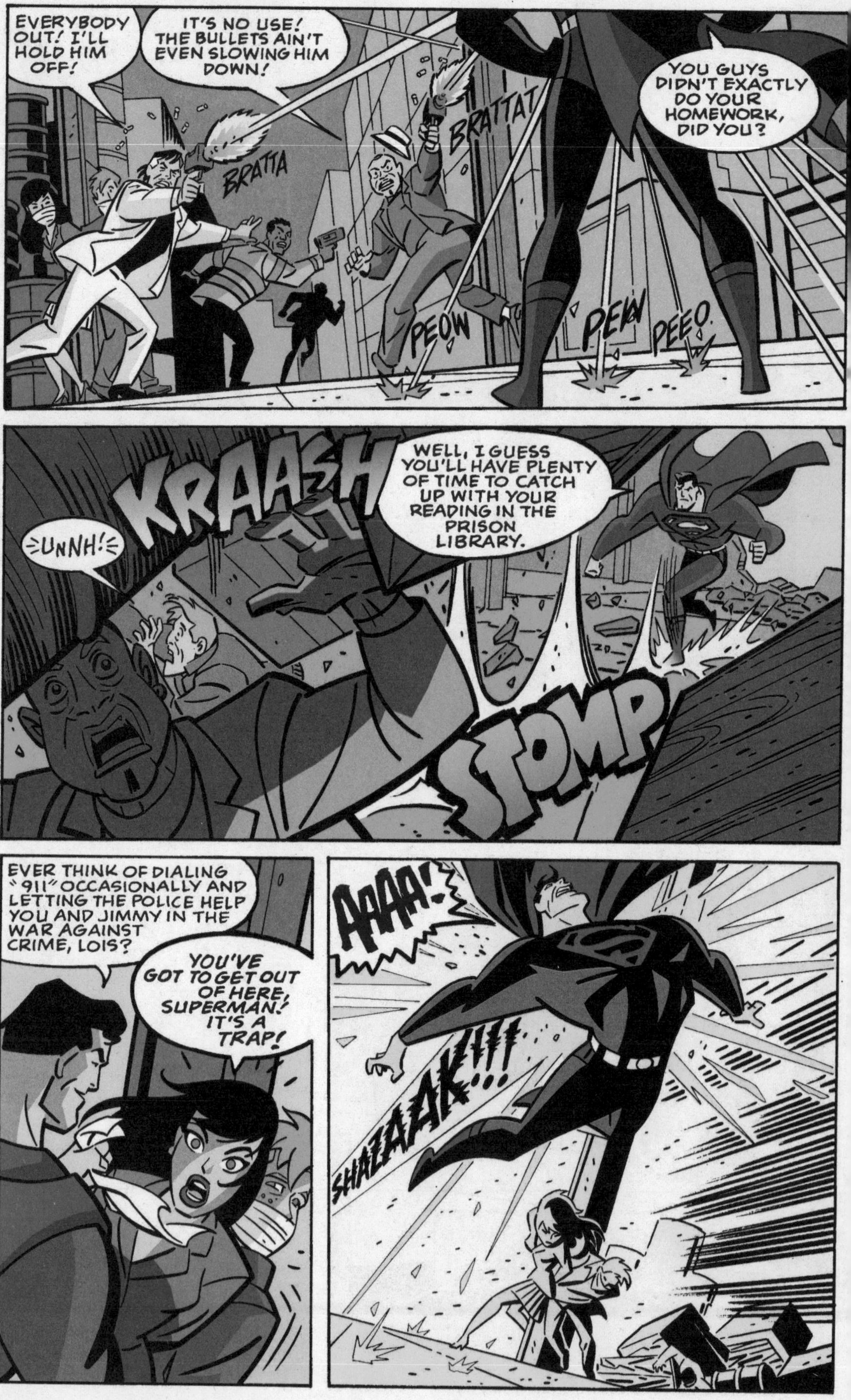
EVERYBODY OUT! I'LL HOLD HIM OFF!
IT'S NO USE! THE BULLETS AIN'T EVEN SLOWING HIM DOWN!
BRATTA
BRATTAT
YOU GUYS DIDN'T EXACTLY DO YOUR HOMEWORK, DID YOU?
PEOW
PEW
PEEO
KRAASH
UNNH!
WELL, I GUESS YOU'LL HAVE PLENTY OF TIME TO CATCH UP WITH YOUR READING IN THE PRISON LIBRARY.
STOMP
EVER THINK OF DIALING "911" OCCASIONALLY AND LETTING THE POLICE HELP YOU AND JIMMY IN THE WAR AGAINST CRIME, LOIS?
YOU'VE GOT TO GET OUT OF HERE, SUPERMAN! IT'S A TRAP!
AAAA!
SHAZAAAK!!!

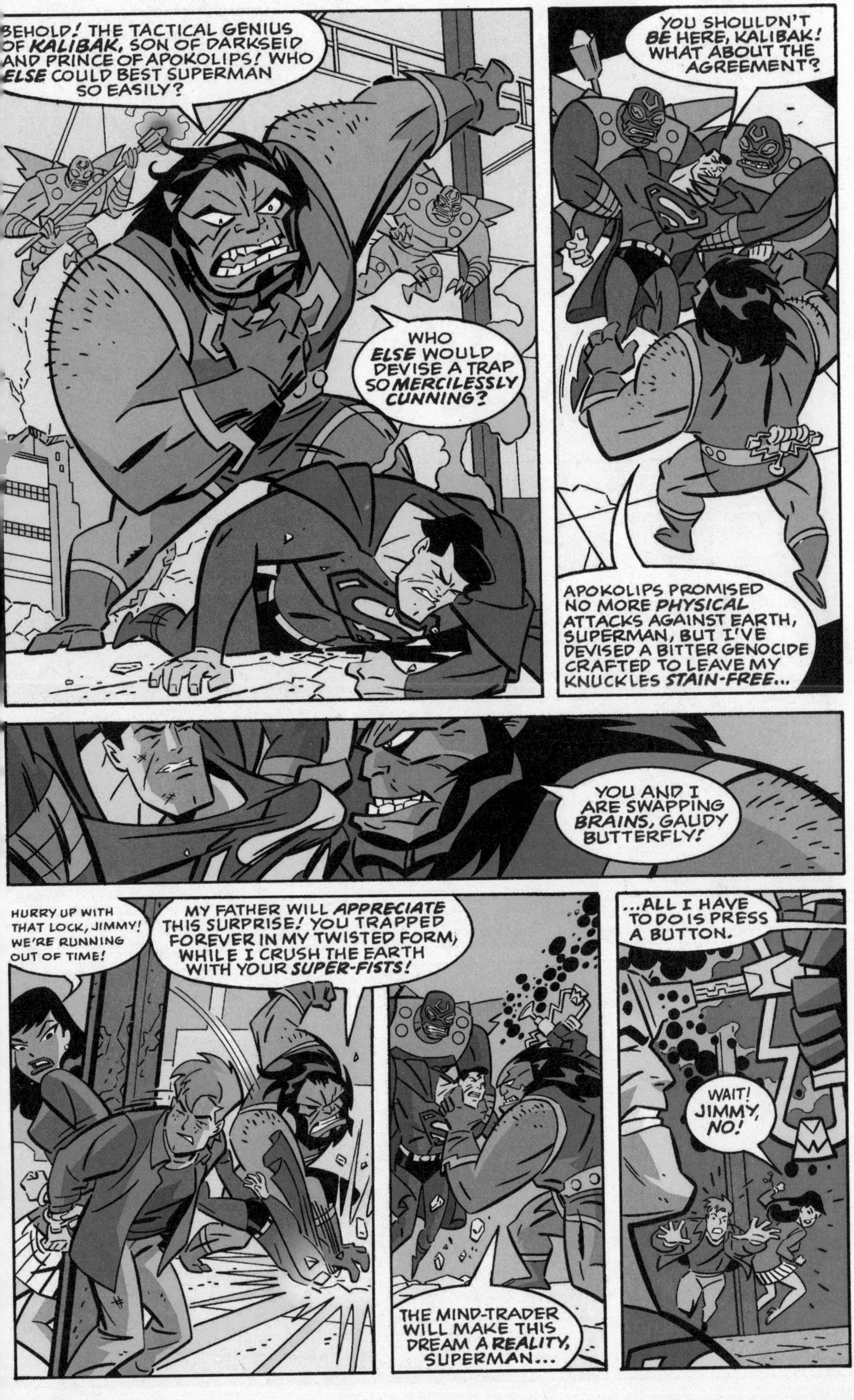
BEHOLD! THE TACTICAL GENIUS OF KALIBAK, SON OF DARKSEID AND PRINCE OF APOKOLIPS! WHO ELSE COULD BEST SUPERMAN SO EASILY?
WHO ELSE WOULD DEVISE A TRAP SO MERCILESSLY CUNNING?
YOU SHOULDN'T BE HERE, KALIBAK! WHAT ABOUT THE AGREEMENT?
APOKOLIPS PROMISED NO MORE PHYSICAL ATTACKS AGAINST EARTH, SUPERMAN, BUT I'VE DEVISED A BITTER GENOCIDE CRAFTED TO LEAVE MY KNUCKLES STAIN-FREE...
YOU AND I ARE SWAPPING BRAINS, GAUDY BUTTERFLY!
HURRY UP WITH THAT LOCK, JIMMY! WE'RE RUNNING OUT OF TIME!
MY FATHER WILL APPRECIATE THIS SURPRISE! YOU TRAPPED FOREVER IN MY TWISTED FORM, WHILE I CRUSH THE EARTH WITH YOUR SUPER-FISTS!
THE MIND-TRADER WILL MAKE THIS DREAM A REALITY, SUPERMAN...
...ALL I HAVE TO DO IS PRESS A BUTTON.
WAIT! JIMMY, NO!

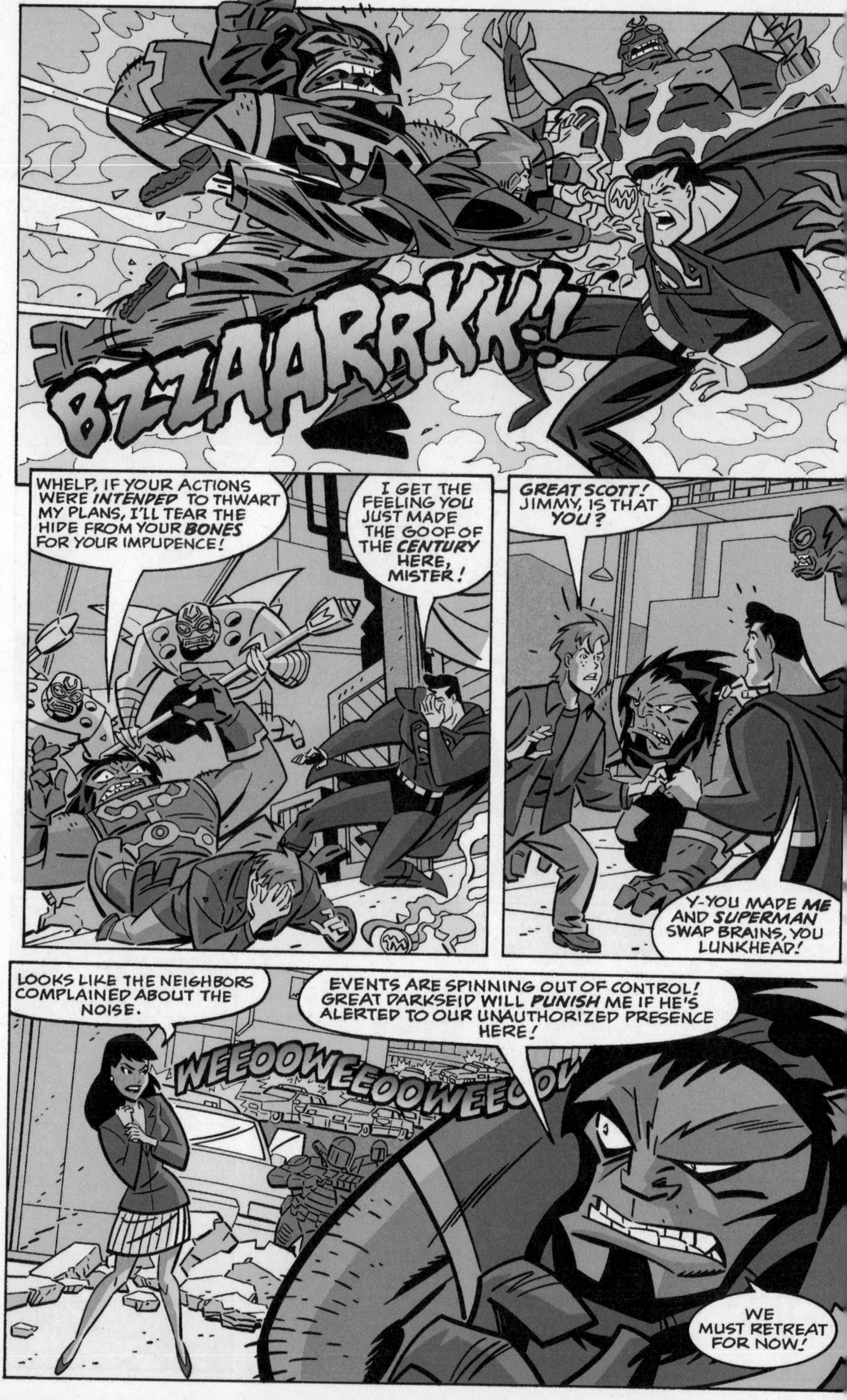
BZZAARRKK!!
WHELP, IF YOUR ACTIONS WERE INTENDED TO THWART MY PLANS, I'LL TEAR THE HIDE FROM YOUR BONES FOR YOUR IMPUDENCE!
I GET THE FEELING YOU JUST MADE THE GOOF OF THE CENTURY HERE, MISTER!
GREAT SCOTT! JIMMY, IS THAT YOU?
Y-YOU MADE ME AND SUPERMAN SWAP BRAINS, YOU LUNKHEAD!
LOOKS LIKE THE NEIGHBORS COMPLAINED ABOUT THE NOISE.
EVENTS ARE SPINNING OUT OF CONTROL! GREAT DARKSEID WILL PUNISH ME IF HE'S ALERTED TO OUR UNAUTHORIZED PRESENCE HERE!
WEEOOWEEOOWEEOO
WE MUST RETREAT FOR NOW!

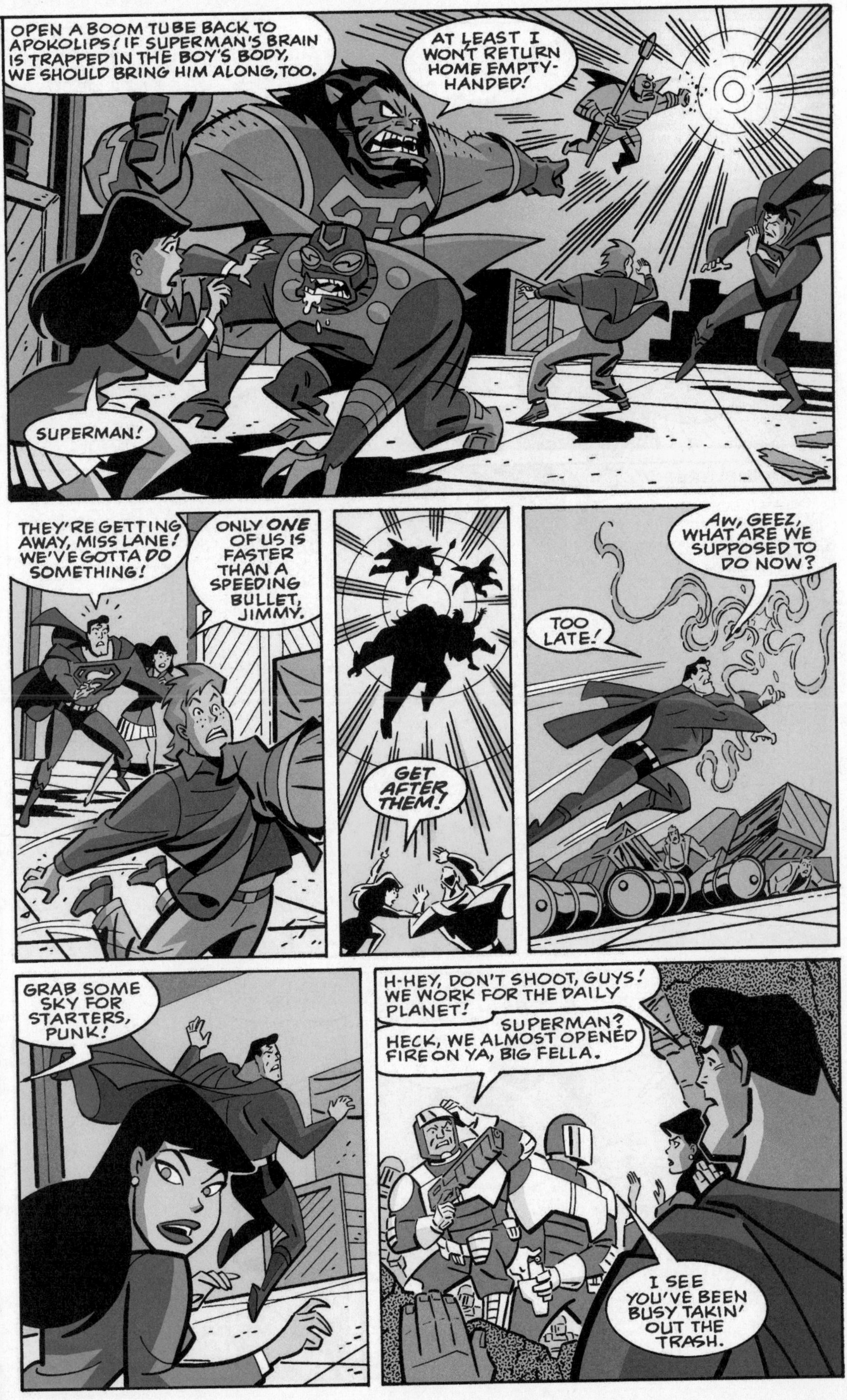
OPEN A BOOM TUBE BACK TO APOKOLIPS! IF SUPERMAN'S BRAIN IS TRAPPED IN THE BOY'S BODY, WE SHOULD BRING HIM ALONG, TOO.
AT LEAST I WON'T RETURN HOME EMPTY-HANDED!
SUPERMAN!
THEY'RE GETTING AWAY, MISS LANE! WE'VE GOTTA DO SOMETHING!
ONLY ONE OF US IS FASTER THAN A SPEEDING BULLET, JIMMY.
GET AFTER THEM!
AW, GEEZ, WHAT ARE WE SUPPOSED TO DO NOW?
TOO LATE!
GRAB SOME SKY FOR STARTERS, PUNK!
H-HEY, DON'T SHOOT, GUYS! WE WORK FOR THE DAILY PLANET!
SUPERMAN? HECK, WE ALMOST OPENED FIRE ON YA, BIG FELLA.
I SEE YOU'VE BEEN BUSY TAKIN' OUT THE TRASH.

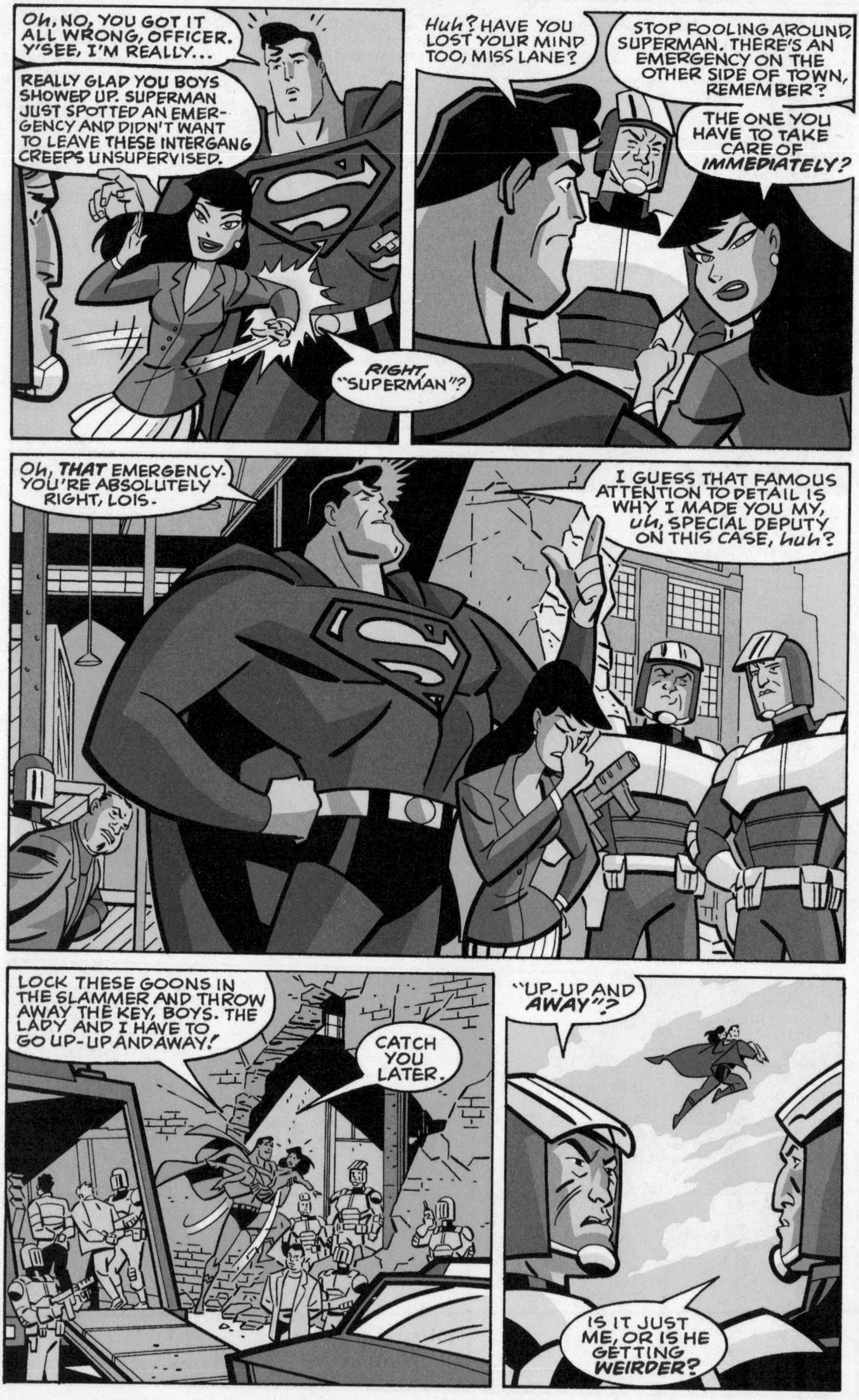
OH, NO, YOU GOT IT ALL WRONG, OFFICER. Y'SEE, I'M REALLY...
REALLY GLAD YOU BOYS SHOWED UP. SUPERMAN JUST SPOTTED AN EMERGENCY AND DIDN'T WANT TO LEAVE THESE INTERGANG CREEPS UNSUPERVISED.
RIGHT, "SUPERMAN"?
HUH? HAVE YOU LOST YOUR MIND TOO, MISS LANE?
STOP FOOLING AROUND, SUPERMAN. THERE'S AN EMERGENCY ON THE OTHER SIDE OF TOWN, REMEMBER?
THE ONE YOU HAVE TO TAKE CARE OF IMMEDIATELY?
OH, THAT EMERGENCY. YOU'RE ABSOLUTELY RIGHT, LOIS.
I GUESS THAT FAMOUS ATTENTION TO DETAIL IS WHY I MADE YOU MY, UH, SPECIAL DEPUTY ON THIS CASE, HUH?
LOCK THESE GOONS IN THE SLAMMER AND THROW AWAY THE KEY, BOYS. THE LADY AND I HAVE TO GO UP-UP AND AWAY!
CATCH YOU LATER.
"UP-UP AND AWAY"?
IS IT JUST ME, OR IS HE GETTING WEIRDER?

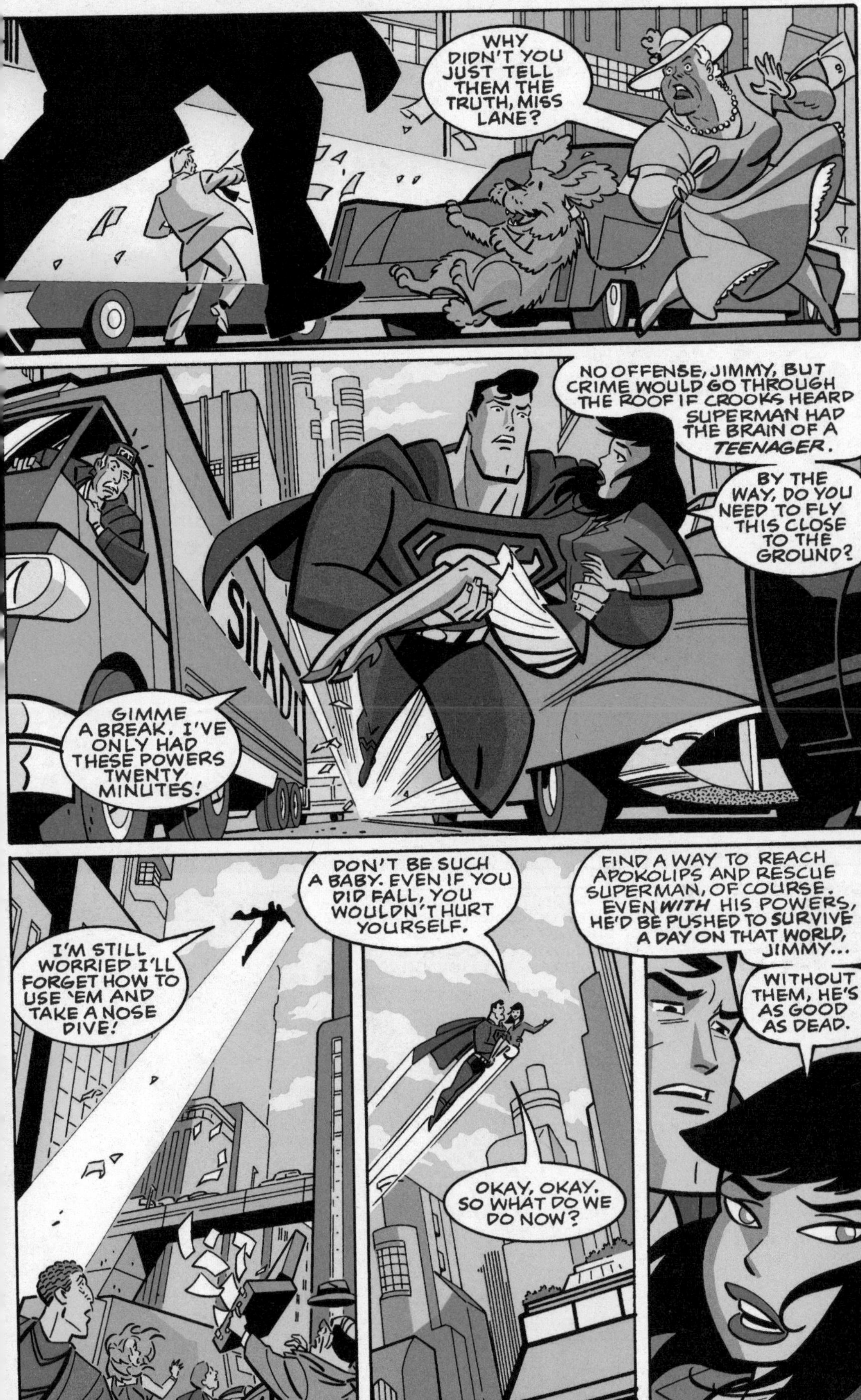
WHY DIDN'T YOU JUST TELL THEM THE TRUTH, MISS LANE?
NO OFFENSE, JIMMY, BUT CRIME WOULD GO THROUGH THE ROOF IF CROOKS HEARD SUPERMAN HAD THE BRAIN OF A TEENAGER.
BY THE WAY, DO YOU NEED TO FLY THIS CLOSE TO THE GROUND?
GIMME A BREAK. I'VE ONLY HAD THESE POWERS TWENTY MINUTES!
SILADI
I'M STILL WORRIED I'LL FORGET HOW TO USE 'EM AND TAKE A NOSE DIVE!
DON'T BE SUCH A BABY. EVEN IF YOU DID FALL, YOU WOULDN'T HURT YOURSELF.
OKAY, OKAY. SO WHAT DO WE DO NOW?
FIND A WAY TO REACH APOKOLIPS AND RESCUE SUPERMAN, OF COURSE. EVEN WITH HIS POWERS, HE'D BE PUSHED TO SURVIVE A DAY ON THAT WORLD, JIMMY...
WITHOUT THEM, HE'S AS GOOD AS DEAD.

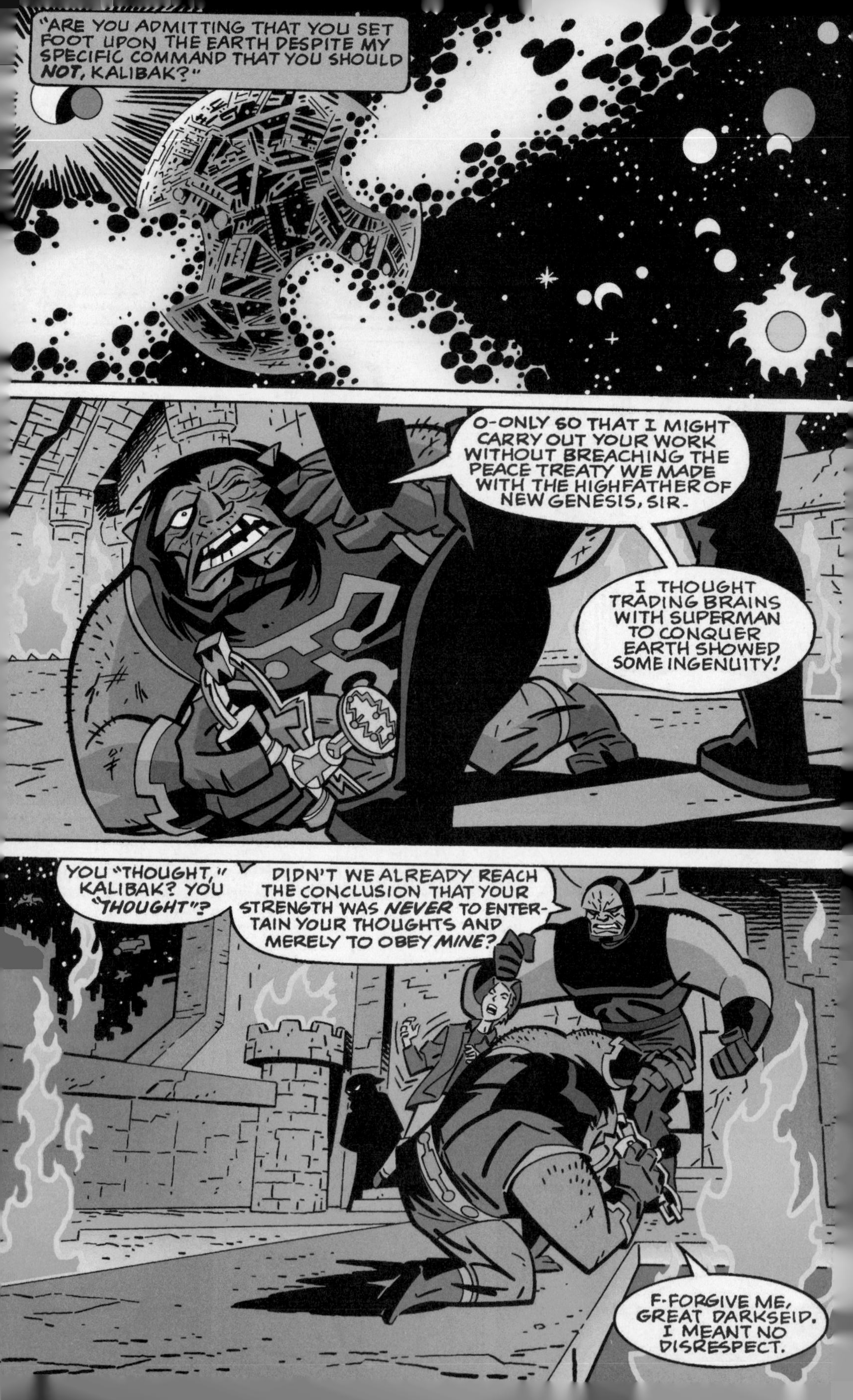
"ARE YOU ADMITTING THAT YOU SET FOOT UPON THE EARTH DESPITE MY SPECIFIC COMMAND THAT YOU SHOULD *NOT*, KALIBAK?"
O-ONLY SO THAT I MIGHT CARRY OUT YOUR WORK WITHOUT BREACHING THE PEACE TREATY WE MADE WITH THE HIGHFATHER OF NEW GENESIS, SIR-
I THOUGHT TRADING BRAINS WITH SUPERMAN TO CONQUER EARTH SHOWED SOME INGENUITY!
YOU "THOUGHT," KALIBAK? YOU "*THOUGHT*"?
DIDN'T WE ALREADY REACH THE CONCLUSION THAT YOUR STRENGTH WAS *NEVER* TO ENTERTAIN YOUR THOUGHTS AND MERELY TO OBEY *MINE*?
F-FORGIVE ME, GREAT DARKSEID. I MEANT NO DISRESPECT.

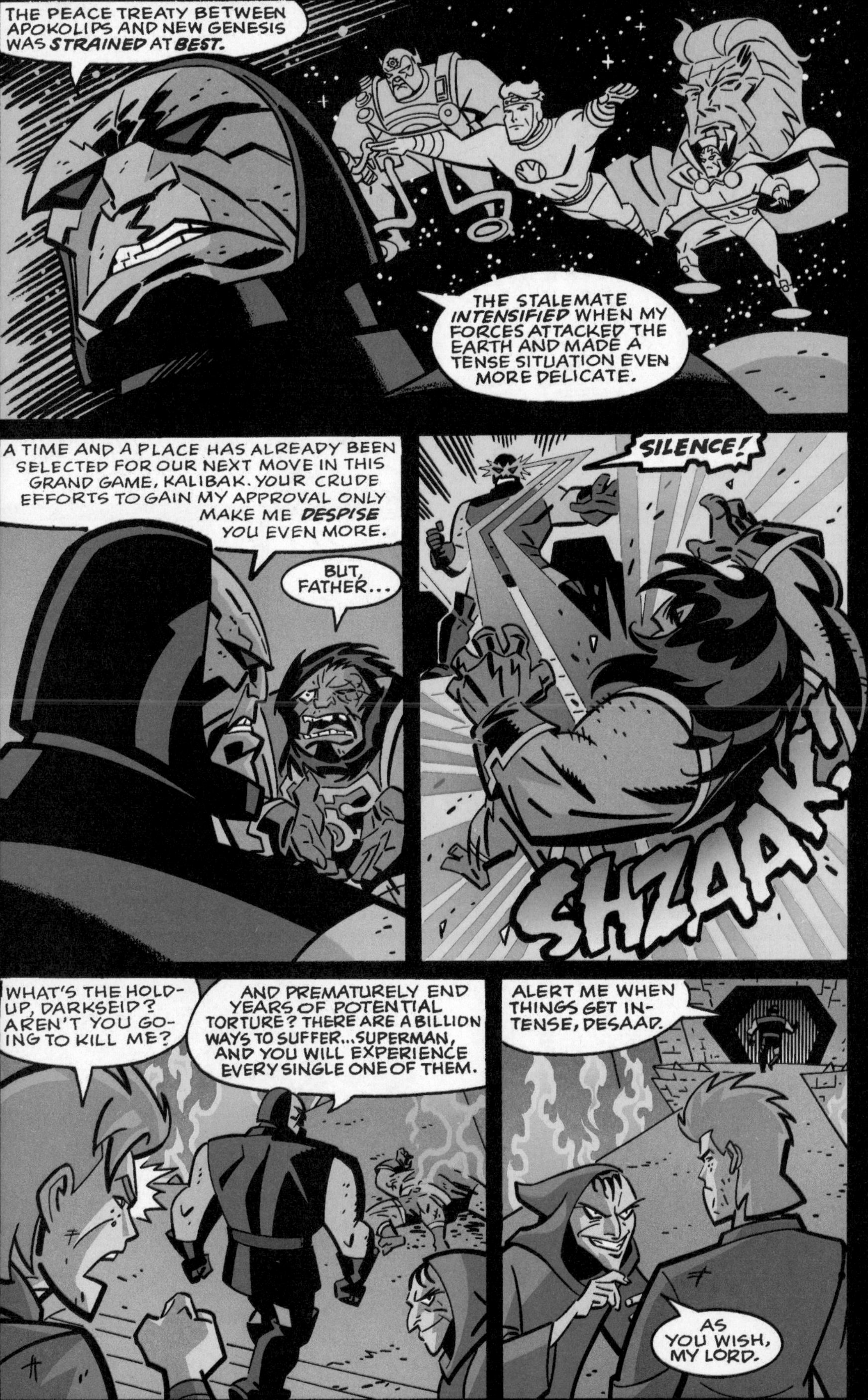
THE PEACE TREATY BETWEEN APOKOLIPS AND NEW GENESIS WAS STRAINED AT BEST.
THE STALEMATE INTENSIFIED WHEN MY FORCES ATTACKED THE EARTH AND MADE A TENSE SITUATION EVEN MORE DELICATE.
A TIME AND A PLACE HAS ALREADY BEEN SELECTED FOR OUR NEXT MOVE IN THIS GRAND GAME, KALIBAK. YOUR CRUDE EFFORTS TO GAIN MY APPROVAL ONLY MAKE ME DESPISE YOU EVEN MORE.
BUT, FATHER...
SILENCE!
SHZAAK!
WHAT'S THE HOLD-UP, DARKSEID? AREN'T YOU GOING TO KILL ME?
AND PREMATURELY END YEARS OF POTENTIAL TORTURE? THERE ARE A BILLION WAYS TO SUFFER...SUPERMAN, AND YOU WILL EXPERIENCE EVERY SINGLE ONE OF THEM.
ALERT ME WHEN THINGS GET INTENSE, DESAAD.
AS YOU WISH, MY LORD.

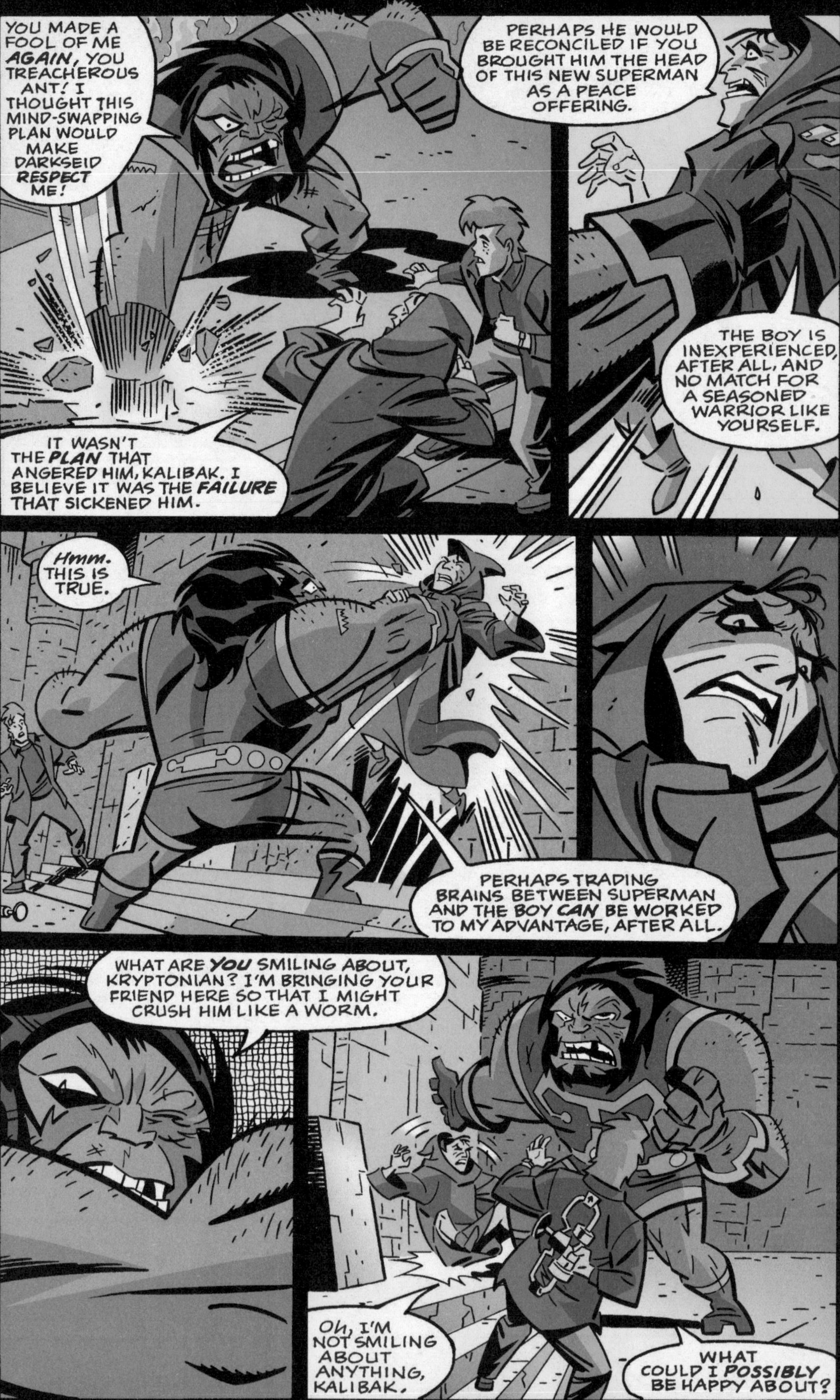

YOU MADE A FOOL OF ME AGAIN, YOU TREACHEROUS ANT! I THOUGHT THIS MIND-SWAPPING PLAN WOULD MAKE DARKSEID RESPECT ME!
IT WASN'T THE PLAN THAT ANGERED HIM, KALIBAK. I BELIEVE IT WAS THE FAILURE THAT SICKENED HIM.
PERHAPS HE WOULD BE RECONCILED IF YOU BROUGHT HIM THE HEAD OF THIS NEW SUPERMAN AS A PEACE OFFERING.
THE BOY IS INEXPERIENCED, AFTER ALL, AND NO MATCH FOR A SEASONED WARRIOR LIKE YOURSELF.
Hmm. THIS IS TRUE.
PERHAPS TRADING BRAINS BETWEEN SUPERMAN AND THE BOY CAN BE WORKED TO MY ADVANTAGE, AFTER ALL.
WHAT ARE YOU SMILING ABOUT, KRYPTONIAN? I'M BRINGING YOUR FRIEND HERE SO THAT I MIGHT CRUSH HIM LIKE A WORM.
Oh, I'M NOT SMILING ABOUT ANYTHING, KALIBAK.
WHAT COULD I POSSIBLY BE HAPPY ABOUT?

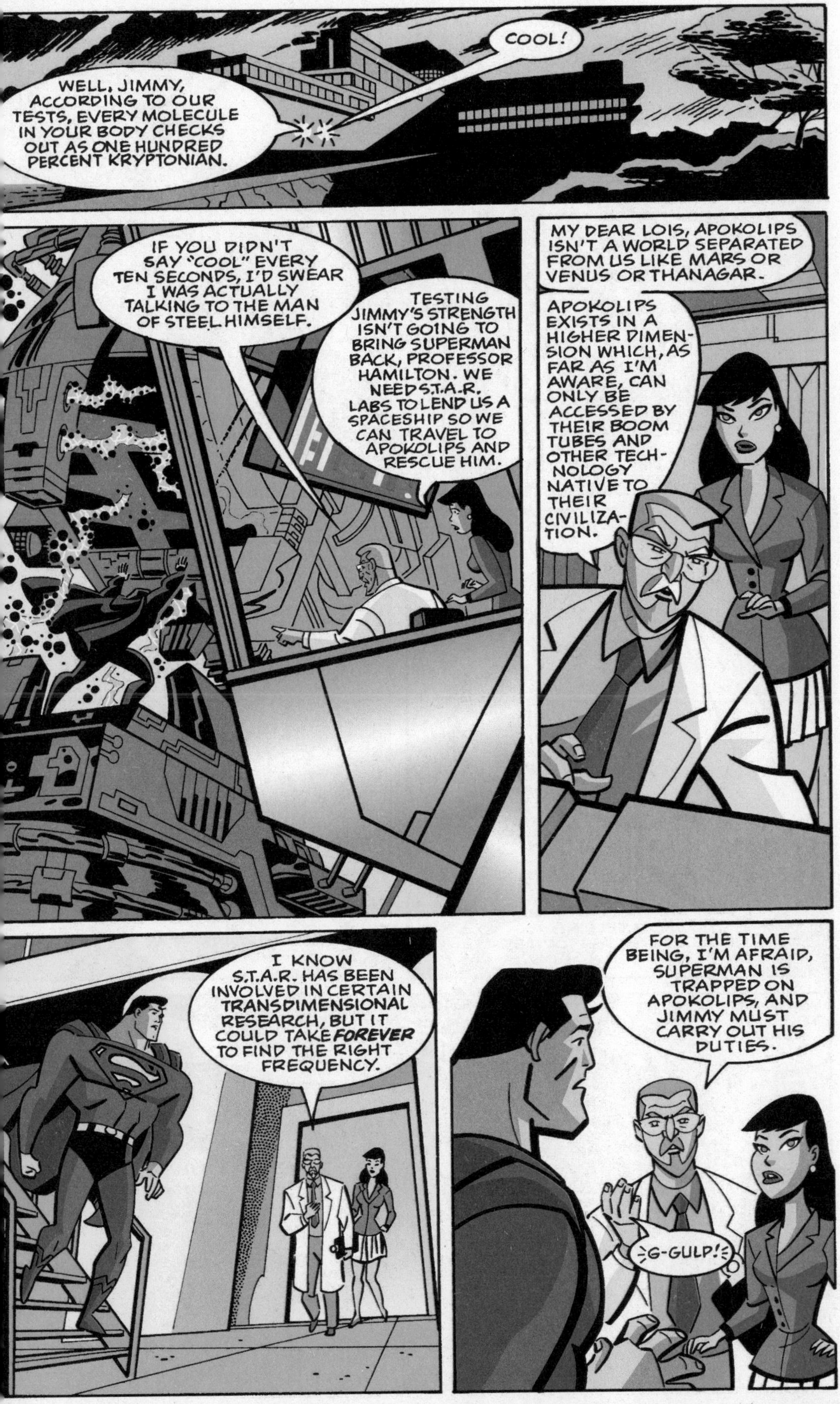

WELL, JIMMY, ACCORDING TO OUR TESTS, EVERY MOLECULE IN YOUR BODY CHECKS OUT AS ONE HUNDRED PERCENT KRYPTONIAN.
COOL!
IF YOU DIDN'T SAY "COOL" EVERY TEN SECONDS, I'D SWEAR I WAS ACTUALLY TALKING TO THE MAN OF STEEL HIMSELF.
TESTING JIMMY'S STRENGTH ISN'T GOING TO BRING SUPERMAN BACK, PROFESSOR HAMILTON. WE NEED S.T.A.R. LABS TO LEND US A SPACESHIP SO WE CAN TRAVEL TO APOKOLIPS AND RESCUE HIM.
MY DEAR LOIS, APOKOLIPS ISN'T A WORLD SEPARATED FROM US LIKE MARS OR VENUS OR THANAGAR.
APOKOLIPS EXISTS IN A HIGHER DIMENSION WHICH, AS FAR AS I'M AWARE, CAN ONLY BE ACCESSED BY THEIR BOOM TUBES AND OTHER TECHNOLOGY NATIVE TO THEIR CIVILIZATION.
I KNOW S.T.A.R. HAS BEEN INVOLVED IN CERTAIN TRANSDIMENSIONAL RESEARCH, BUT IT COULD TAKE FOREVER TO FIND THE RIGHT FREQUENCY.
FOR THE TIME BEING, I'M AFRAID, SUPERMAN IS TRAPPED ON APOKOLIPS, AND JIMMY MUST CARRY OUT HIS DUTIES.
G-GULP!

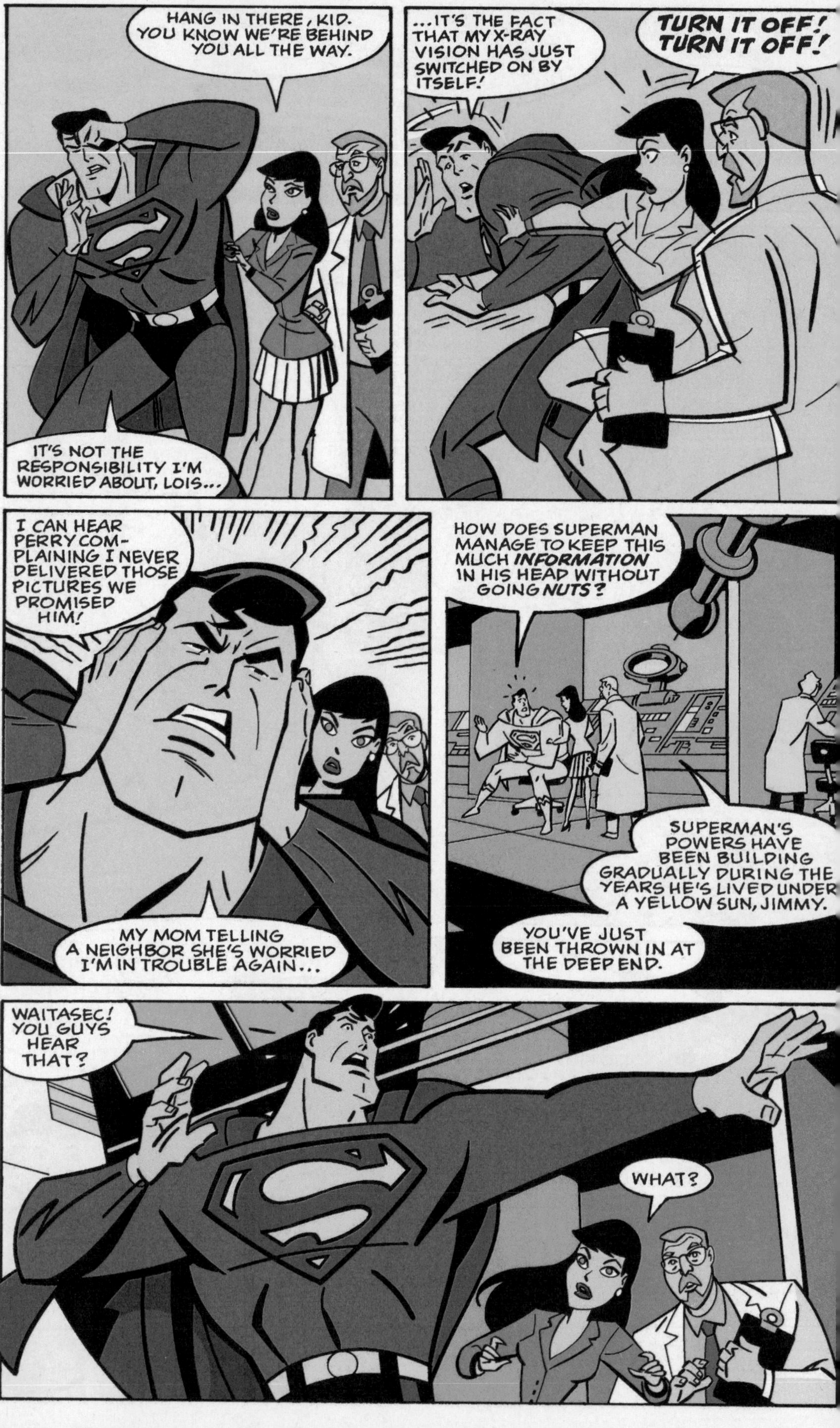
HANG IN THERE, KID. YOU KNOW WE'RE BEHIND YOU ALL THE WAY.
IT'S NOT THE RESPONSIBILITY I'M WORRIED ABOUT, LOIS...
...IT'S THE FACT THAT MY X-RAY VISION HAS JUST SWITCHED ON BY ITSELF!
TURN IT OFF! TURN IT OFF!
I CAN HEAR PERRY COM-PLAINING I NEVER DELIVERED THOSE PICTURES WE PROMISED HIM!
MY MOM TELLING A NEIGHBOR SHE'S WORRIED I'M IN TROUBLE AGAIN...
HOW DOES SUPERMAN MANAGE TO KEEP THIS MUCH INFORMATION IN HIS HEAD WITHOUT GOING NUTS?
SUPERMAN'S POWERS HAVE BEEN BUILDING GRADUALLY DURING THE YEARS HE'S LIVED UNDER A YELLOW SUN, JIMMY.
YOU'VE JUST BEEN THROWN IN AT THE DEEP END.
WAITASEC! YOU GUYS HEAR THAT?
WHAT?

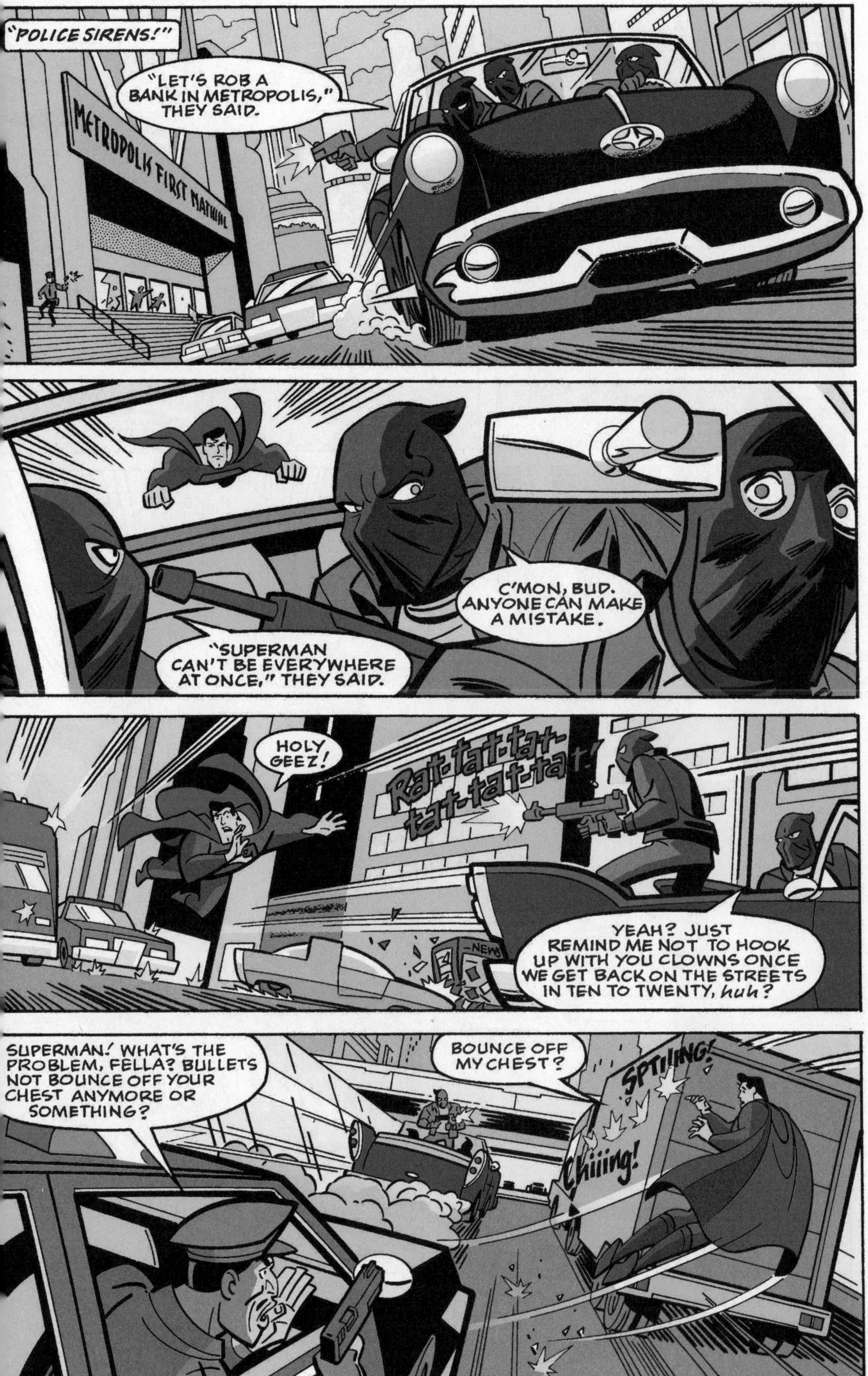
"POLICE SIRENS!"
"LET'S ROB A BANK IN METROPOLIS," THEY SAID.
METROPOLIS FIRST NATIONAL
"SUPERMAN CAN'T BE EVERYWHERE AT ONCE," THEY SAID.
C'MON, BUD. ANYONE CAN MAKE A MISTAKE.
HOLY GEEZ!
Rat-tat-tat-tat-tat-tat-tat!
YEAH? JUST REMIND ME NOT TO HOOK UP WITH YOU CLOWNS ONCE WE GET BACK ON THE STREETS IN TEN TO TWENTY, *huh*?
SUPERMAN! WHAT'S THE PROBLEM, FELLA? BULLETS NOT BOUNCE OFF YOUR CHEST ANYMORE OR SOMETHING?
BOUNCE OFF MY CHEST?
SPTIIING!
Chiiing!

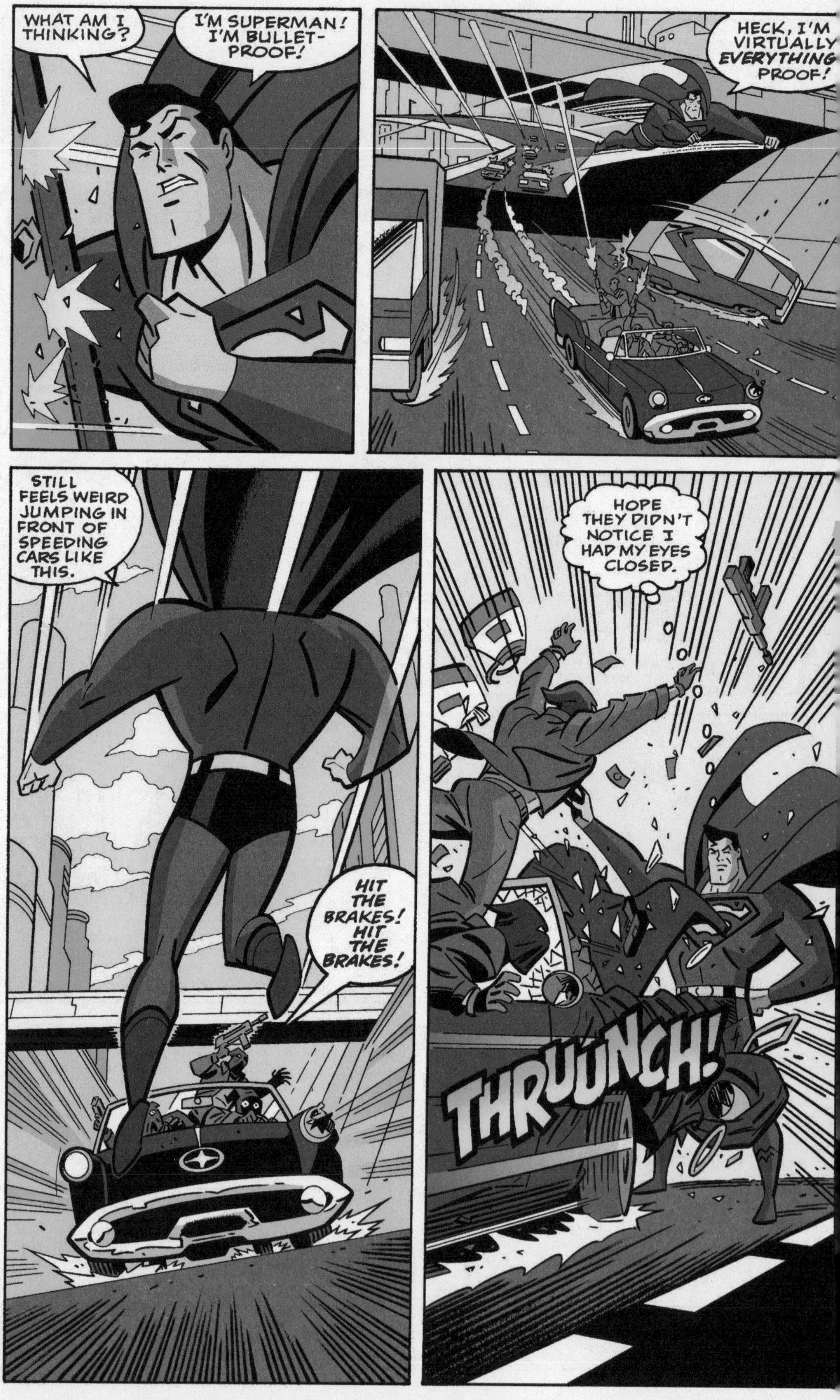
WHAT AM I THINKING?
I'M SUPERMAN! I'M BULLET-PROOF!
HECK, I'M VIRTUALLY EVERYTHING PROOF!
STILL FEELS WEIRD JUMPING IN FRONT OF SPEEDING CARS LIKE THIS.
HIT THE BRAKES! HIT THE BRAKES!
HOPE THEY DIDN'T NOTICE I HAD MY EYES CLOSED.
THRUUNCH!

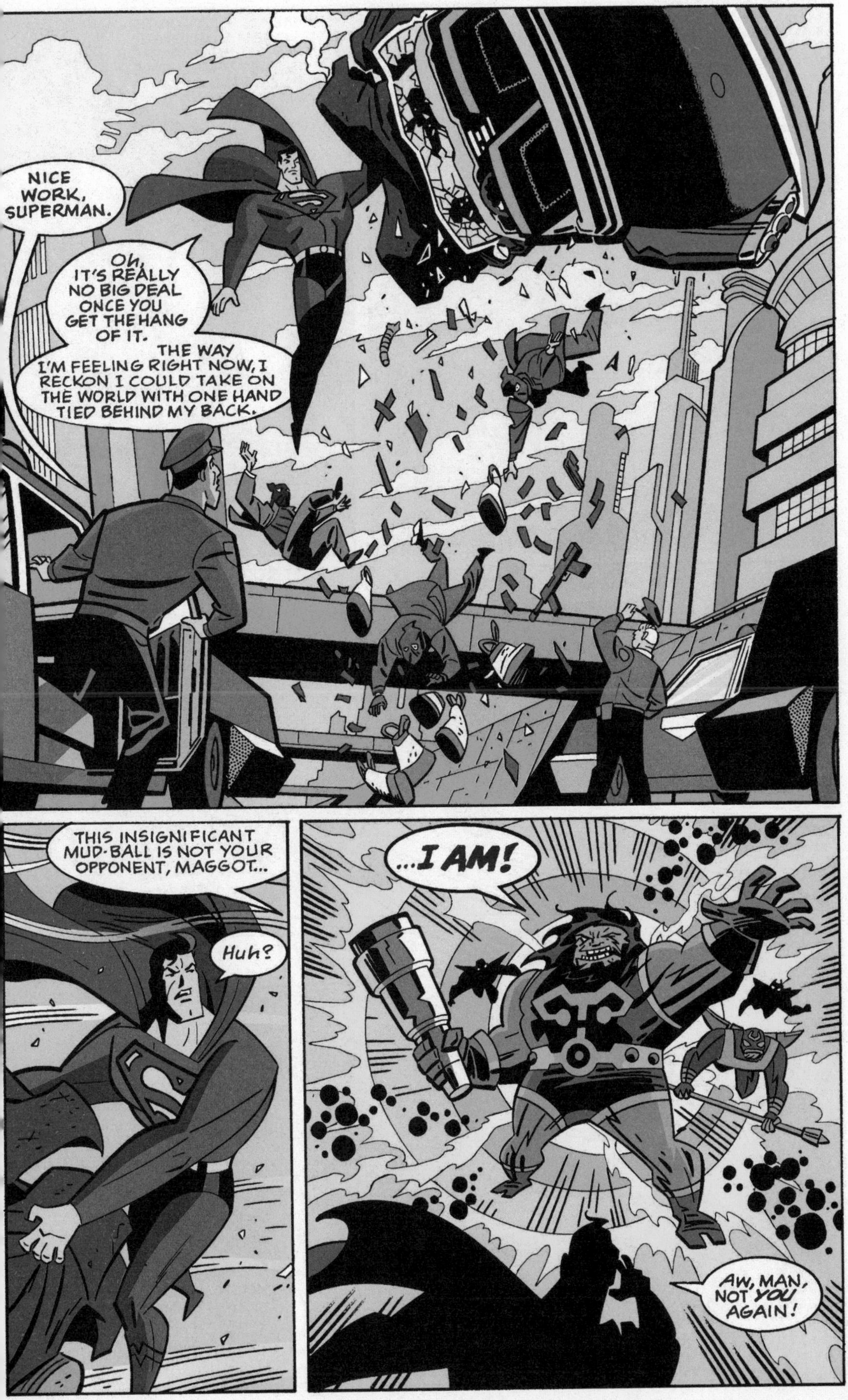
NICE WORK, SUPERMAN.
Oh, IT'S REALLY NO BIG DEAL ONCE YOU GET THE HANG OF IT.
THE WAY I'M FEELING RIGHT NOW, I RECKON I COULD TAKE ON THE WORLD WITH ONE HAND TIED BEHIND MY BACK.
THIS INSIGNIFICANT MUD-BALL IS NOT YOUR OPPONENT, MAGGOT...
Huh?
...I AM!
AW, MAN, NOT YOU AGAIN!

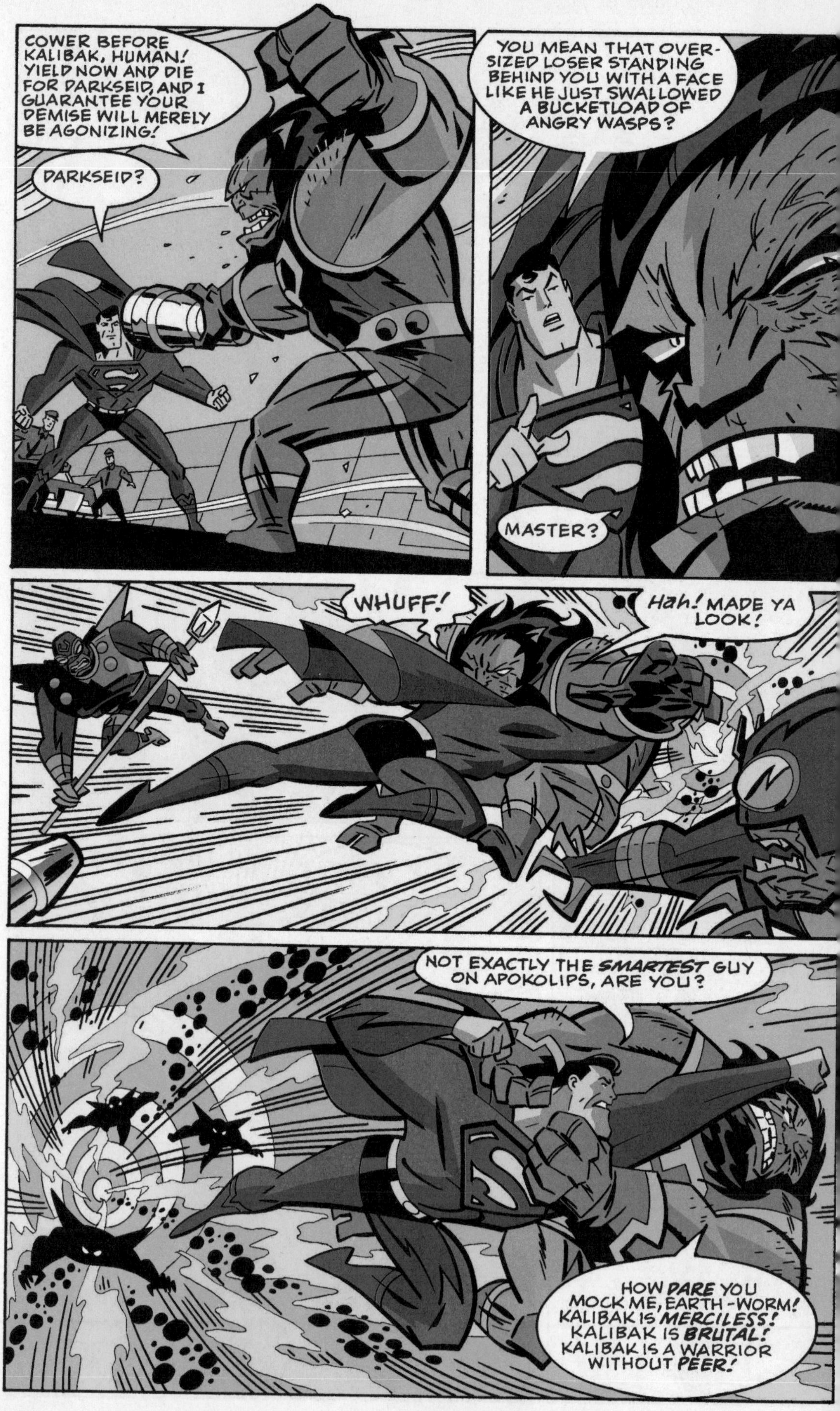
COWER BEFORE KALIBAK, HUMAN! YIELD NOW AND DIE FOR DARKSEID, AND I GUARANTEE YOUR DEMISE WILL MERELY BE AGONIZING!
DARKSEID?
YOU MEAN THAT OVER-SIZED LOSER STANDING BEHIND YOU WITH A FACE LIKE HE JUST SWALLOWED A BUCKETLOAD OF ANGRY WASPS?
MASTER?
WHUFF!
Hah! MADE YA LOOK!
NOT EXACTLY THE SMARTEST GUY ON APOKOLIPS, ARE YOU?
HOW DARE YOU MOCK ME, EARTH-WORM! KALIBAK IS MERCILESS! KALIBAK IS BRUTAL! KALIBAK IS A WARRIOR WITHOUT PEER!

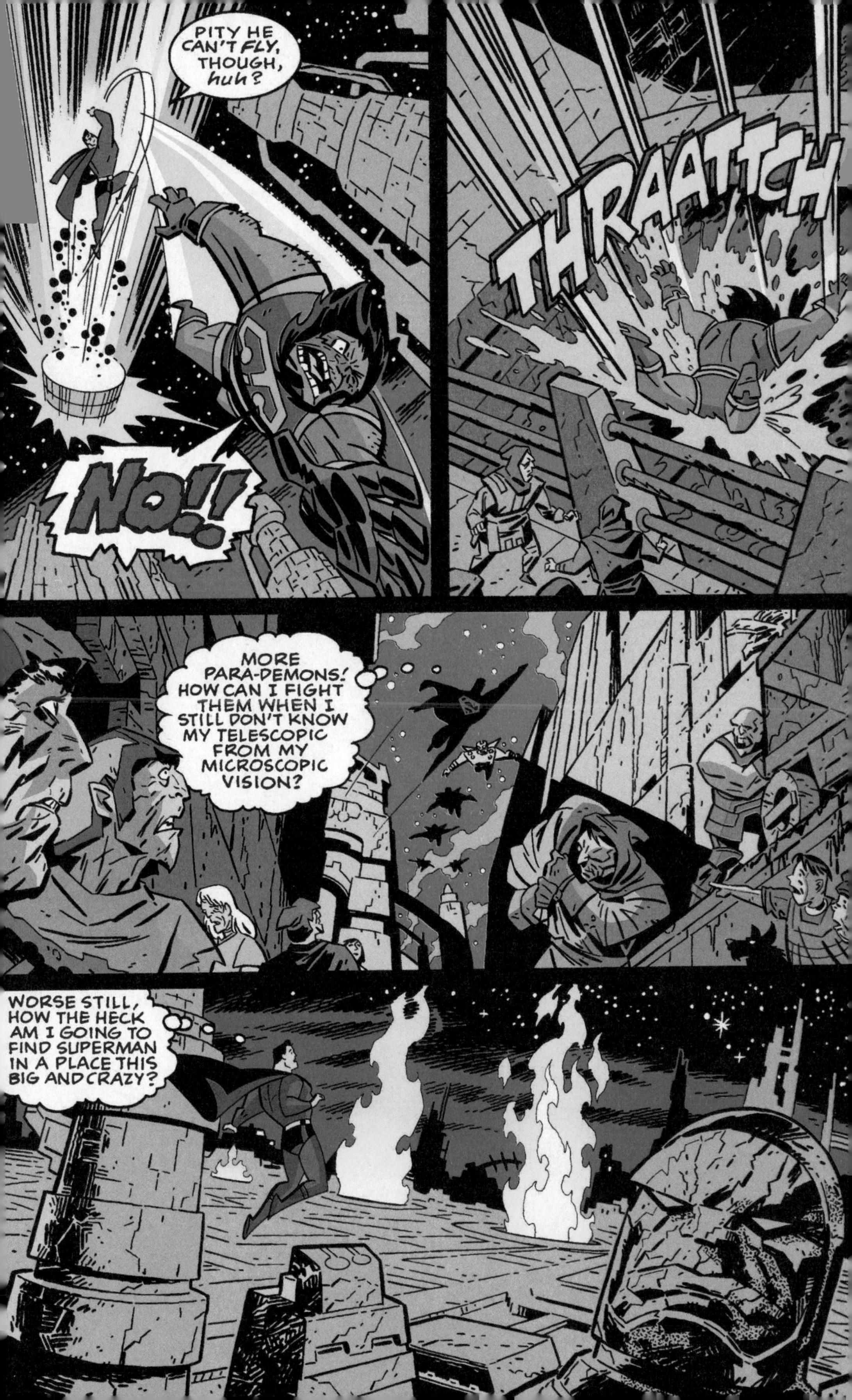
PITY HE CAN'T FLY, THOUGH, huh?
NO...!!
THRAATCH
MORE PARA-DEMONS! HOW CAN I FIGHT THEM WHEN I STILL DON'T KNOW MY TELESCOPIC FROM MY MICROSCOPIC VISION?
WORSE STILL, HOW THE HECK AM I GOING TO FIND SUPERMAN IN A PLACE THIS BIG AND CRAZY?

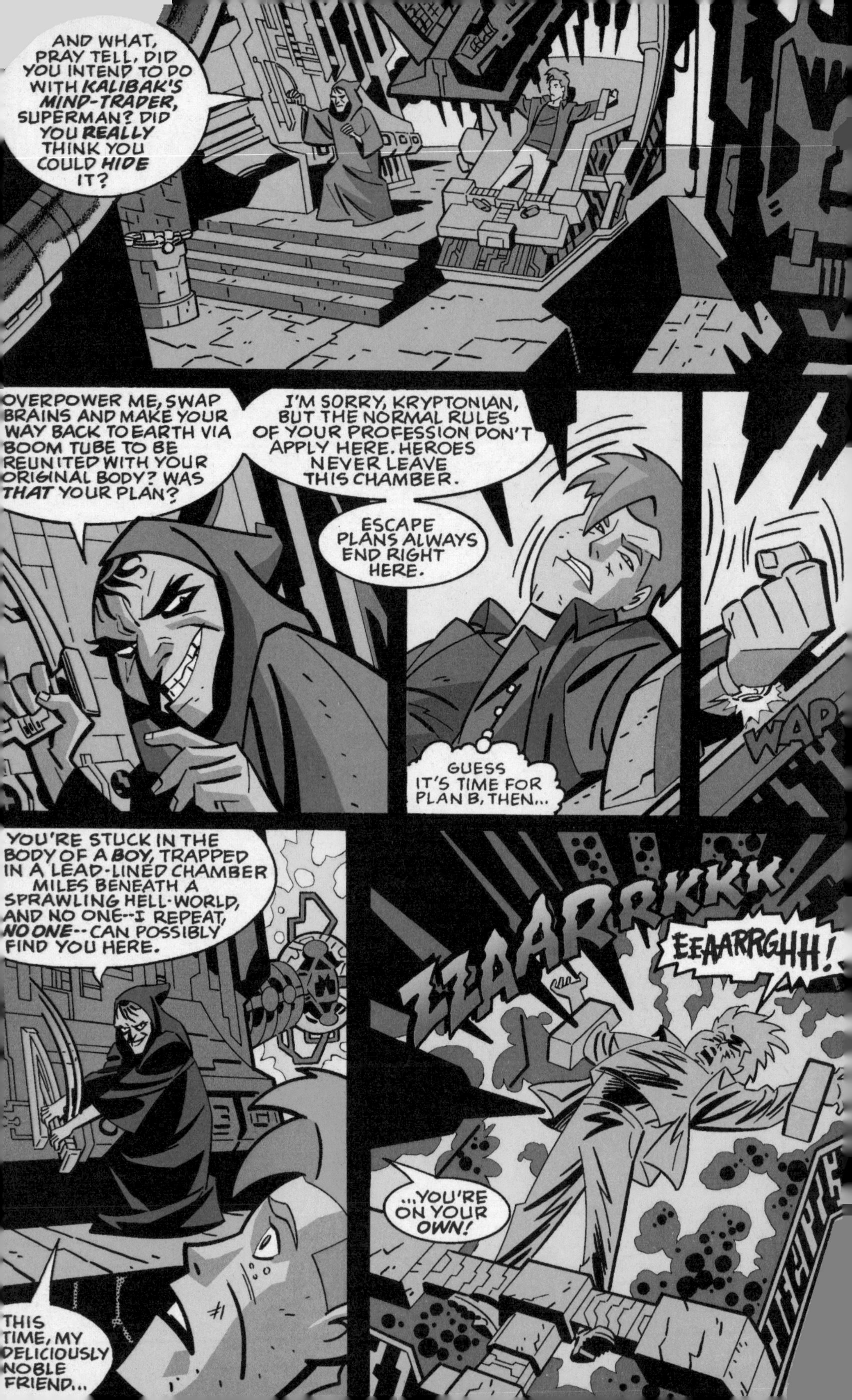
AND WHAT, PRAY TELL, DID YOU INTEND TO DO WITH KALIBAK'S MIND-TRADER, SUPERMAN? DID YOU REALLY THINK YOU COULD HIDE IT?
OVERPOWER ME, SWAP BRAINS AND MAKE YOUR WAY BACK TO EARTH VIA BOOM TUBE TO BE REUNITED WITH YOUR ORIGINAL BODY? WAS THAT YOUR PLAN?
I'M SORRY, KRYPTONIAN, BUT THE NORMAL RULES OF YOUR PROFESSION DON'T APPLY HERE. HEROES NEVER LEAVE THIS CHAMBER.
ESCAPE PLANS ALWAYS END RIGHT HERE.
GUESS IT'S TIME FOR PLAN B, THEN...
WAP
YOU'RE STUCK IN THE BODY OF A BOY, TRAPPED IN A LEAD-LINED CHAMBER MILES BENEATH A SPRAWLING HELL-WORLD, AND NO ONE--I REPEAT, NO ONE--CAN POSSIBLY FIND YOU HERE.
THIS TIME, MY DELICIOUSLY NOBLE FRIEND...
ZZAARRKKKK
EEAARRGHH!
...YOU'RE ON YOUR OWN!

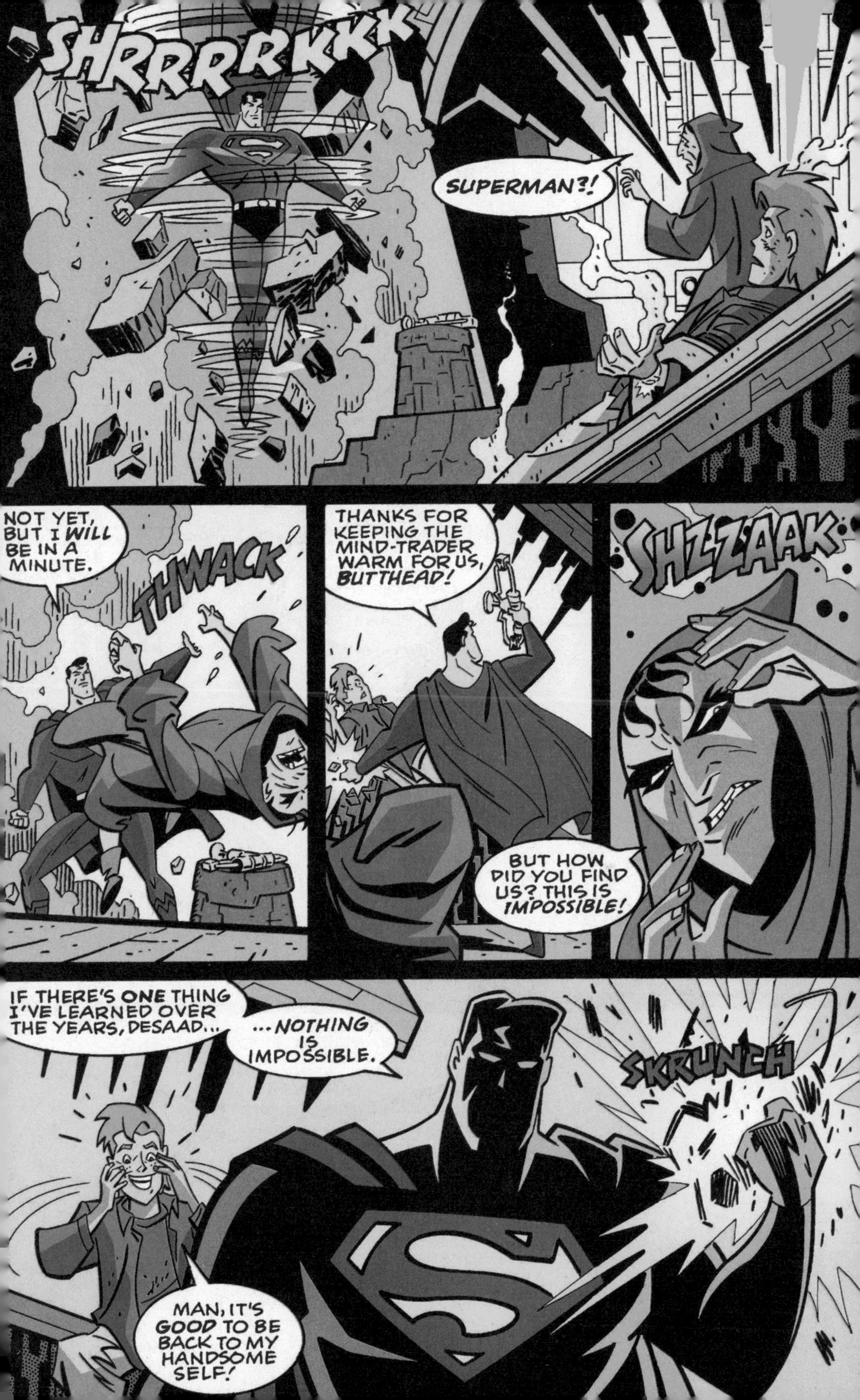
SHRRRRKKK
SUPERMAN?!
NOT YET, BUT I WILL BE IN A MINUTE.
THWACK
THANKS FOR KEEPING THE MIND-TRADER WARM FOR US, BUTTHEAD!
SHZZAAK
BUT HOW DID YOU FIND US? THIS IS IMPOSSIBLE!
IF THERE'S ONE THING I'VE LEARNED OVER THE YEARS, DESAAD...
...NOTHING IS IMPOSSIBLE.
SKRUNCH
MAN, IT'S GOOD TO BE BACK TO MY HANDSOME SELF!

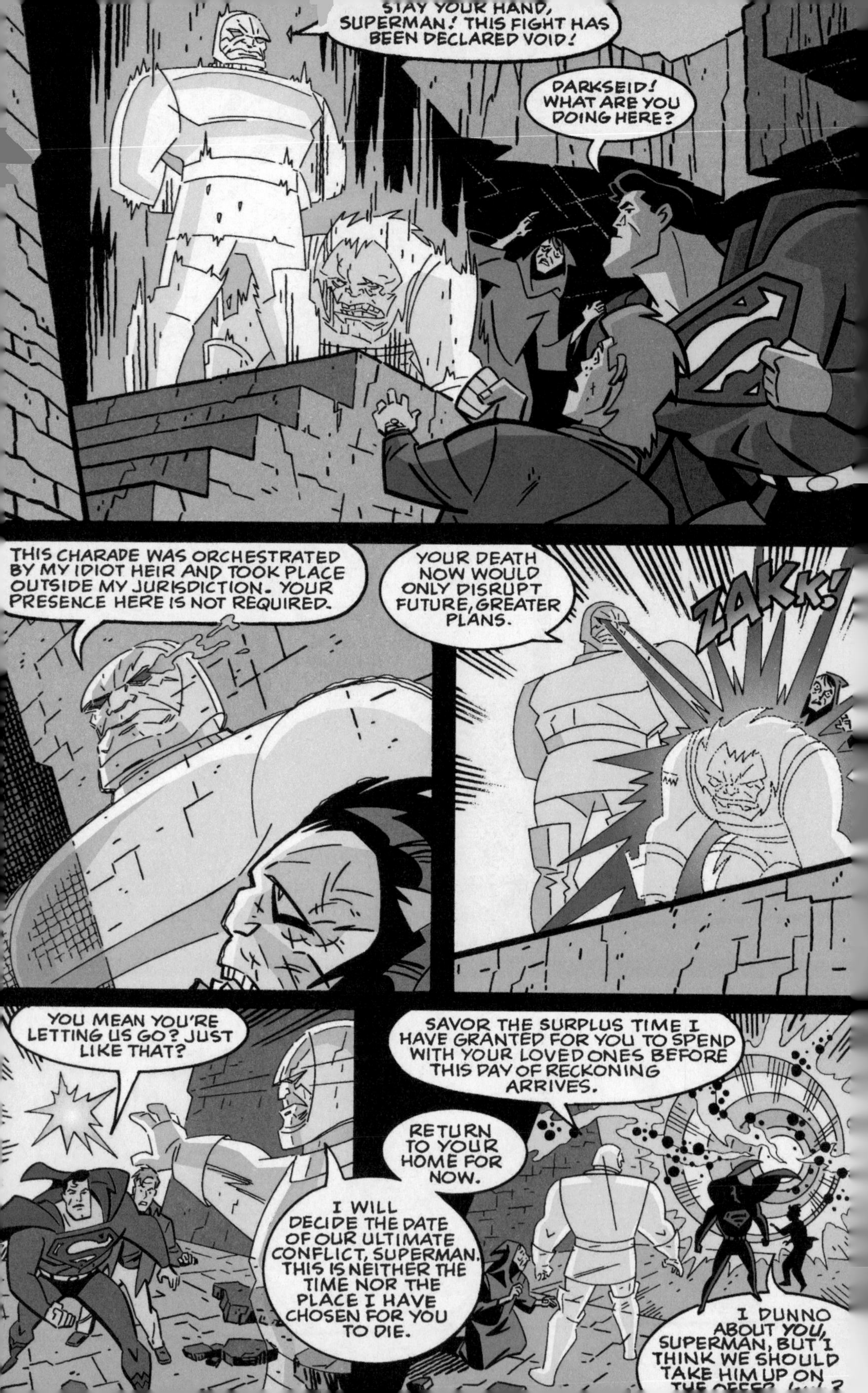
STAY YOUR HAND, SUPERMAN! THIS FIGHT HAS BEEN DECLARED VOID!
DARKSEID! WHAT ARE YOU DOING HERE?
THIS CHARADE WAS ORCHESTRATED BY MY IDIOT HEIR AND TOOK PLACE OUTSIDE MY JURISDICTION. YOUR PRESENCE HERE IS NOT REQUIRED.
YOUR DEATH NOW WOULD ONLY DISRUPT FUTURE, GREATER PLANS.
ZAKK!
YOU MEAN YOU'RE LETTING US GO? JUST LIKE THAT?
SAVOR THE SURPLUS TIME I HAVE GRANTED FOR YOU TO SPEND WITH YOUR LOVED ONES BEFORE THIS DAY OF RECKONING ARRIVES.
RETURN TO YOUR HOME FOR NOW.
I WILL DECIDE THE DATE OF OUR ULTIMATE CONFLICT, SUPERMAN. THIS IS NEITHER THE TIME NOR THE PLACE I HAVE CHOSEN FOR YOU TO DIE.
I DUNNO ABOUT YOU, SUPERMAN, BUT I THINK WE SHOULD TAKE HIM UP ON

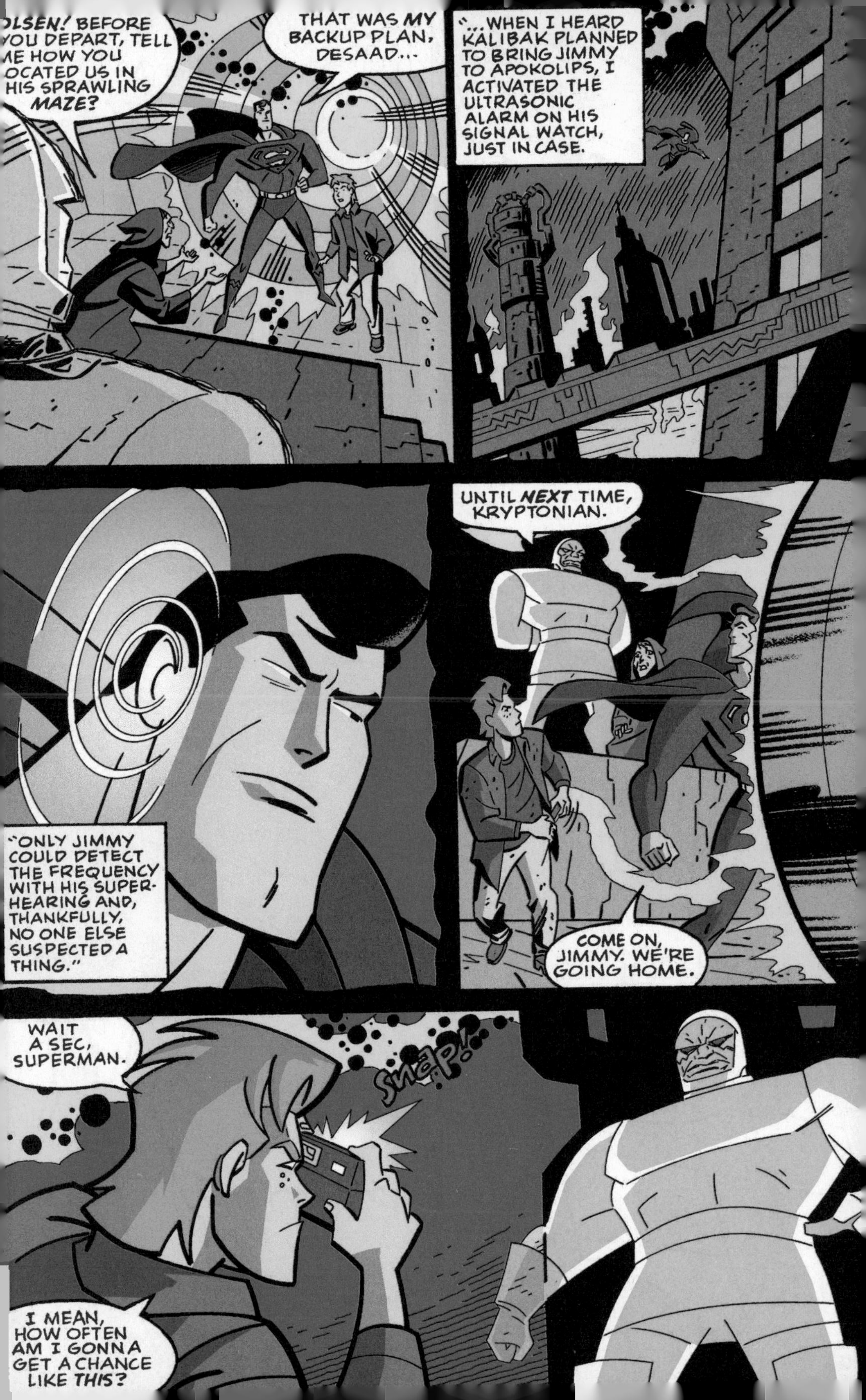
OLSEN! BEFORE YOU DEPART, TELL ME HOW YOU LOCATED US IN HIS SPRAWLING MAZE?
THAT WAS MY BACKUP PLAN, DESAAD...
"...WHEN I HEARD KALIBAK PLANNED TO BRING JIMMY TO APOKOLIPS, I ACTIVATED THE ULTRASONIC ALARM ON HIS SIGNAL WATCH, JUST IN CASE.
"ONLY JIMMY COULD DETECT THE FREQUENCY WITH HIS SUPER-HEARING AND, THANKFULLY, NO ONE ELSE SUSPECTED A THING."
UNTIL NEXT TIME, KRYPTONIAN.
COME ON, JIMMY. WE'RE GOING HOME.
WAIT A SEC, SUPERMAN.
SNAP!
I MEAN, HOW OFTEN AM I GONNA GET A CHANCE LIKE THIS?

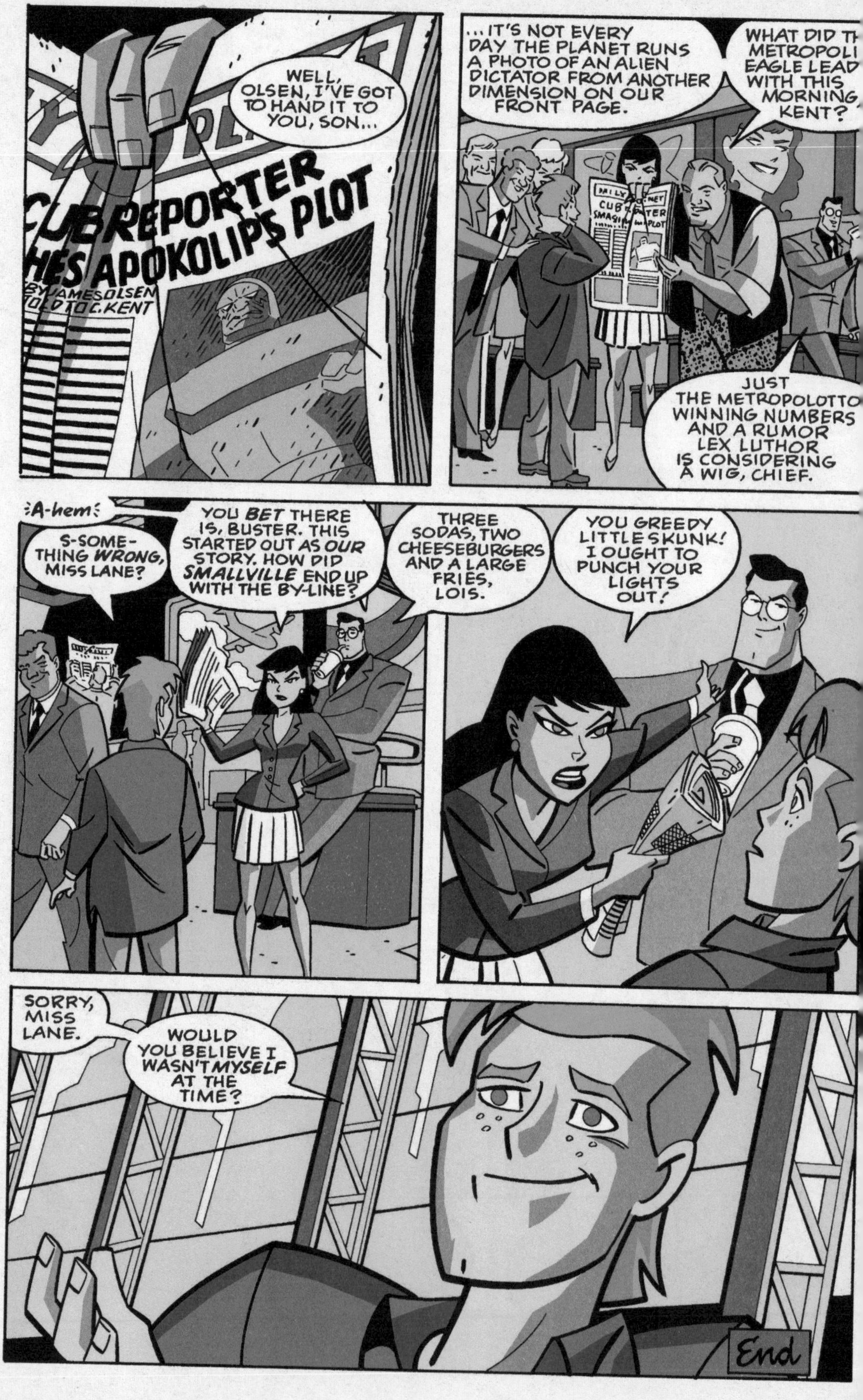

WELL, OLSEN, I'VE GOT TO HAND IT TO YOU, SON...
CUB REPORTER
HES APOKOLIPS PLOT
BY JAMES OLSEN TOLD TO C. KENT
...IT'S NOT EVERY DAY THE PLANET RUNS A PHOTO OF AN ALIEN DICTATOR FROM ANOTHER DIMENSION ON OUR FRONT PAGE.
WHAT DID TH METROPOLI EAGLE LEAD WITH THIS MORNING, KENT?
JUST THE METROPOLOTTO WINNING NUMBERS AND A RUMOR LEX LUTHOR IS CONSIDERING A WIG, CHIEF.
A-hem
S-SOME-THING WRONG, MISS LANE?
YOU BET THERE IS, BUSTER. THIS STARTED OUT AS OUR STORY. HOW DID SMALLVILLE END UP WITH THE BY-LINE?
THREE SODAS, TWO CHEESEBURGERS AND A LARGE FRIES, LOIS.
YOU GREEDY LITTLE SKUNK! I OUGHT TO PUNCH YOUR LIGHTS OUT!
SORRY, MISS LANE.
WOULD YOU BELIEVE I WASN'T MYSELF AT THE TIME?
End

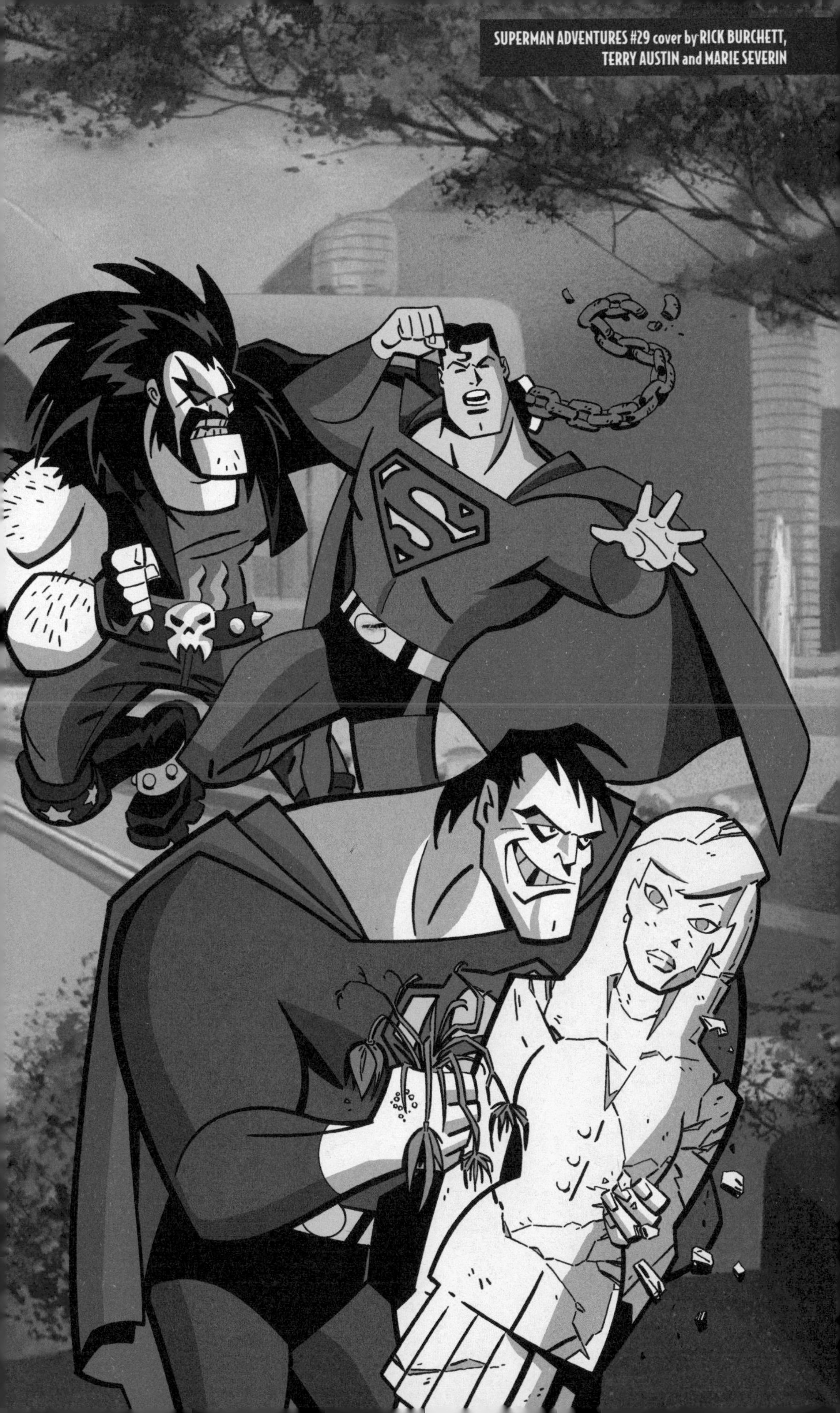

SUPERMAN ADVENTURES #29 cover by RICK BURCHETT, TERRY AUSTIN and MARIE SEVERIN

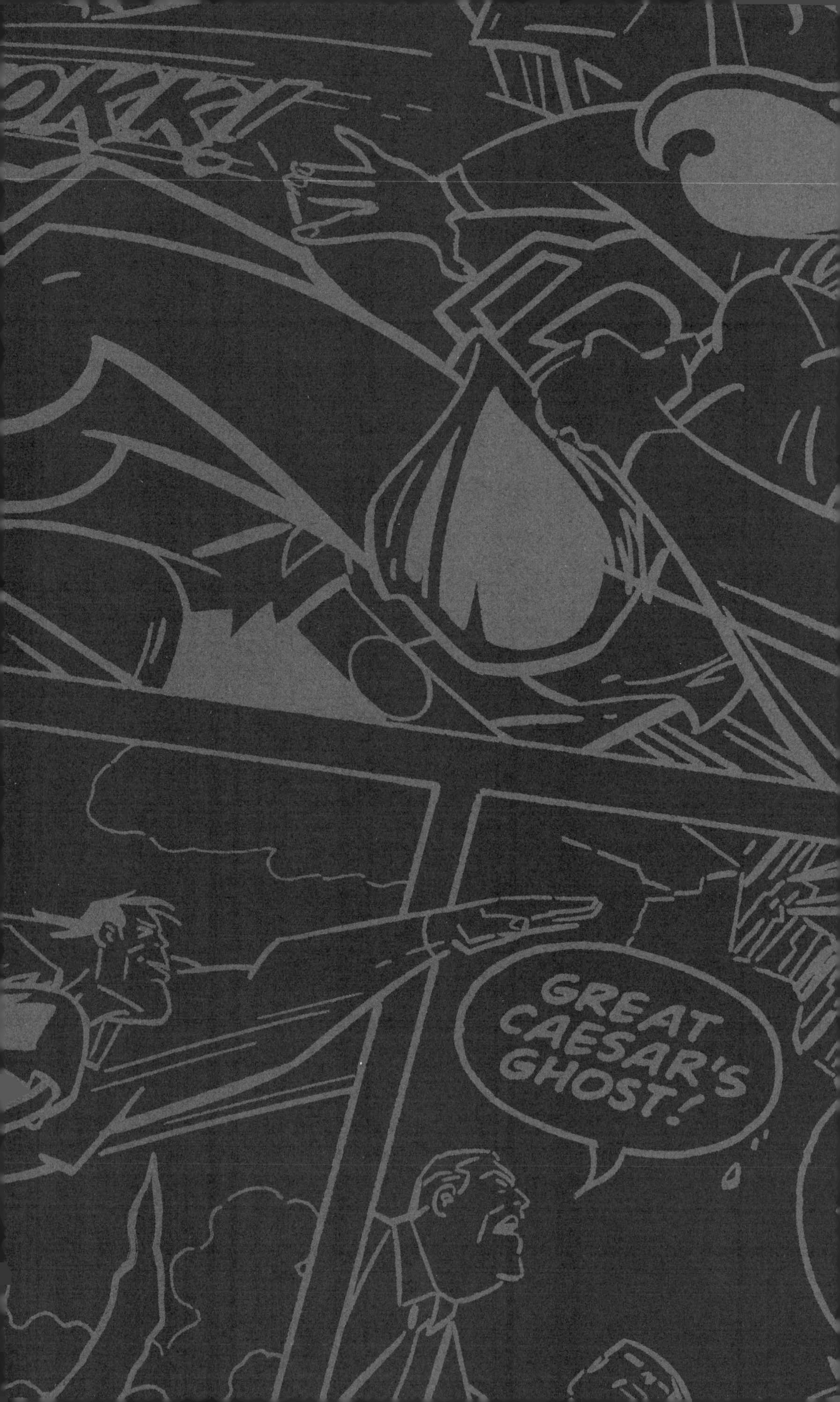
GREAT CAESAR'S GHOST!

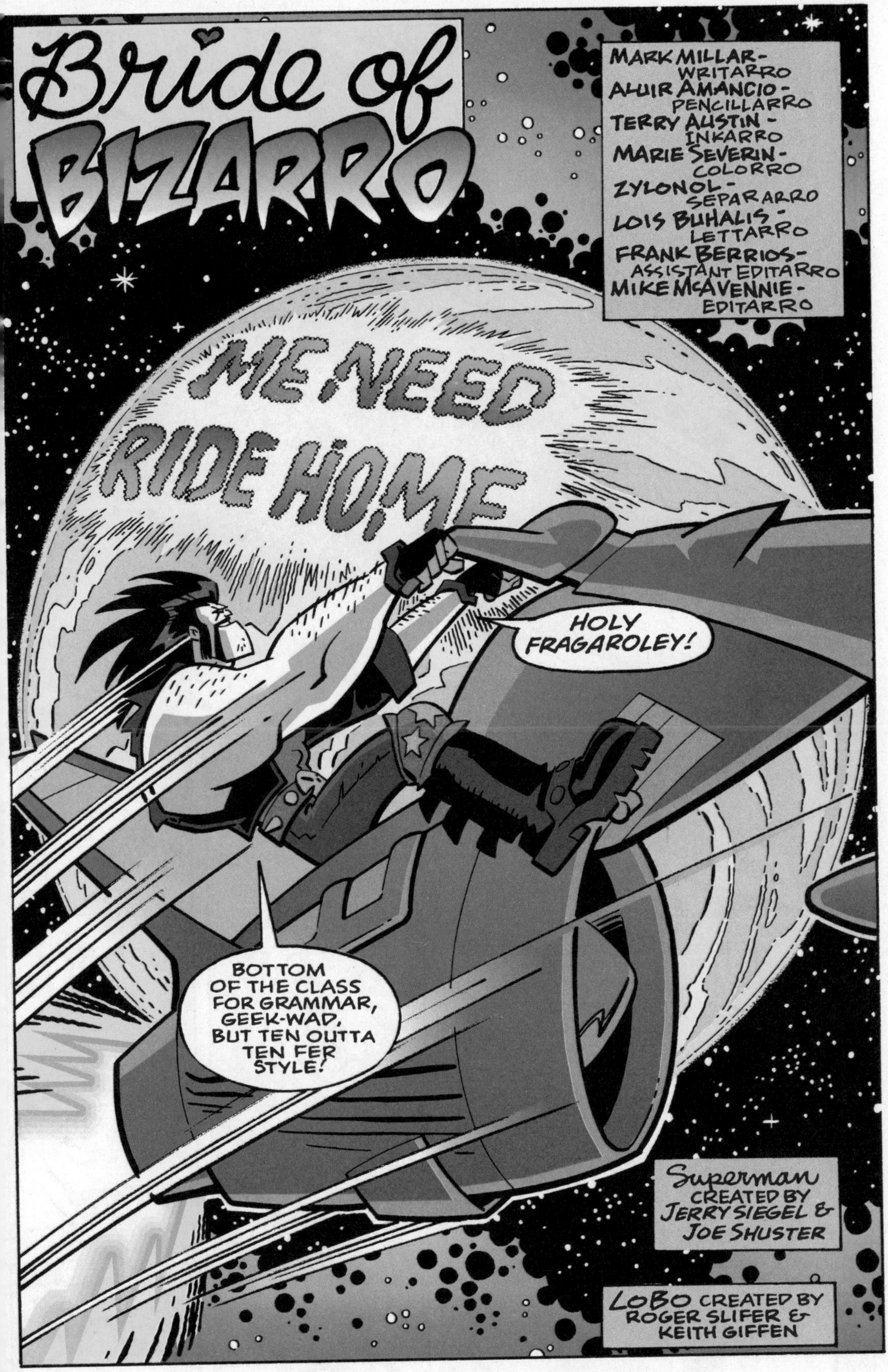

Bride of BIZARRO
MARK MILLAR - WRITARRO
ALUIR AMANCIO - PENCILLARRO
TERRY AUSTIN - INKARRO
MARIE SEVERIN - COLORRO
ZYLONOL - SEPARARRO
LOIS BUHALIS - LETTARRO
FRANK BERRIOS - ASSISTANT EDITARRO
MIKE McAVENNIE - EDITARRO
ME NEED RIDE HOME
HOLY FRAGAROLEY!
BOTTOM OF THE CLASS FOR GRAMMAR, GEEK-WAD, BUT TEN OUTTA TEN FER STYLE!
Superman CREATED BY JERRY SIEGEL & JOE SHUSTER
LOBO CREATED BY ROGER SLIFER & KEITH GIFFEN

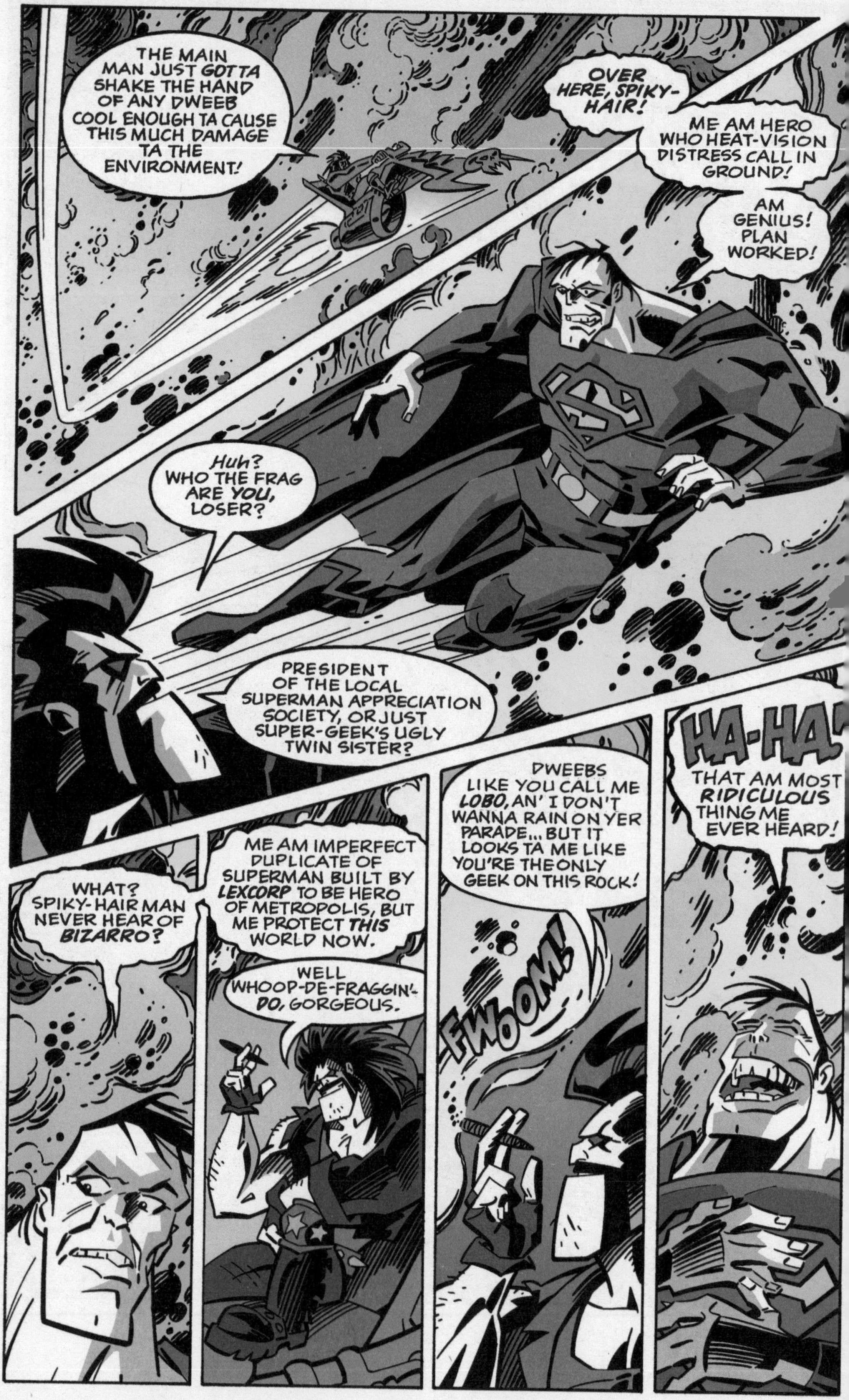
THE MAIN MAN JUST GOTTA SHAKE THE HAND OF ANY DWEEB COOL ENOUGH TA CAUSE THIS MUCH DAMAGE TA THE ENVIRONMENT!
OVER HERE, SPIKY-HAIR!
ME AM HERO WHO HEAT-VISION DISTRESS CALL IN GROUND!
AM GENIUS! PLAN WORKED!
Huh? WHO THE FRAG ARE YOU, LOSER?
PRESIDENT OF THE LOCAL SUPERMAN APPRECIATION SOCIETY, OR JUST SUPER-GEEK'S UGLY TWIN SISTER?
WHAT? SPIKY-HAIR MAN NEVER HEAR OF BIZARRO?
ME AM IMPERFECT DUPLICATE OF SUPERMAN BUILT BY LEXCORP TO BE HERO OF METROPOLIS, BUT ME PROTECT THIS WORLD NOW.
WELL WHOOP-DE-FRAGGIN'-DO, GORGEOUS.
DWEEBS LIKE YOU CALL ME LOBO, AN' I DON'T WANNA RAIN ON YER PARADE... BUT IT LOOKS TA ME LIKE YOU'RE THE ONLY GEEK ON THIS ROCK!
FWOOM!
THAT AM MOST RIDICULOUS THING ME EVER HEARD!

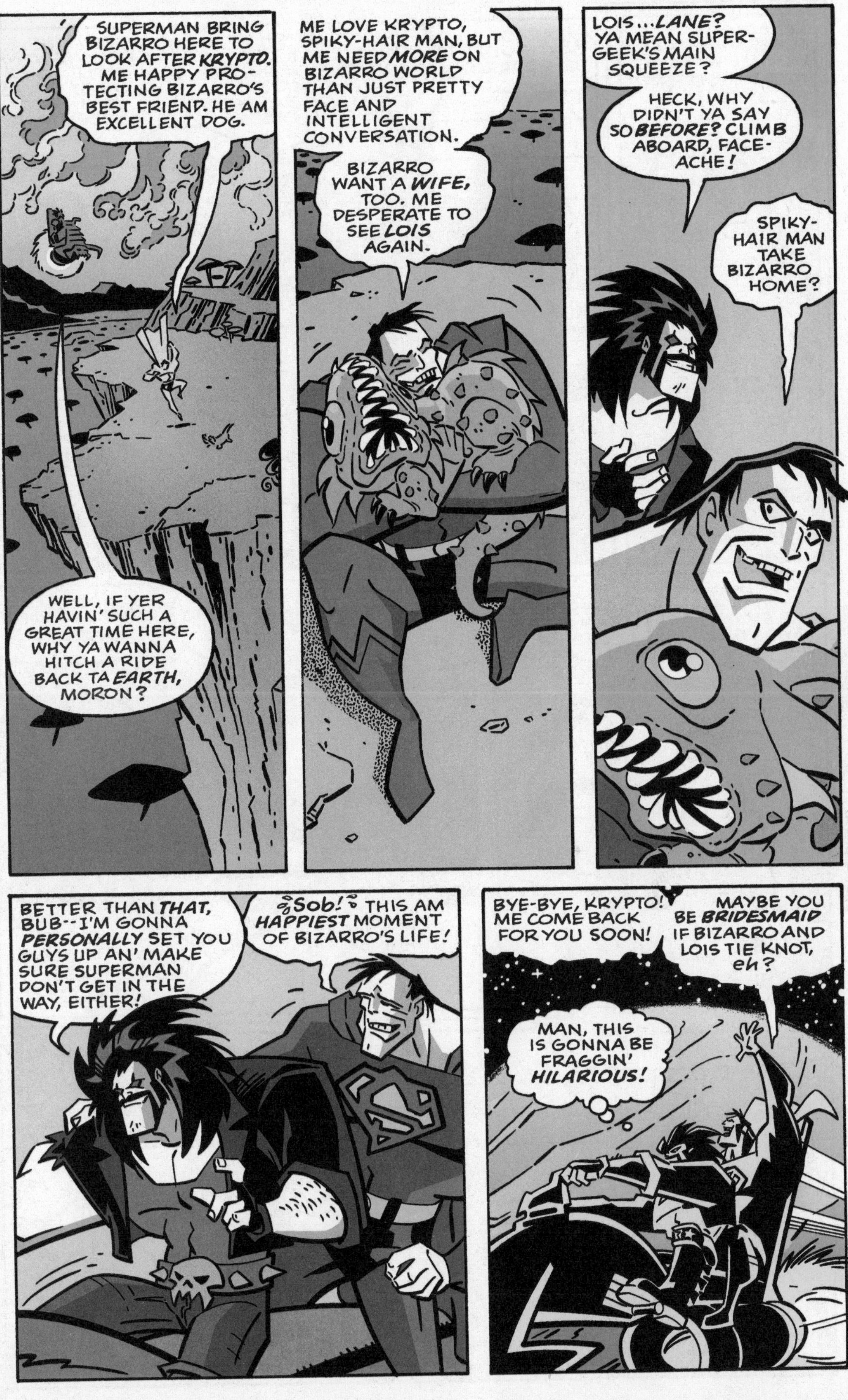
SUPERMAN BRING BIZARRO HERE TO LOOK AFTER KRYPTO. ME HAPPY PROTECTING BIZARRO'S BEST FRIEND. HE AM EXCELLENT DOG.
WELL, IF YER HAVIN' SUCH A GREAT TIME HERE, WHY YA WANNA HITCH A RIDE BACK TA EARTH, MORON?
ME LOVE KRYPTO, SPIKY-HAIR MAN, BUT ME NEED MORE ON BIZARRO WORLD THAN JUST PRETTY FACE AND INTELLIGENT CONVERSATION.
BIZARRO WANT A WIFE, TOO. ME DESPERATE TO SEE LOIS AGAIN.
LOIS...LANE? YA MEAN SUPER-GEEK'S MAIN SQUEEZE?
HECK, WHY DIDN'T YA SAY SO BEFORE? CLIMB ABOARD, FACE-ACHE!
SPIKY-HAIR MAN TAKE BIZARRO HOME?
BETTER THAN THAT, BUB--I'M GONNA PERSONALLY SET YOU GUYS UP AN' MAKE SURE SUPERMAN DON'T GET IN THE WAY, EITHER!
Sob! THIS AM HAPPIEST MOMENT OF BIZARRO'S LIFE!
BYE-BYE, KRYPTO! ME COME BACK FOR YOU SOON!
MAYBE YOU BE BRIDESMAID IF BIZARRO AND LOIS TIE KNOT, eh?
MAN, THIS IS GONNA BE FRAGGIN' HILARIOUS!

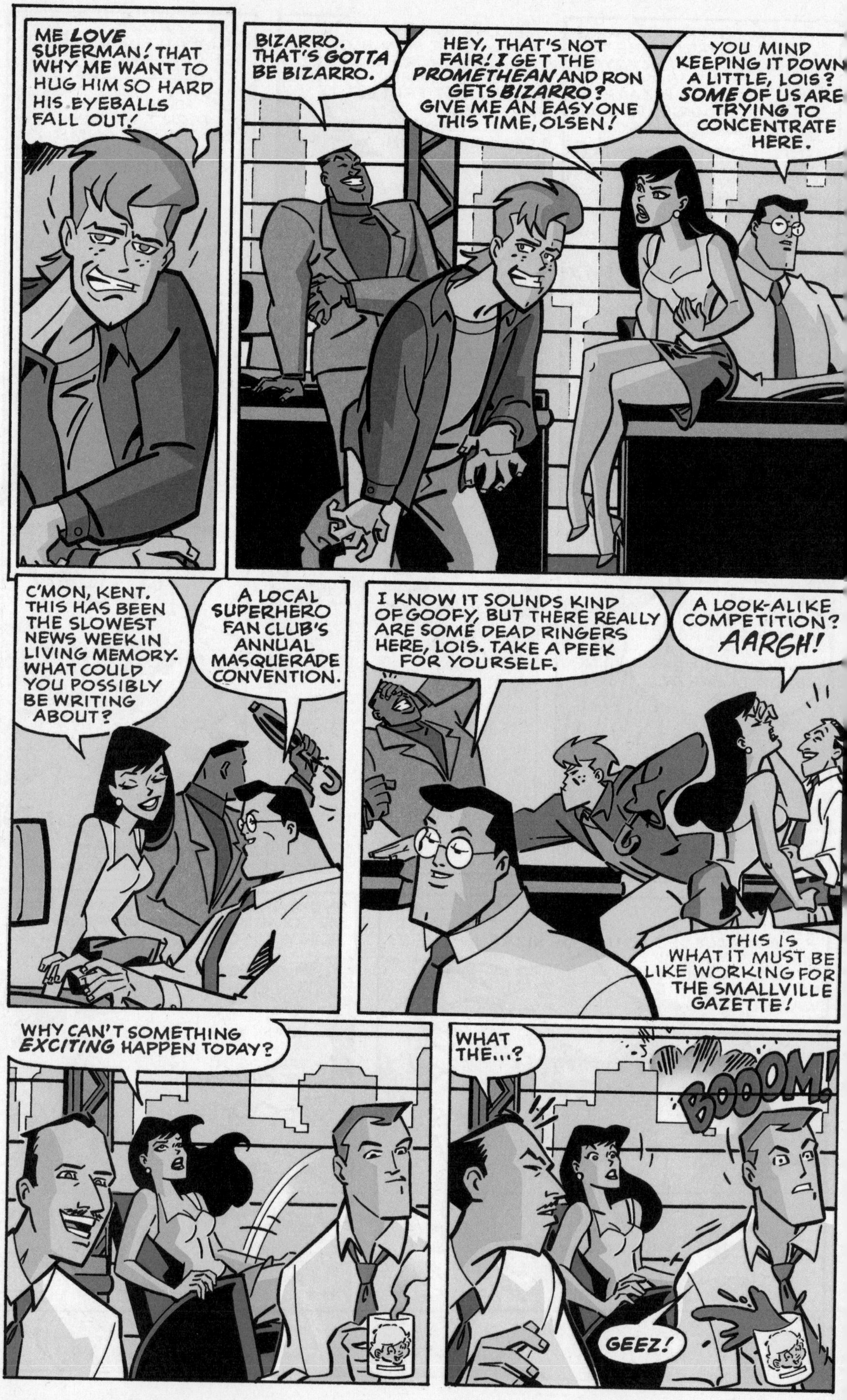

ME LOVE SUPERMAN! THAT WHY ME WANT TO HUG HIM SO HARD HIS EYEBALLS FALL OUT!
BIZARRO. THAT'S GOTTA BE BIZARRO.
HEY, THAT'S NOT FAIR! I GET THE PROMETHEAN AND RON GETS BIZARRO? GIVE ME AN EASY ONE THIS TIME, OLSEN!
YOU MIND KEEPING IT DOWN A LITTLE, LOIS? SOME OF US ARE TRYING TO CONCENTRATE HERE.
C'MON, KENT. THIS HAS BEEN THE SLOWEST NEWS WEEK IN LIVING MEMORY. WHAT COULD YOU POSSIBLY BE WRITING ABOUT?
A LOCAL SUPERHERO FAN CLUB'S ANNUAL MASQUERADE CONVENTION.
I KNOW IT SOUNDS KIND OF GOOFY, BUT THERE REALLY ARE SOME DEAD RINGERS HERE, LOIS. TAKE A PEEK FOR YOURSELF.
A LOOK-ALIKE COMPETITION? AARGH!
THIS IS WHAT IT MUST BE LIKE WORKING FOR THE SMALLVILLE GAZETTE!
WHY CAN'T SOMETHING EXCITING HAPPEN TODAY?
WHAT THE...?
BOOOM!
GEEZ!

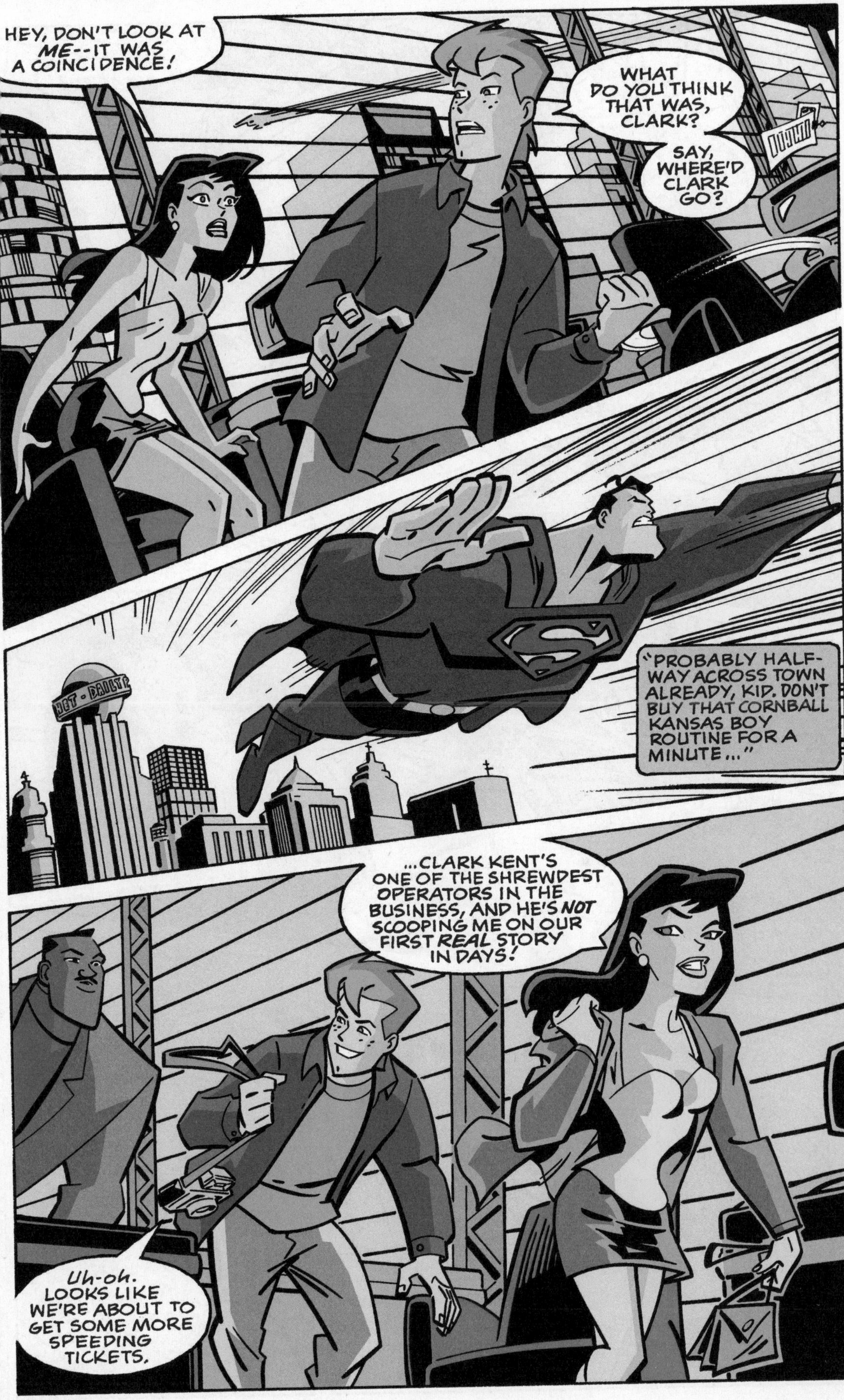
HEY, DON'T LOOK AT *ME*--IT WAS A COINCIDENCE!
WHAT DO YOU THINK THAT WAS, CLARK?
SAY, WHERE'D CLARK GO?
"PROBABLY HALF-WAY ACROSS TOWN ALREADY, KID. DON'T BUY THAT CORNBALL KANSAS BOY ROUTINE FOR A MINUTE..."
...CLARK KENT'S ONE OF THE SHREWDEST OPERATORS IN THE BUSINESS, AND HE'S *NOT* SCOOPING ME ON OUR FIRST *REAL* STORY IN DAYS!
Uh-oh. LOOKS LIKE WE'RE ABOUT TO GET SOME MORE SPEEDING TICKETS.

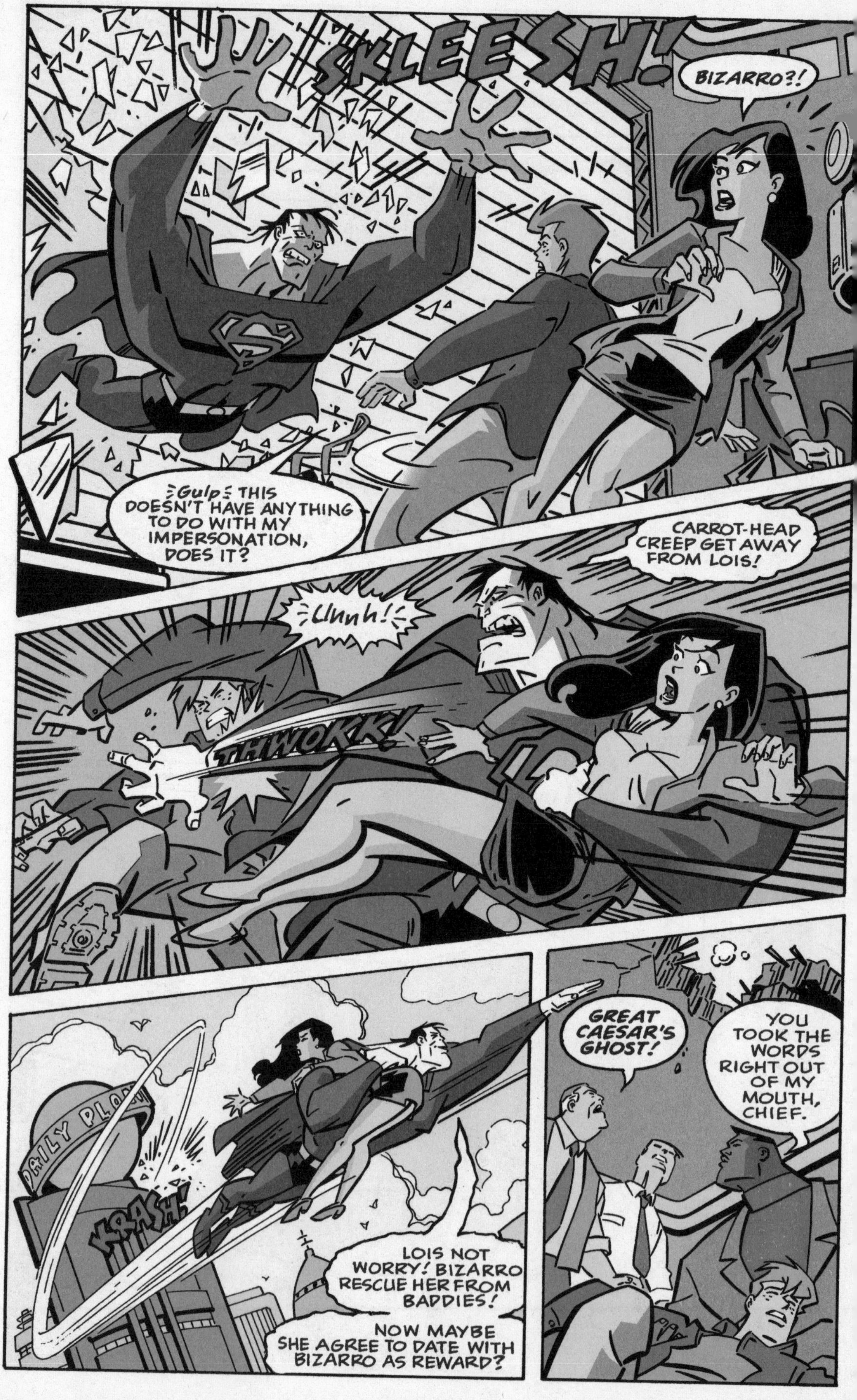
SKLEESH!
BIZARRO?!
Gulp THIS DOESN'T HAVE ANYTHING TO DO WITH MY IMPERSONATION, DOES IT?
CARROT-HEAD CREEP GET AWAY FROM LOIS!
Unnh!
THWOKK!
KRASH!
LOIS NOT WORRY! BIZARRO RESCUE HER FROM BADDIES!
NOW MAYBE SHE AGREE TO DATE WITH BIZARRO AS REWARD?
GREAT CAESAR'S GHOST!
YOU TOOK THE WORDS RIGHT OUT OF MY MOUTH, CHIEF.

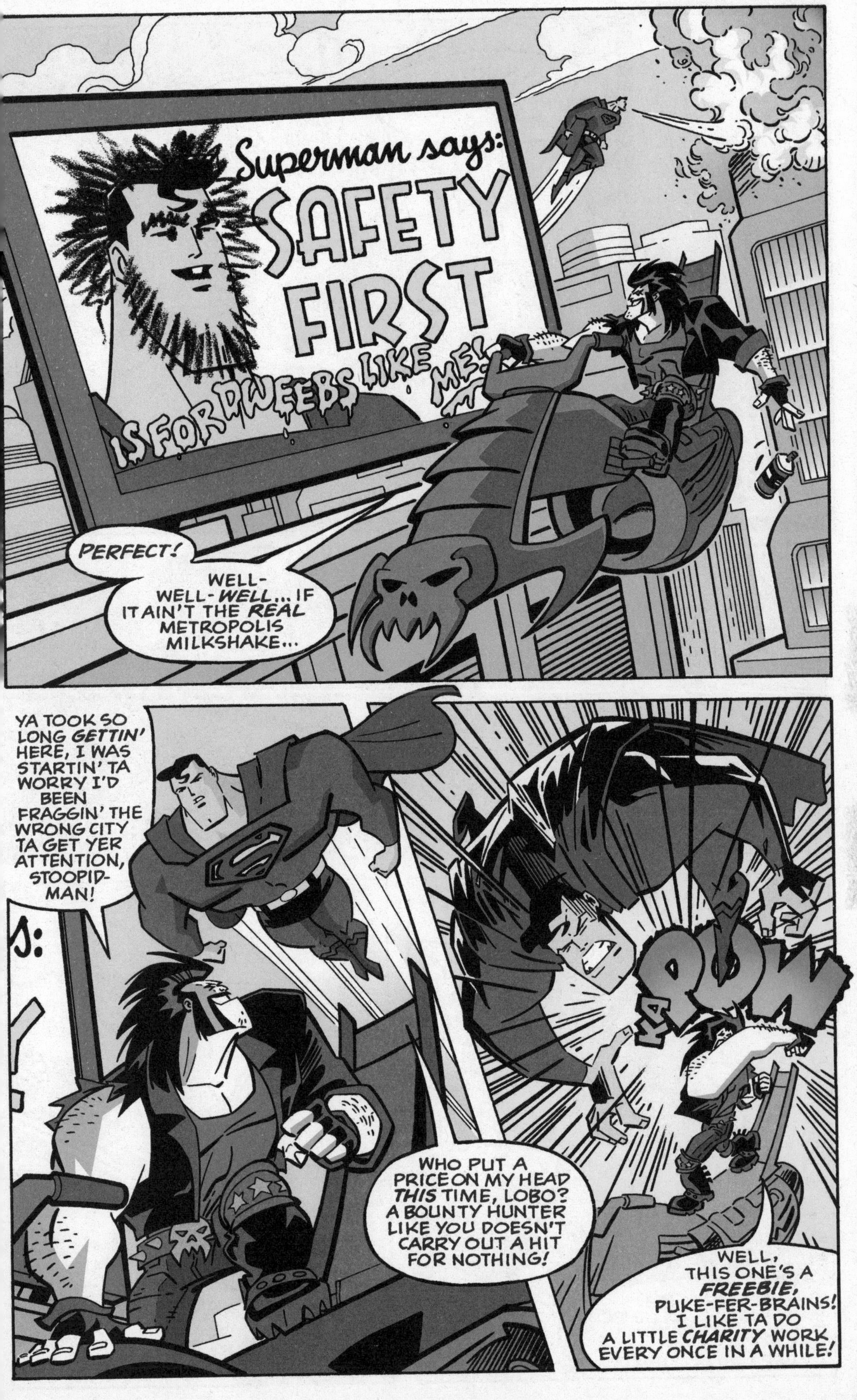

Superman says:
SAFETY FIRST
IS FOR DWEEBS LIKE ME!
PERFECT!
WELL-WELL-WELL... IF IT AIN'T THE REAL METROPOLIS MILKSHAKE...
YA TOOK SO LONG GETTIN' HERE, I WAS STARTIN' TA WORRY I'D BEEN FRAGGIN' THE WRONG CITY TA GET YER ATTENTION, STOOPID-MAN!
KA POW
WHO PUT A PRICE ON MY HEAD THIS TIME, LOBO? A BOUNTY HUNTER LIKE YOU DOESN'T CARRY OUT A HIT FOR NOTHING!
WELL, THIS ONE'S A FREEBIE, PUKE-FER-BRAINS! I LIKE TA DO A LITTLE CHARITY WORK EVERY ONCE IN A WHILE!

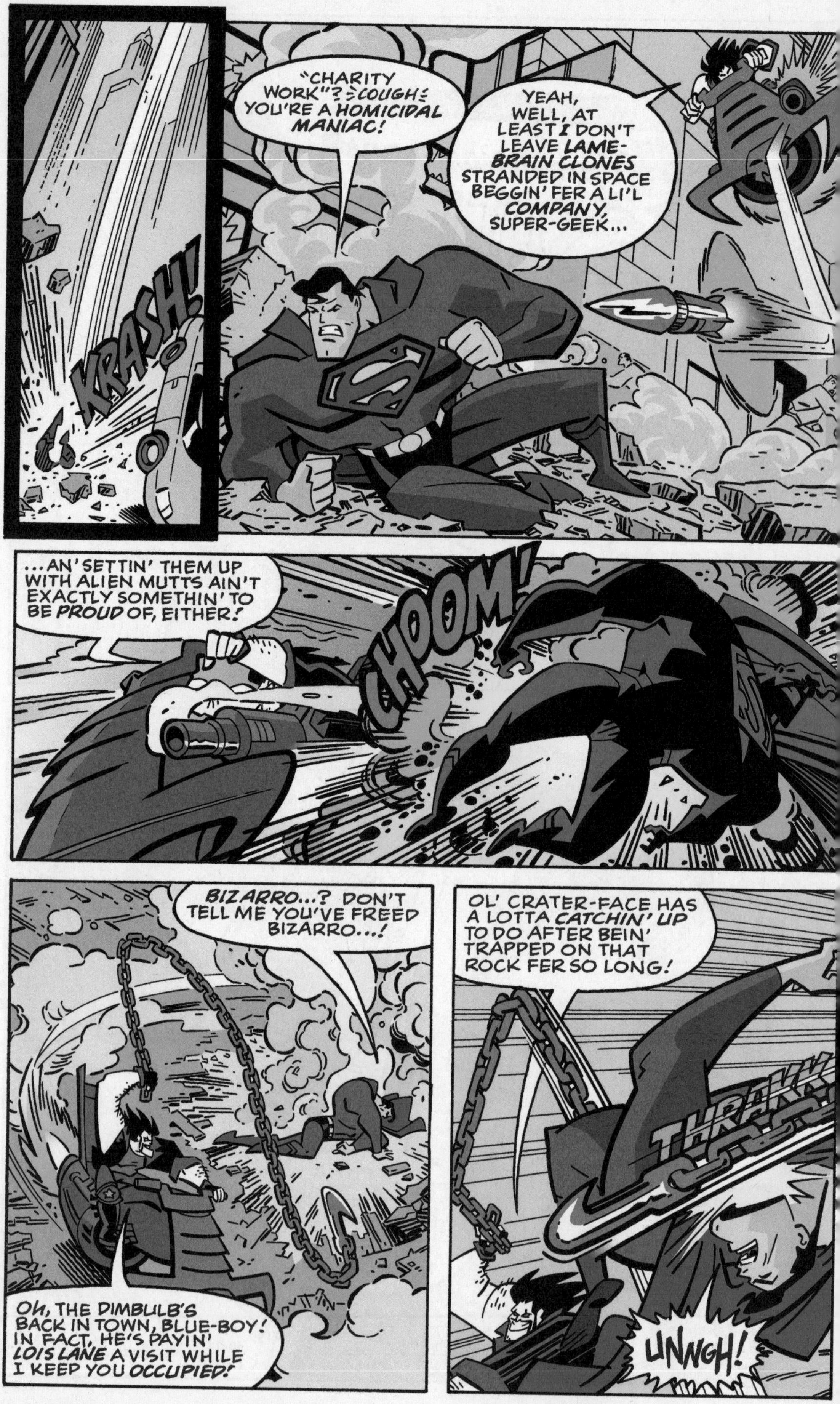
KRASH!
"CHARITY WORK"? COUGH YOU'RE A HOMICIDAL MANIAC!
YEAH, WELL, AT LEAST I DON'T LEAVE LAME-BRAIN CLONES STRANDED IN SPACE BEGGIN' FER A LI'L COMPANY, SUPER-GEEK...
...AN' SETTIN' THEM UP WITH ALIEN MUTTS AIN'T EXACTLY SOMETHIN' TO BE PROUD OF, EITHER!
CHOOM!
BIZARRO...? DON'T TELL ME YOU'VE FREED BIZARRO...!
OH, THE DIMBULB'S BACK IN TOWN, BLUE-BOY! IN FACT, HE'S PAYIN' LOIS LANE A VISIT WHILE I KEEP YOU OCCUPIED!
OL' CRATER-FACE HAS A LOTTA CATCHIN' UP TO DO AFTER BEIN' TRAPPED ON THAT ROCK FER SO LONG!
UNNGH!

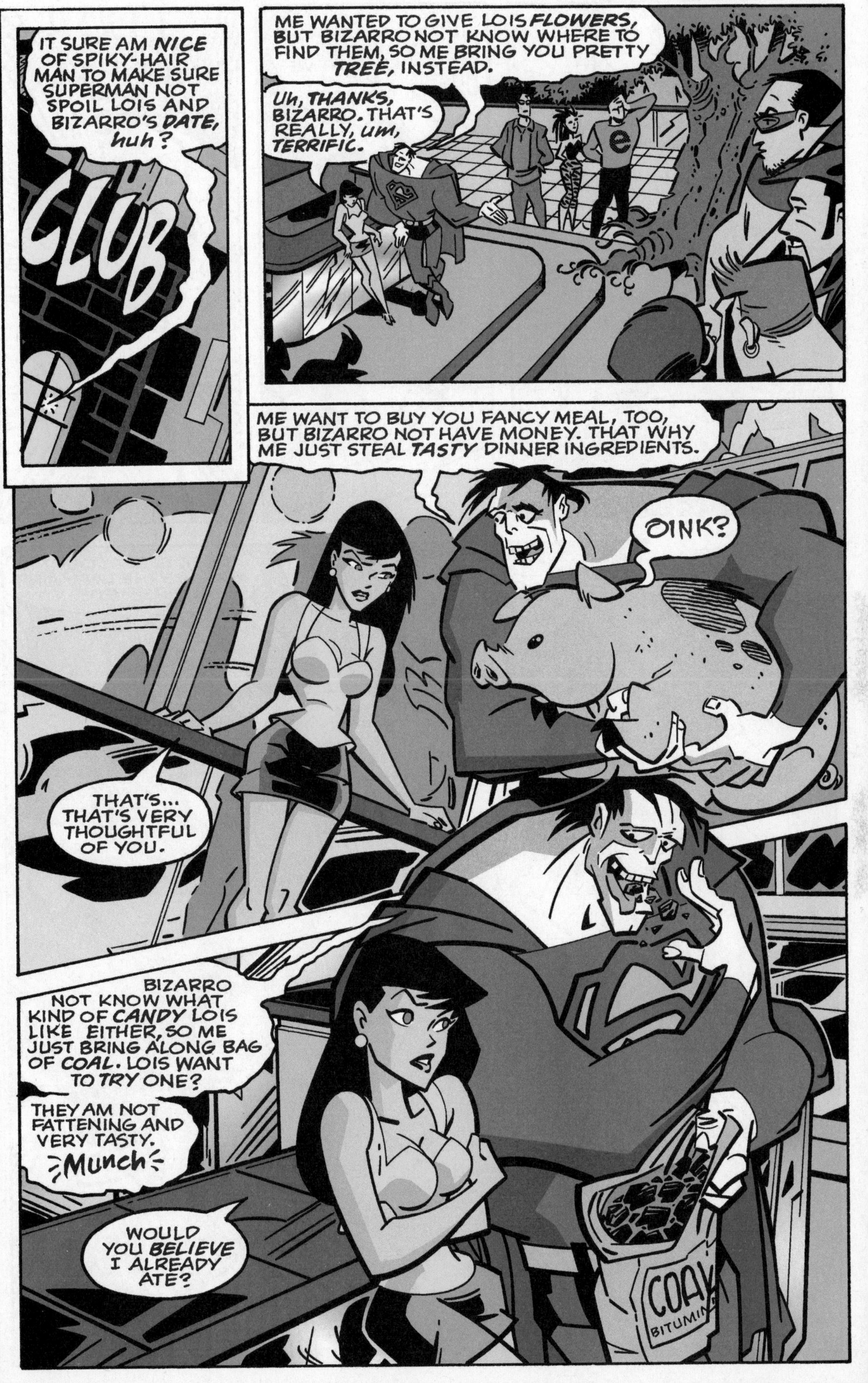

IT SURE AM NICE OF SPIKY-HAIR MAN TO MAKE SURE SUPERMAN NOT SPOIL LOIS AND BIZARRO'S DATE, huh?
CLUB
ME WANTED TO GIVE LOIS FLOWERS, BUT BIZARRO NOT KNOW WHERE TO FIND THEM, SO ME BRING YOU PRETTY TREE, INSTEAD.
Uh, THANKS, BIZARRO. THAT'S REALLY, um, TERRIFIC.
ME WANT TO BUY YOU FANCY MEAL, TOO, BUT BIZARRO NOT HAVE MONEY. THAT WHY ME JUST STEAL TASTY DINNER INGREDIENTS.
OINK?
THAT'S... THAT'S VERY THOUGHTFUL OF YOU.
BIZARRO NOT KNOW WHAT KIND OF CANDY LOIS LIKE EITHER, SO ME JUST BRING ALONG BAG OF COAL. LOIS WANT TO TRY ONE?
THEY AM NOT FATTENING AND VERY TASTY.
Munch
WOULD YOU BELIEVE I ALREADY ATE?

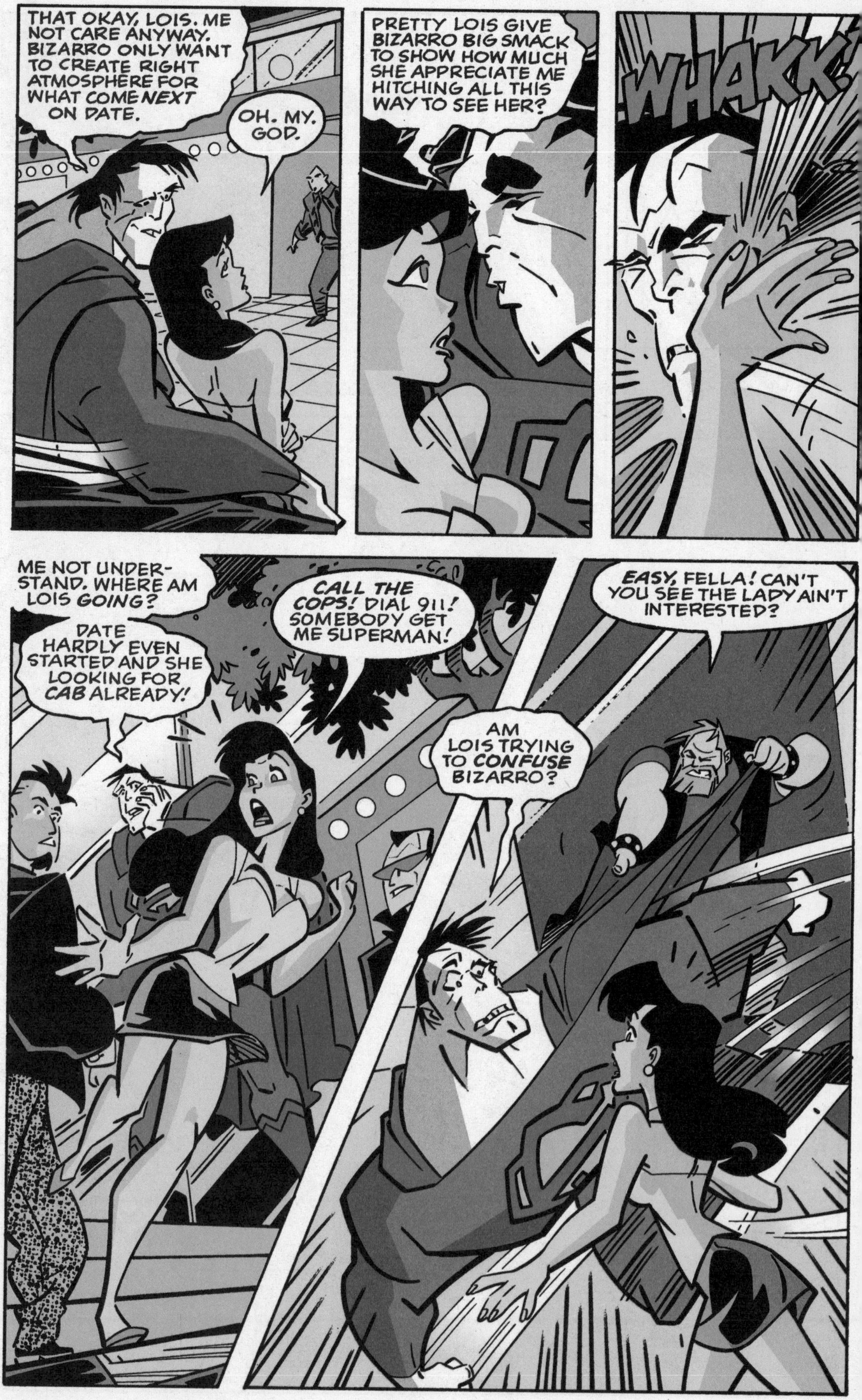
THAT OKAY, LOIS. ME NOT CARE ANYWAY. BIZARRO ONLY WANT TO CREATE RIGHT ATMOSPHERE FOR WHAT COME NEXT ON DATE.
OH. MY. GOD.
PRETTY LOIS GIVE BIZARRO BIG SMACK TO SHOW HOW MUCH SHE APPRECIATE ME HITCHING ALL THIS WAY TO SEE HER?
WHAKK!
ME NOT UNDER-STAND. WHERE AM LOIS GOING?
DATE HARDLY EVEN STARTED AND SHE LOOKING FOR CAB ALREADY!
CALL THE COPS! DIAL 911! SOMEBODY GET ME SUPERMAN!
EASY, FELLA! CAN'T YOU SEE THE LADY AIN'T INTERESTED?
AM LOIS TRYING TO CONFUSE BIZARRO?

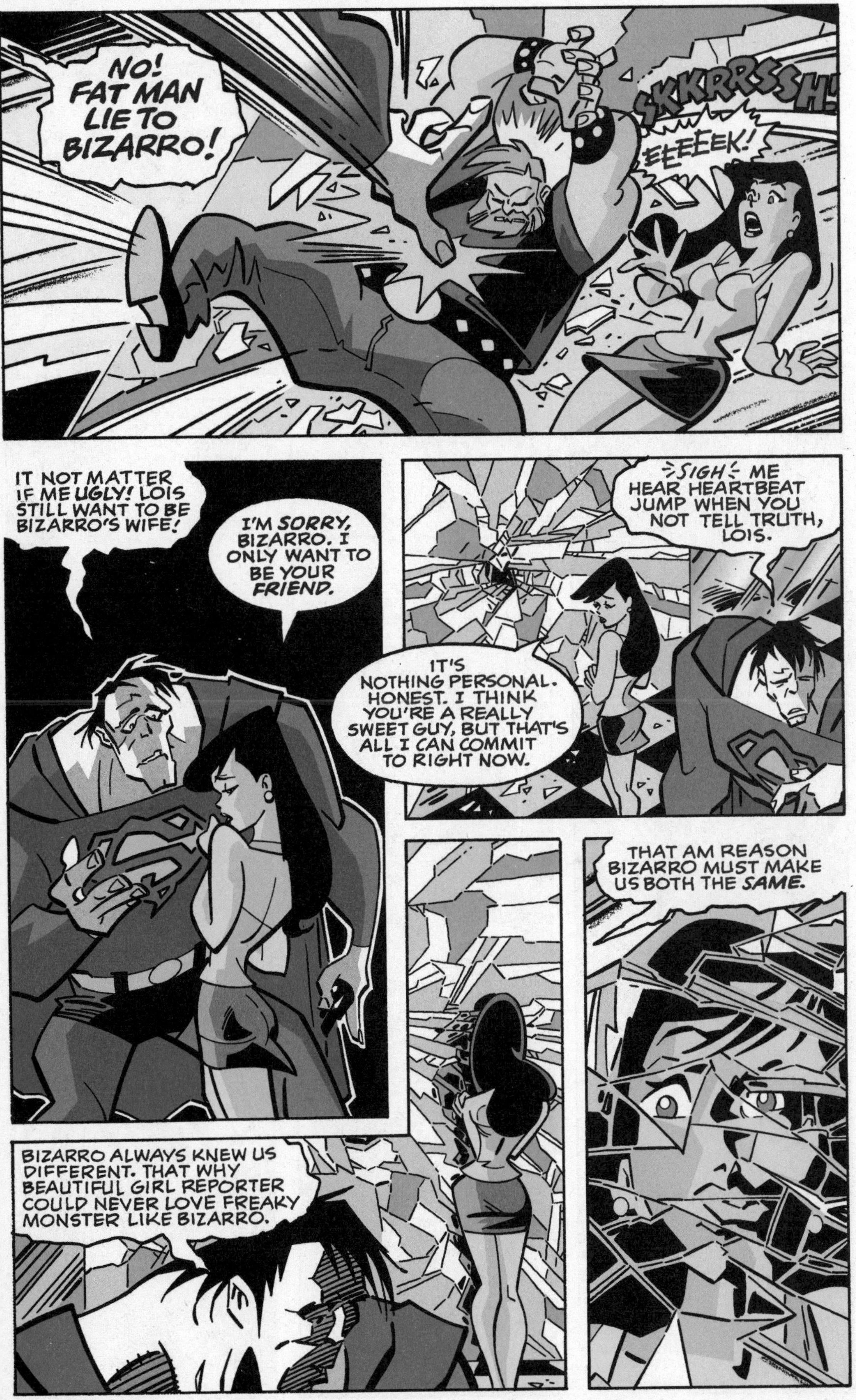
NO! FAT MAN LIE TO BIZARRO!
SKKRRSSH!
EEEEEK!
IT NOT MATTER IF ME UGLY! LOIS STILL WANT TO BE BIZARRO'S WIFE!
I'M SORRY, BIZARRO. I ONLY WANT TO BE YOUR FRIEND.
IT'S NOTHING PERSONAL. HONEST. I THINK YOU'RE A REALLY SWEET GUY, BUT THAT'S ALL I CAN COMMIT TO RIGHT NOW.
SIGH ME HEAR HEARTBEAT JUMP WHEN YOU NOT TELL TRUTH, LOIS.
BIZARRO ALWAYS KNEW US DIFFERENT. THAT WHY BEAUTIFUL GIRL REPORTER COULD NEVER LOVE FREAKY MONSTER LIKE BIZARRO.
THAT AM REASON BIZARRO MUST MAKE US BOTH THE SAME.

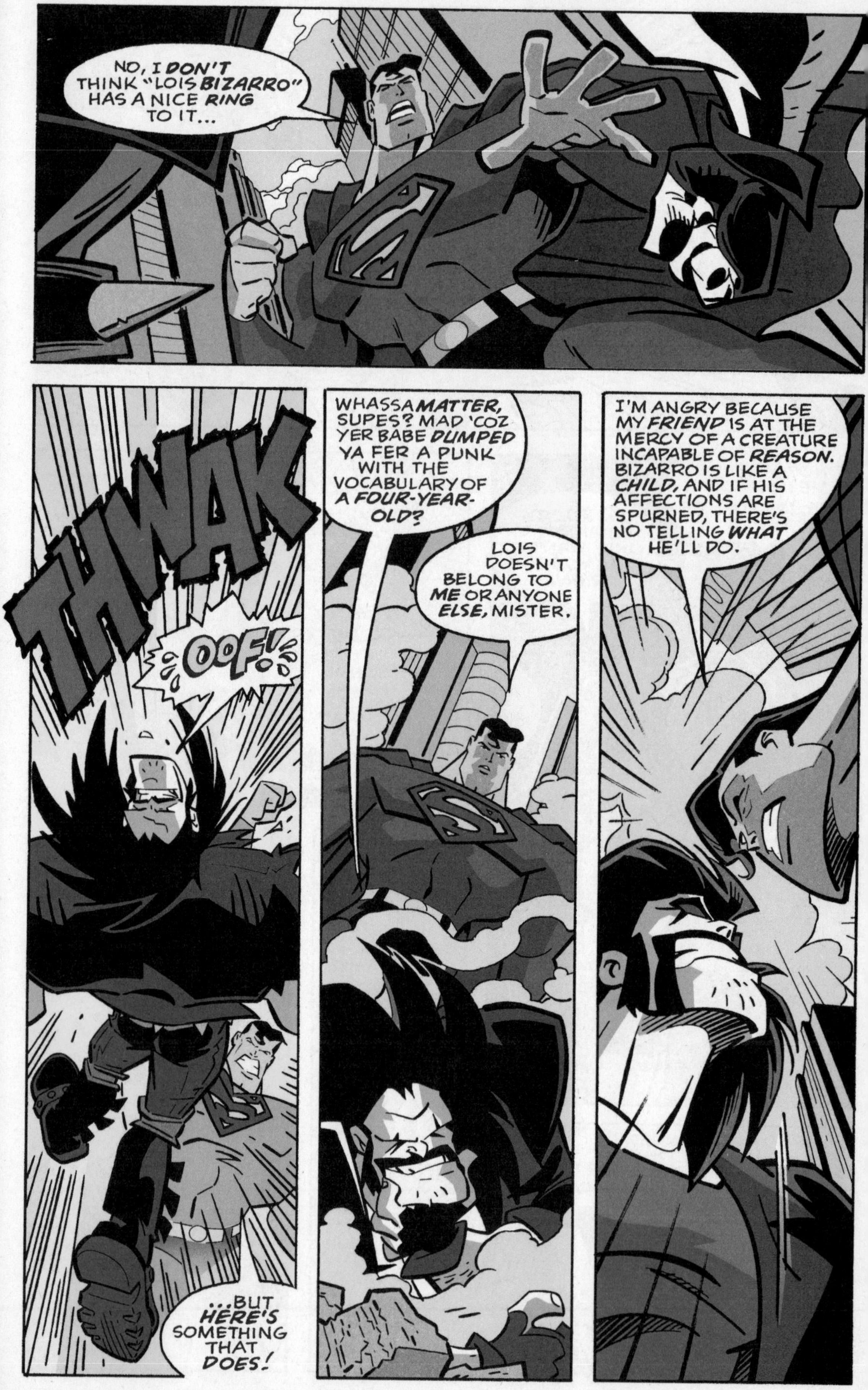

NO, I DON'T THINK "LOIS BIZARRO" HAS A NICE RING TO IT...
THWAK
OOF!
...BUT HERE'S SOMETHING THAT DOES!
WHASSA MATTER, SUPES? MAD 'COZ YER BABE DUMPED YA FER A PUNK WITH THE VOCABULARY OF A FOUR-YEAR-OLD?
LOIS DOESN'T BELONG TO ME OR ANYONE ELSE, MISTER.
I'M ANGRY BECAUSE MY FRIEND IS AT THE MERCY OF A CREATURE INCAPABLE OF REASON. BIZARRO IS LIKE A CHILD, AND IF HIS AFFECTIONS ARE SPURNED, THERE'S NO TELLING WHAT HE'LL DO.

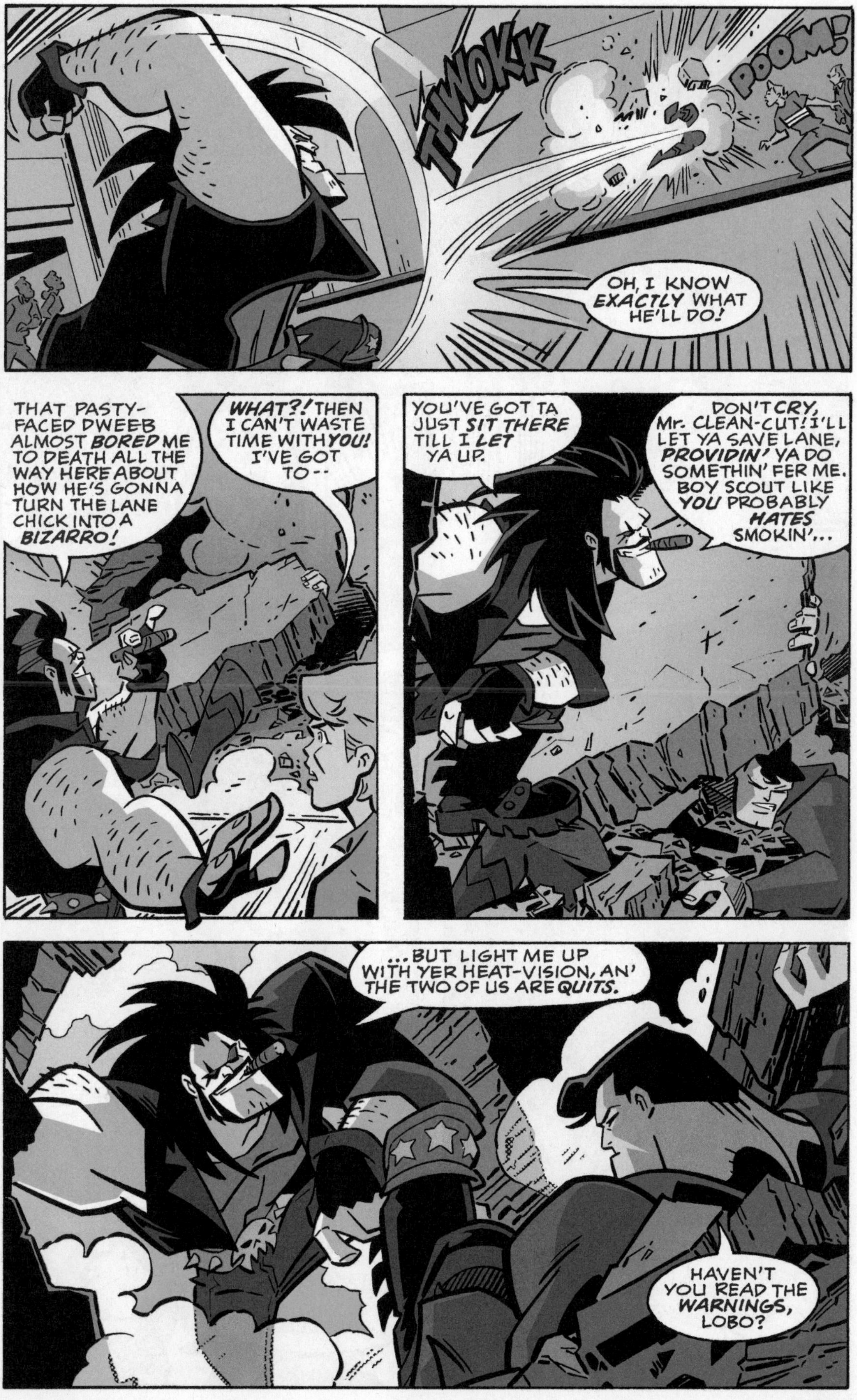
THWOKK
POOM!
OH, I KNOW EXACTLY WHAT HE'LL DO!
THAT PASTY-FACED DWEEB ALMOST BORED ME TO DEATH ALL THE WAY HERE ABOUT HOW HE'S GONNA TURN THE LANE CHICK INTO A BIZARRO!
WHAT?! THEN I CAN'T WASTE TIME WITH YOU! I'VE GOT TO--
YOU'VE GOT TA JUST SIT THERE TILL I LET YA UP.
DON'T CRY, Mr. CLEAN-CUT! I'LL LET YA SAVE LANE, PROVIDIN' YA DO SOMETHIN' FER ME. BOY SCOUT LIKE YOU PROBABLY HATES SMOKIN'...
...BUT LIGHT ME UP WITH YER HEAT-VISION, AN' THE TWO OF US ARE QUITS.
HAVEN'T YOU READ THE WARNINGS, LOBO?

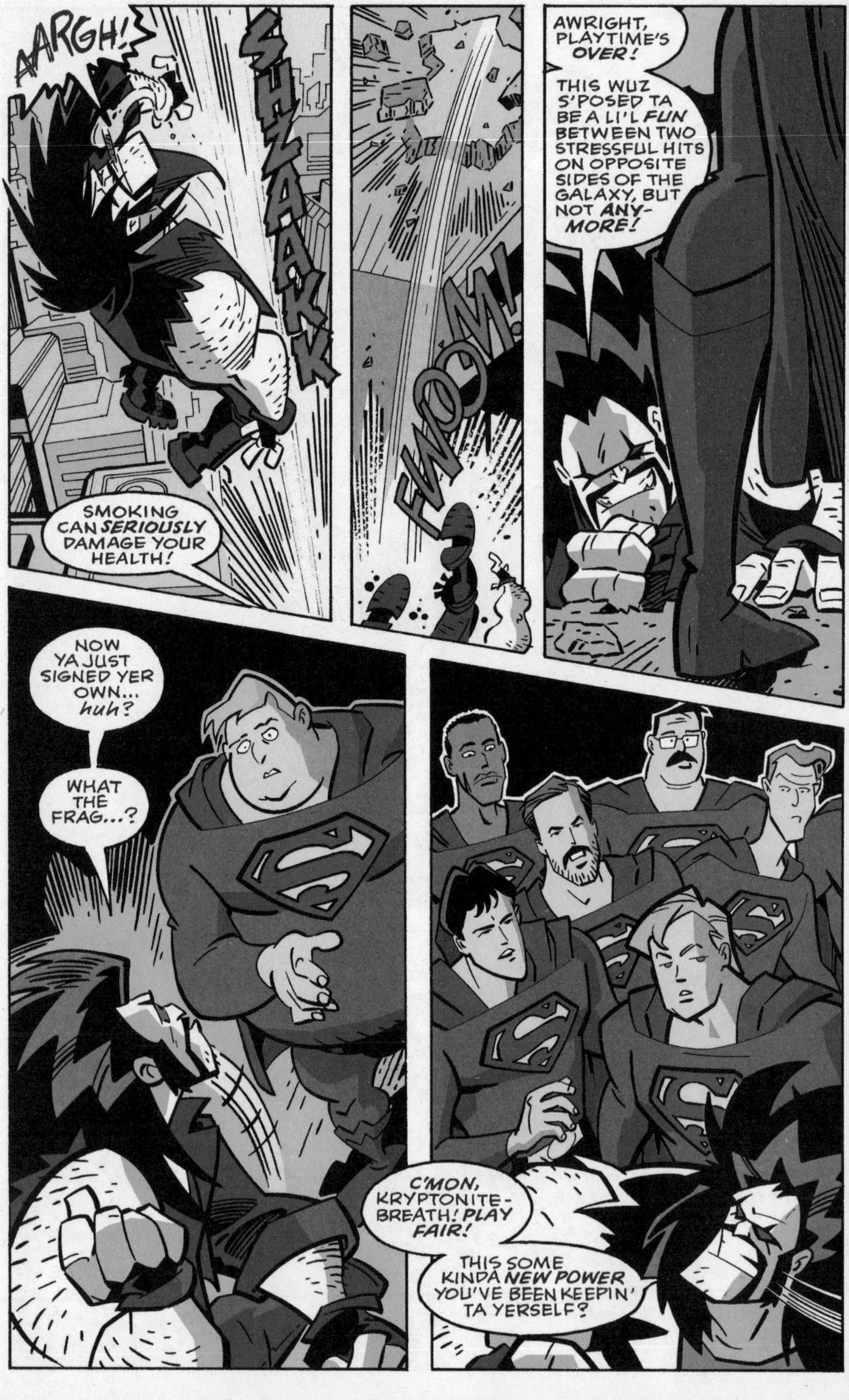
AARGH!
SHZAAKK
SMOKING CAN SERIOUSLY DAMAGE YOUR HEALTH!
FWOOOM!
AWRIGHT, PLAYTIME'S OVER!
THIS WUZ S'POSED TA BE A LI'L FUN BETWEEN TWO STRESSFUL HITS ON OPPOSITE SIDES OF THE GALAXY, BUT NOT ANY-MORE!
NOW YA JUST SIGNED YER OWN... huh?
WHAT THE FRAG...?
C'MON, KRYPTONITE-BREATH! PLAY FAIR!
THIS SOME KINDA NEW POWER YOU'VE BEEN KEEPIN' TA YERSELF?

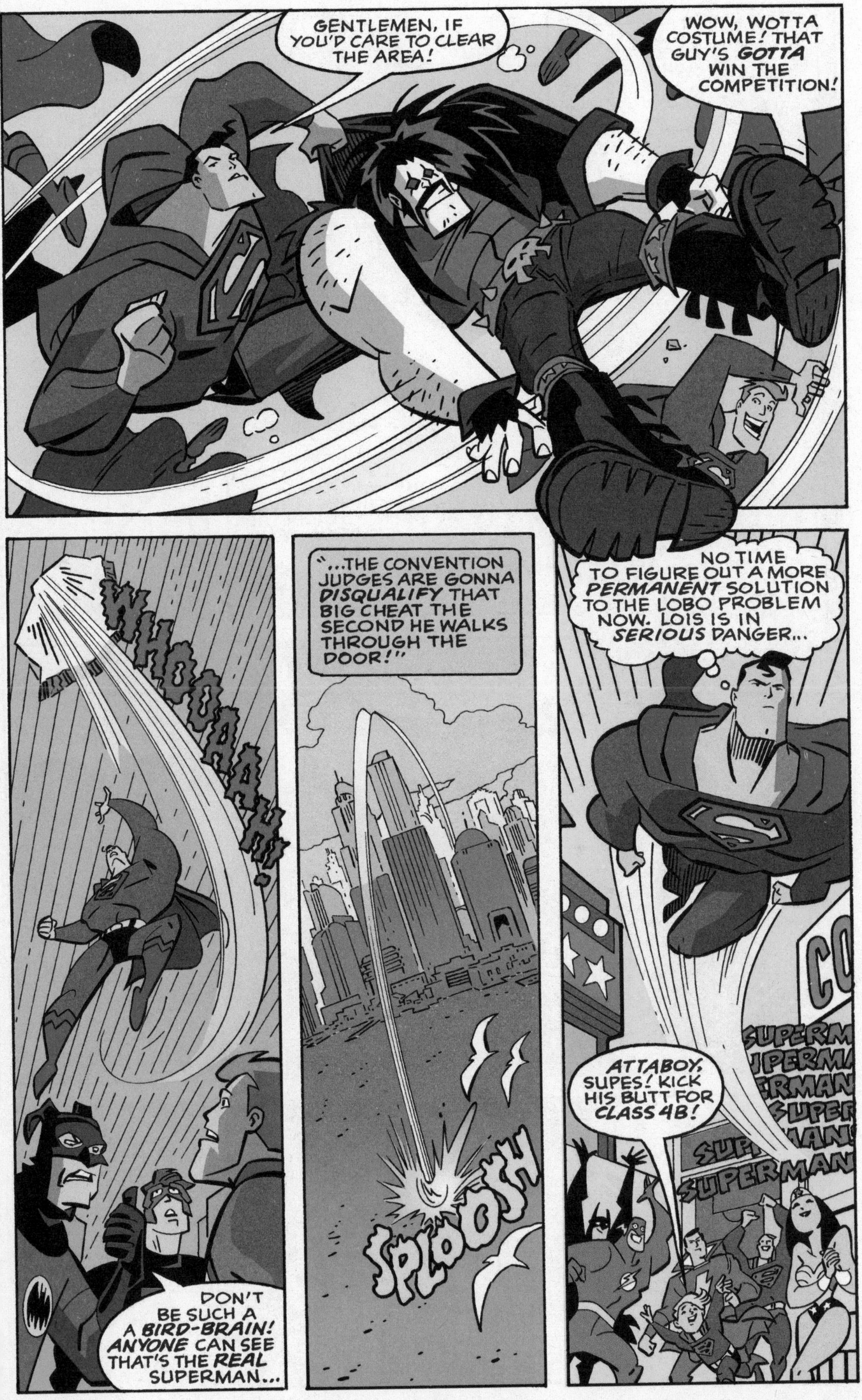
GENTLEMEN, IF YOU'D CARE TO CLEAR THE AREA!
WOW, WOTTA COSTUME! THAT GUY'S GOTTA WIN THE COMPETITION!
WHOOAAAH!!
DON'T BE SUCH A A BIRD-BRAIN! ANYONE CAN SEE THAT'S THE REAL SUPERMAN...
"...THE CONVENTION JUDGES ARE GONNA DISQUALIFY THAT BIG CHEAT THE SECOND HE WALKS THROUGH THE DOOR!"
SPLOOSH
NO TIME TO FIGURE OUT A MORE PERMANENT SOLUTION TO THE LOBO PROBLEM NOW. LOIS IS IN SERIOUS DANGER...
ATTABOY, SUPES! KICK HIS BUTT FOR CLASS 4B!

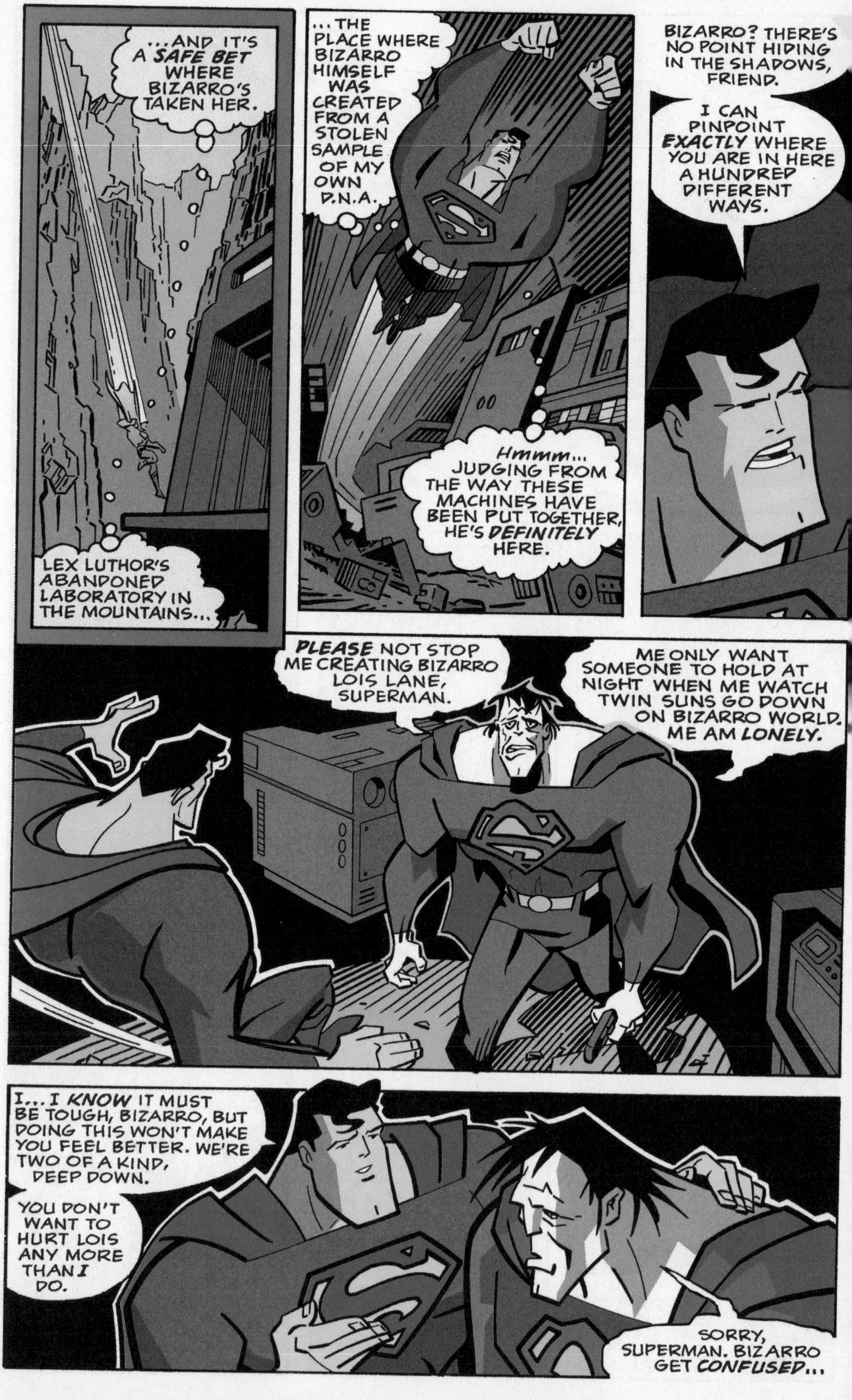
...AND IT'S A SAFE BET WHERE BIZARRO'S TAKEN HER.
LEX LUTHOR'S ABANDONED LABORATORY IN THE MOUNTAINS...
...THE PLACE WHERE BIZARRO HIMSELF WAS CREATED FROM A STOLEN SAMPLE OF MY OWN D.N.A.
Hmmm... JUDGING FROM THE WAY THESE MACHINES HAVE BEEN PUT TOGETHER, HE'S DEFINITELY HERE.
BIZARRO? THERE'S NO POINT HIDING IN THE SHADOWS, FRIEND.
I CAN PINPOINT EXACTLY WHERE YOU ARE IN HERE A HUNDRED DIFFERENT WAYS.
PLEASE NOT STOP ME CREATING BIZARRO LOIS LANE, SUPERMAN.
ME ONLY WANT SOMEONE TO HOLD AT NIGHT WHEN ME WATCH TWIN SUNS GO DOWN ON BIZARRO WORLD. ME AM LONELY.
I... I KNOW IT MUST BE TOUGH, BIZARRO, BUT DOING THIS WON'T MAKE YOU FEEL BETTER. WE'RE TWO OF A KIND, DEEP DOWN.
YOU DON'T WANT TO HURT LOIS ANY MORE THAN I DO.
SORRY, SUPERMAN. BIZARRO GET CONFUSED...

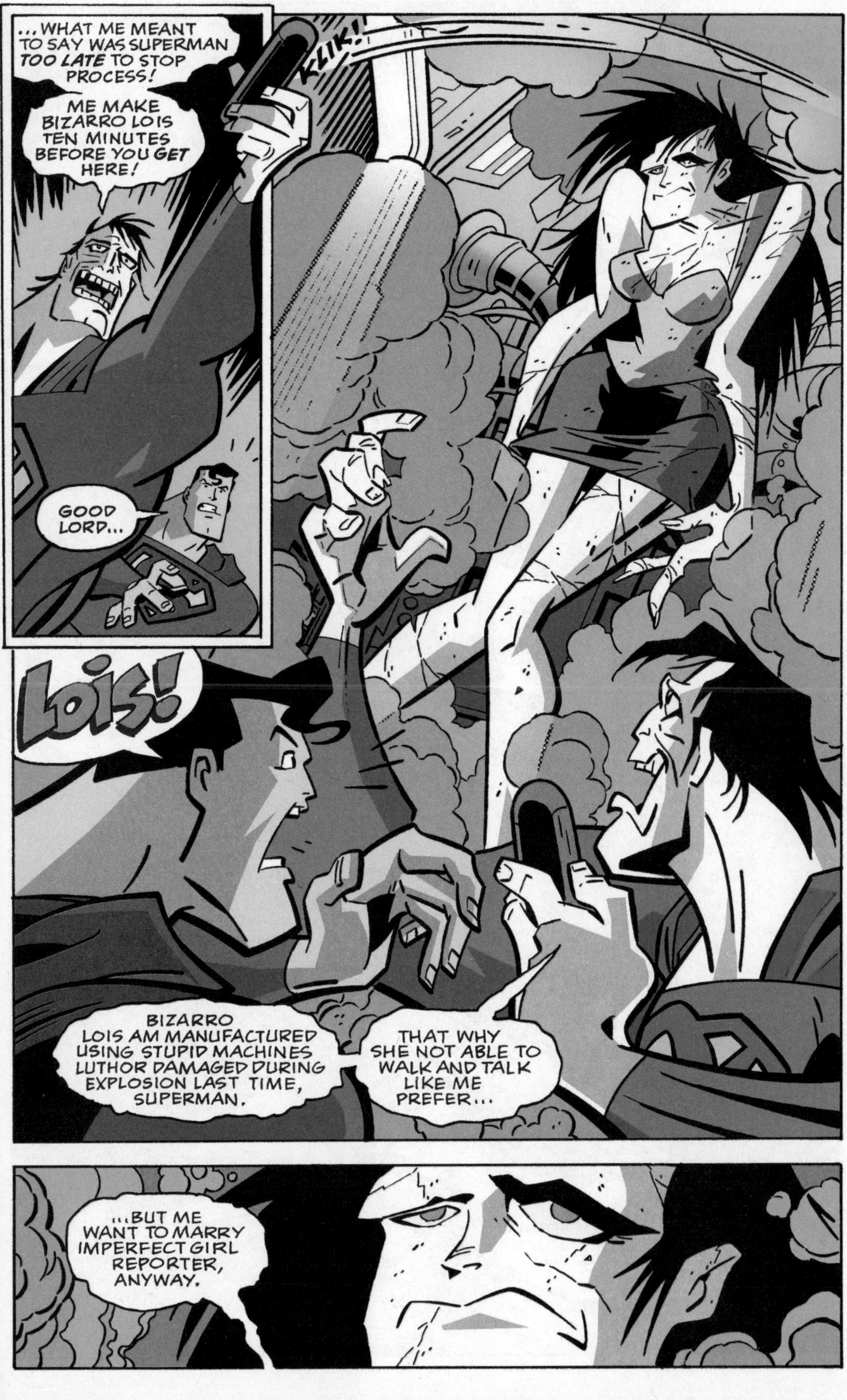
...WHAT ME MEANT TO SAY WAS SUPERMAN TOO LATE TO STOP PROCESS!
KLIK!
ME MAKE BIZARRO LOIS TEN MINUTES BEFORE YOU GET HERE!
GOOD LORD...
LOIS!
BIZARRO LOIS AM MANUFACTURED USING STUPID MACHINES LUTHOR DAMAGED DURING EXPLOSION LAST TIME, SUPERMAN.
THAT WHY SHE NOT ABLE TO WALK AND TALK LIKE ME PREFER...
...BUT ME WANT TO MARRY IMPERFECT GIRL REPORTER, ANYWAY.

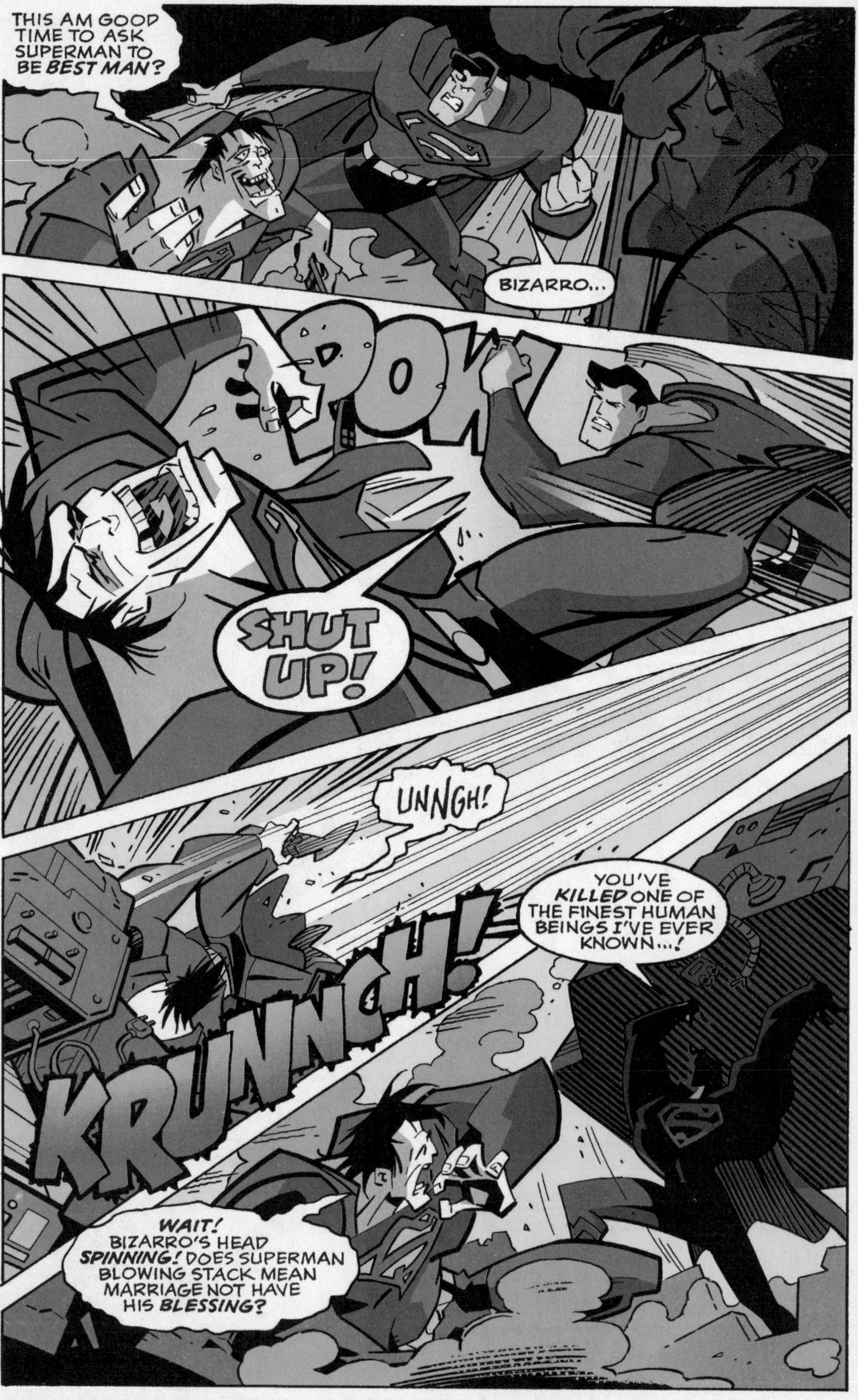
THIS AM GOOD TIME TO ASK SUPERMAN TO BE BEST MAN?
BIZARRO...
POW
SHUT UP!
UNNGH!
YOU'VE KILLED ONE OF THE FINEST HUMAN BEINGS I'VE EVER KNOWN...!
KRUNNCH!
WAIT! BIZARRO'S HEAD SPINNING! DOES SUPERMAN BLOWING STACK MEAN MARRIAGE NOT HAVE HIS BLESSING?

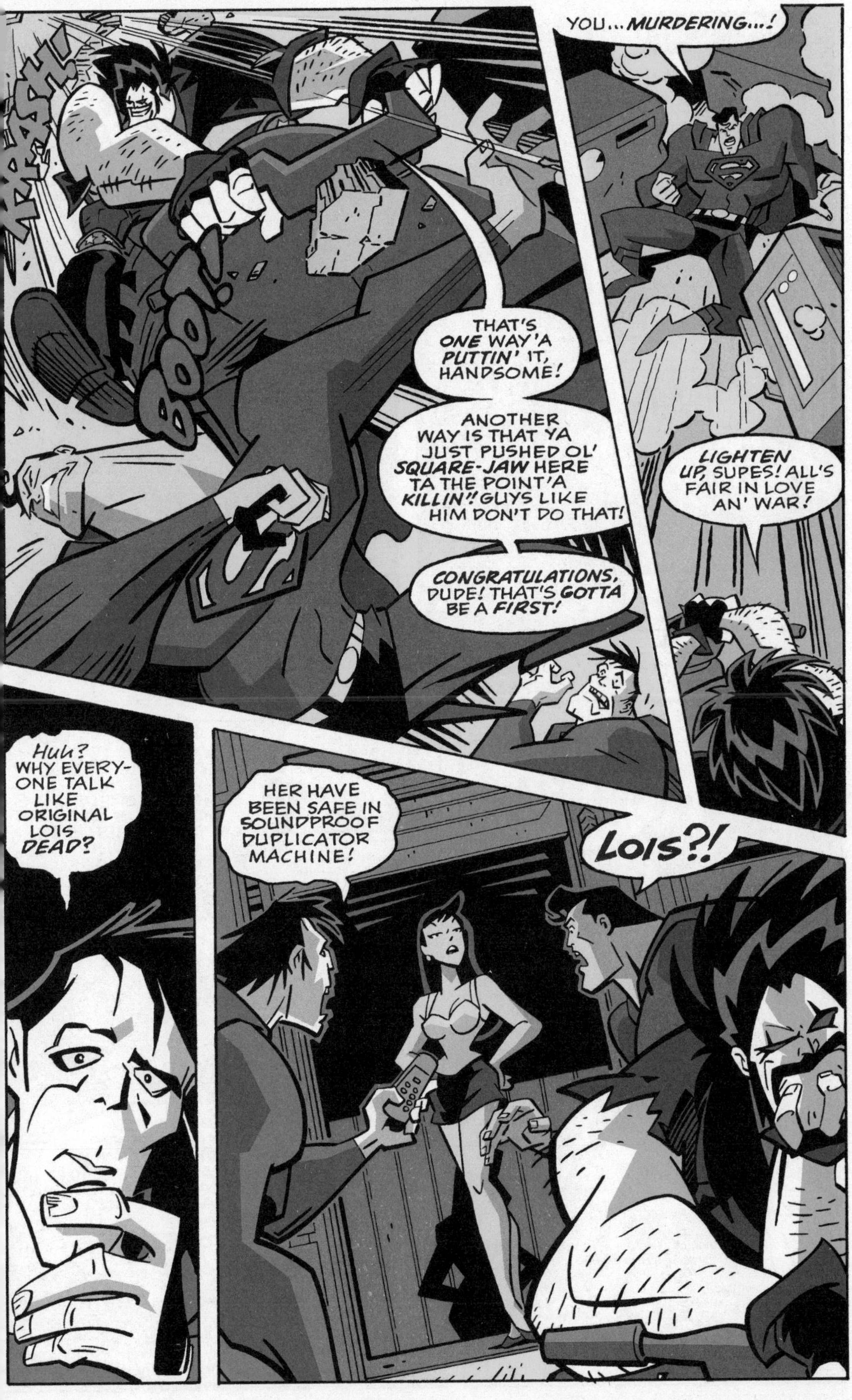
KRASH!
BOOOOM
YOU... MURDERING...!
THAT'S ONE WAY'A PUTTIN' IT, HANDSOME!
ANOTHER WAY IS THAT YA JUST PUSHED OL' SQUARE-JAW HERE TA THE POINT'A KILLIN'! GUYS LIKE HIM DON'T DO THAT!
CONGRATULATIONS, DUDE! THAT'S GOTTA BE A FIRST!
LIGHTEN UP, SUPES! ALL'S FAIR IN LOVE AN' WAR!
Huh? WHY EVERY-ONE TALK LIKE ORIGINAL LOIS DEAD?
HER HAVE BEEN SAFE IN SOUNDPROOF DUPLICATOR MACHINE!
LOIS?!

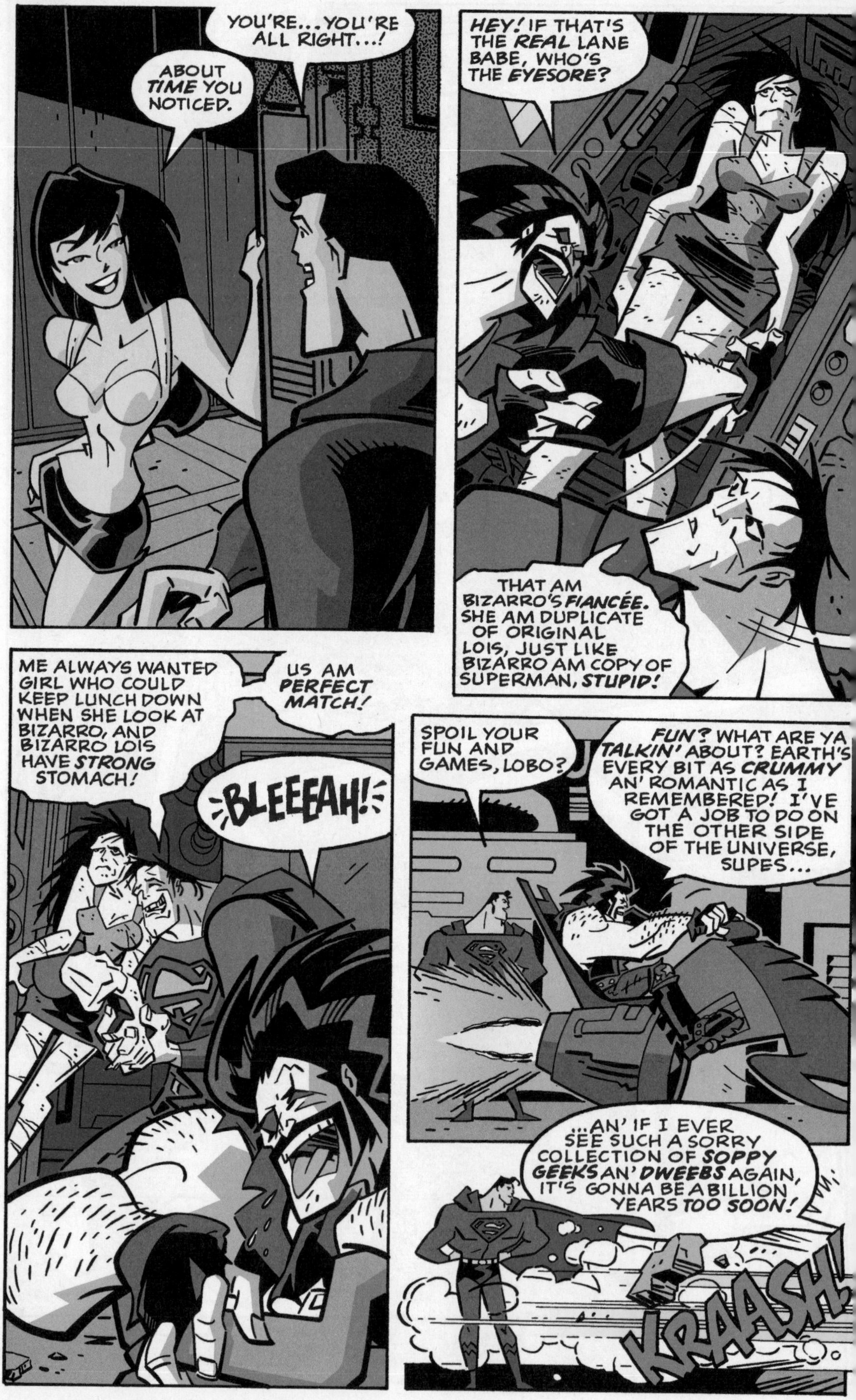
YOU'RE...YOU'RE ALL RIGHT...!
ABOUT TIME YOU NOTICED.
HEY! IF THAT'S THE REAL LANE BABE, WHO'S THE EYESORE?
THAT AM BIZARRO'S FIANCÉE. SHE AM DUPLICATE OF ORIGINAL LOIS, JUST LIKE BIZARRO AM COPY OF SUPERMAN, STUPID!
ME ALWAYS WANTED GIRL WHO COULD KEEP LUNCH DOWN WHEN SHE LOOK AT BIZARRO, AND BIZARRO LOIS HAVE STRONG STOMACH!
US AM PERFECT MATCH!
BLEEEAH!
SPOIL YOUR FUN AND GAMES, LOBO?
FUN? WHAT ARE YA TALKIN' ABOUT? EARTH'S EVERY BIT AS CRUMMY AN' ROMANTIC AS I REMEMBERED! I'VE GOT A JOB TO DO ON THE OTHER SIDE OF THE UNIVERSE, SUPES...
...AN' IF I EVER SEE SUCH A SORRY COLLECTION OF SOPPY GEEKS AN' DWEEBS AGAIN, IT'S GONNA BE A BILLION YEARS TOO SOON!
KRAASH!

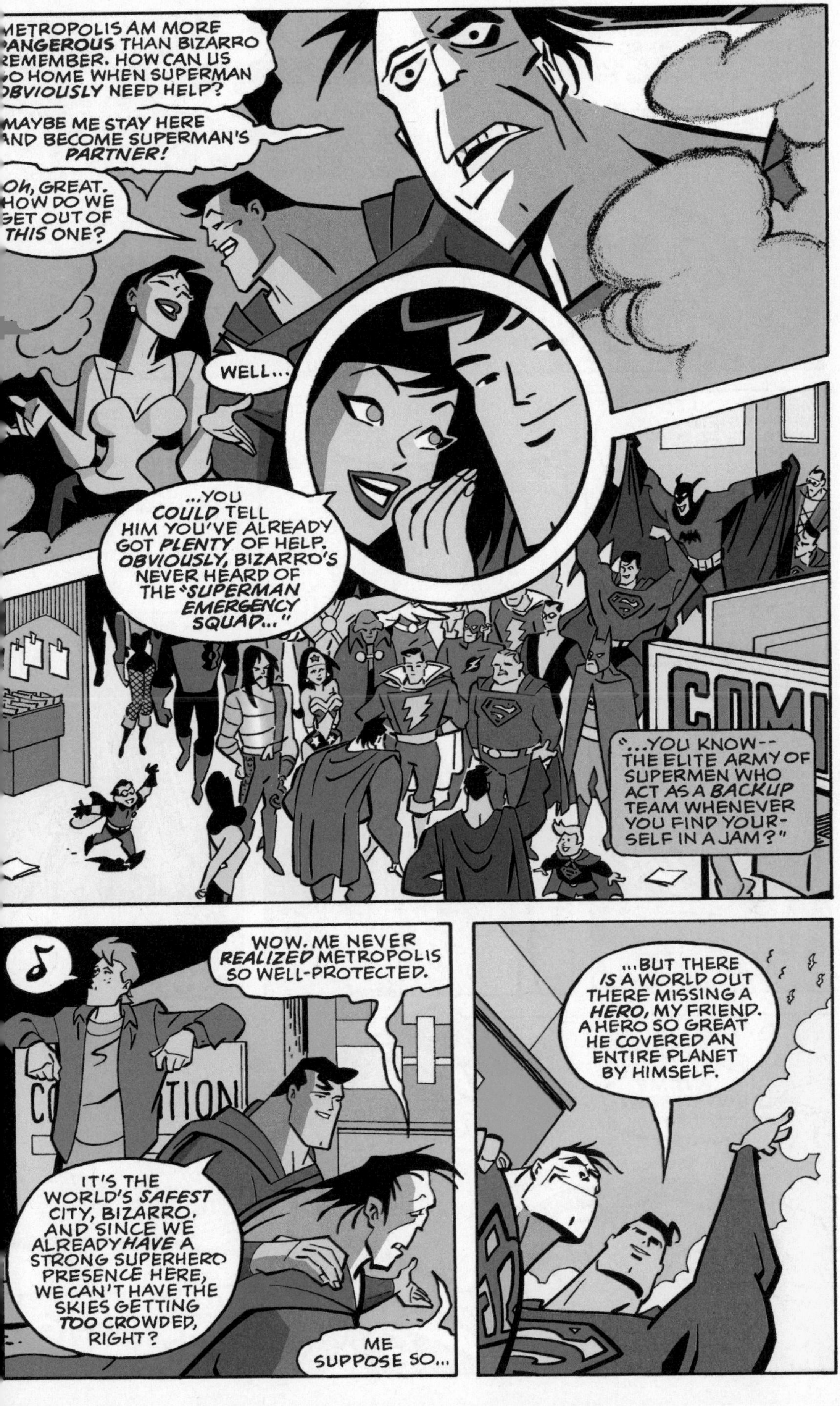
METROPOLIS AM MORE DANGEROUS THAN BIZARRO REMEMBER. HOW CAN US GO HOME WHEN SUPERMAN OBVIOUSLY NEED HELP?
MAYBE ME STAY HERE AND BECOME SUPERMAN'S PARTNER!
Oh, GREAT. HOW DO WE GET OUT OF THIS ONE?
WELL...
...YOU COULD TELL HIM YOU'VE ALREADY GOT PLENTY OF HELP. OBVIOUSLY, BIZARRO'S NEVER HEARD OF THE "SUPERMAN EMERGENCY SQUAD..."
COMI
"...YOU KNOW-- THE ELITE ARMY OF SUPERMEN WHO ACT AS A BACKUP TEAM WHENEVER YOU FIND YOURSELF IN A JAM?"
WOW. ME NEVER REALIZED METROPOLIS SO WELL-PROTECTED.
IT'S THE WORLD'S SAFEST CITY, BIZARRO. AND SINCE WE ALREADY HAVE A STRONG SUPERHERO PRESENCE HERE, WE CAN'T HAVE THE SKIES GETTING TOO CROWDED, RIGHT?
ME SUPPOSE SO...
...BUT THERE IS A WORLD OUT THERE MISSING A HERO, MY FRIEND. A HERO SO GREAT HE COVERED AN ENTIRE PLANET BY HIMSELF.

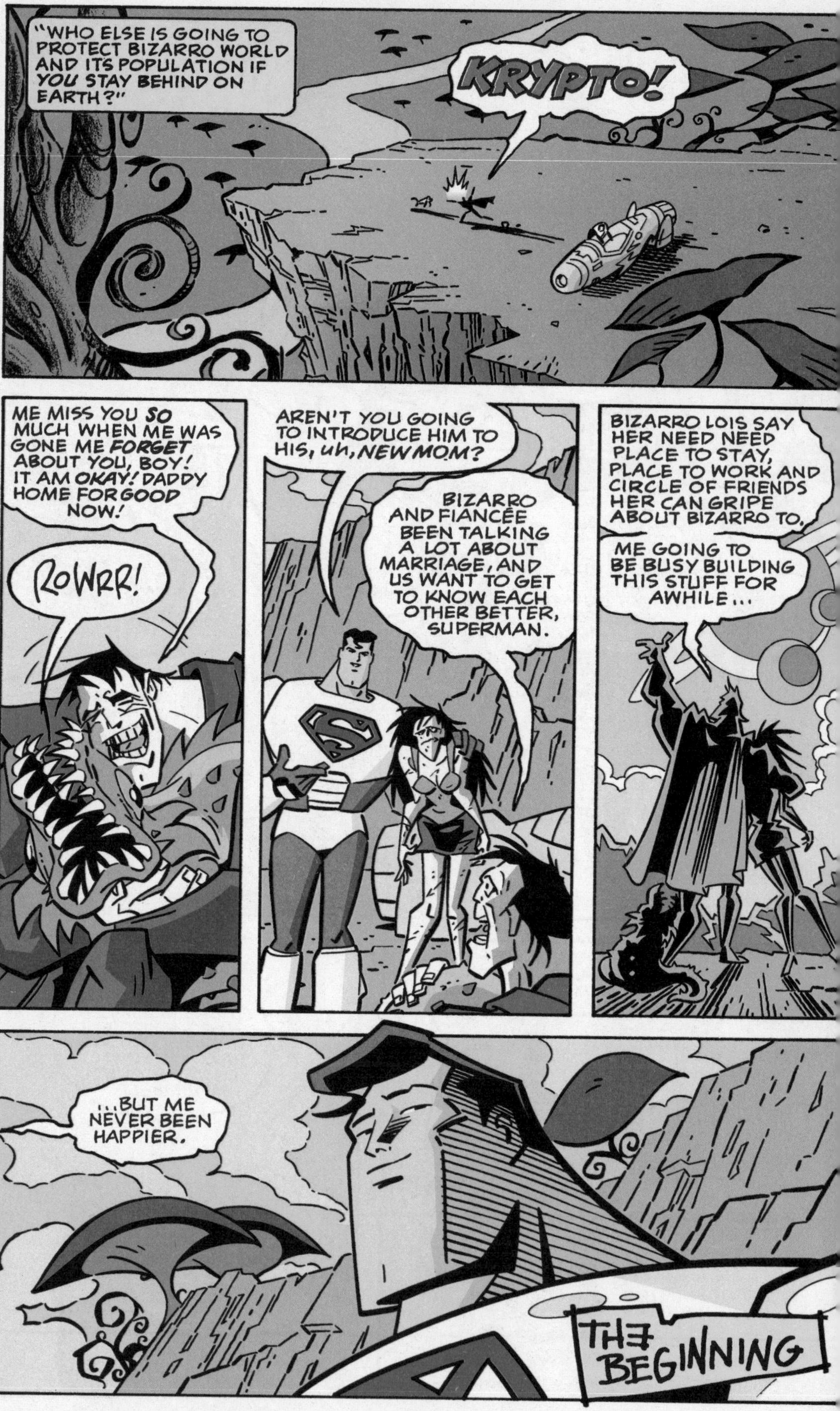
"WHO ELSE IS GOING TO PROTECT BIZARRO WORLD AND ITS POPULATION IF *YOU* STAY BEHIND ON EARTH?"
KRYPTO!
ME MISS YOU **SO** MUCH WHEN ME WAS GONE ME ***FORGET*** ABOUT YOU, BOY! IT AM ***OKAY!*** DADDY HOME FOR **GOOD** NOW!
ROWRR!
AREN'T YOU GOING TO INTRODUCE HIM TO HIS, *uh*, ***NEW MOM?***
BIZARRO AND FIANCÉE BEEN TALKING A LOT ABOUT MARRIAGE, AND US WANT TO GET TO KNOW EACH OTHER BETTER, SUPERMAN.
BIZARRO LOIS SAY HER NEED NEED PLACE TO STAY, PLACE TO WORK AND CIRCLE OF FRIENDS HER CAN GRIPE ABOUT BIZARRO TO.
ME GOING TO BE BUSY BUILDING THIS STUFF FOR AWHILE...
...BUT ME NEVER BEEN HAPPIER.
THƎ BEGINNING

SUPERMAN ADVENTURES #30 cover by MIKE MANLEY, TERRY AUSTIN and MARIE SEVERIN

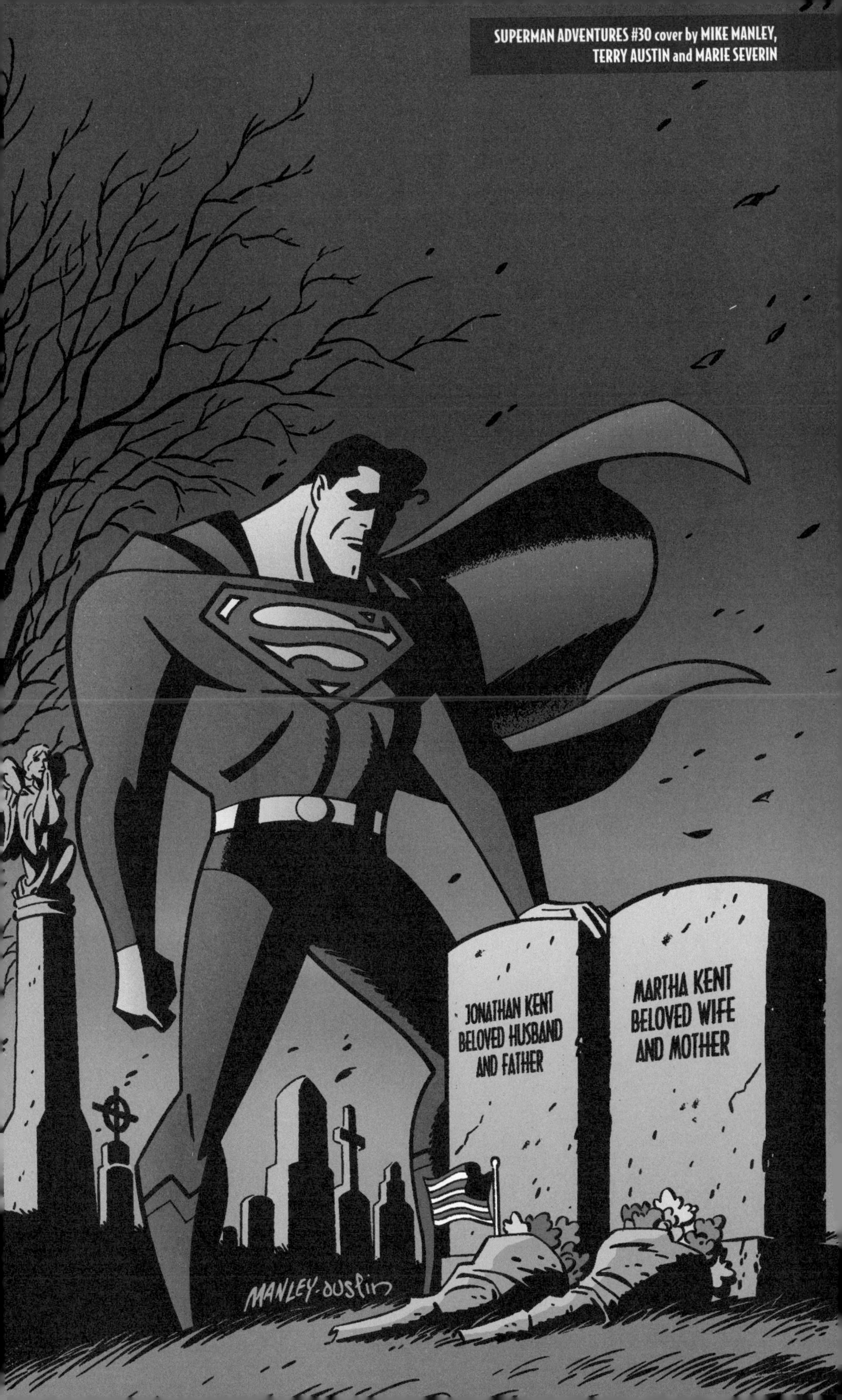

JONATHAN KENT
BELOVED HUSBAND
AND FATHER
MARTHA KENT
BELOVED WIFE
AND MOTHER
MANLEY-austin

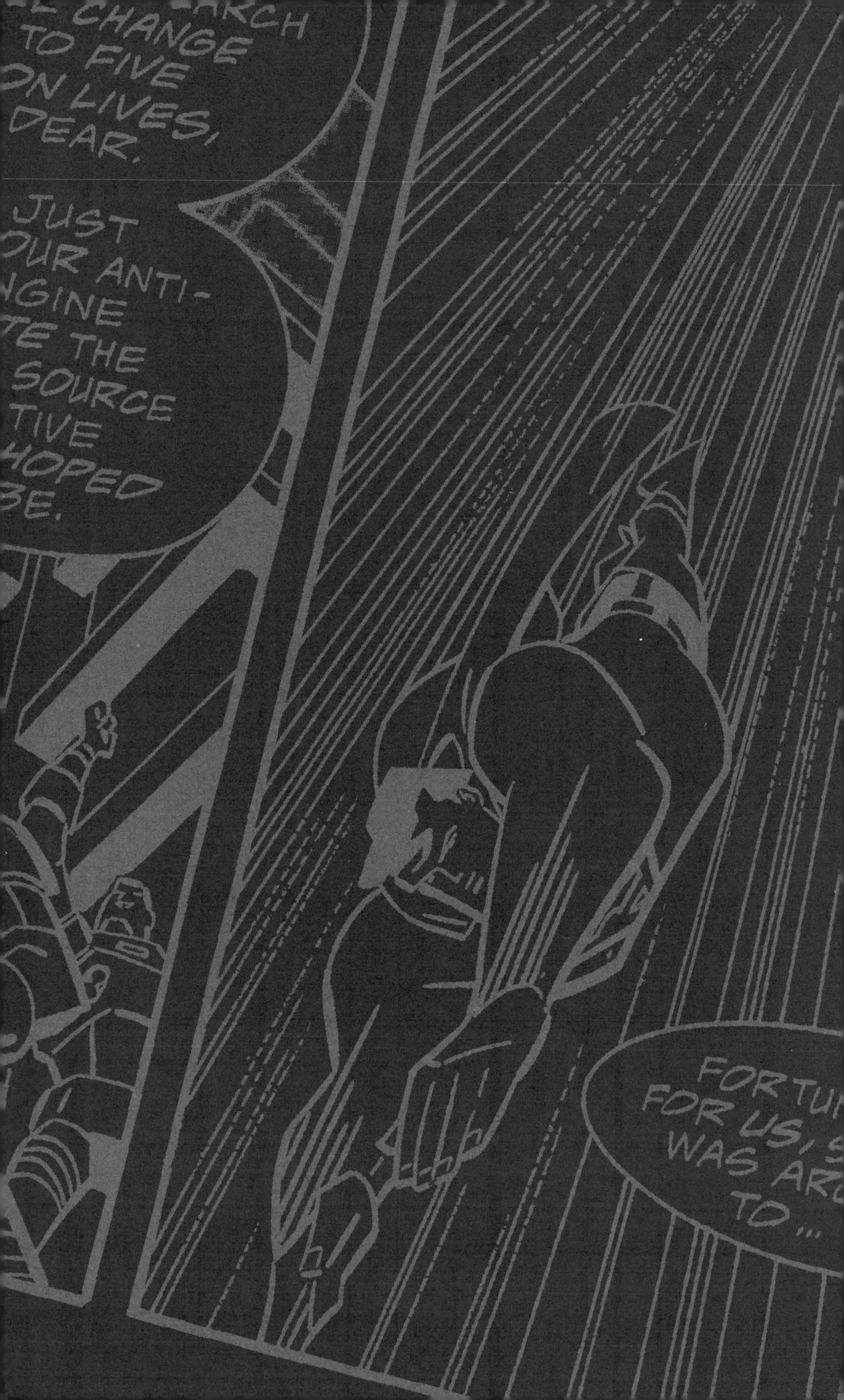
TO CHANGE
FIVE
LIVES,
DEAR.
JUST
ANTI-
THE
SOURCE
HOPED
FOR US,
WAS
TO...

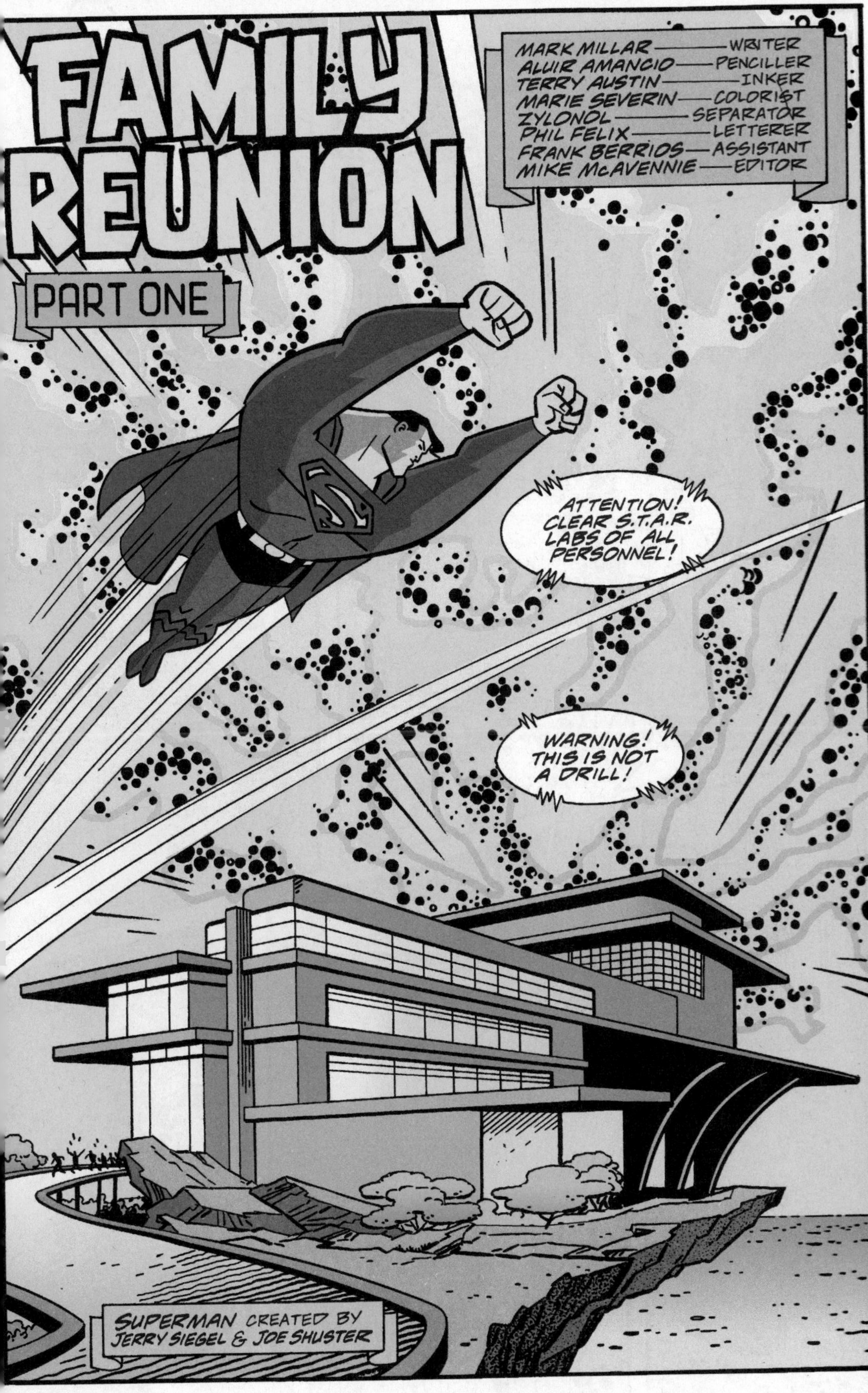
FAMILY REUNION
PART ONE
MARK MILLAR—WRITER
ALUIR AMANCIO—PENCILLER
TERRY AUSTIN—INKER
MARIE SEVERIN—COLORIST
ZYLONOL—SEPARATOR
PHIL FELIX—LETTERER
FRANK BERRIOS—ASSISTANT
MIKE McAVENNIE—EDITOR
ATTENTION! CLEAR S.T.A.R. LABS OF ALL PERSONNEL!
WARNING! THIS IS NOT A DRILL!
SUPERMAN CREATED BY JERRY SIEGEL & JOE SHUSTER

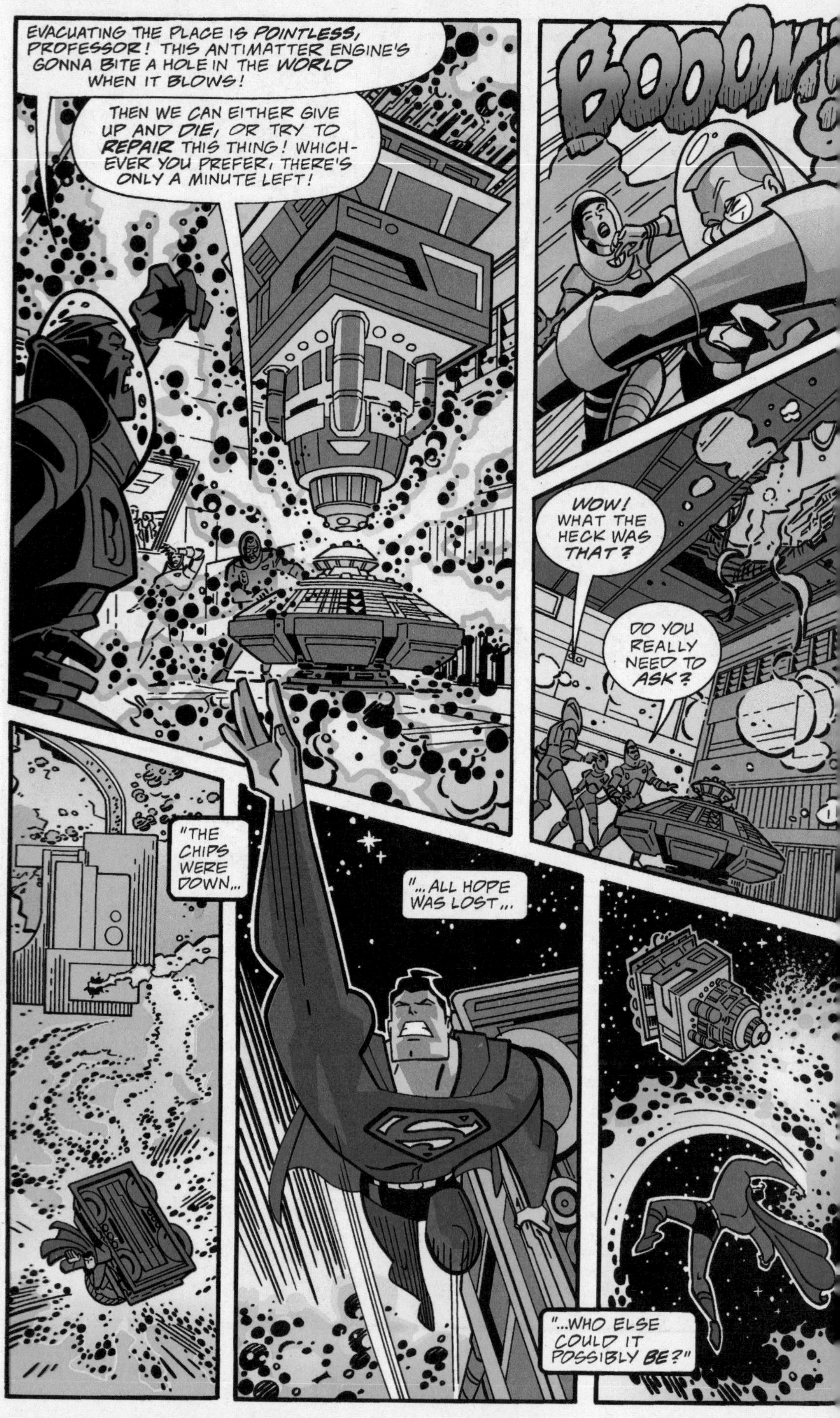
EVACUATING THE PLACE IS POINTLESS, PROFESSOR! THIS ANTIMATTER ENGINE'S GONNA BITE A HOLE IN THE WORLD WHEN IT BLOWS!
THEN WE CAN EITHER GIVE UP AND DIE, OR TRY TO REPAIR THIS THING! WHICH-EVER YOU PREFER, THERE'S ONLY A MINUTE LEFT!
BOOOM
WOW! WHAT THE HECK WAS THAT?
DO YOU REALLY NEED TO ASK?
"THE CHIPS WERE DOWN...
"...ALL HOPE WAS LOST...
"...WHO ELSE COULD IT POSSIBLY BE?"

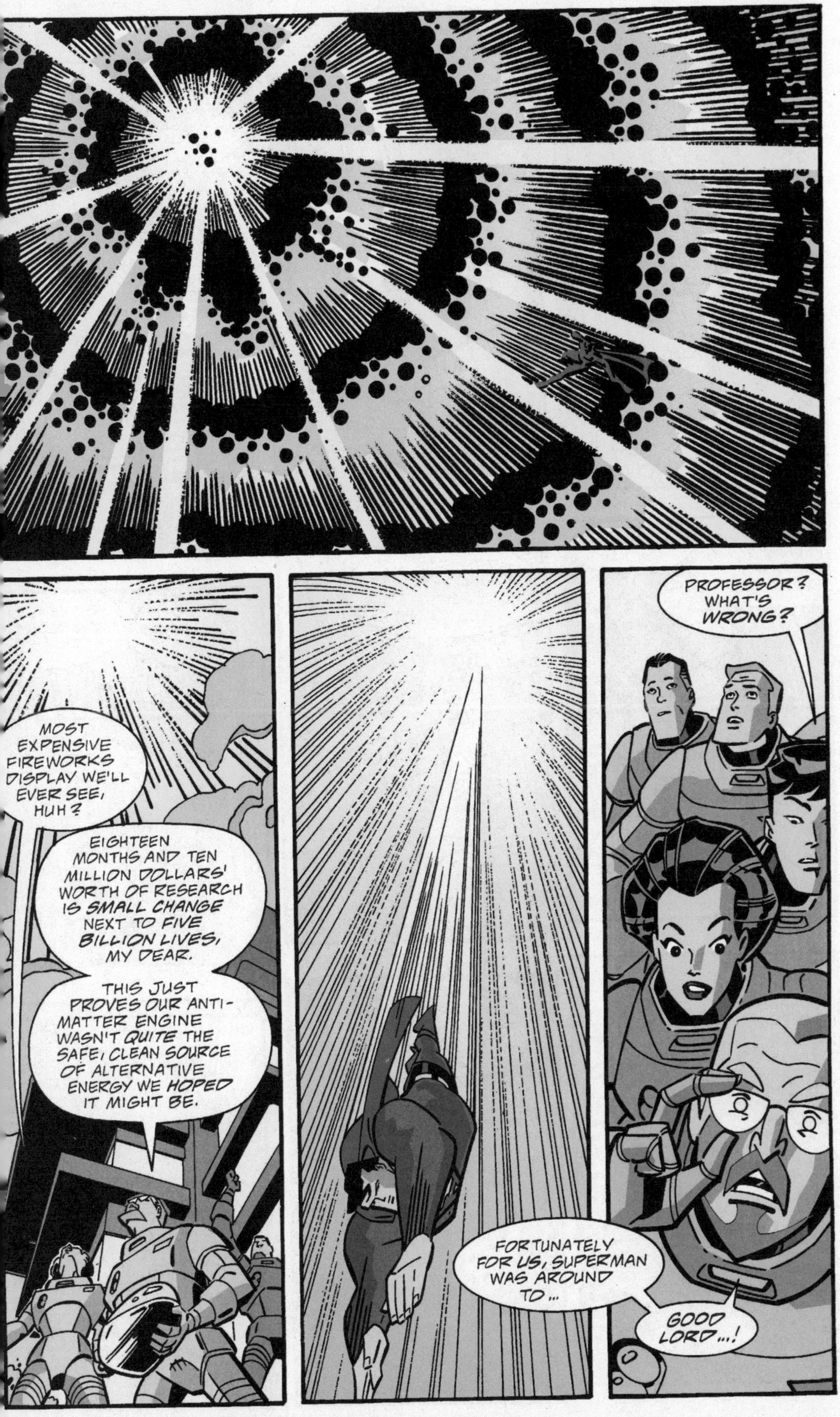
MOST EXPENSIVE FIREWORKS DISPLAY WE'LL EVER SEE, HUH?
EIGHTEEN MONTHS AND TEN MILLION DOLLARS' WORTH OF RESEARCH IS SMALL CHANGE NEXT TO FIVE BILLION LIVES, MY DEAR.
THIS JUST PROVES OUR ANTI-MATTER ENGINE WASN'T QUITE THE SAFE, CLEAN SOURCE OF ALTERNATIVE ENERGY WE HOPED IT MIGHT BE.
FORTUNATELY FOR US, SUPERMAN WAS AROUND TO...
GOOD LORD...!
PROFESSOR? WHAT'S WRONG?

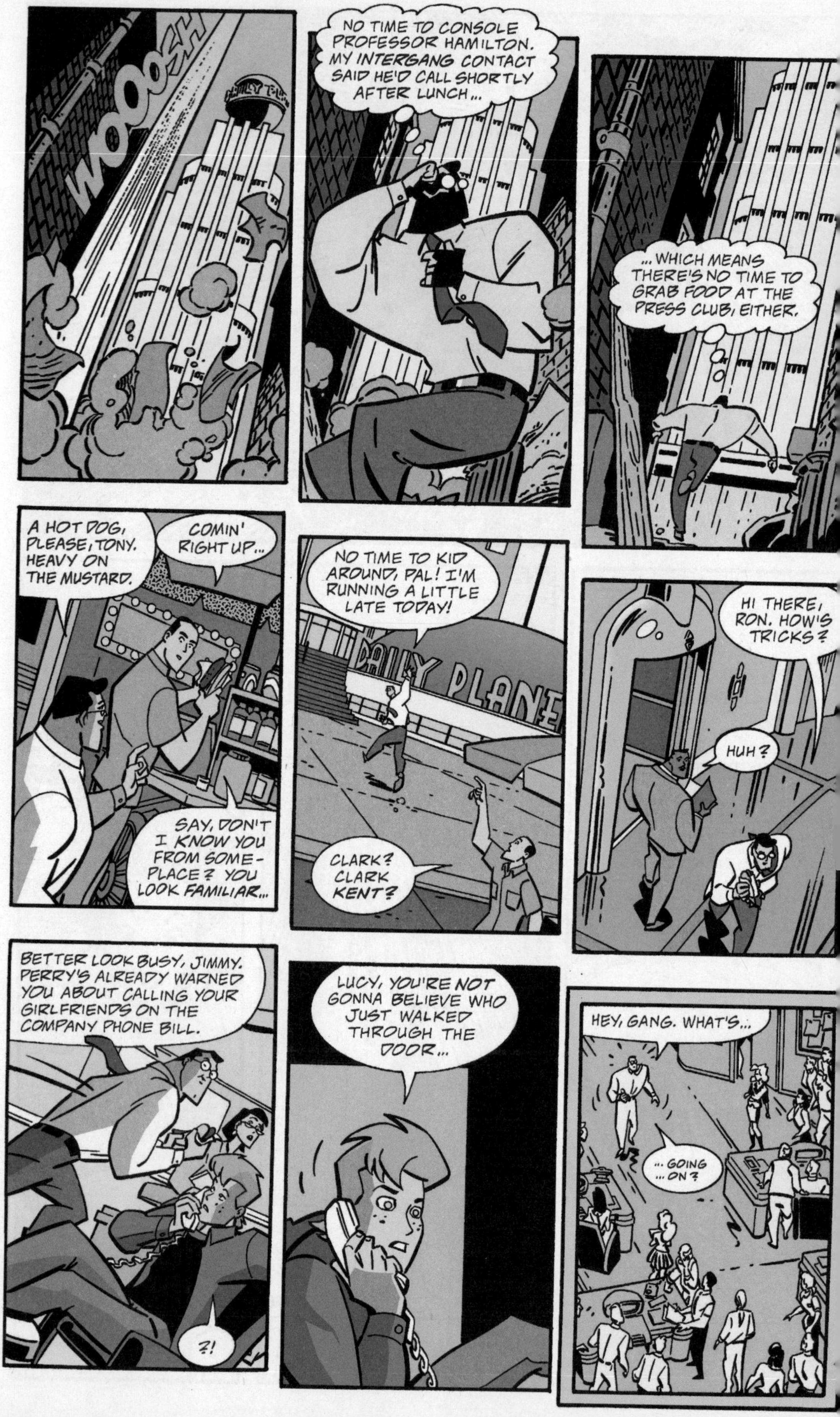

WOOOSH
NO TIME TO CONSOLE PROFESSOR HAMILTON. MY INTERGANG CONTACT SAID HE'D CALL SHORTLY AFTER LUNCH...
...WHICH MEANS THERE'S NO TIME TO GRAB FOOD AT THE PRESS CLUB, EITHER.
A HOT DOG, PLEASE, TONY. HEAVY ON THE MUSTARD.
COMIN' RIGHT UP...
SAY, DON'T I KNOW YOU FROM SOME-PLACE? YOU LOOK FAMILIAR...
NO TIME TO KID AROUND, PAL! I'M RUNNING A LITTLE LATE TODAY!
DAILY PLANE
CLARK? CLARK KENT?
HI THERE, RON. HOW'S TRICKS?
HUH?
BETTER LOOK BUSY, JIMMY. PERRY'S ALREADY WARNED YOU ABOUT CALLING YOUR GIRLFRIENDS ON THE COMPANY PHONE BILL.
?!
LUCY, YOU'RE NOT GONNA BELIEVE WHO JUST WALKED THROUGH THE DOOR...
HEY, GANG. WHAT'S...
...GOING ON?

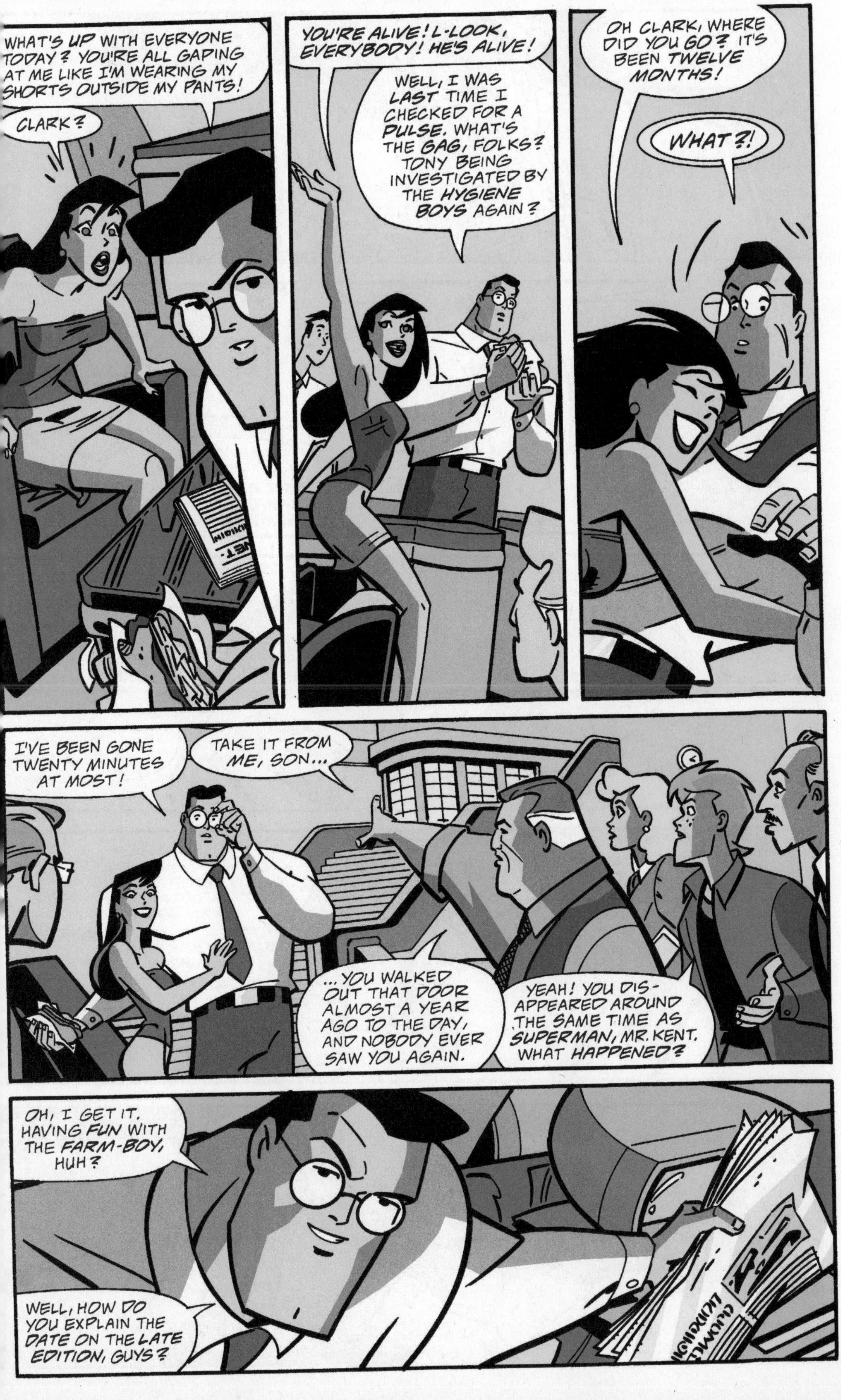
WHAT'S UP WITH EVERYONE TODAY? YOU'RE ALL GAPING AT ME LIKE I'M WEARING MY SHORTS OUTSIDE MY PANTS!
CLARK?
YOU'RE ALIVE! L-LOOK, EVERYBODY! HE'S ALIVE!
WELL, I WAS LAST TIME I CHECKED FOR A PULSE. WHAT'S THE GAG, FOLKS? TONY BEING INVESTIGATED BY THE HYGIENE BOYS AGAIN?
OH CLARK, WHERE DID YOU GO? IT'S BEEN TWELVE MONTHS!
WHAT?!
I'VE BEEN GONE TWENTY MINUTES AT MOST!
TAKE IT FROM ME, SON...
...YOU WALKED OUT THAT DOOR ALMOST A YEAR AGO TO THE DAY, AND NOBODY EVER SAW YOU AGAIN.
YEAH! YOU DIS-APPEARED AROUND THE SAME TIME AS SUPERMAN, MR. KENT. WHAT HAPPENED?
OH, I GET IT. HAVING FUN WITH THE FARM-BOY, HUH?
WELL, HOW DO YOU EXPLAIN THE DATE ON THE LATE EDITION, GUYS?

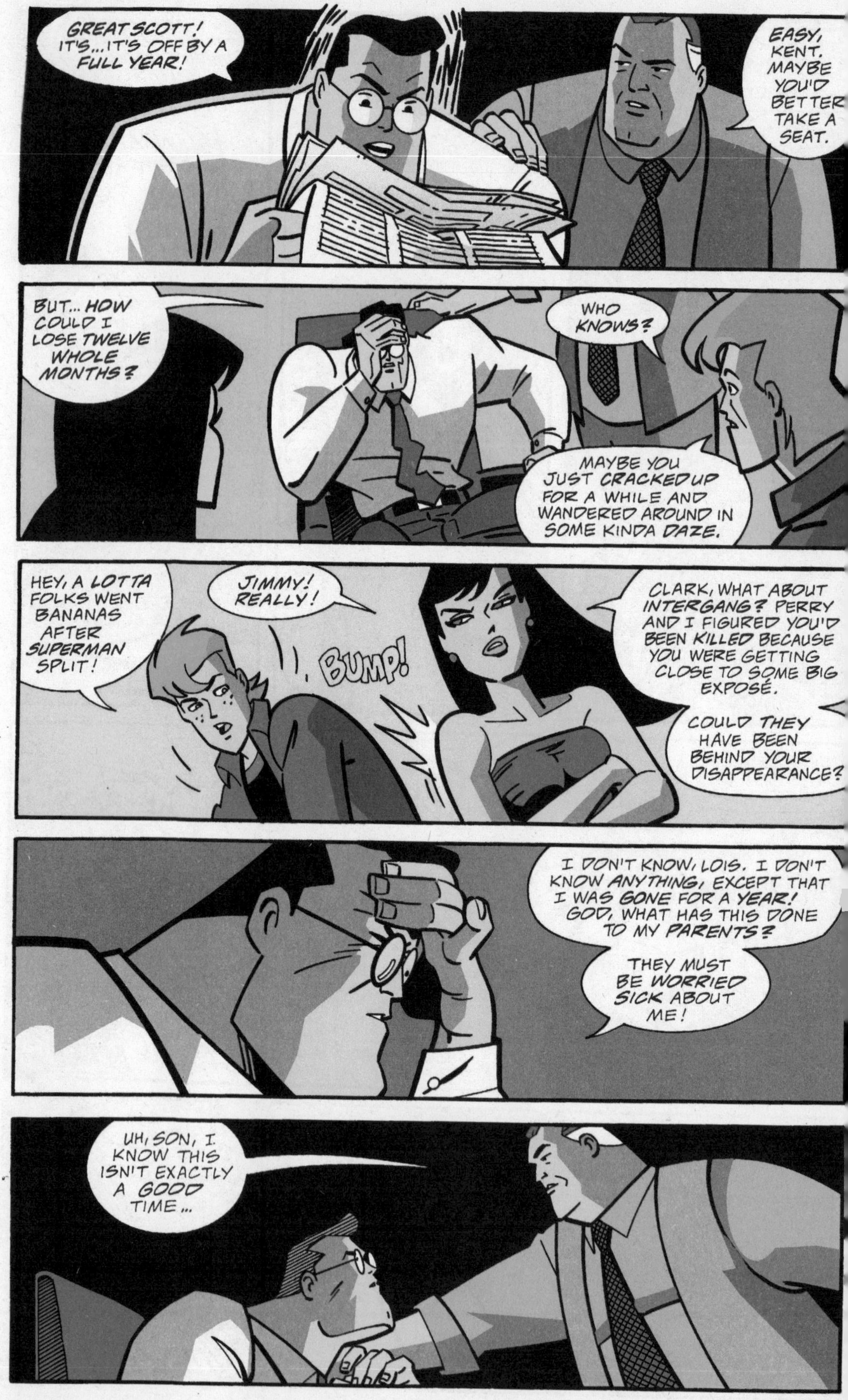

GREAT SCOTT! IT'S... IT'S OFF BY A FULL YEAR!
EASY, KENT. MAYBE YOU'D BETTER TAKE A SEAT.
BUT... HOW COULD I LOSE TWELVE WHOLE MONTHS?
WHO KNOWS?
MAYBE YOU JUST CRACKED UP FOR A WHILE AND WANDERED AROUND IN SOME KINDA DAZE.
HEY, A LOTTA FOLKS WENT BANANAS AFTER SUPERMAN SPLIT!
JIMMY! REALLY!
BUMP!
CLARK, WHAT ABOUT INTERGANG? PERRY AND I FIGURED YOU'D BEEN KILLED BECAUSE YOU WERE GETTING CLOSE TO SOME BIG EXPOSÉ.
COULD THEY HAVE BEEN BEHIND YOUR DISAPPEARANCE?
I DON'T KNOW, LOIS. I DON'T KNOW ANYTHING, EXCEPT THAT I WAS GONE FOR A YEAR! GOD, WHAT HAS THIS DONE TO MY PARENTS?
THEY MUST BE WORRIED SICK ABOUT ME!
UH, SON, I KNOW THIS ISN'T EXACTLY A GOOD TIME...

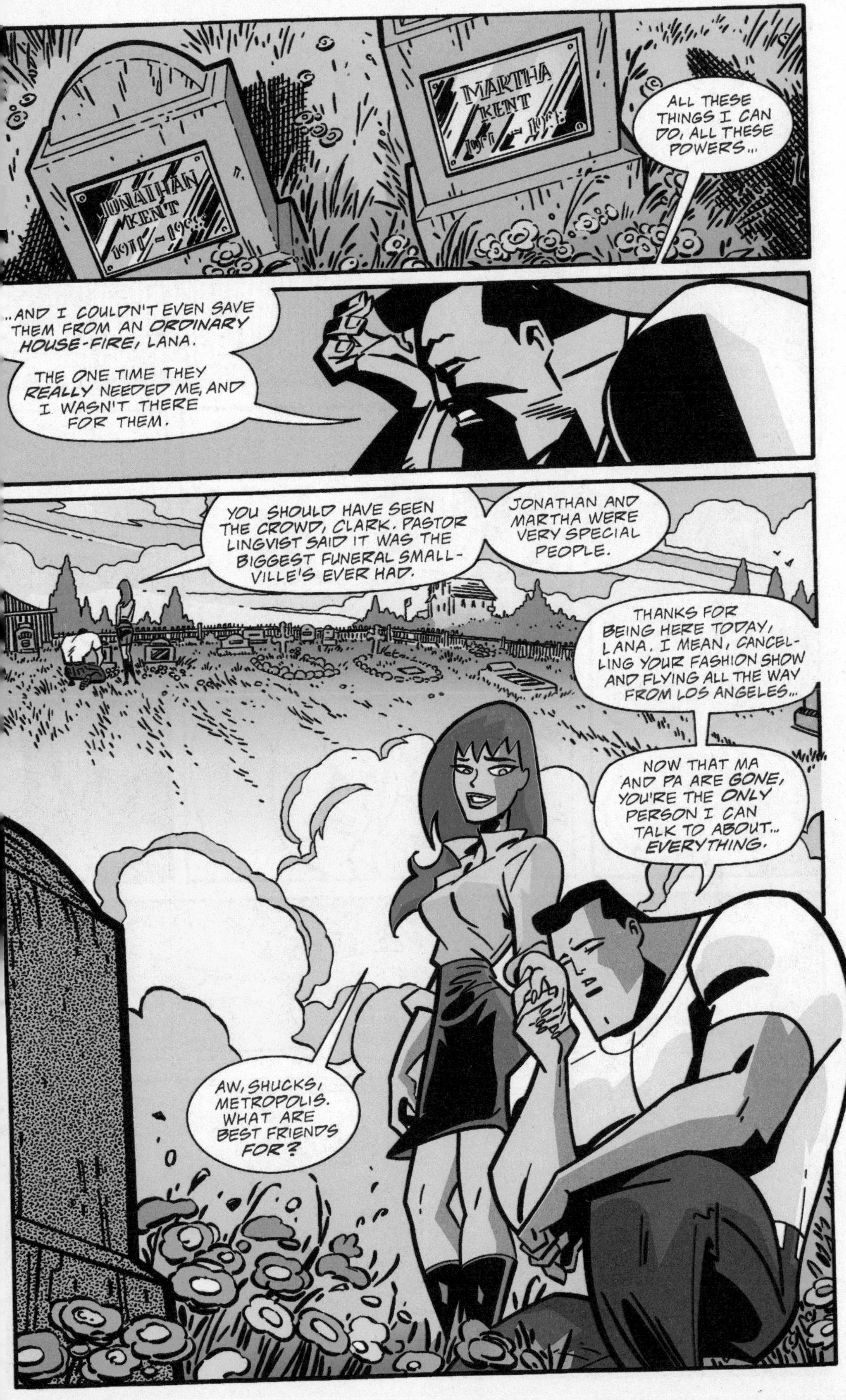
MARTHA KENT
JONATHAN KENT
ALL THESE THINGS I CAN DO, ALL THESE POWERS...
...AND I COULDN'T EVEN SAVE THEM FROM AN ORDINARY HOUSE-FIRE, LANA.
THE ONE TIME THEY REALLY NEEDED ME, AND I WASN'T THERE FOR THEM.
YOU SHOULD HAVE SEEN THE CROWD, CLARK. PASTOR LINGVIST SAID IT WAS THE BIGGEST FUNERAL SMALLVILLE'S EVER HAD.
JONATHAN AND MARTHA WERE VERY SPECIAL PEOPLE.
THANKS FOR BEING HERE TODAY, LANA. I MEAN, CANCELLING YOUR FASHION SHOW AND FLYING ALL THE WAY FROM LOS ANGELES...
NOW THAT MA AND PA ARE GONE, YOU'RE THE ONLY PERSON I CAN TALK TO ABOUT... EVERYTHING.
AW, SHUCKS, METROPOLIS. WHAT ARE BEST FRIENDS FOR?

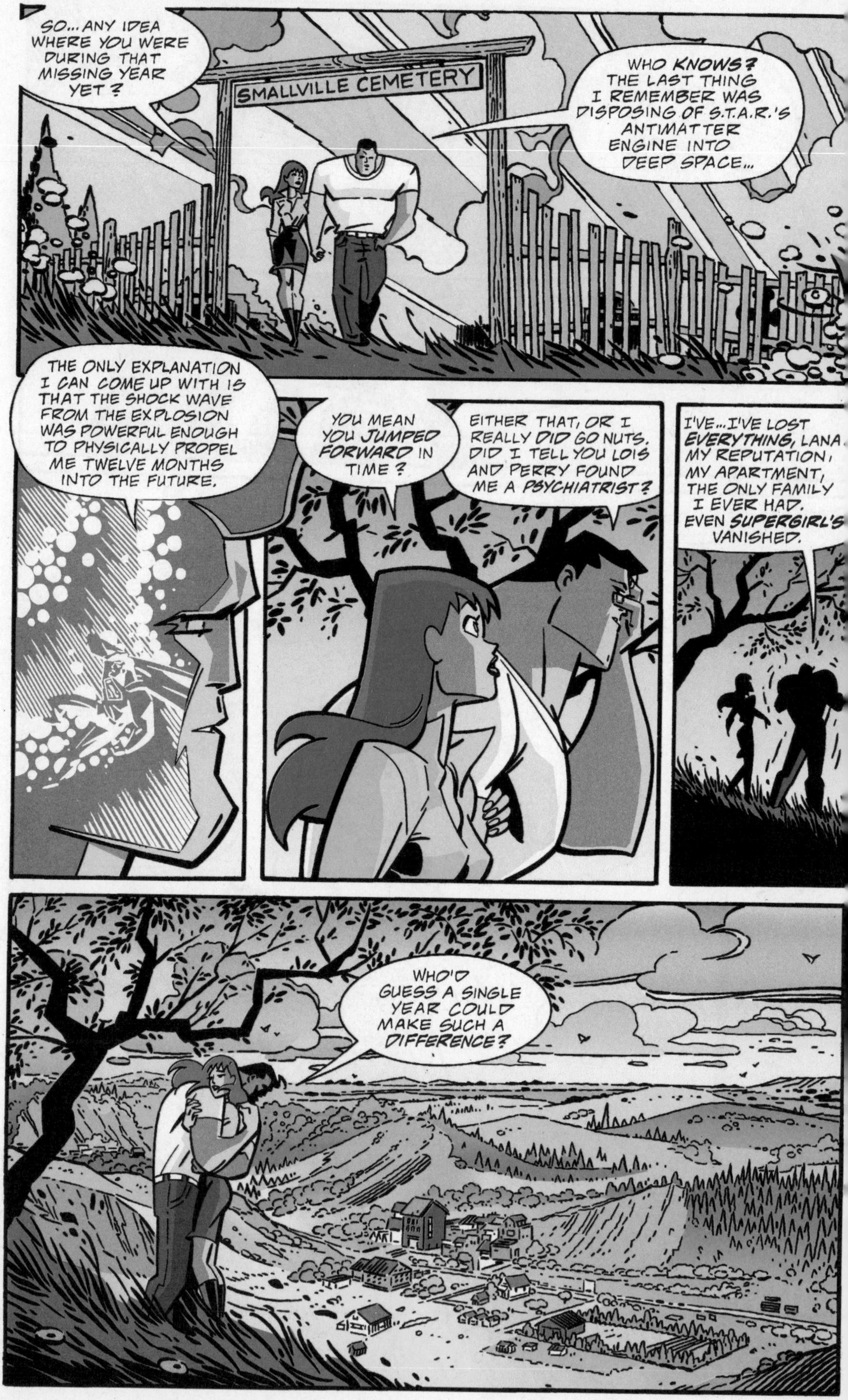
SO... ANY IDEA WHERE YOU WERE DURING THAT MISSING YEAR YET?
SMALLVILLE CEMETERY
WHO KNOWS? THE LAST THING I REMEMBER WAS DISPOSING OF S.T.A.R.'S ANTIMATTER ENGINE INTO DEEP SPACE...
THE ONLY EXPLANATION I CAN COME UP WITH IS THAT THE SHOCK WAVE FROM THE EXPLOSION WAS POWERFUL ENOUGH TO PHYSICALLY PROPEL ME TWELVE MONTHS INTO THE FUTURE.
YOU MEAN YOU JUMPED FORWARD IN TIME?
EITHER THAT, OR I REALLY DID GO NUTS. DID I TELL YOU LOIS AND PERRY FOUND ME A PSYCHIATRIST?
I'VE... I'VE LOST EVERYTHING, LANA. MY REPUTATION, MY APARTMENT, THE ONLY FAMILY I EVER HAD. EVEN SUPERGIRL'S VANISHED.
WHO'D GUESS A SINGLE YEAR COULD MAKE SUCH A DIFFERENCE?

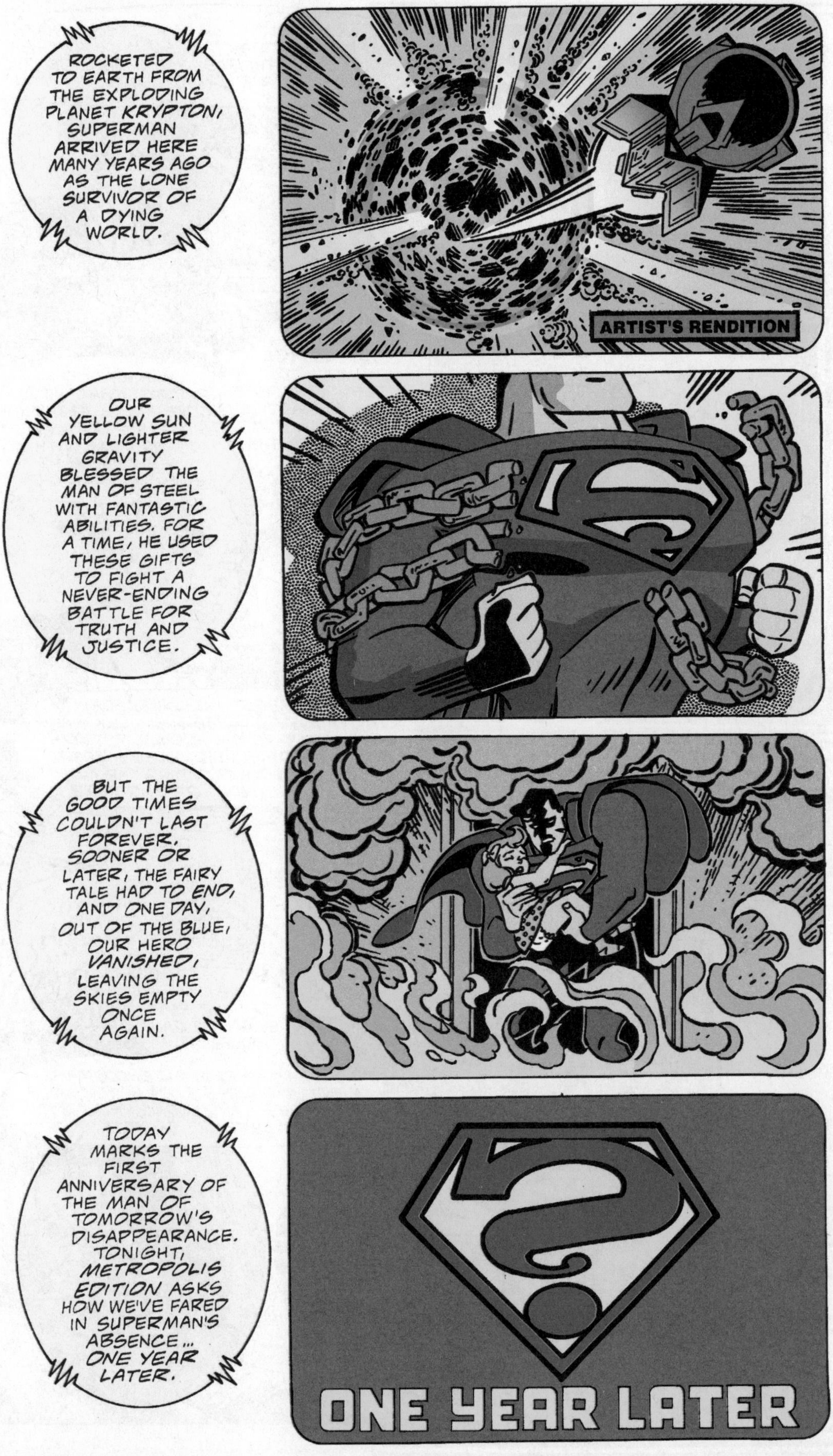
ROCKETED TO EARTH FROM THE EXPLODING PLANET KRYPTON, SUPERMAN ARRIVED HERE MANY YEARS AGO AS THE LONE SURVIVOR OF A DYING WORLD.
ARTIST'S RENDITION
OUR YELLOW SUN AND LIGHTER GRAVITY BLESSED THE MAN OF STEEL WITH FANTASTIC ABILITIES. FOR A TIME, HE USED THESE GIFTS TO FIGHT A NEVER-ENDING BATTLE FOR TRUTH AND JUSTICE.
BUT THE GOOD TIMES COULDN'T LAST FOREVER. SOONER OR LATER, THE FAIRY TALE HAD TO END, AND ONE DAY, OUT OF THE BLUE, OUR HERO VANISHED, LEAVING THE SKIES EMPTY ONCE AGAIN.
TODAY MARKS THE FIRST ANNIVERSARY OF THE MAN OF TOMORROW'S DISAPPEARANCE. TONIGHT, METROPOLIS EDITION ASKS HOW WE'VE FARED IN SUPERMAN'S ABSENCE... ONE YEAR LATER.
ONE YEAR LATER

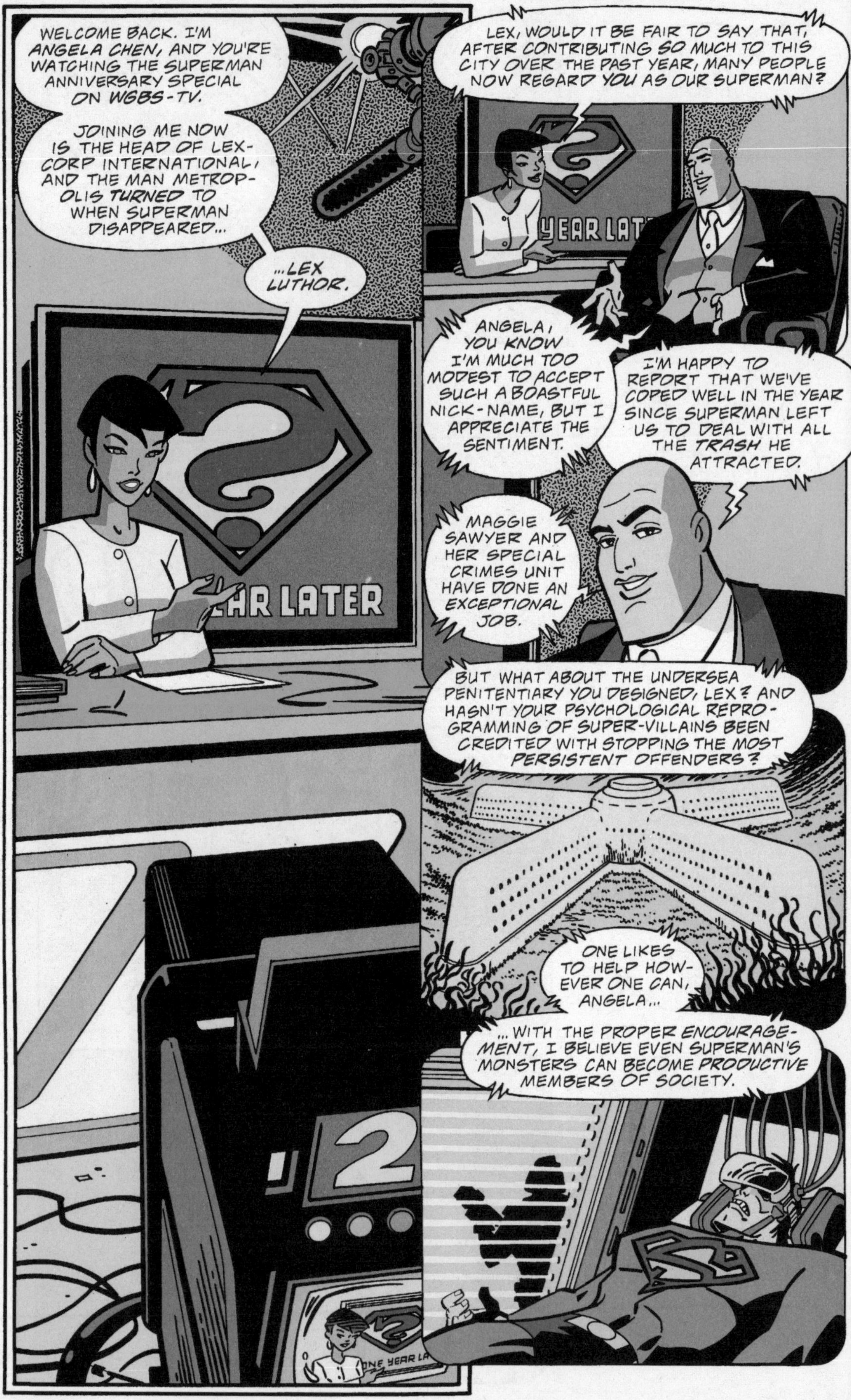
WELCOME BACK. I'M ANGELA CHEN, AND YOU'RE WATCHING THE SUPERMAN ANNIVERSARY SPECIAL ON WGBS-TV.
JOINING ME NOW IS THE HEAD OF LEX-CORP INTERNATIONAL, AND THE MAN METROP-OLIS TURNED TO WHEN SUPERMAN DISAPPEARED...
...LEX LUTHOR.
YEAR LATER
LEX, WOULD IT BE FAIR TO SAY THAT, AFTER CONTRIBUTING SO MUCH TO THIS CITY OVER THE PAST YEAR, MANY PEOPLE NOW REGARD YOU AS OUR SUPERMAN?
ANGELA, YOU KNOW I'M MUCH TOO MODEST TO ACCEPT SUCH A BOASTFUL NICK-NAME, BUT I APPRECIATE THE SENTIMENT.
I'M HAPPY TO REPORT THAT WE'VE COPED WELL IN THE YEAR SINCE SUPERMAN LEFT US TO DEAL WITH ALL THE TRASH HE ATTRACTED.
MAGGIE SAWYER AND HER SPECIAL CRIMES UNIT HAVE DONE AN EXCEPTIONAL JOB.
BUT WHAT ABOUT THE UNDERSEA PENITENTIARY YOU DESIGNED, LEX? AND HASN'T YOUR PSYCHOLOGICAL REPRO-GRAMMING OF SUPER-VILLAINS BEEN CREDITED WITH STOPPING THE MOST PERSISTENT OFFENDERS?
ONE LIKES TO HELP HOW-EVER ONE CAN, ANGELA...
...WITH THE PROPER ENCOURAGE-MENT, I BELIEVE EVEN SUPERMAN'S MONSTERS CAN BECOME PRODUCTIVE MEMBERS OF SOCIETY.
2
ONE YEAR LA

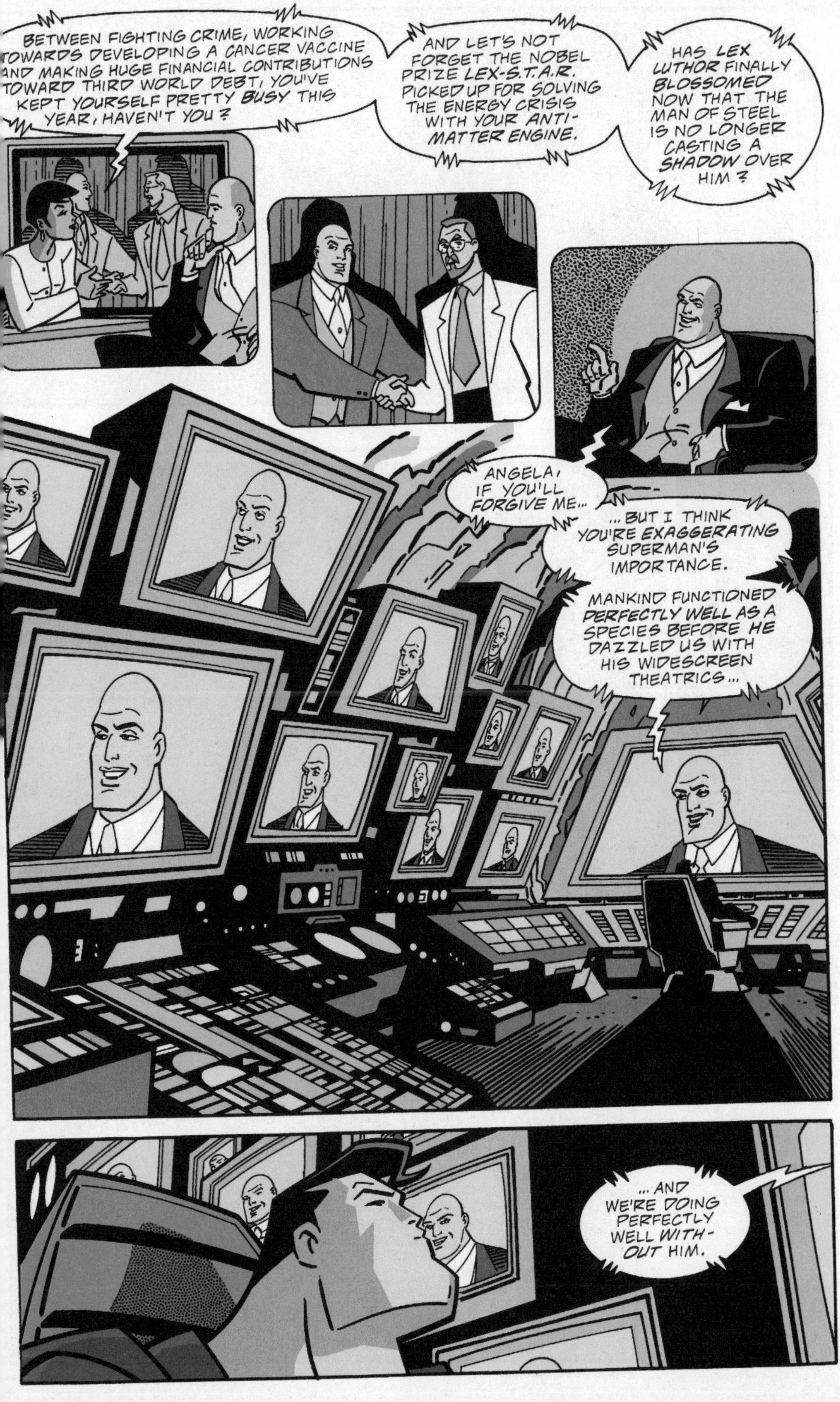
BETWEEN FIGHTING CRIME, WORKING TOWARDS DEVELOPING A CANCER VACCINE AND MAKING HUGE FINANCIAL CONTRIBUTIONS TOWARD THIRD WORLD DEBT, YOU'VE KEPT YOURSELF PRETTY BUSY THIS YEAR, HAVEN'T YOU?
AND LET'S NOT FORGET THE NOBEL PRIZE LEX-S.T.A.R. PICKED UP FOR SOLVING THE ENERGY CRISIS WITH YOUR ANTI-MATTER ENGINE.
HAS LEX LUTHOR FINALLY BLOSSOMED NOW THAT THE MAN OF STEEL IS NO LONGER CASTING A SHADOW OVER HIM?
ANGELA, IF YOU'LL FORGIVE ME...
...BUT I THINK YOU'RE EXAGGERATING SUPERMAN'S IMPORTANCE.
MANKIND FUNCTIONED PERFECTLY WELL AS A SPECIES BEFORE HE DAZZLED US WITH HIS WIDESCREEN THEATRICS...
...AND WE'RE DOING PERFECTLY WELL WITHOUT HIM.

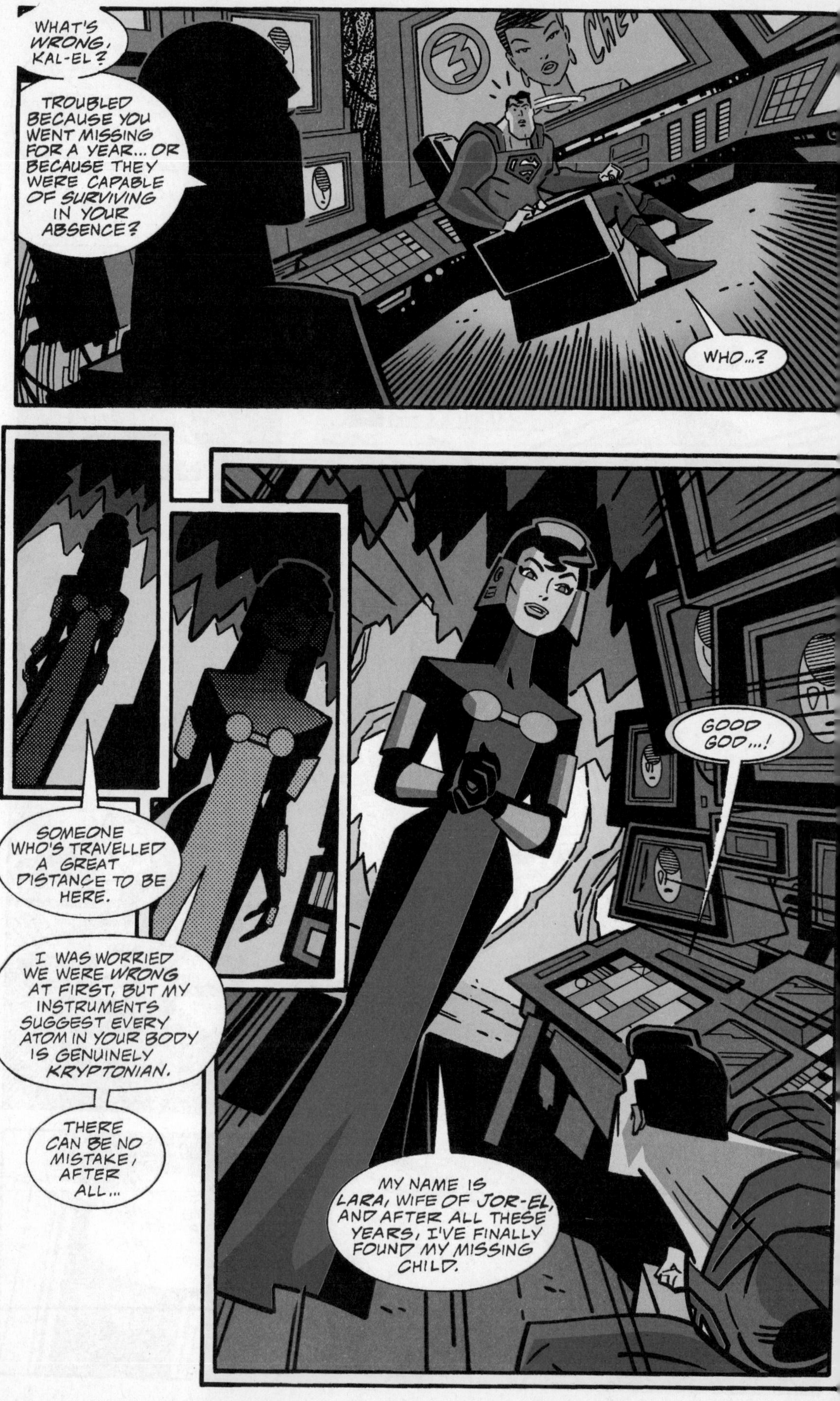
WHAT'S WRONG, KAL-EL?
TROUBLED BECAUSE YOU WENT MISSING FOR A YEAR... OR BECAUSE THEY WERE CAPABLE OF SURVIVING IN YOUR ABSENCE?
WHO...?
SOMEONE WHO'S TRAVELLED A GREAT DISTANCE TO BE HERE.
I WAS WORRIED WE WERE WRONG AT FIRST, BUT MY INSTRUMENTS SUGGEST EVERY ATOM IN YOUR BODY IS GENUINELY KRYPTONIAN.
THERE CAN BE NO MISTAKE, AFTER ALL...
GOOD GOD...!
MY NAME IS LARA, WIFE OF JOR-EL, AND AFTER ALL THESE YEARS, I'VE FINALLY FOUND MY MISSING CHILD.

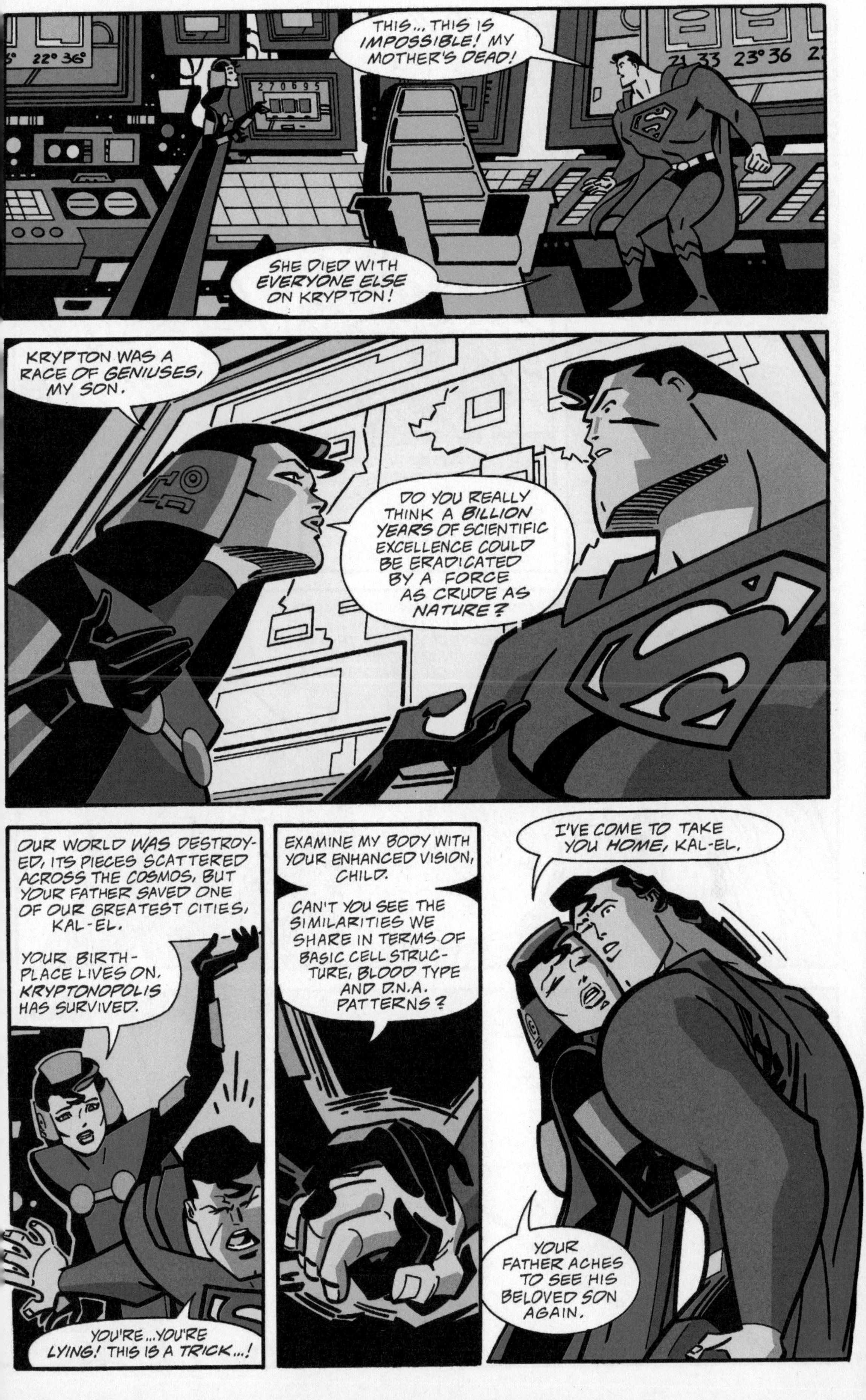
THIS... THIS IS IMPOSSIBLE! MY MOTHER'S DEAD!
SHE DIED WITH EVERYONE ELSE ON KRYPTON!
KRYPTON WAS A RACE OF GENIUSES, MY SON.
DO YOU REALLY THINK A BILLION YEARS OF SCIENTIFIC EXCELLENCE COULD BE ERADICATED BY A FORCE AS CRUDE AS NATURE?
OUR WORLD WAS DESTROYED, ITS PIECES SCATTERED ACROSS THE COSMOS, BUT YOUR FATHER SAVED ONE OF OUR GREATEST CITIES, KAL-EL.
YOUR BIRTHPLACE LIVES ON. KRYPTONOPOLIS HAS SURVIVED.
YOU'RE...YOU'RE LYING! THIS IS A TRICK...!
EXAMINE MY BODY WITH YOUR ENHANCED VISION, CHILD.
CAN'T YOU SEE THE SIMILARITIES WE SHARE IN TERMS OF BASIC CELL STRUCTURE, BLOOD TYPE AND D.N.A. PATTERNS?
I'VE COME TO TAKE YOU HOME, KAL-EL.
YOUR FATHER ACHES TO SEE HIS BELOVED SON AGAIN.

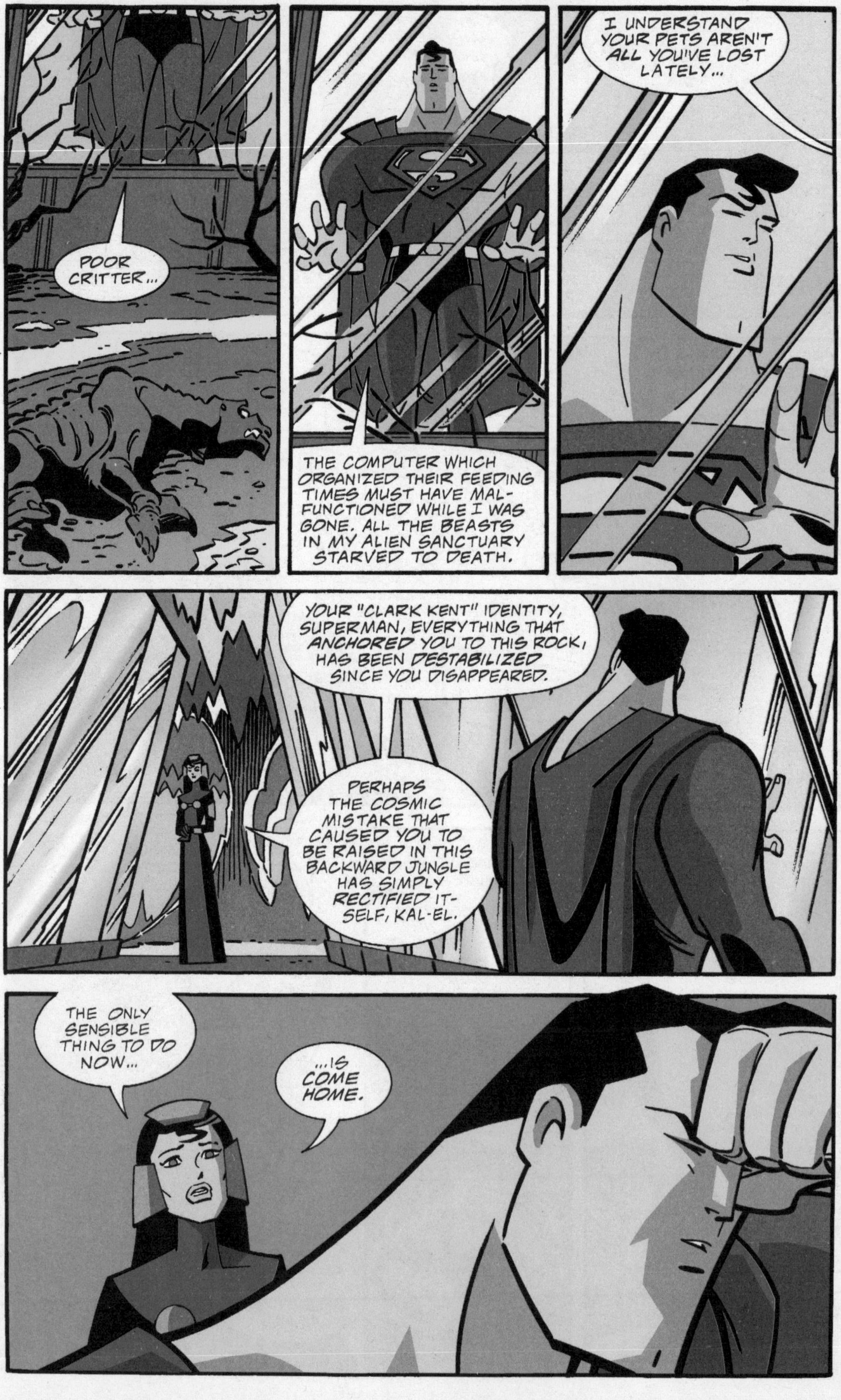
POOR CRITTER...
THE COMPUTER WHICH ORGANIZED THEIR FEEDING TIMES MUST HAVE MAL-FUNCTIONED WHILE I WAS GONE. ALL THE BEASTS IN MY ALIEN SANCTUARY STARVED TO DEATH.
I UNDERSTAND YOUR PETS AREN'T ALL YOU'VE LOST LATELY...
YOUR "CLARK KENT" IDENTITY, SUPERMAN, EVERYTHING THAT ANCHORED YOU TO THIS ROCK, HAS BEEN DESTABILIZED SINCE YOU DISAPPEARED.
PERHAPS THE COSMIC MISTAKE THAT CAUSED YOU TO BE RAISED IN THIS BACKWARD JUNGLE HAS SIMPLY RECTIFIED IT-SELF, KAL-EL.
THE ONLY SENSIBLE THING TO DO NOW...
...IS COME HOME.

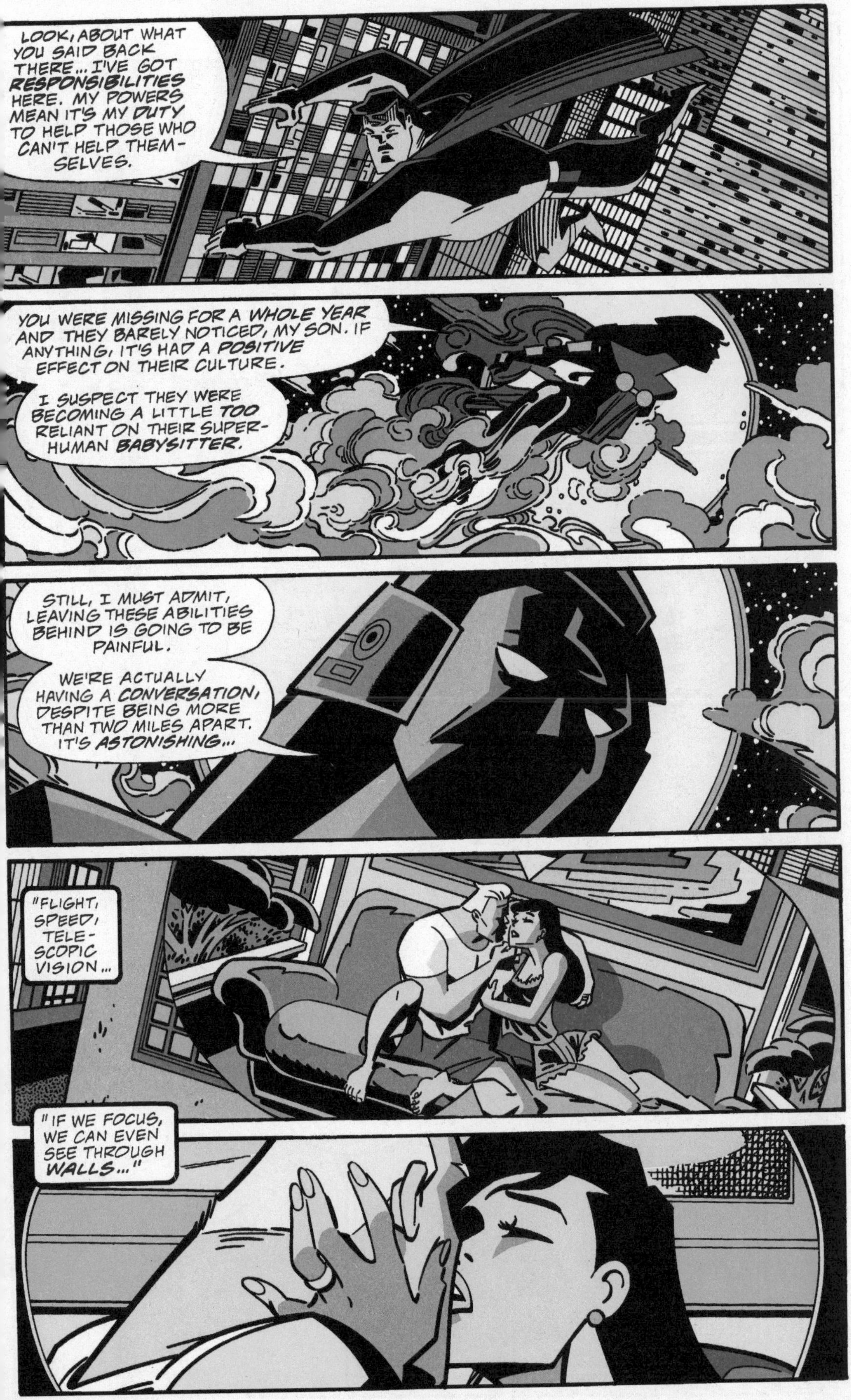
LOOK, ABOUT WHAT YOU SAID BACK THERE... I'VE GOT RESPONSIBILITIES HERE. MY POWERS MEAN IT'S MY DUTY TO HELP THOSE WHO CAN'T HELP THEM-SELVES.
YOU WERE MISSING FOR A WHOLE YEAR AND THEY BARELY NOTICED, MY SON. IF ANYTHING, IT'S HAD A POSITIVE EFFECT ON THEIR CULTURE.
I SUSPECT THEY WERE BECOMING A LITTLE TOO RELIANT ON THEIR SUPER-HUMAN BABYSITTER.
STILL, I MUST ADMIT, LEAVING THESE ABILITIES BEHIND IS GOING TO BE PAINFUL.
WE'RE ACTUALLY HAVING A CONVERSATION, DESPITE BEING MORE THAN TWO MILES APART. IT'S ASTONISHING...
"FLIGHT, SPEED, TELE-SCOPIC VISION...
"IF WE FOCUS, WE CAN EVEN SEE THROUGH WALLS..."

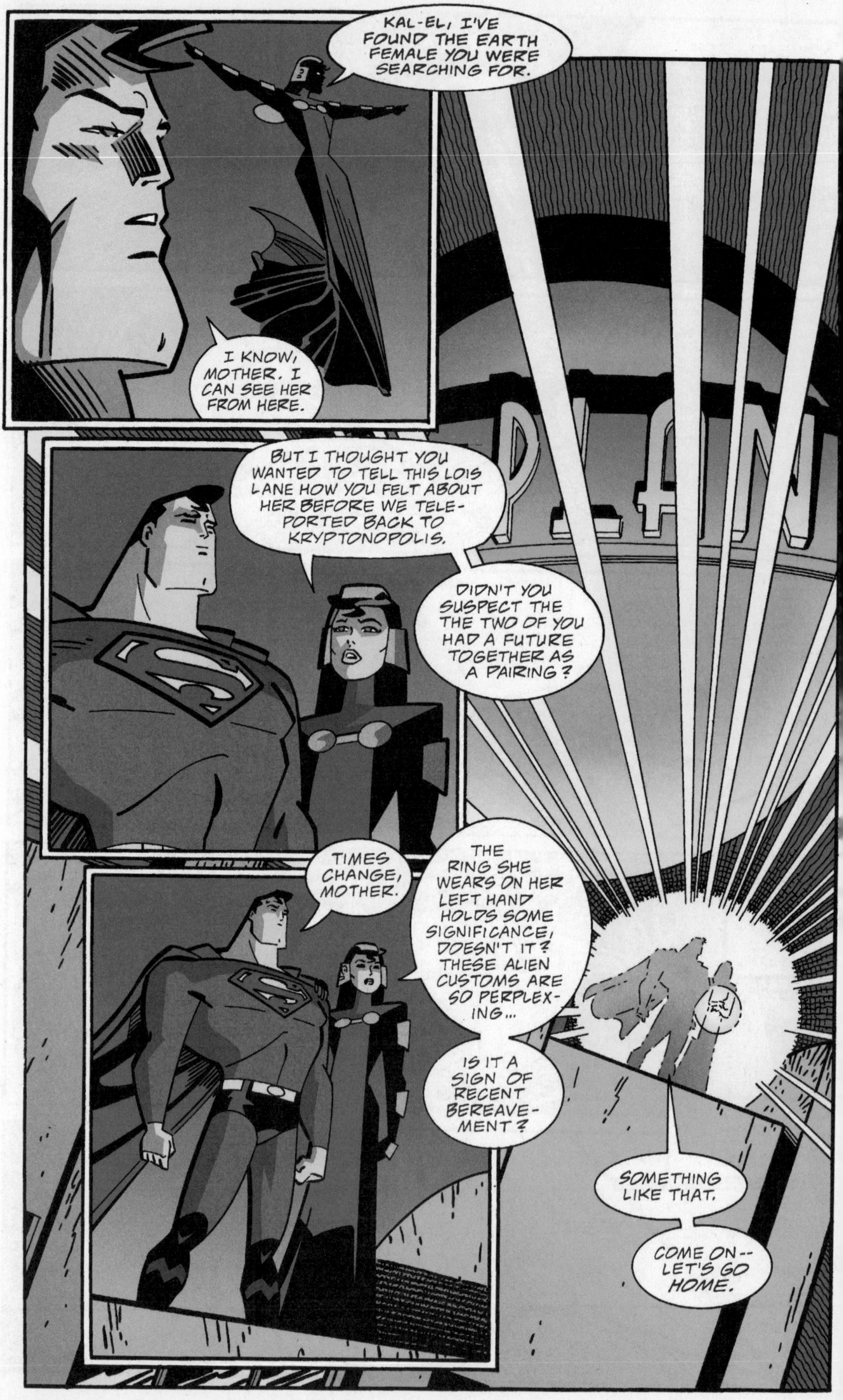

KAL-EL, I'VE FOUND THE EARTH FEMALE YOU WERE SEARCHING FOR.
I KNOW, MOTHER. I CAN SEE HER FROM HERE.
BUT I THOUGHT YOU WANTED TO TELL THIS LOIS LANE HOW YOU FELT ABOUT HER BEFORE WE TELE-PORTED BACK TO KRYPTONOPOLIS.
DIDN'T YOU SUSPECT THE THE TWO OF YOU HAD A FUTURE TOGETHER AS A PAIRING?
TIMES CHANGE, MOTHER.
THE RING SHE WEARS ON HER LEFT HAND HOLDS SOME SIGNIFICANCE, DOESN'T IT? THESE ALIEN CUSTOMS ARE SO PERPLEX-ING...
IS IT A SIGN OF RECENT BEREAVE-MENT?
SOMETHING LIKE THAT.
COME ON-- LET'S GO HOME.

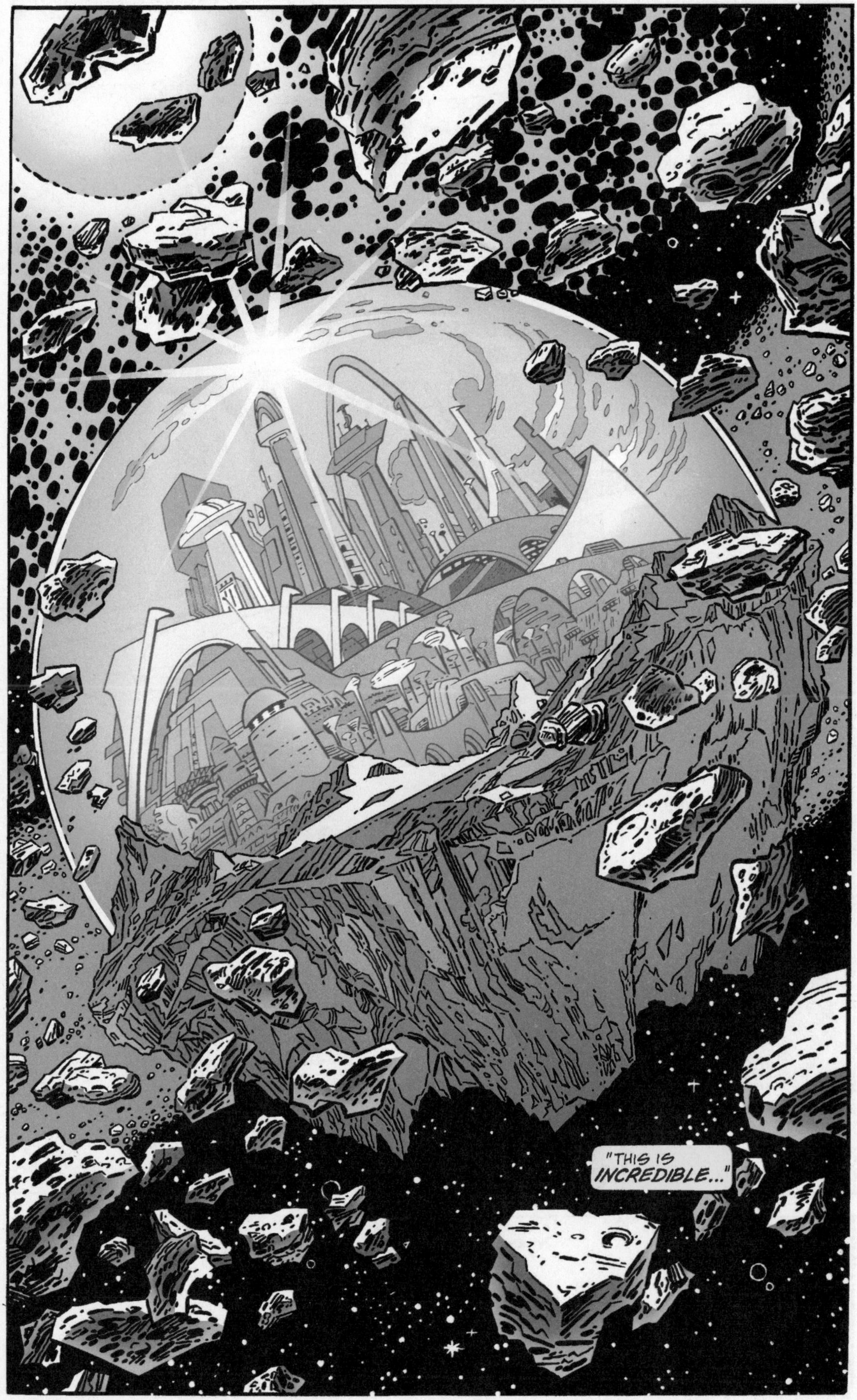
"THIS IS INCREDIBLE..."

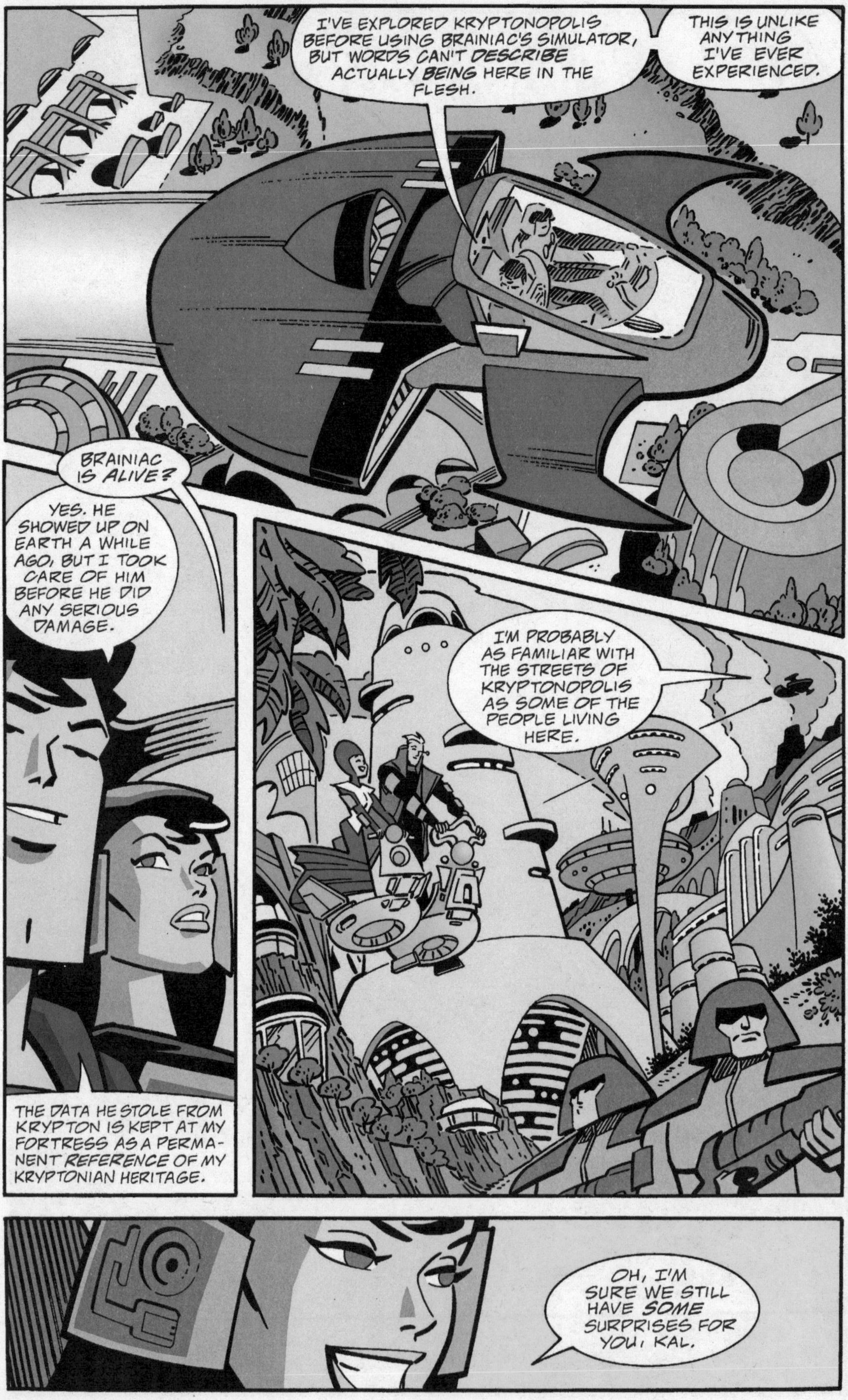
I'VE EXPLORED KRYPTONOPOLIS BEFORE USING BRAINIAC'S SIMULATOR, BUT WORDS CAN'T DESCRIBE ACTUALLY BEING HERE IN THE FLESH.
THIS IS UNLIKE ANYTHING I'VE EVER EXPERIENCED.
BRAINIAC IS ALIVE?
YES. HE SHOWED UP ON EARTH A WHILE AGO, BUT I TOOK CARE OF HIM BEFORE HE DID ANY SERIOUS DAMAGE.
THE DATA HE STOLE FROM KRYPTON IS KEPT AT MY FORTRESS AS A PERMANENT REFERENCE OF MY KRYPTONIAN HERITAGE.
I'M PROBABLY AS FAMILIAR WITH THE STREETS OF KRYPTONOPOLIS AS SOME OF THE PEOPLE LIVING HERE.
OH, I'M SURE WE STILL HAVE SOME SURPRISES FOR YOU, KAL.

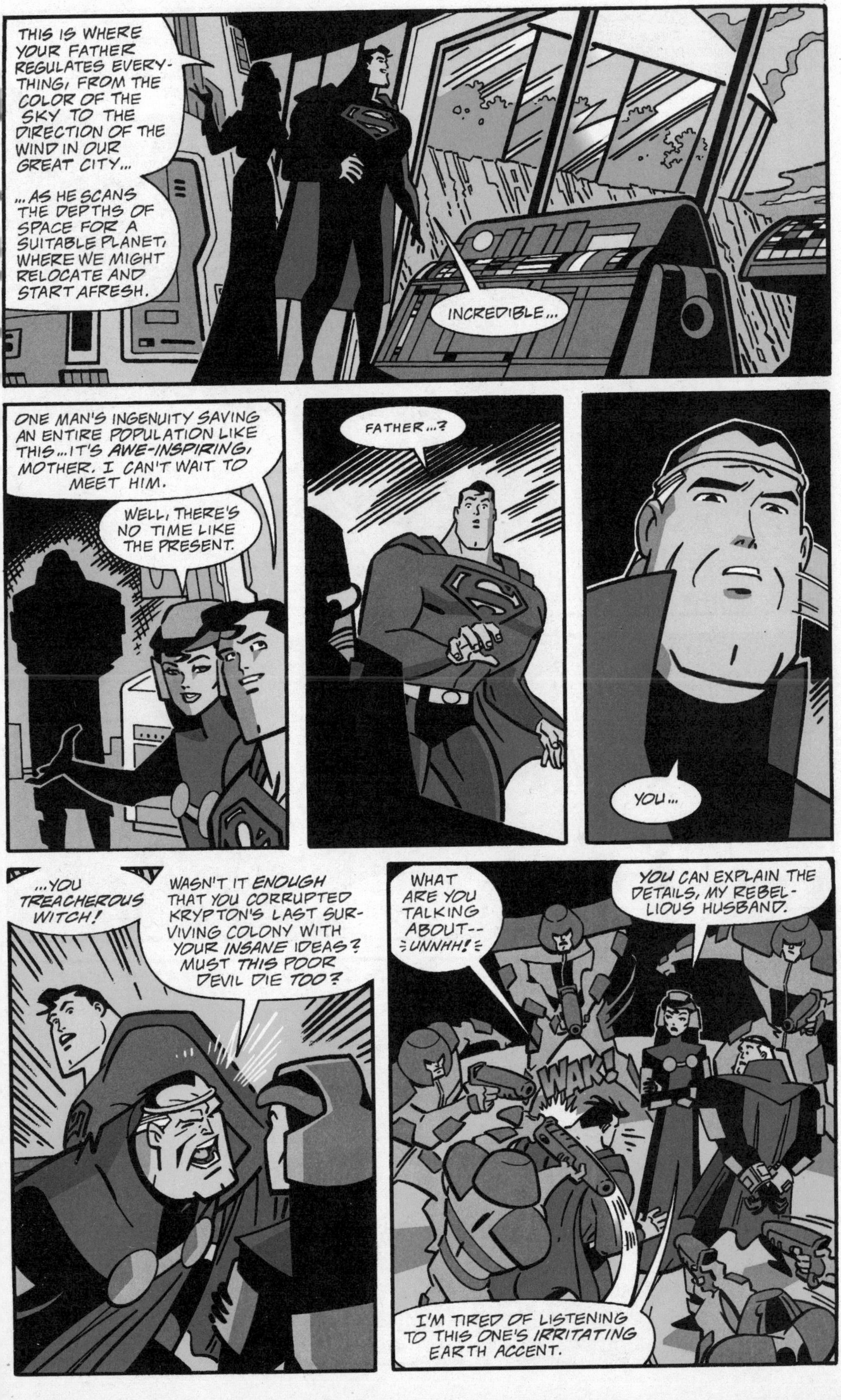
THIS IS WHERE YOUR FATHER REGULATES EVERYTHING, FROM THE COLOR OF THE SKY TO THE DIRECTION OF THE WIND IN OUR GREAT CITY...
...AS HE SCANS THE DEPTHS OF SPACE FOR A SUITABLE PLANET, WHERE WE MIGHT RELOCATE AND START AFRESH.
INCREDIBLE...
ONE MAN'S INGENUITY SAVING AN ENTIRE POPULATION LIKE THIS...IT'S AWE-INSPIRING, MOTHER. I CAN'T WAIT TO MEET HIM.
WELL, THERE'S NO TIME LIKE THE PRESENT.
FATHER...?
YOU...
...YOU TREACHEROUS WITCH!
WASN'T IT ENOUGH THAT YOU CORRUPTED KRYPTON'S LAST SURVIVING COLONY WITH YOUR INSANE IDEAS? MUST THIS POOR DEVIL DIE TOO?
WHAT ARE YOU TALKING ABOUT-- UNNHH!
YOU CAN EXPLAIN THE DETAILS, MY REBELLIOUS HUSBAND.
WAK!
I'M TIRED OF LISTENING TO THIS ONE'S IRRITATING EARTH ACCENT.

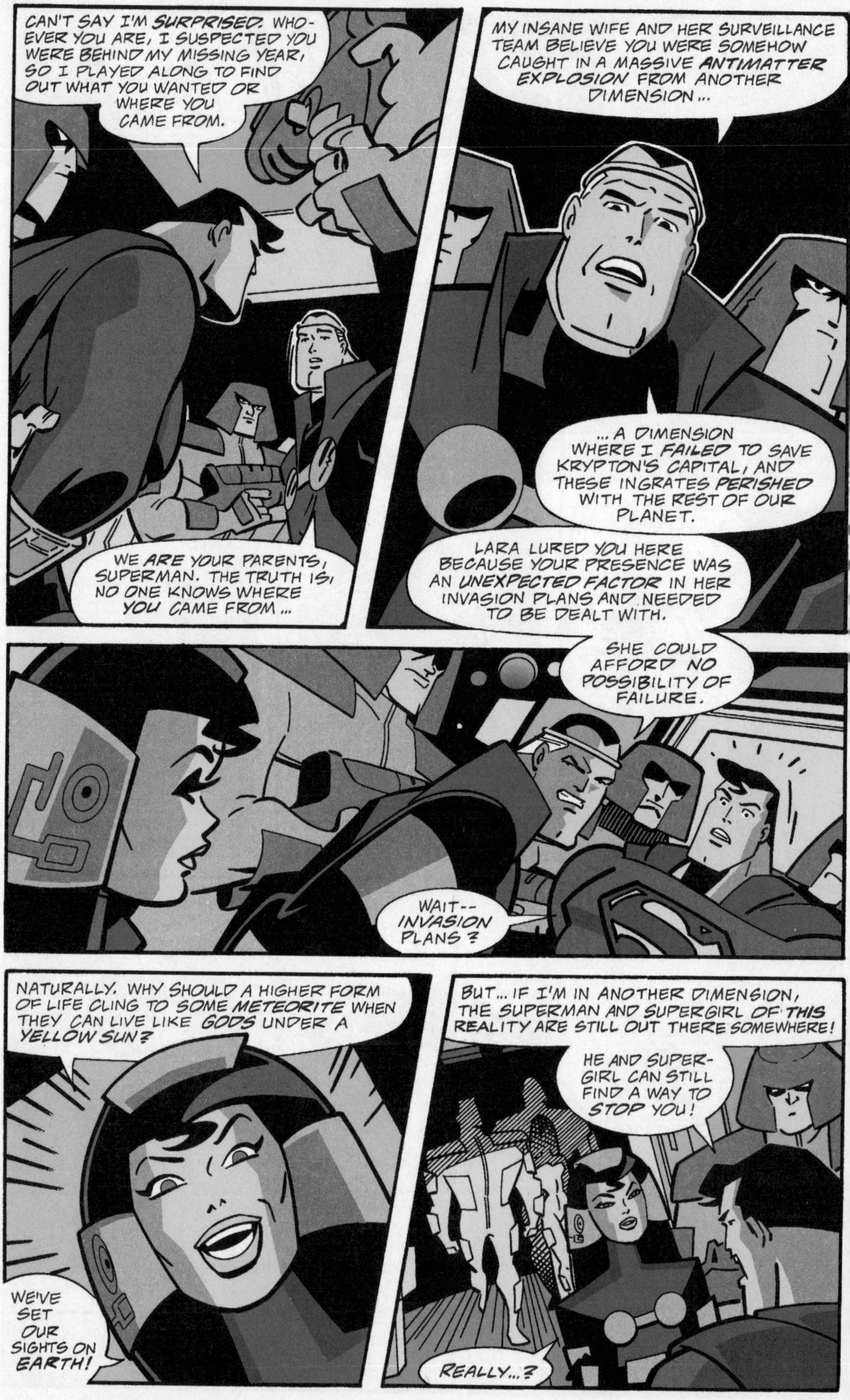

CAN'T SAY I'M SURPRISED. WHO-EVER YOU ARE, I SUSPECTED YOU WERE BEHIND MY MISSING YEAR, SO I PLAYED ALONG TO FIND OUT WHAT YOU WANTED OR WHERE YOU CAME FROM.
WE ARE YOUR PARENTS, SUPERMAN. THE TRUTH IS, NO ONE KNOWS WHERE YOU CAME FROM...
MY INSANE WIFE AND HER SURVEILLANCE TEAM BELIEVE YOU WERE SOMEHOW CAUGHT IN A MASSIVE ANTIMATTER EXPLOSION FROM ANOTHER DIMENSION...
...A DIMENSION WHERE I FAILED TO SAVE KRYPTON'S CAPITAL, AND THESE INGRATES PERISHED WITH THE REST OF OUR PLANET.
LARA LURED YOU HERE BECAUSE YOUR PRESENCE WAS AN UNEXPECTED FACTOR IN HER INVASION PLANS AND NEEDED TO BE DEALT WITH.
SHE COULD AFFORD NO POSSIBILITY OF FAILURE.
WAIT-- INVASION PLANS?
NATURALLY. WHY SHOULD A HIGHER FORM OF LIFE CLING TO SOME METEORITE WHEN THEY CAN LIVE LIKE GODS UNDER A YELLOW SUN?
WE'VE SET OUR SIGHTS ON EARTH!
BUT... IF I'M IN ANOTHER DIMENSION, THE SUPERMAN AND SUPERGIRL OF THIS REALITY ARE STILL OUT THERE SOMEWHERE!
HE AND SUPER-GIRL CAN STILL FIND A WAY TO STOP YOU!
REALLY...?

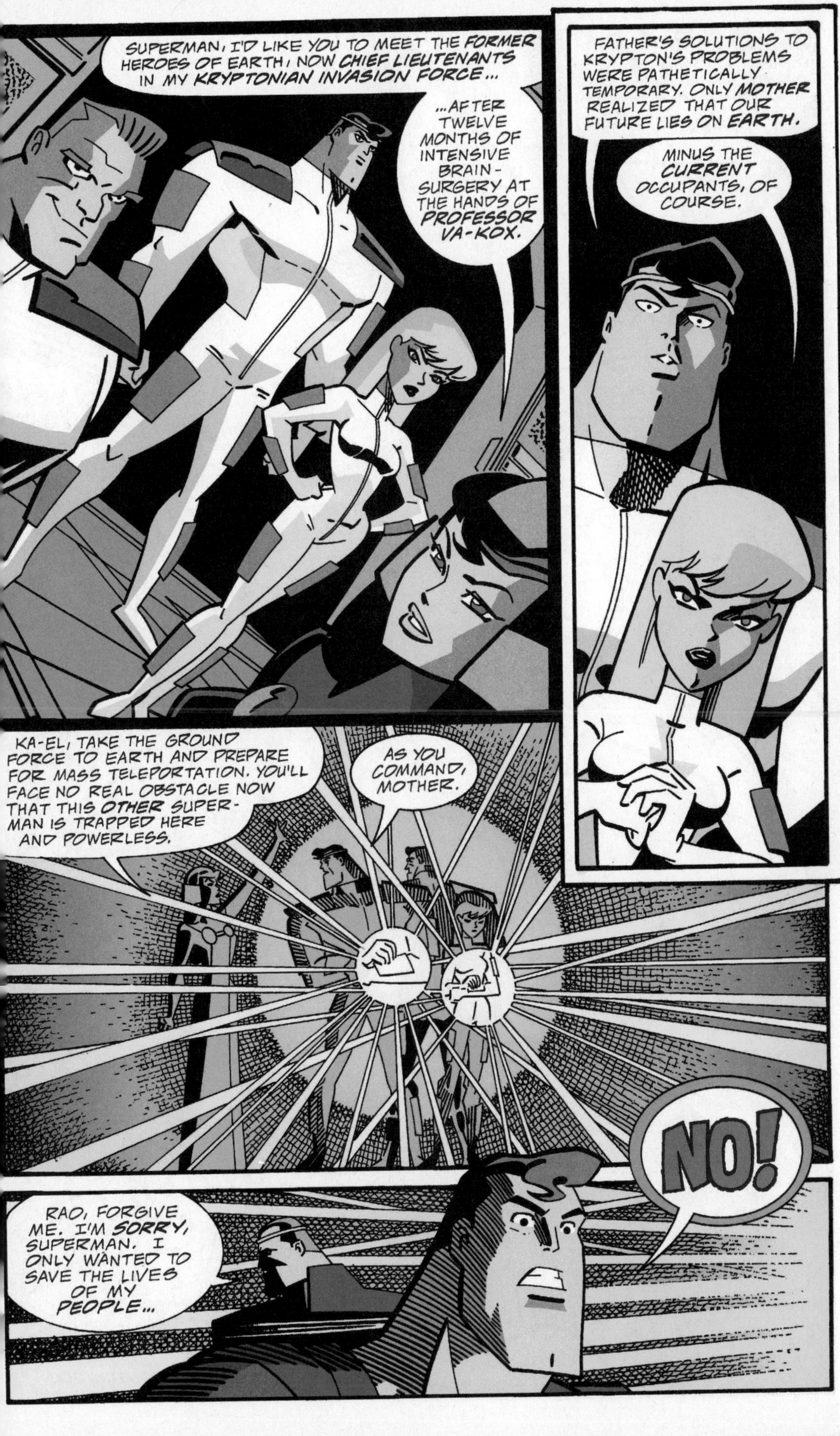
SUPERMAN, I'D LIKE YOU TO MEET THE FORMER HEROES OF EARTH, NOW CHIEF LIEUTENANTS IN MY KRYPTONIAN INVASION FORCE...
...AFTER TWELVE MONTHS OF INTENSIVE BRAIN-SURGERY AT THE HANDS OF PROFESSOR VA-KOX.
FATHER'S SOLUTIONS TO KRYPTON'S PROBLEMS WERE PATHETICALLY TEMPORARY. ONLY MOTHER REALIZED THAT OUR FUTURE LIES ON EARTH.
MINUS THE CURRENT OCCUPANTS, OF COURSE.
KA-EL, TAKE THE GROUND FORCE TO EARTH AND PREPARE FOR MASS TELEPORTATION. YOU'LL FACE NO REAL OBSTACLE NOW THAT THIS OTHER SUPERMAN IS TRAPPED HERE AND POWERLESS.
AS YOU COMMAND, MOTHER.
RAO, FORGIVE ME. I'M SORRY, SUPERMAN. I ONLY WANTED TO SAVE THE LIVES OF MY PEOPLE...
NO!

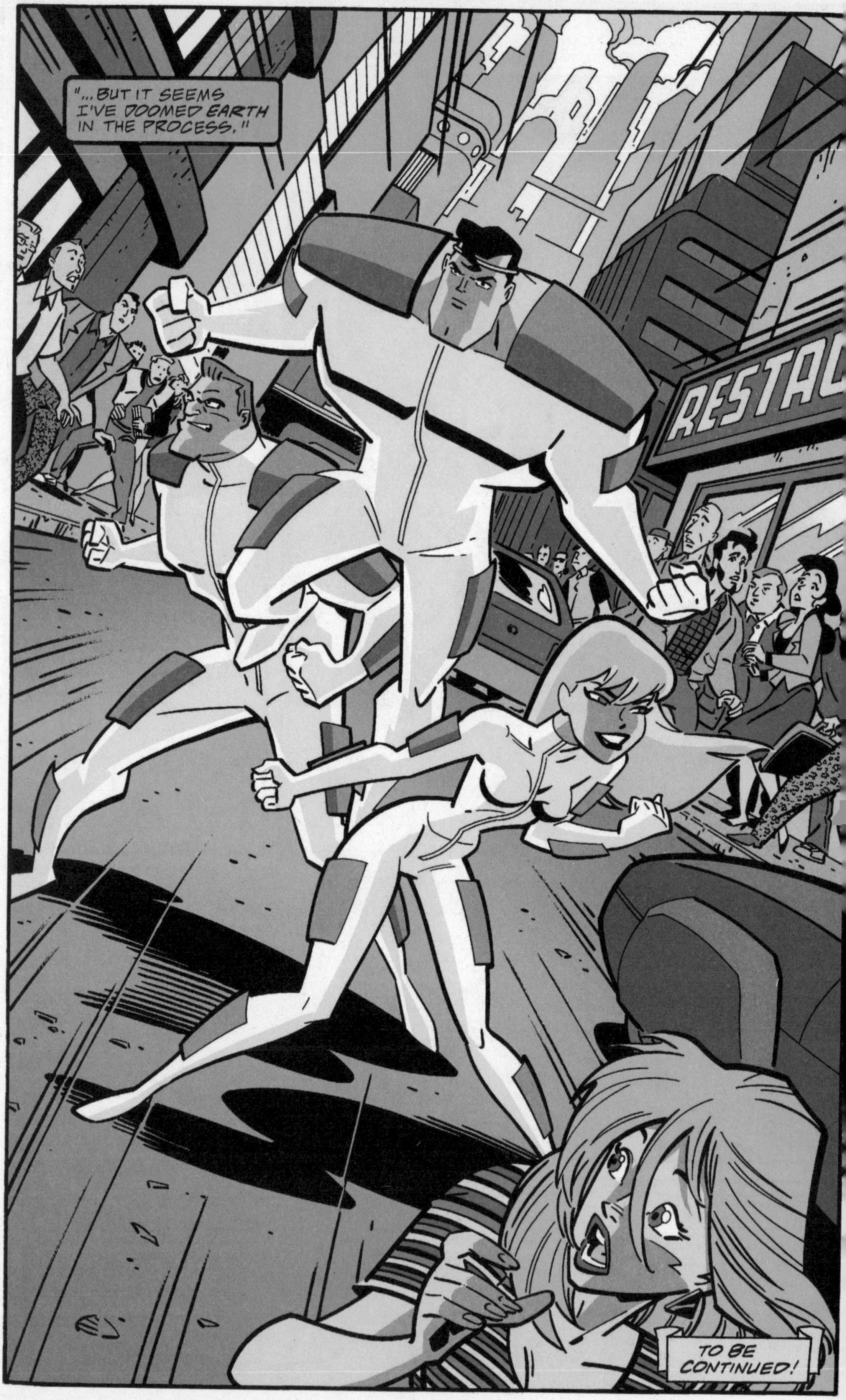
"...BUT IT SEEMS I'VE DOOMED EARTH IN THE PROCESS."
RESTAU
TO BE CONTINUED!

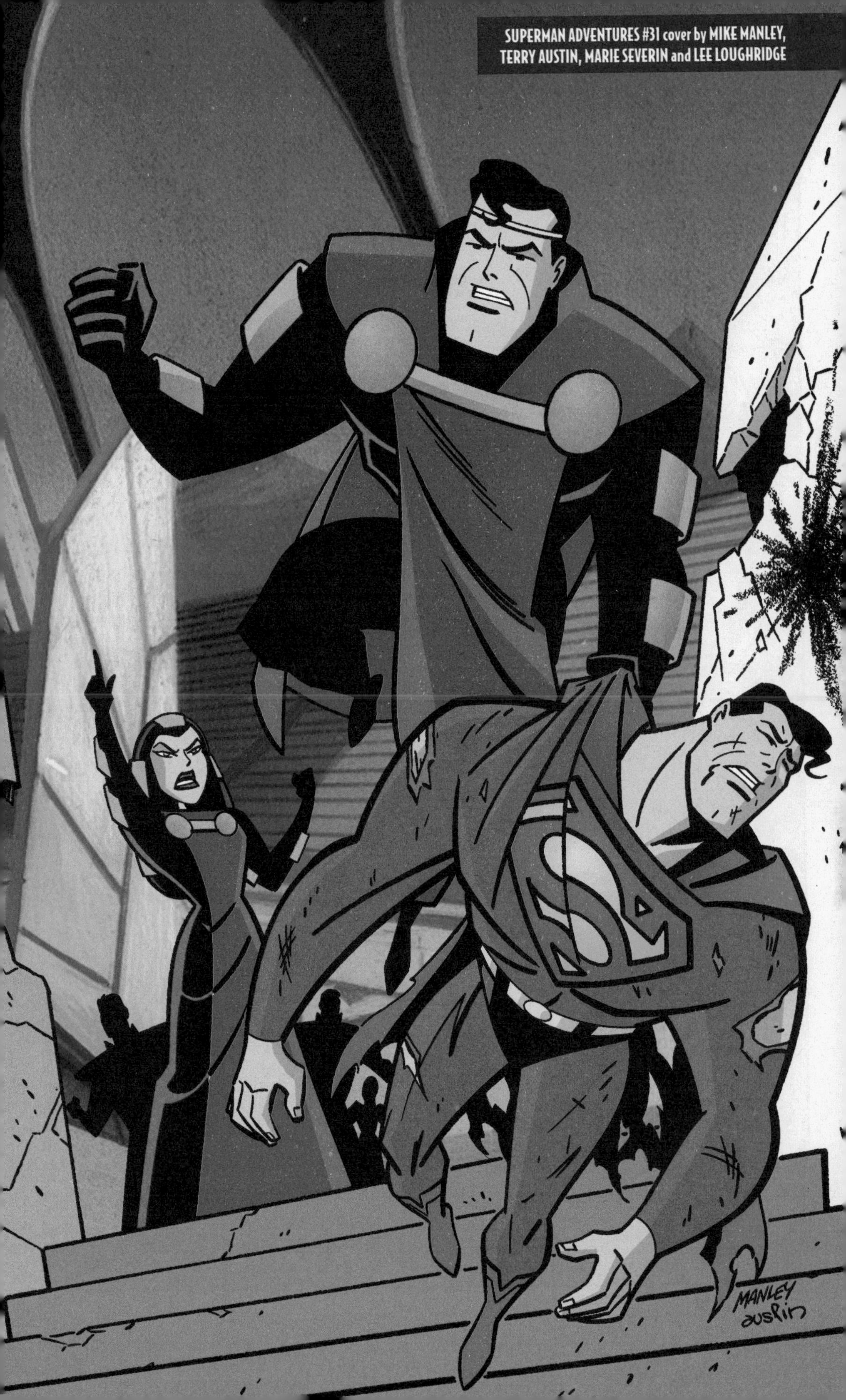
MANLEY
austin

SUPERMAN ADVENTURES #31 cover by MIKE MANLEY, TERRY AUSTIN, MARIE SEVERIN and LEE LOUGHRIDGE

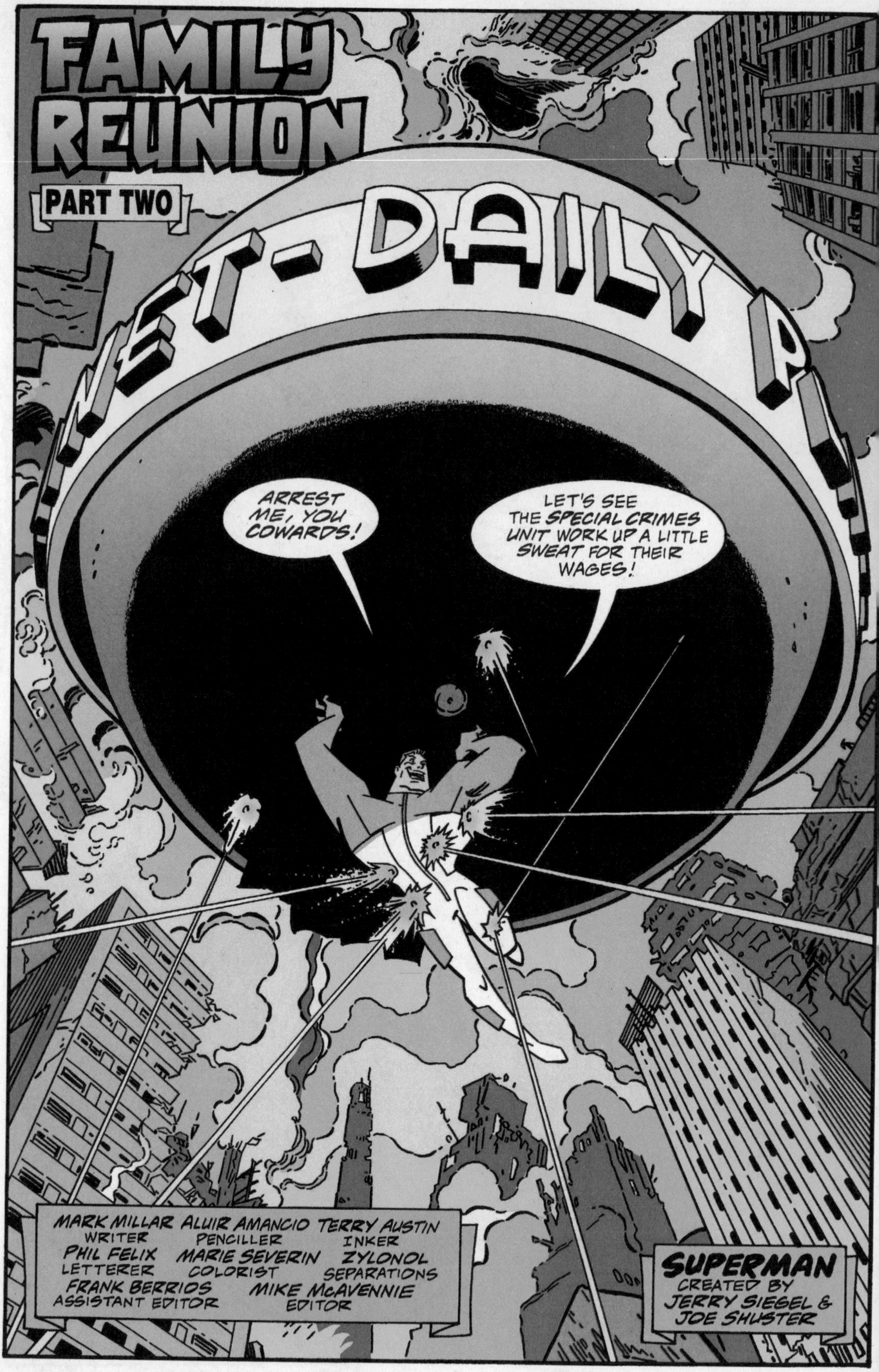
FAMILY REUNION
PART TWO
-DAILY P
ARREST ME, YOU COWARDS!
LET'S SEE THE SPECIAL CRIMES UNIT WORK UP A LITTLE SWEAT FOR THEIR WAGES!
MARK MILLAR WRITER
ALUIR AMANCIO PENCILLER
TERRY AUSTIN INKER
PHIL FELIX LETTERER
MARIE SEVERIN COLORIST
ZYLONOL SEPARATIONS
FRANK BERRIOS ASSISTANT EDITOR
MIKE McAVENNIE EDITOR
SUPERMAN CREATED BY JERRY SIEGEL & JOE SHUSTER

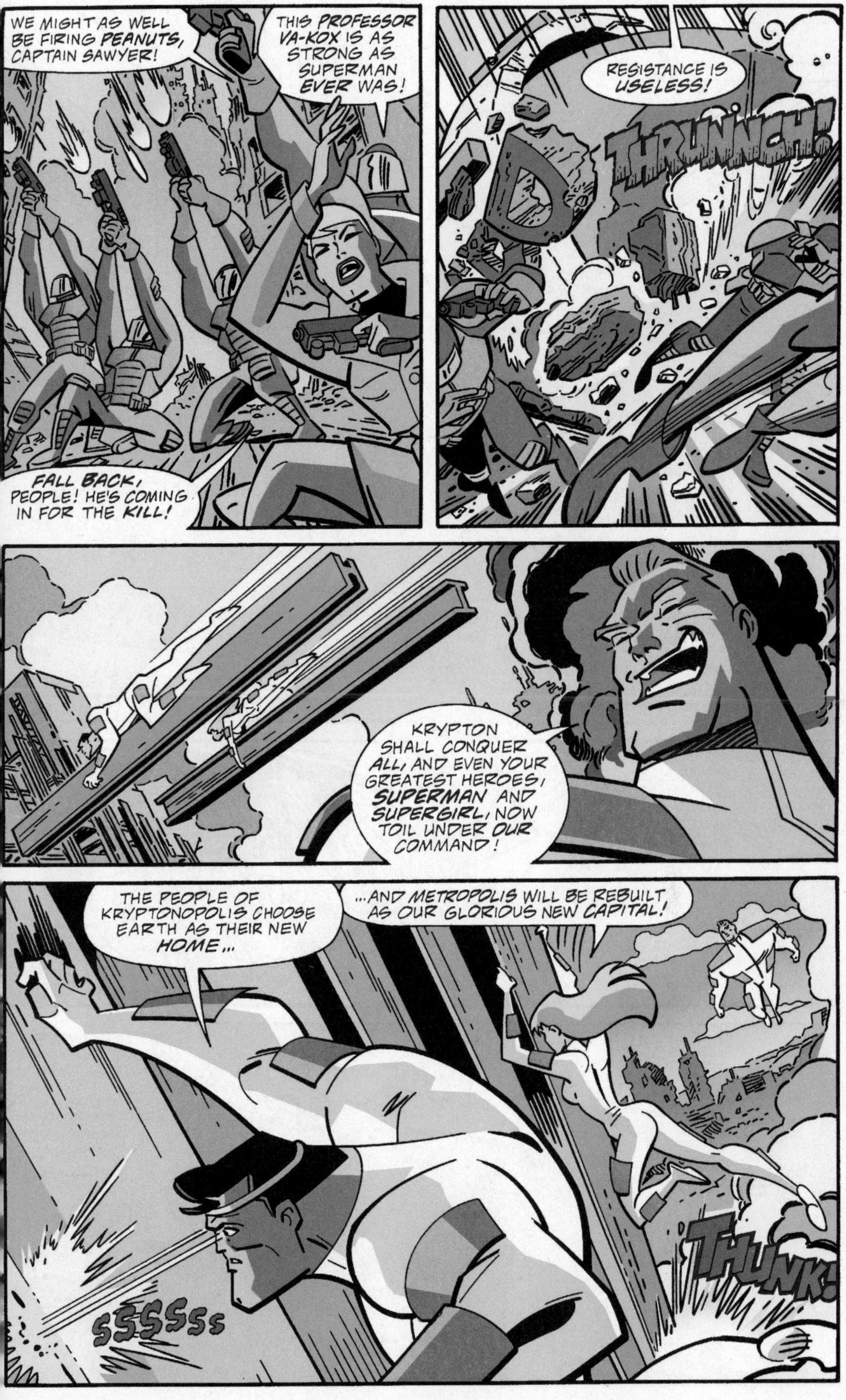
WE MIGHT AS WELL BE FIRING PEANUTS, CAPTAIN SAWYER!
THIS PROFESSOR VA-KOX IS AS STRONG AS SUPERMAN EVER WAS!
FALL BACK, PEOPLE! HE'S COMING IN FOR THE KILL!
RESISTANCE IS USELESS!
THRUNNCH!
KRYPTON SHALL CONQUER ALL, AND EVEN YOUR GREATEST HEROES, SUPERMAN AND SUPERGIRL, NOW TOIL UNDER OUR COMMAND!
THE PEOPLE OF KRYPTONOPOLIS CHOOSE EARTH AS THEIR NEW HOME...
...AND METROPOLIS WILL BE REBUILT AS OUR GLORIOUS NEW CAPITAL!
THUNK!
SSSSSSS

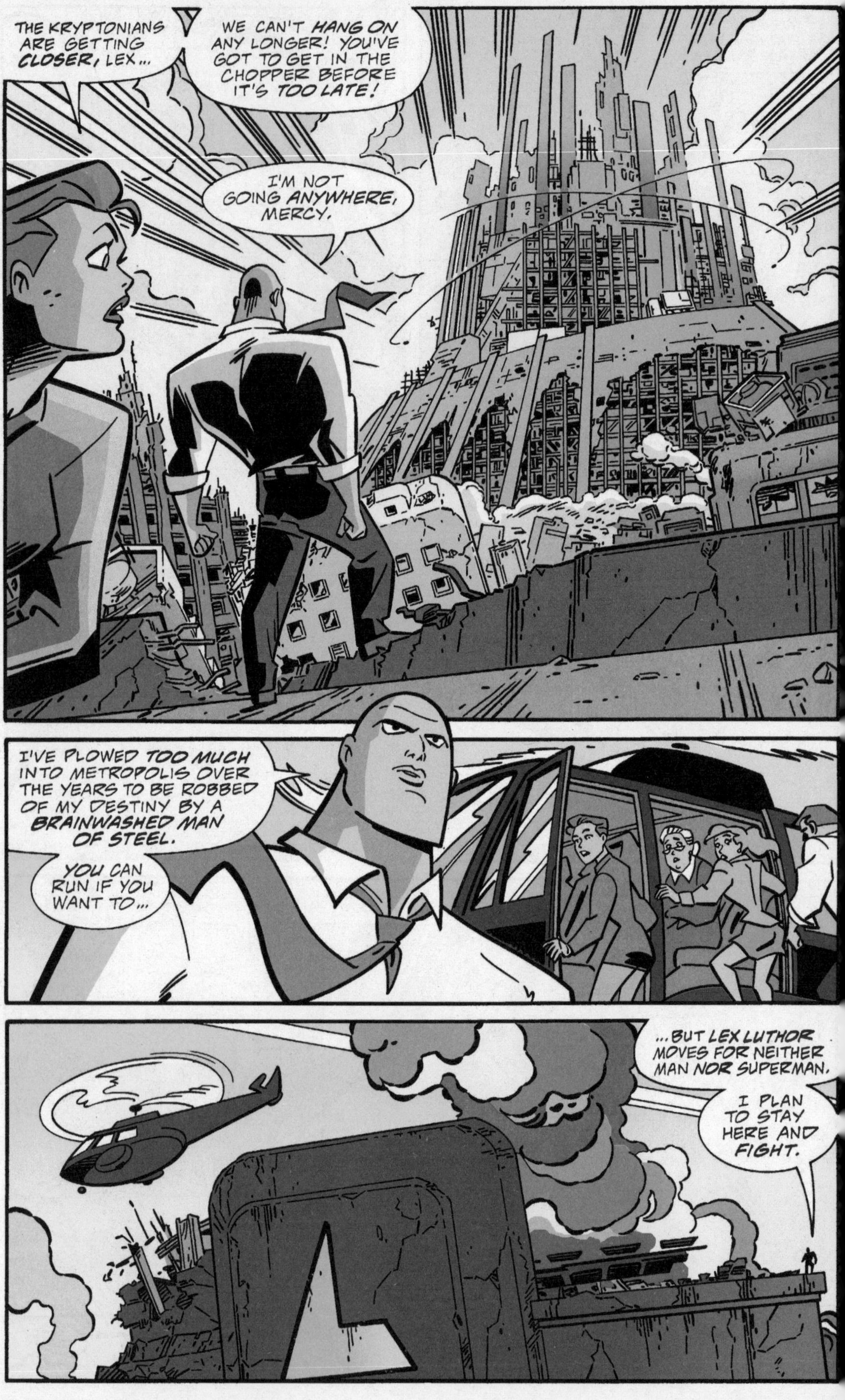
THE KRYPTONIANS ARE GETTING CLOSER, LEX...
WE CAN'T HANG ON ANY LONGER! YOU'VE GOT TO GET IN THE CHOPPER BEFORE IT'S TOO LATE!
I'M NOT GOING ANYWHERE, MERCY.
I'VE PLOWED TOO MUCH INTO METROPOLIS OVER THE YEARS TO BE ROBBED OF MY DESTINY BY A BRAINWASHED MAN OF STEEL.
YOU CAN RUN IF YOU WANT TO...
...BUT LEX LUTHOR MOVES FOR NEITHER MAN NOR SUPERMAN.
I PLAN TO STAY HERE AND FIGHT.

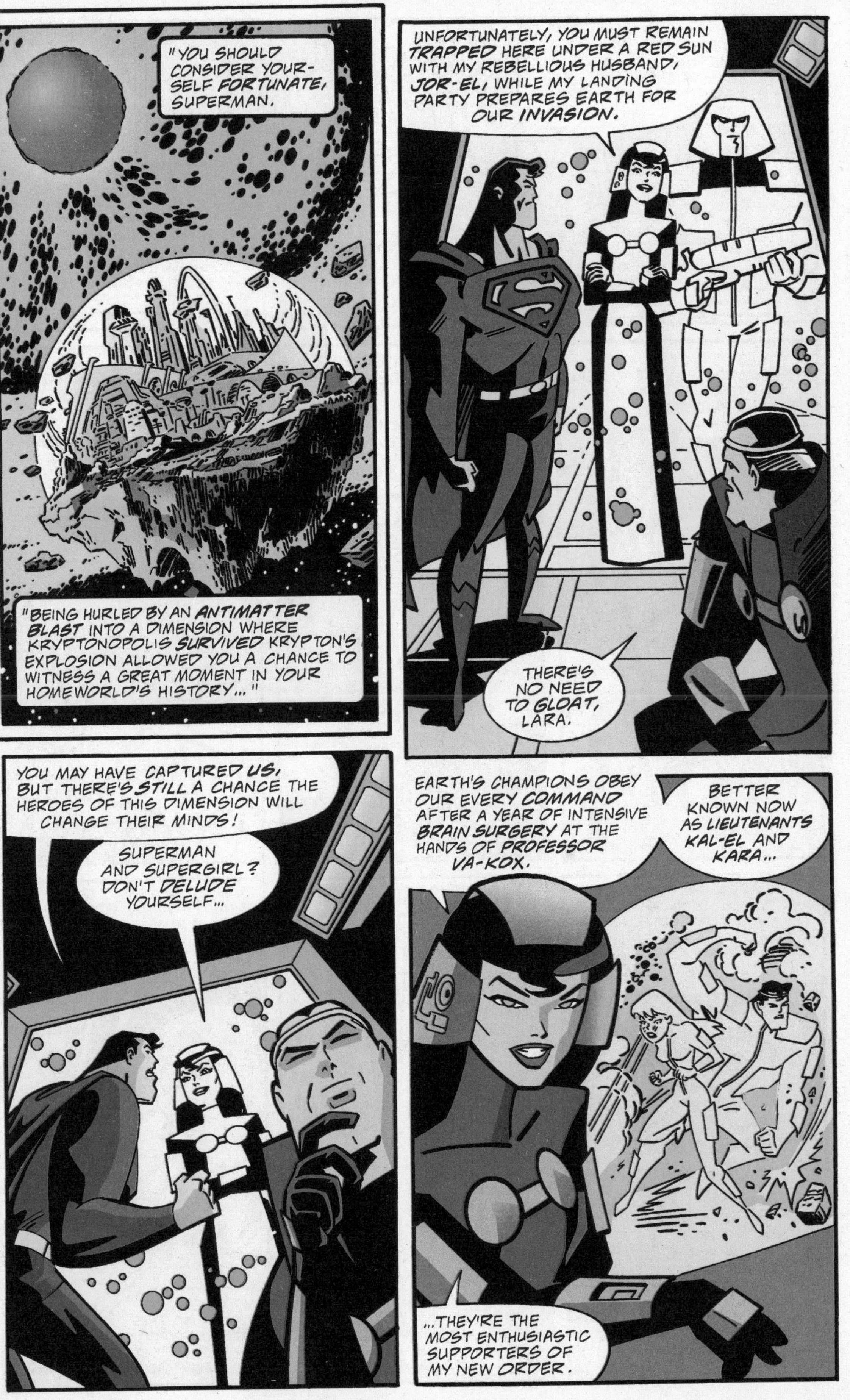
"YOU SHOULD CONSIDER YOURSELF FORTUNATE, SUPERMAN.
"BEING HURLED BY AN ANTIMATTER BLAST INTO A DIMENSION WHERE KRYPTONOPOLIS SURVIVED KRYPTON'S EXPLOSION ALLOWED YOU A CHANCE TO WITNESS A GREAT MOMENT IN YOUR HOMEWORLD'S HISTORY..."
UNFORTUNATELY, YOU MUST REMAIN TRAPPED HERE UNDER A RED SUN WITH MY REBELLIOUS HUSBAND, JOR-EL, WHILE MY LANDING PARTY PREPARES EARTH FOR OUR INVASION.
THERE'S NO NEED TO GLOAT, LARA.
YOU MAY HAVE CAPTURED US, BUT THERE'S STILL A CHANCE THE HEROES OF THIS DIMENSION WILL CHANGE THEIR MINDS!
SUPERMAN AND SUPERGIRL? DON'T DELUDE YOURSELF...
EARTH'S CHAMPIONS OBEY OUR EVERY COMMAND AFTER A YEAR OF INTENSIVE BRAIN SURGERY AT THE HANDS OF PROFESSOR VA-KOX.
BETTER KNOWN NOW AS LIEUTENANTS KAL-EL AND KARA...
...THEY'RE THE MOST ENTHUSIASTIC SUPPORTERS OF MY NEW ORDER.

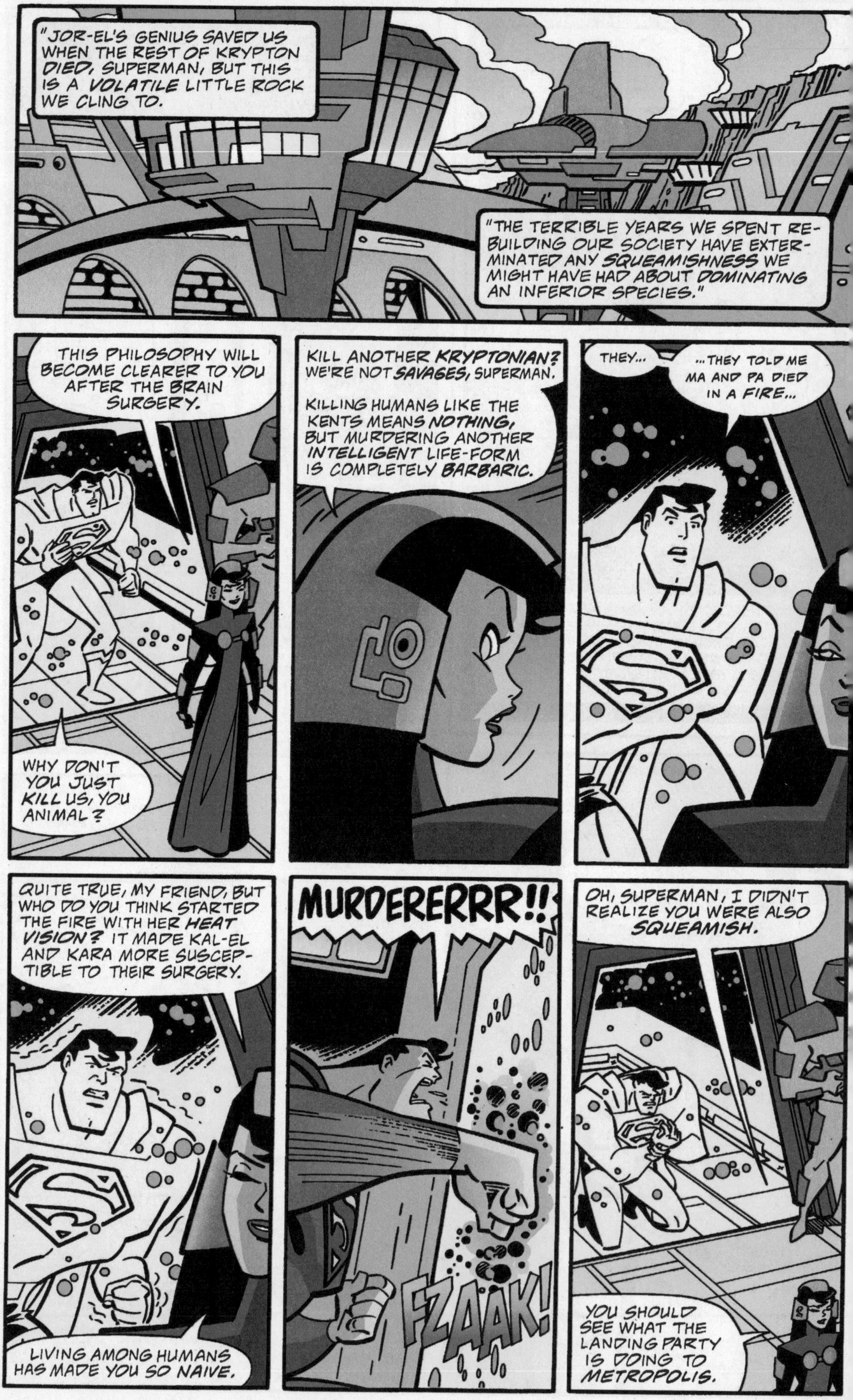
"JOR-EL'S GENIUS SAVED US WHEN THE REST OF KRYPTON DIED, SUPERMAN, BUT THIS IS A VOLATILE LITTLE ROCK WE CLING TO.
"THE TERRIBLE YEARS WE SPENT RE-BUILDING OUR SOCIETY HAVE EXTER-MINATED ANY SQUEAMISHNESS WE MIGHT HAVE HAD ABOUT DOMINATING AN INFERIOR SPECIES."
THIS PHILOSOPHY WILL BECOME CLEARER TO YOU AFTER THE BRAIN SURGERY.
WHY DON'T YOU JUST KILL US, YOU ANIMAL?
KILL ANOTHER KRYPTONIAN? WE'RE NOT SAVAGES, SUPERMAN.
KILLING HUMANS LIKE THE KENTS MEANS NOTHING, BUT MURDERING ANOTHER INTELLIGENT LIFE-FORM IS COMPLETELY BARBARIC.
THEY...
...THEY TOLD ME MA AND PA DIED IN A FIRE...
QUITE TRUE, MY FRIEND, BUT WHO DO YOU THINK STARTED THE FIRE WITH HER HEAT VISION? IT MADE KAL-EL AND KARA MORE SUSCEP-TIBLE TO THEIR SURGERY.
LIVING AMONG HUMANS HAS MADE YOU SO NAIVE.
MURDERERRR!!
FZAAK!
OH, SUPERMAN, I DIDN'T REALIZE YOU WERE ALSO SQUEAMISH.
YOU SHOULD SEE WHAT THE LANDING PARTY IS DOING TO METROPOLIS.

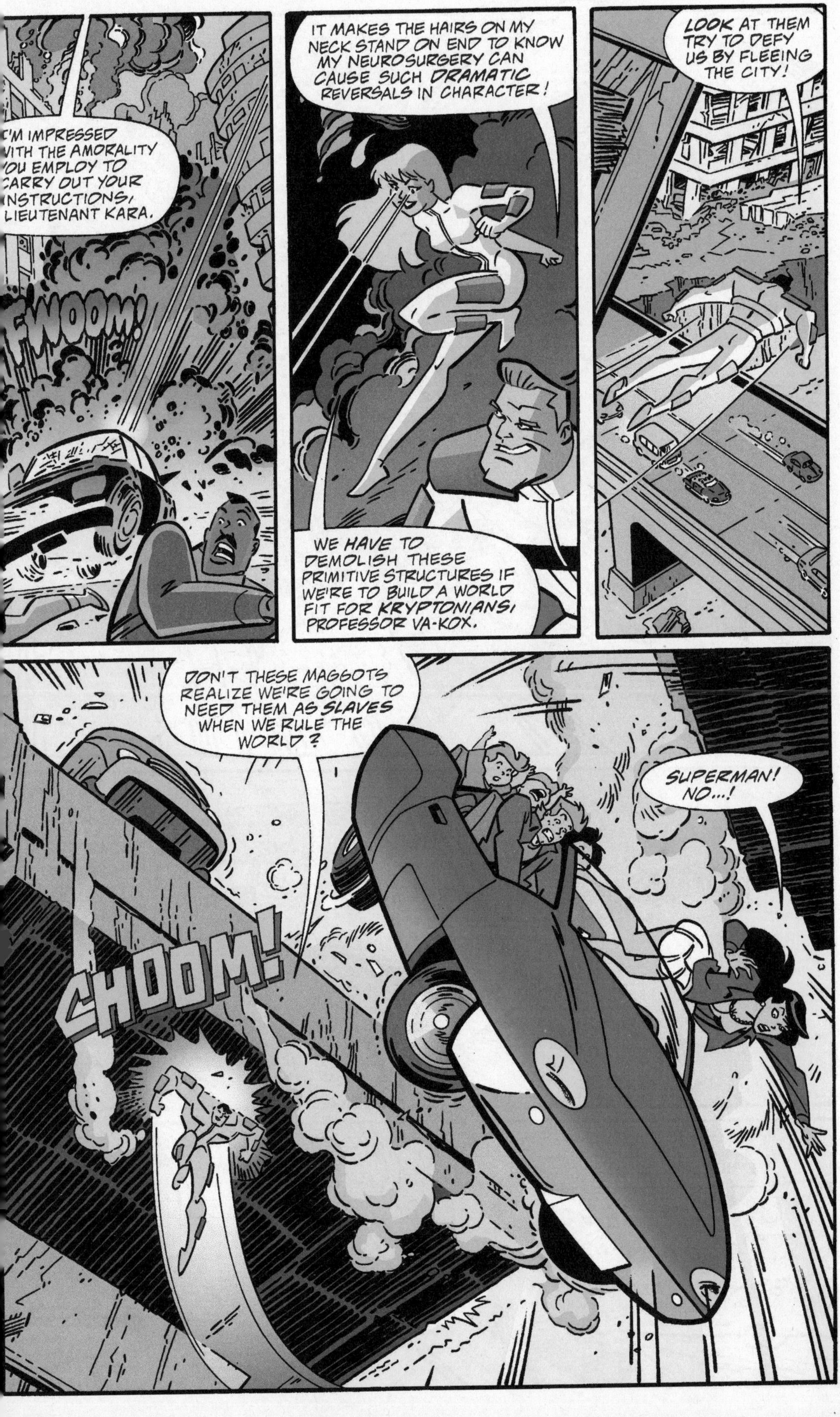
I'M IMPRESSED WITH THE AMORALITY YOU EMPLOY TO CARRY OUT YOUR INSTRUCTIONS, LIEUTENANT KARA.
FWOOM!
IT MAKES THE HAIRS ON MY NECK STAND ON END TO KNOW MY NEUROSURGERY CAN CAUSE SUCH DRAMATIC REVERSALS IN CHARACTER!
WE HAVE TO DEMOLISH THESE PRIMITIVE STRUCTURES IF WE'RE TO BUILD A WORLD FIT FOR KRYPTONIANS, PROFESSOR VA-KOX.
LOOK AT THEM TRY TO DEFY US BY FLEEING THE CITY!
DON'T THESE MAGGOTS REALIZE WE'RE GOING TO NEED THEM AS SLAVES WHEN WE RULE THE WORLD?
SUPERMAN! NO...!
CHOOM!

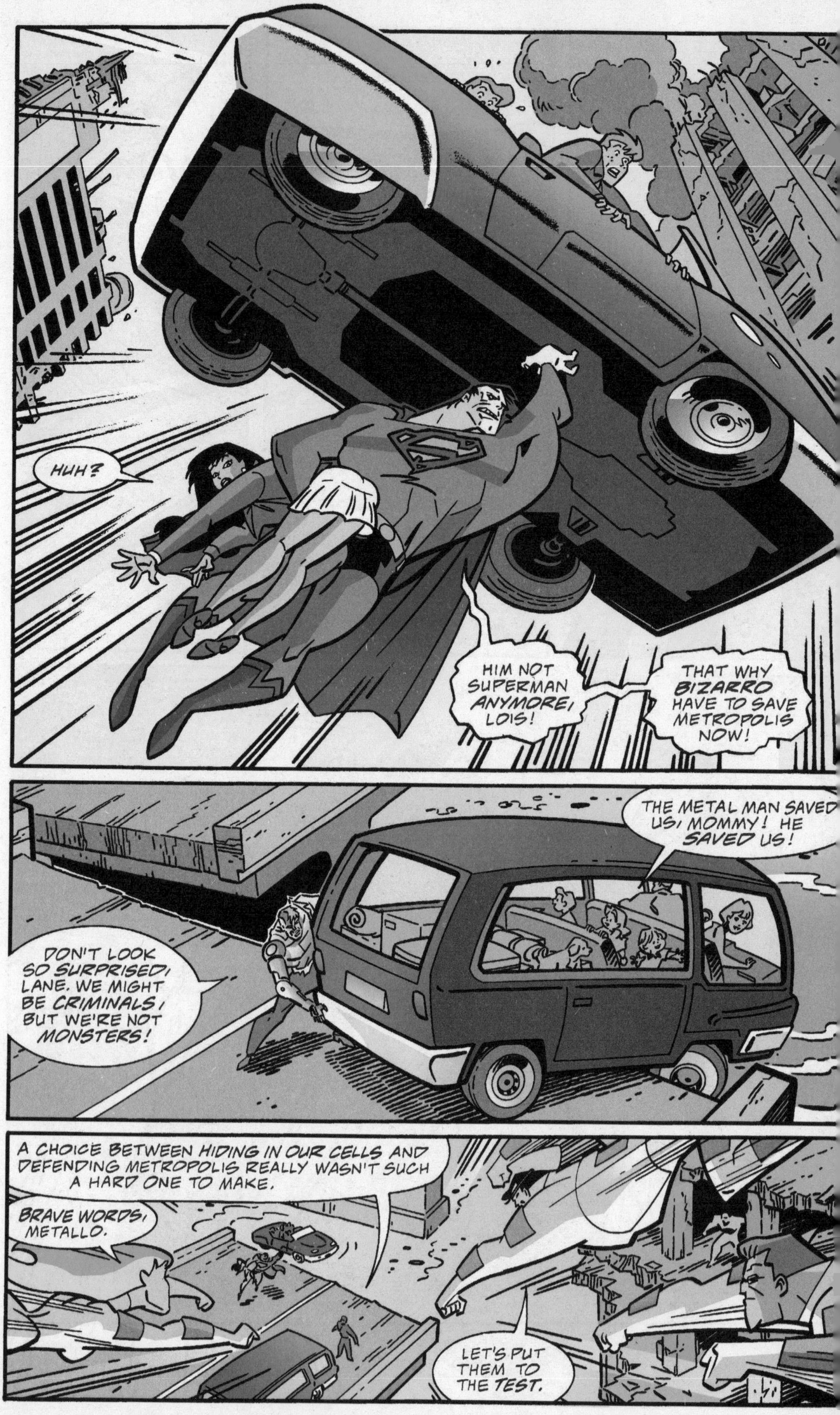
HUH?
HIM NOT SUPERMAN ANYMORE, LOIS!
THAT WHY BIZARRO HAVE TO SAVE METROPOLIS NOW!
THE METAL MAN SAVED US, MOMMY! HE SAVED US!
DON'T LOOK SO SURPRISED, LANE. WE MIGHT BE CRIMINALS, BUT WE'RE NOT MONSTERS!
A CHOICE BETWEEN HIDING IN OUR CELLS AND DEFENDING METROPOLIS REALLY WASN'T SUCH A HARD ONE TO MAKE.
BRAVE WORDS, METALLO.
LET'S PUT THEM TO THE TEST.

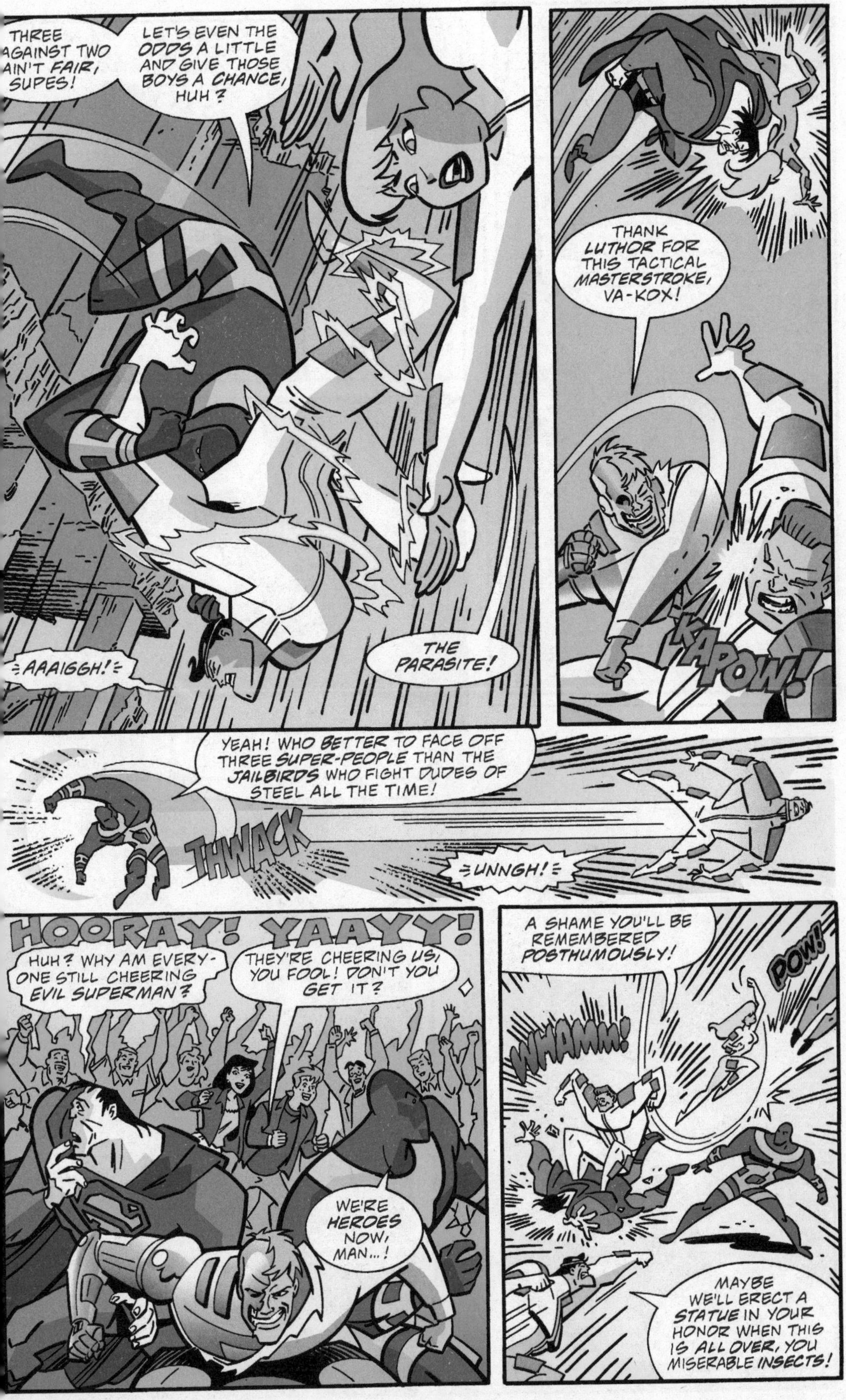
THREE AGAINST TWO AIN'T FAIR, SUPES!
LET'S EVEN THE ODDS A LITTLE AND GIVE THOSE BOYS A CHANCE, HUH?
AAAIGGH!
THE PARASITE!
THANK LUTHOR FOR THIS TACTICAL MASTERSTROKE, VA-KOX!
KAPOW!
YEAH! WHO BETTER TO FACE OFF THREE SUPER-PEOPLE THAN THE JAILBIRDS WHO FIGHT DUDES OF STEEL ALL THE TIME!
THWACK
UNNGH!
HOORAY! YAAYY!
HUH? WHY AM EVERY-ONE STILL CHEERING EVIL SUPERMAN?
THEY'RE CHEERING US, YOU FOOL! DON'T YOU GET IT?
WE'RE HEROES NOW, MAN...!
A SHAME YOU'LL BE REMEMBERED POSTHUMOUSLY!
POW!
WHAMM!
MAYBE WE'LL ERECT A STATUE IN YOUR HONOR WHEN THIS IS ALL OVER, YOU MISERABLE INSECTS!

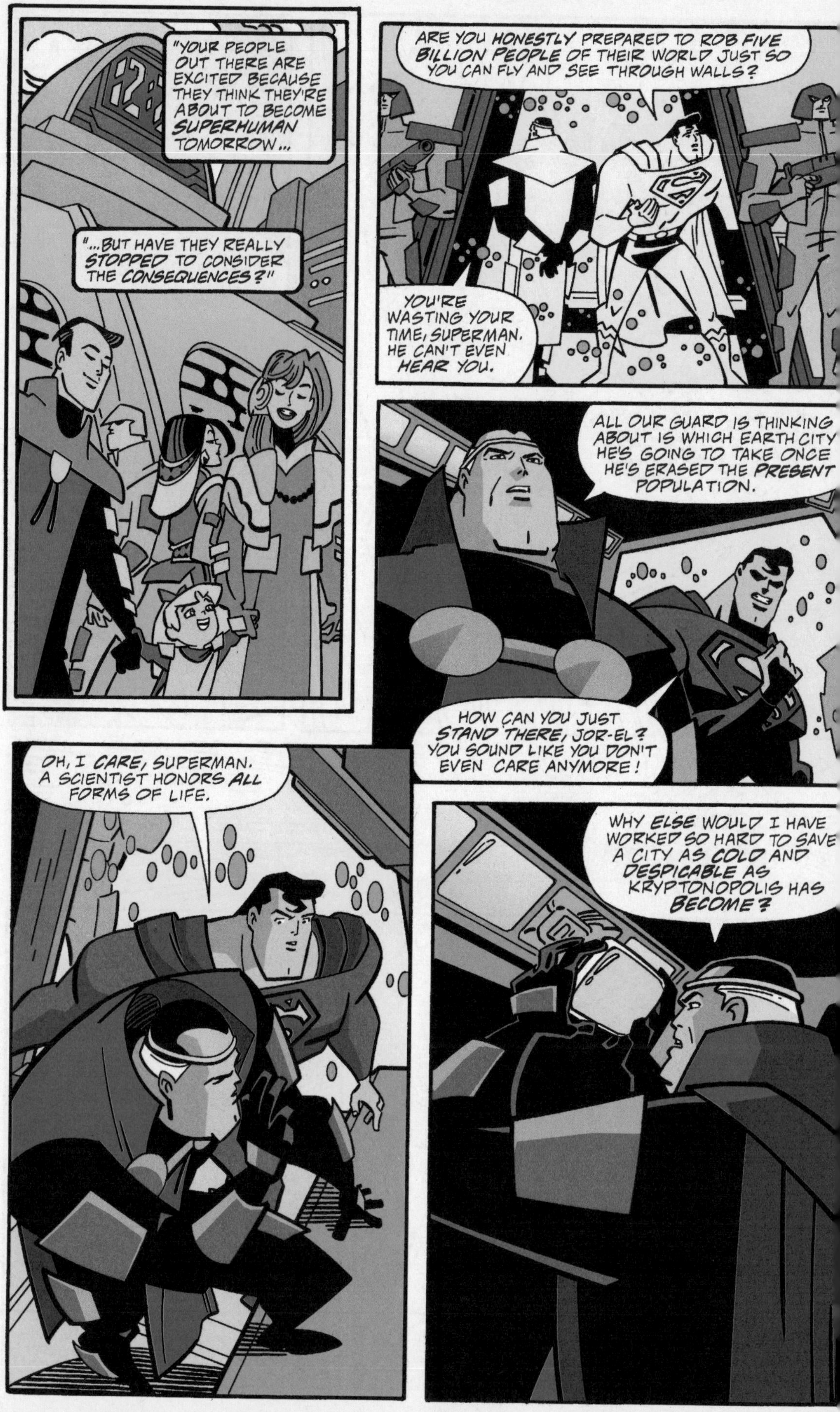
"YOUR PEOPLE OUT THERE ARE EXCITED BECAUSE THEY THINK THEY'RE ABOUT TO BECOME SUPERHUMAN TOMORROW...
"...BUT HAVE THEY REALLY STOPPED TO CONSIDER THE CONSEQUENCES?"
ARE YOU HONESTLY PREPARED TO ROB FIVE BILLION PEOPLE OF THEIR WORLD JUST SO YOU CAN FLY AND SEE THROUGH WALLS?
YOU'RE WASTING YOUR TIME, SUPERMAN. HE CAN'T EVEN HEAR YOU.
ALL OUR GUARD IS THINKING ABOUT IS WHICH EARTH CITY HE'S GOING TO TAKE ONCE HE'S ERASED THE PRESENT POPULATION.
HOW CAN YOU JUST STAND THERE, JOR-EL? YOU SOUND LIKE YOU DON'T EVEN CARE ANYMORE!
OH, I CARE, SUPERMAN. A SCIENTIST HONORS ALL FORMS OF LIFE.
WHY ELSE WOULD I HAVE WORKED SO HARD TO SAVE A CITY AS COLD AND DESPICABLE AS KRYPTONOPOLIS HAS BECOME?

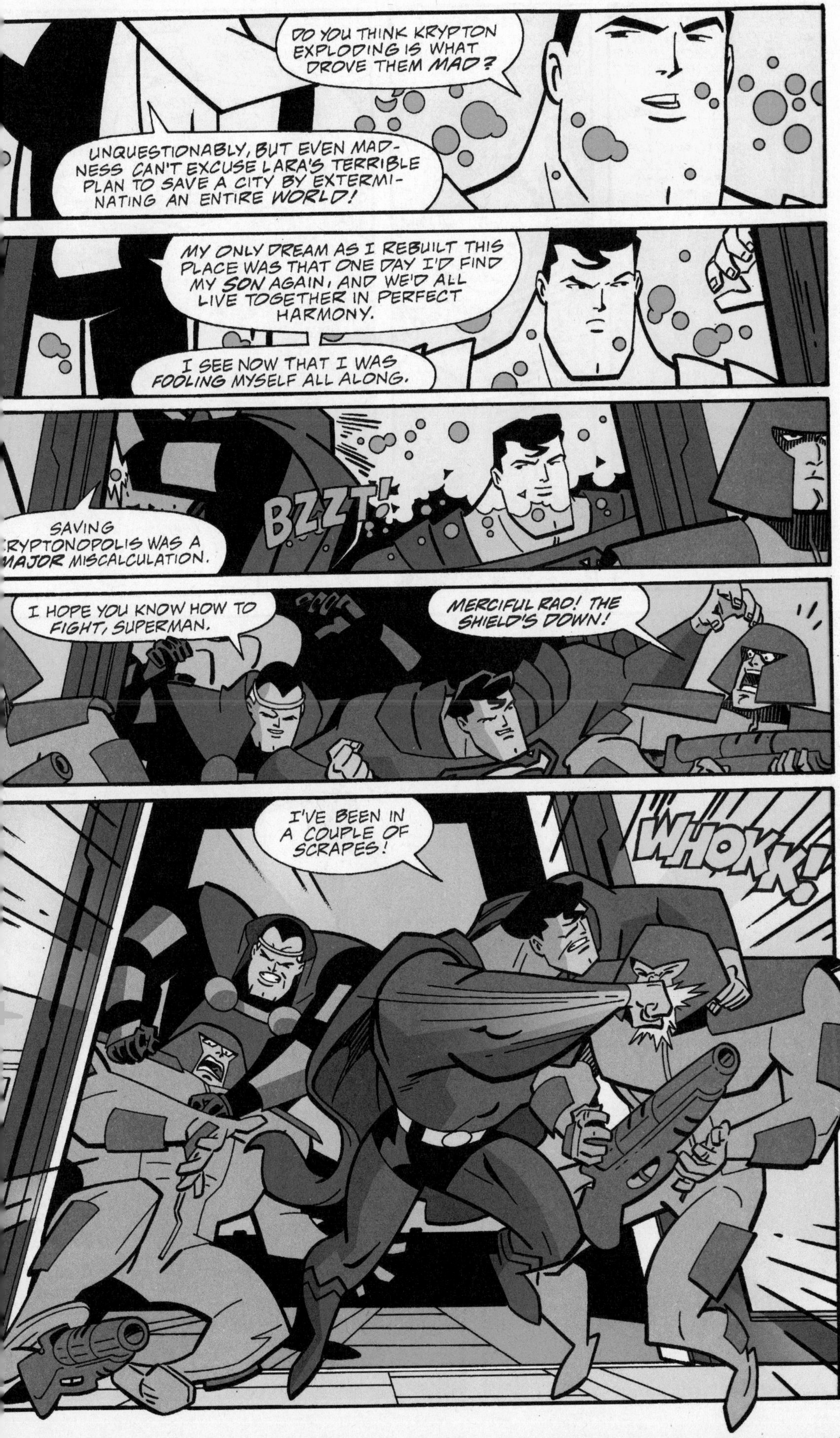
DO YOU THINK KRYPTON EXPLODING IS WHAT DROVE THEM MAD?
UNQUESTIONABLY, BUT EVEN MADNESS CAN'T EXCUSE LARA'S TERRIBLE PLAN TO SAVE A CITY BY EXTERMINATING AN ENTIRE WORLD!
MY ONLY DREAM AS I REBUILT THIS PLACE WAS THAT ONE DAY I'D FIND MY SON AGAIN, AND WE'D ALL LIVE TOGETHER IN PERFECT HARMONY.
I SEE NOW THAT I WAS FOOLING MYSELF ALL ALONG.
BZZZT!
SAVING KRYPTONOPOLIS WAS A MAJOR MISCALCULATION.
I HOPE YOU KNOW HOW TO FIGHT, SUPERMAN.
MERCIFUL RAO! THE SHIELD'S DOWN!
I'VE BEEN IN A COUPLE OF SCRAPES!
WHOKK!

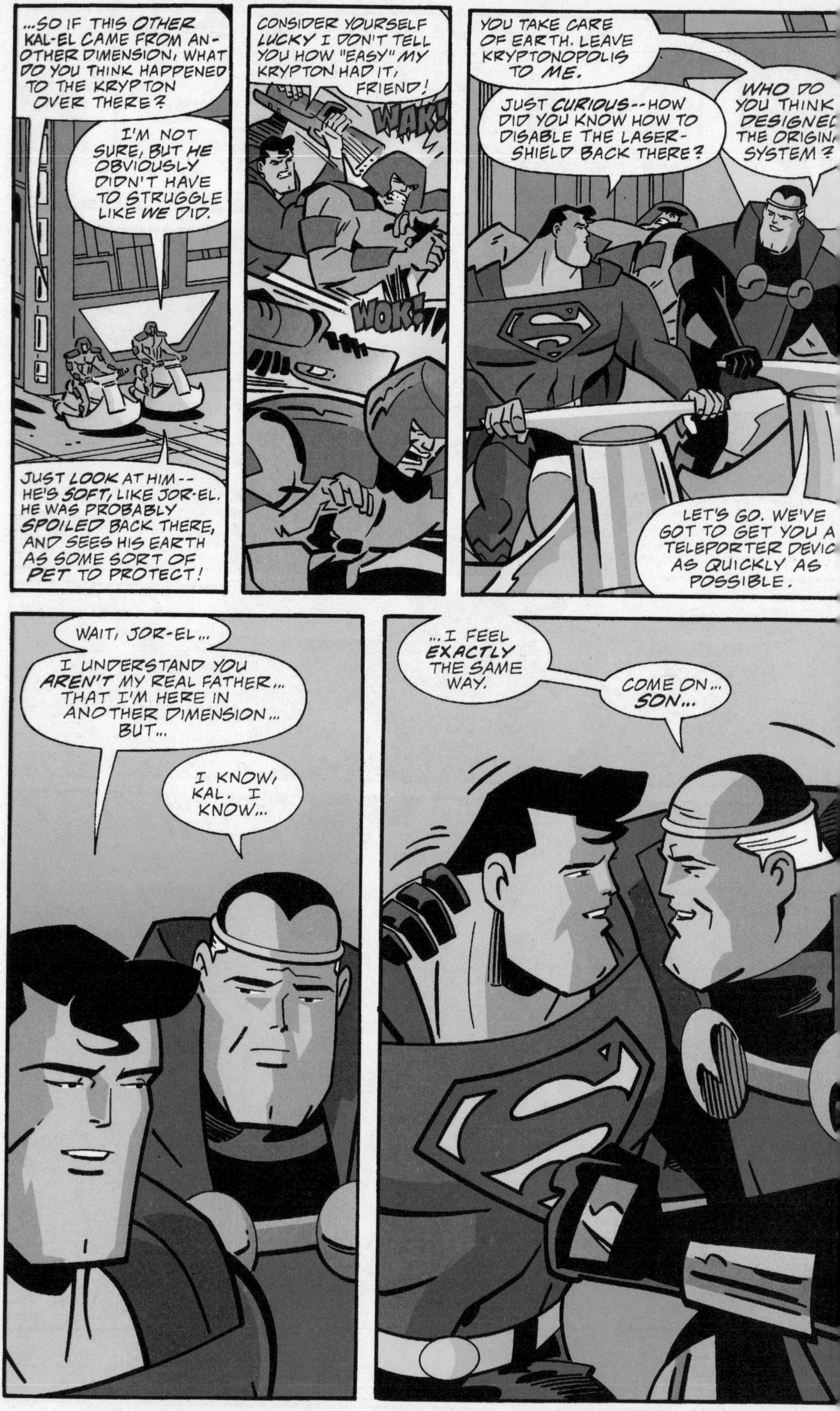
...SO IF THIS OTHER KAL-EL CAME FROM ANOTHER DIMENSION, WHAT DO YOU THINK HAPPENED TO THE KRYPTON OVER THERE?
I'M NOT SURE, BUT HE OBVIOUSLY DIDN'T HAVE TO STRUGGLE LIKE WE DID.
JUST LOOK AT HIM--HE'S SOFT, LIKE JOR-EL. HE WAS PROBABLY SPOILED BACK THERE, AND SEES HIS EARTH AS SOME SORT OF PET TO PROTECT!
CONSIDER YOURSELF LUCKY I DON'T TELL YOU HOW "EASY" MY KRYPTON HAD IT, FRIEND!
WAK!
WOK!
YOU TAKE CARE OF EARTH. LEAVE KRYPTONOPOLIS TO ME.
JUST CURIOUS--HOW DID YOU KNOW HOW TO DISABLE THE LASER-SHIELD BACK THERE?
WHO DO YOU THINK DESIGNED THE ORIGIN SYSTEM?
LET'S GO. WE'VE GOT TO GET YOU A TELEPORTER DEVIC AS QUICKLY AS POSSIBLE.
WAIT, JOR-EL...
I UNDERSTAND YOU AREN'T MY REAL FATHER... THAT I'M HERE IN ANOTHER DIMENSION... BUT...
I KNOW, KAL. I KNOW...
...I FEEL EXACTLY THE SAME WAY.
COME ON... SON...

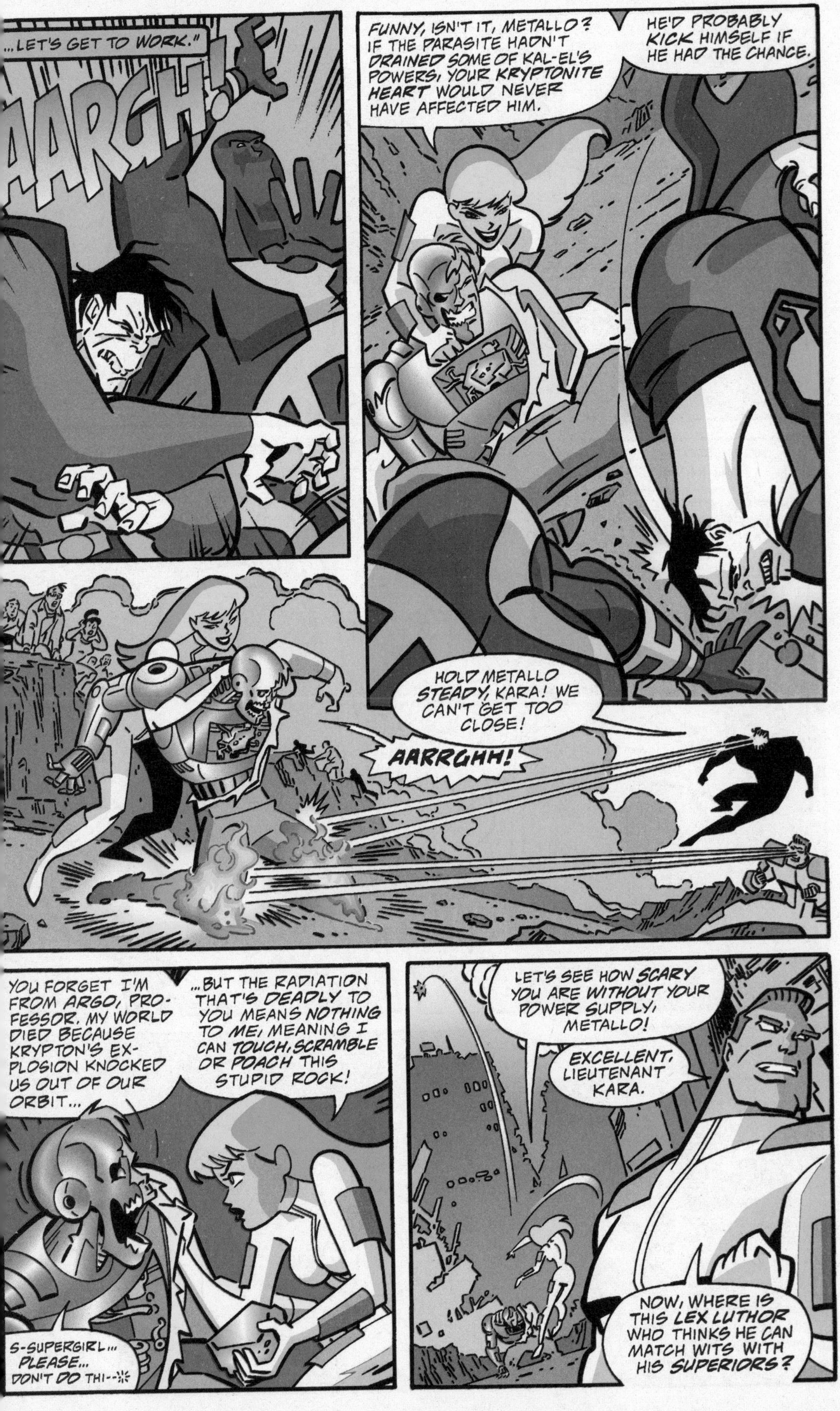
...LET'S GET TO WORK."
AARGH!!
FUNNY, ISN'T IT, METALLO? IF THE PARASITE HADN'T DRAINED SOME OF KAL-EL'S POWERS, YOUR KRYPTONITE HEART WOULD NEVER HAVE AFFECTED HIM.
HE'D PROBABLY KICK HIMSELF IF HE HAD THE CHANCE.
HOLD METALLO STEADY, KARA! WE CAN'T GET TOO CLOSE!
AARRGHH!
YOU FORGET I'M FROM ARGO, PRO-FESSOR. MY WORLD DIED BECAUSE KRYPTON'S EX-PLOSION KNOCKED US OUT OF OUR ORBIT...
...BUT THE RADIATION THAT'S DEADLY TO YOU MEANS NOTHING TO ME, MEANING I CAN TOUCH, SCRAMBLE OR POACH THIS STUPID ROCK!
S-SUPERGIRL... PLEASE... DON'T DO THI--
LET'S SEE HOW SCARY YOU ARE WITHOUT YOUR POWER SUPPLY, METALLO!
EXCELLENT, LIEUTENANT KARA.
NOW, WHERE IS THIS LEX LUTHOR WHO THINKS HE CAN MATCH WITS WITH HIS SUPERIORS?

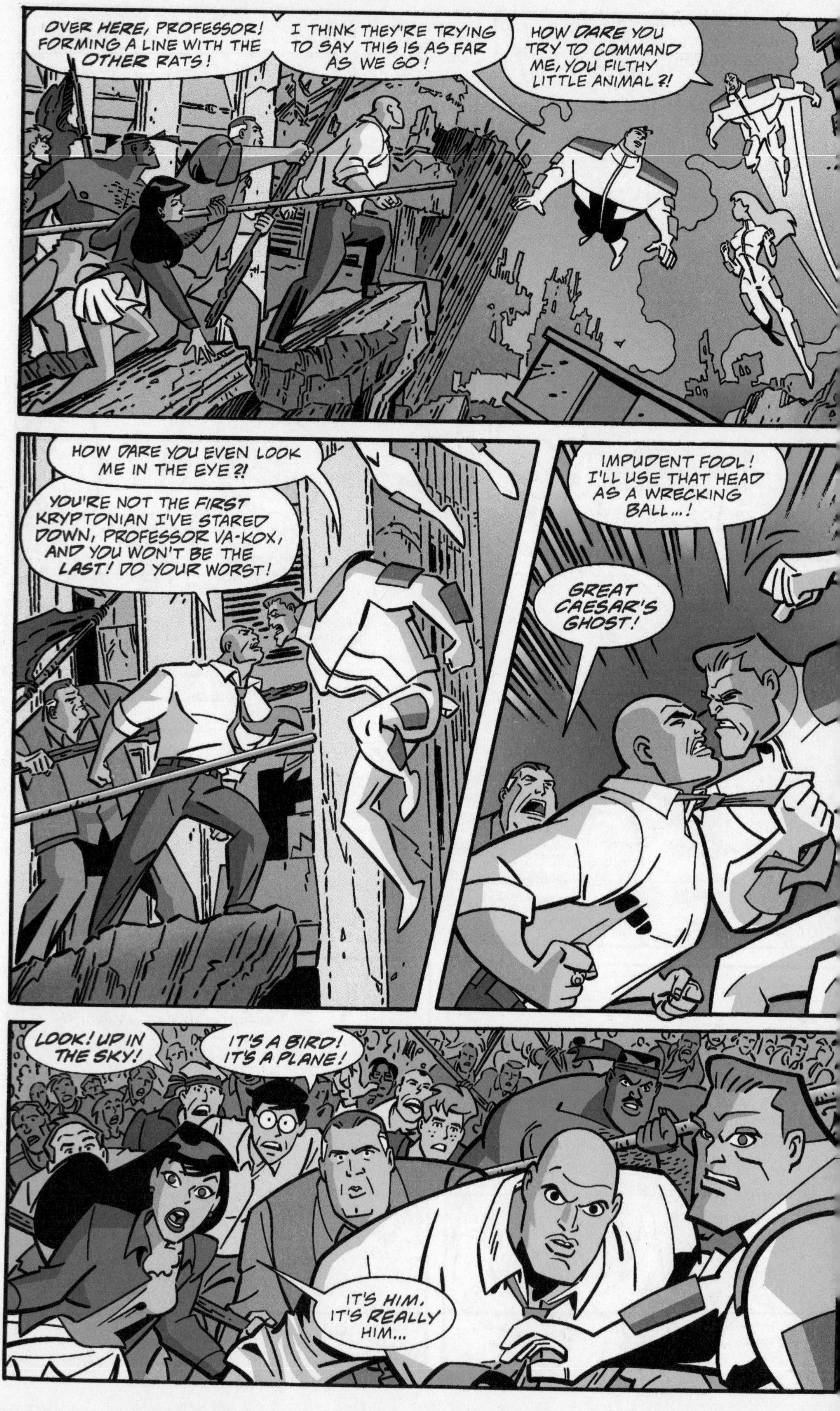

OVER HERE, PROFESSOR! FORMING A LINE WITH THE OTHER RATS!
I THINK THEY'RE TRYING TO SAY THIS IS AS FAR AS WE GO!
HOW DARE YOU TRY TO COMMAND ME, YOU FILTHY LITTLE ANIMAL?!
HOW DARE YOU EVEN LOOK ME IN THE EYE?!
YOU'RE NOT THE FIRST KRYPTONIAN I'VE STARED DOWN, PROFESSOR VA-KOX, AND YOU WON'T BE THE LAST! DO YOUR WORST!
IMPUDENT FOOL! I'LL USE THAT HEAD AS A WRECKING BALL...!
GREAT CAESAR'S GHOST!
LOOK! UP IN THE SKY!
IT'S A BIRD! IT'S A PLANE!
IT'S HIM. IT'S REALLY HIM...

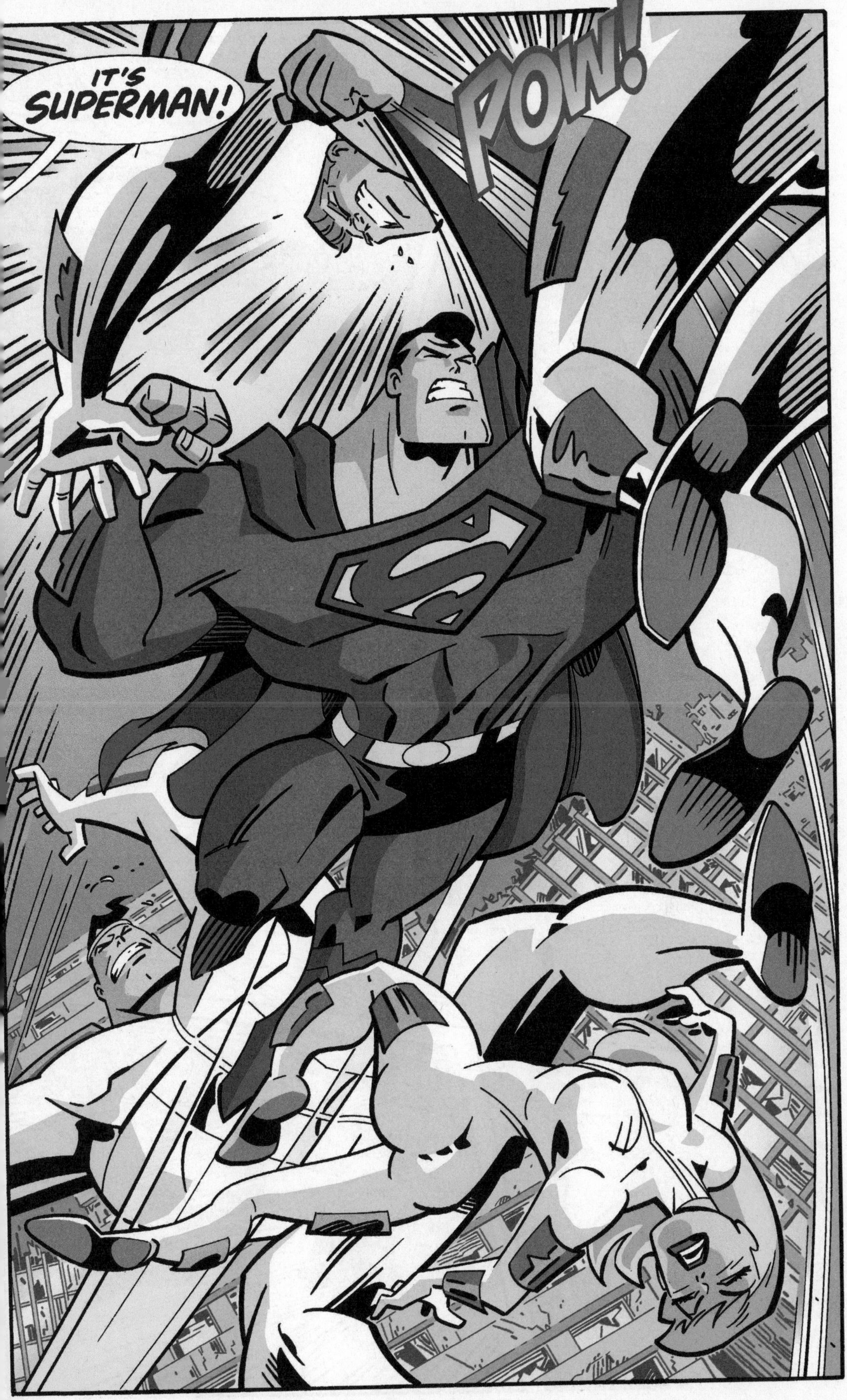
IT'S SUPERMAN!
POW!

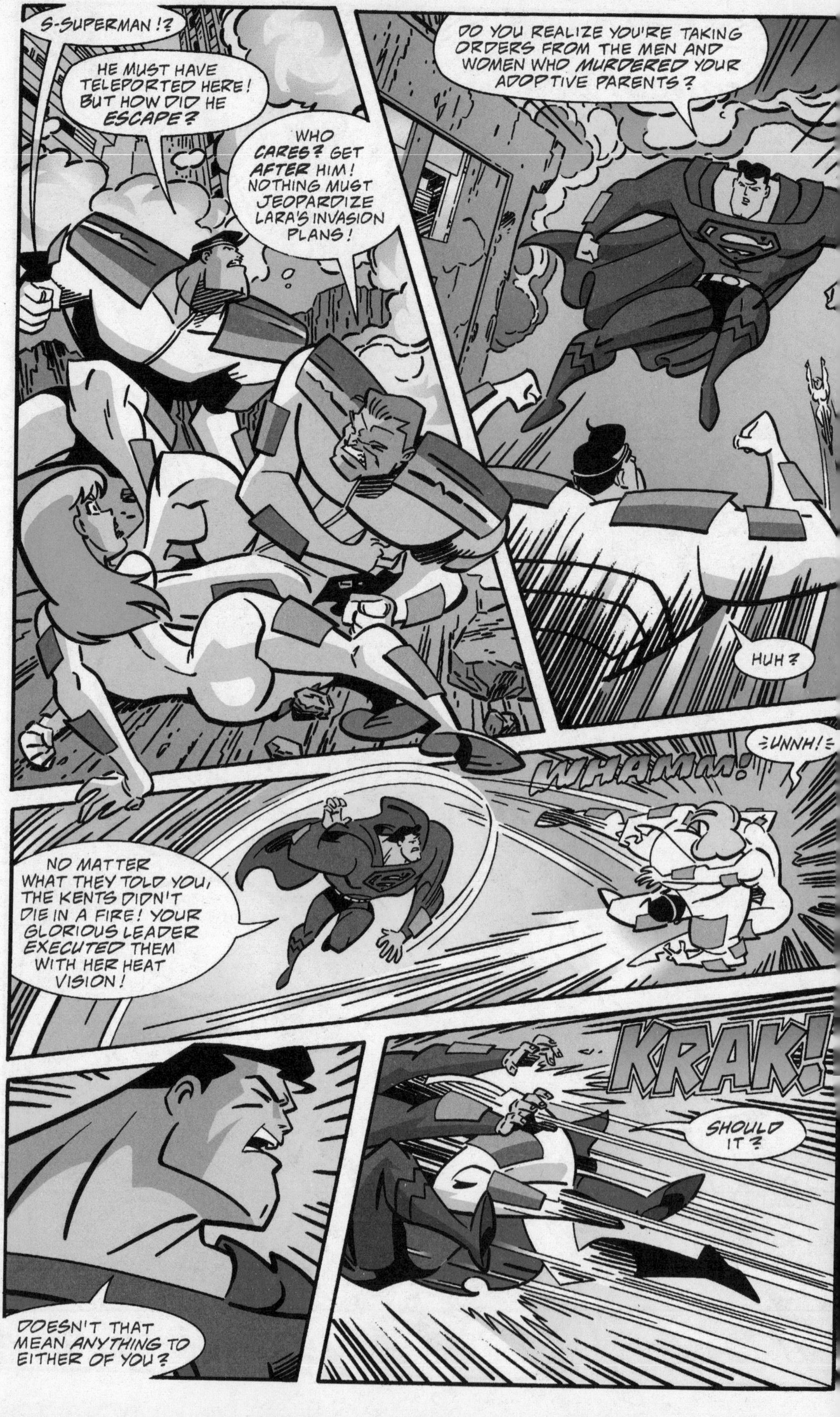
S-SUPERMAN !?
HE MUST HAVE TELEPORTED HERE! BUT HOW DID HE ESCAPE?
WHO CARES? GET AFTER HIM! NOTHING MUST JEOPARDIZE LARA'S INVASION PLANS!
DO YOU REALIZE YOU'RE TAKING ORDERS FROM THE MEN AND WOMEN WHO MURDERED YOUR ADOPTIVE PARENTS?
HUH?
WHAMM!
UNNH!
NO MATTER WHAT THEY TOLD YOU, THE KENTS DIDN'T DIE IN A FIRE! YOUR GLORIOUS LEADER EXECUTED THEM WITH HER HEAT VISION!
DOESN'T THAT MEAN ANYTHING TO EITHER OF YOU?
KRAK!
SHOULD IT?

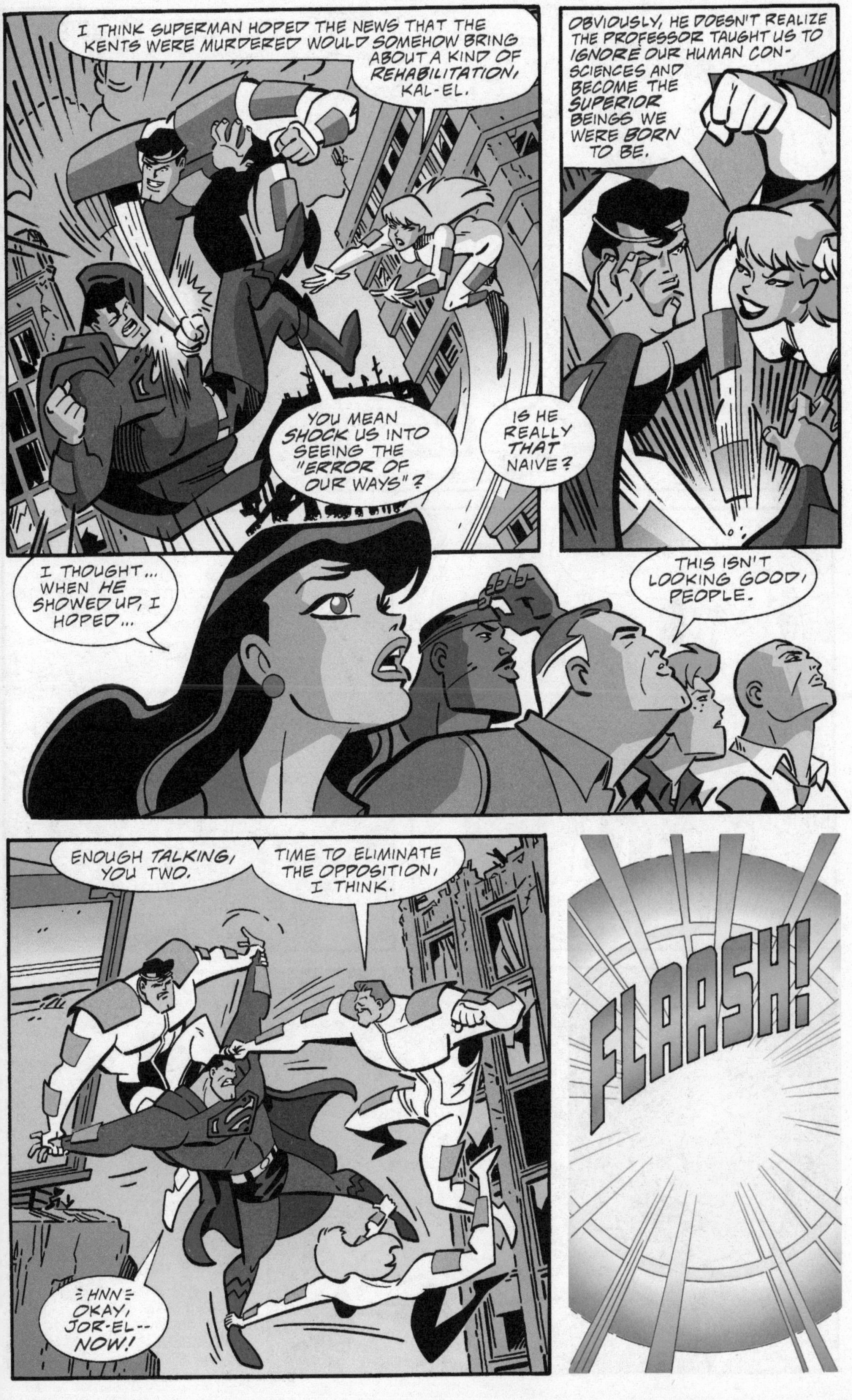

I THINK SUPERMAN HOPED THE NEWS THAT THE KENTS WERE MURDERED WOULD SOMEHOW BRING ABOUT A KIND OF REHABILITATION, KAL-EL.
YOU MEAN SHOCK US INTO SEEING THE "ERROR OF OUR WAYS"?
IS HE REALLY THAT NAIVE?
OBVIOUSLY, HE DOESN'T REALIZE THE PROFESSOR TAUGHT US TO IGNORE OUR HUMAN CON-SCIENCES AND BECOME THE SUPERIOR BEINGS WE WERE BORN TO BE.
I THOUGHT... WHEN HE SHOWED UP, I HOPED...
THIS ISN'T LOOKING GOOD, PEOPLE.
ENOUGH TALKING, YOU TWO.
TIME TO ELIMINATE THE OPPOSITION, I THINK.
HNN OKAY, JOR-EL-- NOW!
FLAASH!

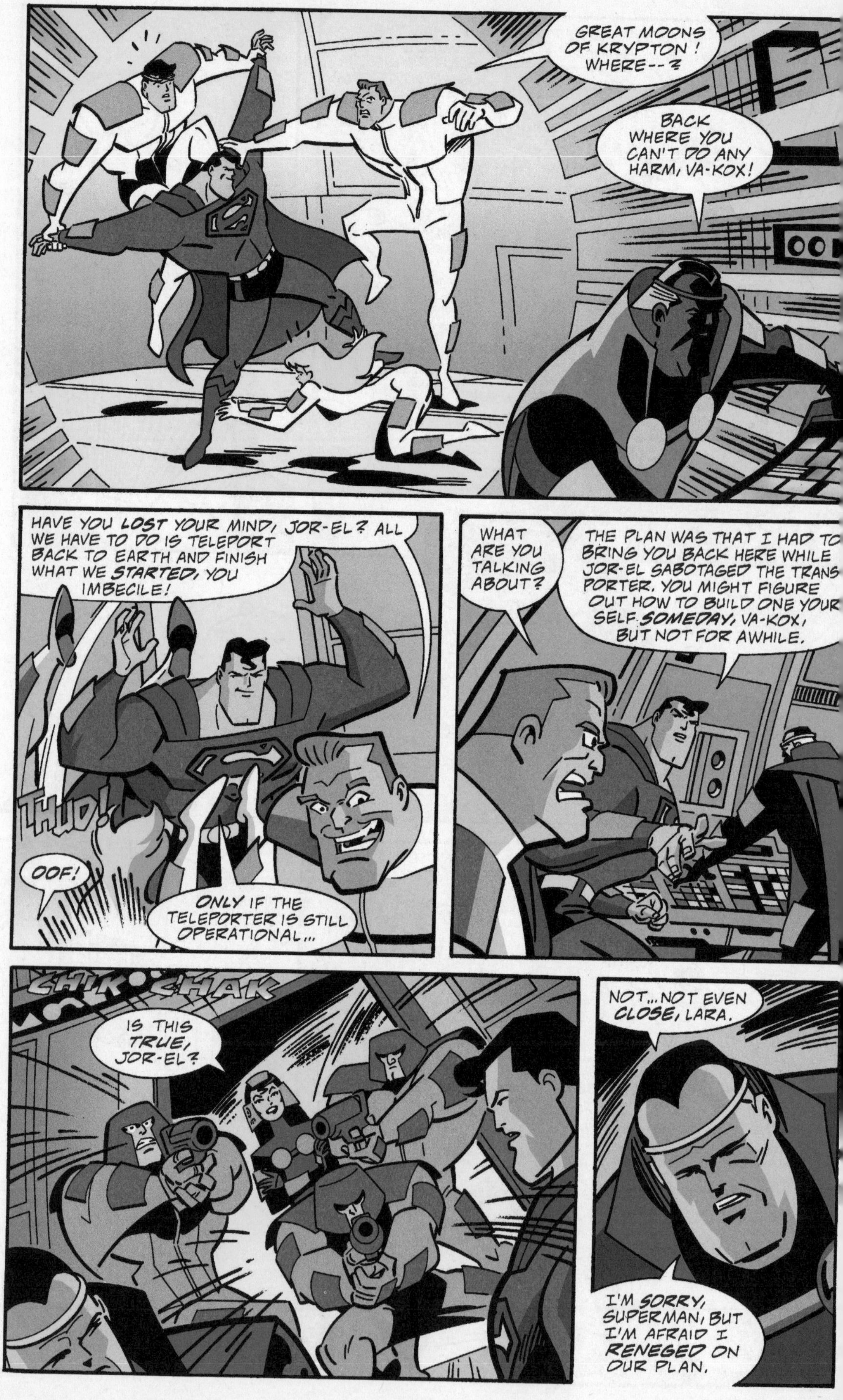
GREAT MOONS OF KRYPTON! WHERE--?
BACK WHERE YOU CAN'T DO ANY HARM, VA-KOX!
HAVE YOU LOST YOUR MIND, JOR-EL? ALL WE HAVE TO DO IS TELEPORT BACK TO EARTH AND FINISH WHAT WE STARTED, YOU IMBECILE!
THUD!
OOF!
ONLY IF THE TELEPORTER IS STILL OPERATIONAL...
WHAT ARE YOU TALKING ABOUT?
THE PLAN WAS THAT I HAD TO BRING YOU BACK HERE WHILE JOR-EL SABOTAGED THE TRANSPORTER. YOU MIGHT FIGURE OUT HOW TO BUILD ONE YOURSELF SOMEDAY, VA-KOX, BUT NOT FOR AWHILE.
CHIK-CHAK
IS THIS TRUE, JOR-EL?
NOT...NOT EVEN CLOSE, LARA.
I'M SORRY, SUPERMAN, BUT I'M AFRAID I RENEGED ON OUR PLAN.

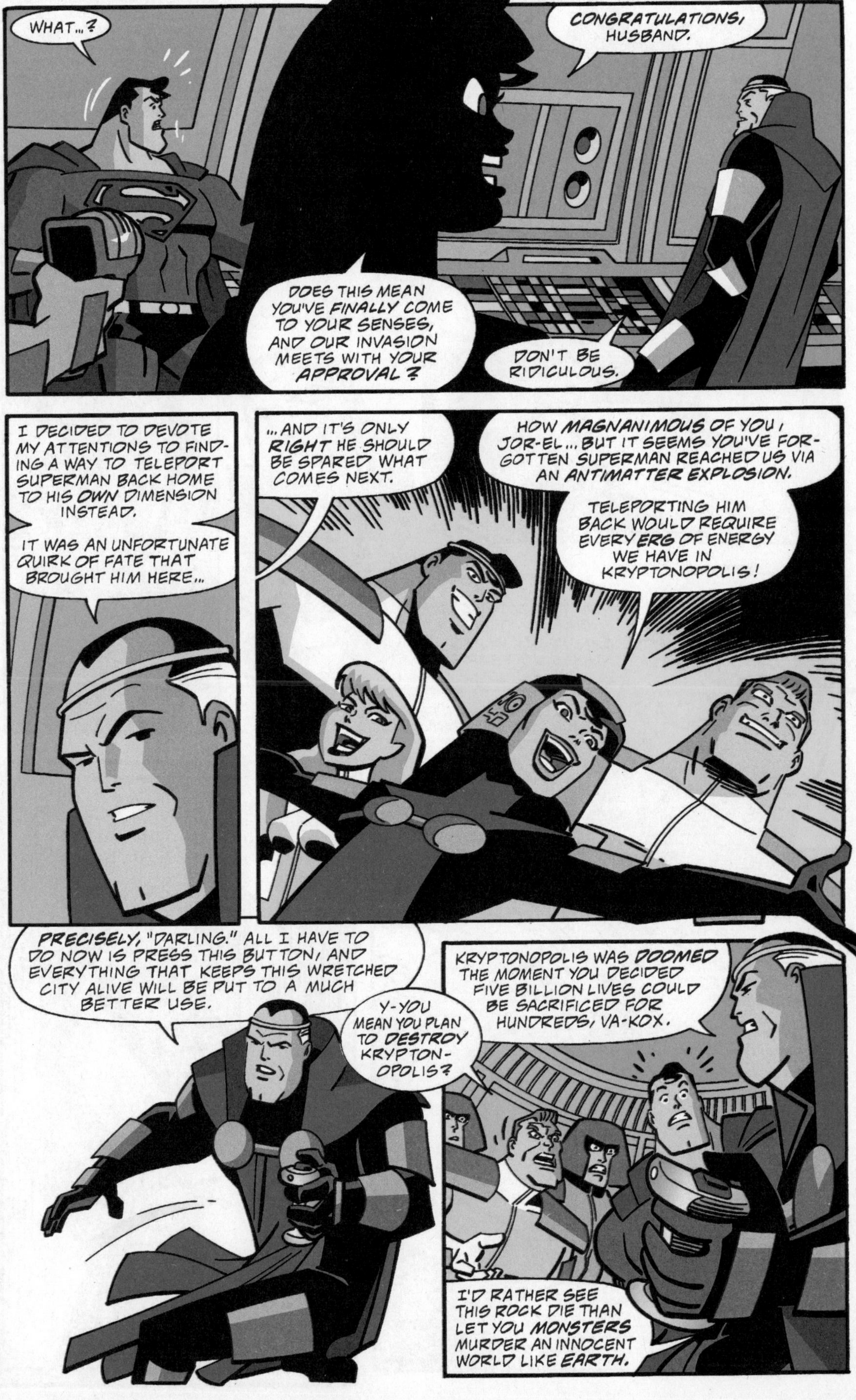

WHAT...?
CONGRATULATIONS, HUSBAND.
DOES THIS MEAN YOU'VE FINALLY COME TO YOUR SENSES, AND OUR INVASION MEETS WITH YOUR APPROVAL?
DON'T BE RIDICULOUS.
I DECIDED TO DEVOTE MY ATTENTIONS TO FINDING A WAY TO TELEPORT SUPERMAN BACK HOME TO HIS OWN DIMENSION INSTEAD.
IT WAS AN UNFORTUNATE QUIRK OF FATE THAT BROUGHT HIM HERE...
...AND IT'S ONLY RIGHT HE SHOULD BE SPARED WHAT COMES NEXT.
HOW MAGNANIMOUS OF YOU, JOR-EL... BUT IT SEEMS YOU'VE FORGOTTEN SUPERMAN REACHED US VIA AN ANTIMATTER EXPLOSION.
TELEPORTING HIM BACK WOULD REQUIRE EVERY ERG OF ENERGY WE HAVE IN KRYPTONOPOLIS!
PRECISELY, "DARLING." ALL I HAVE TO DO NOW IS PRESS THIS BUTTON, AND EVERYTHING THAT KEEPS THIS WRETCHED CITY ALIVE WILL BE PUT TO A MUCH BETTER USE.
Y-YOU MEAN YOU PLAN TO DESTROY KRYPTONOPOLIS?
KRYPTONOPOLIS WAS DOOMED THE MOMENT YOU DECIDED FIVE BILLION LIVES COULD BE SACRIFICED FOR HUNDREDS, VA-KOX.
I'D RATHER SEE THIS ROCK DIE THAN LET YOU MONSTERS MURDER AN INNOCENT WORLD LIKE EARTH.

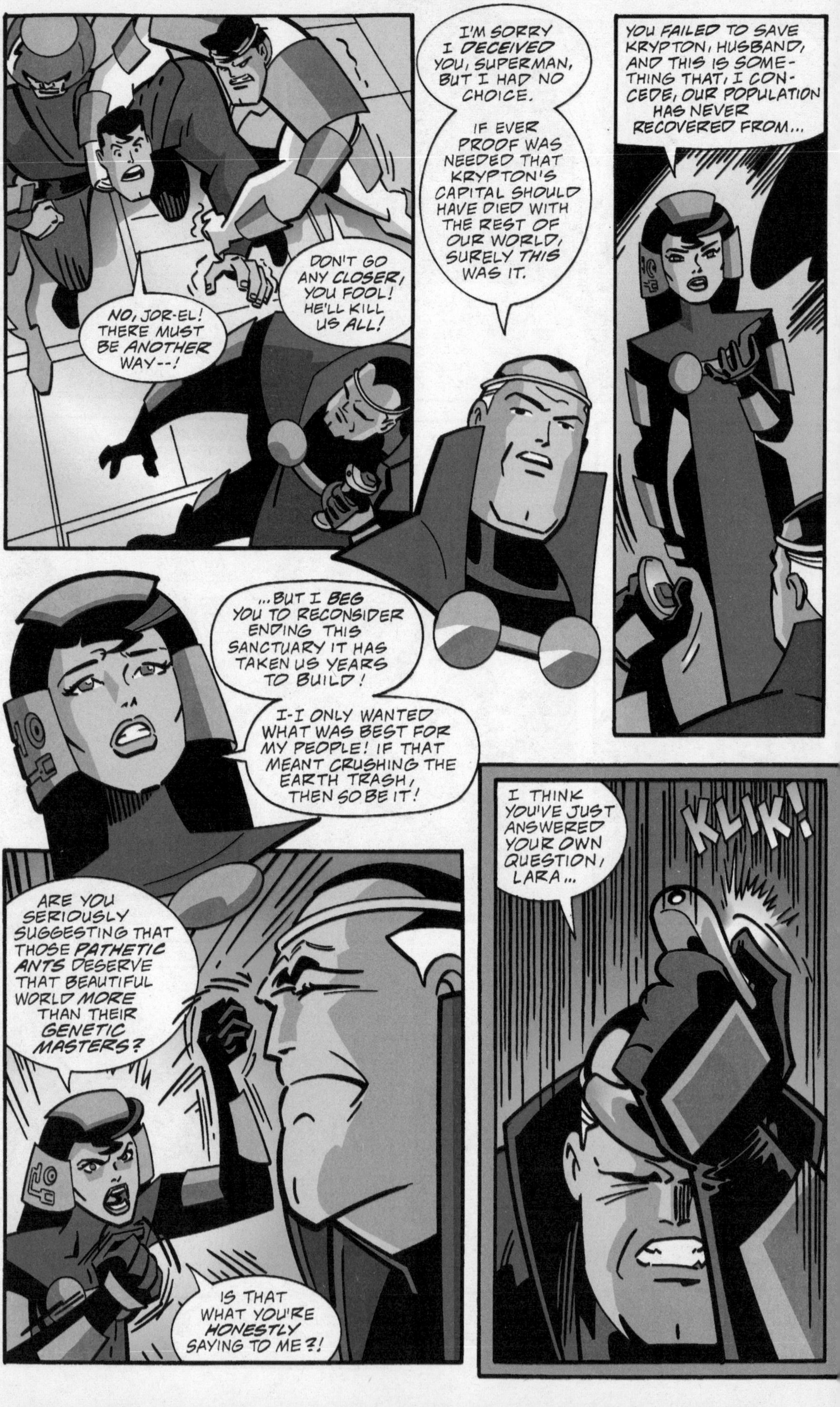

NO, JOR-EL! THERE MUST BE ANOTHER WAY--!
DON'T GO ANY CLOSER, YOU FOOL! HE'LL KILL US ALL!
I'M SORRY I DECEIVED YOU, SUPERMAN, BUT I HAD NO CHOICE.
IF EVER PROOF WAS NEEDED THAT KRYPTON'S CAPITAL SHOULD HAVE DIED WITH THE REST OF OUR WORLD, SURELY THIS WAS IT.
YOU FAILED TO SAVE KRYPTON, HUSBAND, AND THIS IS SOMETHING THAT, I CONCEDE, OUR POPULATION HAS NEVER RECOVERED FROM...
...BUT I BEG YOU TO RECONSIDER ENDING THIS SANCTUARY IT HAS TAKEN US YEARS TO BUILD!
I-I ONLY WANTED WHAT WAS BEST FOR MY PEOPLE! IF THAT MEANT CRUSHING THE EARTH TRASH, THEN SO BE IT!
ARE YOU SERIOUSLY SUGGESTING THAT THOSE PATHETIC ANTS DESERVE THAT BEAUTIFUL WORLD MORE THAN THEIR GENETIC MASTERS?
IS THAT WHAT YOU'RE HONESTLY SAYING TO ME?!
I THINK YOU'VE JUST ANSWERED YOUR OWN QUESTION, LARA...
KLIK!

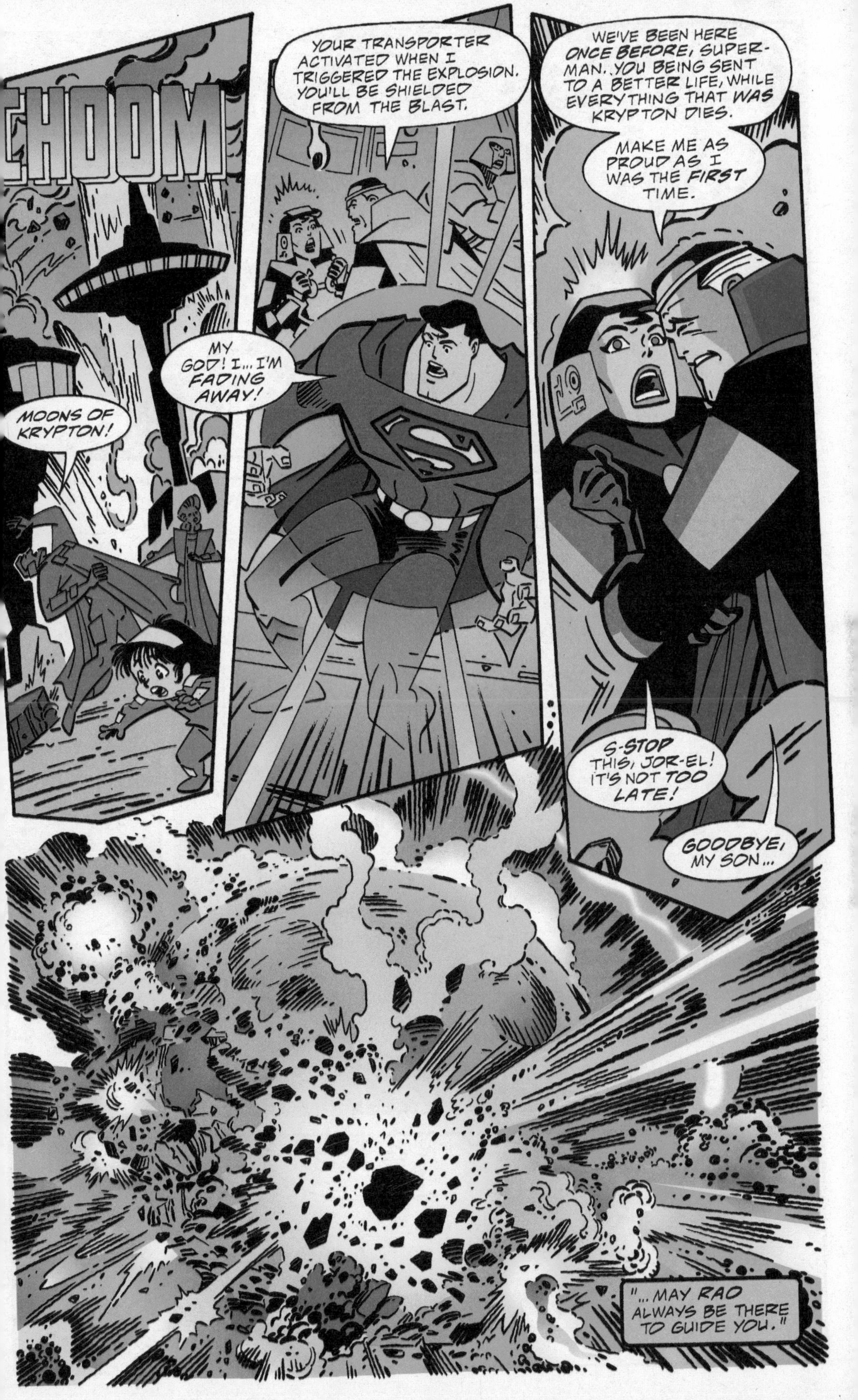
CHOOM
MOONS OF KRYPTON!
YOUR TRANSPORTER ACTIVATED WHEN I TRIGGERED THE EXPLOSION. YOU'LL BE SHIELDED FROM THE BLAST.
MY GOD! I... I'M FADING AWAY!
WE'VE BEEN HERE ONCE BEFORE, SUPERMAN. YOU BEING SENT TO A BETTER LIFE, WHILE EVERYTHING THAT WAS KRYPTON DIES.
MAKE ME AS PROUD AS I WAS THE FIRST TIME.
S-STOP THIS, JOR-EL! IT'S NOT TOO LATE!
GOODBYE, MY SON...
"...MAY RAO ALWAYS BE THERE TO GUIDE YOU."

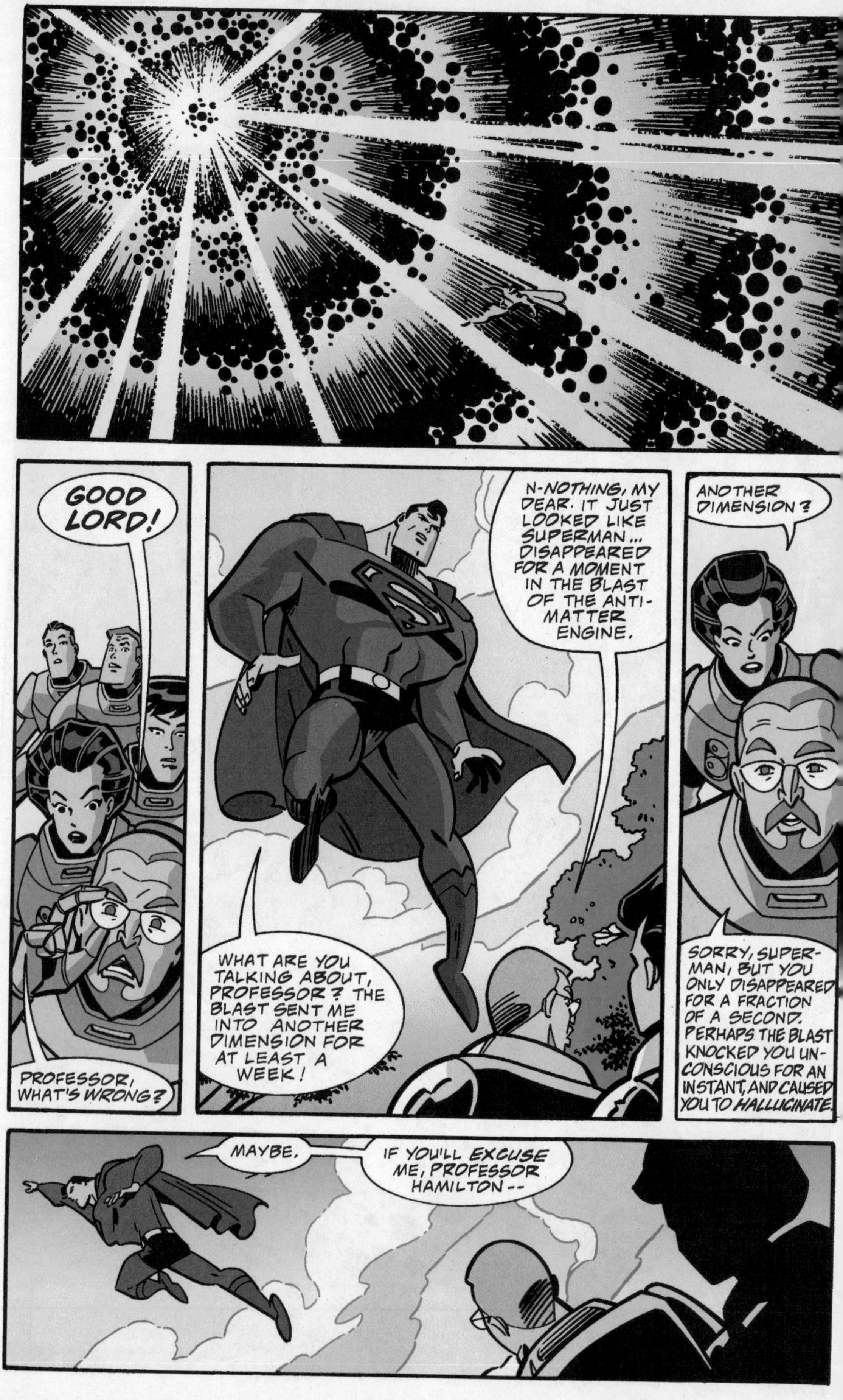
GOOD LORD!
PROFESSOR, WHAT'S WRONG?
N-NOTHING, MY DEAR. IT JUST LOOKED LIKE SUPERMAN... DISAPPEARED FOR A MOMENT IN THE BLAST OF THE ANTI-MATTER ENGINE.
WHAT ARE YOU TALKING ABOUT, PROFESSOR? THE BLAST SENT ME INTO ANOTHER DIMENSION FOR AT LEAST A WEEK!
ANOTHER DIMENSION?
SORRY, SUPER-MAN, BUT YOU ONLY DISAPPEARED FOR A FRACTION OF A SECOND. PERHAPS THE BLAST KNOCKED YOU UN-CONSCIOUS FOR AN INSTANT, AND CAUSED YOU TO HALLUCINATE.
MAYBE.
IF YOU'LL EXCUSE ME, PROFESSOR HAMILTON--

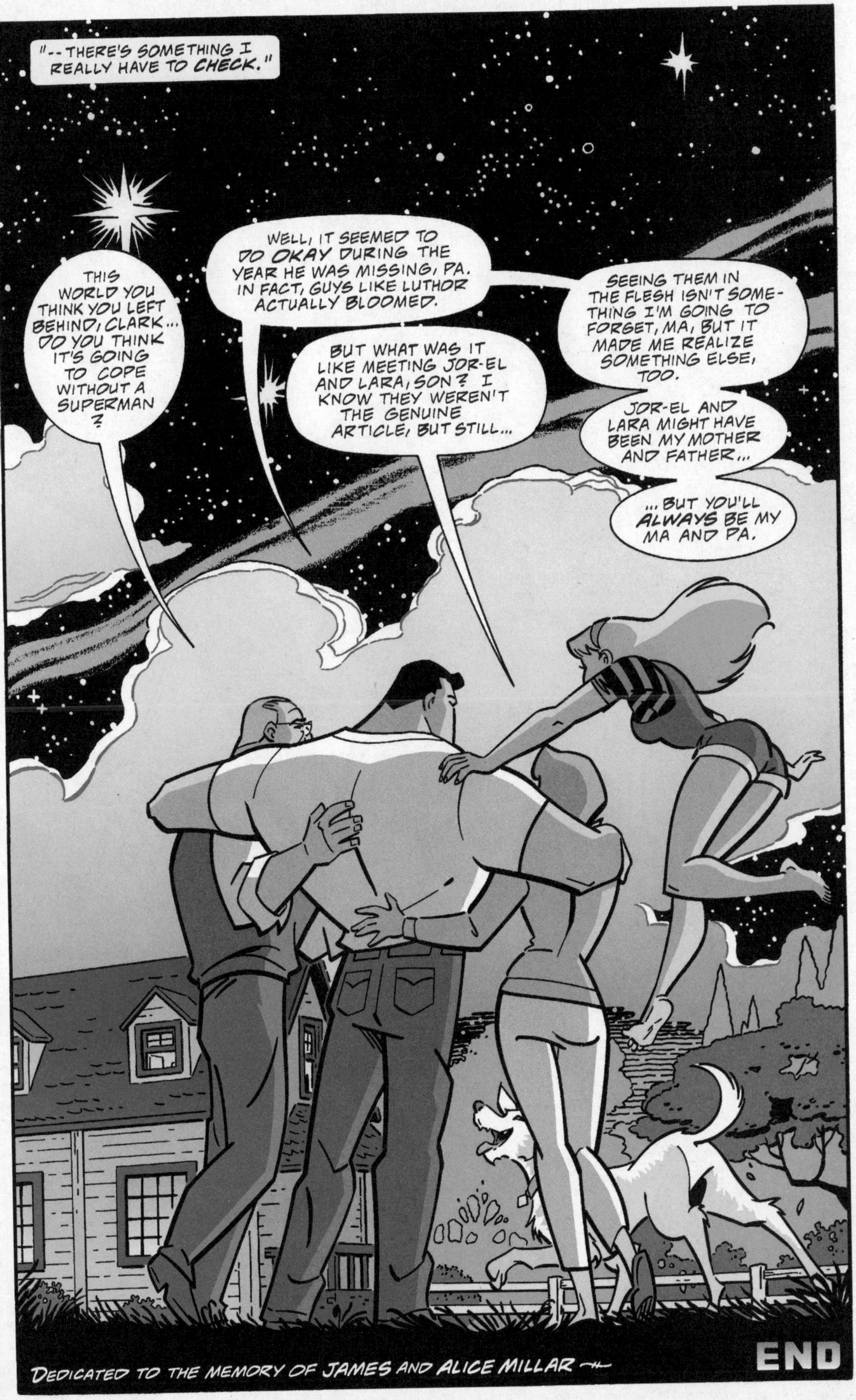
"-- THERE'S SOMETHING I REALLY HAVE TO CHECK."
THIS WORLD YOU THINK YOU LEFT BEHIND, CLARK... DO YOU THINK IT'S GOING TO COPE WITHOUT A SUPERMAN ?
WELL, IT SEEMED TO DO OKAY DURING THE YEAR HE WAS MISSING, PA. IN FACT, GUYS LIKE LUTHOR ACTUALLY BLOOMED.
BUT WHAT WAS IT LIKE MEETING JOR-EL AND LARA, SON ? I KNOW THEY WEREN'T THE GENUINE ARTICLE, BUT STILL...
SEEING THEM IN THE FLESH ISN'T SOMETHING I'M GOING TO FORGET, MA, BUT IT MADE ME REALIZE SOMETHING ELSE, TOO.
JOR-EL AND LARA MIGHT HAVE BEEN MY MOTHER AND FATHER...
...BUT YOU'LL ALWAYS BE MY MA AND PA.
DEDICATED TO THE MEMORY OF JAMES AND ALICE MILLAR —
END

SUPERMAN ADVENTURES #32 cover by MIKE MANLEY, TERRY AUSTIN and MARIE SEVERIN

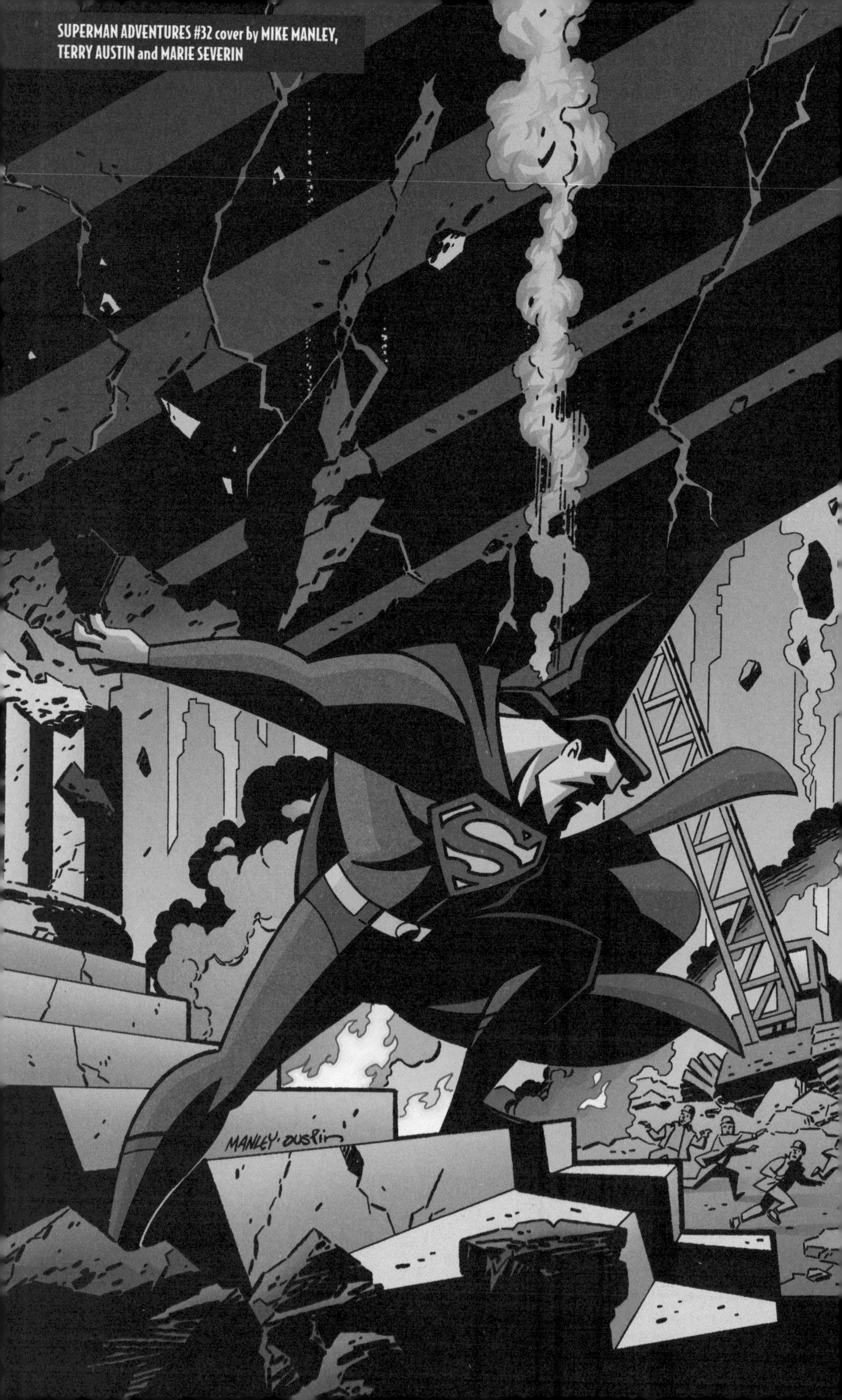

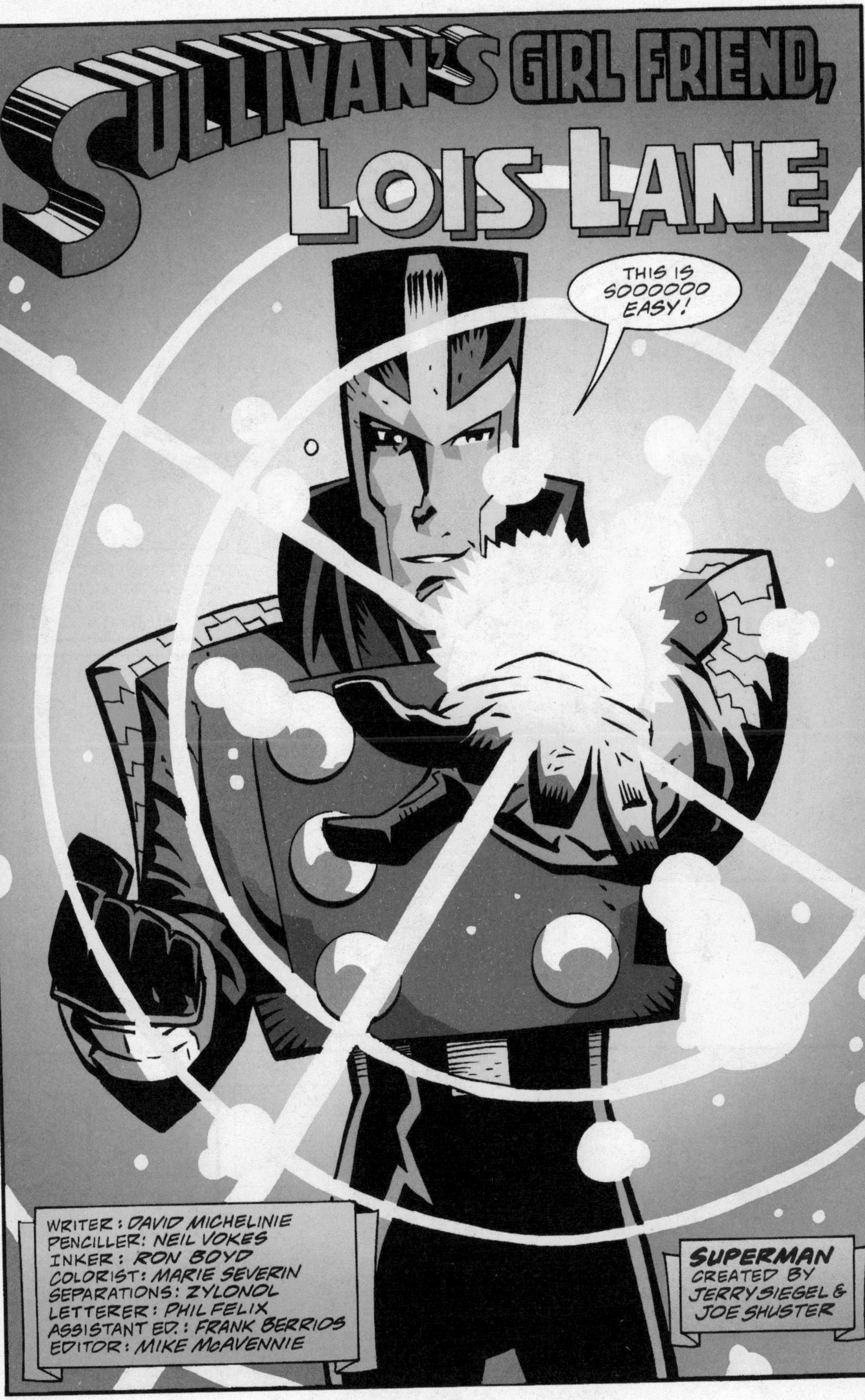
SULLIVAN'S GIRL FRIEND, LOIS LANE
THIS IS SOOOOOO EASY!
WRITER: DAVID MICHELINIE
PENCILLER: NEIL VOKES
INKER: RON BOYD
COLORIST: MARIE SEVERIN
SEPARATIONS: ZYLONOL
LETTERER: PHIL FELIX
ASSISTANT ED.: FRANK BERRIOS
EDITOR: MIKE McAVENNIE
SUPERMAN CREATED BY JERRY SIEGEL & JOE SHUSTER

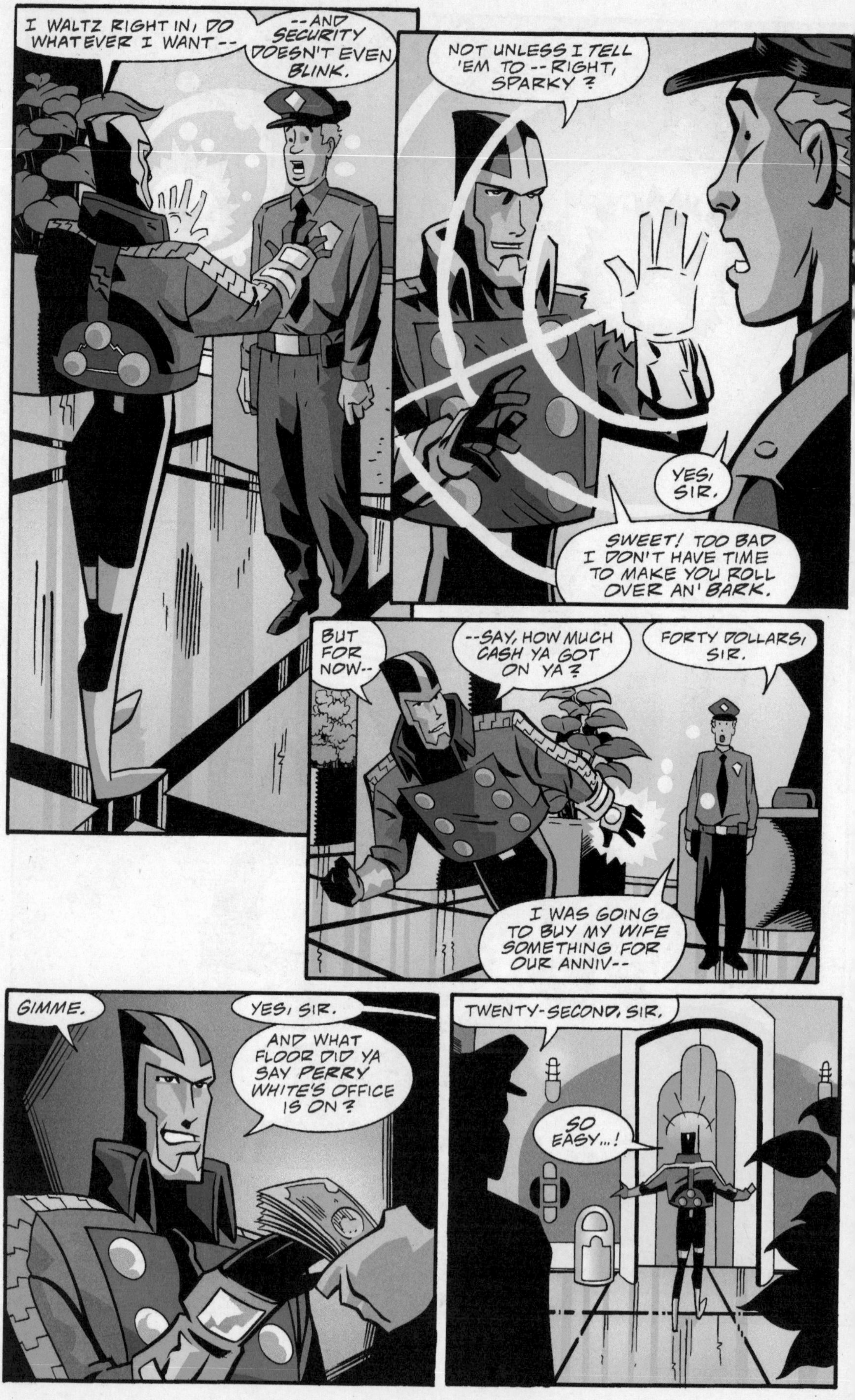
I WALTZ RIGHT IN, DO WHATEVER I WANT --
-- AND SECURITY DOESN'T EVEN BLINK.
NOT UNLESS I TELL 'EM TO -- RIGHT, SPARKY?
YES, SIR.
SWEET! TOO BAD I DON'T HAVE TIME TO MAKE YOU ROLL OVER AN' BARK.
BUT FOR NOW--
--SAY, HOW MUCH CASH YA GOT ON YA?
FORTY DOLLARS, SIR.
I WAS GOING TO BUY MY WIFE SOMETHING FOR OUR ANNIV--
GIMME.
YES, SIR.
AND WHAT FLOOR DID YA SAY PERRY WHITE'S OFFICE IS ON?
TWENTY-SECOND, SIR.
SO EASY...!

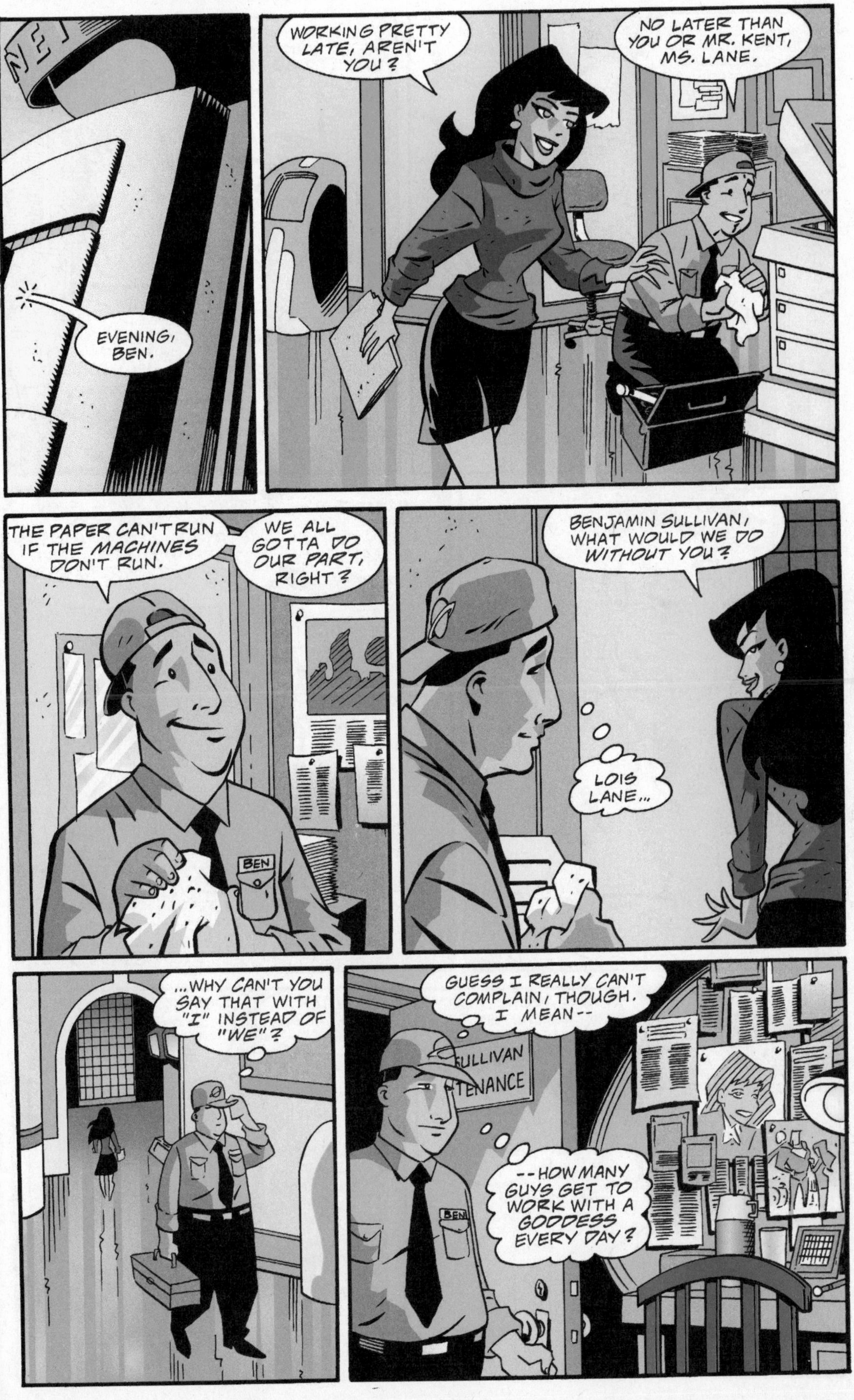
EVENING, BEN.
WORKING PRETTY LATE, AREN'T YOU?
NO LATER THAN YOU OR MR. KENT, MS. LANE.
THE PAPER CAN'T RUN IF THE MACHINES DON'T RUN.
WE ALL GOTTA DO OUR PART, RIGHT?
BEN
BENJAMIN SULLIVAN, WHAT WOULD WE DO WITHOUT YOU?
LOIS LANE...
...WHY CAN'T YOU SAY THAT WITH "I" INSTEAD OF "WE"?
GUESS I REALLY CAN'T COMPLAIN, THOUGH. I MEAN--
SULLIVAN
TENANCE
--HOW MANY GUYS GET TO WORK WITH A GODDESS EVERY DAY?
BEN

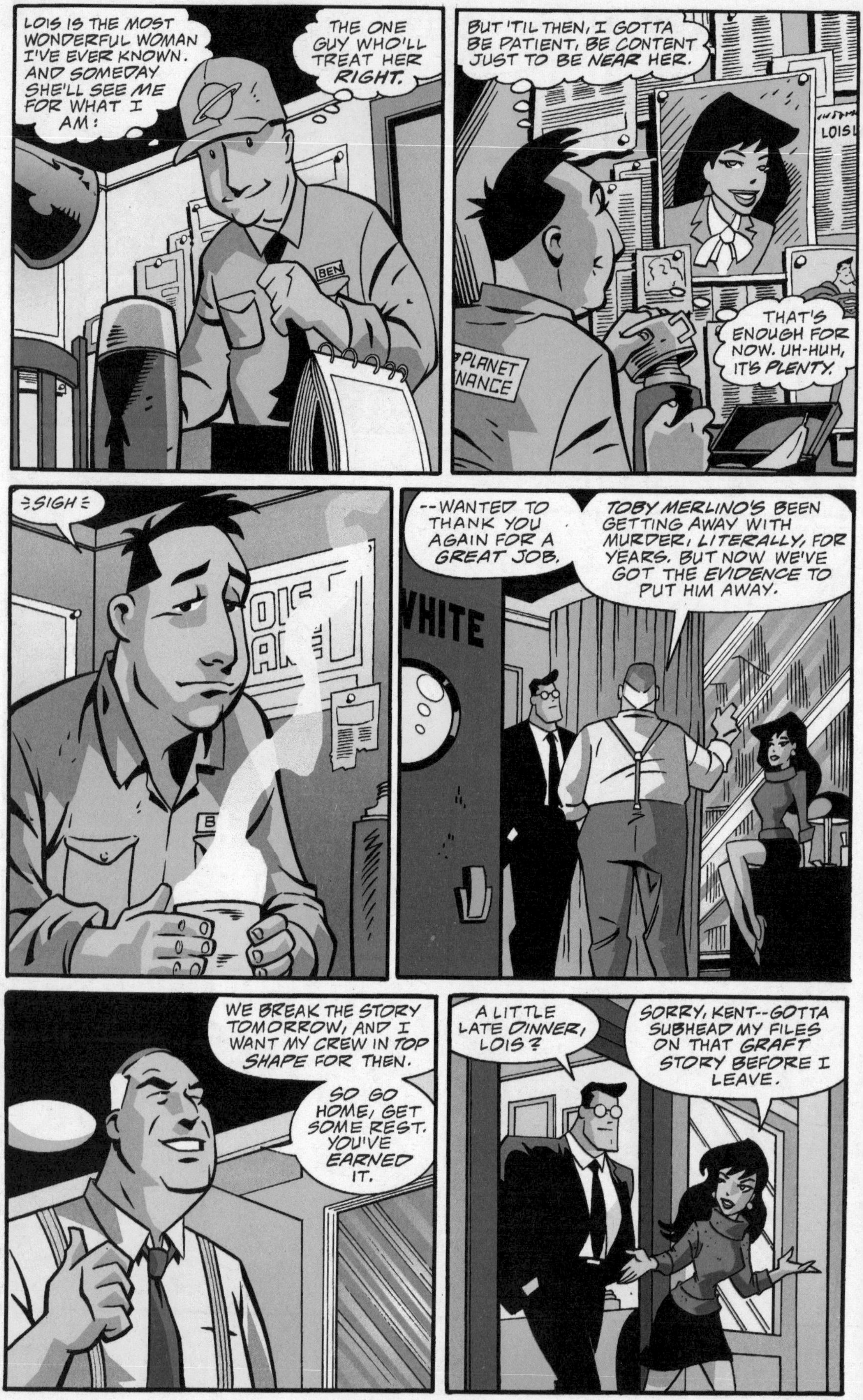
LOIS IS THE MOST WONDERFUL WOMAN I'VE EVER KNOWN. AND SOMEDAY SHE'LL SEE ME FOR WHAT I AM:
THE ONE GUY WHO'LL TREAT HER RIGHT.
BEN
BUT 'TIL THEN, I GOTTA BE PATIENT, BE CONTENT JUST TO BE NEAR HER.
LOIS L
PLANET
NANCE
THAT'S ENOUGH FOR NOW. UH-HUH, IT'S PLENTY.
SIGH
--WANTED TO THANK YOU AGAIN FOR A GREAT JOB.
TOBY MERLINO'S BEEN GETTING AWAY WITH MURDER, LITERALLY, FOR YEARS. BUT NOW WE'VE GOT THE EVIDENCE TO PUT HIM AWAY.
WHITE
WE BREAK THE STORY TOMORROW, AND I WANT MY CREW IN TOP SHAPE FOR THEN.
SO GO HOME, GET SOME REST. YOU'VE EARNED IT.
A LITTLE LATE DINNER, LOIS?
SORRY, KENT--GOTTA SUBHEAD MY FILES ON THAT GRAFT STORY BEFORE I LEAVE.

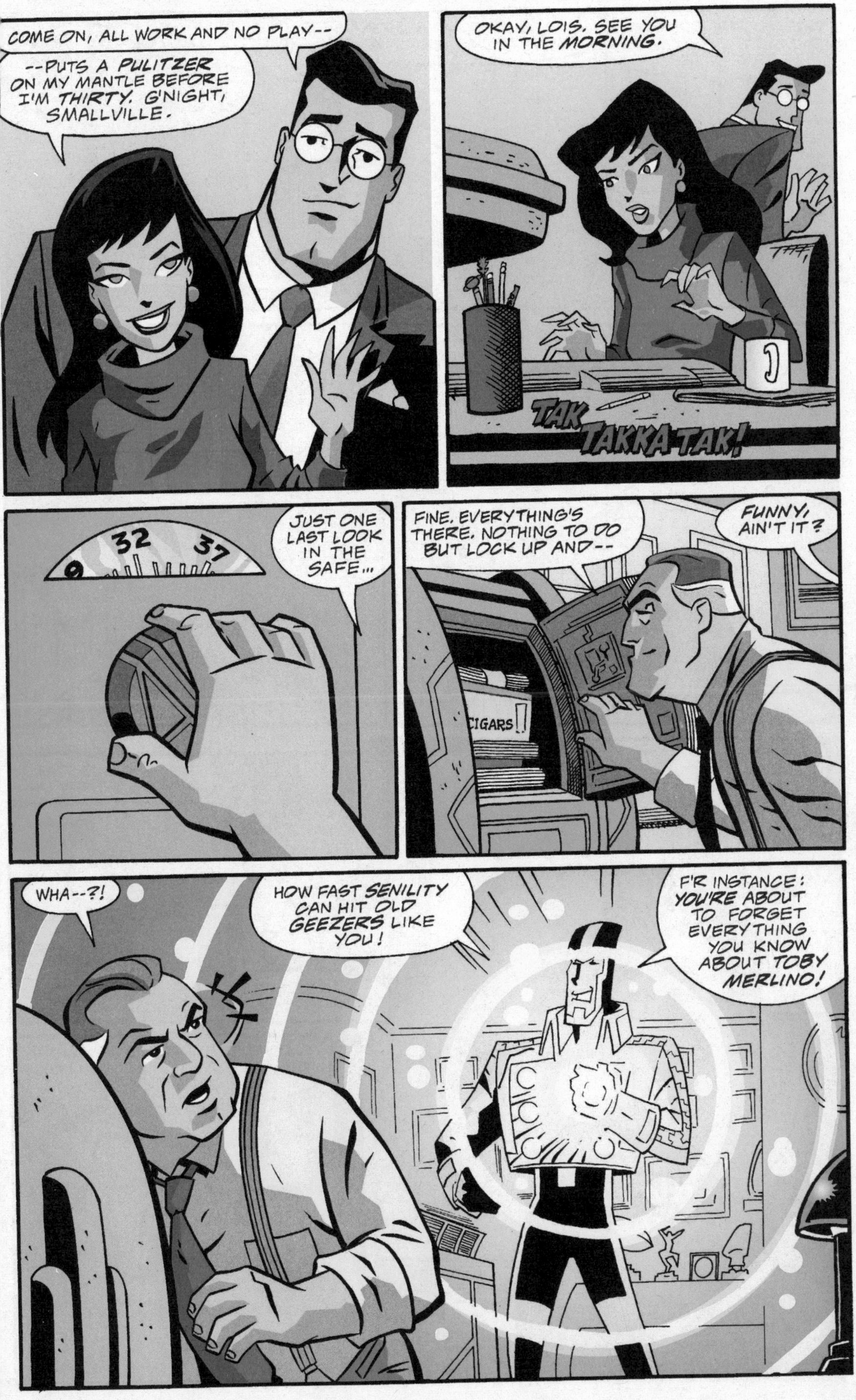
COME ON, ALL WORK AND NO PLAY--
--PUTS A PULITZER ON MY MANTLE BEFORE I'M THIRTY. G'NIGHT, SMALLVILLE.
OKAY, LOIS. SEE YOU IN THE MORNING.
TAK TAKKA TAK!
0 32 37
JUST ONE LAST LOOK IN THE SAFE...
FINE. EVERYTHING'S THERE. NOTHING TO DO BUT LOCK UP AND--
FUNNY, AIN'T IT?
CIGARS
WHA--?!
HOW FAST SENILITY CAN HIT OLD GEEZERS LIKE YOU!
F'R INSTANCE: YOU'RE ABOUT TO FORGET EVERYTHING YOU KNOW ABOUT TOBY MERLINO!

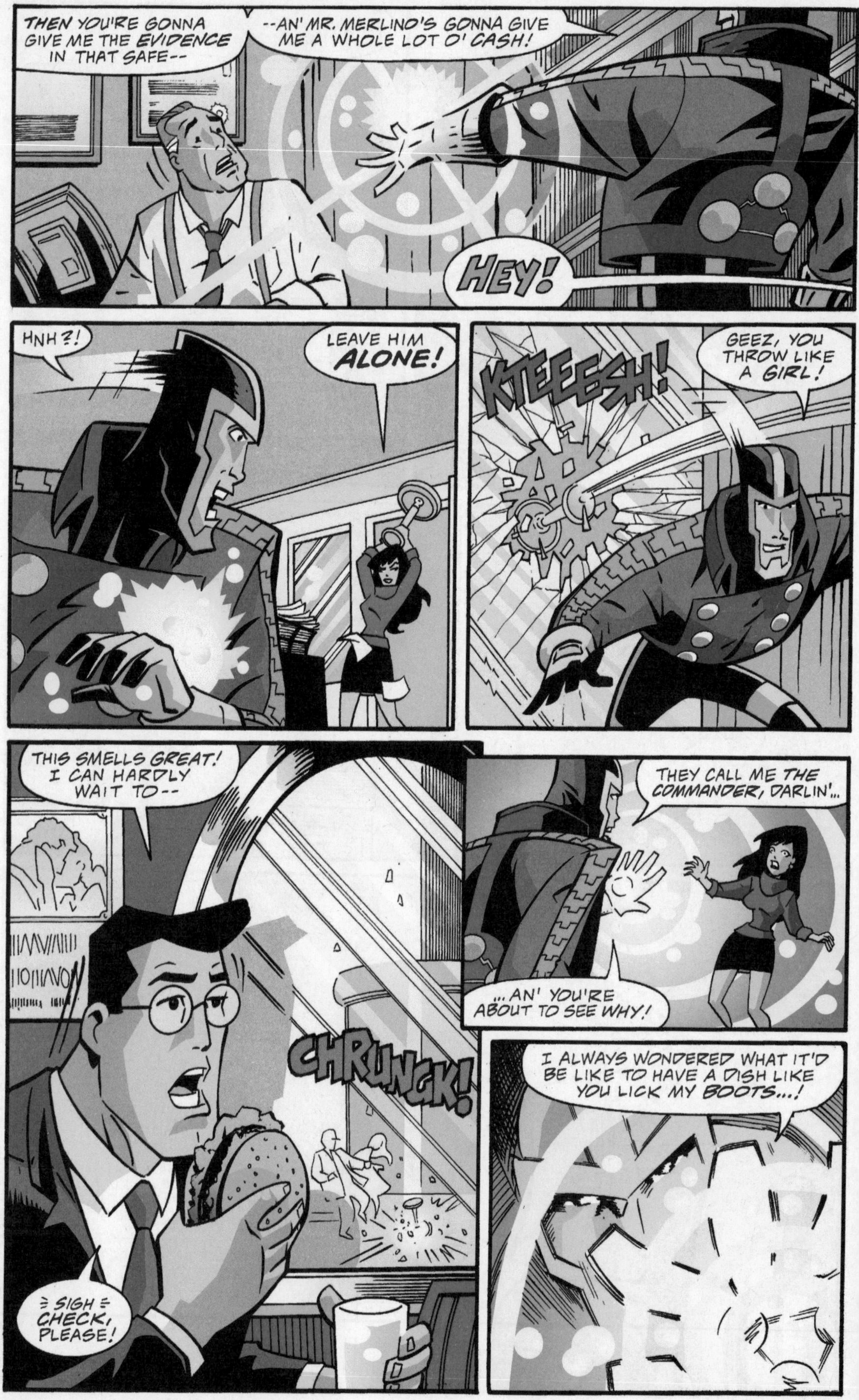
THEN YOU'RE GONNA GIVE ME THE EVIDENCE IN THAT SAFE--
--AN' MR. MERLINO'S GONNA GIVE ME A WHOLE LOT O' CASH!
HEY!
HNH?!
LEAVE HIM ALONE!
KTEEEESH!
GEEZ, YOU THROW LIKE A GIRL!
THIS SMELLS GREAT! I CAN HARDLY WAIT TO--
CHRUNGK!
SIGH
CHECK, PLEASE!
THEY CALL ME THE COMMANDER, DARLIN'...
...AN' YOU'RE ABOUT TO SEE WHY!
I ALWAYS WONDERED WHAT IT'D BE LIKE TO HAVE A DISH LIKE YOU LICK MY BOOTS...!

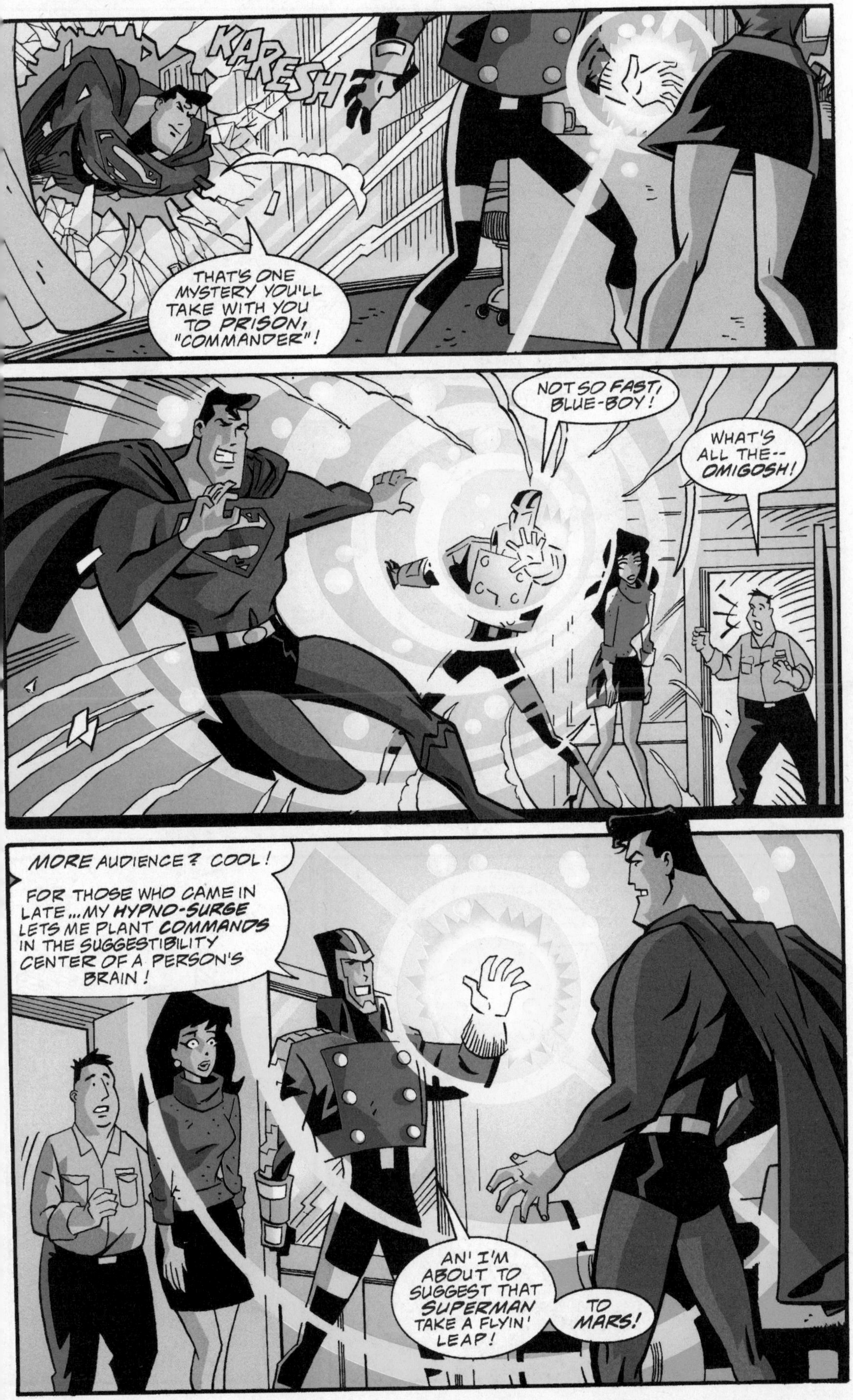
KARESH
THAT'S ONE MYSTERY YOU'LL TAKE WITH YOU TO PRISON, "COMMANDER"!
NOT SO FAST, BLUE-BOY!
WHAT'S ALL THE-- OMIGOSH!
MORE AUDIENCE? COOL!
FOR THOSE WHO CAME IN LATE... MY HYPNO-SURGE LETS ME PLANT COMMANDS IN THE SUGGESTIBILITY CENTER OF A PERSON'S BRAIN!
AN' I'M ABOUT TO SUGGEST THAT SUPERMAN TAKE A FLYIN' LEAP!
TO MARS!

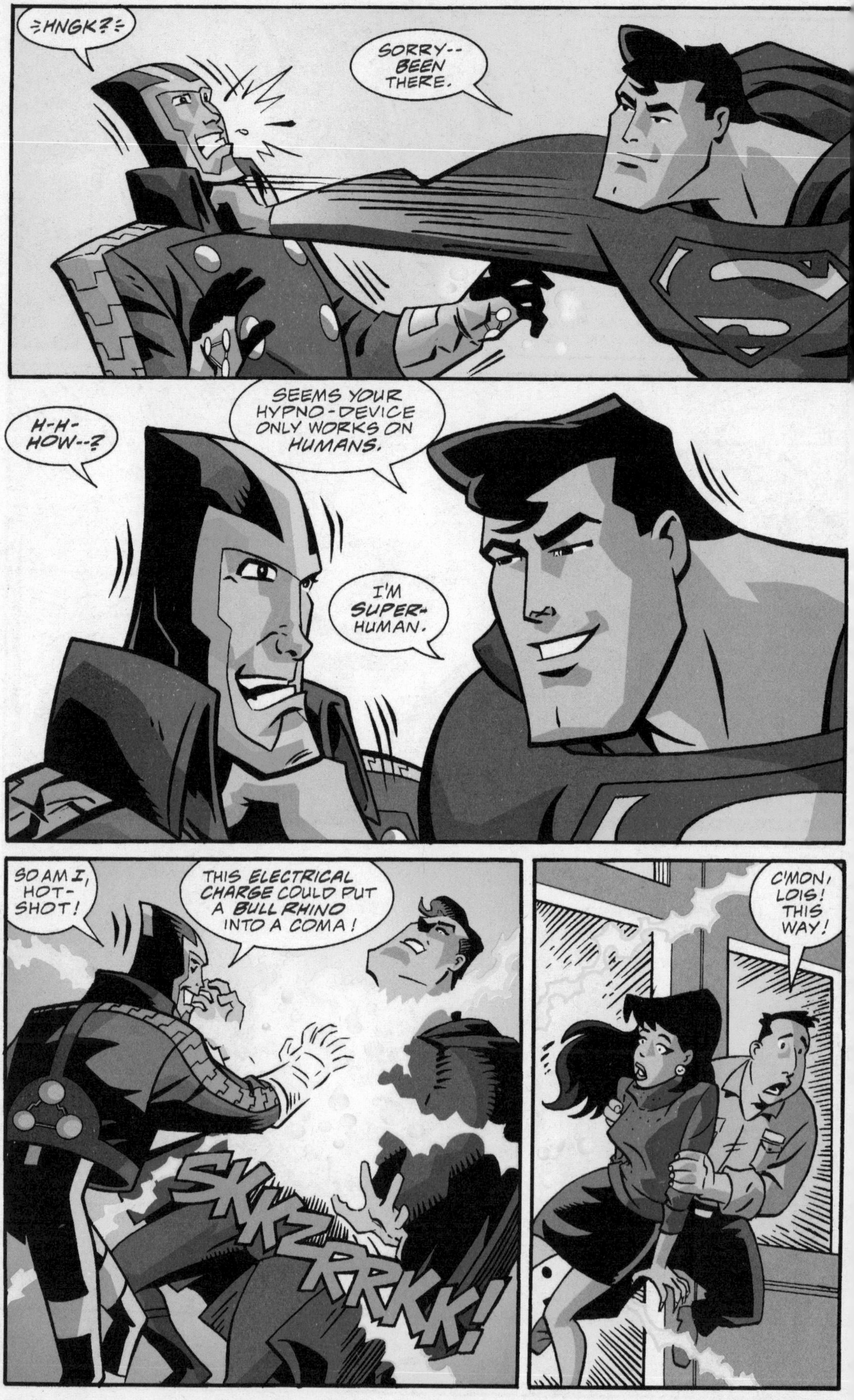
HNGK?
SORRY-- BEEN THERE.
H-H-HOW--?
SEEMS YOUR HYPNO-DEVICE ONLY WORKS ON HUMANS.
I'M SUPER-HUMAN.
SO AM I, HOT-SHOT!
THIS ELECTRICAL CHARGE COULD PUT A BULL RHINO INTO A COMA!
SKKZRRKK!
C'MON, LOIS! THIS WAY!

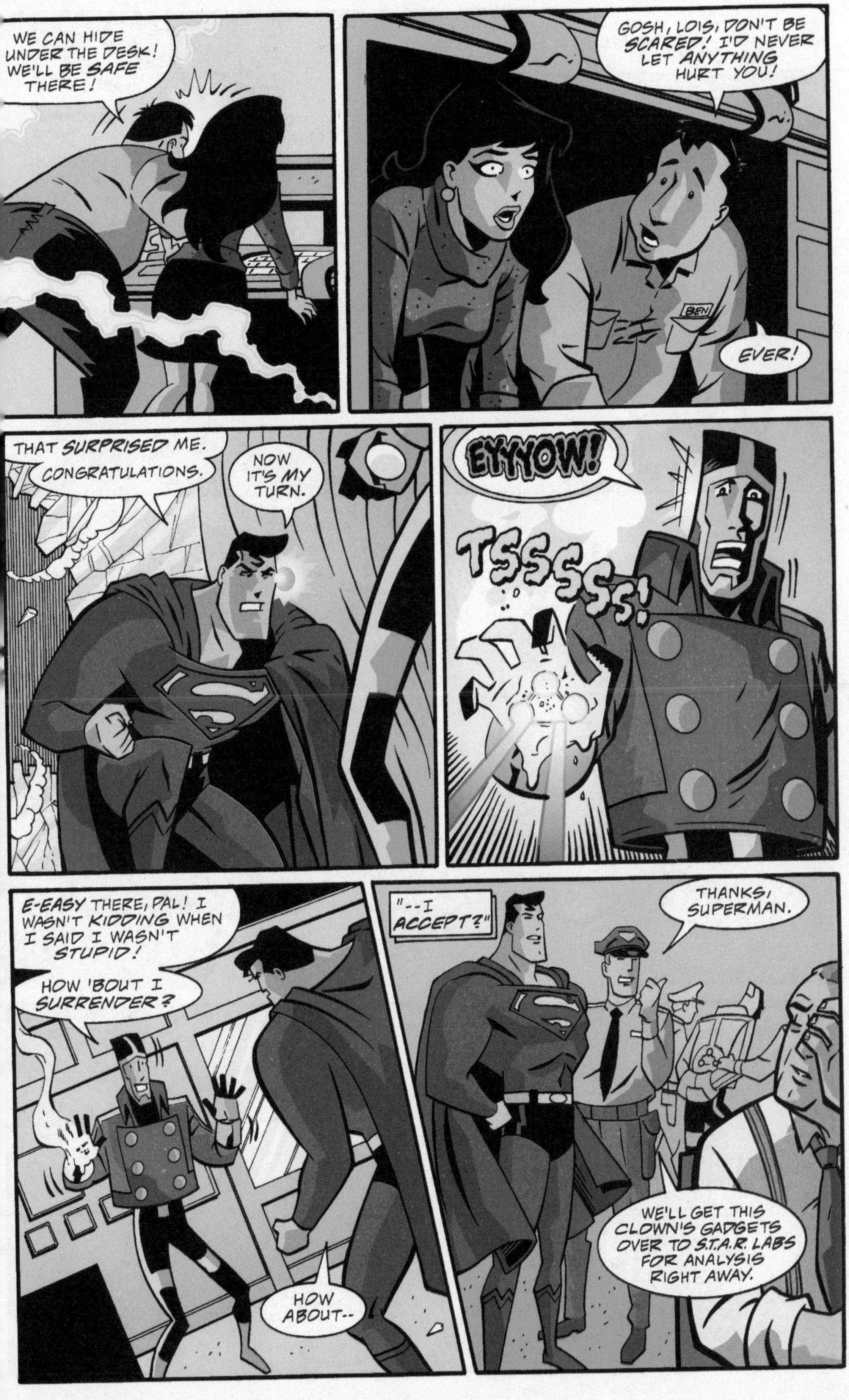
WE CAN HIDE UNDER THE DESK! WE'LL BE SAFE THERE!
GOSH, LOIS, DON'T BE SCARED! I'D NEVER LET ANYTHING HURT YOU!
EVER!
BEN
THAT SURPRISED ME. CONGRATULATIONS.
NOW IT'S MY TURN.
EYYYOW!
TSSSSSS!
E-EASY THERE, PAL! I WASN'T KIDDING WHEN I SAID I WASN'T STUPID!
HOW 'BOUT I SURRENDER?
HOW ABOUT--
"--I ACCEPT?"
THANKS, SUPERMAN.
WE'LL GET THIS CLOWN'S GADGETS OVER TO S.T.A.R. LABS FOR ANALYSIS RIGHT AWAY.

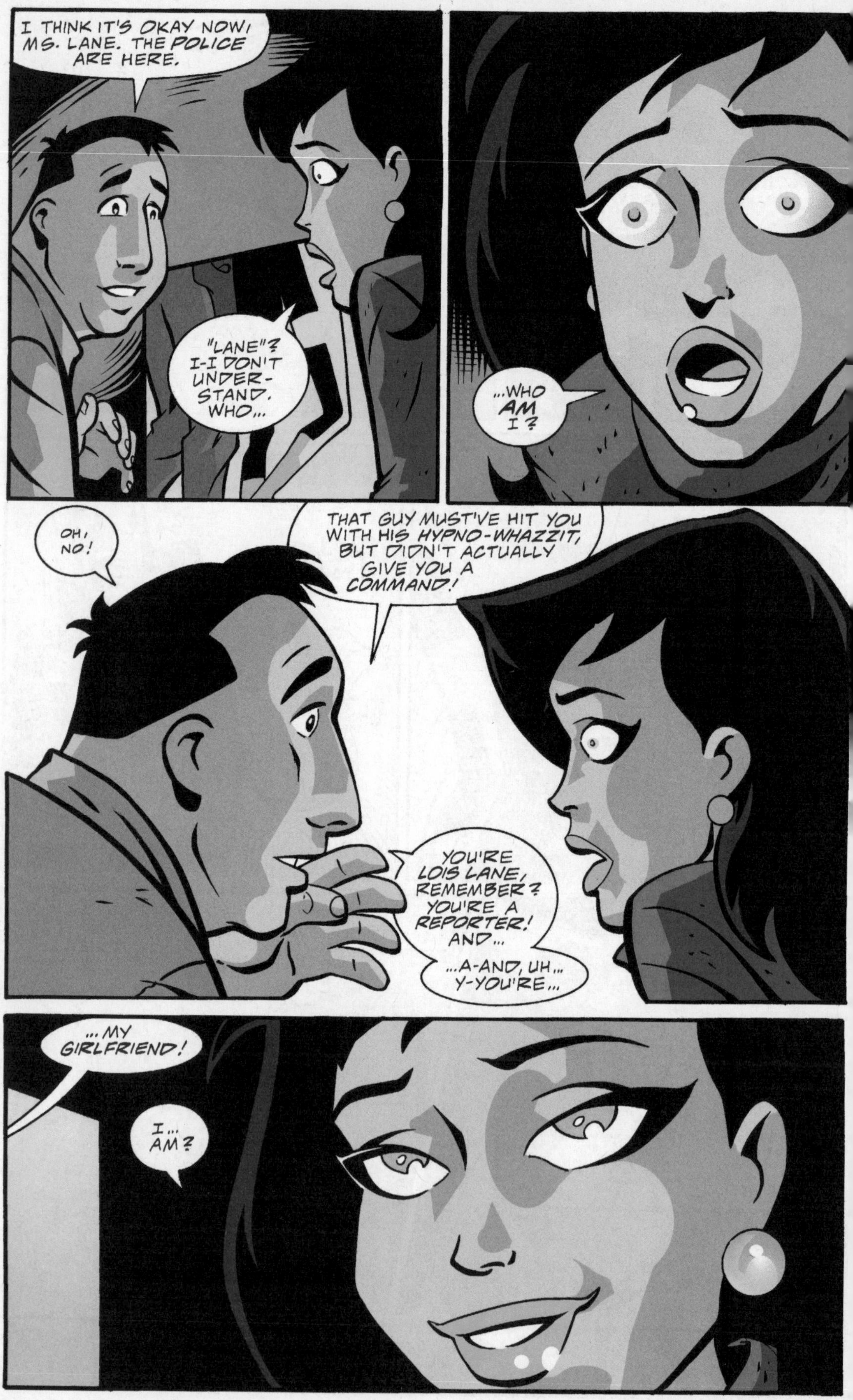
I THINK IT'S OKAY NOW, MS. LANE. THE POLICE ARE HERE.
"LANE"? I-I DON'T UNDER-STAND. WHO...
...WHO AM I?
OH, NO!
THAT GUY MUST'VE HIT YOU WITH HIS HYPNO-WHAZZIT, BUT DIDN'T ACTUALLY GIVE YOU A COMMAND!
YOU'RE LOIS LANE, REMEMBER? YOU'RE A REPORTER! AND...
...A-AND, UH... Y-YOU'RE...
...MY GIRLFRIEND!
I... AM?

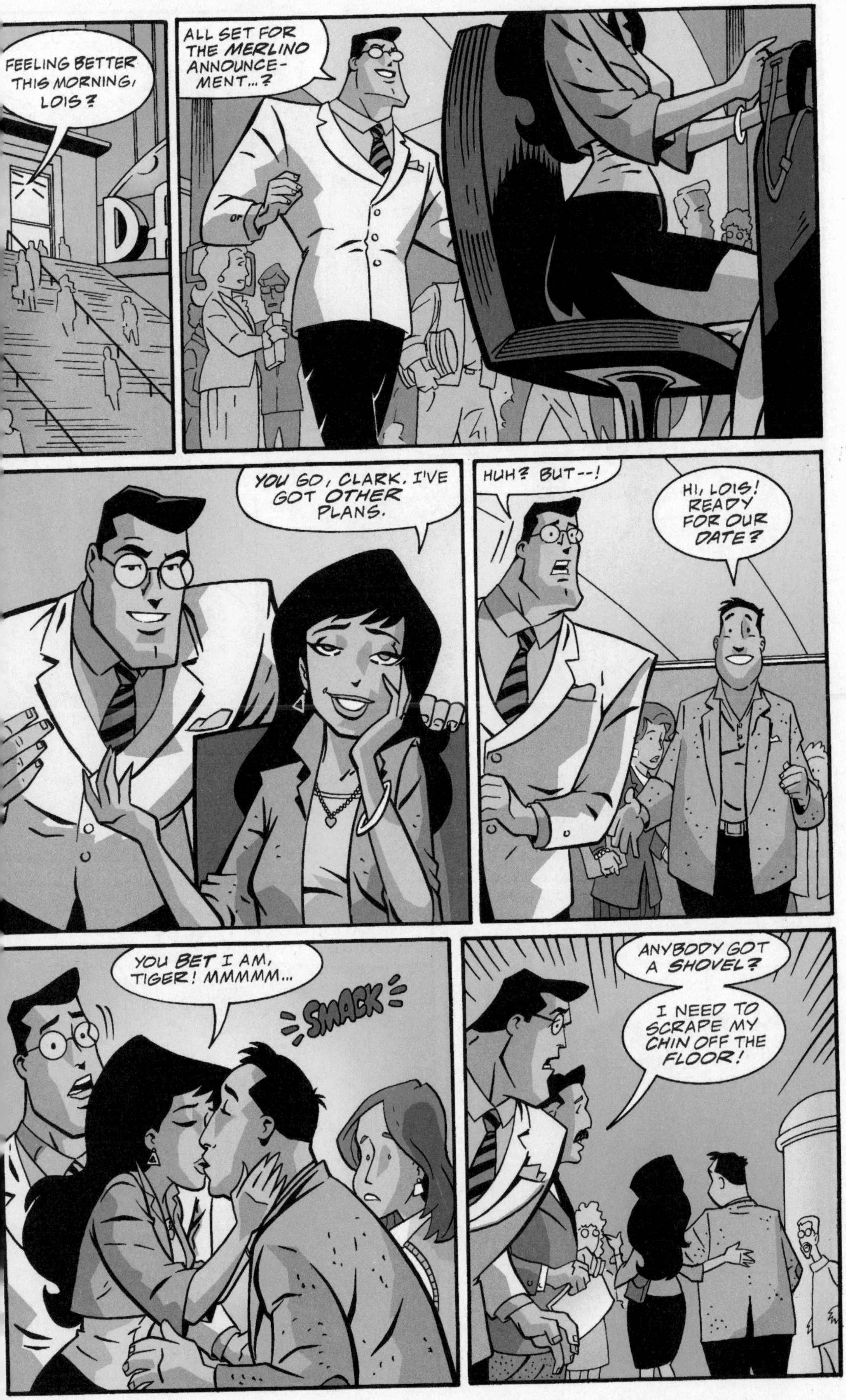
FEELING BETTER THIS MORNING, LOIS?
ALL SET FOR THE MERLINO ANNOUNCE-MENT...?
YOU GO, CLARK. I'VE GOT OTHER PLANS.
HUH? BUT--!
HI, LOIS! READY FOR OUR DATE?
YOU BET I AM, TIGER! MMMMM...
SMACK
ANYBODY GOT A SHOVEL?
I NEED TO SCRAPE MY CHIN OFF THE FLOOR!

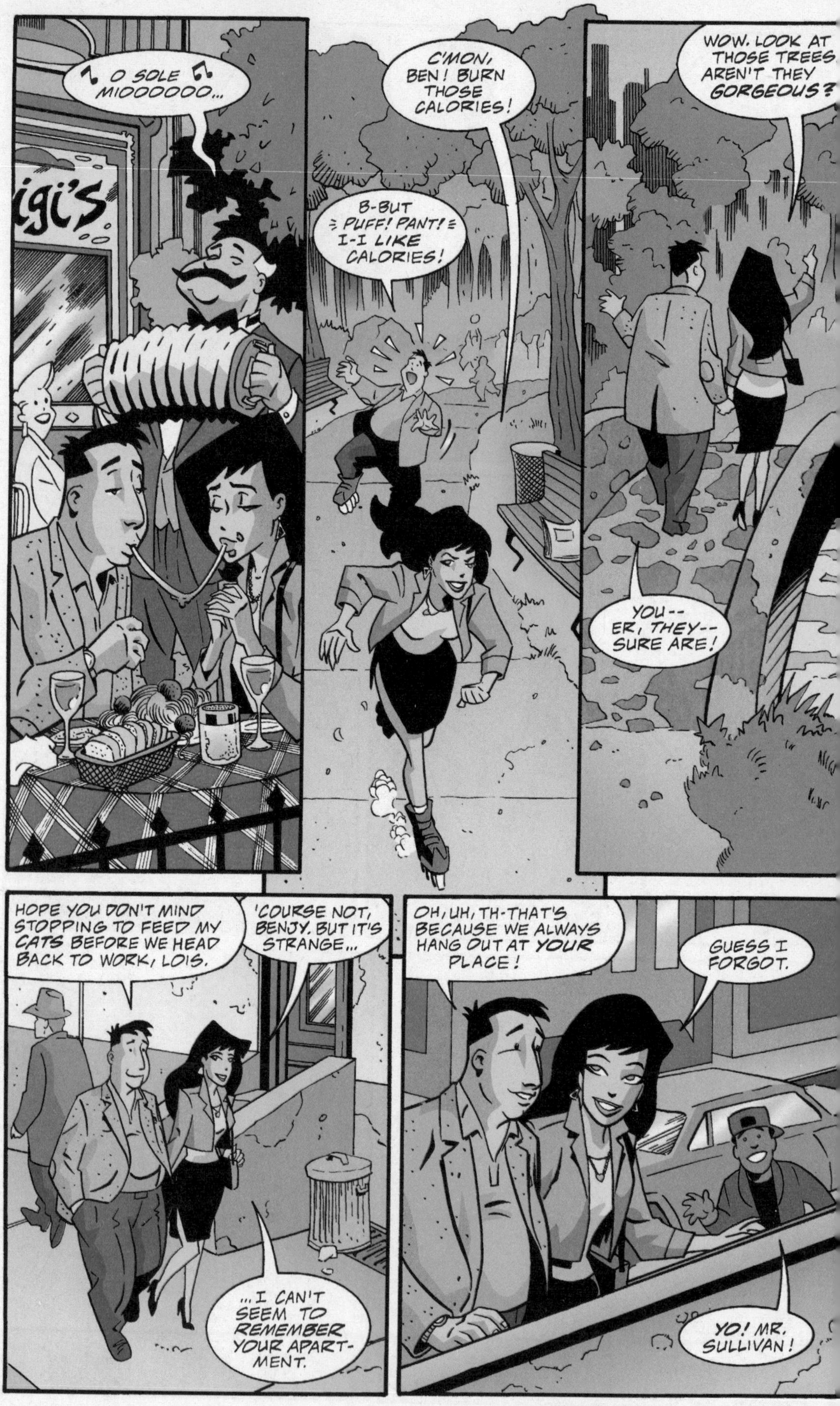

O SOLE MIOOOOOO...
igi's
C'MON, BEN! BURN THOSE CALORIES!
B-BUT PUFF! PANT! I-I LIKE CALORIES!
WOW. LOOK AT THOSE TREES. AREN'T THEY GORGEOUS?
YOU-- ER, THEY-- SURE ARE!
HOPE YOU DON'T MIND STOPPING TO FEED MY CATS BEFORE WE HEAD BACK TO WORK, LOIS.
'COURSE NOT, BENJY. BUT IT'S STRANGE...
...I CAN'T SEEM TO REMEMBER YOUR APARTMENT.
OH, UH, TH-THAT'S BECAUSE WE ALWAYS HANG OUT AT YOUR PLACE!
GUESS I FORGOT.
YO! MR. SULLIVAN!

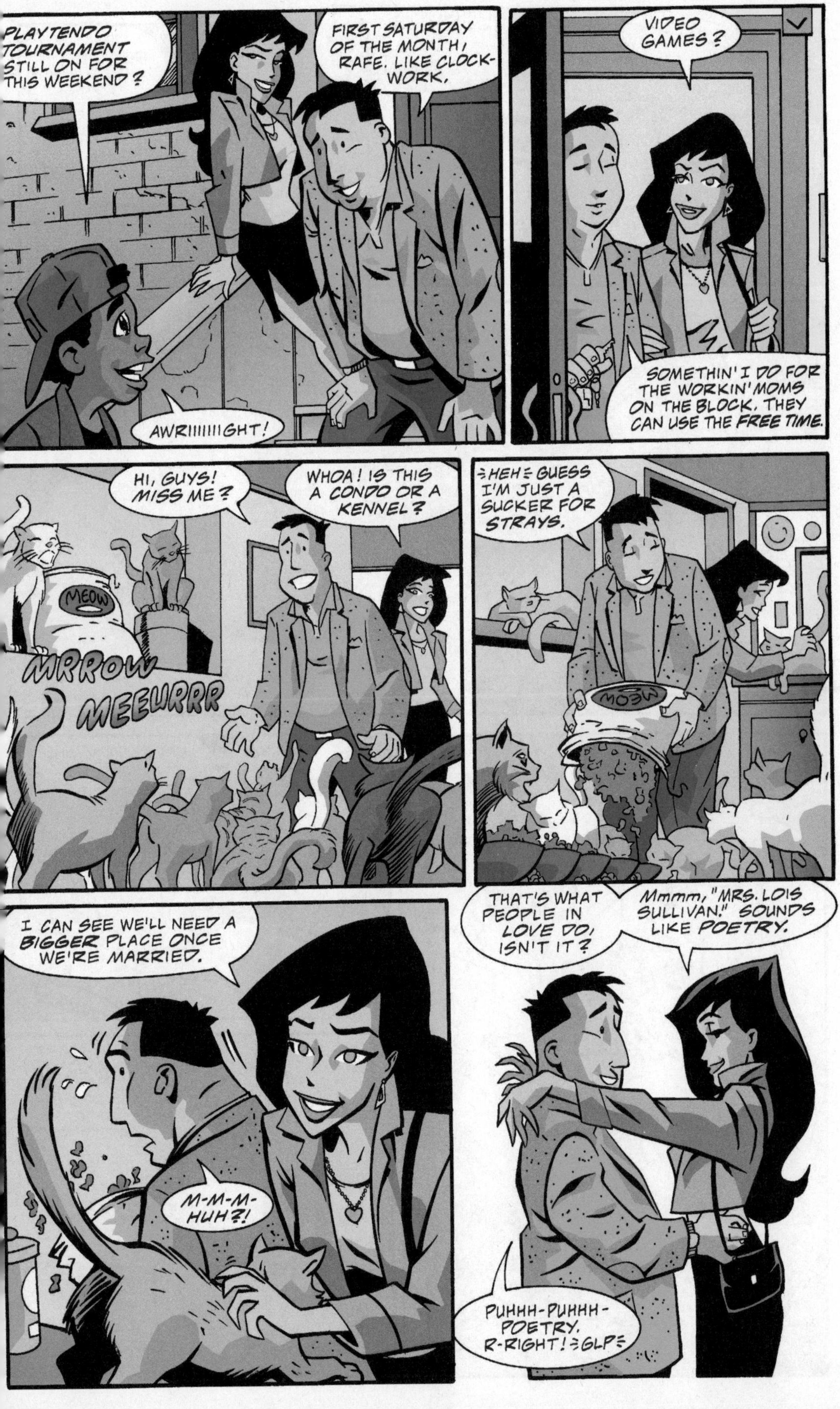
PLAYTENDO TOURNAMENT STILL ON FOR THIS WEEKEND?
FIRST SATURDAY OF THE MONTH, RAFE. LIKE CLOCK-WORK.
AWRIIIIIIIGHT!
VIDEO GAMES?
SOMETHIN' I DO FOR THE WORKIN' MOMS ON THE BLOCK. THEY CAN USE THE FREE TIME.
HI, GUYS! MISS ME?
WHOA! IS THIS A CONDO OR A KENNEL?
MEOW
MRROW
MEEURRR
=HEH= GUESS I'M JUST A SUCKER FOR STRAYS.
MEOW
I CAN SEE WE'LL NEED A BIGGER PLACE ONCE WE'RE MARRIED.
M-M-M-HUH?!
THAT'S WHAT PEOPLE IN LOVE DO, ISN'T IT?
Mmmm, "MRS. LOIS SULLIVAN." SOUNDS LIKE POETRY.
PUHHH-PUHHH-POETRY. R-RIGHT! =GLP=

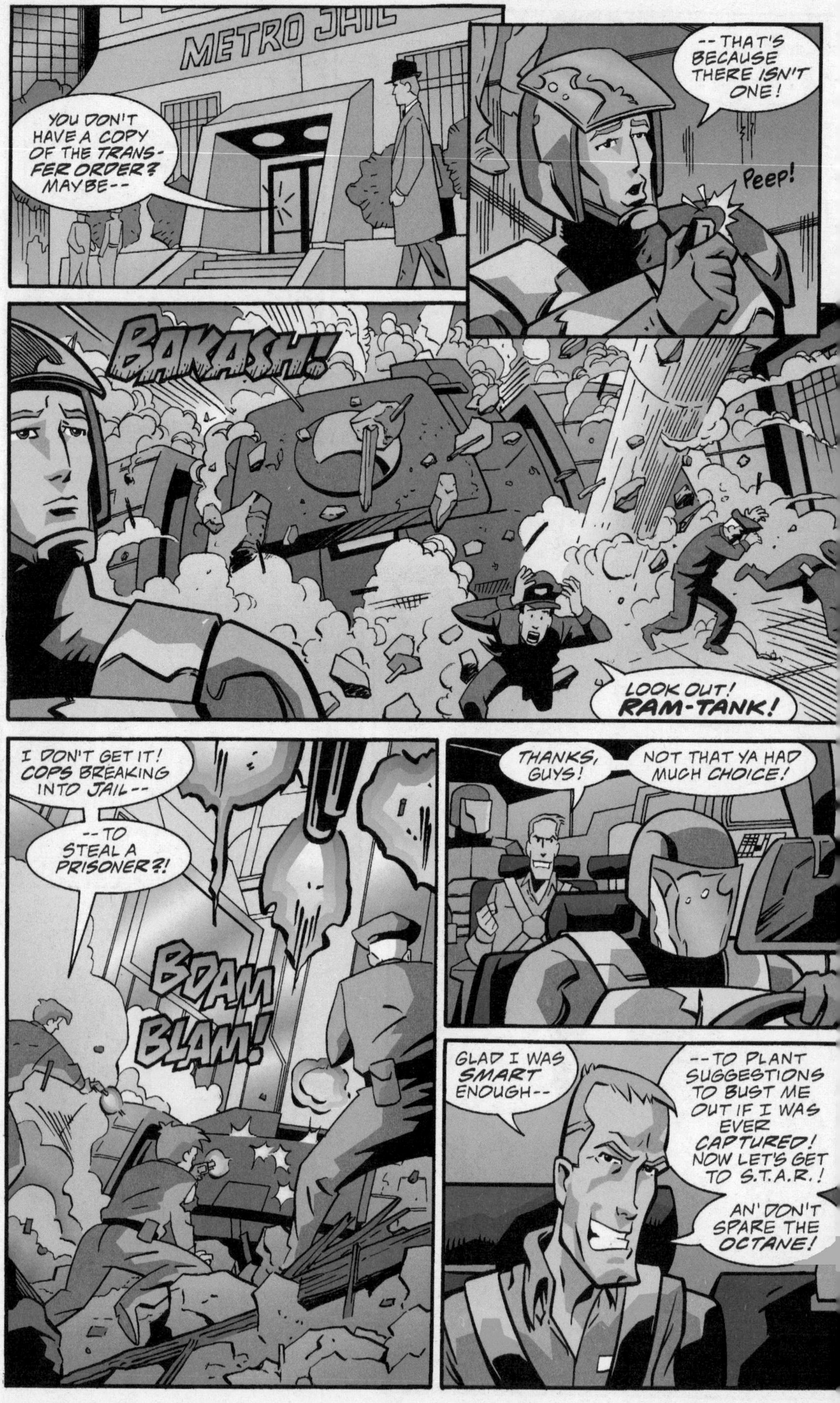
METRO JAIL
YOU DON'T HAVE A COPY OF THE TRANSFER ORDER? MAYBE--
--THAT'S BECAUSE THERE ISN'T ONE!
Peep!
BAKASH!
LOOK OUT! RAM-TANK!
I DON'T GET IT! COPS BREAKING INTO JAIL--
--TO STEAL A PRISONER?!
BOAM BLAM!
THANKS, GUYS!
NOT THAT YA HAD MUCH CHOICE!
GLAD I WAS SMART ENOUGH--
--TO PLANT SUGGESTIONS TO BUST ME OUT IF I WAS EVER CAPTURED! NOW LET'S GET TO S.T.A.R.!
AN' DON'T SPARE THE OCTANE!

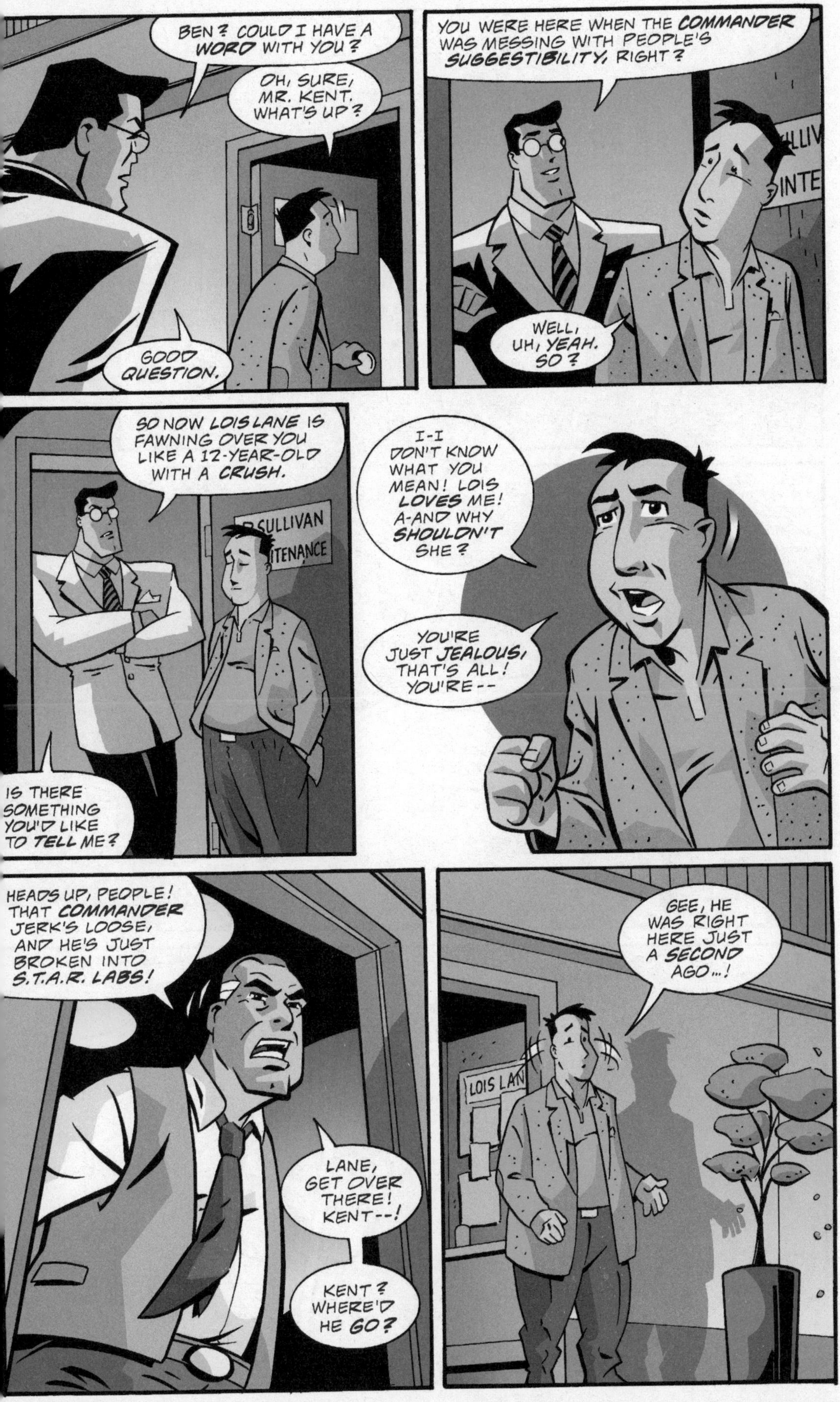
BEN? COULD I HAVE A WORD WITH YOU?
OH, SURE, MR. KENT. WHAT'S UP?
GOOD QUESTION.
YOU WERE HERE WHEN THE COMMANDER WAS MESSING WITH PEOPLE'S SUGGESTIBILITY, RIGHT?
WELL, UH, YEAH. SO?
SO NOW LOIS LANE IS FAWNING OVER YOU LIKE A 12-YEAR-OLD WITH A CRUSH.
SULLIVAN
ITENANCE
IS THERE SOMETHING YOU'D LIKE TO TELL ME?
I-I DON'T KNOW WHAT YOU MEAN! LOIS LOVES ME! A-AND WHY SHOULDN'T SHE?
YOU'RE JUST JEALOUS, THAT'S ALL! YOU'RE--
HEADS UP, PEOPLE! THAT COMMANDER JERK'S LOOSE, AND HE'S JUST BROKEN INTO S.T.A.R. LABS!
LANE, GET OVER THERE! KENT--!
KENT? WHERE'D HE GO?
GEE, HE WAS RIGHT HERE JUST A SECOND AGO...!
LOIS LAN

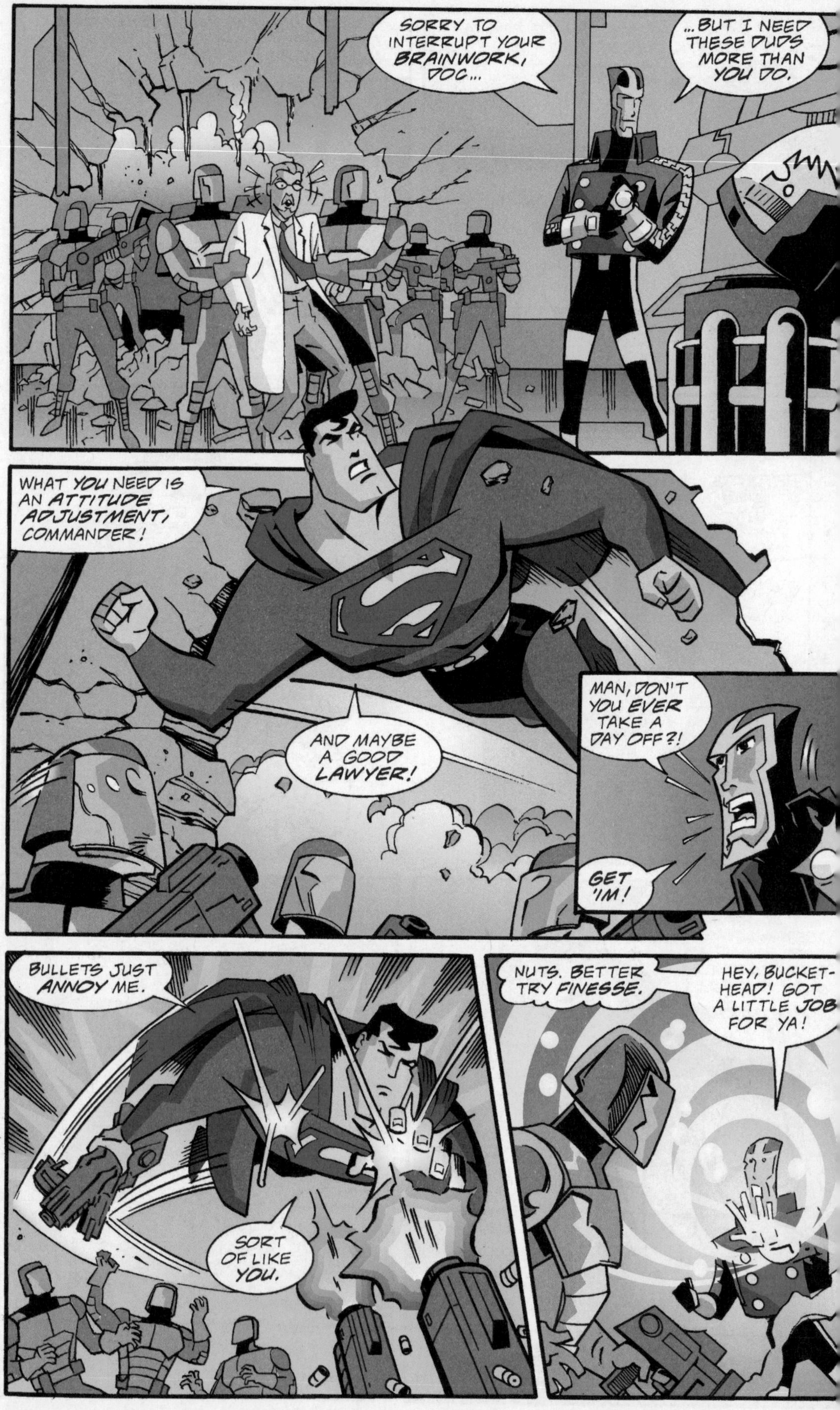
SORRY TO INTERRUPT YOUR BRAINWORK, DOC...
...BUT I NEED THESE DUDS MORE THAN YOU DO.
WHAT YOU NEED IS AN ATTITUDE ADJUSTMENT, COMMANDER!
AND MAYBE A GOOD LAWYER!
MAN, DON'T YOU EVER TAKE A DAY OFF?!
GET 'IM!
BULLETS JUST ANNOY ME.
SORT OF LIKE YOU.
NUTS. BETTER TRY FINESSE.
HEY, BUCKET-HEAD! GOT A LITTLE JOB FOR YA!

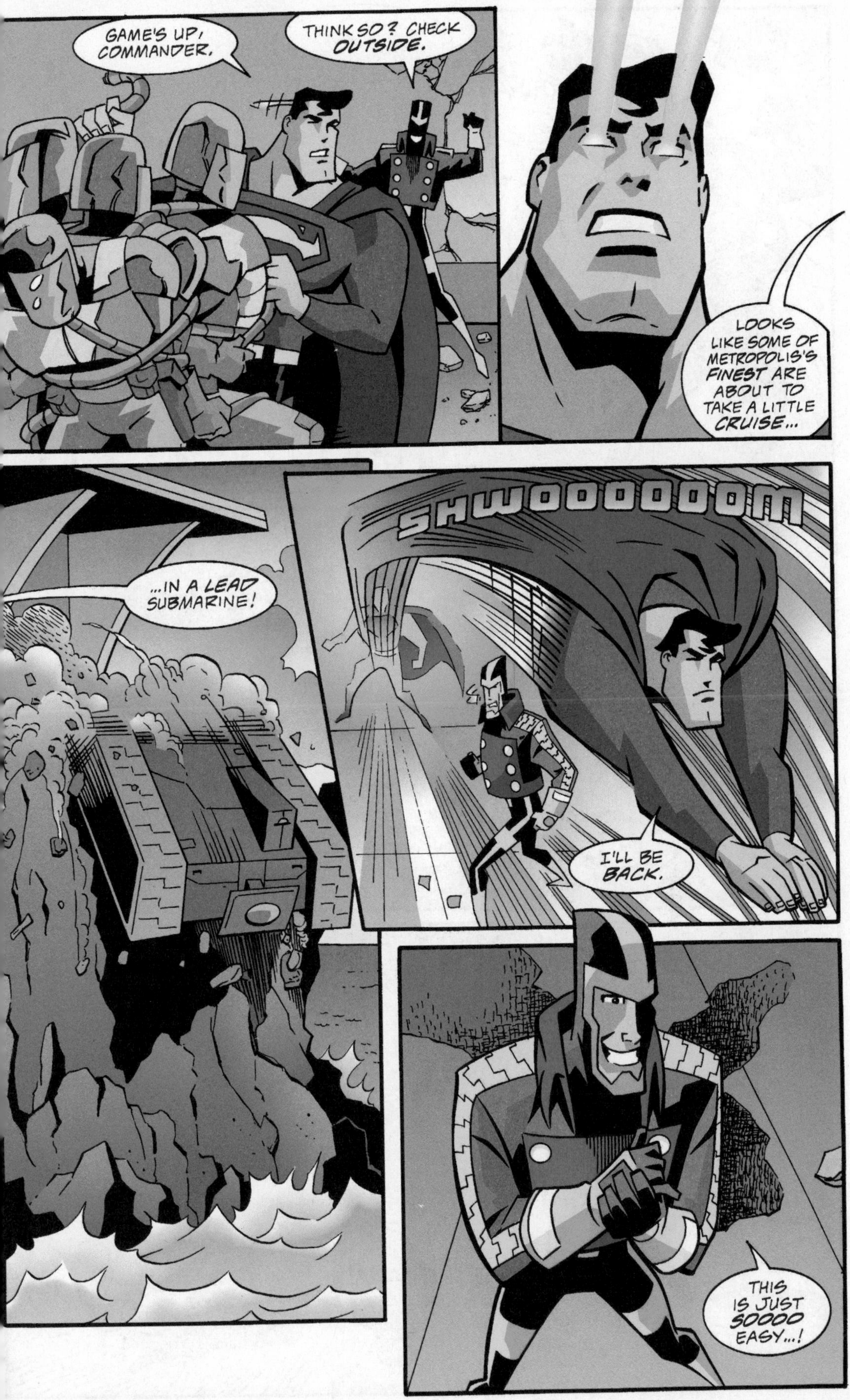
GAME'S UP, COMMANDER.
THINK SO? CHECK OUTSIDE.
LOOKS LIKE SOME OF METROPOLIS'S FINEST ARE ABOUT TO TAKE A LITTLE CRUISE...
...IN A LEAD SUBMARINE!
SHWOOOOOOOM
I'LL BE BACK.
THIS IS JUST SOOOO EASY...!

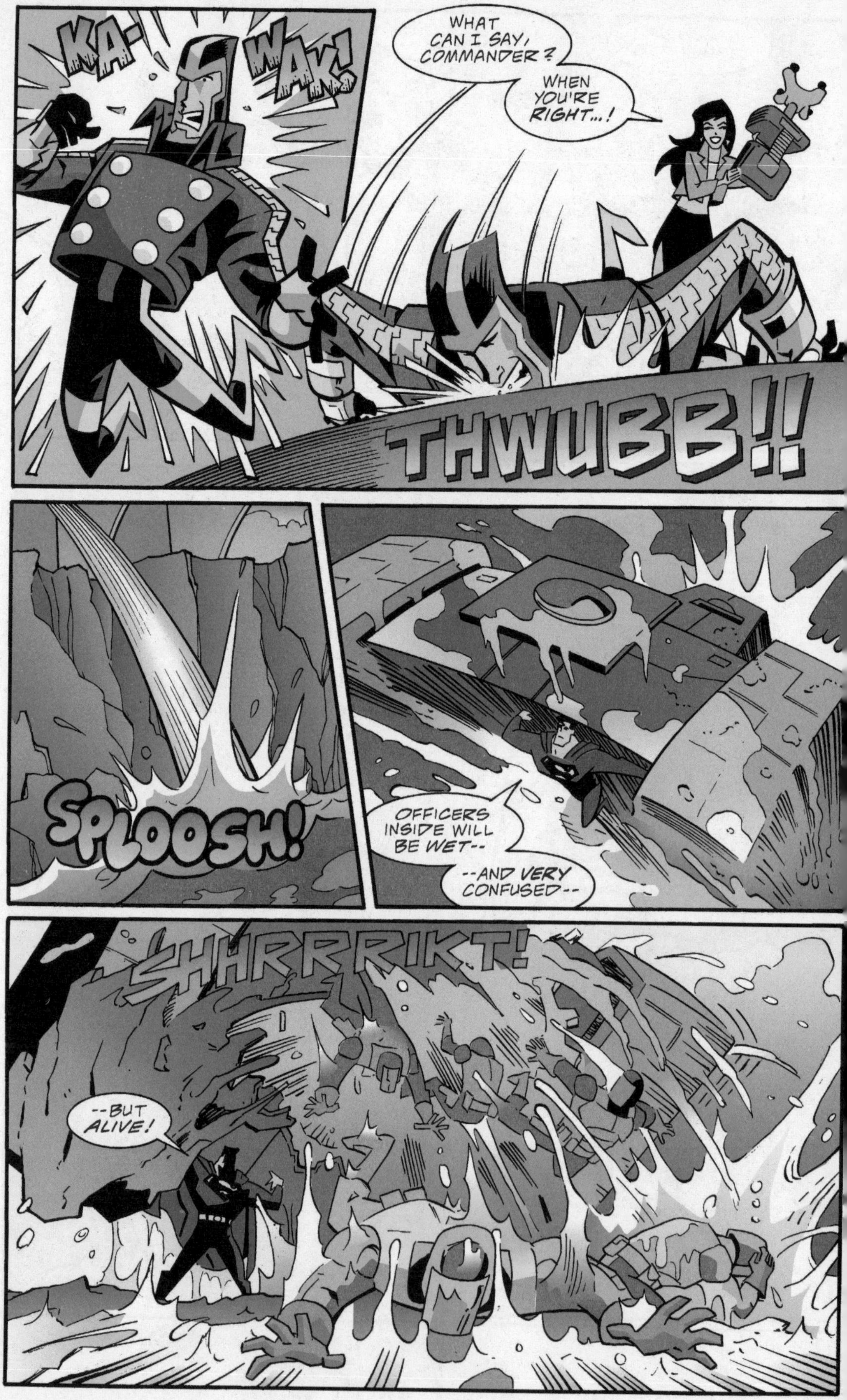
KA-WAK!
WHAT CAN I SAY, COMMANDER?
WHEN YOU'RE RIGHT...!
THWUBB!!
SPLOOSH!
OFFICERS INSIDE WILL BE WET--
--AND VERY CONFUSED--
SHHRRRIKT!
--BUT ALIVE!

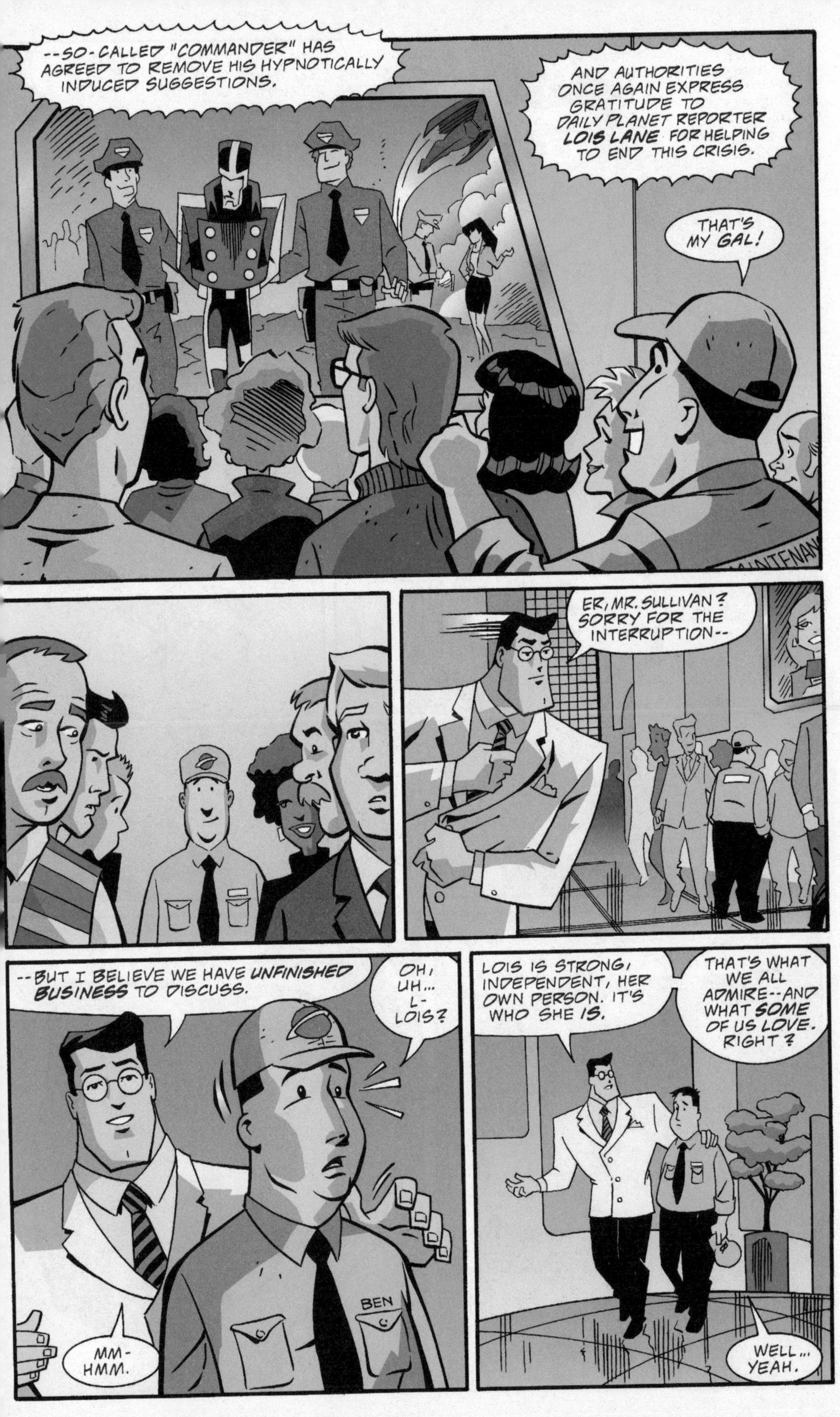
--SO-CALLED "COMMANDER" HAS AGREED TO REMOVE HIS HYPNOTICALLY INDUCED SUGGESTIONS.
AND AUTHORITIES ONCE AGAIN EXPRESS GRATITUDE TO DAILY PLANET REPORTER LOIS LANE FOR HELPING TO END THIS CRISIS.
THAT'S MY GAL!
ER, MR. SULLIVAN? SORRY FOR THE INTERRUPTION--
--BUT I BELIEVE WE HAVE UNFINISHED BUSINESS TO DISCUSS.
OH, UH... L-LOIS?
MM-HMM.
BEN
LOIS IS STRONG, INDEPENDENT, HER OWN PERSON. IT'S WHO SHE IS.
THAT'S WHAT WE ALL ADMIRE--AND WHAT SOME OF US LOVE. RIGHT?
WELL... YEAH.

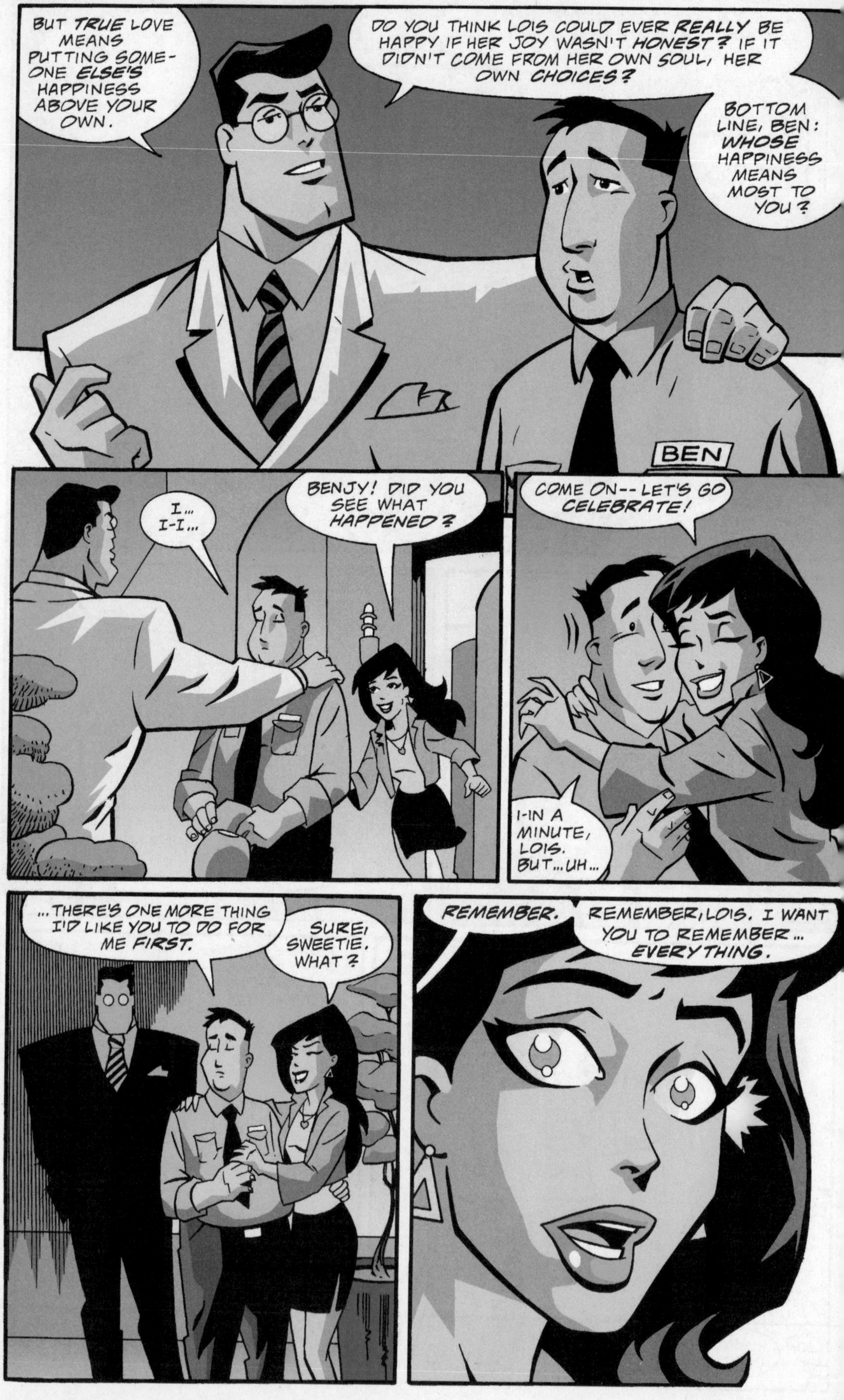
BUT TRUE LOVE MEANS PUTTING SOME-ONE ELSE'S HAPPINESS ABOVE YOUR OWN.
DO YOU THINK LOIS COULD EVER REALLY BE HAPPY IF HER JOY WASN'T HONEST? IF IT DIDN'T COME FROM HER OWN SOUL, HER OWN CHOICES?
BOTTOM LINE, BEN: WHOSE HAPPINESS MEANS MOST TO YOU?
BEN
I... I-I...
BENJY! DID YOU SEE WHAT HAPPENED?
COME ON-- LET'S GO CELEBRATE!
I-IN A MINUTE, LOIS. BUT...UH...
...THERE'S ONE MORE THING I'D LIKE YOU TO DO FOR ME FIRST.
SURE, SWEETIE. WHAT?
REMEMBER.
REMEMBER, LOIS. I WANT YOU TO REMEMBER... EVERYTHING.

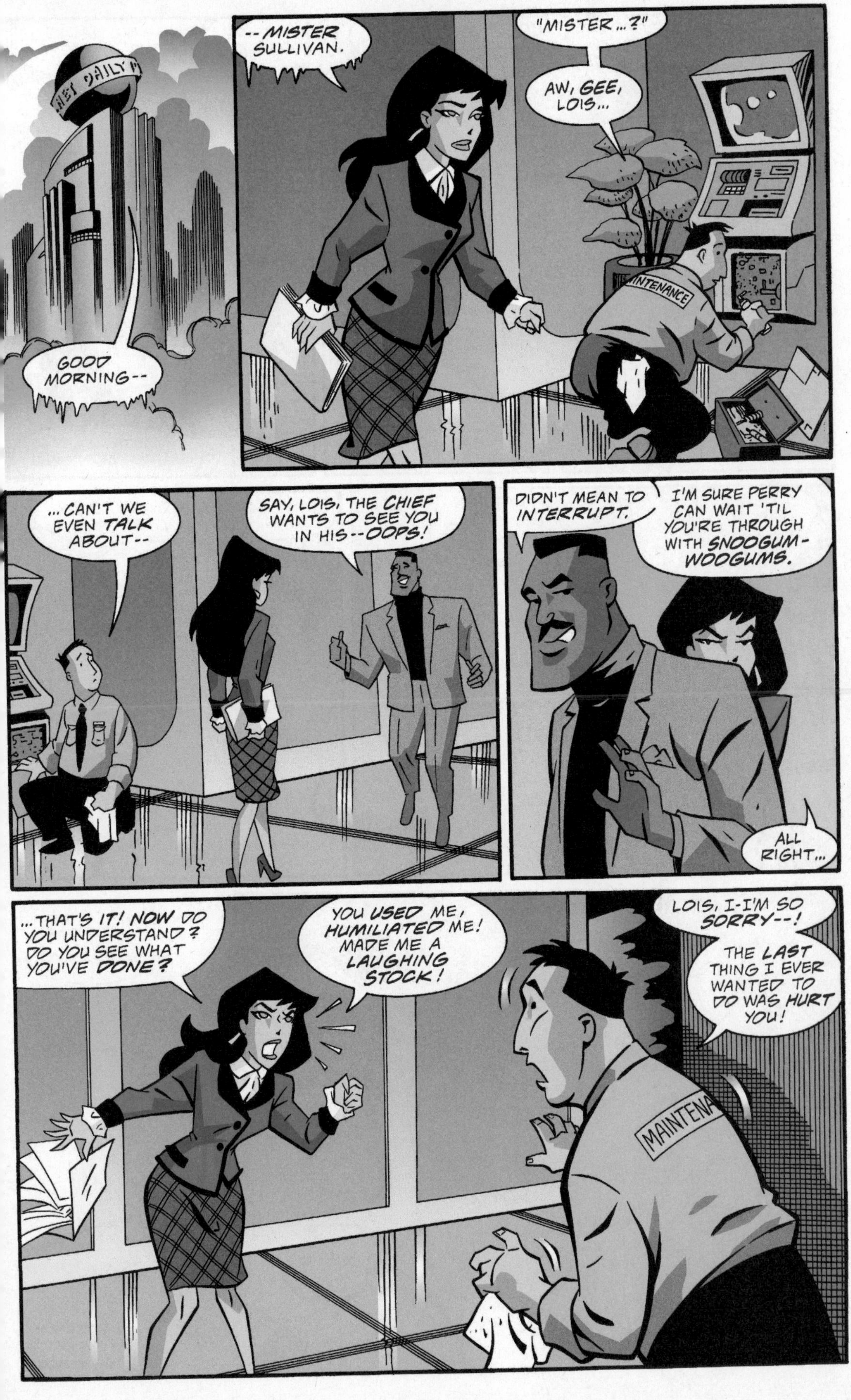
DAILY PLANET
GOOD MORNING--
--MISTER SULLIVAN.
"MISTER...?"
AW, GEE, LOIS...
INTENANCE
...CAN'T WE EVEN TALK ABOUT--
SAY, LOIS, THE CHIEF WANTS TO SEE YOU IN HIS--OOPS!
DIDN'T MEAN TO INTERRUPT.
I'M SURE PERRY CAN WAIT 'TIL YOU'RE THROUGH WITH SNOOGUM-WOOGUMS.
ALL RIGHT...
...THAT'S IT! NOW DO YOU UNDERSTAND? DO YOU SEE WHAT YOU'VE DONE?
YOU USED ME, HUMILIATED ME! MADE ME A LAUGHING STOCK!
LOIS, I-I'M SO SORRY--!
THE LAST THING I EVER WANTED TO DO WAS HURT YOU!
MAINTENA

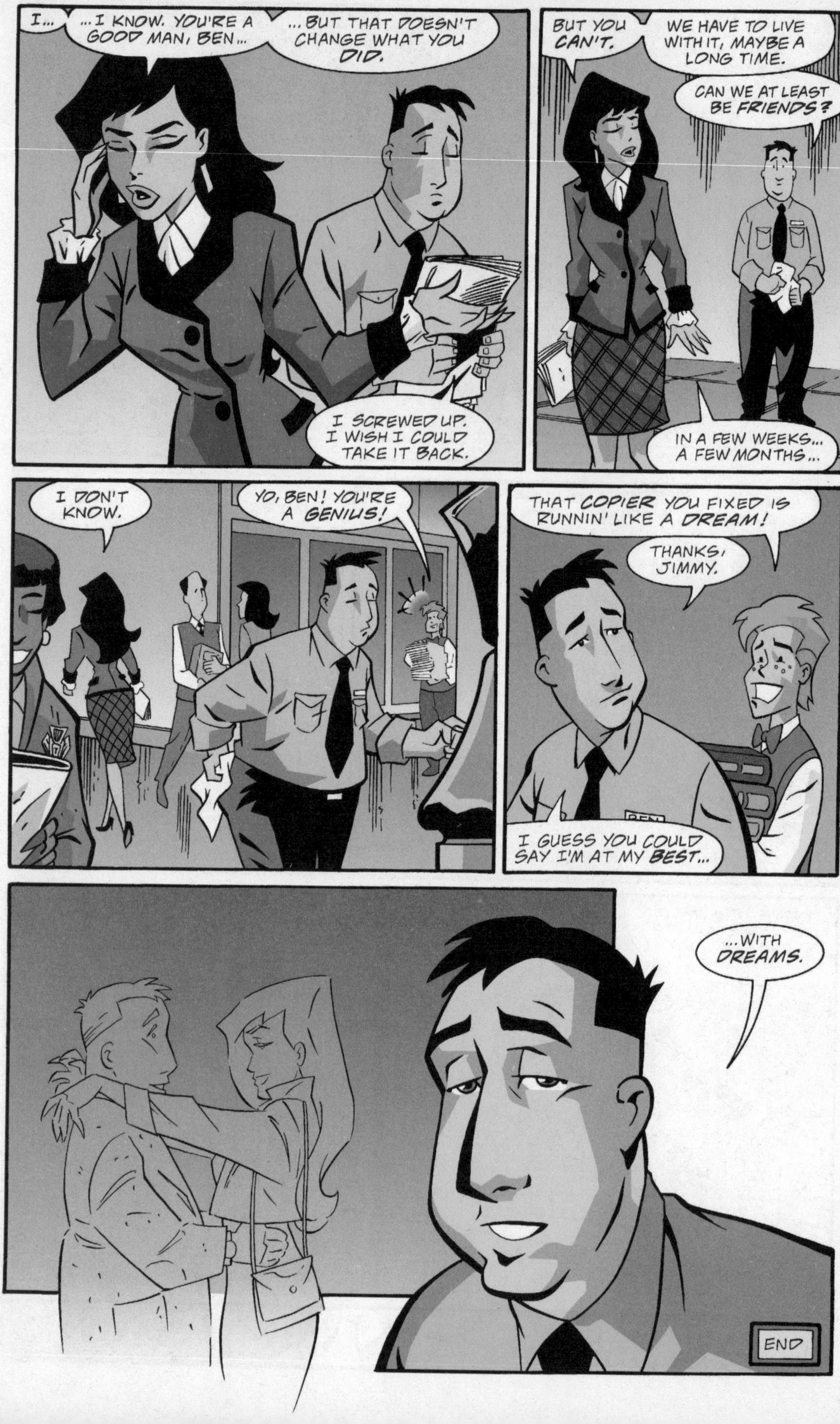
I...
...I KNOW. YOU'RE A GOOD MAN, BEN...
...BUT THAT DOESN'T CHANGE WHAT YOU DID.
I SCREWED UP. I WISH I COULD TAKE IT BACK.
BUT YOU CAN'T.
WE HAVE TO LIVE WITH IT, MAYBE A LONG TIME.
CAN WE AT LEAST BE FRIENDS?
IN A FEW WEEKS... A FEW MONTHS...
I DON'T KNOW.
YO, BEN! YOU'RE A GENIUS!
THAT COPIER YOU FIXED IS RUNNIN' LIKE A DREAM!
THANKS, JIMMY.
I GUESS YOU COULD SAY I'M AT MY BEST...
...WITH DREAMS.
END

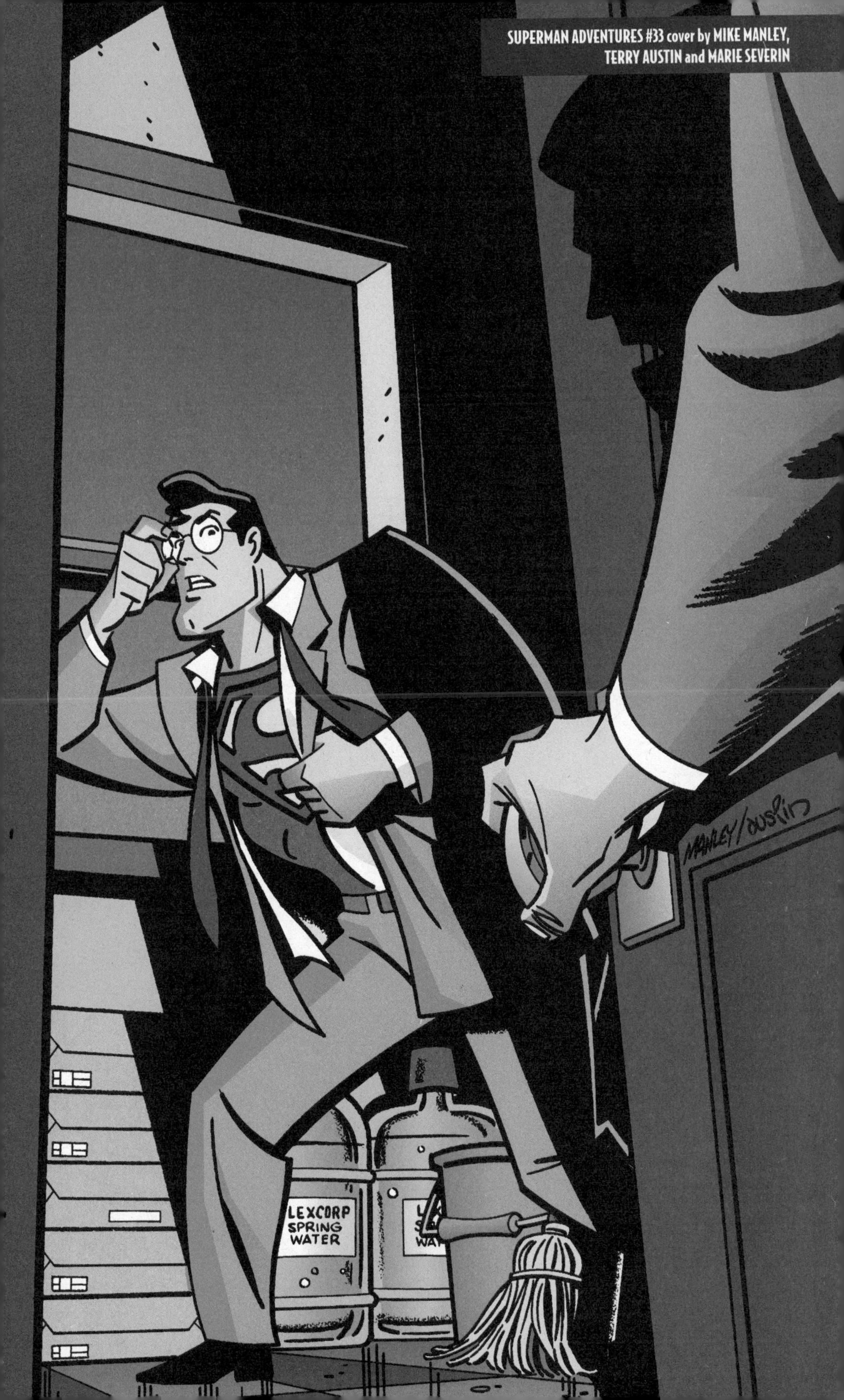
MANLEY/austin
LEXCORP
SPRING
WATER
SUPERMAN ADVENTURES #33 cover by MIKE MANLEY,
TERRY AUSTIN and MARIE SEVERIN

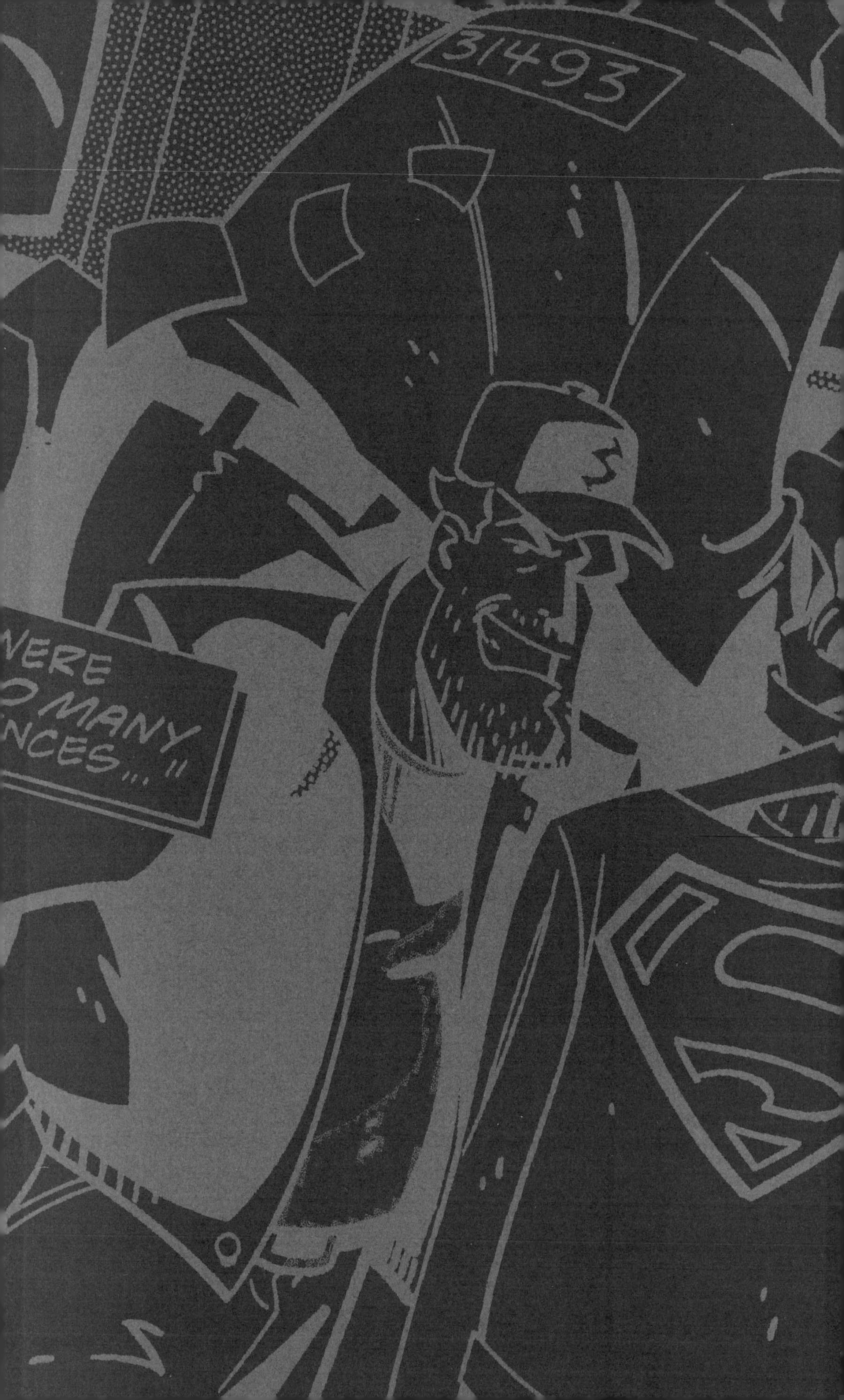
31493
NERE
O MANY
NCES... !!

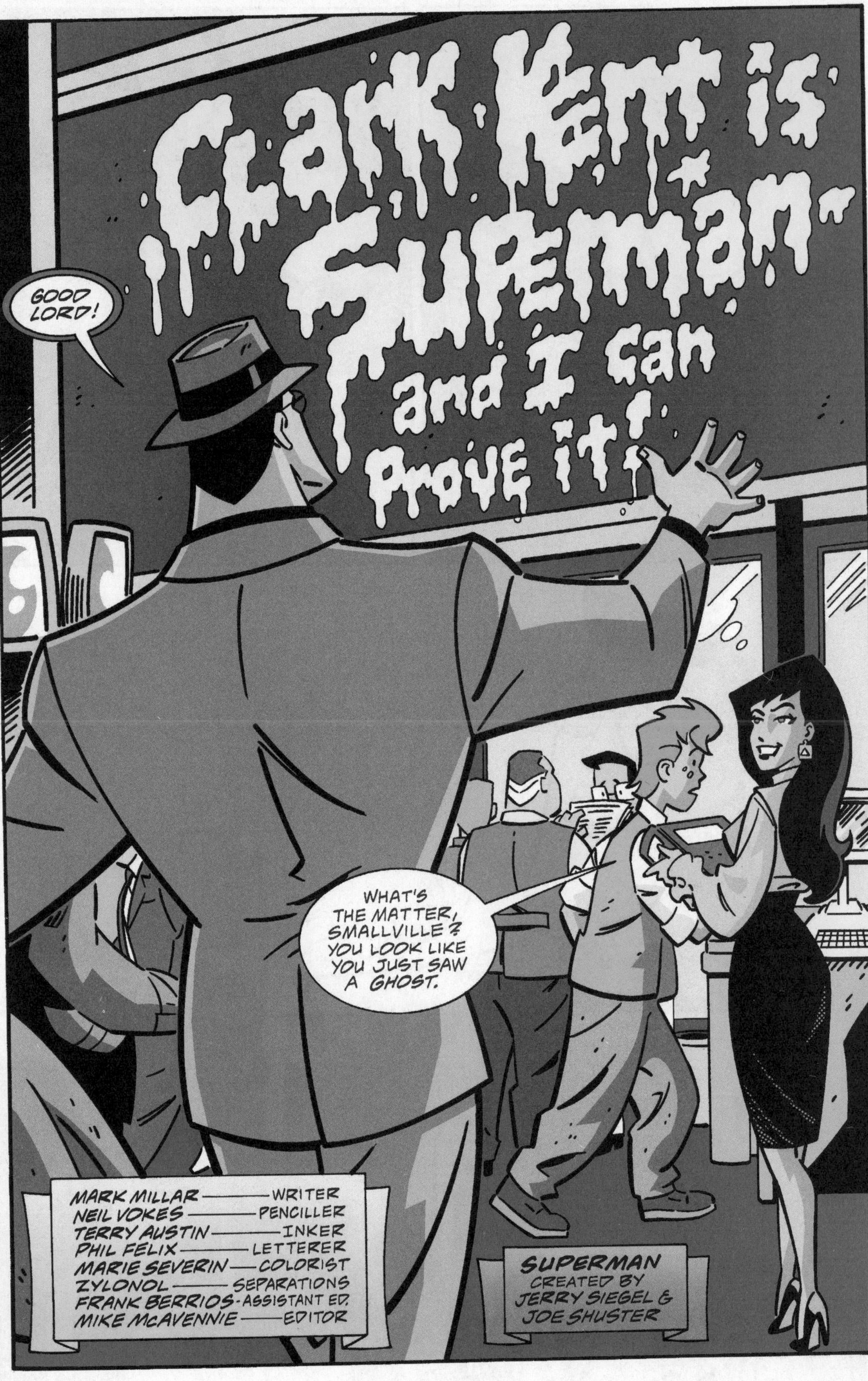

"CLARK KENT IS SUPERMAN" AND I CAN PROVE IT!
GOOD LORD!
WHAT'S THE MATTER, SMALLVILLE? YOU LOOK LIKE YOU JUST SAW A GHOST.
MARK MILLAR—WRITER
NEIL VOKES—PENCILLER
TERRY AUSTIN—INKER
PHIL FELIX—LETTERER
MARIE SEVERIN—COLORIST
ZYLONOL—SEPARATIONS
FRANK BERRIOS-ASSISTANT ED.
MIKE McAVENNIE—EDITOR
SUPERMAN CREATED BY JERRY SIEGEL & JOE SHUSTER

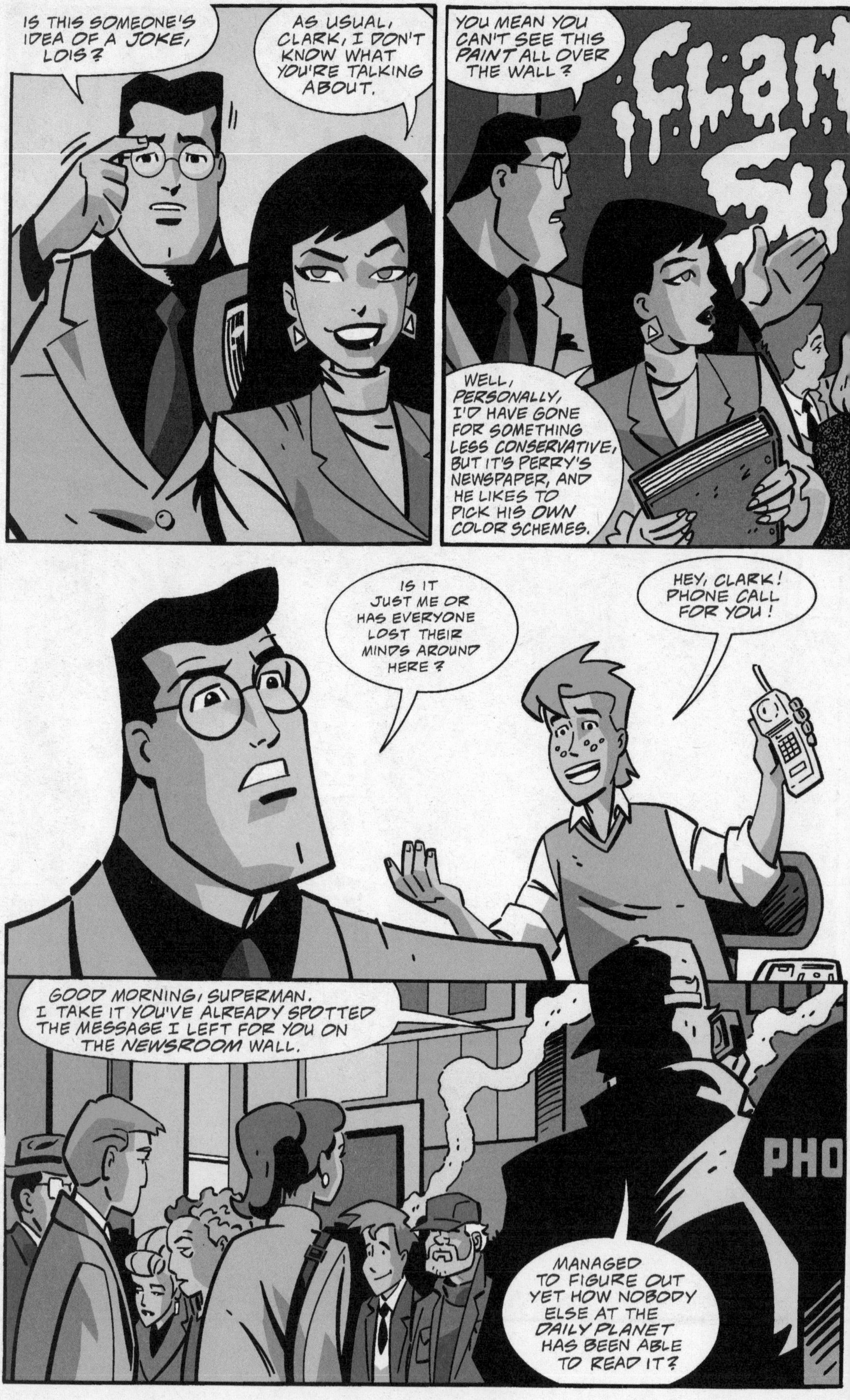
IS THIS SOMEONE'S IDEA OF A JOKE, LOIS?
AS USUAL, CLARK, I DON'T KNOW WHAT YOU'RE TALKING ABOUT.
YOU MEAN YOU CAN'T SEE THIS PAINT ALL OVER THE WALL?
WELL, PERSONALLY, I'D HAVE GONE FOR SOMETHING LESS CONSERVATIVE, BUT IT'S PERRY'S NEWSPAPER, AND HE LIKES TO PICK HIS OWN COLOR SCHEMES.
IS IT JUST ME OR HAS EVERYONE LOST THEIR MINDS AROUND HERE?
HEY, CLARK! PHONE CALL FOR YOU!
GOOD MORNING, SUPERMAN. I TAKE IT YOU'VE ALREADY SPOTTED THE MESSAGE I LEFT FOR YOU ON THE NEWSROOM WALL.
MANAGED TO FIGURE OUT YET HOW NOBODY ELSE AT THE DAILY PLANET HAS BEEN ABLE TO READ IT?
PHO

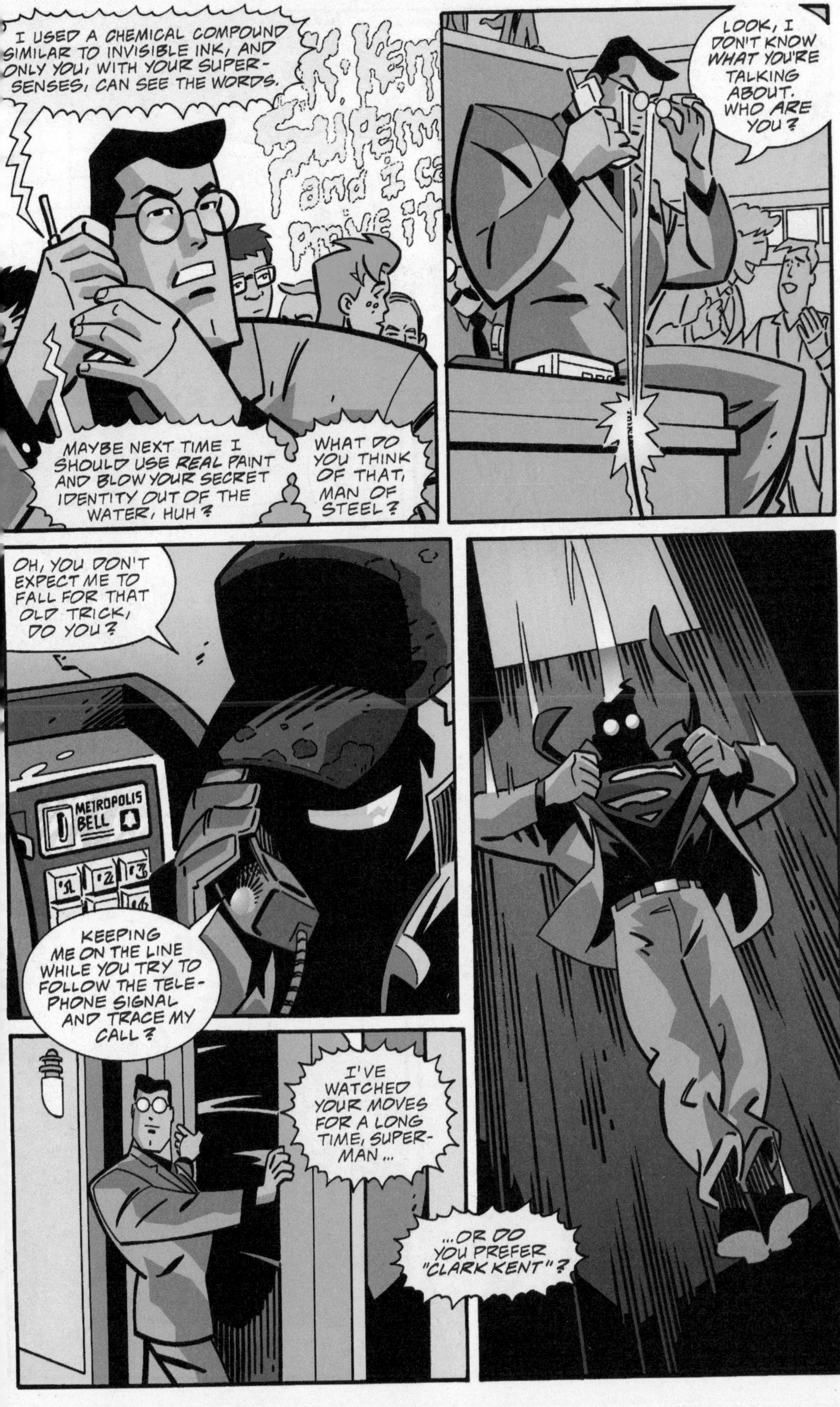
I USED A CHEMICAL COMPOUND SIMILAR TO INVISIBLE INK, AND ONLY YOU, WITH YOUR SUPER-SENSES, CAN SEE THE WORDS.
MAYBE NEXT TIME I SHOULD USE REAL PAINT AND BLOW YOUR SECRET IDENTITY OUT OF THE WATER, HUH?
WHAT DO YOU THINK OF THAT, MAN OF STEEL?
LOOK, I DON'T KNOW WHAT YOU'RE TALKING ABOUT. WHO ARE YOU?
OH, YOU DON'T EXPECT ME TO FALL FOR THAT OLD TRICK, DO YOU?
METROPOLIS BELL
KEEPING ME ON THE LINE WHILE YOU TRY TO FOLLOW THE TELE-PHONE SIGNAL AND TRACE MY CALL?
I'VE WATCHED YOUR MOVES FOR A LONG TIME, SUPER-MAN...
...OR DO YOU PREFER "CLARK KENT"?

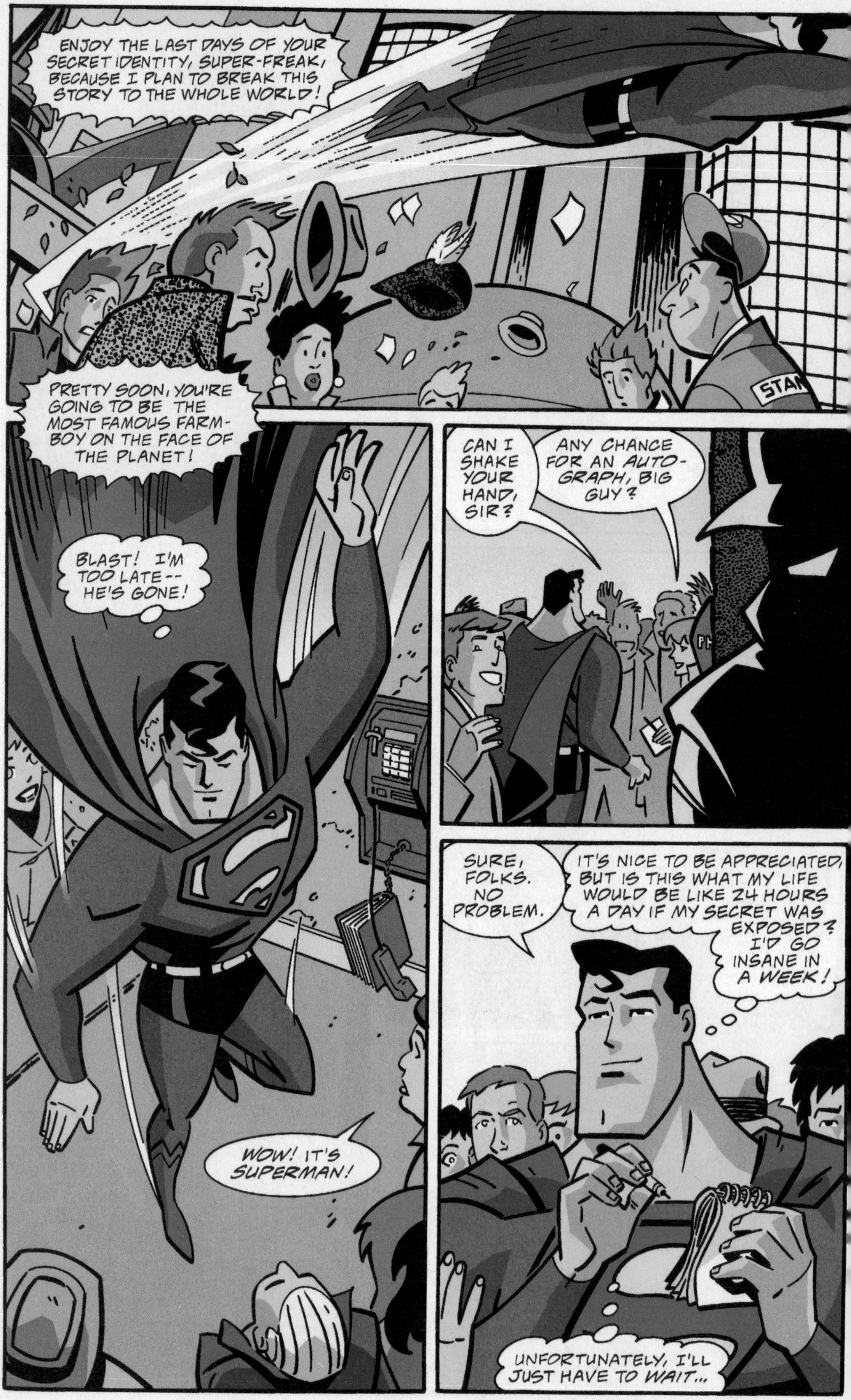
ENJOY THE LAST DAYS OF YOUR SECRET IDENTITY, SUPER-FREAK, BECAUSE I PLAN TO BREAK THIS STORY TO THE WHOLE WORLD!
PRETTY SOON, YOU'RE GOING TO BE THE MOST FAMOUS FARM-BOY ON THE FACE OF THE PLANET!
BLAST! I'M TOO LATE-- HE'S GONE!
WOW! IT'S SUPERMAN!
CAN I SHAKE YOUR HAND, SIR?
ANY CHANCE FOR AN AUTO-GRAPH, BIG GUY?
SURE, FOLKS. NO PROBLEM.
IT'S NICE TO BE APPRECIATED, BUT IS THIS WHAT MY LIFE WOULD BE LIKE 24 HOURS A DAY IF MY SECRET WAS EXPOSED? I'D GO INSANE IN A WEEK!
UNFORTUNATELY, I'LL JUST HAVE TO WAIT...

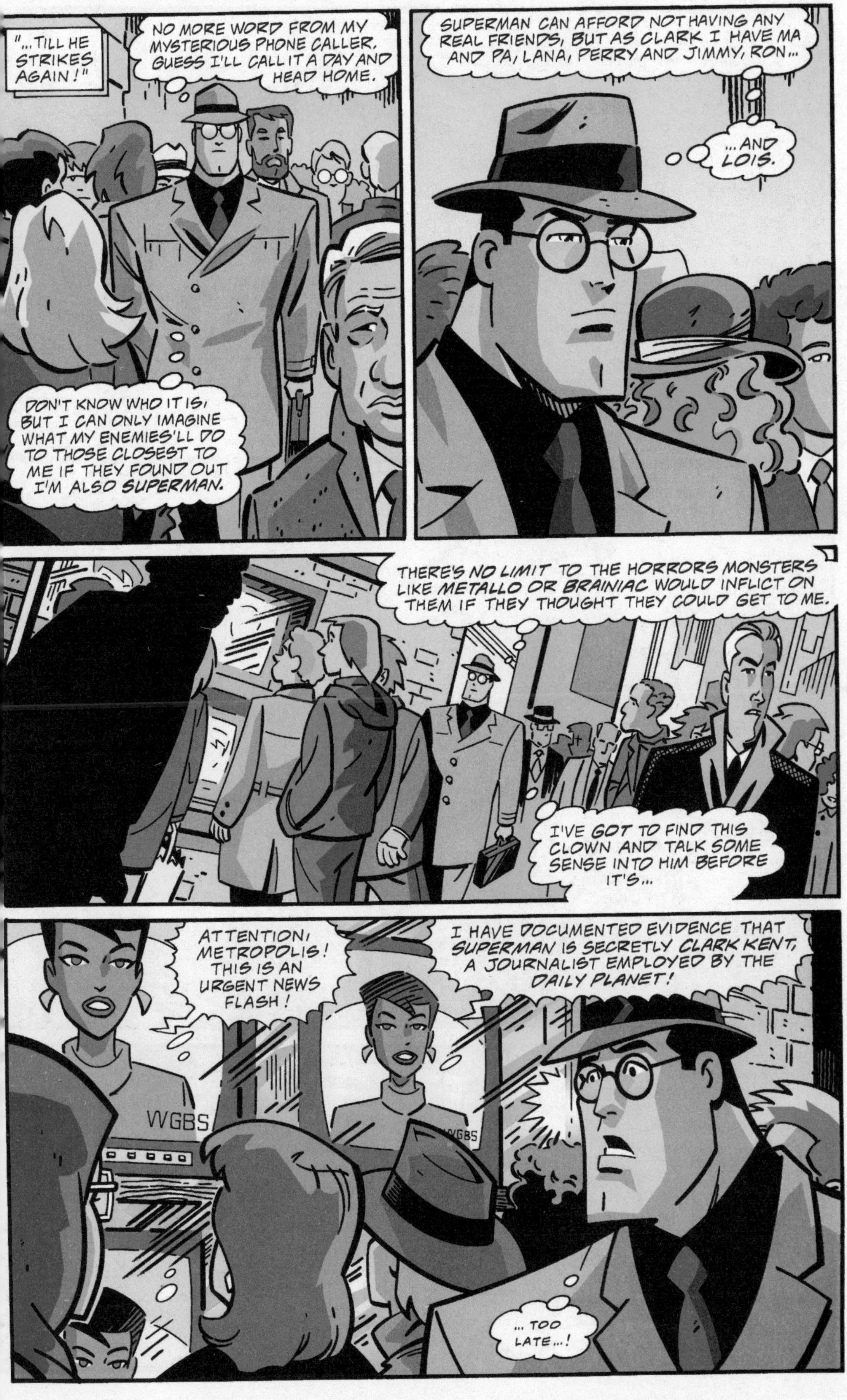

"...TILL HE STRIKES AGAIN!"
NO MORE WORD FROM MY MYSTERIOUS PHONE CALLER. GUESS I'LL CALL IT A DAY AND HEAD HOME.
DON'T KNOW WHO IT IS, BUT I CAN ONLY IMAGINE WHAT MY ENEMIES'LL DO TO THOSE CLOSEST TO ME IF THEY FOUND OUT I'M ALSO SUPERMAN.
SUPERMAN CAN AFFORD NOT HAVING ANY REAL FRIENDS, BUT AS CLARK I HAVE MA AND PA, LANA, PERRY AND JIMMY, RON...
...AND LOIS.
THERE'S NO LIMIT TO THE HORRORS MONSTERS LIKE METALLO OR BRAINIAC WOULD INFLICT ON THEM IF THEY THOUGHT THEY COULD GET TO ME.
I'VE GOT TO FIND THIS CLOWN AND TALK SOME SENSE INTO HIM BEFORE IT'S...
ATTENTION, METROPOLIS! THIS IS AN URGENT NEWS FLASH!
I HAVE DOCUMENTED EVIDENCE THAT SUPERMAN IS SECRETLY CLARK KENT, A JOURNALIST EMPLOYED BY THE DAILY PLANET!
WGBS
WGBS
...TOO LATE...!

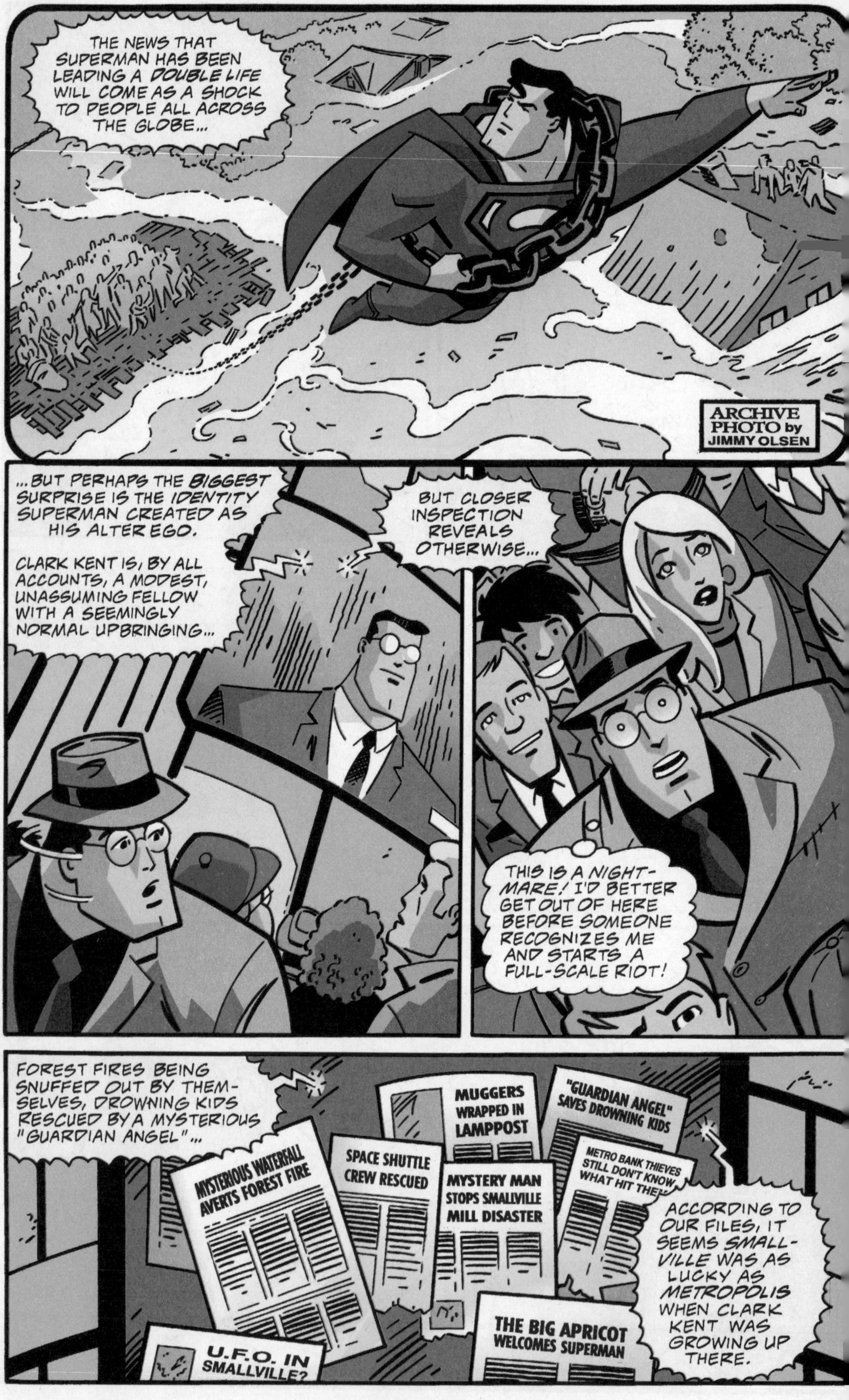
THE NEWS THAT SUPERMAN HAS BEEN LEADING A DOUBLE LIFE WILL COME AS A SHOCK TO PEOPLE ALL ACROSS THE GLOBE...
ARCHIVE PHOTO by JIMMY OLSEN
...BUT PERHAPS THE BIGGEST SURPRISE IS THE IDENTITY SUPERMAN CREATED AS HIS ALTER EGO.
CLARK KENT IS, BY ALL ACCOUNTS, A MODEST, UNASSUMING FELLOW WITH A SEEMINGLY NORMAL UPBRINGING...
BUT CLOSER INSPECTION REVEALS OTHERWISE...
THIS IS A NIGHT-MARE! I'D BETTER GET OUT OF HERE BEFORE SOMEONE RECOGNIZES ME AND STARTS A FULL-SCALE RIOT!
FOREST FIRES BEING SNUFFED OUT BY THEM-SELVES, DROWNING KIDS RESCUED BY A MYSTERIOUS "GUARDIAN ANGEL"...
MUGGERS WRAPPED IN LAMPPOST
"GUARDIAN ANGEL" SAVES DROWNING KIDS
MYSTERIOUS WATERFALL AVERTS FOREST FIRE
SPACE SHUTTLE CREW RESCUED
MYSTERY MAN STOPS SMALLVILLE MILL DISASTER
METRO BANK THIEVES STILL DON'T KNOW WHAT HIT THEM
U.F.O. IN SMALLVILLE?
THE BIG APRICOT WELCOMES SUPERMAN
ACCORDING TO OUR FILES, IT SEEMS SMALL-VILLE WAS AS LUCKY AS METROPOLIS WHEN CLARK KENT WAS GROWING UP THERE.

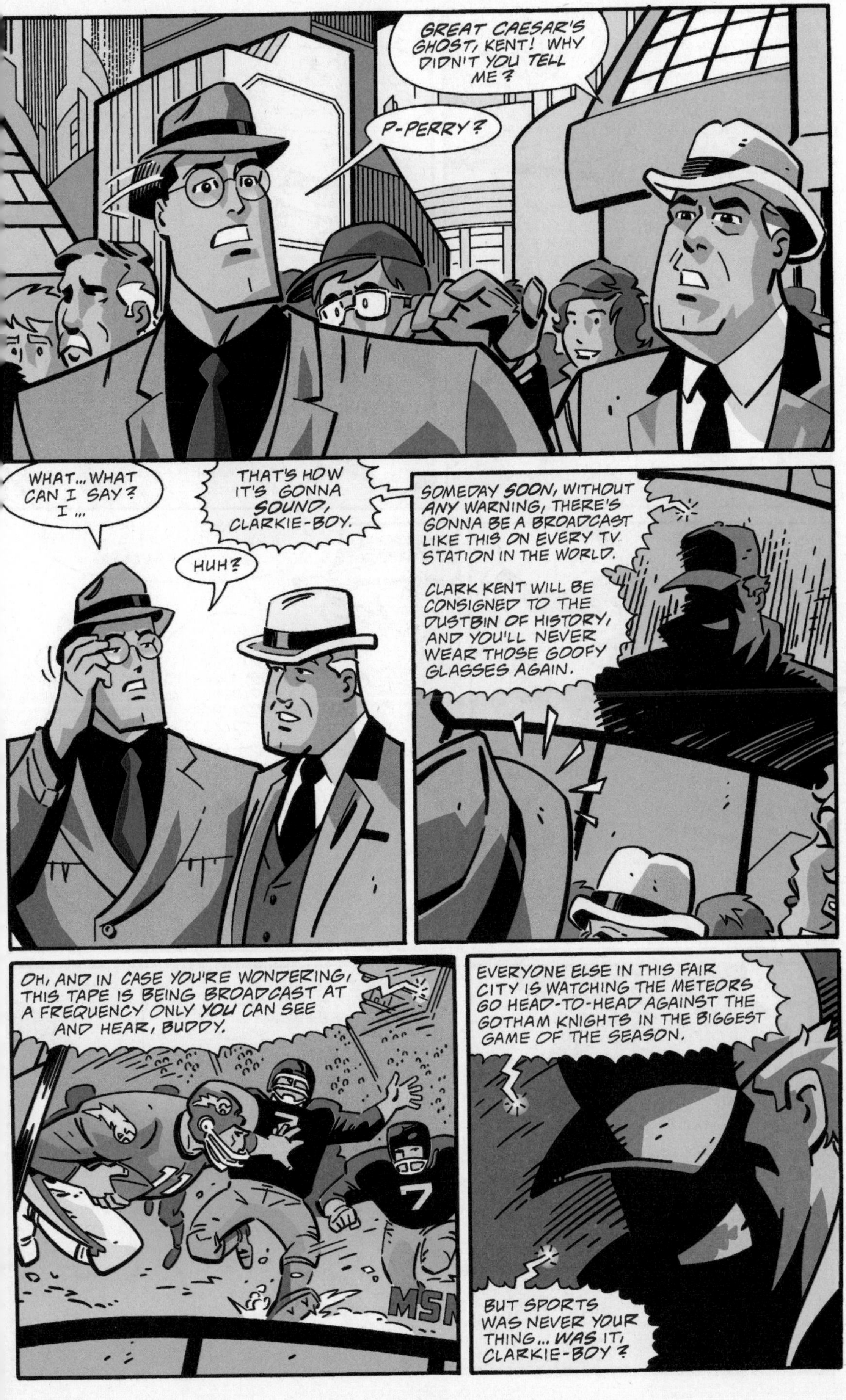
GREAT CAESAR'S GHOST, KENT! WHY DIDN'T YOU TELL ME?
P-PERRY?
WHAT... WHAT CAN I SAY? I...
THAT'S HOW IT'S GONNA SOUND, CLARKIE-BOY.
HUH?
SOMEDAY SOON, WITHOUT ANY WARNING, THERE'S GONNA BE A BROADCAST LIKE THIS ON EVERY TV STATION IN THE WORLD.
CLARK KENT WILL BE CONSIGNED TO THE DUSTBIN OF HISTORY, AND YOU'LL NEVER WEAR THOSE GOOFY GLASSES AGAIN.
OH, AND IN CASE YOU'RE WONDERING, THIS TAPE IS BEING BROADCAST AT A FREQUENCY ONLY YOU CAN SEE AND HEAR, BUDDY.
EVERYONE ELSE IN THIS FAIR CITY IS WATCHING THE METEORS GO HEAD-TO-HEAD AGAINST THE GOTHAM KNIGHTS IN THE BIGGEST GAME OF THE SEASON.
BUT SPORTS WAS NEVER YOUR THING... WAS IT, CLARKIE-BOY?

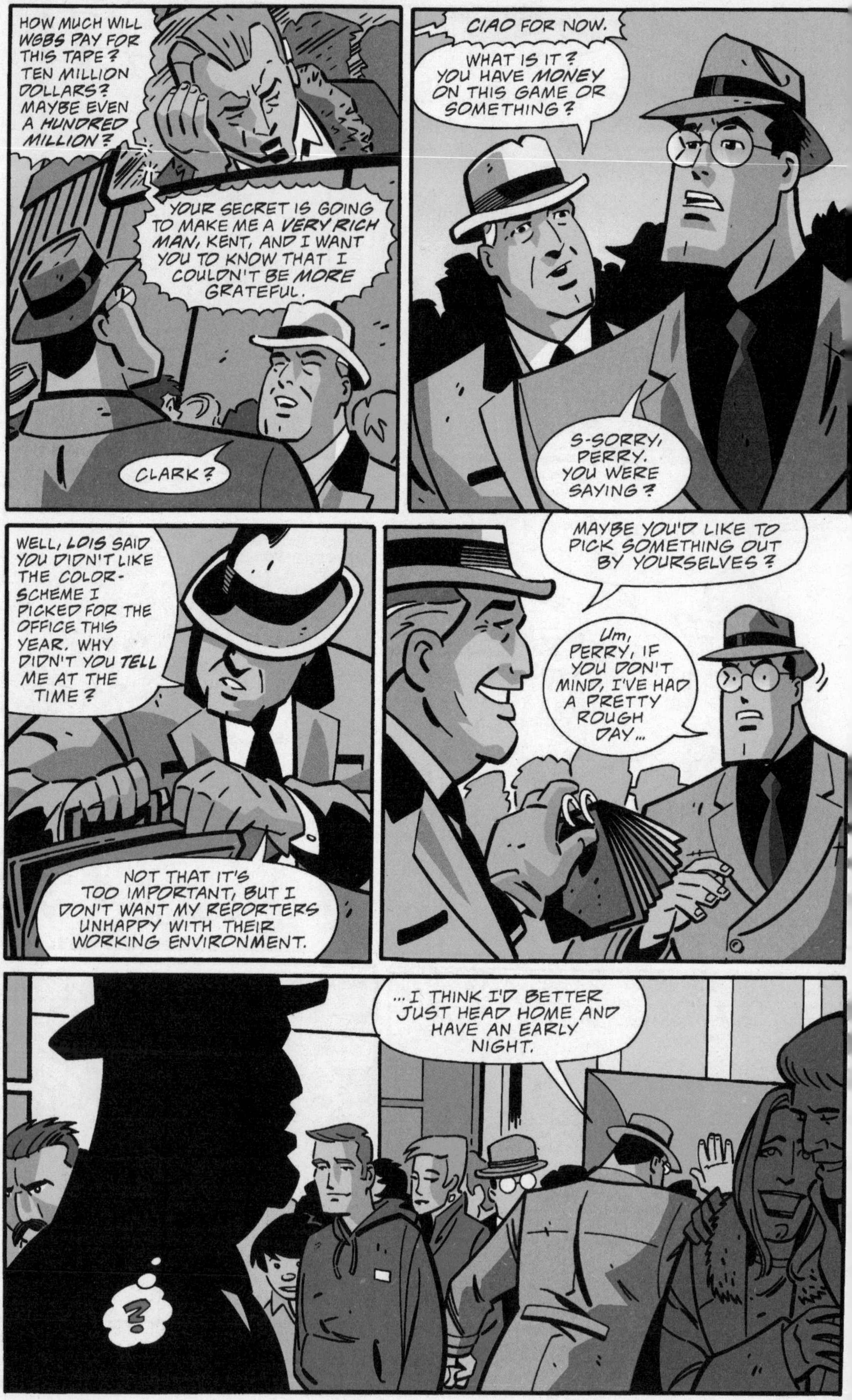
HOW MUCH WILL WGBS PAY FOR THIS TAPE? TEN MILLION DOLLARS? MAYBE EVEN A HUNDRED MILLION?
YOUR SECRET IS GOING TO MAKE ME A VERY RICH MAN, KENT, AND I WANT YOU TO KNOW THAT I COULDN'T BE MORE GRATEFUL.
CLARK?
CIAO FOR NOW.
WHAT IS IT? YOU HAVE MONEY ON THIS GAME OR SOMETHING?
S-SORRY, PERRY. YOU WERE SAYING?
WELL, LOIS SAID YOU DIDN'T LIKE THE COLOR-SCHEME I PICKED FOR THE OFFICE THIS YEAR. WHY DIDN'T YOU TELL ME AT THE TIME?
NOT THAT IT'S TOO IMPORTANT, BUT I DON'T WANT MY REPORTERS UNHAPPY WITH THEIR WORKING ENVIRONMENT.
MAYBE YOU'D LIKE TO PICK SOMETHING OUT BY YOURSELVES?
Um, PERRY, IF YOU DON'T MIND, I'VE HAD A PRETTY ROUGH DAY...
...I THINK I'D BETTER JUST HEAD HOME AND HAVE AN EARLY NIGHT.
?

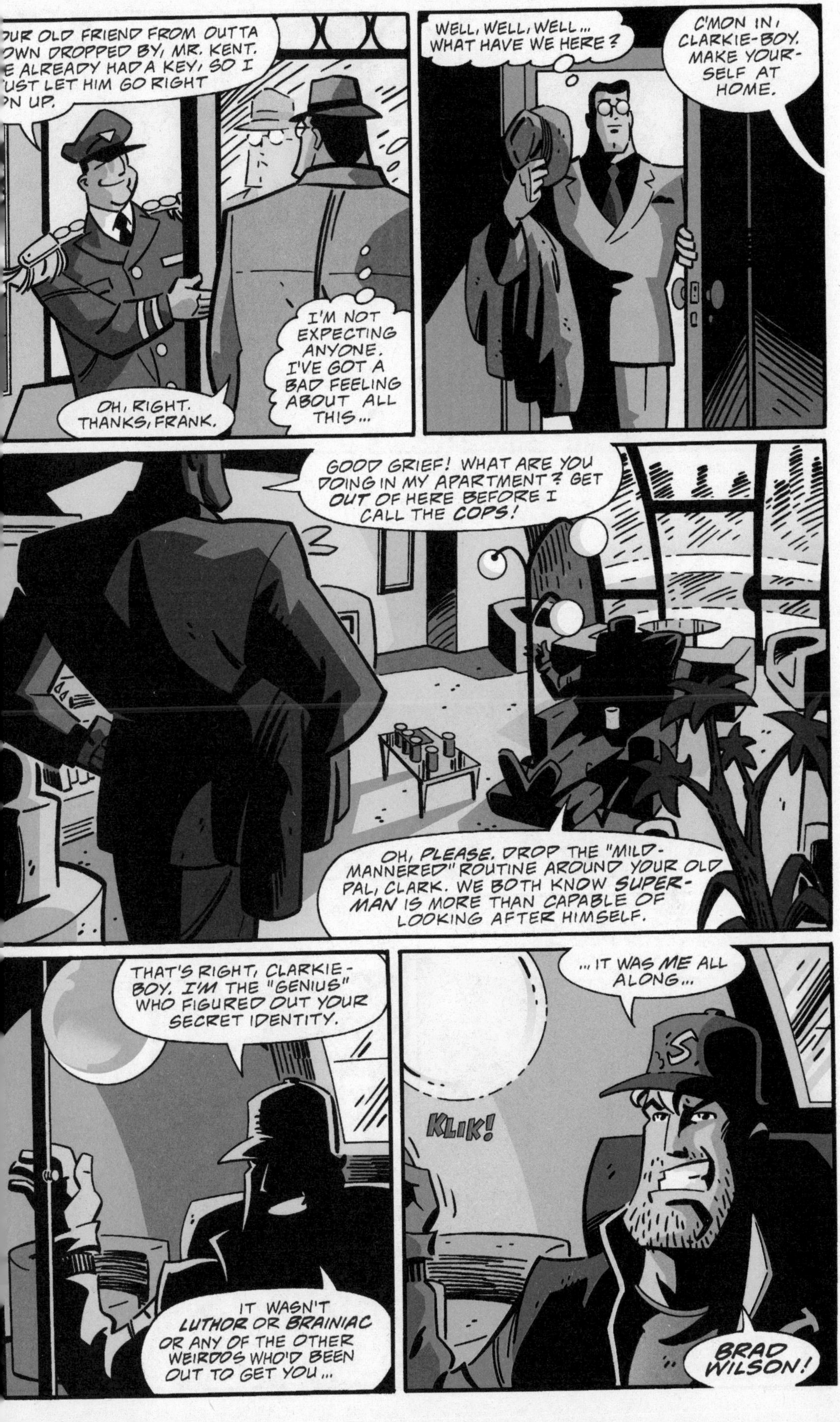
OUR OLD FRIEND FROM OUTTA TOWN DROPPED BY, MR. KENT. HE ALREADY HAD A KEY, SO I JUST LET HIM GO RIGHT ON UP.
OH, RIGHT. THANKS, FRANK.
I'M NOT EXPECTING ANYONE. I'VE GOT A BAD FEELING ABOUT ALL THIS...
WELL, WELL, WELL... WHAT HAVE WE HERE?
C'MON IN, CLARKIE-BOY. MAKE YOURSELF AT HOME.
GOOD GRIEF! WHAT ARE YOU DOING IN MY APARTMENT? GET OUT OF HERE BEFORE I CALL THE COPS!
OH, PLEASE. DROP THE "MILD-MANNERED" ROUTINE AROUND YOUR OLD PAL, CLARK. WE BOTH KNOW SUPERMAN IS MORE THAN CAPABLE OF LOOKING AFTER HIMSELF.
THAT'S RIGHT, CLARKIE-BOY. I'M THE "GENIUS" WHO FIGURED OUT YOUR SECRET IDENTITY.
IT WASN'T LUTHOR OR BRAINIAC OR ANY OF THE OTHER WEIRDOS WHO'D BEEN OUT TO GET YOU...
...IT WAS ME ALL ALONG...
KLIK!
BRAD WILSON!

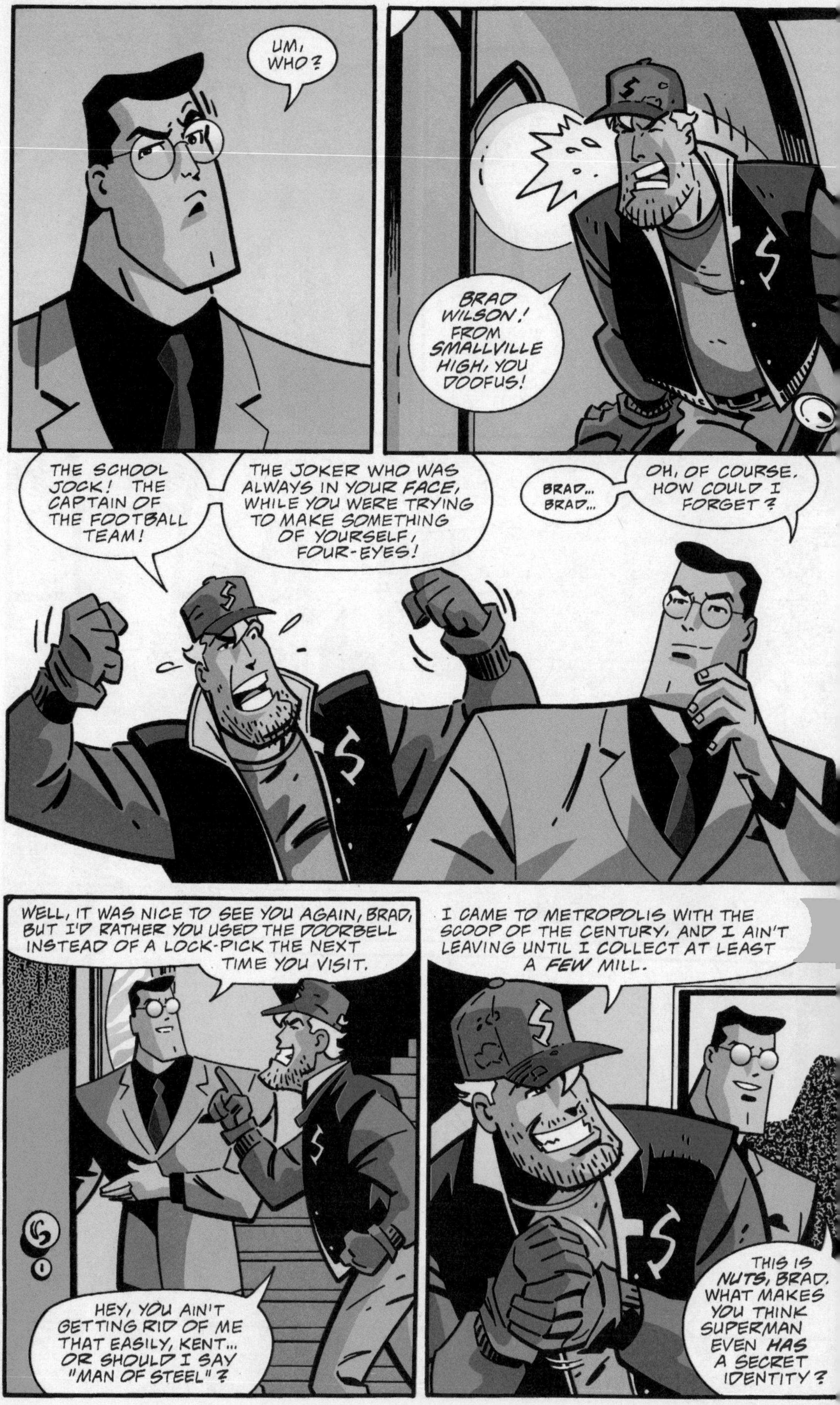
UM, WHO?
BRAD WILSON! FROM SMALLVILLE HIGH, YOU DOOFUS!
THE SCHOOL JOCK! THE CAPTAIN OF THE FOOTBALL TEAM!
THE JOKER WHO WAS ALWAYS IN YOUR FACE, WHILE YOU WERE TRYING TO MAKE SOMETHING OF YOURSELF, FOUR-EYES!
BRAD... BRAD...
OH, OF COURSE. HOW COULD I FORGET?
WELL, IT WAS NICE TO SEE YOU AGAIN, BRAD, BUT I'D RATHER YOU USED THE DOORBELL INSTEAD OF A LOCK-PICK THE NEXT TIME YOU VISIT.
HEY, YOU AIN'T GETTING RID OF ME THAT EASILY, KENT... OR SHOULD I SAY "MAN OF STEEL"?
I CAME TO METROPOLIS WITH THE SCOOP OF THE CENTURY, AND I AIN'T LEAVING UNTIL I COLLECT AT LEAST A FEW MILL.
THIS IS NUTS, BRAD. WHAT MAKES YOU THINK SUPERMAN EVEN HAS A SECRET IDENTITY?

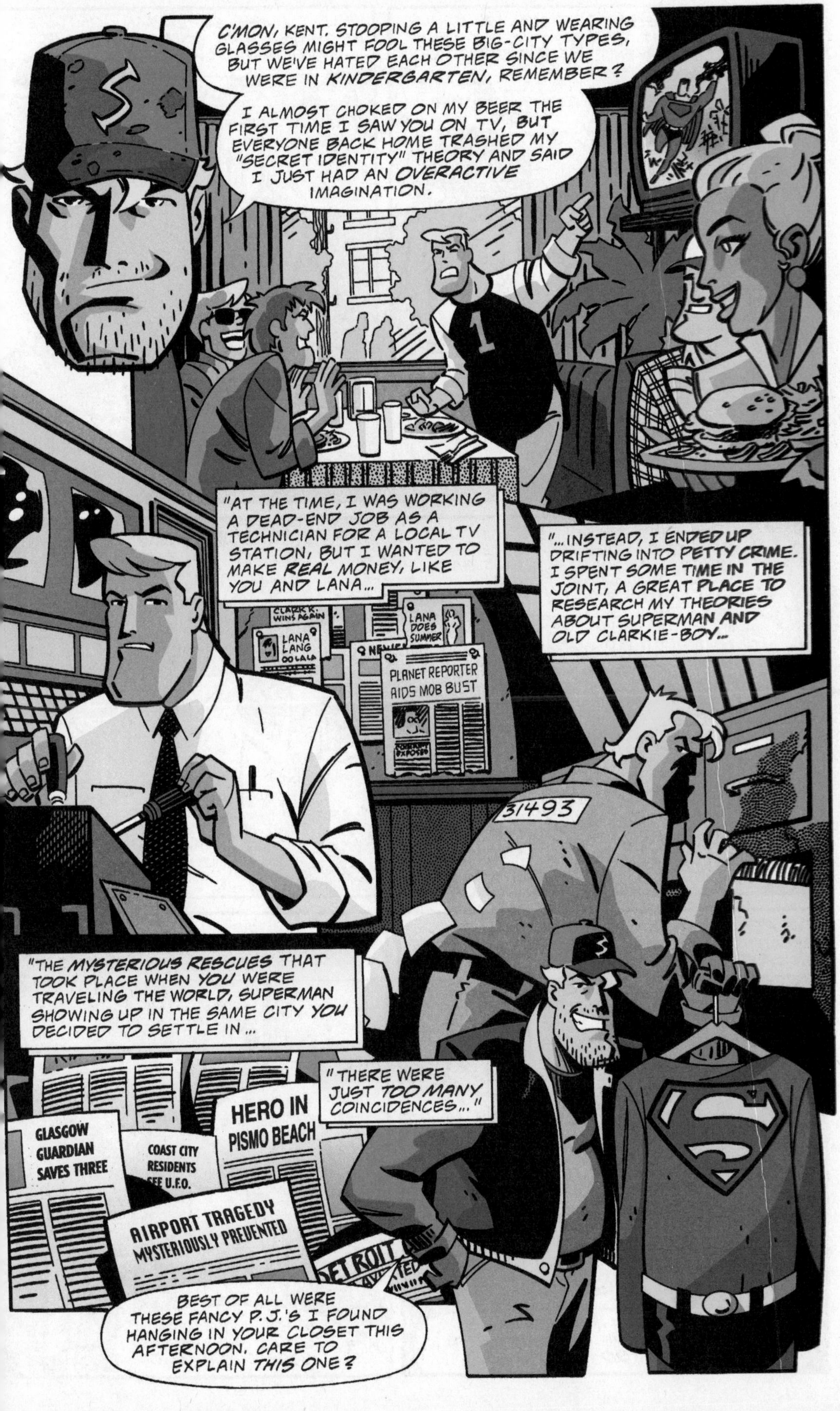

C'MON, KENT. STOOPING A LITTLE AND WEARING GLASSES MIGHT FOOL THESE BIG-CITY TYPES, BUT WE'VE HATED EACH OTHER SINCE WE WERE IN KINDERGARTEN, REMEMBER?
I ALMOST CHOKED ON MY BEER THE FIRST TIME I SAW YOU ON TV, BUT EVERYONE BACK HOME TRASHED MY "SECRET IDENTITY" THEORY AND SAID I JUST HAD AN OVERACTIVE IMAGINATION.
"AT THE TIME, I WAS WORKING A DEAD-END JOB AS A TECHNICIAN FOR A LOCAL TV STATION, BUT I WANTED TO MAKE REAL MONEY, LIKE YOU AND LANA...
CLARK K. WINS AGAIN
LANA LANG OO LA LA
LANA DOES SUMMER
PLANET REPORTER AIDS MOB BUST
"...INSTEAD, I ENDED UP DRIFTING INTO PETTY CRIME. I SPENT SOME TIME IN THE JOINT, A GREAT PLACE TO RESEARCH MY THEORIES ABOUT SUPERMAN AND OLD CLARKIE-BOY...
31493
"THE MYSTERIOUS RESCUES THAT TOOK PLACE WHEN YOU WERE TRAVELING THE WORLD, SUPERMAN SHOWING UP IN THE SAME CITY YOU DECIDED TO SETTLE IN...
"THERE WERE JUST TOO MANY COINCIDENCES..."
HERO IN PISMO BEACH
GLASGOW GUARDIAN SAVES THREE
COAST CITY RESIDENTS SEE U.F.O.
AIRPORT TRAGEDY MYSTERIOUSLY PREVENTED
DETROIT
BEST OF ALL WERE THESE FANCY P. J.'S I FOUND HANGING IN YOUR CLOSET THIS AFTERNOON. CARE TO EXPLAIN THIS ONE?

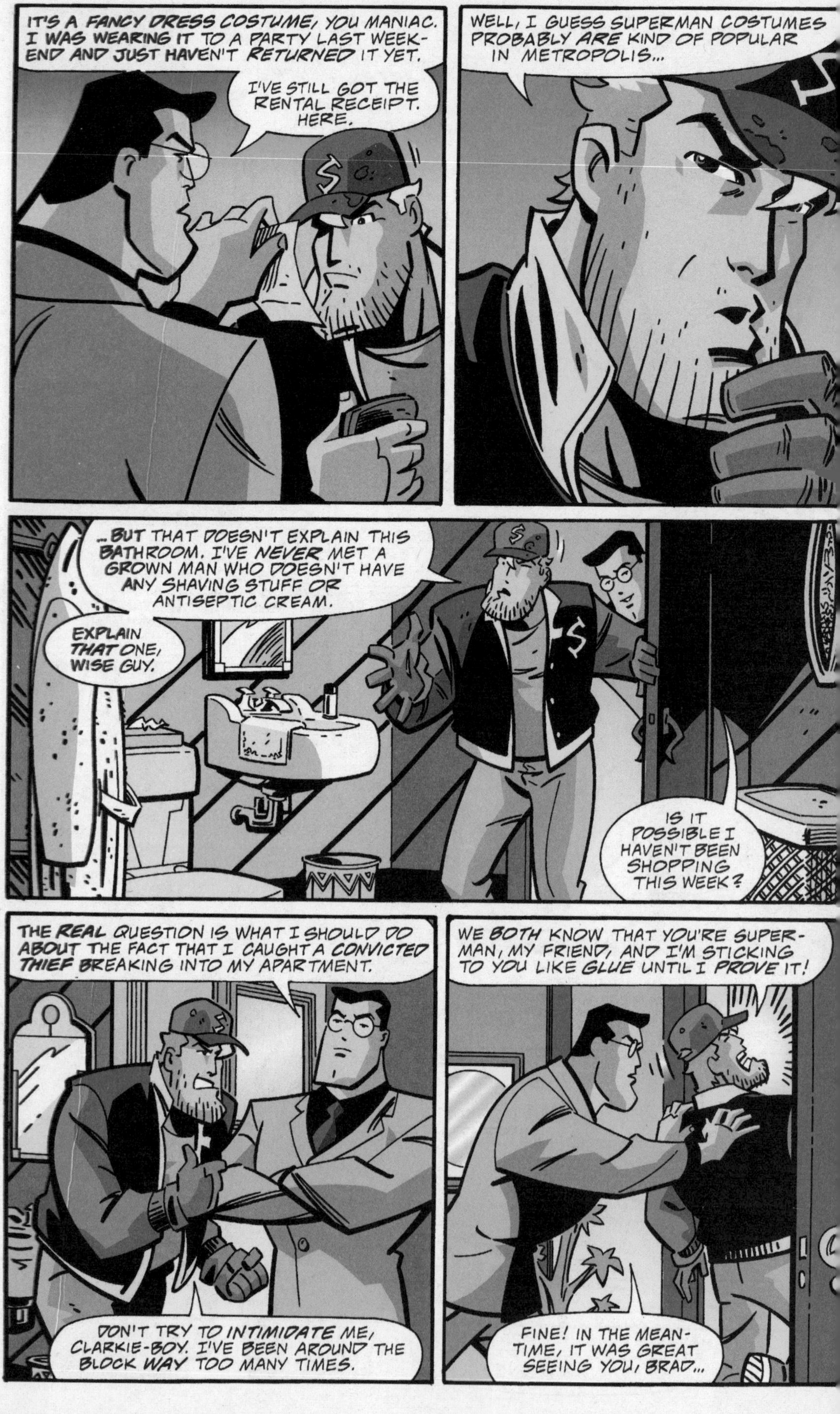

IT'S A FANCY DRESS COSTUME, YOU MANIAC. I WAS WEARING IT TO A PARTY LAST WEEK-END AND JUST HAVEN'T RETURNED IT YET.
I'VE STILL GOT THE RENTAL RECEIPT. HERE.
WELL, I GUESS SUPERMAN COSTUMES PROBABLY ARE KIND OF POPULAR IN METROPOLIS...
...BUT THAT DOESN'T EXPLAIN THIS BATHROOM. I'VE NEVER MET A GROWN MAN WHO DOESN'T HAVE ANY SHAVING STUFF OR ANTISEPTIC CREAM.
EXPLAIN THAT ONE, WISE GUY.
IS IT POSSIBLE I HAVEN'T BEEN SHOPPING THIS WEEK?
THE REAL QUESTION IS WHAT I SHOULD DO ABOUT THE FACT THAT I CAUGHT A CONVICTED THIEF BREAKING INTO MY APARTMENT.
DON'T TRY TO INTIMIDATE ME, CLARKIE-BOY. I'VE BEEN AROUND THE BLOCK WAY TOO MANY TIMES.
WE BOTH KNOW THAT YOU'RE SUPER-MAN, MY FRIEND, AND I'M STICKING TO YOU LIKE GLUE UNTIL I PROVE IT!
FINE! IN THE MEAN-TIME, IT WAS GREAT SEEING YOU, BRAD...

"...BUT DON'T HURRY BACK!"

SO, I HEARD A RUMOR YOU'VE SET UP SOME KIND OF MAJOR INTERVIEW FOR THE FINANCIAL PAGES, CLARK.

IS IT TRUE *LEXCORP'S* CLOSE TO SIGNING A DEAL WITH *WAYNETECH ELECTRONICS* OVER IN GOTHAM CITY?

SORRY, JIMMY--

--UNTIL I GET ALL THE *FACTS*, I CAN'T COMMENT ON THAT ONE.

BE CAREFUL AROUND THAT *LUTHOR* GUY, CLARKIE-BOY. FOR A "GREAT HUMANITARIAN," HE *SCARES* THE *LIFE* OUTTA ME.

MAYBE ONE CROOK CAN JUST *SMELL* ANOTHER, HUH?

EXCUSE ME, JIMMY...

...MY FRIEND AND I NEED A WORD IN *PRIVATE*.

WHAT'S *WRONG*, KENT? ANNOYED CUZ I'M TAILING YOU AROUND AND MAKING SURE YOU CAN'T CHANGE INTO SUPERMAN?

WONDERING WHAT YOU'RE GONNA DO IF AN EMERGENCY POPS UP?

WEEDOWEEDOWEEDOWEEDO

OOH, TALK ABOUT *TIMING!*

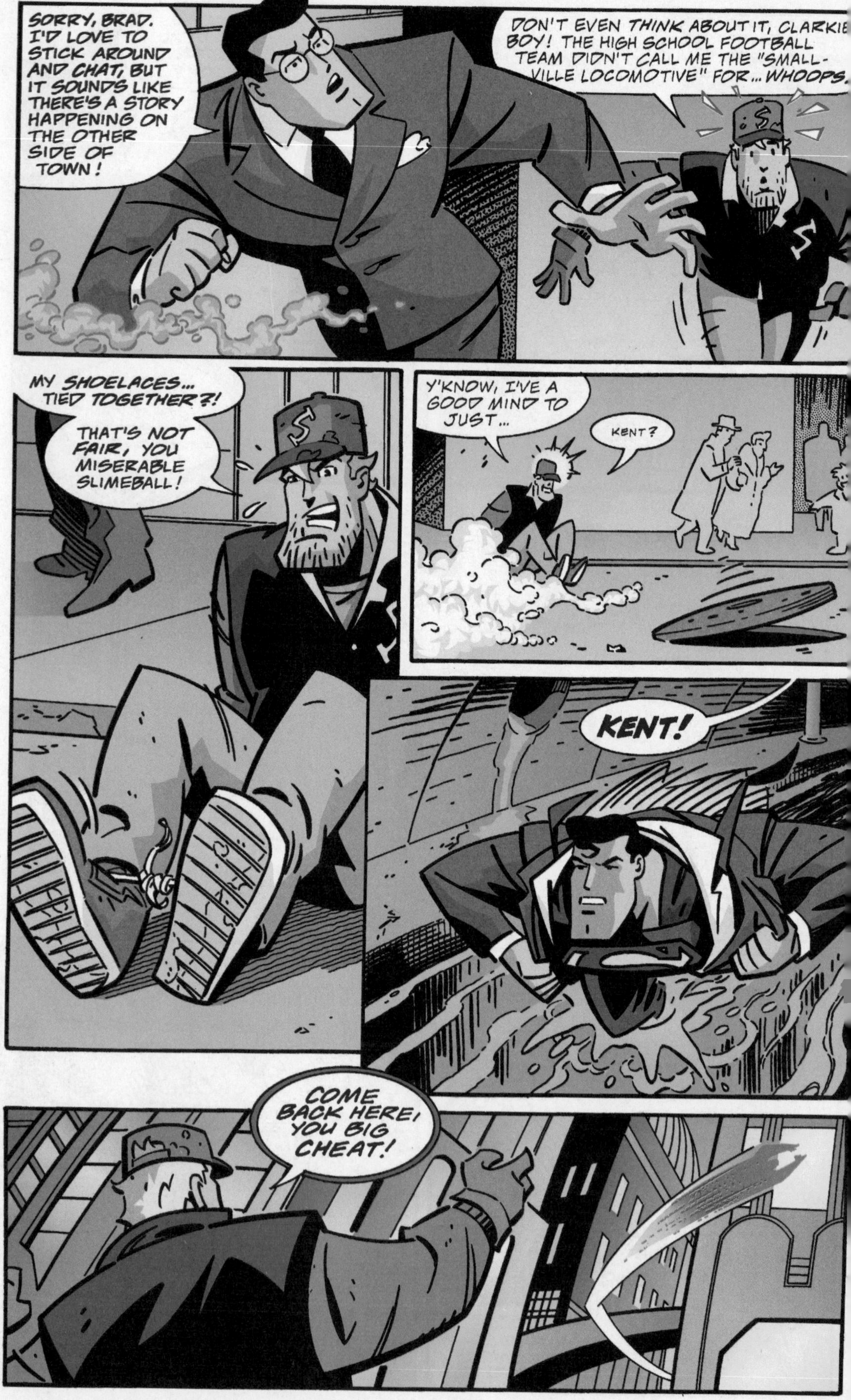

SORRY, BRAD. I'D LOVE TO STICK AROUND AND CHAT, BUT IT SOUNDS LIKE THERE'S A STORY HAPPENING ON THE OTHER SIDE OF TOWN!
DON'T EVEN THINK ABOUT IT, CLARKIE BOY! THE HIGH SCHOOL FOOTBALL TEAM DIDN'T CALL ME THE "SMALL-VILLE LOCOMOTIVE" FOR... WHOOPS.
MY SHOELACES... TIED TOGETHER?!
THAT'S NOT FAIR, YOU MISERABLE SLIMEBALL!
Y'KNOW, I'VE A GOOD MIND TO JUST...
KENT?
KENT!
COME BACK HERE, YOU BIG CHEAT!

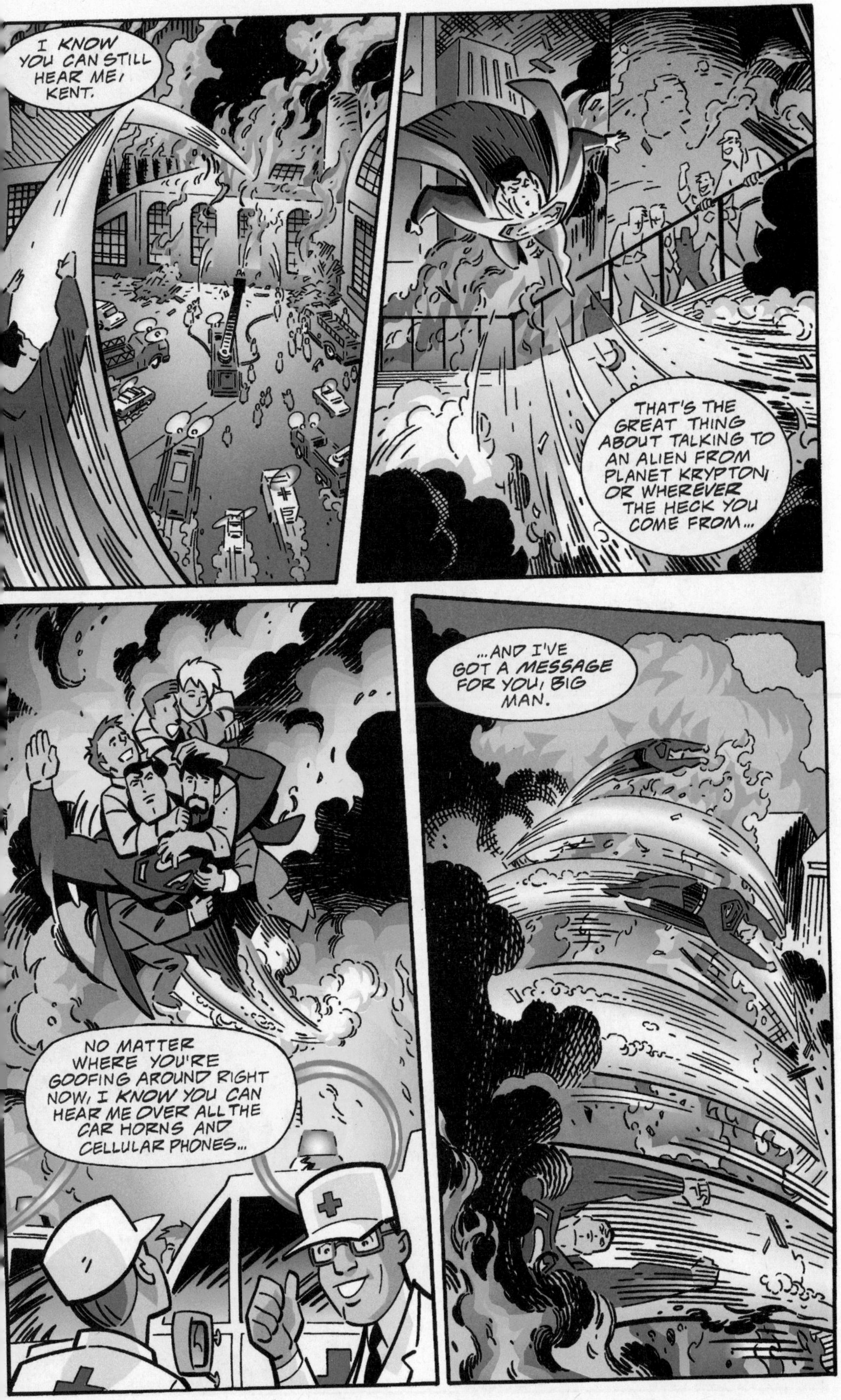
I KNOW YOU CAN STILL HEAR ME, KENT.
THAT'S THE GREAT THING ABOUT TALKING TO AN ALIEN FROM PLANET KRYPTON, OR WHEREVER THE HECK YOU COME FROM...
NO MATTER WHERE YOU'RE GOOFING AROUND RIGHT NOW, I KNOW YOU CAN HEAR ME OVER ALL THE CAR HORNS AND CELLULAR PHONES...
...AND I'VE GOT A MESSAGE FOR YOU, BIG MAN.

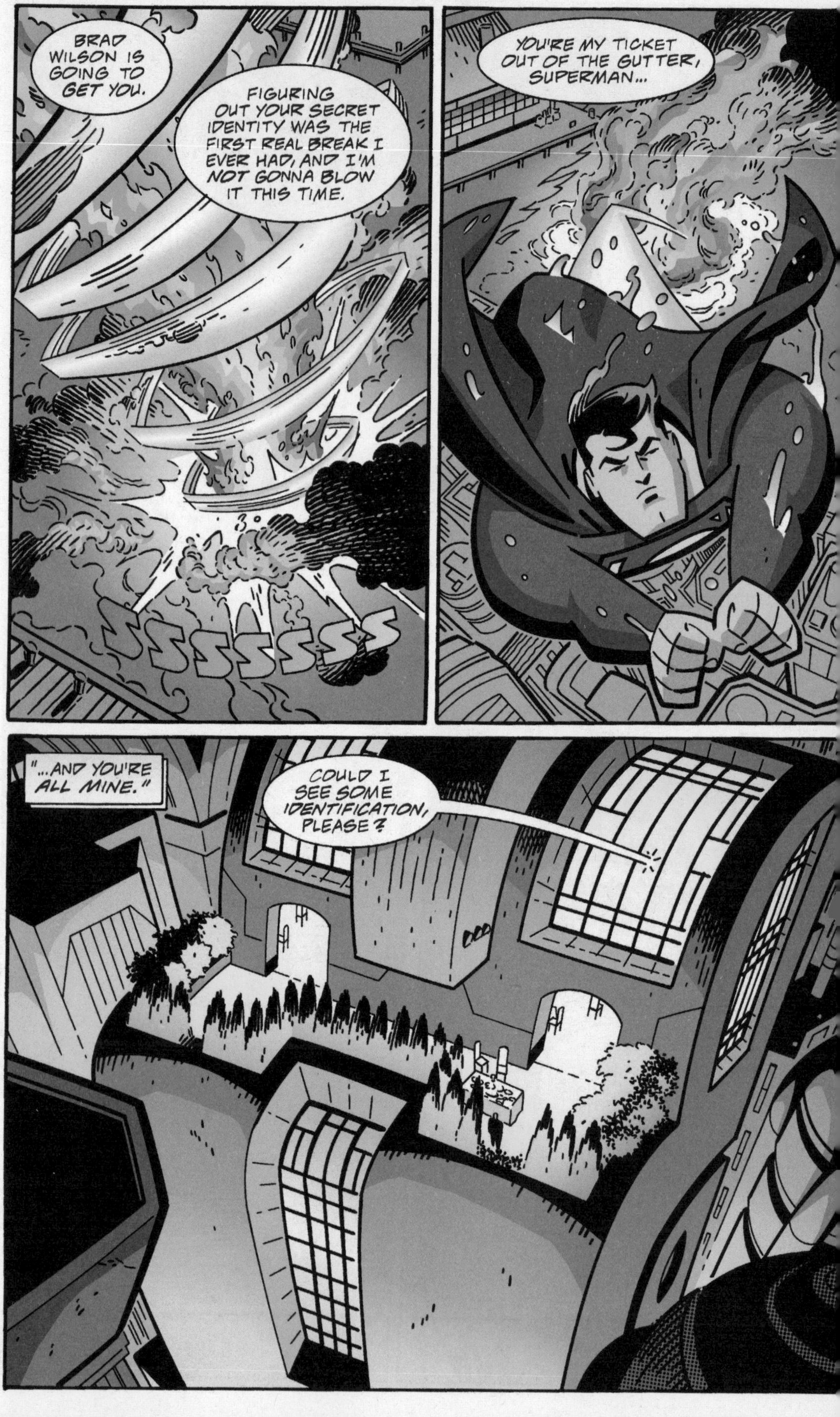
BRAD WILSON IS GOING TO GET YOU.
FIGURING OUT YOUR SECRET IDENTITY WAS THE FIRST REAL BREAK I EVER HAD, AND I'M NOT GONNA BLOW IT THIS TIME.
SSSSSS
YOU'RE MY TICKET OUT OF THE GUTTER, SUPERMAN...
"...AND YOU'RE ALL MINE."
COULD I SEE SOME IDENTIFICATION, PLEASE?

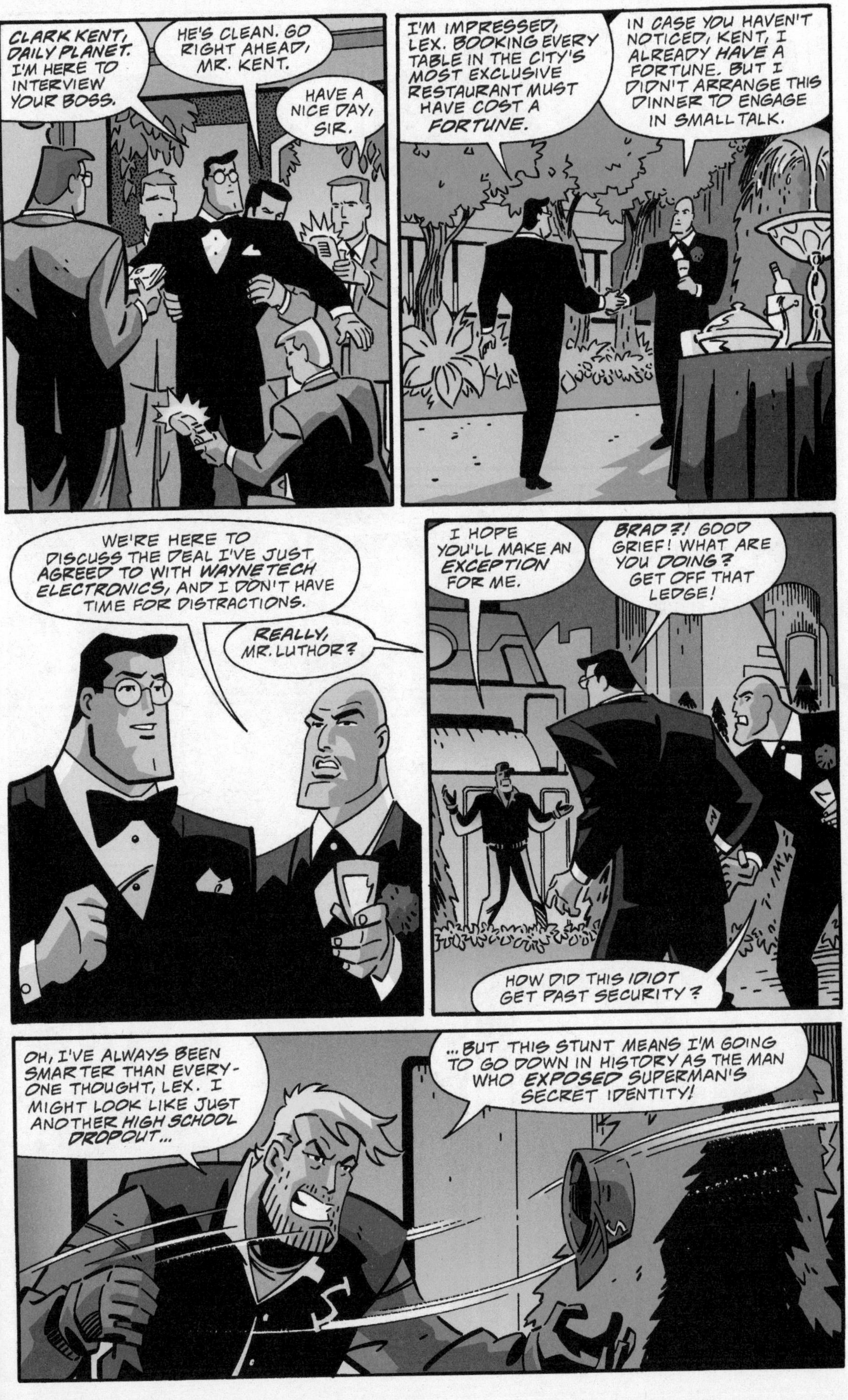
CLARK KENT, DAILY PLANET. I'M HERE TO INTERVIEW YOUR BOSS.
HE'S CLEAN. GO RIGHT AHEAD, MR. KENT.
HAVE A NICE DAY, SIR.
I'M IMPRESSED, LEX. BOOKING EVERY TABLE IN THE CITY'S MOST EXCLUSIVE RESTAURANT MUST HAVE COST A FORTUNE.
IN CASE YOU HAVEN'T NOTICED, KENT, I ALREADY HAVE A FORTUNE. BUT I DIDN'T ARRANGE THIS DINNER TO ENGAGE IN SMALL TALK.
WE'RE HERE TO DISCUSS THE DEAL I'VE JUST AGREED TO WITH WAYNETECH ELECTRONICS, AND I DON'T HAVE TIME FOR DISTRACTIONS.
REALLY, MR. LUTHOR?
I HOPE YOU'LL MAKE AN EXCEPTION FOR ME.
BRAD?! GOOD GRIEF! WHAT ARE YOU DOING? GET OFF THAT LEDGE!
HOW DID THIS IDIOT GET PAST SECURITY?
OH, I'VE ALWAYS BEEN SMARTER THAN EVERY-ONE THOUGHT, LEX. I MIGHT LOOK LIKE JUST ANOTHER HIGH SCHOOL DROPOUT...
...BUT THIS STUNT MEANS I'M GOING TO GO DOWN IN HISTORY AS THE MAN WHO EXPOSED SUPERMAN'S SECRET IDENTITY!

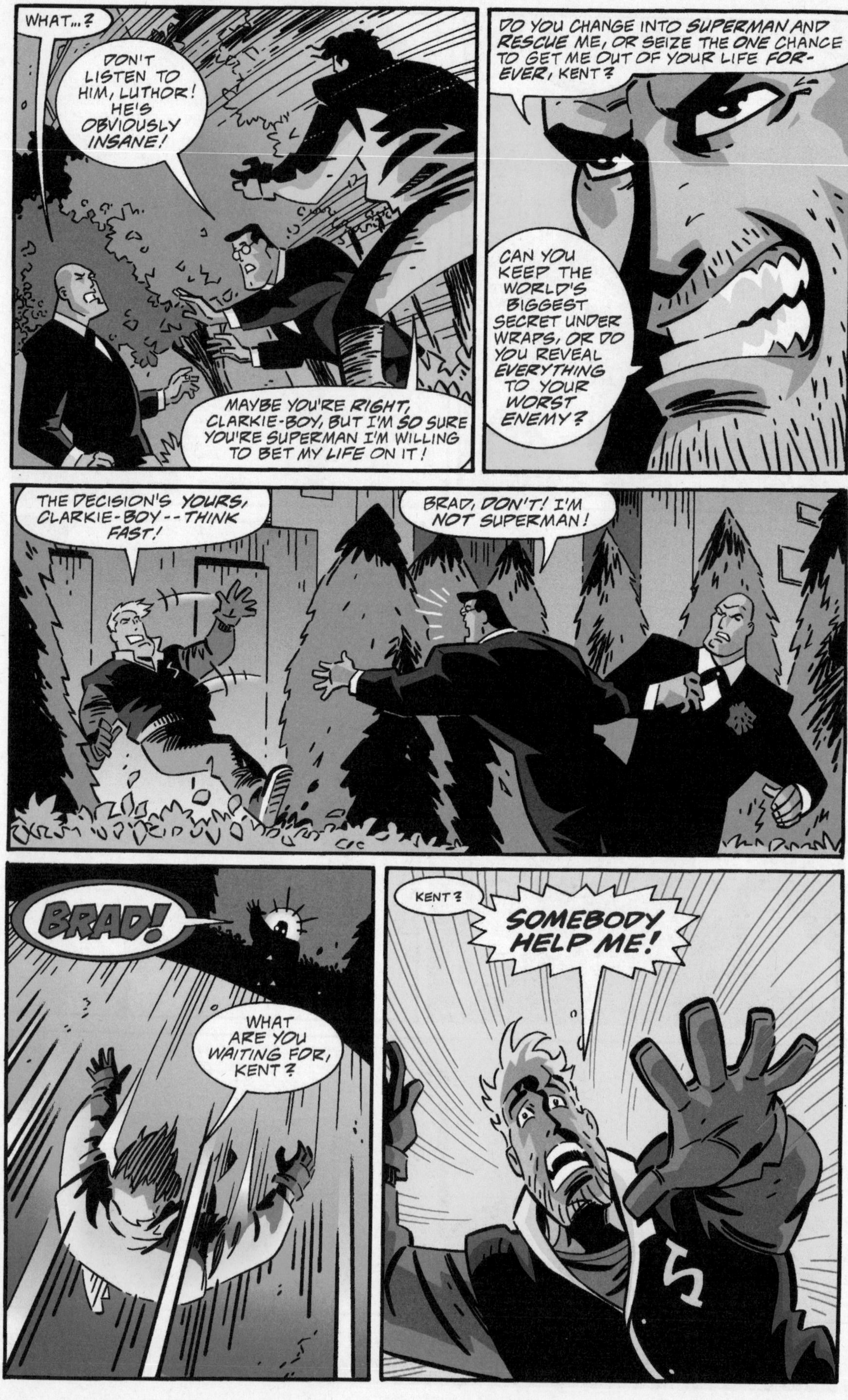
WHAT...?
DON'T LISTEN TO HIM, LUTHOR! HE'S OBVIOUSLY INSANE!
MAYBE YOU'RE RIGHT, CLARKIE-BOY, BUT I'M SO SURE YOU'RE SUPERMAN I'M WILLING TO BET MY LIFE ON IT!
DO YOU CHANGE INTO SUPERMAN AND RESCUE ME, OR SEIZE THE ONE CHANCE TO GET ME OUT OF YOUR LIFE FOR-EVER, KENT?
CAN YOU KEEP THE WORLD'S BIGGEST SECRET UNDER WRAPS, OR DO YOU REVEAL EVERYTHING TO YOUR WORST ENEMY?
THE DECISION'S YOURS, CLARKIE-BOY--THINK FAST!
BRAD, DON'T! I'M NOT SUPERMAN!
BRAD!
WHAT ARE YOU WAITING FOR, KENT?
KENT?
SOMEBODY HELP ME!

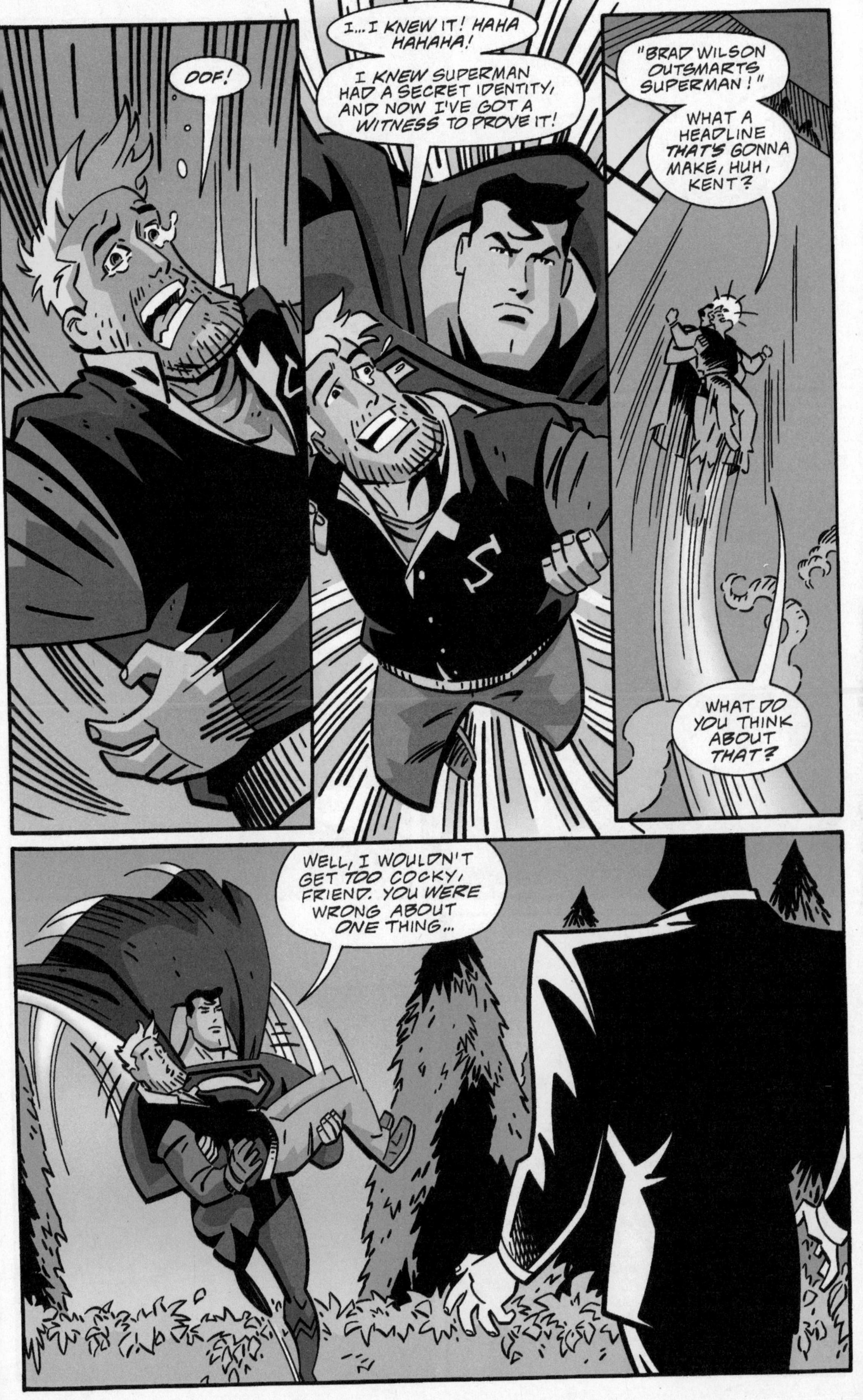
OOF!
I... I KNEW IT! HAHA HAHAHA!
I KNEW SUPERMAN HAD A SECRET IDENTITY, AND NOW I'VE GOT A WITNESS TO PROVE IT!
"BRAD WILSON OUTSMARTS SUPERMAN!"
WHAT A HEADLINE THAT'S GONNA MAKE, HUH, KENT?
WHAT DO YOU THINK ABOUT THAT?
WELL, I WOULDN'T GET TOO COCKY, FRIEND. YOU WERE WRONG ABOUT ONE THING...

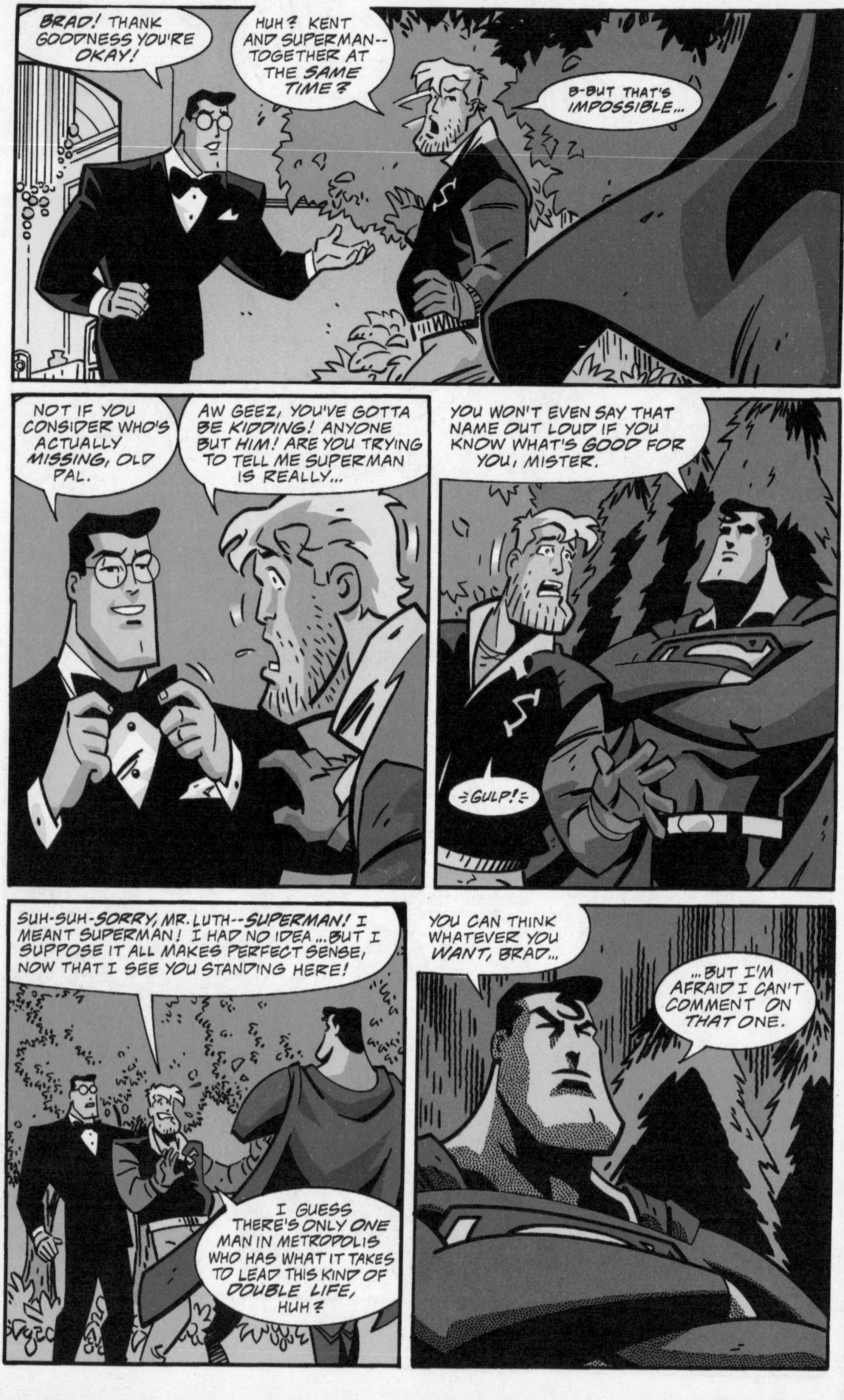
BRAD! THANK GOODNESS YOU'RE OKAY!
HUH? KENT AND SUPERMAN-- TOGETHER AT THE SAME TIME?
B-BUT THAT'S IMPOSSIBLE...
NOT IF YOU CONSIDER WHO'S ACTUALLY MISSING, OLD PAL.
AW GEEZ, YOU'VE GOTTA BE KIDDING! ANYONE BUT HIM! ARE YOU TRYING TO TELL ME SUPERMAN IS REALLY...
YOU WON'T EVEN SAY THAT NAME OUT LOUD IF YOU KNOW WHAT'S GOOD FOR YOU, MISTER.
GULP!
SUH-SUH-SORRY, MR. LUTH--SUPERMAN! I MEANT SUPERMAN! I HAD NO IDEA ...BUT I SUPPOSE IT ALL MAKES PERFECT SENSE, NOW THAT I SEE YOU STANDING HERE!
I GUESS THERE'S ONLY ONE MAN IN METROPOLIS WHO HAS WHAT IT TAKES TO LEAD THIS KIND OF DOUBLE LIFE, HUH?
YOU CAN THINK WHATEVER YOU WANT, BRAD...
...BUT I'M AFRAID I CAN'T COMMENT ON THAT ONE.

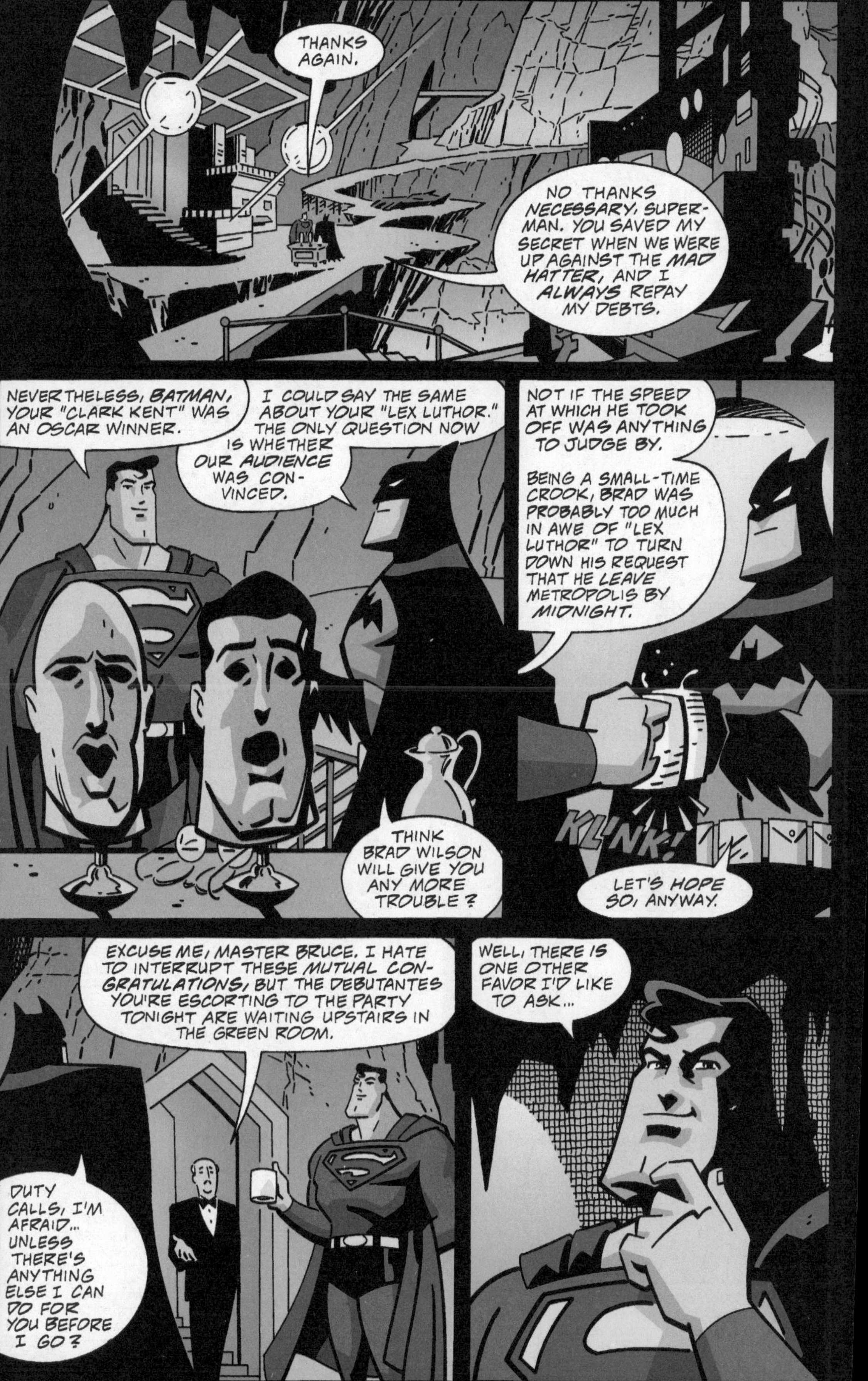
THANKS AGAIN.
NO THANKS NECESSARY, SUPERMAN. YOU SAVED MY SECRET WHEN WE WERE UP AGAINST THE MAD HATTER, AND I ALWAYS REPAY MY DEBTS.
NEVERTHELESS, BATMAN, YOUR "CLARK KENT" WAS AN OSCAR WINNER.
I COULD SAY THE SAME ABOUT YOUR "LEX LUTHOR." THE ONLY QUESTION NOW IS WHETHER OUR AUDIENCE WAS CONVINCED.
THINK BRAD WILSON WILL GIVE YOU ANY MORE TROUBLE?
NOT IF THE SPEED AT WHICH HE TOOK OFF WAS ANYTHING TO JUDGE BY.
BEING A SMALL-TIME CROOK, BRAD WAS PROBABLY TOO MUCH IN AWE OF "LEX LUTHOR" TO TURN DOWN HIS REQUEST THAT HE LEAVE METROPOLIS BY MIDNIGHT.
KLINK!
LET'S HOPE SO, ANYWAY.
EXCUSE ME, MASTER BRUCE. I HATE TO INTERRUPT THESE MUTUAL CONGRATULATIONS, BUT THE DEBUTANTES YOU'RE ESCORTING TO THE PARTY TONIGHT ARE WAITING UPSTAIRS IN THE GREEN ROOM.
DUTY CALLS, I'M AFRAID... UNLESS THERE'S ANYTHING ELSE I CAN DO FOR YOU BEFORE I GO?
WELL, THERE IS ONE OTHER FAVOR I'D LIKE TO ASK...

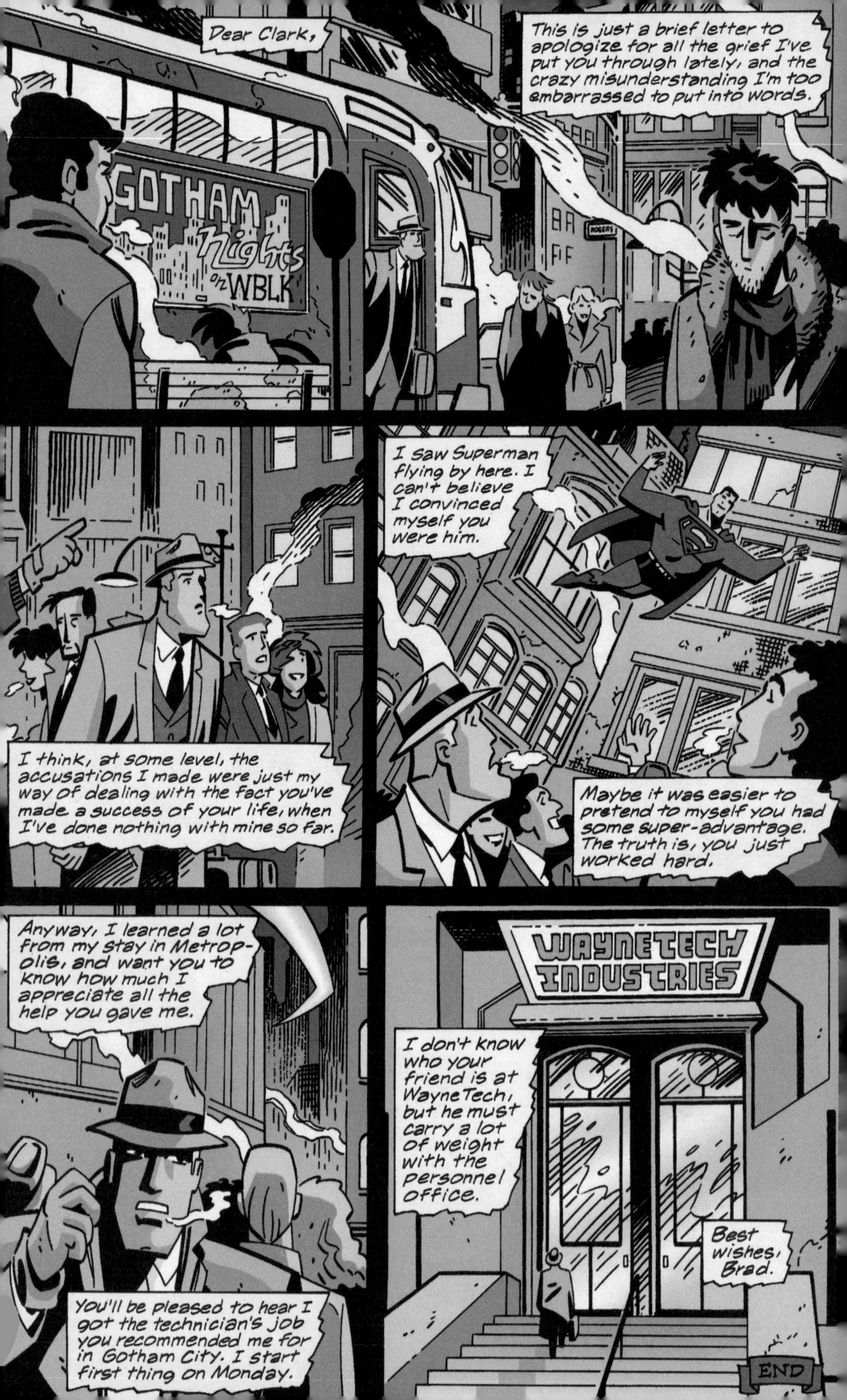
Dear Clark,
This is just a brief letter to apologize for all the grief I've put you through lately, and the crazy misunderstanding I'm too embarrassed to put into words.
GOTHAM Nights on WBLK
ROGERS
I saw Superman flying by here. I can't believe I convinced myself you were him.
I think, at some level, the accusations I made were just my way of dealing with the fact you've made a success of your life, when I've done nothing with mine so far.
Maybe it was easier to pretend to myself you had some super-advantage. The truth is, you just worked hard.
Anyway, I learned a lot from my stay in Metropolis, and want you to know how much I appreciate all the help you gave me.
You'll be pleased to hear I got the technician's job you recommended me for in Gotham City. I start first thing on Monday.
WAYNETECH INDUSTRIES
I don't know who your friend is at WayneTech, but he must carry a lot of weight with the personnel office.
Best wishes, Brad.
END

SUPERMAN ADVENTURES #34 cover by MIKE MANLEY, TERRY AUSTIN and MARIE SEVERIN

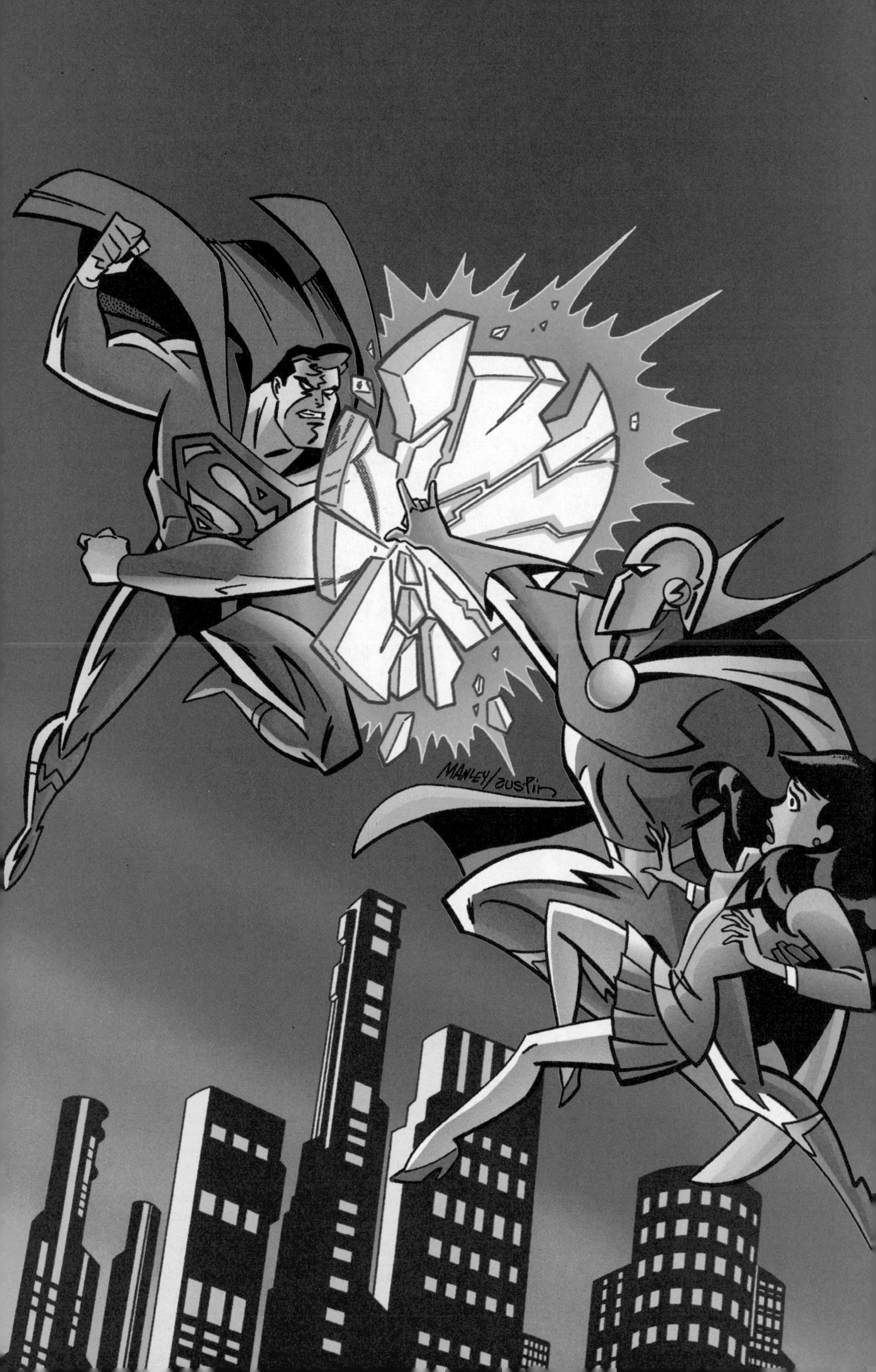

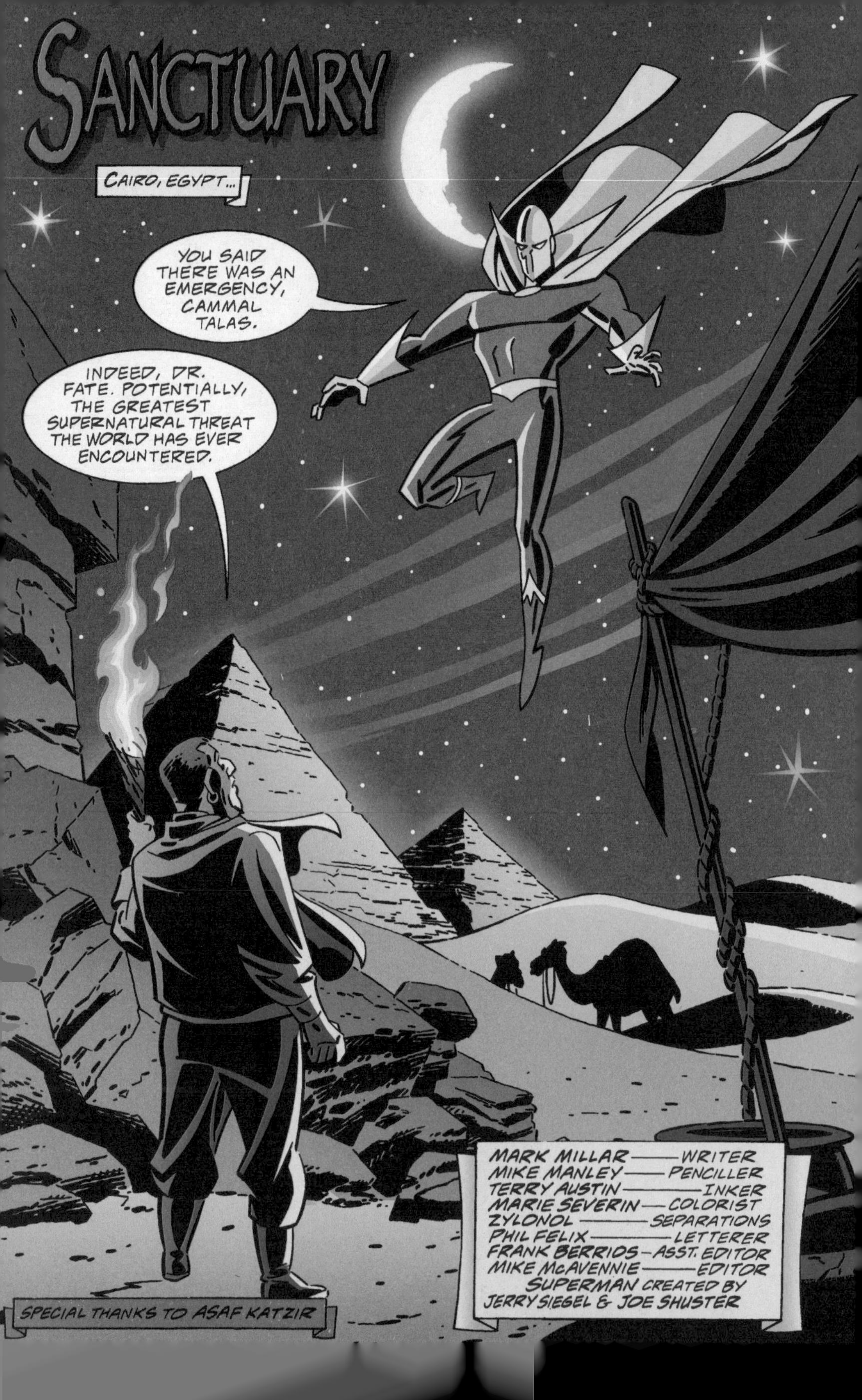
SANCTUARY
CAIRO, EGYPT...
YOU SAID THERE WAS AN EMERGENCY, CAMMAL TALAS.
INDEED, DR. FATE. POTENTIALLY, THE GREATEST SUPERNATURAL THREAT THE WORLD HAS EVER ENCOUNTERED.
MARK MILLAR—WRITER
MIKE MANLEY—PENCILLER
TERRY AUSTIN—INKER
MARIE SEVERIN—COLORIST
ZYLONOL—SEPARATIONS
PHIL FELIX—LETTERER
FRANK BERRIOS—ASST. EDITOR
MIKE McAVENNIE—EDITOR
SUPERMAN CREATED BY JERRY SIEGEL & JOE SHUSTER
SPECIAL THANKS TO ASAF KATZIR

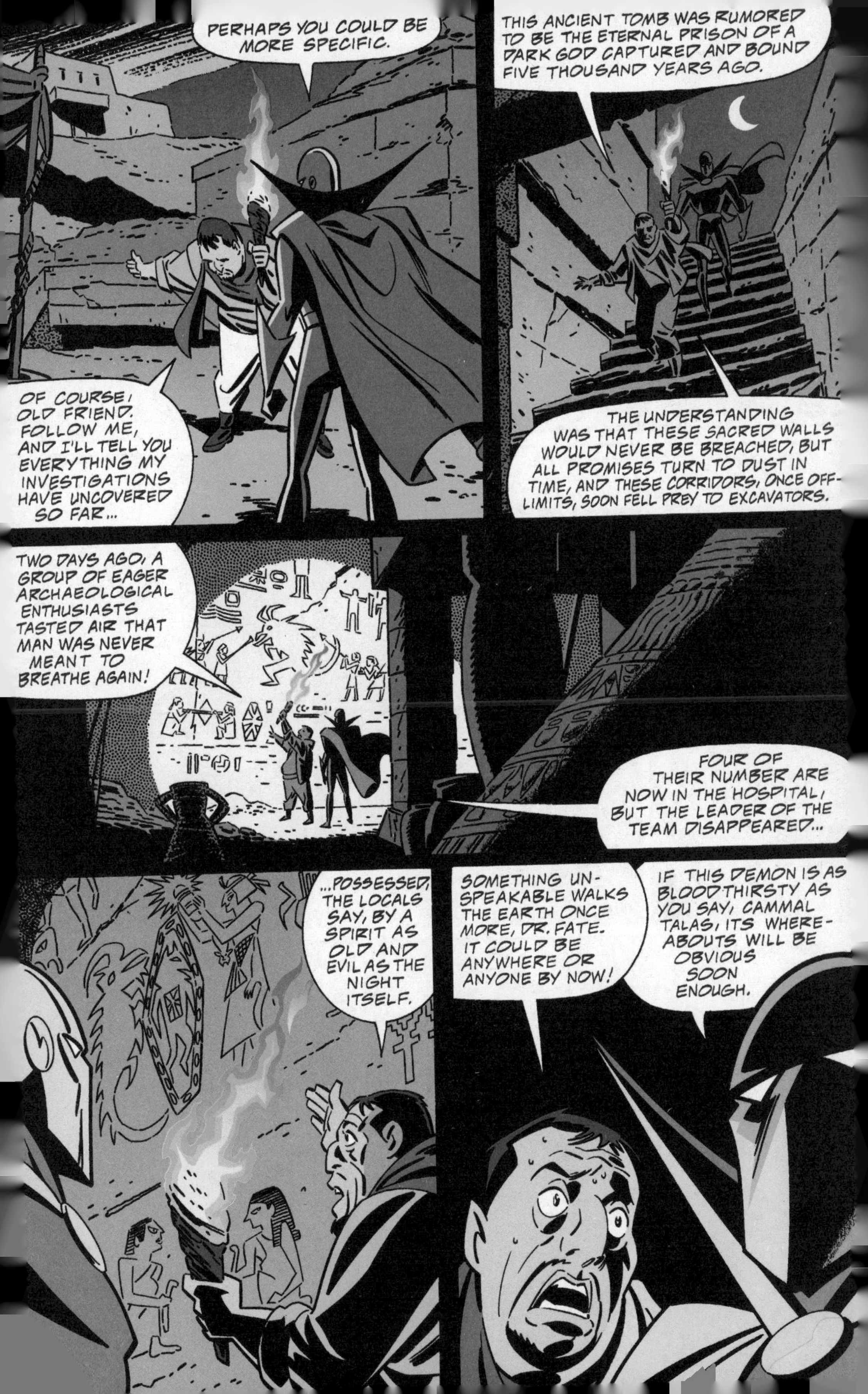
PERHAPS YOU COULD BE MORE SPECIFIC.
OF COURSE, OLD FRIEND. FOLLOW ME, AND I'LL TELL YOU EVERYTHING MY INVESTIGATIONS HAVE UNCOVERED SO FAR...
THIS ANCIENT TOMB WAS RUMORED TO BE THE ETERNAL PRISON OF A DARK GOD CAPTURED AND BOUND FIVE THOUSAND YEARS AGO.
THE UNDERSTANDING WAS THAT THESE SACRED WALLS WOULD NEVER BE BREACHED, BUT ALL PROMISES TURN TO DUST IN TIME, AND THESE CORRIDORS, ONCE OFF-LIMITS, SOON FELL PREY TO EXCAVATORS.
TWO DAYS AGO, A GROUP OF EAGER ARCHAEOLOGICAL ENTHUSIASTS TASTED AIR THAT MAN WAS NEVER MEANT TO BREATHE AGAIN!
FOUR OF THEIR NUMBER ARE NOW IN THE HOSPITAL, BUT THE LEADER OF THE TEAM DISAPPEARED...
...POSSESSED, THE LOCALS SAY, BY A SPIRIT AS OLD AND EVIL AS THE NIGHT ITSELF.
SOMETHING UN-SPEAKABLE WALKS THE EARTH ONCE MORE, DR. FATE. IT COULD BE ANYWHERE OR ANYONE BY NOW!
IF THIS DEMON IS AS BLOODTHIRSTY AS YOU SAY, CAMMAL TALAS, ITS WHERE-ABOUTS WILL BE OBVIOUS SOON ENOUGH.

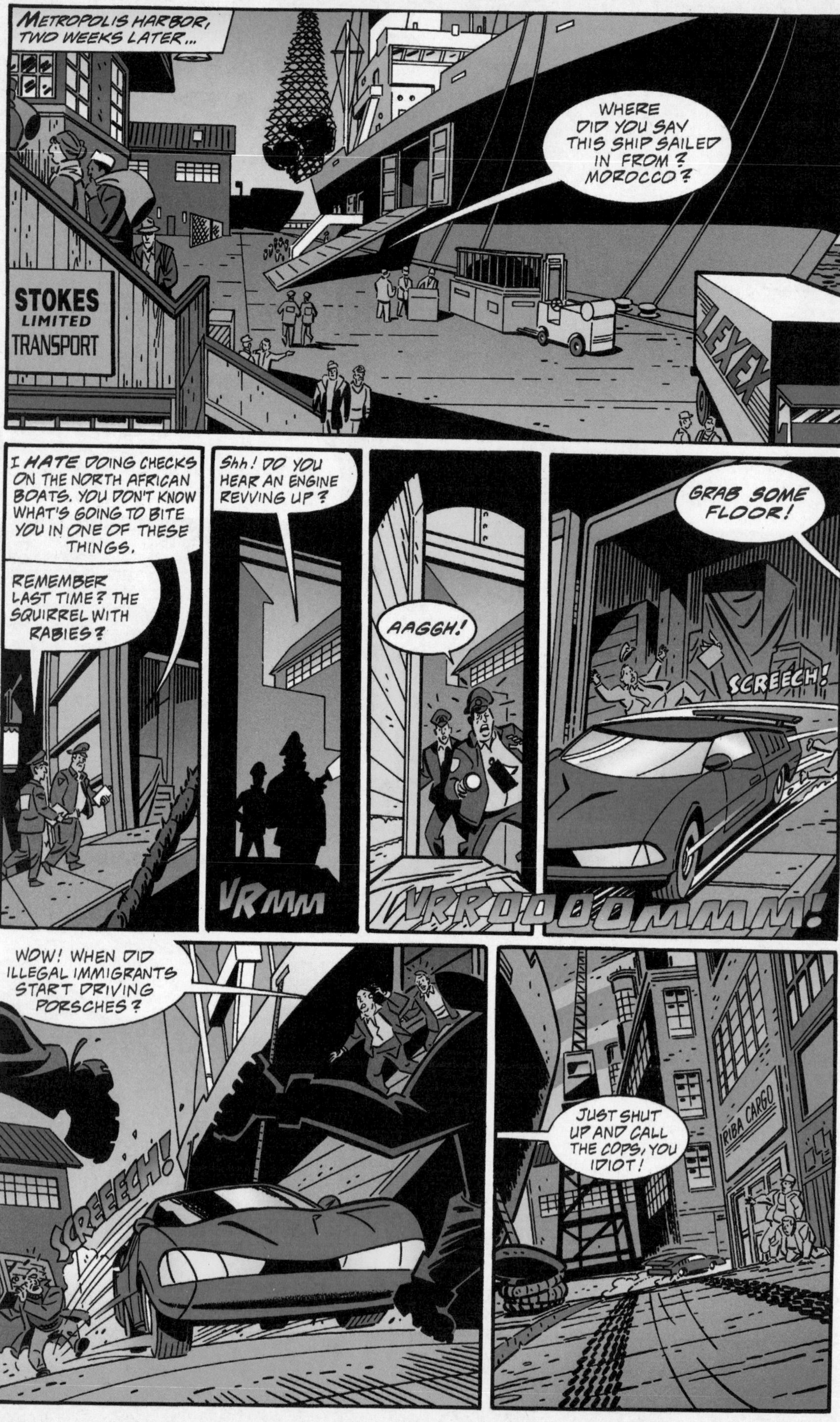

METROPOLIS HARBOR, TWO WEEKS LATER...
WHERE DID YOU SAY THIS SHIP SAILED IN FROM? MOROCCO?
STOKES LIMITED TRANSPORT
LEXEX
I HATE DOING CHECKS ON THE NORTH AFRICAN BOATS. YOU DON'T KNOW WHAT'S GOING TO BITE YOU IN ONE OF THESE THINGS.
REMEMBER LAST TIME? THE SQUIRREL WITH RABIES?
Shh! DO YOU HEAR AN ENGINE REVVING UP?
VRMM
AAGGH!
GRAB SOME FLOOR!
SCREECH!
VRROOOOOMMMM!
WOW! WHEN DID ILLEGAL IMMIGRANTS START DRIVING PORSCHES?
SCREEECH!
JUST SHUT UP AND CALL THE COPS, YOU IDIOT!
RIBA CARGO

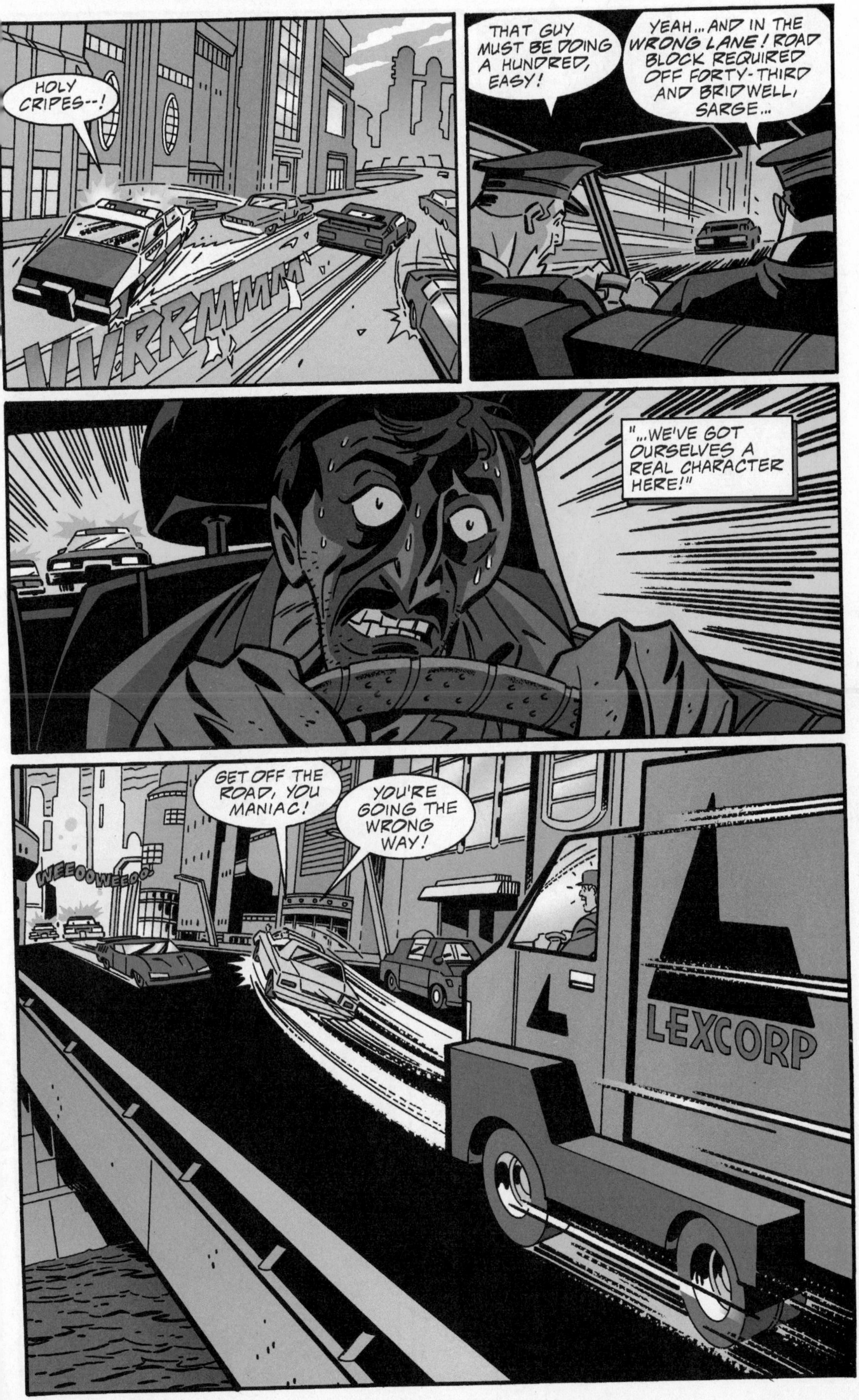
HOLY CRIPES--!
VVRRMMMM
THAT GUY MUST BE DOING A HUNDRED, EASY!
YEAH... AND IN THE WRONG LANE! ROAD BLOCK REQUIRED OFF FORTY-THIRD AND BRIDWELL, SARGE...
"...WE'VE GOT OURSELVES A REAL CHARACTER HERE!"
WEEOOWEEOO
GET OFF THE ROAD, YOU MANIAC!
YOU'RE GOING THE WRONG WAY!
LEXCORP

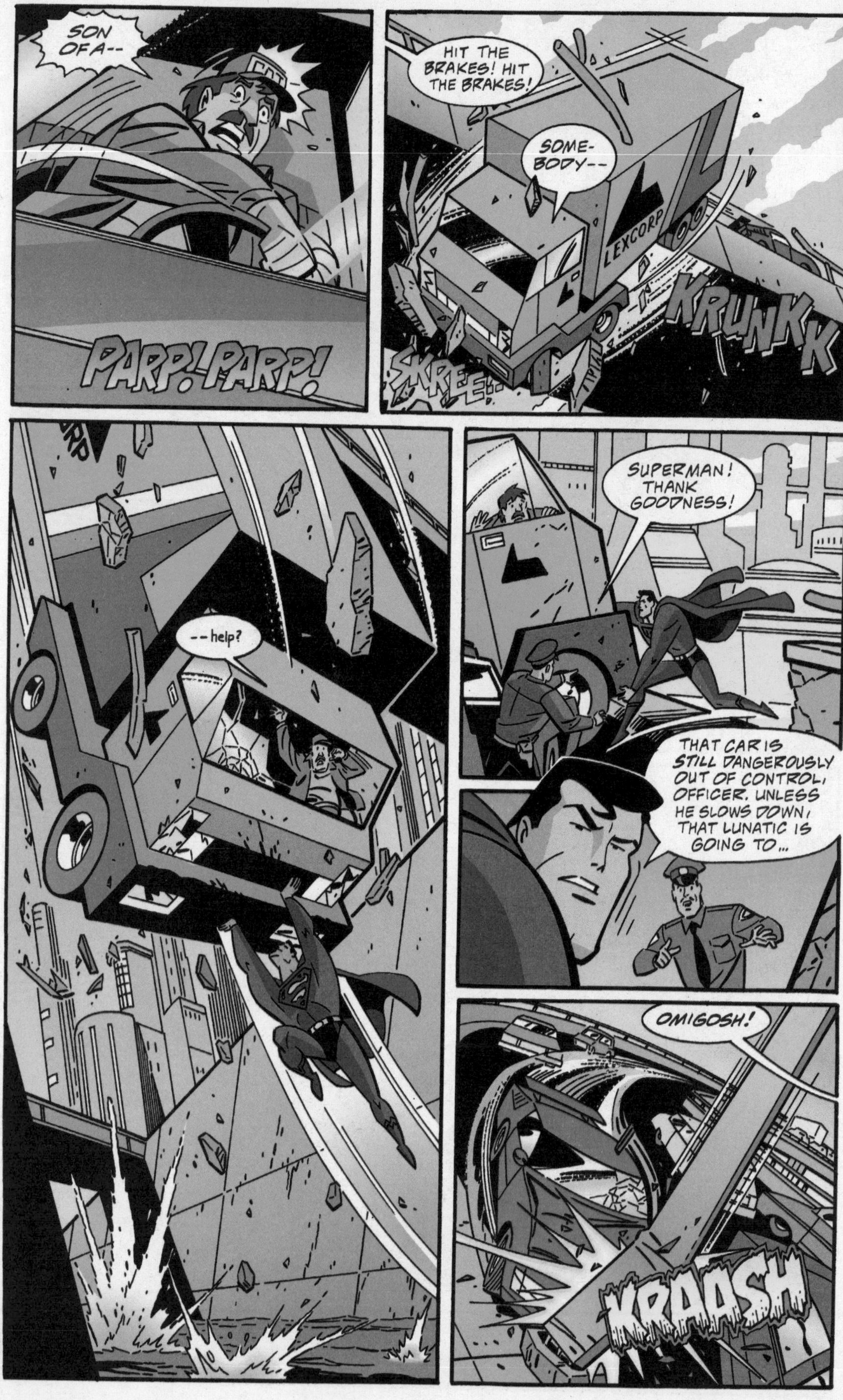
SON OF A--
PARP! PARP!
HIT THE BRAKES! HIT THE BRAKES!
SOME-BODY--
LEXCORP
KRUNKK
SKREE!!
--help?
SUPERMAN! THANK GOODNESS!
THAT CAR IS STILL DANGEROUSLY OUT OF CONTROL, OFFICER. UNLESS HE SLOWS DOWN, THAT LUNATIC IS GOING TO...
OMIGOSH!
KRAASH

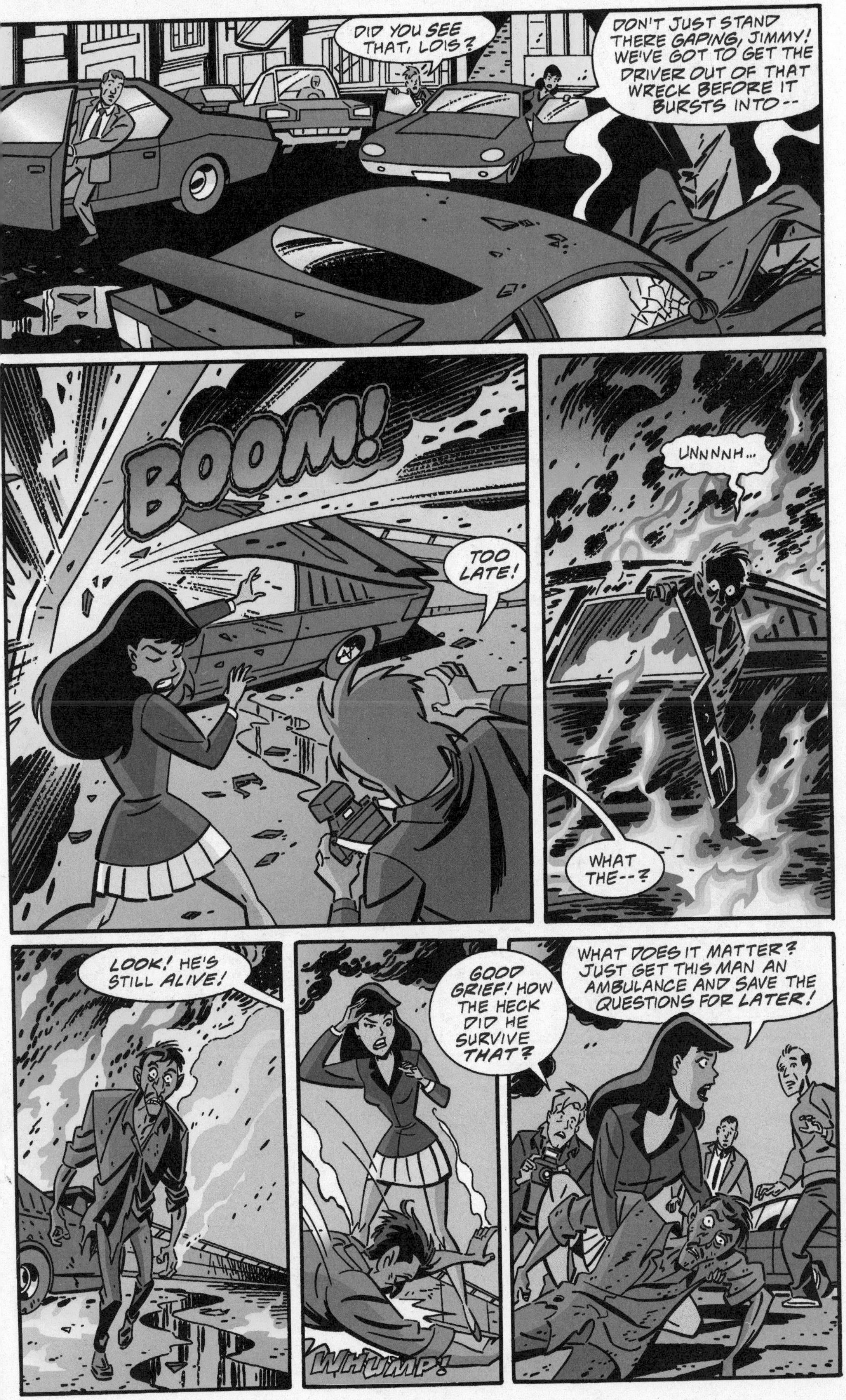

DID YOU SEE THAT, LOIS?
DON'T JUST STAND THERE GAPING, JIMMY! WE'VE GOT TO GET THE DRIVER OUT OF THAT WRECK BEFORE IT BURSTS INTO--
BOOM!
TOO LATE!
UNNNNH...
WHAT THE--?
LOOK! HE'S STILL ALIVE!
GOOD GRIEF! HOW THE HECK DID HE SURVIVE THAT?
WHUMP!
WHAT DOES IT MATTER? JUST GET THIS MAN AN AMBULANCE AND SAVE THE QUESTIONS FOR LATER!

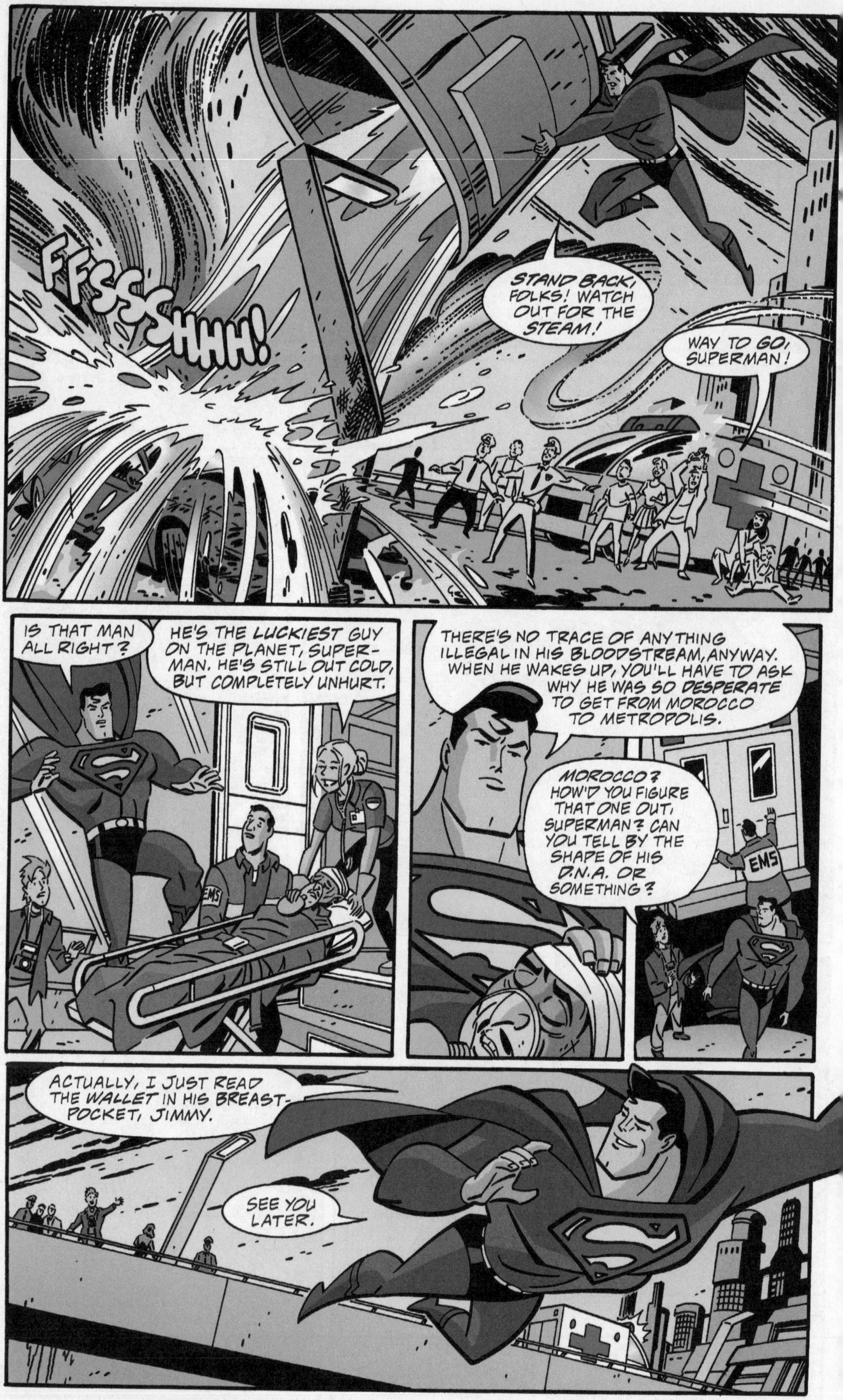
FFSSSHHH!
STAND BACK, FOLKS! WATCH OUT FOR THE STEAM!
WAY TO GO, SUPERMAN!
IS THAT MAN ALL RIGHT?
HE'S THE LUCKIEST GUY ON THE PLANET, SUPER-MAN. HE'S STILL OUT COLD, BUT COMPLETELY UNHURT.
THERE'S NO TRACE OF ANYTHING ILLEGAL IN HIS BLOODSTREAM, ANYWAY. WHEN HE WAKES UP, YOU'LL HAVE TO ASK WHY HE WAS SO DESPERATE TO GET FROM MOROCCO TO METROPOLIS.
MOROCCO? HOW'D YOU FIGURE THAT ONE OUT, SUPERMAN? CAN YOU TELL BY THE SHAPE OF HIS D.N.A. OR SOMETHING?
EMS
ACTUALLY, I JUST READ THE WALLET IN HIS BREAST-POCKET, JIMMY.
SEE YOU LATER.

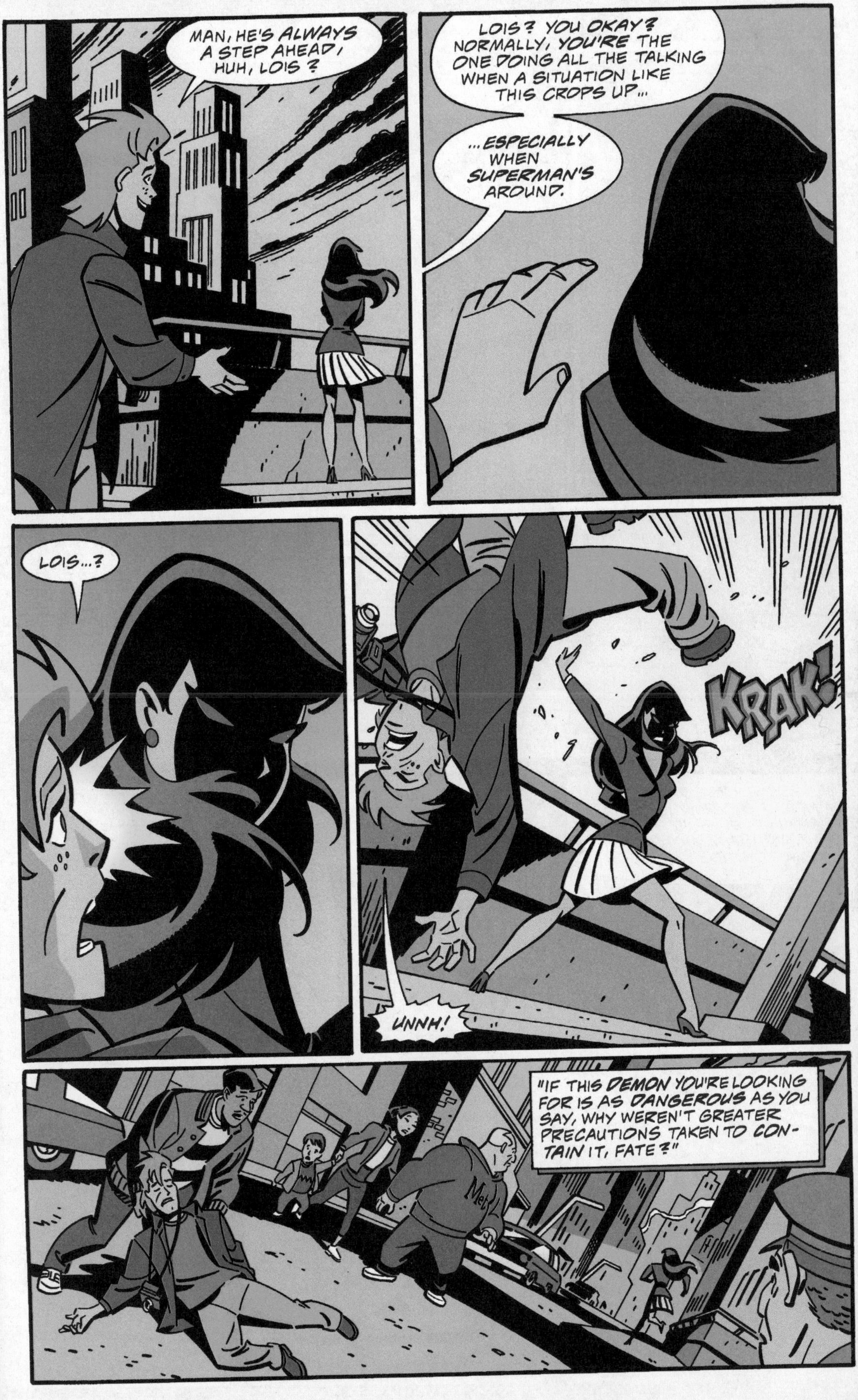
MAN, HE'S ALWAYS A STEP AHEAD, HUH, LOIS?
LOIS? YOU OKAY? NORMALLY, YOU'RE THE ONE DOING ALL THE TALKING WHEN A SITUATION LIKE THIS CROPS UP...
...ESPECIALLY WHEN SUPERMAN'S AROUND.
LOIS...?
KRAK!
UNNH!
"IF THIS DEMON YOU'RE LOOKING FOR IS AS DANGEROUS AS YOU SAY, WHY WEREN'T GREATER PRECAUTIONS TAKEN TO CONTAIN IT, FATE?"

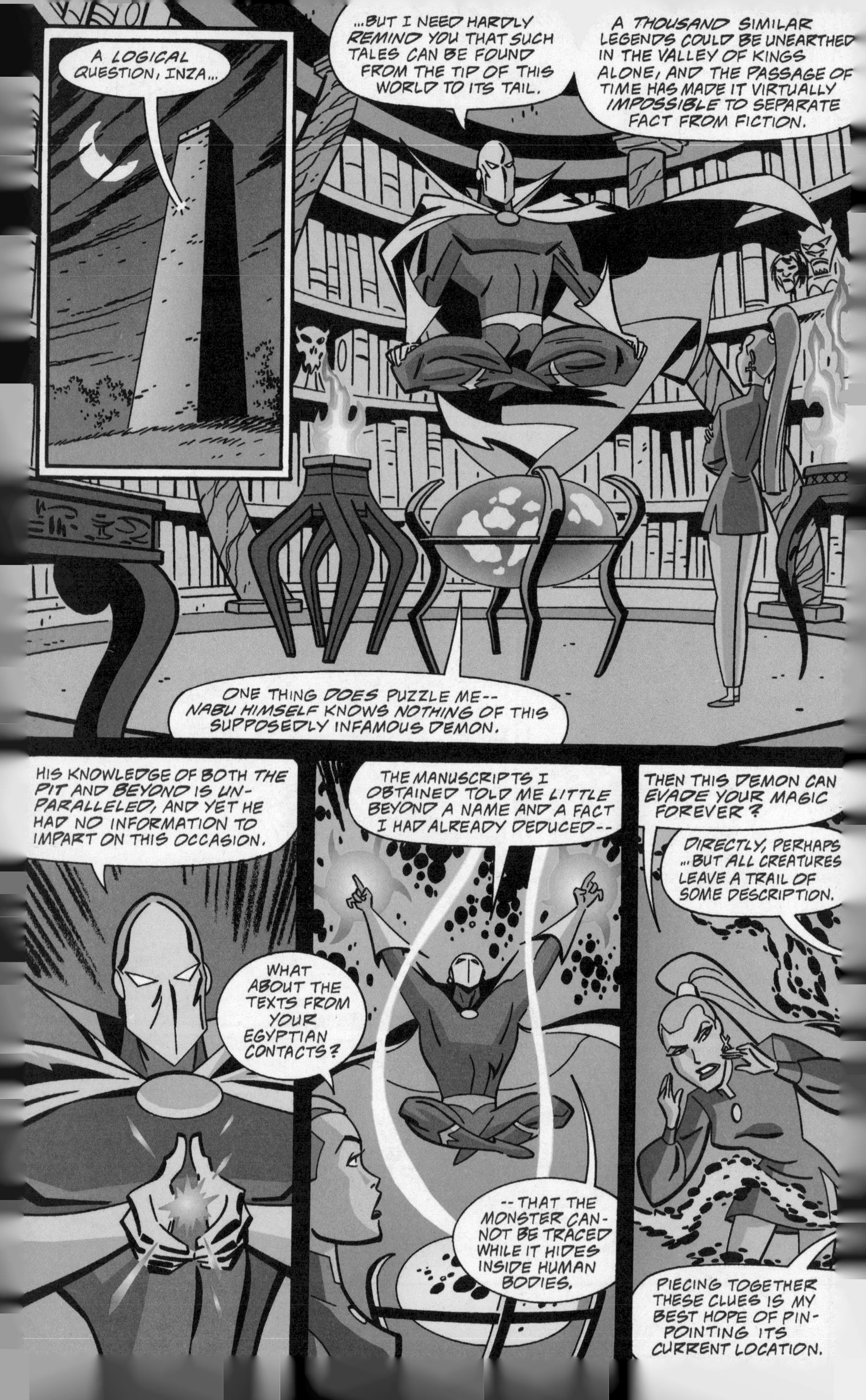
A LOGICAL QUESTION, INZA...
...BUT I NEED HARDLY REMIND YOU THAT SUCH TALES CAN BE FOUND FROM THE TIP OF THIS WORLD TO ITS TAIL.
A THOUSAND SIMILAR LEGENDS COULD BE UNEARTHED IN THE VALLEY OF KINGS ALONE, AND THE PASSAGE OF TIME HAS MADE IT VIRTUALLY IMPOSSIBLE TO SEPARATE FACT FROM FICTION.
ONE THING DOES PUZZLE ME-- NABU HIMSELF KNOWS NOTHING OF THIS SUPPOSEDLY INFAMOUS DEMON.
HIS KNOWLEDGE OF BOTH THE PIT AND BEYOND IS UN-PARALLELED, AND YET HE HAD NO INFORMATION TO IMPART ON THIS OCCASION.
WHAT ABOUT THE TEXTS FROM YOUR EGYPTIAN CONTACTS?
THE MANUSCRIPTS I OBTAINED TOLD ME LITTLE BEYOND A NAME AND A FACT I HAD ALREADY DEDUCED--
--THAT THE MONSTER CAN-NOT BE TRACED WHILE IT HIDES INSIDE HUMAN BODIES.
THEN THIS DEMON CAN EVADE YOUR MAGIC FOREVER?
DIRECTLY, PERHAPS ...BUT ALL CREATURES LEAVE A TRAIL OF SOME DESCRIPTION.
PIECING TOGETHER THESE CLUES IS MY BEST HOPE OF PIN-POINTING ITS CURRENT LOCATION.

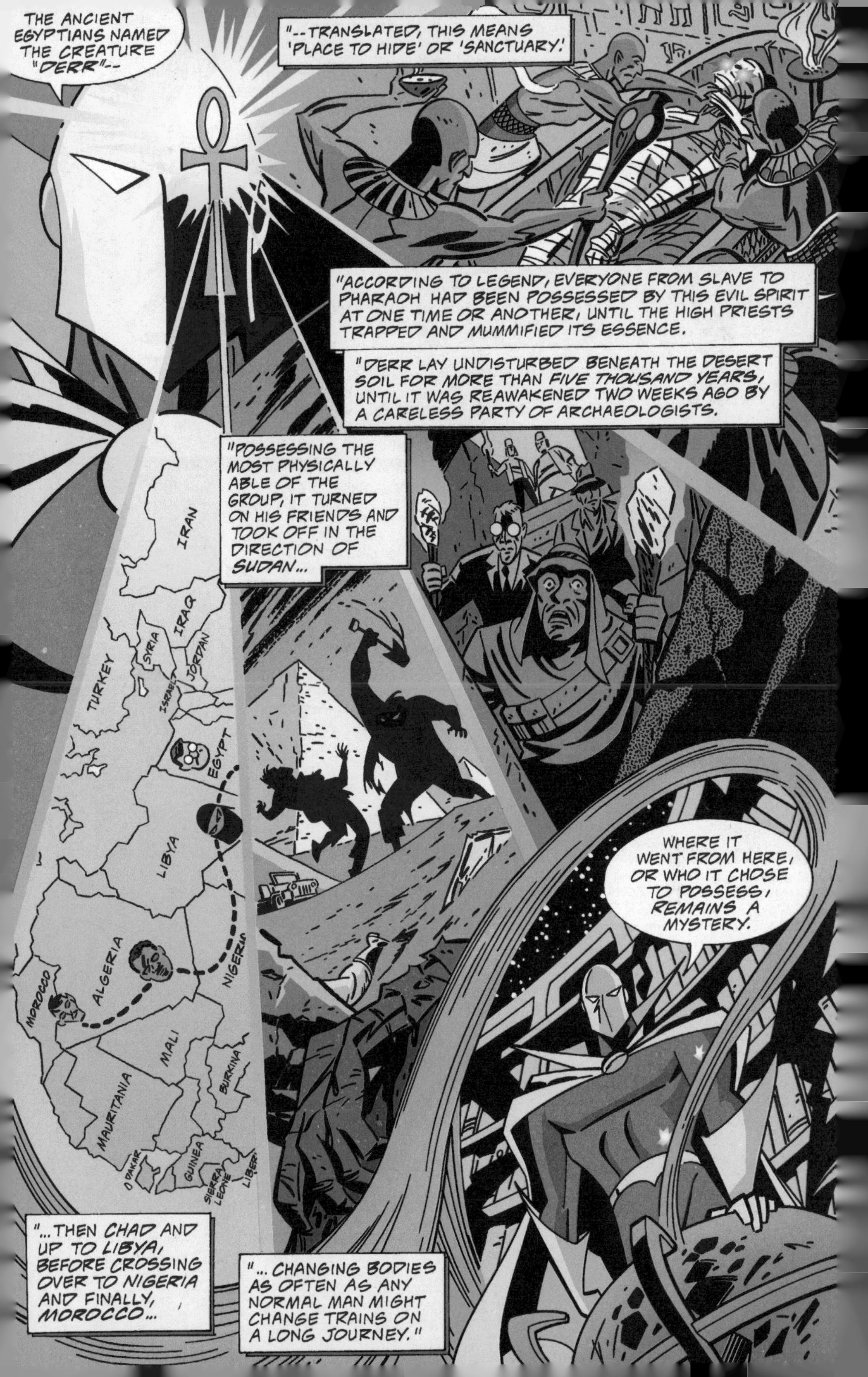
THE ANCIENT EGYPTIANS NAMED THE CREATURE "DERR"--
"--TRANSLATED, THIS MEANS 'PLACE TO HIDE' OR 'SANCTUARY.'
"ACCORDING TO LEGEND, EVERYONE FROM SLAVE TO PHARAOH HAD BEEN POSSESSED BY THIS EVIL SPIRIT AT ONE TIME OR ANOTHER, UNTIL THE HIGH PRIESTS TRAPPED AND MUMMIFIED ITS ESSENCE.
"DERR LAY UNDISTURBED BENEATH THE DESERT SOIL FOR MORE THAN FIVE THOUSAND YEARS, UNTIL IT WAS REAWAKENED TWO WEEKS AGO BY A CARELESS PARTY OF ARCHAEOLOGISTS.
"POSSESSING THE MOST PHYSICALLY ABLE OF THE GROUP, IT TURNED ON HIS FRIENDS AND TOOK OFF IN THE DIRECTION OF SUDAN...
IRAN
IRAQ
SYRIA
JORDAN
TURKEY
ISRAEL
EGYPT
LIBYA
ALGERIA
MOROCCO
MALI
MAURITANIA
BURKINA
DAKAR
GUINEA
SIERRA LEONE
"...THEN CHAD AND UP TO LIBYA, BEFORE CROSSING OVER TO NIGERIA AND FINALLY, MOROCCO...
"...CHANGING BODIES AS OFTEN AS ANY NORMAL MAN MIGHT CHANGE TRAINS ON A LONG JOURNEY."
WHERE IT WENT FROM HERE, OR WHO IT CHOSE TO POSSESS, REMAINS A MYSTERY.

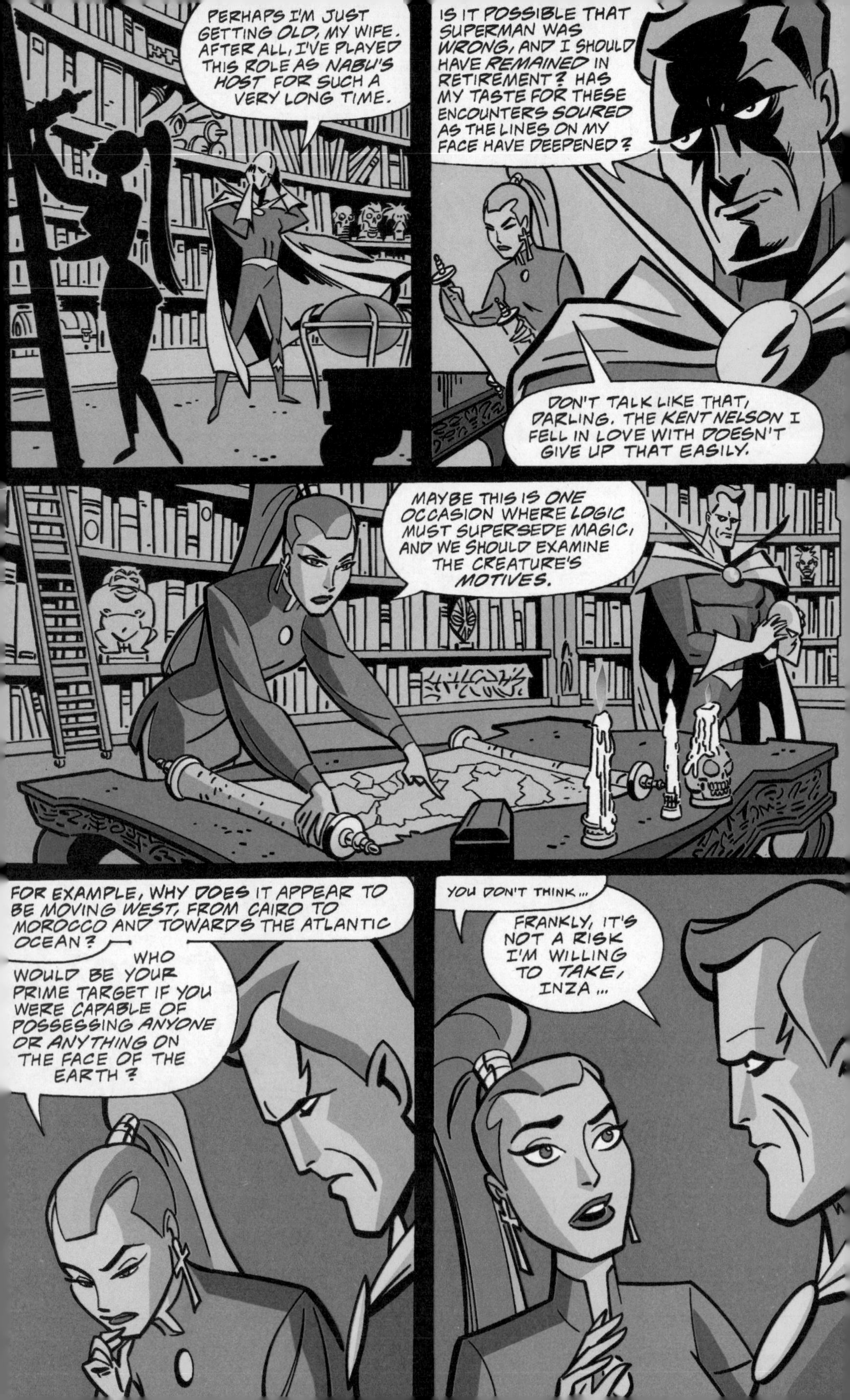
PERHAPS I'M JUST GETTING OLD, MY WIFE. AFTER ALL, I'VE PLAYED THIS ROLE AS NABU'S HOST FOR SUCH A VERY LONG TIME.
IS IT POSSIBLE THAT SUPERMAN WAS WRONG, AND I SHOULD HAVE REMAINED IN RETIREMENT? HAS MY TASTE FOR THESE ENCOUNTERS SOURED AS THE LINES ON MY FACE HAVE DEEPENED?
DON'T TALK LIKE THAT, DARLING. THE KENT NELSON I FELL IN LOVE WITH DOESN'T GIVE UP THAT EASILY.
MAYBE THIS IS ONE OCCASION WHERE LOGIC MUST SUPERSEDE MAGIC, AND WE SHOULD EXAMINE THE CREATURE'S MOTIVES.
FOR EXAMPLE, WHY DOES IT APPEAR TO BE MOVING WEST, FROM CAIRO TO MOROCCO AND TOWARDS THE ATLANTIC OCEAN?
WHO WOULD BE YOUR PRIME TARGET IF YOU WERE CAPABLE OF POSSESSING ANYONE OR ANYTHING ON THE FACE OF THE EARTH?
YOU DON'T THINK...
FRANKLY, IT'S NOT A RISK I'M WILLING TO TAKE, INZA...

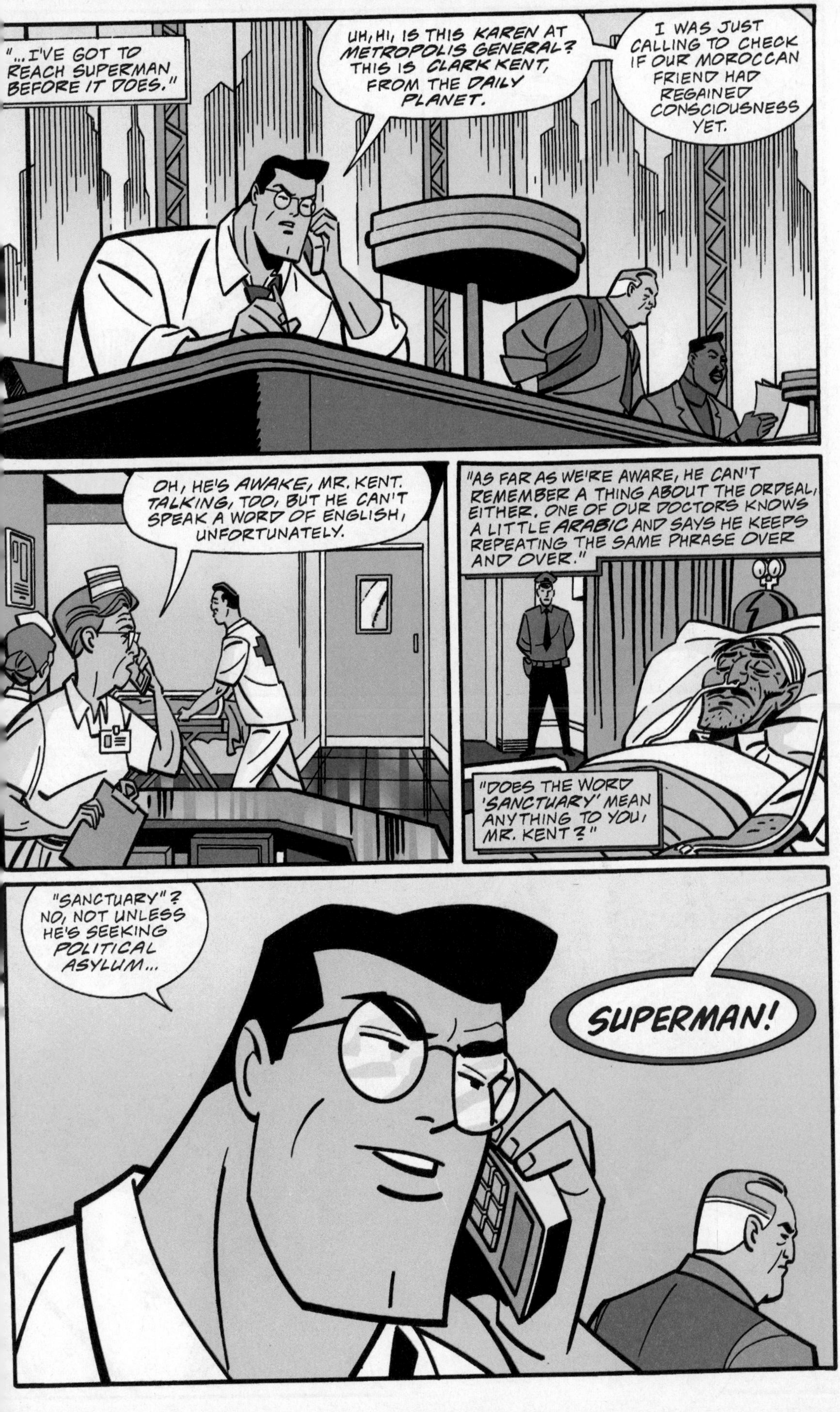
"...I'VE GOT TO REACH SUPERMAN BEFORE IT DOES."
UH, HI, IS THIS KAREN AT METROPOLIS GENERAL? THIS IS CLARK KENT, FROM THE DAILY PLANET.
I WAS JUST CALLING TO CHECK IF OUR MOROCCAN FRIEND HAD REGAINED CONSCIOUSNESS YET.
OH, HE'S AWAKE, MR. KENT. TALKING, TOO, BUT HE CAN'T SPEAK A WORD OF ENGLISH, UNFORTUNATELY.
"AS FAR AS WE'RE AWARE, HE CAN'T REMEMBER A THING ABOUT THE ORDEAL, EITHER. ONE OF OUR DOCTORS KNOWS A LITTLE ARABIC AND SAYS HE KEEPS REPEATING THE SAME PHRASE OVER AND OVER."
"DOES THE WORD 'SANCTUARY' MEAN ANYTHING TO YOU, MR. KENT?"
"SANCTUARY"? NO, NOT UNLESS HE'S SEEKING POLITICAL ASYLUM...
SUPERMAN!

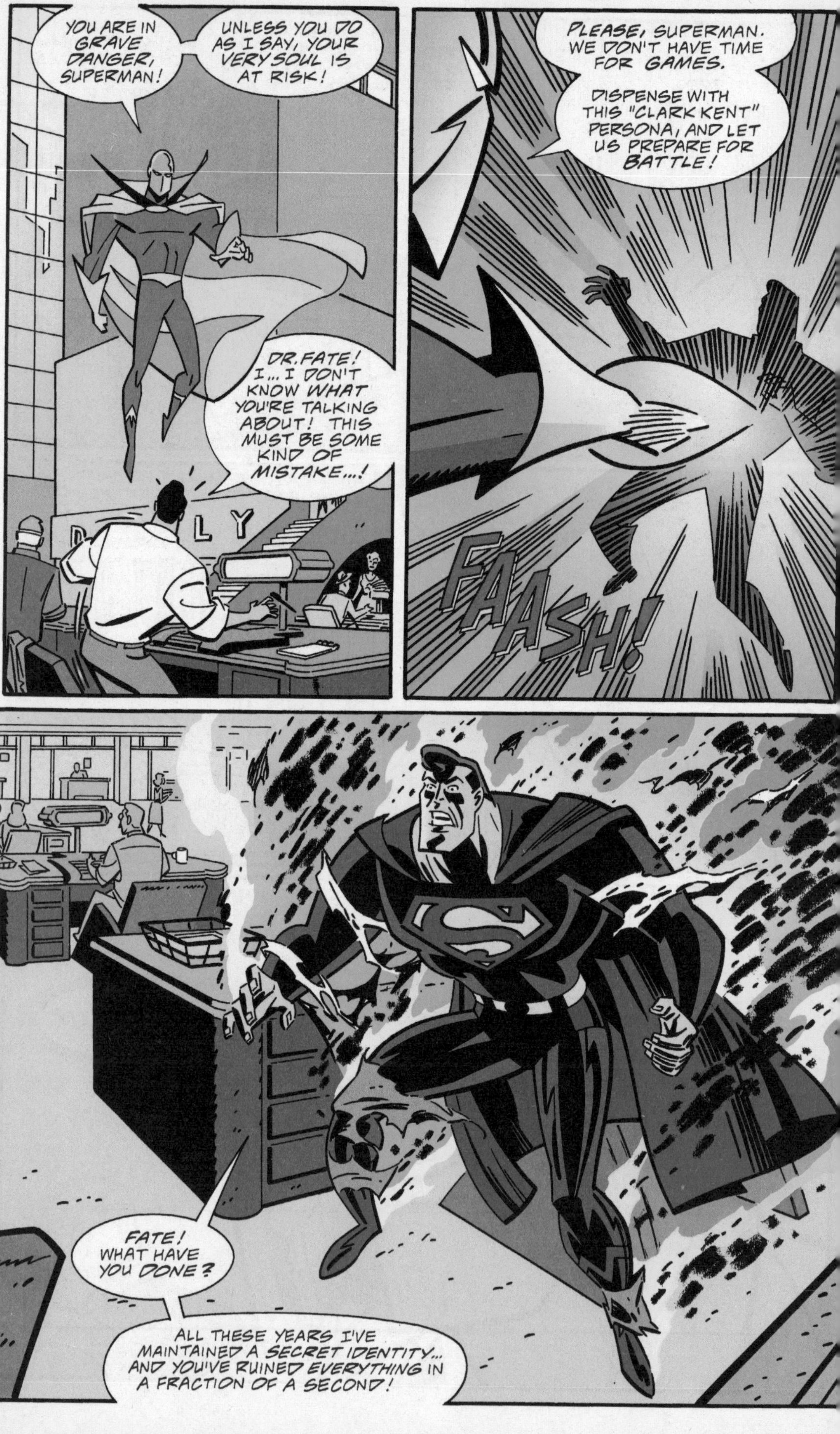
YOU ARE IN GRAVE DANGER, SUPERMAN!
UNLESS YOU DO AS I SAY, YOUR VERY SOUL IS AT RISK!
DR. FATE! I... I DON'T KNOW WHAT YOU'RE TALKING ABOUT! THIS MUST BE SOME KIND OF MISTAKE...!
PLEASE, SUPERMAN. WE DON'T HAVE TIME FOR GAMES.
DISPENSE WITH THIS "CLARK KENT" PERSONA, AND LET US PREPARE FOR BATTLE!
FAASH!
FATE! WHAT HAVE YOU DONE?
ALL THESE YEARS I'VE MAINTAINED A SECRET IDENTITY... AND YOU'VE RUINED EVERYTHING IN A FRACTION OF A SECOND!

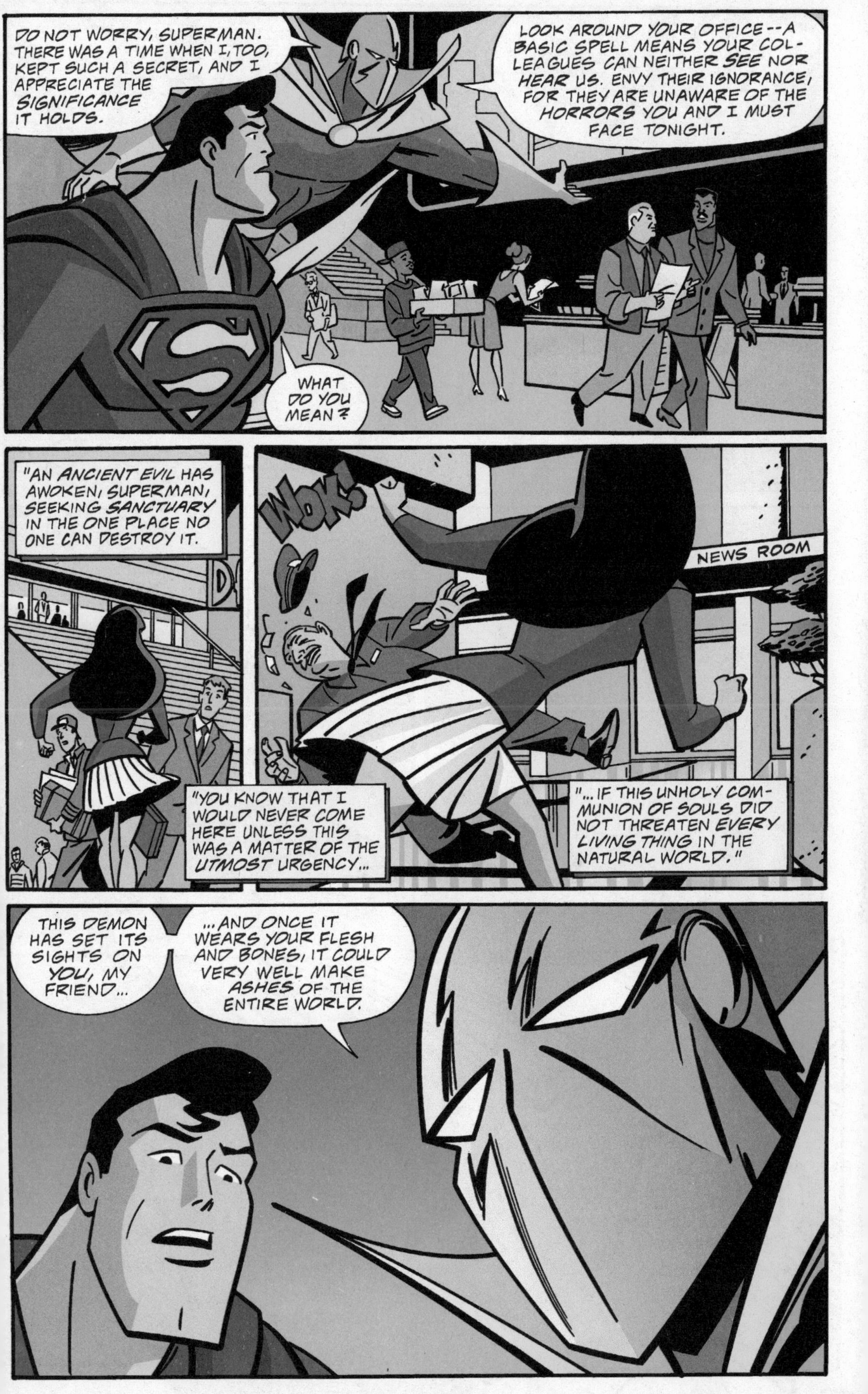
DO NOT WORRY, SUPERMAN. THERE WAS A TIME WHEN I, TOO, KEPT SUCH A SECRET, AND I APPRECIATE THE SIGNIFICANCE IT HOLDS.
LOOK AROUND YOUR OFFICE--A BASIC SPELL MEANS YOUR COLLEAGUES CAN NEITHER SEE NOR HEAR US. ENVY THEIR IGNORANCE, FOR THEY ARE UNAWARE OF THE HORRORS YOU AND I MUST FACE TONIGHT.
WHAT DO YOU MEAN?
"AN ANCIENT EVIL HAS AWOKEN, SUPERMAN, SEEKING SANCTUARY IN THE ONE PLACE NO ONE CAN DESTROY IT.
WOK!
NEWS ROOM
"YOU KNOW THAT I WOULD NEVER COME HERE UNLESS THIS WAS A MATTER OF THE UTMOST URGENCY...
"...IF THIS UNHOLY COMMUNION OF SOULS DID NOT THREATEN EVERY LIVING THING IN THE NATURAL WORLD."
THIS DEMON HAS SET ITS SIGHTS ON YOU, MY FRIEND...
...AND ONCE IT WEARS YOUR FLESH AND BONES, IT COULD VERY WELL MAKE ASHES OF THE ENTIRE WORLD.

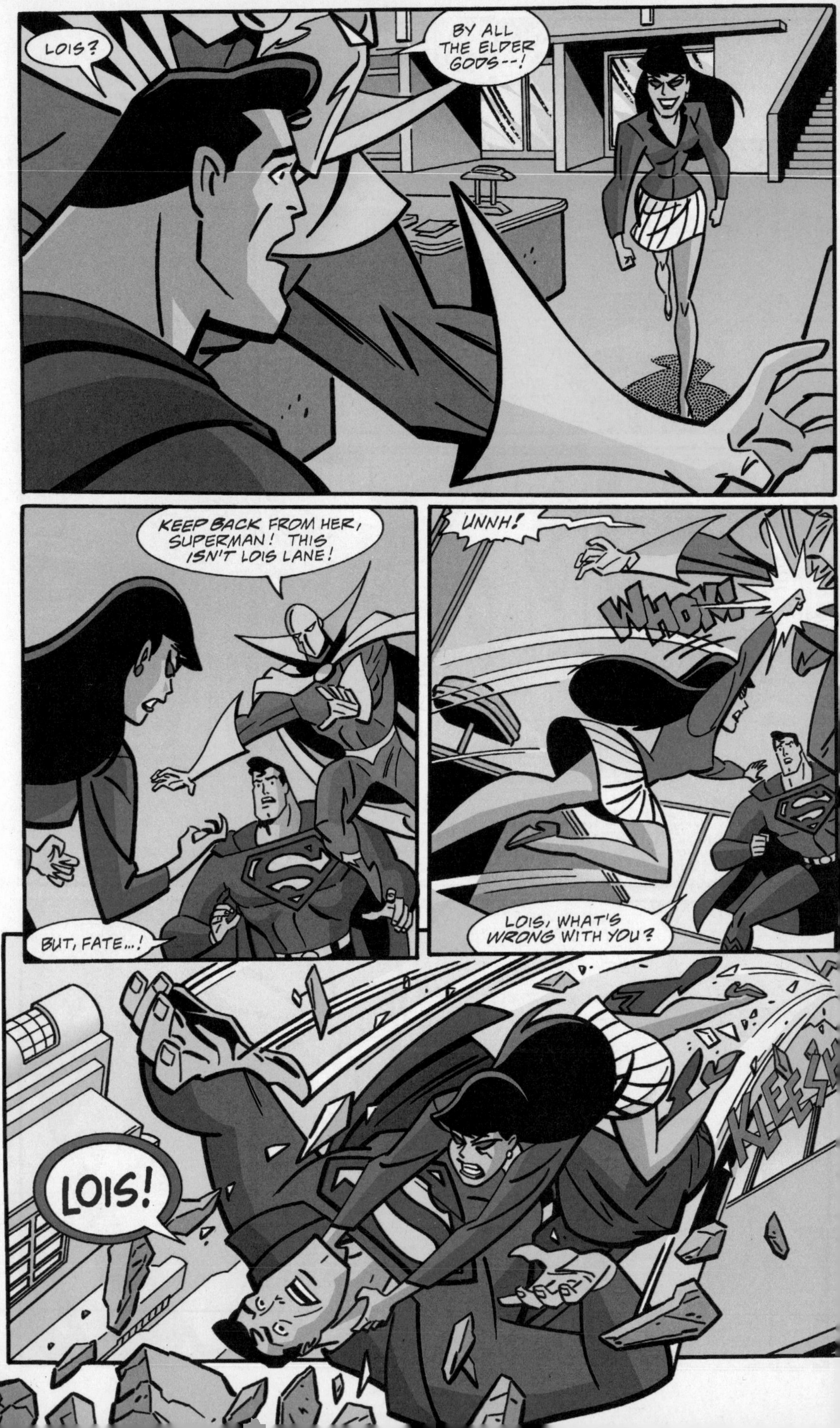

LOIS?
BY ALL THE ELDER GODS--!
KEEP BACK FROM HER, SUPERMAN! THIS ISN'T LOIS LANE!
BUT, FATE...!
UNNH!
WHOM!
LOIS, WHAT'S WRONG WITH YOU?
LOIS!

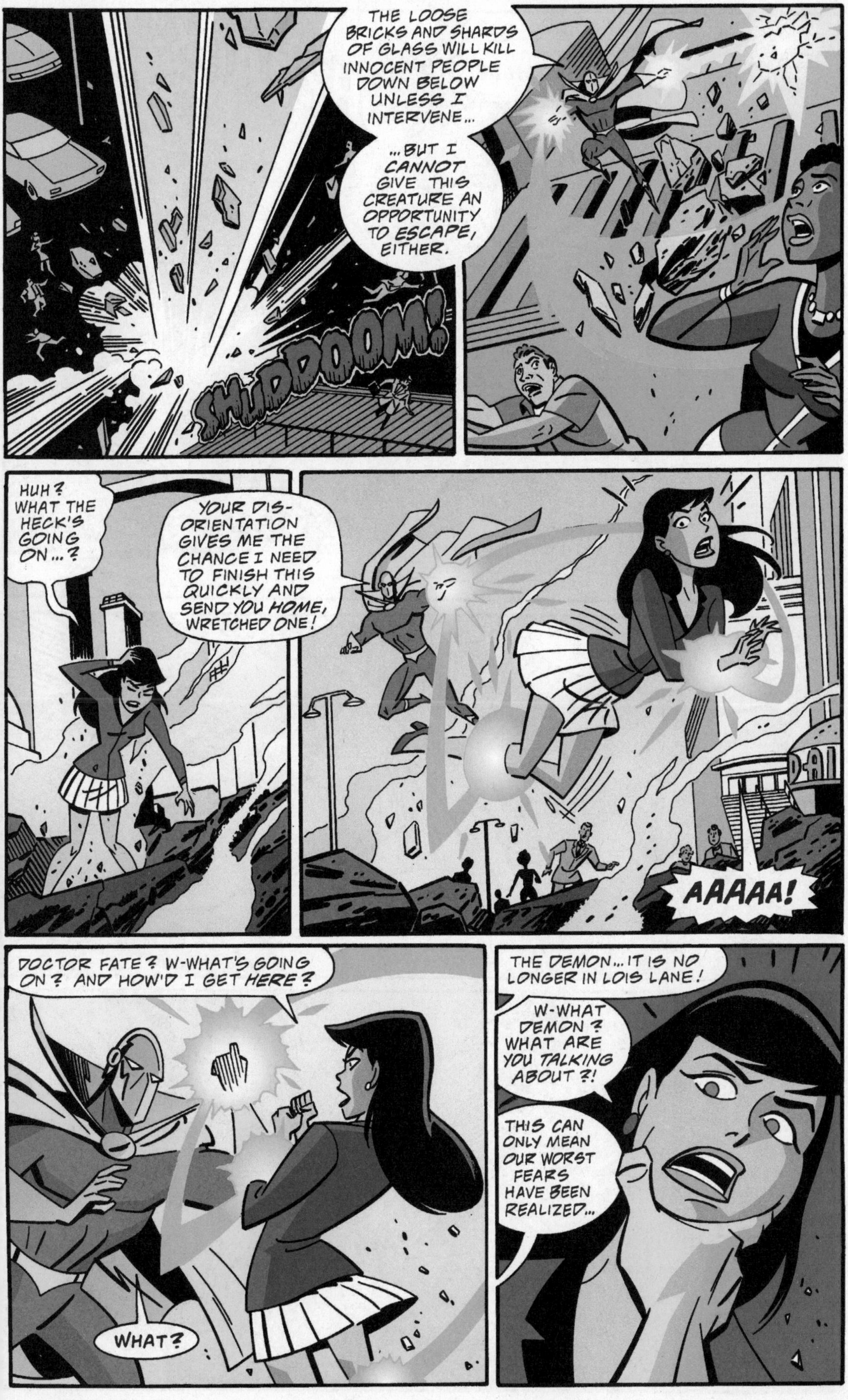
SHUDDOOM!
THE LOOSE BRICKS AND SHARDS OF GLASS WILL KILL INNOCENT PEOPLE DOWN BELOW UNLESS I INTERVENE...
...BUT I CANNOT GIVE THIS CREATURE AN OPPORTUNITY TO ESCAPE, EITHER.
HUH? WHAT THE HECK'S GOING ON...?
YOUR DIS-ORIENTATION GIVES ME THE CHANCE I NEED TO FINISH THIS QUICKLY AND SEND YOU HOME, WRETCHED ONE!
AAAAA!
DOCTOR FATE? W-WHAT'S GOING ON? AND HOW'D I GET HERE?
WHAT?
THE DEMON... IT IS NO LONGER IN LOIS LANE!
W-WHAT DEMON? WHAT ARE YOU TALKING ABOUT?!
THIS CAN ONLY MEAN OUR WORST FEARS HAVE BEEN REALIZED...

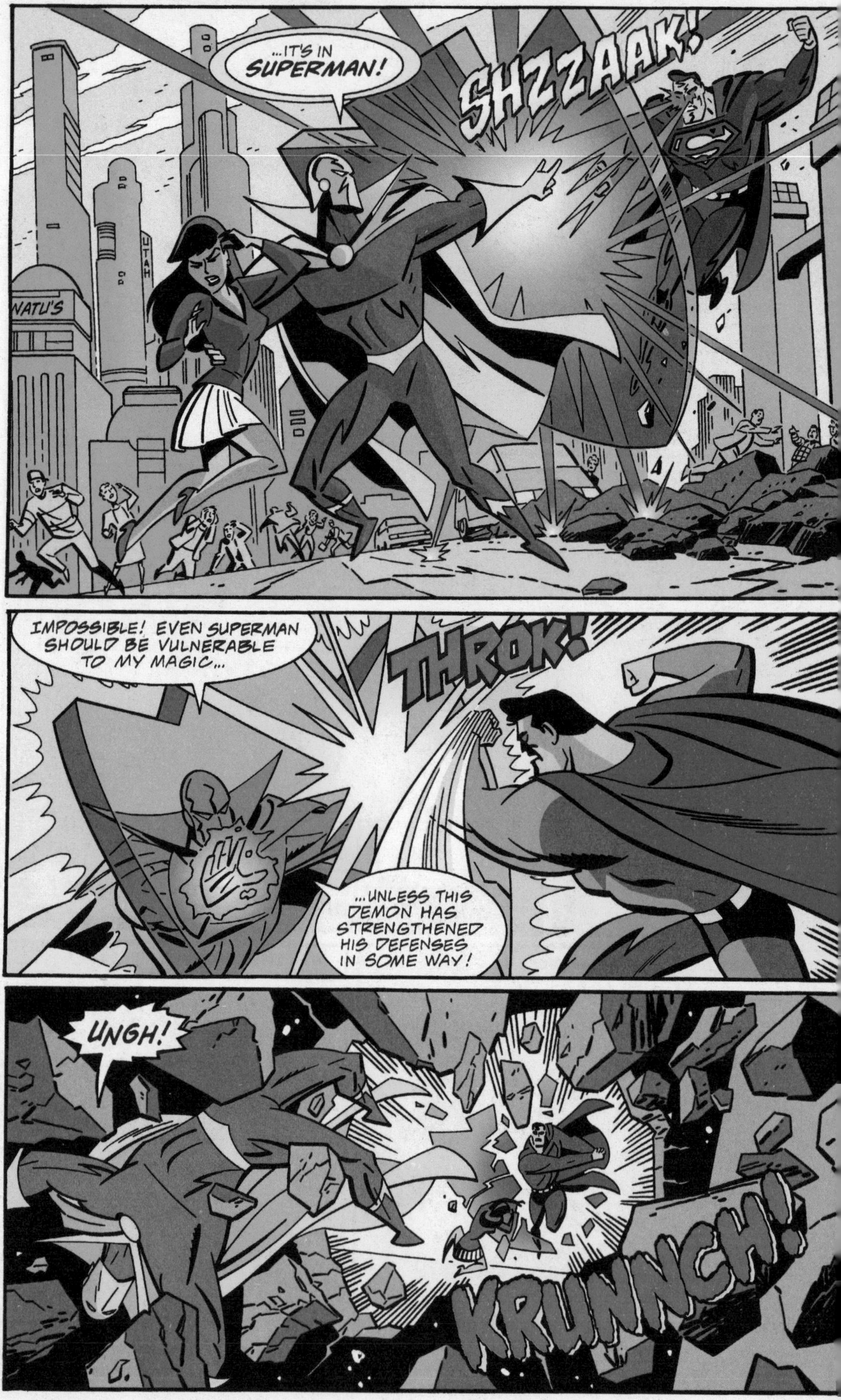
...IT'S IN SUPERMAN!
SHZZAAK!
IMPOSSIBLE! EVEN SUPERMAN SHOULD BE VULNERABLE TO MY MAGIC...
THROK!
...UNLESS THIS DEMON HAS STRENGTHENED HIS DEFENSES IN SOME WAY!
UNGH!
KRUNNCH!

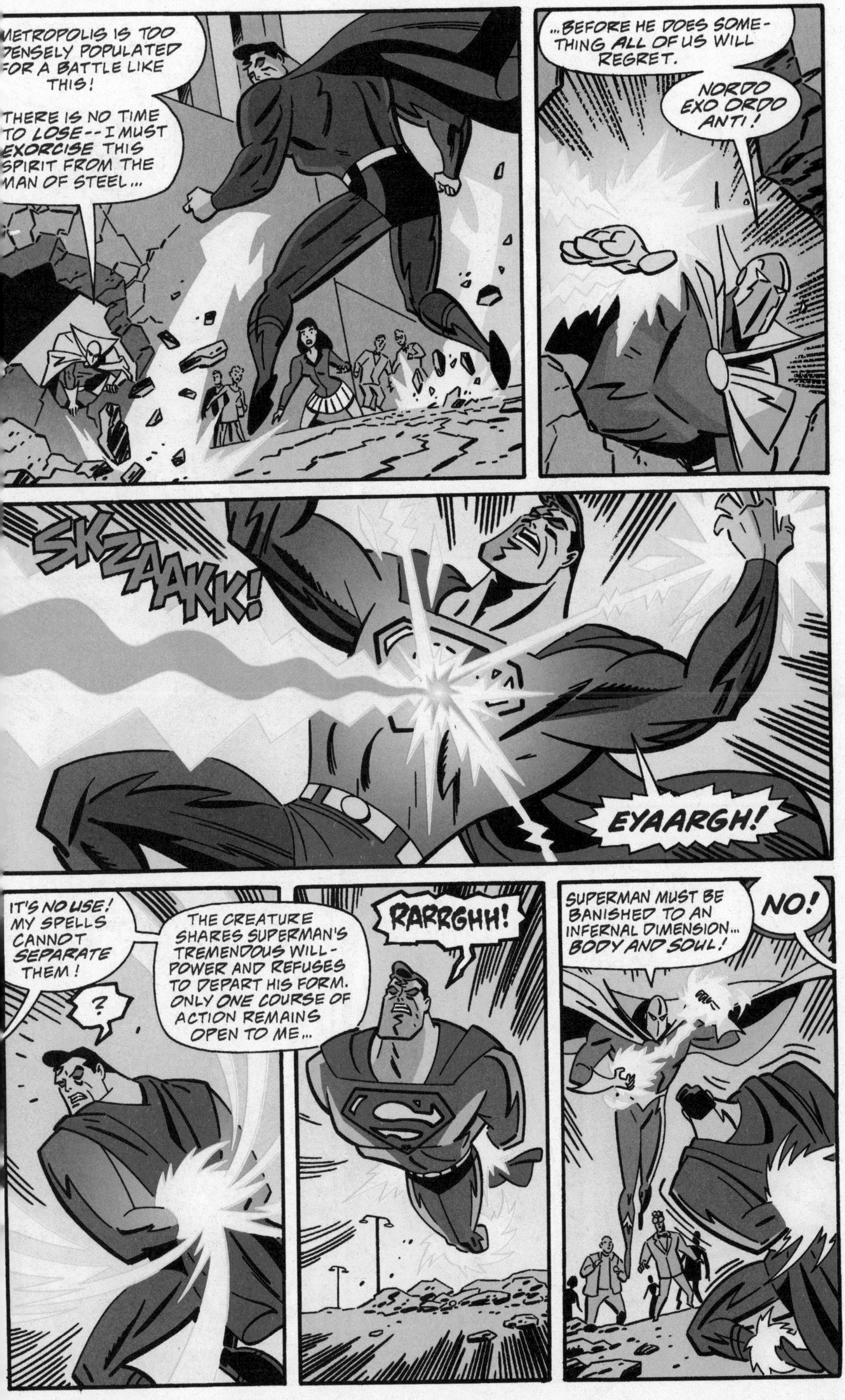

METROPOLIS IS TOO DENSELY POPULATED FOR A BATTLE LIKE THIS!
THERE IS NO TIME TO LOSE--I MUST EXORCISE THIS SPIRIT FROM THE MAN OF STEEL...
...BEFORE HE DOES SOMETHING ALL OF US WILL REGRET.
NORDO EXO ORDO ANTI!
SKZAAKK!
EYAARGH!
IT'S NO USE! MY SPELLS CANNOT SEPARATE THEM!
?
THE CREATURE SHARES SUPERMAN'S TREMENDOUS WILL-POWER AND REFUSES TO DEPART HIS FORM. ONLY ONE COURSE OF ACTION REMAINS OPEN TO ME...
RARRGHH!
SUPERMAN MUST BE BANISHED TO AN INFERNAL DIMENSION... BODY AND SOUL!
NO!

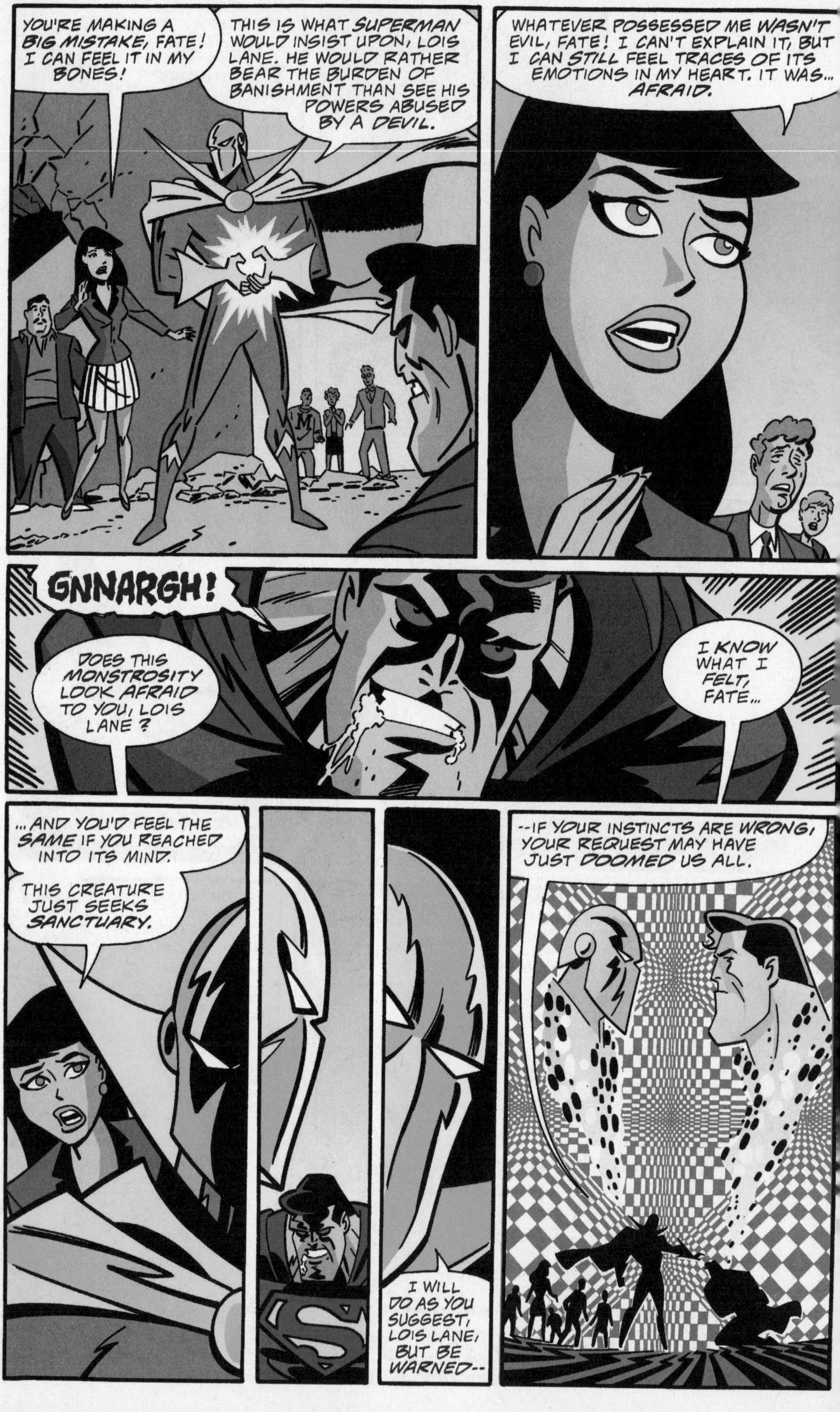
YOU'RE MAKING A BIG MISTAKE, FATE! I CAN FEEL IT IN MY BONES!
THIS IS WHAT SUPERMAN WOULD INSIST UPON, LOIS LANE. HE WOULD RATHER BEAR THE BURDEN OF BANISHMENT THAN SEE HIS POWERS ABUSED BY A DEVIL.
WHATEVER POSSESSED ME WASN'T EVIL, FATE! I CAN'T EXPLAIN IT, BUT I CAN STILL FEEL TRACES OF ITS EMOTIONS IN MY HEART. IT WAS... AFRAID.
GNNARGH!
DOES THIS MONSTROSITY LOOK AFRAID TO YOU, LOIS LANE?
I KNOW WHAT I FELT, FATE...
...AND YOU'D FEEL THE SAME IF YOU REACHED INTO ITS MIND.
THIS CREATURE JUST SEEKS SANCTUARY.
I WILL DO AS YOU SUGGEST, LOIS LANE, BUT BE WARNED--
--IF YOUR INSTINCTS ARE WRONG, YOUR REQUEST MAY HAVE JUST DOOMED US ALL.

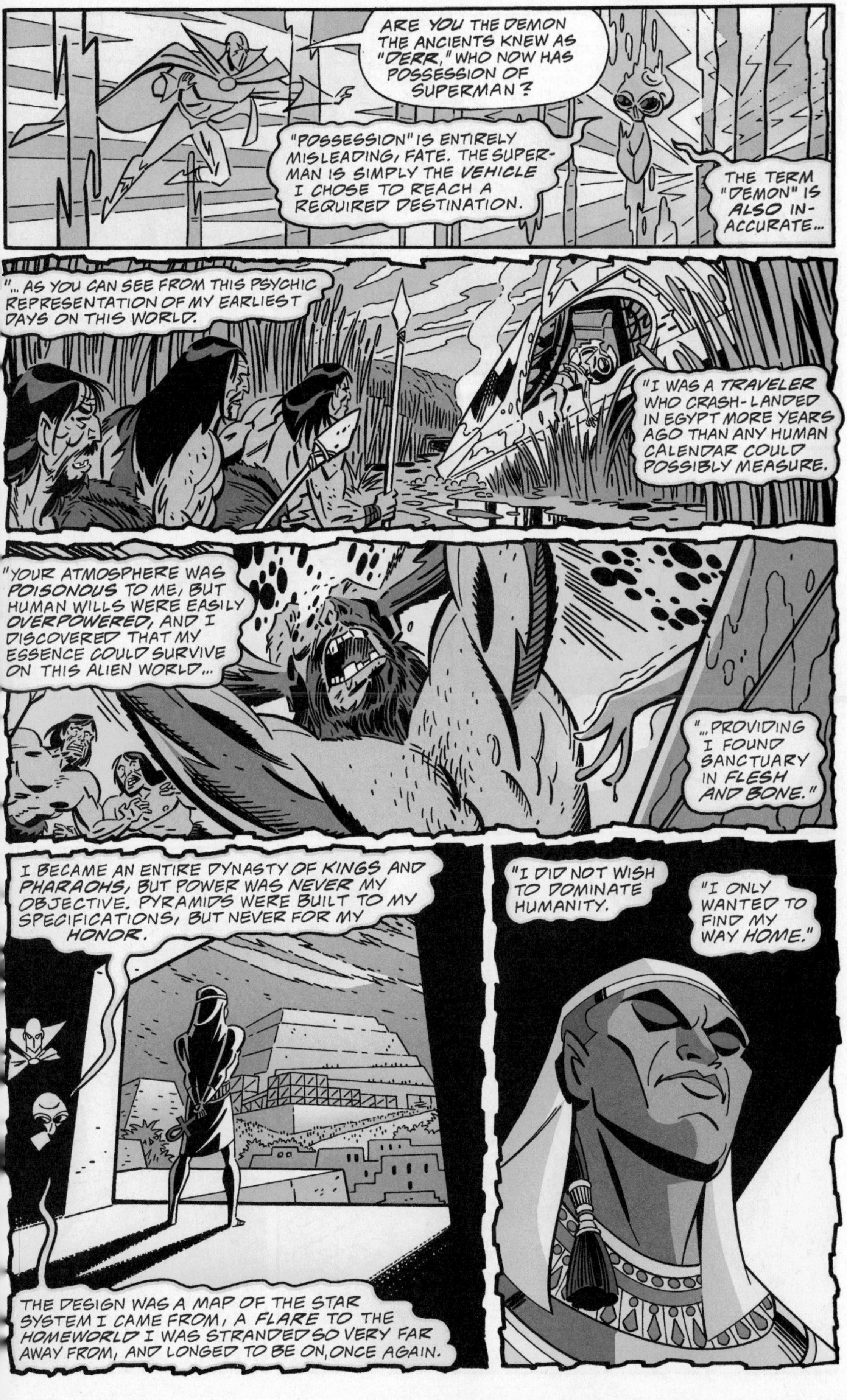
ARE YOU THE DEMON THE ANCIENTS KNEW AS "DERR," WHO NOW HAS POSSESSION OF SUPERMAN?
"POSSESSION" IS ENTIRELY MISLEADING, FATE. THE SUPER-MAN IS SIMPLY THE VEHICLE I CHOSE TO REACH A REQUIRED DESTINATION.
THE TERM "DEMON" IS ALSO IN-ACCURATE...
"...AS YOU CAN SEE FROM THIS PSYCHIC REPRESENTATION OF MY EARLIEST DAYS ON THIS WORLD.
"I WAS A TRAVELER WHO CRASH-LANDED IN EGYPT MORE YEARS AGO THAN ANY HUMAN CALENDAR COULD POSSIBLY MEASURE.
"YOUR ATMOSPHERE WAS POISONOUS TO ME, BUT HUMAN WILLS WERE EASILY OVERPOWERED, AND I DISCOVERED THAT MY ESSENCE COULD SURVIVE ON THIS ALIEN WORLD...
"...PROVIDING I FOUND SANCTUARY IN FLESH AND BONE."
I BECAME AN ENTIRE DYNASTY OF KINGS AND PHARAOHS, BUT POWER WAS NEVER MY OBJECTIVE. PYRAMIDS WERE BUILT TO MY SPECIFICATIONS, BUT NEVER FOR MY HONOR.
THE DESIGN WAS A MAP OF THE STAR SYSTEM I CAME FROM, A FLARE TO THE HOMEWORLD I WAS STRANDED SO VERY FAR AWAY FROM, AND LONGED TO BE ON, ONCE AGAIN.
"I DID NOT WISH TO DOMINATE HUMANITY.
"I ONLY WANTED TO FIND MY WAY HOME."

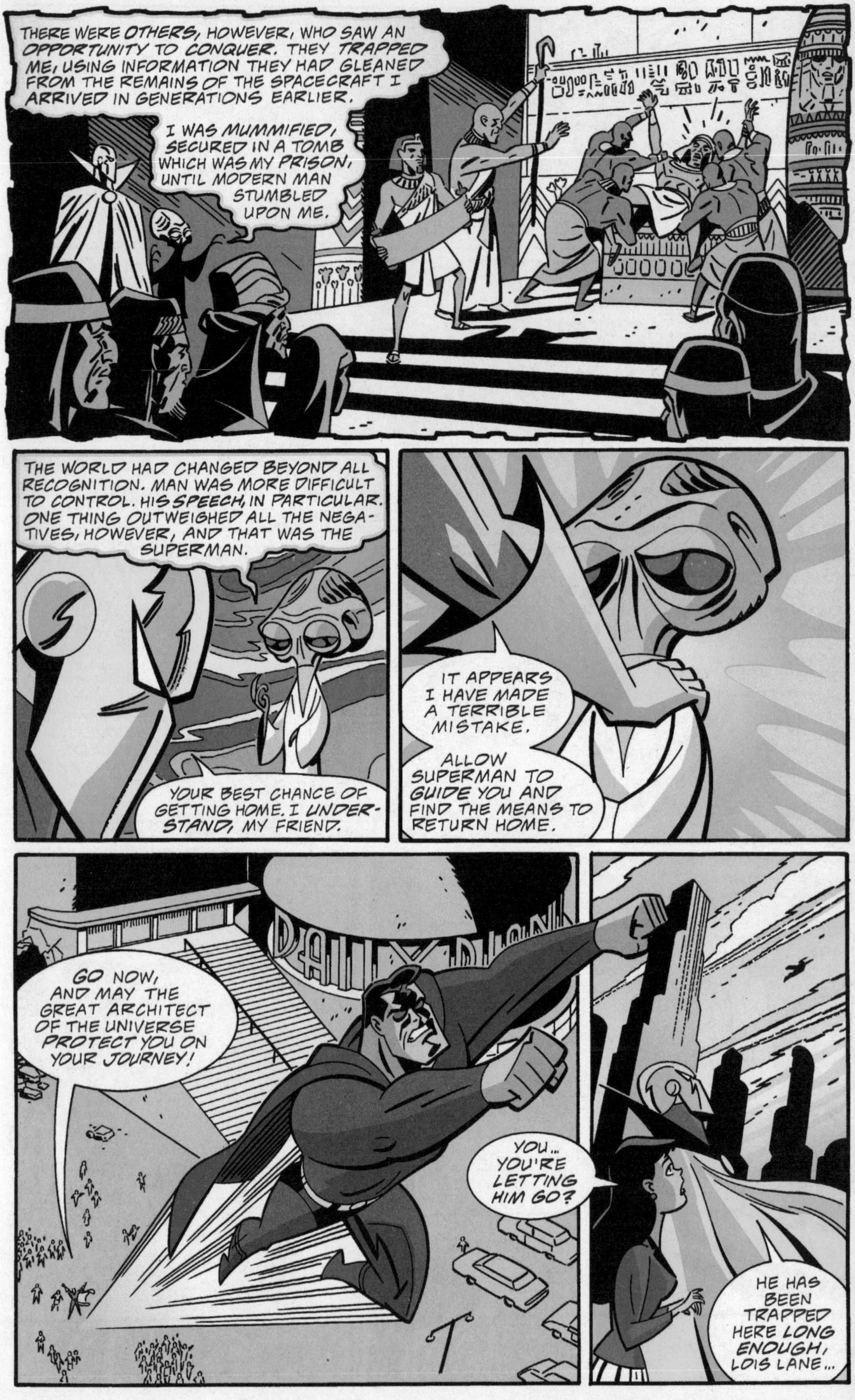
THERE WERE OTHERS, HOWEVER, WHO SAW AN OPPORTUNITY TO CONQUER. THEY TRAPPED ME, USING INFORMATION THEY HAD GLEANED FROM THE REMAINS OF THE SPACECRAFT I ARRIVED IN GENERATIONS EARLIER.
I WAS MUMMIFIED, SECURED IN A TOMB WHICH WAS MY PRISON, UNTIL MODERN MAN STUMBLED UPON ME.
THE WORLD HAD CHANGED BEYOND ALL RECOGNITION. MAN WAS MORE DIFFICULT TO CONTROL. HIS SPEECH, IN PARTICULAR. ONE THING OUTWEIGHED ALL THE NEGATIVES, HOWEVER, AND THAT WAS THE SUPERMAN.
YOUR BEST CHANCE OF GETTING HOME. I UNDERSTAND, MY FRIEND.
IT APPEARS I HAVE MADE A TERRIBLE MISTAKE.
ALLOW SUPERMAN TO GUIDE YOU AND FIND THE MEANS TO RETURN HOME.
GO NOW, AND MAY THE GREAT ARCHITECT OF THE UNIVERSE PROTECT YOU ON YOUR JOURNEY!
YOU... YOU'RE LETTING HIM GO?
HE HAS BEEN TRAPPED HERE LONG ENOUGH, LOIS LANE...

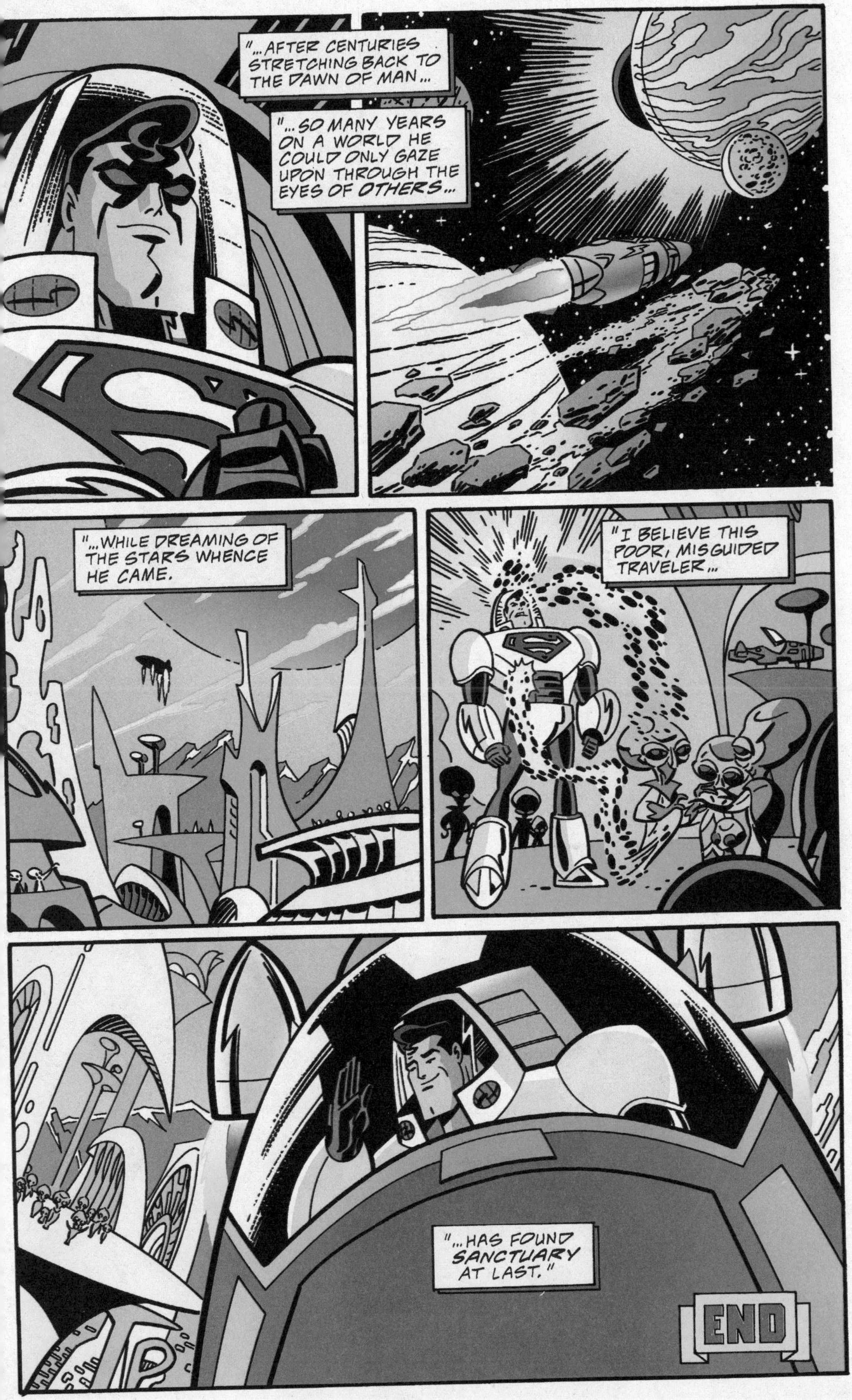
"...AFTER CENTURIES STRETCHING BACK TO THE DAWN OF MAN...
"...SO MANY YEARS ON A WORLD HE COULD ONLY GAZE UPON THROUGH THE EYES OF OTHERS...
"...WHILE DREAMING OF THE STARS WHENCE HE CAME.
"I BELIEVE THIS POOR, MISGUIDED TRAVELER...
"...HAS FOUND SANCTUARY AT LAST."
END

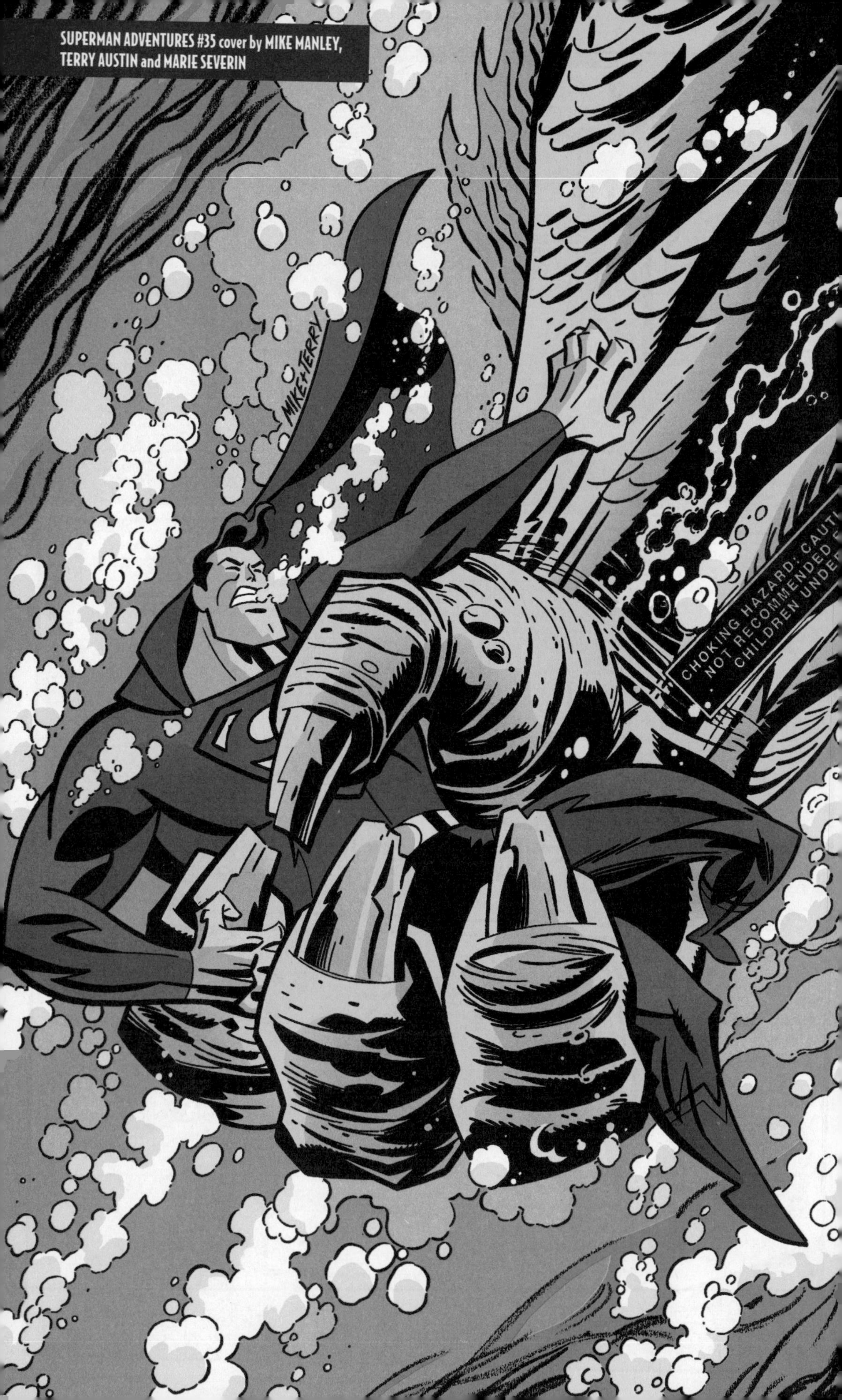
MIKE+TERRY
CHOKING HAZARD: CAUTI
NOT RECOMMENDED
CHILDREN UNDE

SUPERMAN ADVENTURES #35 cover by MIKE MANLEY, TERRY AUSTIN and MARIE SEVERIN

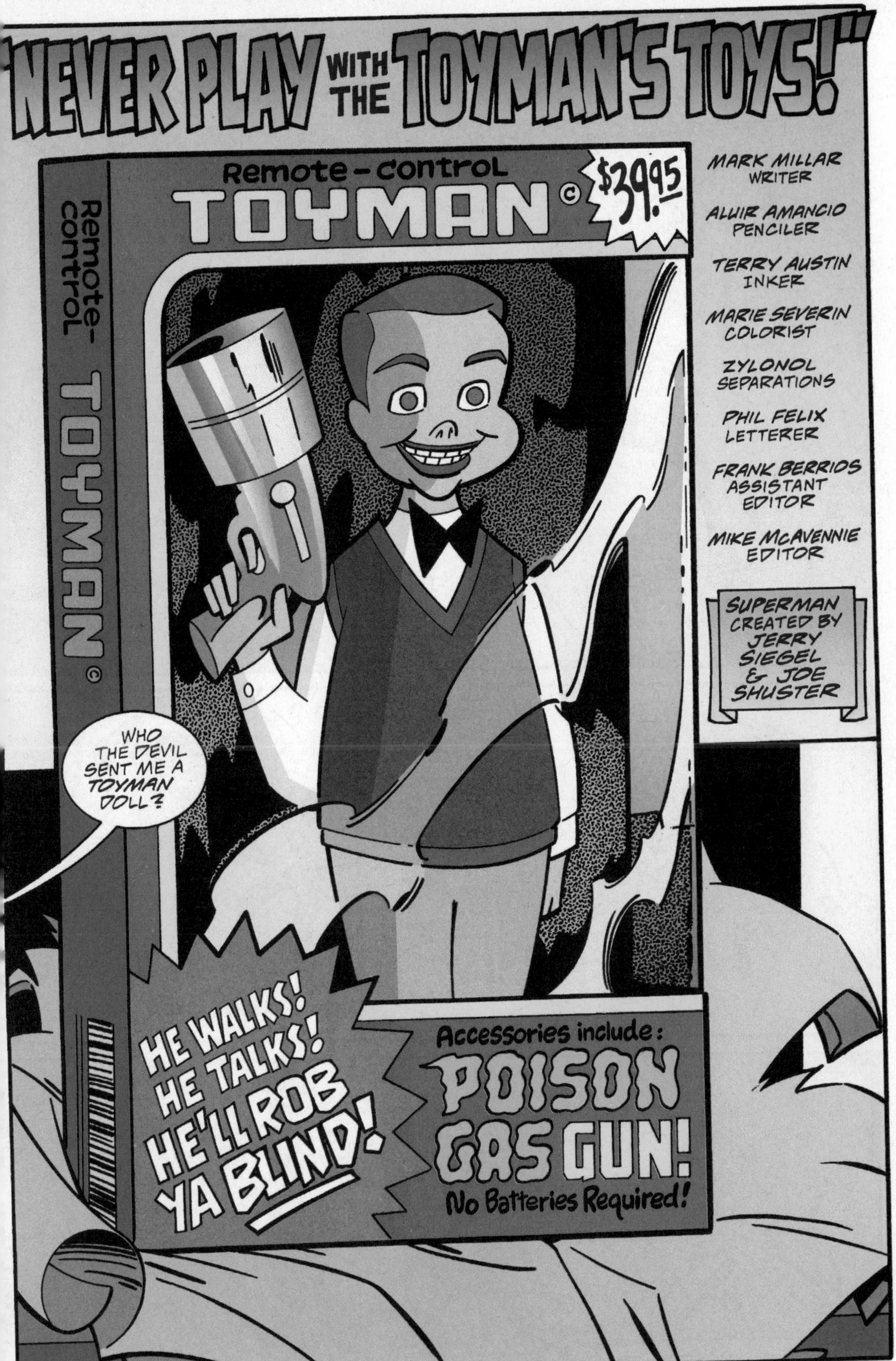
"NEVER PLAY WITH THE TOYMAN'S TOYS!"
Remote-control TOYMAN ©
$39.95
Remote-control TOYMAN ©
MARK MILLAR WRITER
ALUIR AMANCIO PENCILER
TERRY AUSTIN INKER
MARIE SEVERIN COLORIST
ZYLONOL SEPARATIONS
PHIL FELIX LETTERER
FRANK BERRIOS ASSISTANT EDITOR
MIKE McAVENNIE EDITOR
SUPERMAN CREATED BY JERRY SIEGEL & JOE SHUSTER
WHO THE DEVIL SENT ME A TOYMAN DOLL?
HE WALKS! HE TALKS! HE'LL ROB YA BLIND!
Accessories include: POISON GAS GUN!
No Batteries Required!

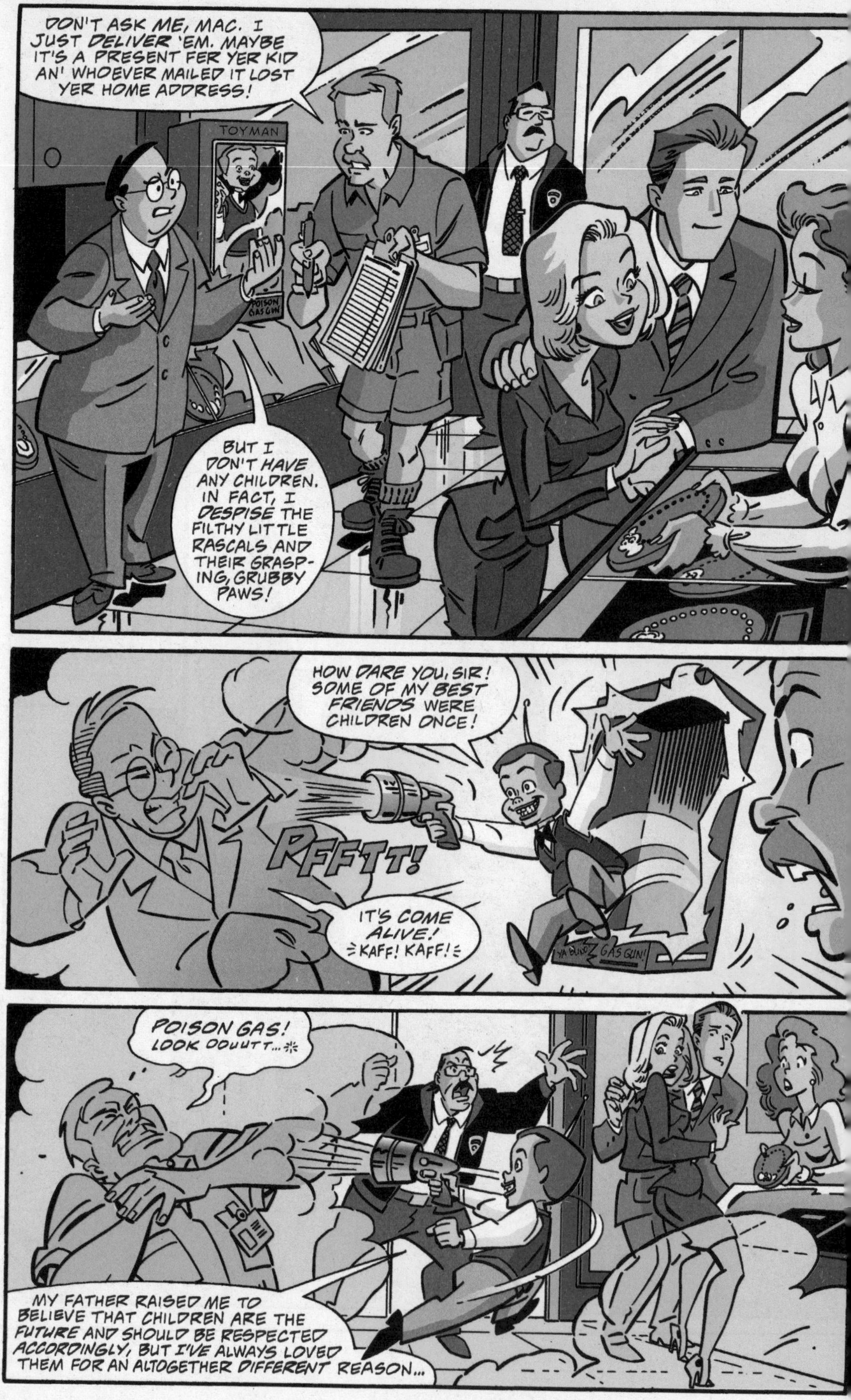
DON'T ASK ME, MAC. I JUST DELIVER 'EM. MAYBE IT'S A PRESENT FER YER KID AN' WHOEVER MAILED IT LOST YER HOME ADDRESS!
TOYMAN
POISON GAS GUN
BUT I DON'T HAVE ANY CHILDREN. IN FACT, I DESPISE THE FILTHY LITTLE RASCALS AND THEIR GRASPING, GRUBBY PAWS!
HOW DARE YOU, SIR! SOME OF MY BEST FRIENDS WERE CHILDREN ONCE!
PFFTTT!
IT'S COME ALIVE! KAFF! KAFF!
GAS GUN!
POISON GAS! LOOK OOUUTT...
MY FATHER RAISED ME TO BELIEVE THAT CHILDREN ARE THE FUTURE AND SHOULD BE RESPECTED ACCORDINGLY, BUT I'VE ALWAYS LOVED THEM FOR AN ALTOGETHER DIFFERENT REASON...

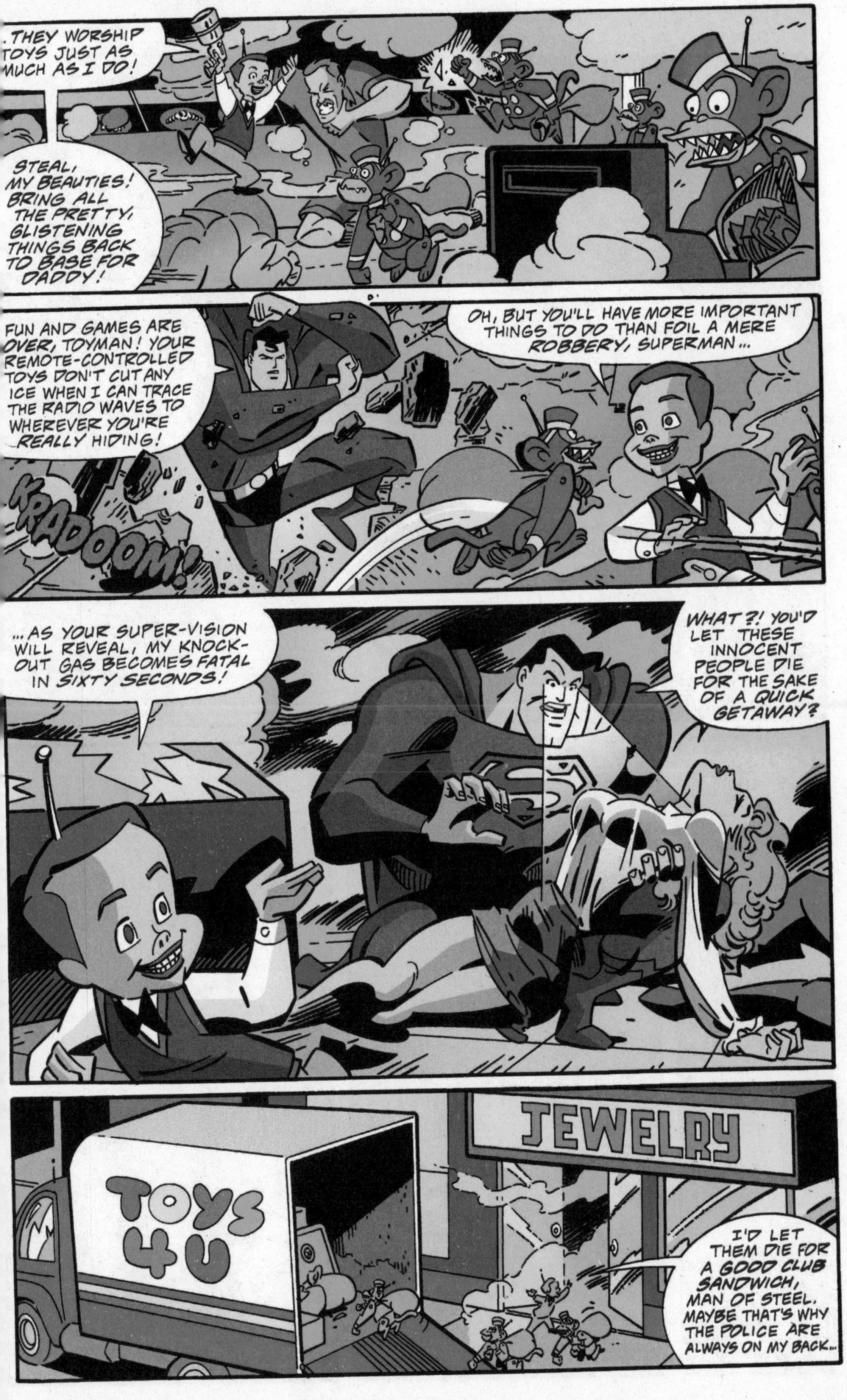
...THEY WORSHIP TOYS JUST AS MUCH AS I DO!
STEAL, MY BEAUTIES! BRING ALL THE PRETTY, GLISTENING THINGS BACK TO BASE FOR DADDY!
FUN AND GAMES ARE OVER, TOYMAN! YOUR REMOTE-CONTROLLED TOYS DON'T CUT ANY ICE WHEN I CAN TRACE THE RADIO WAVES TO WHEREVER YOU'RE REALLY HIDING!
KRADOOOM!
OH, BUT YOU'LL HAVE MORE IMPORTANT THINGS TO DO THAN FOIL A MERE ROBBERY, SUPERMAN...
...AS YOUR SUPER-VISION WILL REVEAL, MY KNOCK-OUT GAS BECOMES FATAL IN SIXTY SECONDS!
WHAT?! YOU'D LET THESE INNOCENT PEOPLE DIE FOR THE SAKE OF A QUICK GETAWAY?
TOYS 4 U
JEWELRY
I'D LET THEM DIE FOR A GOOD CLUB SANDWICH, MAN OF STEEL. MAYBE THAT'S WHY THE POLICE ARE ALWAYS ON MY BACK...

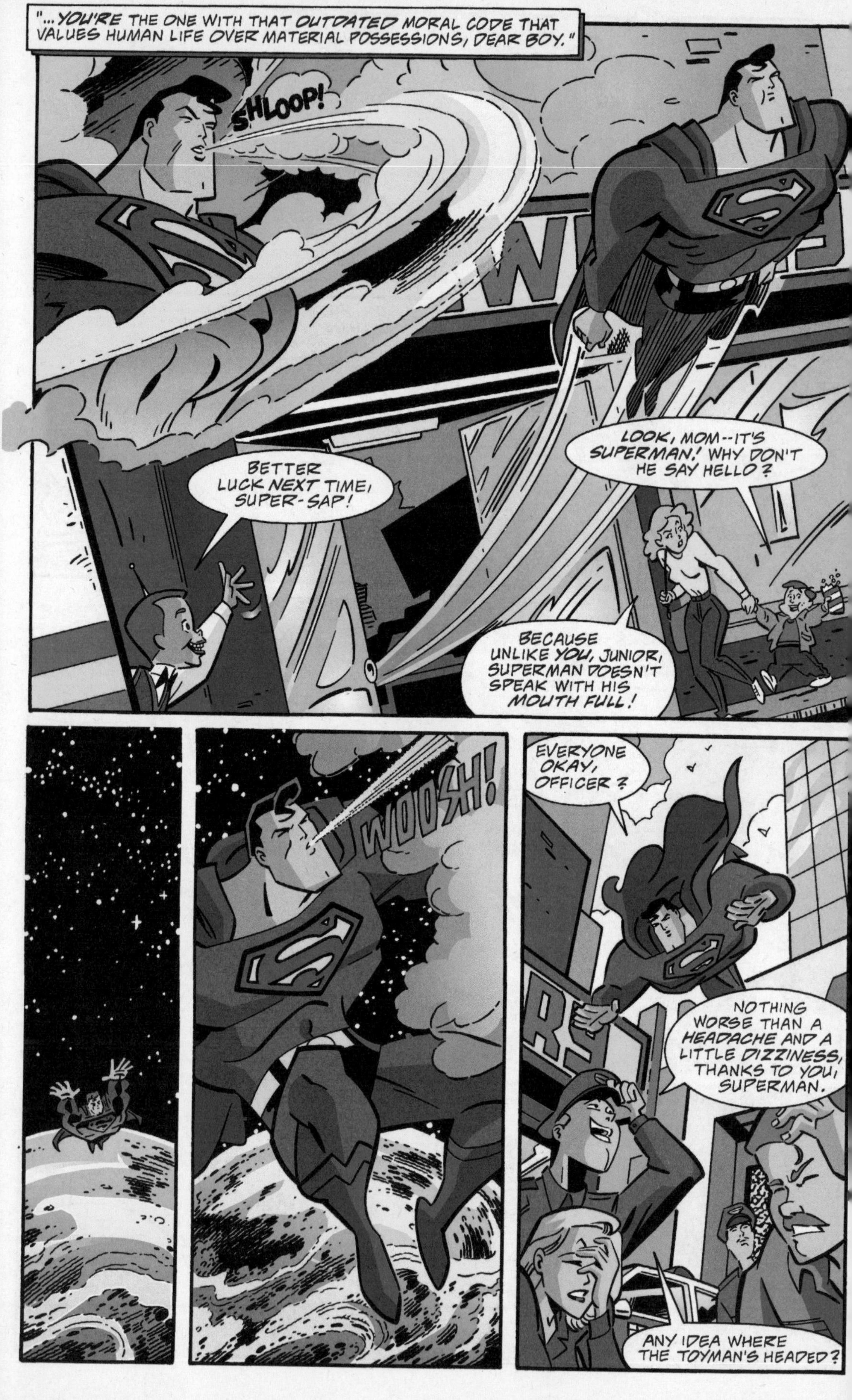
"...YOU'RE THE ONE WITH THAT OUTDATED MORAL CODE THAT VALUES HUMAN LIFE OVER MATERIAL POSSESSIONS, DEAR BOY."
SHLOOP!
BETTER LUCK NEXT TIME, SUPER-SAP!
LOOK, MOM--IT'S SUPERMAN! WHY DON'T HE SAY HELLO?
BECAUSE UNLIKE YOU, JUNIOR, SUPERMAN DOESN'T SPEAK WITH HIS MOUTH FULL!
WOOSH!
EVERYONE OKAY, OFFICER?
NOTHING WORSE THAN A HEADACHE AND A LITTLE DIZZINESS, THANKS TO YOU, SUPERMAN.
ANY IDEA WHERE THE TOYMAN'S HEADED?

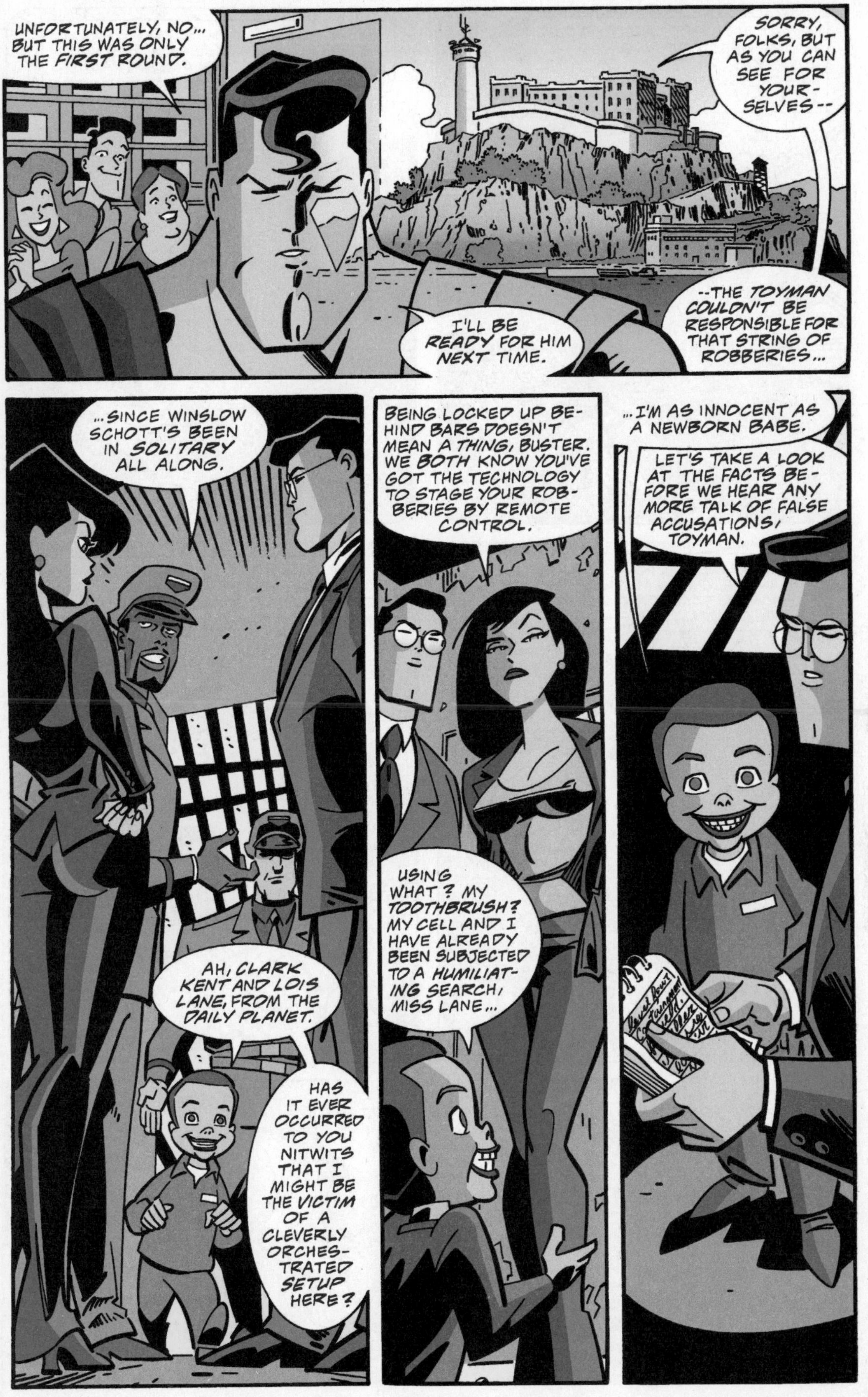
UNFORTUNATELY, NO... BUT THIS WAS ONLY THE *FIRST ROUND.*
I'LL BE *READY* FOR HIM *NEXT* TIME.
SORRY, FOLKS, BUT AS YOU CAN SEE FOR YOUR-SELVES--
--THE *TOYMAN COULDN'T* BE RESPONSIBLE FOR THAT STRING OF ROBBERIES...
...SINCE WINSLOW SCHOTT'S BEEN IN *SOLITARY* ALL ALONG.
AH, *CLARK KENT* AND *LOIS LANE,* FROM THE *DAILY PLANET.*
HAS IT EVER OCCURRED TO YOU NITWITS THAT I MIGHT BE THE *VICTIM* OF A CLEVERLY ORCHES-TRATED *SETUP* HERE?
BEING LOCKED UP BE-HIND BARS DOESN'T MEAN A *THING,* BUSTER. WE *BOTH* KNOW YOU'VE GOT THE TECHNOLOGY TO STAGE YOUR ROB-BERIES BY REMOTE CONTROL.
USING WHAT? MY *TOOTHBRUSH?* MY CELL AND I HAVE ALREADY BEEN SUBJECTED TO A *HUMILIAT-ING* SEARCH, MISS LANE...
...I'M AS INNOCENT AS A NEWBORN BABE.
LET'S TAKE A LOOK AT THE FACTS BE-FORE WE HEAR ANY MORE TALK OF FALSE ACCUSATIONS, TOYMAN.

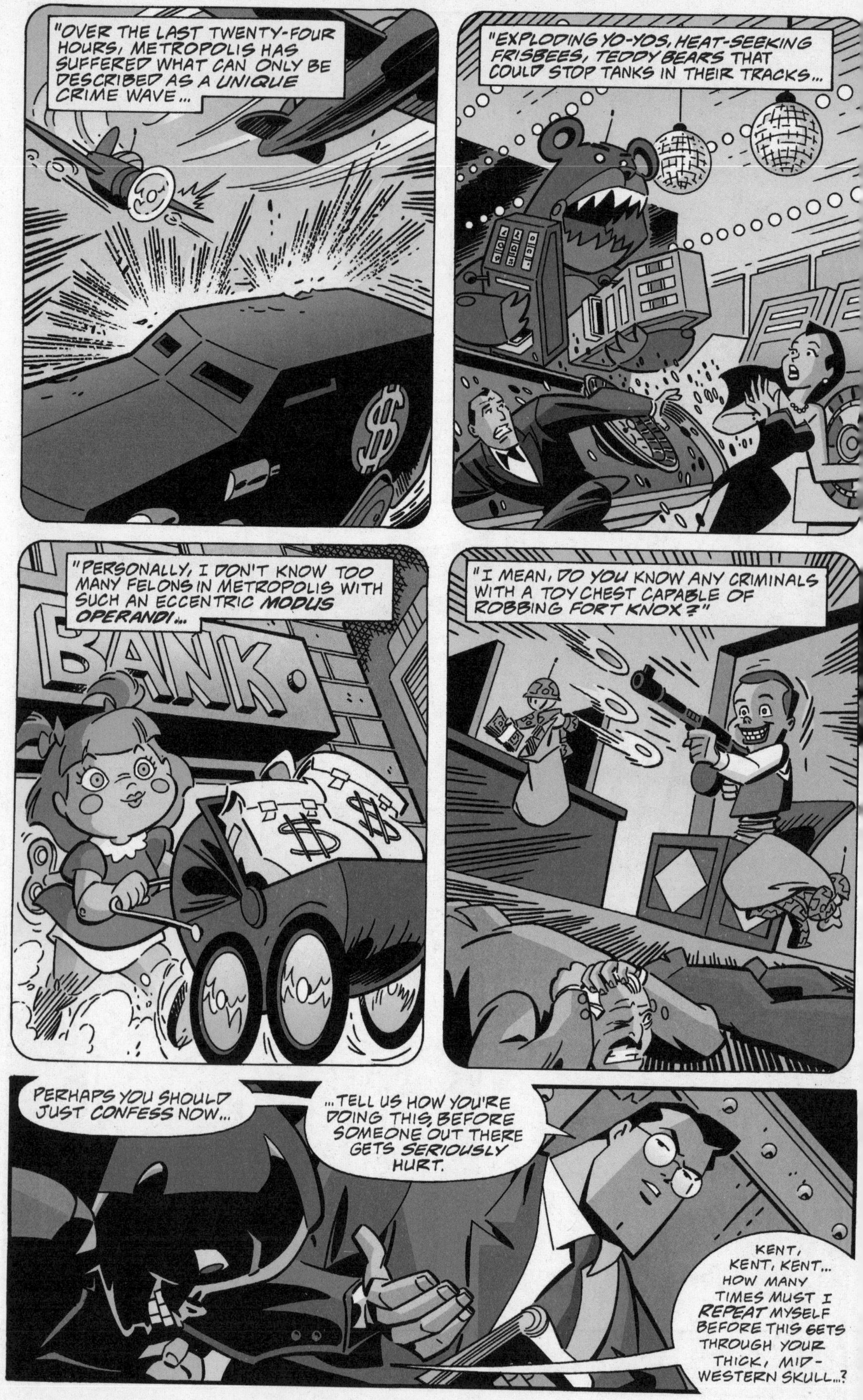
"OVER THE LAST TWENTY-FOUR HOURS, METROPOLIS HAS SUFFERED WHAT CAN ONLY BE DESCRIBED AS A *UNIQUE* CRIME WAVE...
"EXPLODING YO-YOS, HEAT-SEEKING FRISBEES, *TEDDY BEARS* THAT COULD STOP TANKS IN THEIR TRACKS...
"PERSONALLY, I DON'T KNOW TOO MANY FELONS IN METROPOLIS WITH SUCH AN ECCENTRIC ***MODUS OPERANDI***...
BANK
"I MEAN, *DO YOU* KNOW ANY CRIMINALS WITH A TOY CHEST CAPABLE OF ROBBING *FORT KNOX?*"
PERHAPS YOU SHOULD JUST *CONFESS* NOW...
...TELL US HOW YOU'RE DOING THIS, BEFORE SOMEONE OUT THERE GETS *SERIOUSLY* HURT.
KENT, KENT, KENT... HOW MANY TIMES MUST I *REPEAT* MYSELF BEFORE THIS GETS THROUGH YOUR THICK, MID-WESTERN SKULL...?

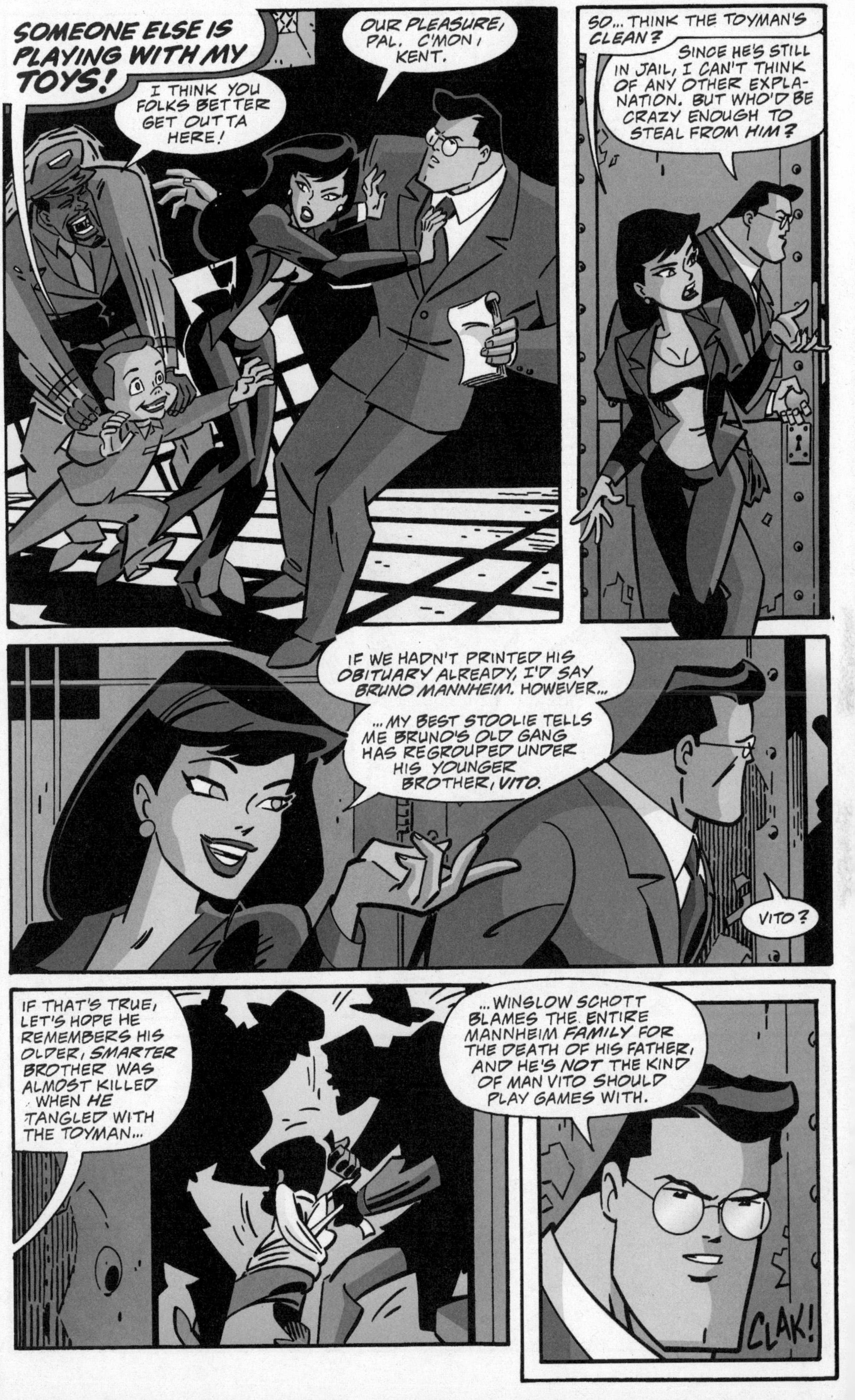
SOMEONE ELSE IS PLAYING WITH MY TOYS!
I THINK YOU FOLKS BETTER GET OUTTA HERE!
OUR PLEASURE, PAL. C'MON, KENT.
SO... THINK THE TOYMAN'S CLEAN?
SINCE HE'S STILL IN JAIL, I CAN'T THINK OF ANY OTHER EXPLANATION. BUT WHO'D BE CRAZY ENOUGH TO STEAL FROM HIM?
IF WE HADN'T PRINTED HIS OBITUARY ALREADY, I'D SAY BRUNO MANNHEIM. HOWEVER...
...MY BEST STOOLIE TELLS ME BRUNO'S OLD GANG HAS REGROUPED UNDER HIS YOUNGER BROTHER, VITO.
VITO?
IF THAT'S TRUE, LET'S HOPE HE REMEMBERS HIS OLDER, SMARTER BROTHER WAS ALMOST KILLED WHEN HE TANGLED WITH THE TOYMAN...
...WINSLOW SCHOTT BLAMES THE ENTIRE MANNHEIM FAMILY FOR THE DEATH OF HIS FATHER, AND HE'S NOT THE KIND OF MAN VITO SHOULD PLAY GAMES WITH.
CLAK!

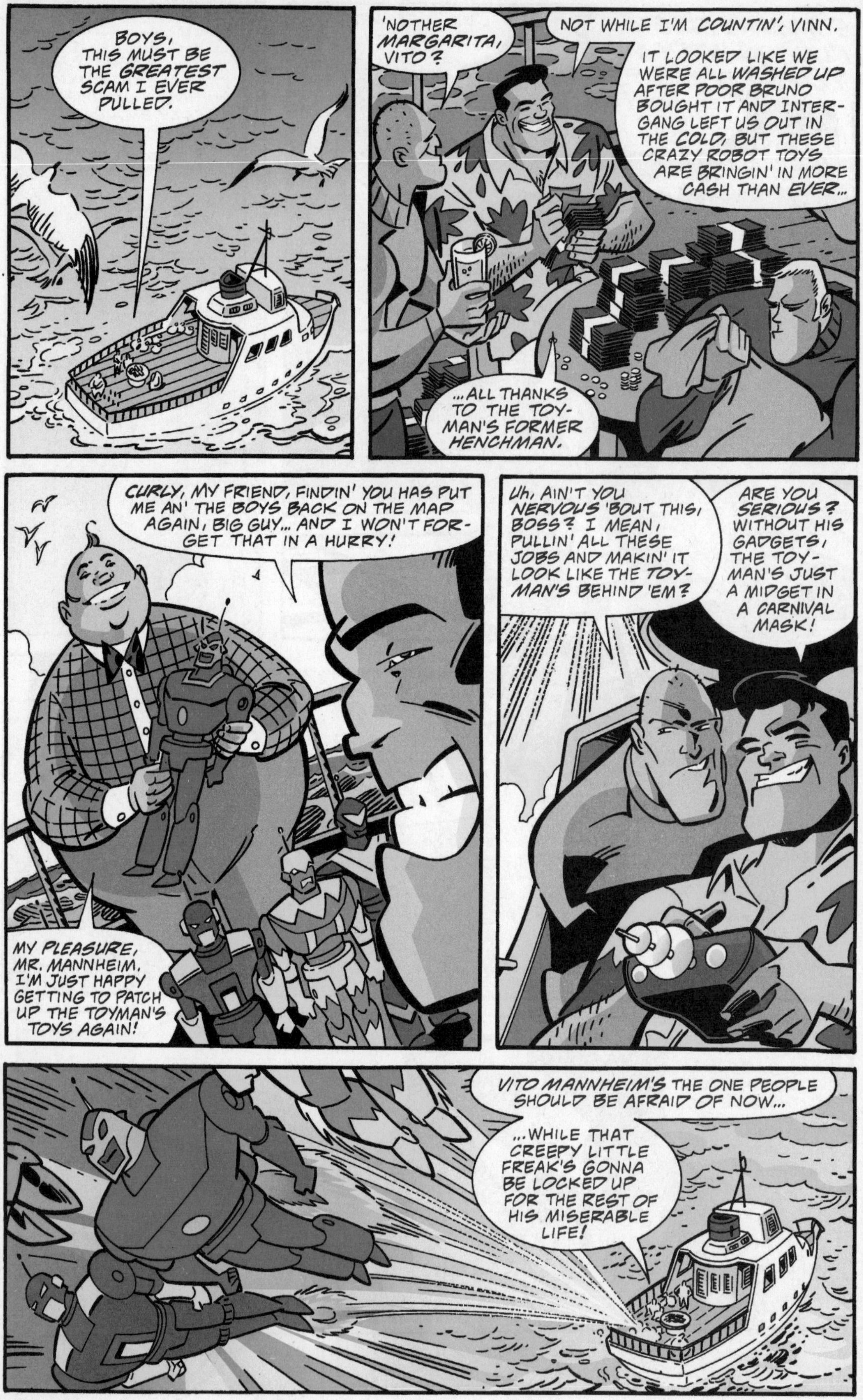
BOYS, THIS MUST BE THE GREATEST SCAM I EVER PULLED.
'NOTHER MARGARITA, VITO?
NOT WHILE I'M COUNTIN', VINN.
IT LOOKED LIKE WE WERE ALL WASHED UP AFTER POOR BRUNO BOUGHT IT AND INTERGANG LEFT US OUT IN THE COLD, BUT THESE CRAZY ROBOT TOYS ARE BRINGIN' IN MORE CASH THAN EVER...
...ALL THANKS TO THE TOYMAN'S FORMER HENCHMAN.
CURLY, MY FRIEND, FINDIN' YOU HAS PUT ME AN' THE BOYS BACK ON THE MAP AGAIN, BIG GUY... AND I WON'T FORGET THAT IN A HURRY!
MY PLEASURE, MR. MANNHEIM. I'M JUST HAPPY GETTING TO PATCH UP THE TOYMAN'S TOYS AGAIN!
UH, AIN'T YOU NERVOUS 'BOUT THIS, BOSS? I MEAN, PULLIN' ALL THESE JOBS AND MAKIN' IT LOOK LIKE THE TOYMAN'S BEHIND 'EM?
ARE YOU SERIOUS? WITHOUT HIS GADGETS, THE TOYMAN'S JUST A MIDGET IN A CARNIVAL MASK!
VITO MANNHEIM'S THE ONE PEOPLE SHOULD BE AFRAID OF NOW...
...WHILE THAT CREEPY LITTLE FREAK'S GONNA BE LOCKED UP FOR THE REST OF HIS MISERABLE LIFE!

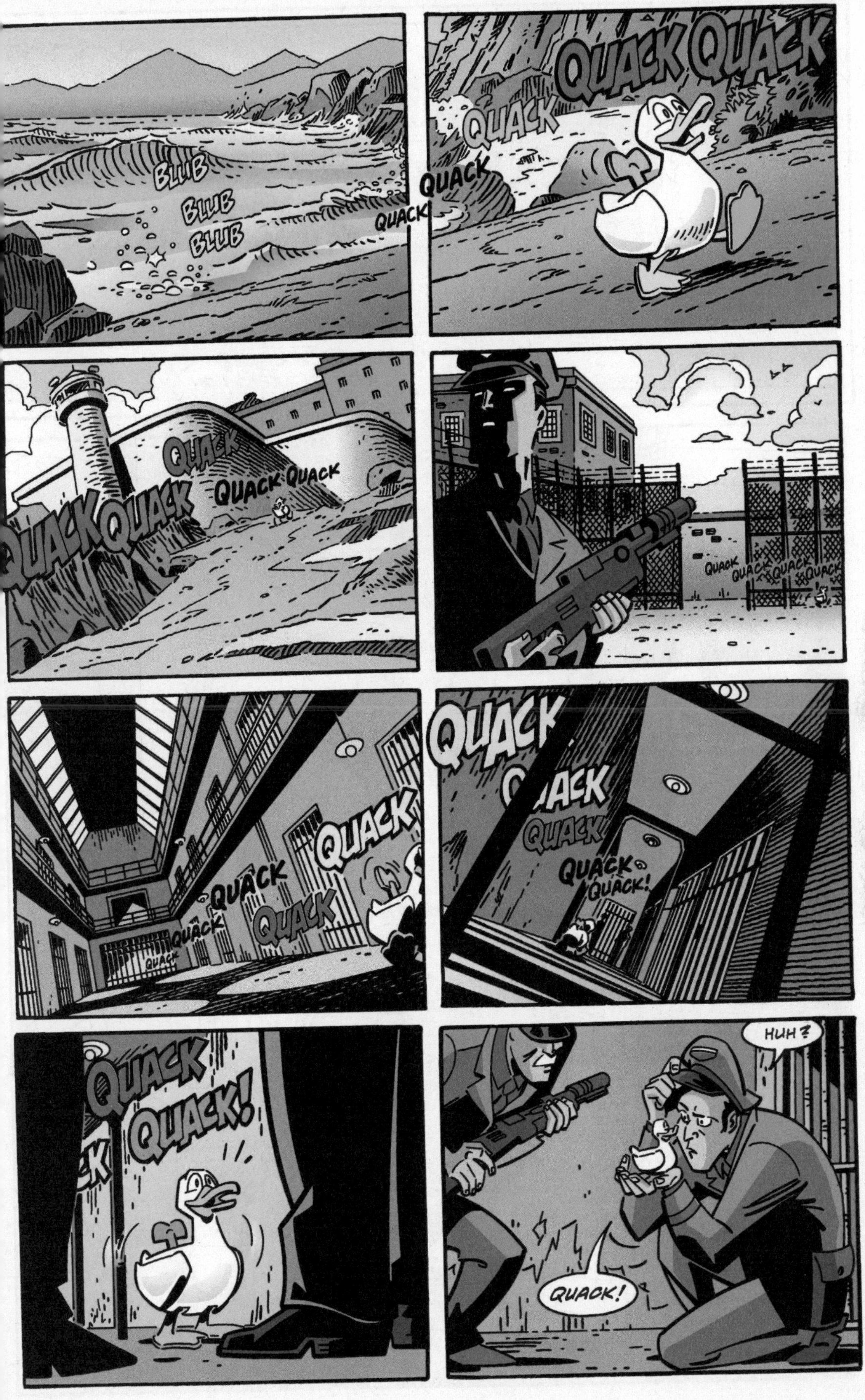
BLUB
BLUB
BLUB
QUACK
QUACK
QUACK
QUACK QUACK
QUACK
QUACK
QUACK QUACK
QUACK QUACK
QUACK
QUACK
QUACK
QUACK
QUACK
QUACK
QUACK
QUACK
QUACK
QUACK
QUACK
QUACK!
QUACK
QUACK!
HUH?
QUACK!

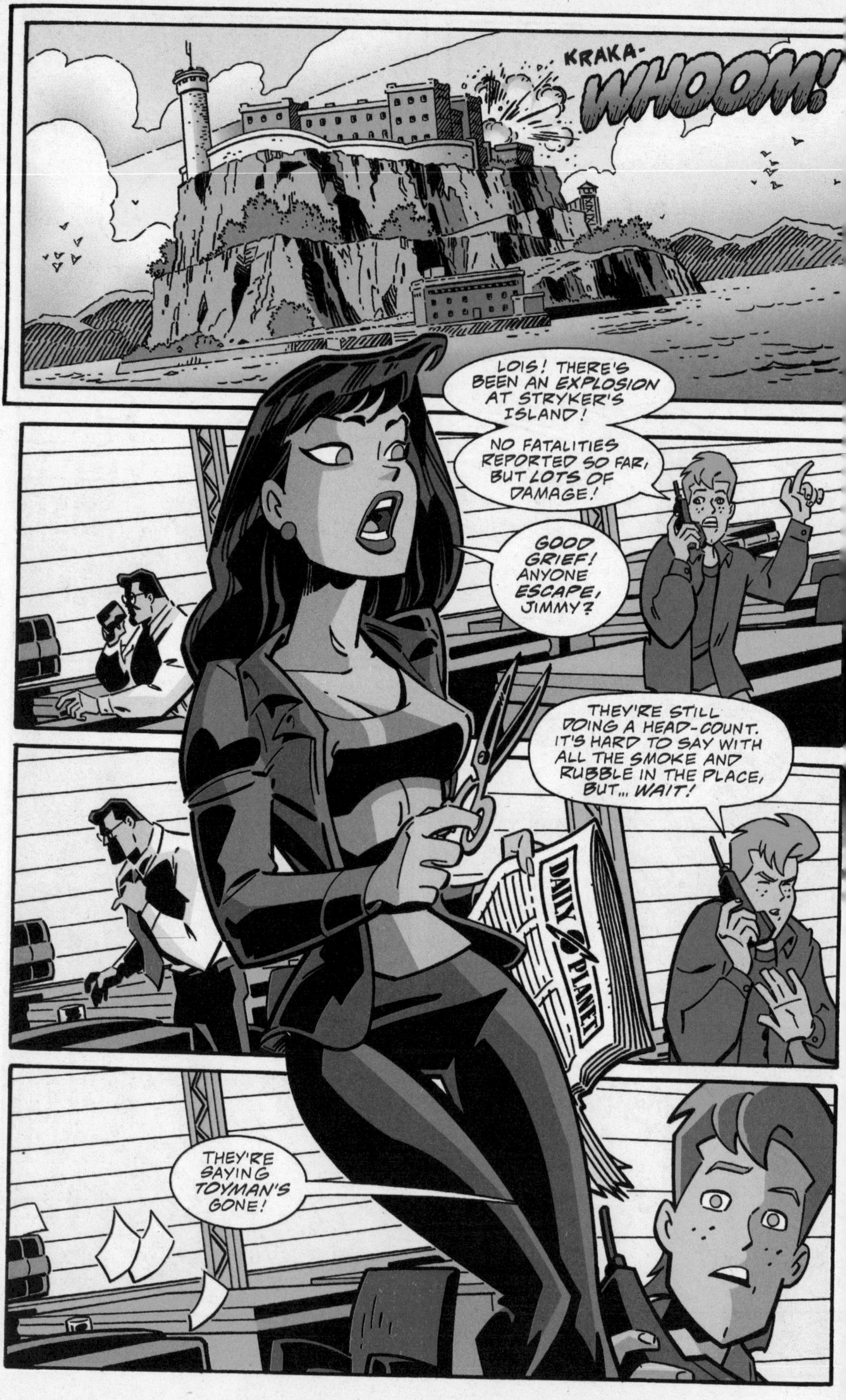

KRAKA-WHOOM!
LOIS! THERE'S BEEN AN EXPLOSION AT STRYKER'S ISLAND!
NO FATALITIES REPORTED SO FAR, BUT LOTS OF DAMAGE!
GOOD GRIEF! ANYONE ESCAPE, JIMMY?
THEY'RE STILL DOING A HEAD-COUNT. IT'S HARD TO SAY WITH ALL THE SMOKE AND RUBBLE IN THE PLACE, BUT... WAIT!
DAILY PLANET
THEY'RE SAYING TOYMAN'S GONE!

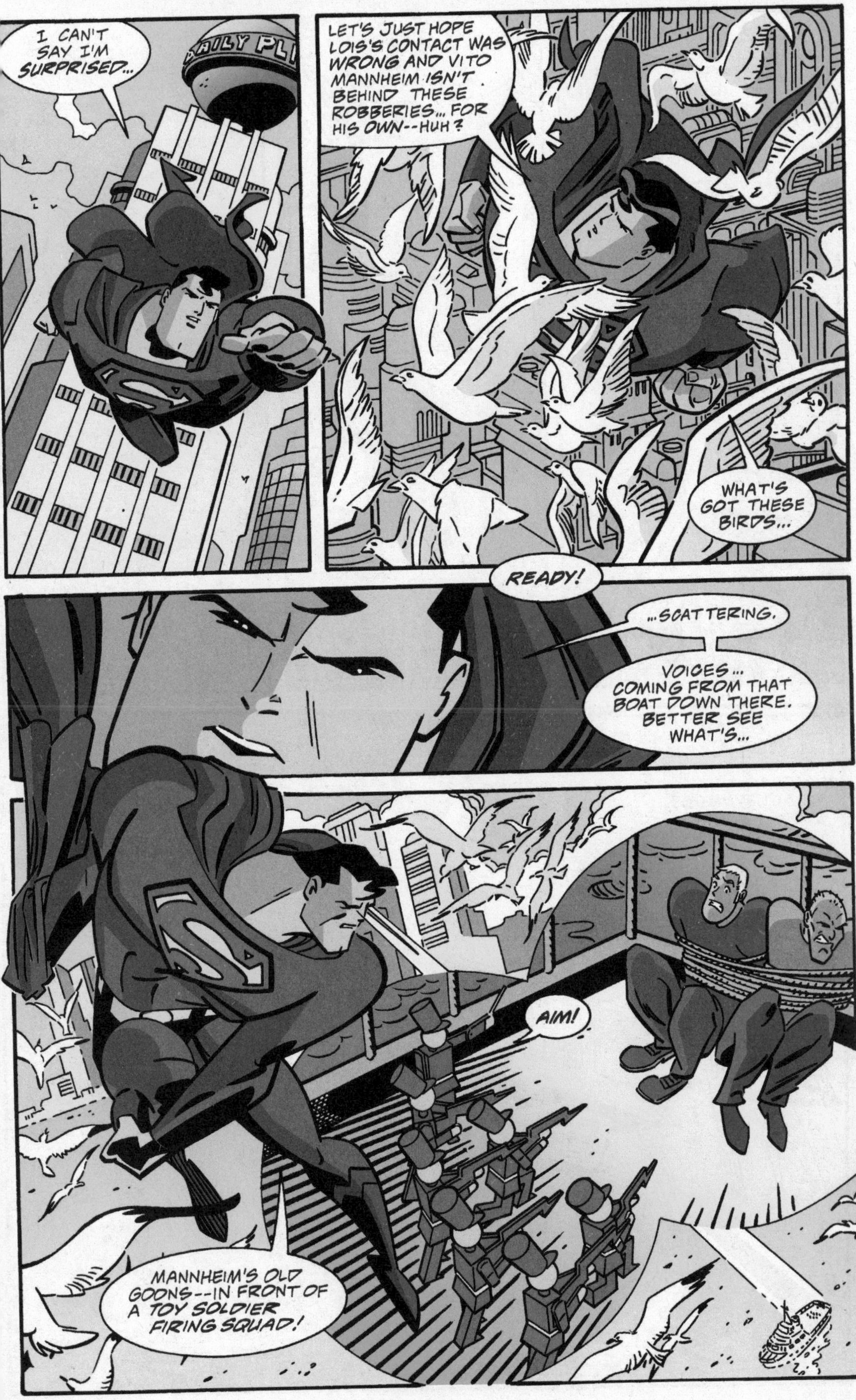
I CAN'T SAY I'M SURPRISED...
DAILY PL
LET'S JUST HOPE LOIS'S CONTACT WAS WRONG AND VITO MANNHEIM ISN'T BEHIND THESE ROBBERIES... FOR HIS OWN--HUH?
WHAT'S GOT THESE BIRDS...
READY!
...SCATTERING.
VOICES... COMING FROM THAT BOAT DOWN THERE. BETTER SEE WHAT'S...
AIM!
MANNHEIM'S OLD GOONS--IN FRONT OF A TOY SOLDIER FIRING SQUAD!

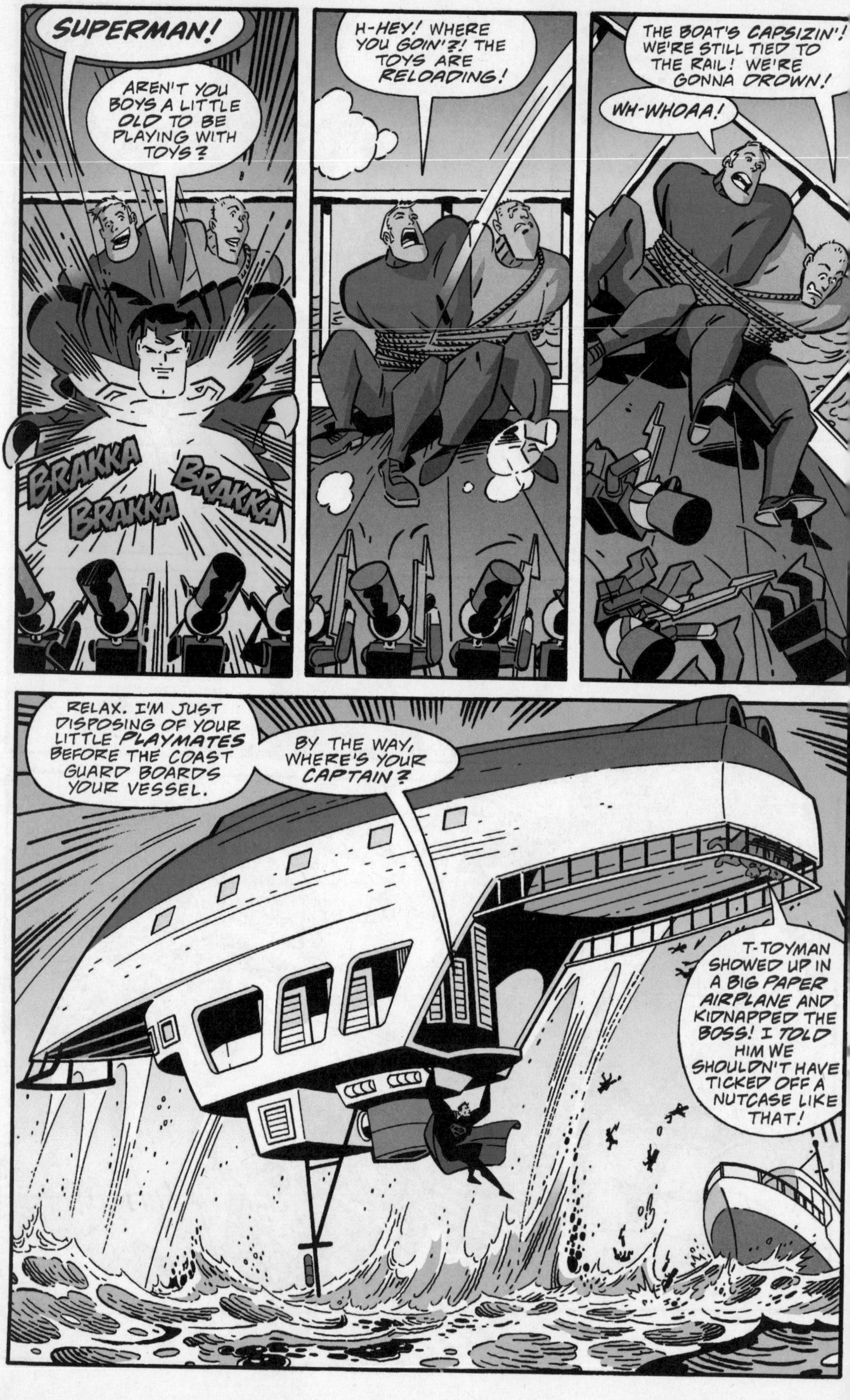
SUPERMAN!
AREN'T YOU BOYS A LITTLE OLD TO BE PLAYING WITH TOYS?
BRAKKA
BRAKKA
BRAKKA
H-HEY! WHERE YOU GOIN'?! THE TOYS ARE RELOADING!
THE BOAT'S CAPSIZIN'! WE'RE STILL TIED TO THE RAIL! WE'RE GONNA DROWN!
WH-WHOAA!
RELAX. I'M JUST DISPOSING OF YOUR LITTLE PLAYMATES BEFORE THE COAST GUARD BOARDS YOUR VESSEL.
BY THE WAY, WHERE'S YOUR CAPTAIN?
T-TOYMAN SHOWED UP IN A BIG PAPER AIRPLANE AND KIDNAPPED THE BOSS! I TOLD HIM WE SHOULDN'T HAVE TICKED OFF A NUTCASE LIKE THAT!

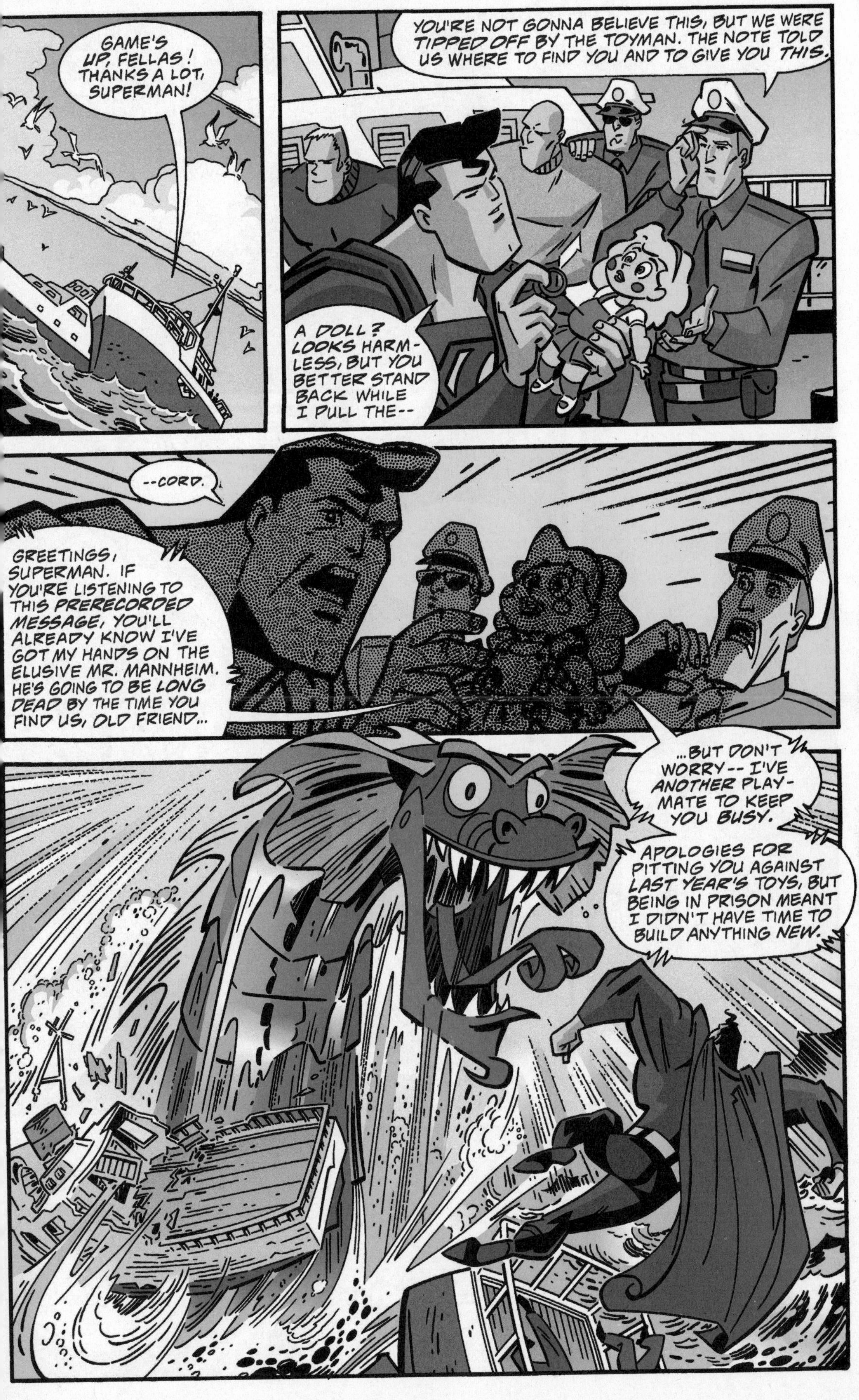
GAME'S UP, FELLAS! THANKS A LOT, SUPERMAN!
YOU'RE NOT GONNA BELIEVE THIS, BUT WE WERE TIPPED OFF BY THE TOYMAN. THE NOTE TOLD US WHERE TO FIND YOU AND TO GIVE YOU THIS.
A DOLL? LOOKS HARMLESS, BUT YOU BETTER STAND BACK WHILE I PULL THE--
--CORD.
GREETINGS, SUPERMAN. IF YOU'RE LISTENING TO THIS PRERECORDED MESSAGE, YOU'LL ALREADY KNOW I'VE GOT MY HANDS ON THE ELUSIVE MR. MANNHEIM. HE'S GOING TO BE LONG DEAD BY THE TIME YOU FIND US, OLD FRIEND...
...BUT DON'T WORRY-- I'VE ANOTHER PLAYMATE TO KEEP YOU BUSY.
APOLOGIES FOR PITTING YOU AGAINST LAST YEAR'S TOYS, BUT BEING IN PRISON MEANT I DIDN'T HAVE TIME TO BUILD ANYTHING NEW.

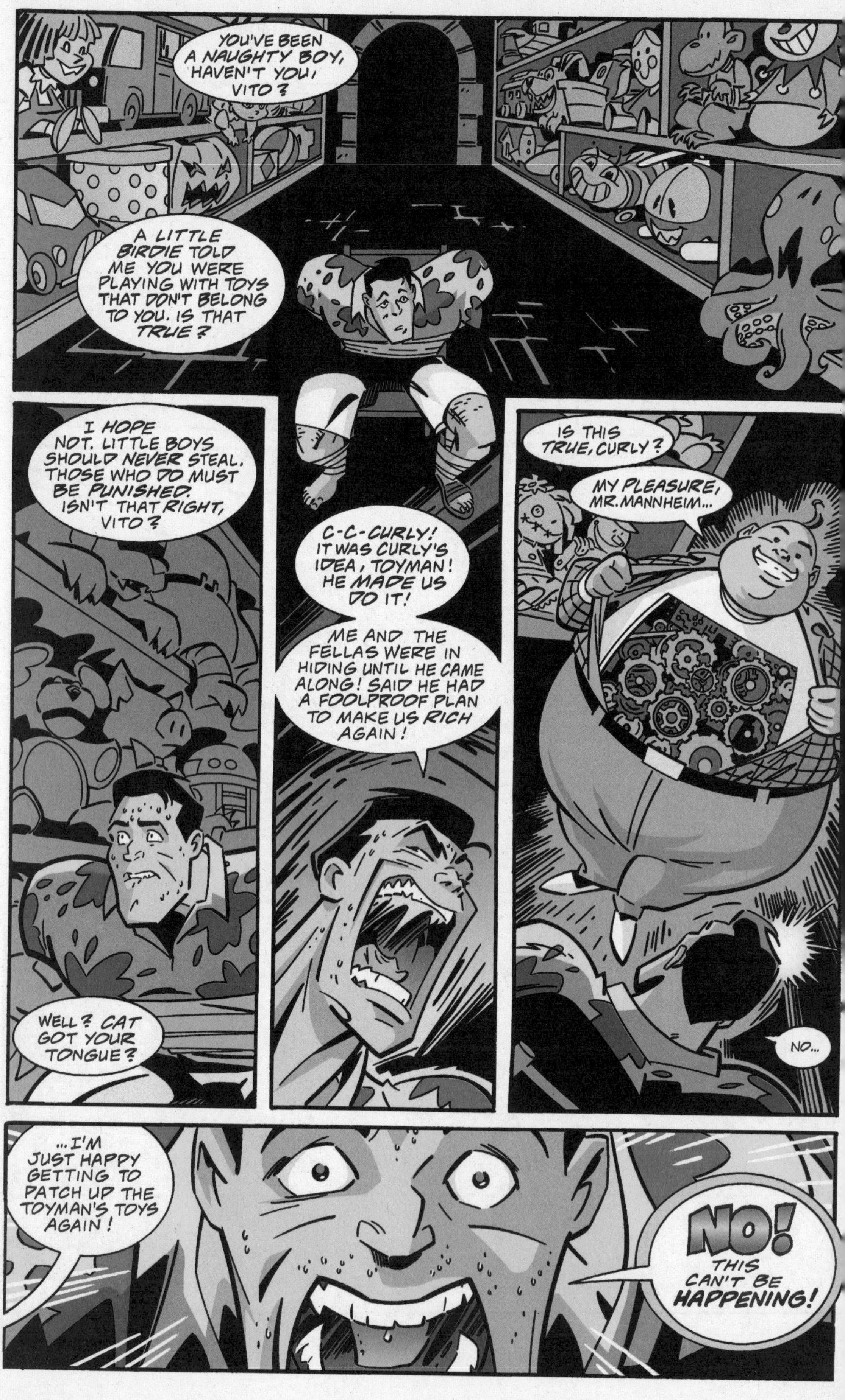
YOU'VE BEEN A NAUGHTY BOY, HAVEN'T YOU, VITO?
A LITTLE BIRDIE TOLD ME YOU WERE PLAYING WITH TOYS THAT DON'T BELONG TO YOU. IS THAT TRUE?
I HOPE NOT. LITTLE BOYS SHOULD NEVER STEAL. THOSE WHO DO MUST BE PUNISHED. ISN'T THAT RIGHT, VITO?
WELL? CAT GOT YOUR TONGUE?
C-C-CURLY! IT WAS CURLY'S IDEA, TOYMAN! HE MADE US DO IT!
ME AND THE FELLAS WERE IN HIDING UNTIL HE CAME ALONG! SAID HE HAD A FOOLPROOF PLAN TO MAKE US RICH AGAIN!
IS THIS TRUE, CURLY?
MY PLEASURE, MR. MANNHEIM...
NO...
...I'M JUST HAPPY GETTING TO PATCH UP THE TOYMAN'S TOYS AGAIN!
NO! THIS CAN'T BE HAPPENING!

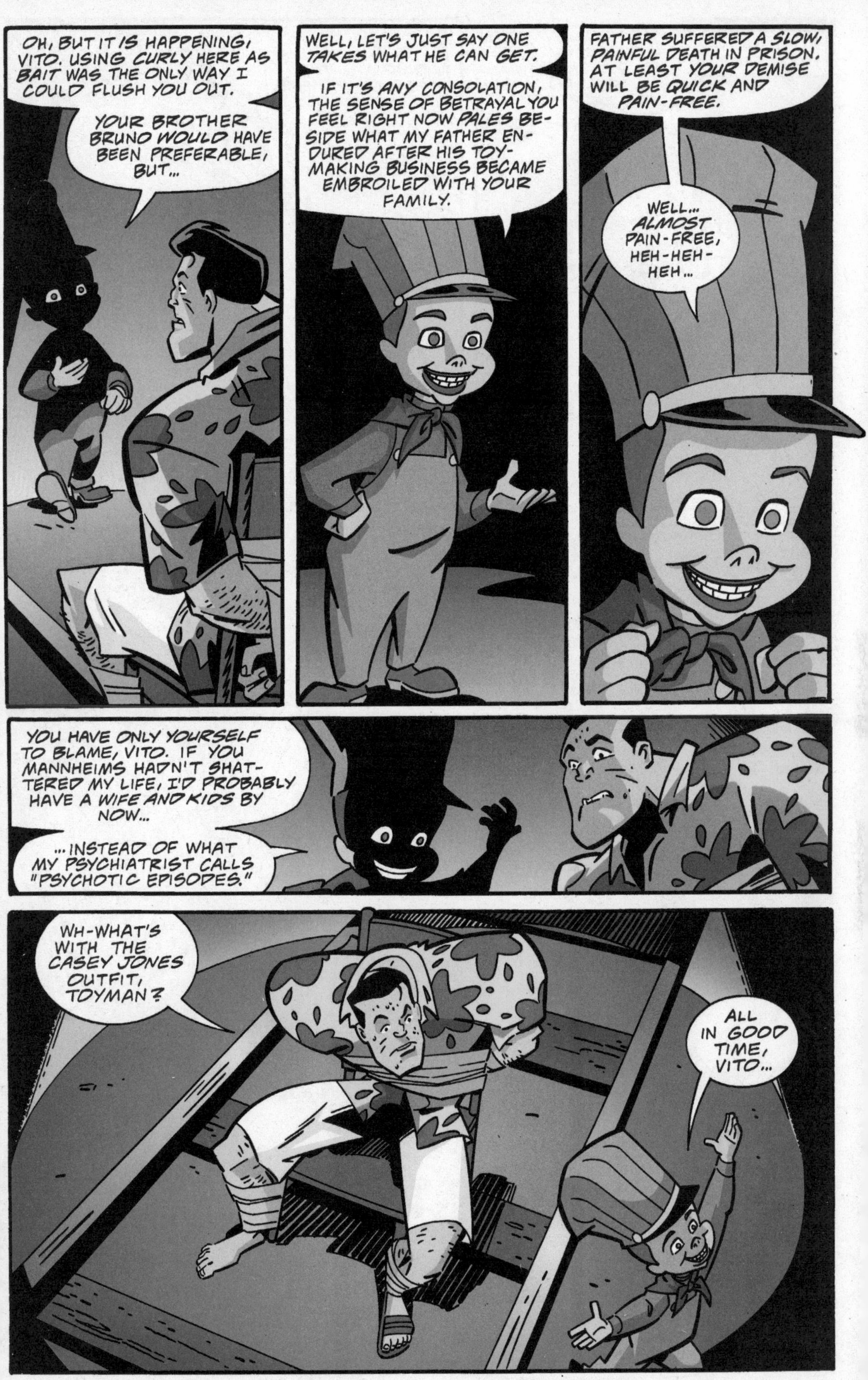
OH, BUT IT IS HAPPENING, VITO. USING CURLY HERE AS BAIT WAS THE ONLY WAY I COULD FLUSH YOU OUT.
YOUR BROTHER BRUNO WOULD HAVE BEEN PREFERABLE, BUT...
WELL, LET'S JUST SAY ONE TAKES WHAT HE CAN GET.
IF IT'S ANY CONSOLATION, THE SENSE OF BETRAYAL YOU FEEL RIGHT NOW PALES BESIDE WHAT MY FATHER ENDURED AFTER HIS TOY-MAKING BUSINESS BECAME EMBROILED WITH YOUR FAMILY.
FATHER SUFFERED A SLOW, PAINFUL DEATH IN PRISON. AT LEAST YOUR DEMISE WILL BE QUICK AND PAIN-FREE.
WELL... ALMOST PAIN-FREE, HEH-HEH-HEH...
YOU HAVE ONLY YOURSELF TO BLAME, VITO. IF YOU MANNHEIMS HADN'T SHATTERED MY LIFE, I'D PROBABLY HAVE A WIFE AND KIDS BY NOW...
...INSTEAD OF WHAT MY PSYCHIATRIST CALLS "PSYCHOTIC EPISODES."
WH-WHAT'S WITH THE CASEY JONES OUTFIT, TOYMAN?
ALL IN GOOD TIME, VITO...

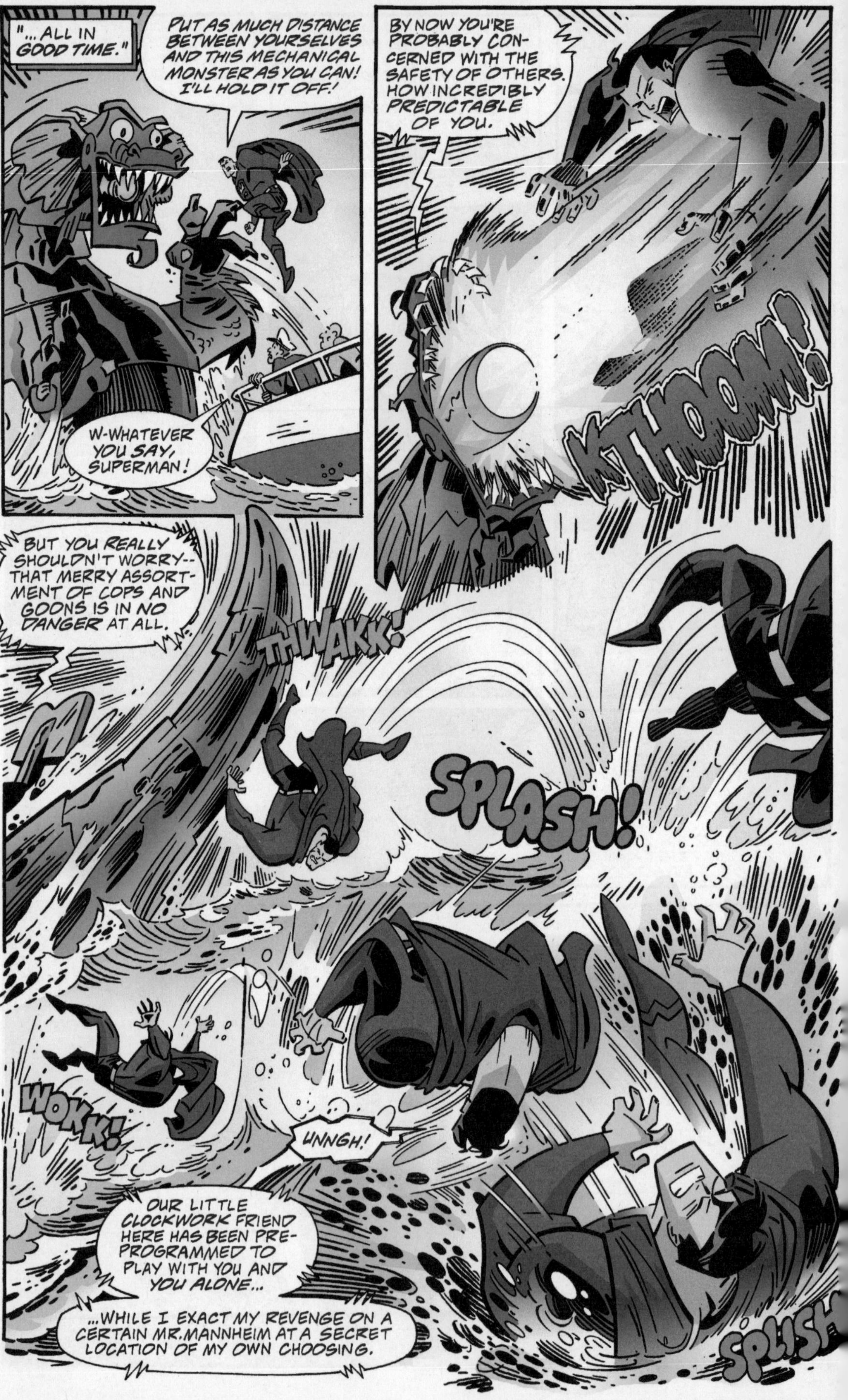
"...ALL IN GOOD TIME."
PUT AS MUCH DISTANCE BETWEEN YOURSELVES AND THIS MECHANICAL MONSTER AS YOU CAN! I'LL HOLD IT OFF!
W-WHATEVER YOU SAY, SUPERMAN!
BY NOW YOU'RE PROBABLY CONCERNED WITH THE SAFETY OF OTHERS. HOW INCREDIBLY PREDICTABLE OF YOU.
KTHOOM!
BUT YOU REALLY SHOULDN'T WORRY-- THAT MERRY ASSORTMENT OF COPS AND GOONS IS IN NO DANGER AT ALL.
THWAKK!
SPLASH!
WOKK!
UNNGH!
OUR LITTLE CLOCKWORK FRIEND HERE HAS BEEN PRE-PROGRAMMED TO PLAY WITH YOU AND YOU ALONE...
...WHILE I EXACT MY REVENGE ON A CERTAIN MR. MANNHEIM AT A SECRET LOCATION OF MY OWN CHOOSING.
SPLISH

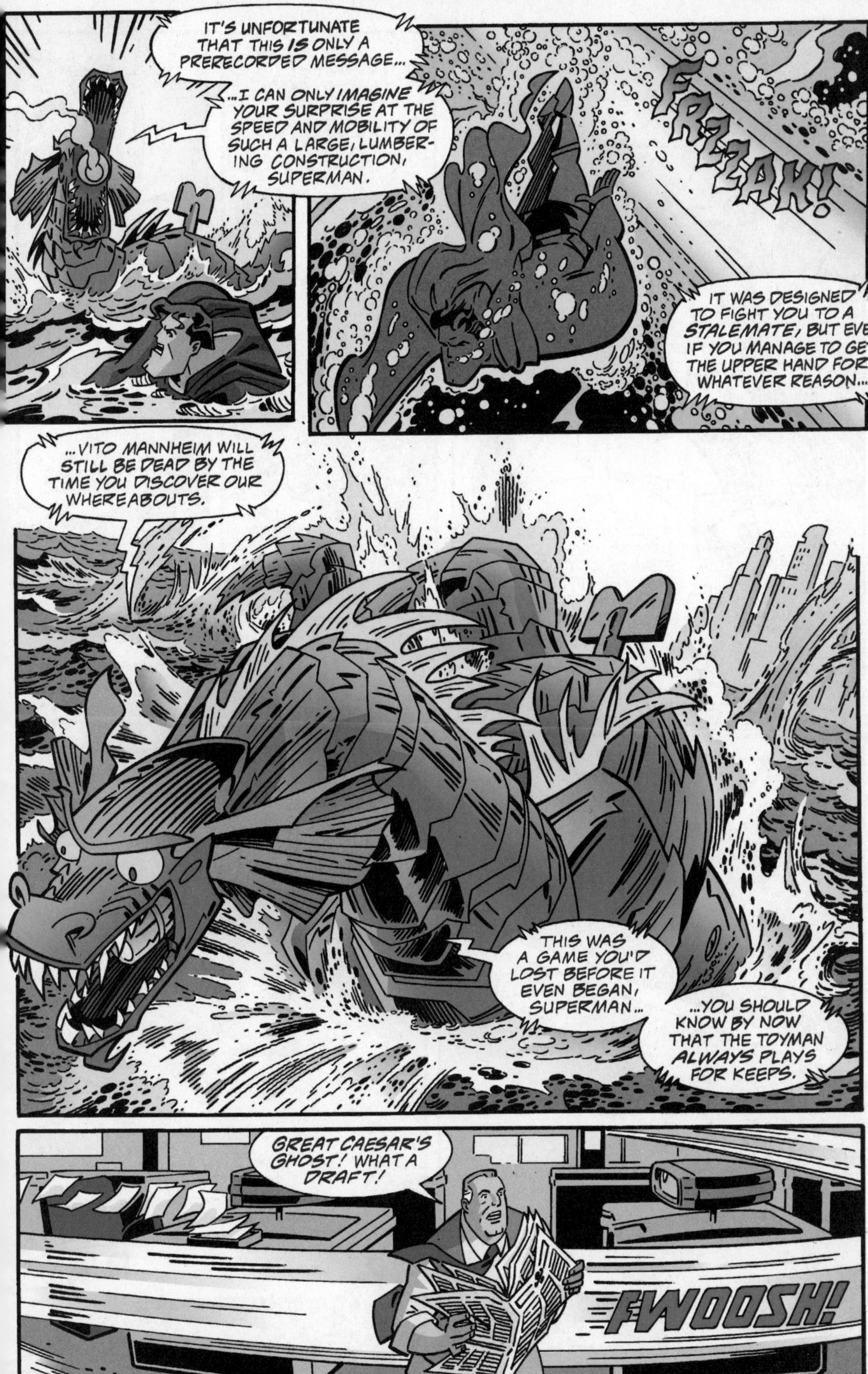
IT'S UNFORTUNATE THAT THIS IS ONLY A PRERECORDED MESSAGE...
...I CAN ONLY IMAGINE YOUR SURPRISE AT THE SPEED AND MOBILITY OF SUCH A LARGE, LUMBERING CONSTRUCTION, SUPERMAN.
FRZZAK!
IT WAS DESIGNED TO FIGHT YOU TO A STALEMATE; BUT EVEN IF YOU MANAGE TO GET THE UPPER HAND FOR WHATEVER REASON...
...VITO MANNHEIM WILL STILL BE DEAD BY THE TIME YOU DISCOVER OUR WHEREABOUTS.
THIS WAS A GAME YOU'D LOST BEFORE IT EVEN BEGAN, SUPERMAN...
...YOU SHOULD KNOW BY NOW THAT THE TOYMAN ALWAYS PLAYS FOR KEEPS.
GREAT CAESAR'S GHOST! WHAT A DRAFT!
FWOOSH!

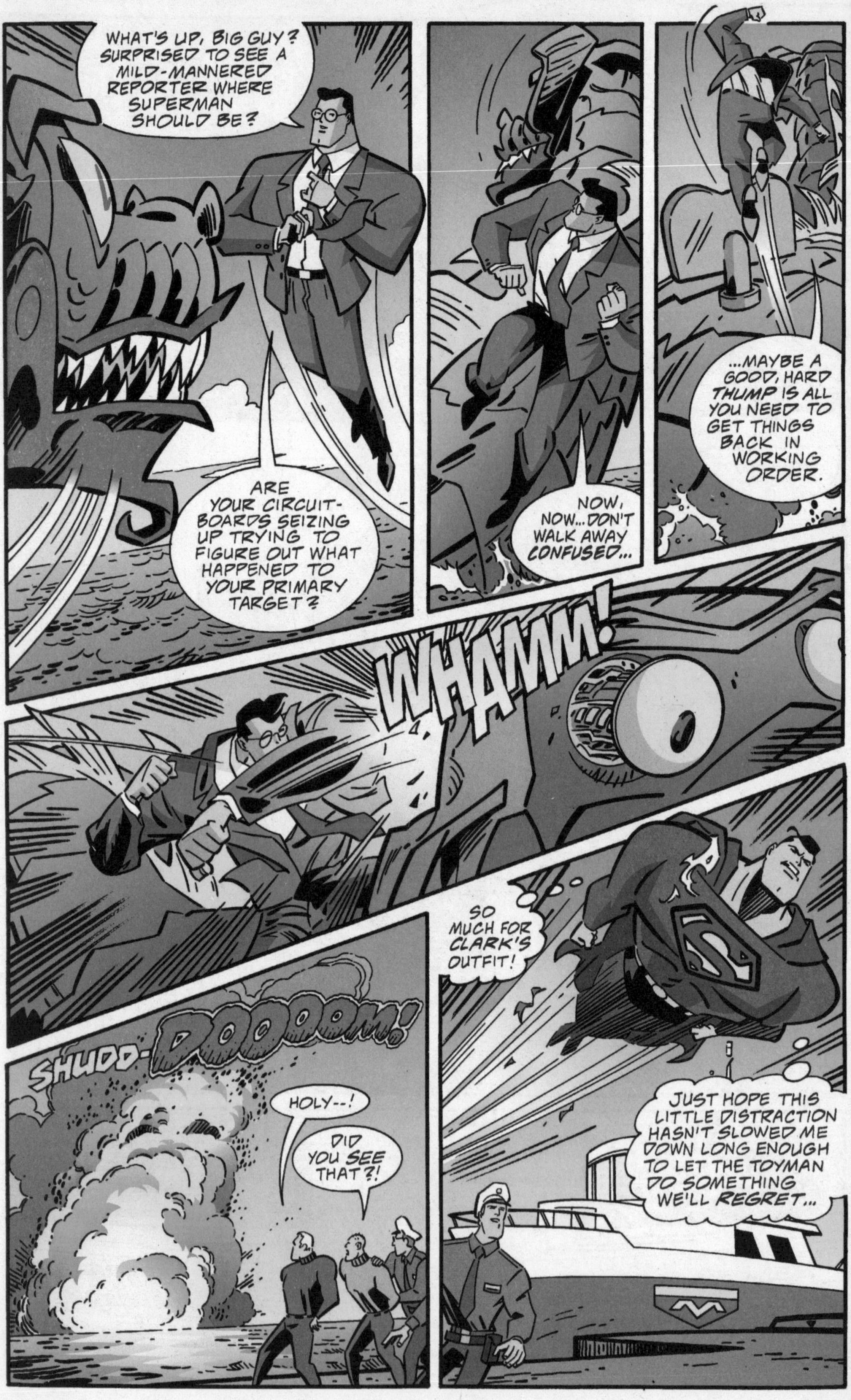
WHAT'S UP, BIG GUY? SURPRISED TO SEE A MILD-MANNERED REPORTER WHERE SUPERMAN SHOULD BE?
ARE YOUR CIRCUIT-BOARDS SEIZING UP TRYING TO FIGURE OUT WHAT HAPPENED TO YOUR PRIMARY TARGET?
NOW, NOW...DON'T WALK AWAY CONFUSED...
...MAYBE A GOOD, HARD THUMP IS ALL YOU NEED TO GET THINGS BACK IN WORKING ORDER.
WHAMM!
SO MUCH FOR CLARK'S OUTFIT!
SHUDD-DOOOOOM!
HOLY--!
DID YOU SEE THAT?!
JUST HOPE THIS LITTLE DISTRACTION HASN'T SLOWED ME DOWN LONG ENOUGH TO LET THE TOYMAN DO SOMETHING WE'LL REGRET...

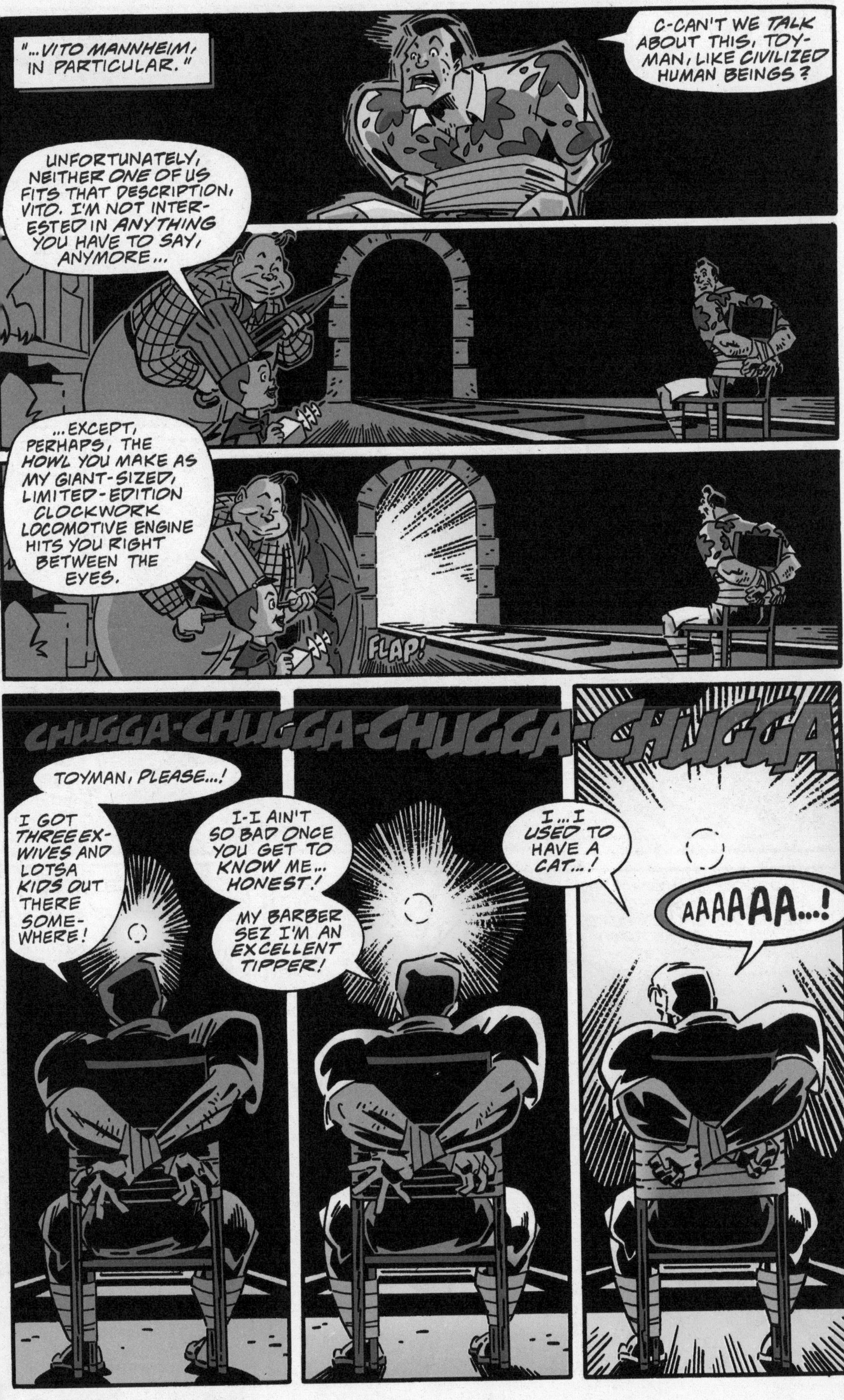
"...VITO MANNHEIM, IN PARTICULAR."
C-CAN'T WE TALK ABOUT THIS, TOY-MAN, LIKE CIVILIZED HUMAN BEINGS?
UNFORTUNATELY, NEITHER ONE OF US FITS THAT DESCRIPTION, VITO. I'M NOT INTER-ESTED IN ANYTHING YOU HAVE TO SAY, ANYMORE...
...EXCEPT, PERHAPS, THE HOWL YOU MAKE AS MY GIANT-SIZED, LIMITED-EDITION CLOCKWORK LOCOMOTIVE ENGINE HITS YOU RIGHT BETWEEN THE EYES.
FLAP!
CHUGGA-CHUGGA-CHUGGA-CHUGGA
TOYMAN, PLEASE...!
I GOT THREE EX-WIVES AND LOTSA KIDS OUT THERE SOME-WHERE!
I-I AIN'T SO BAD ONCE YOU GET TO KNOW ME... HONEST!
MY BARBER SEZ I'M AN EXCELLENT TIPPER!
I...I USED TO HAVE A CAT...!
AAAAAA...!

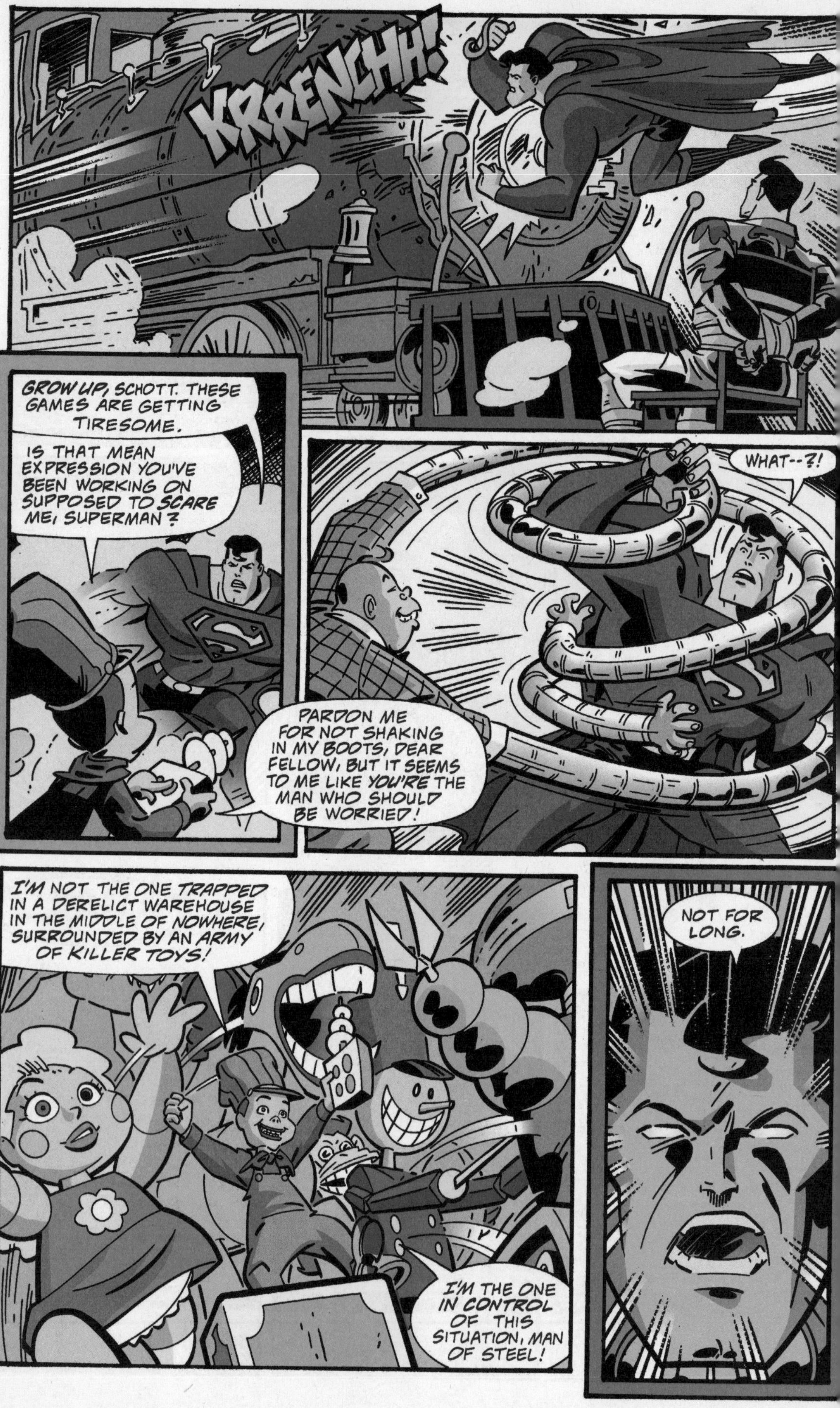
KRRENCHH!
GROW UP, SCHOTT. THESE GAMES ARE GETTING TIRESOME.
IS THAT MEAN EXPRESSION YOU'VE BEEN WORKING ON SUPPOSED TO SCARE ME, SUPERMAN?
WHAT--?!
PARDON ME FOR NOT SHAKING IN MY BOOTS, DEAR FELLOW, BUT IT SEEMS TO ME LIKE YOU'RE THE MAN WHO SHOULD BE WORRIED!
I'M NOT THE ONE TRAPPED IN A DERELICT WAREHOUSE IN THE MIDDLE OF NOWHERE, SURROUNDED BY AN ARMY OF KILLER TOYS!
I'M THE ONE IN CONTROL OF THIS SITUATION, MAN OF STEEL!
NOT FOR LONG.

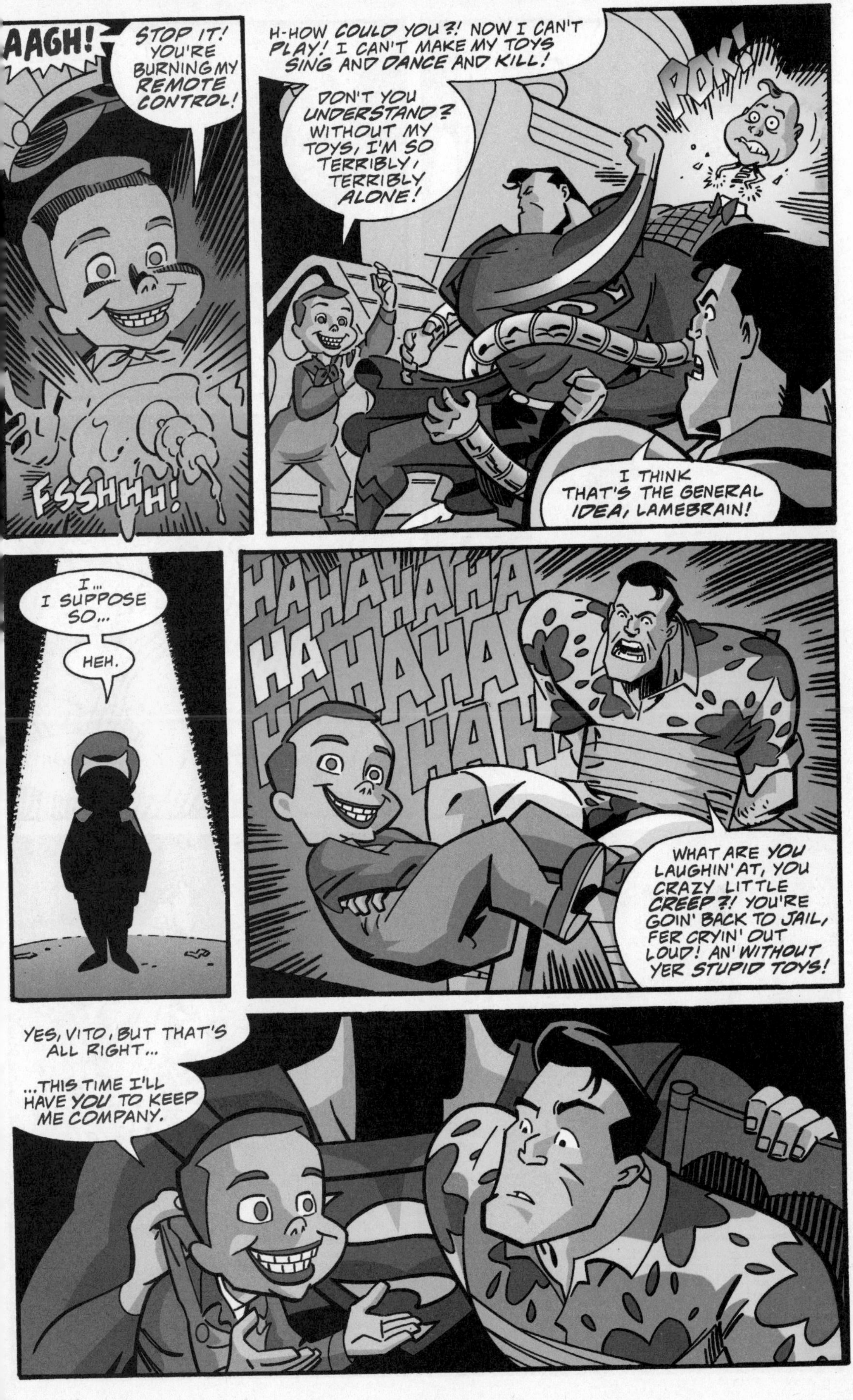
AAGH!
STOP IT! YOU'RE BURNING MY REMOTE CONTROL!
FSSHHHH!
H-HOW COULD YOU?! NOW I CAN'T PLAY! I CAN'T MAKE MY TOYS SING AND DANCE AND KILL!
DON'T YOU UNDERSTAND? WITHOUT MY TOYS, I'M SO TERRIBLY, TERRIBLY ALONE!
POK!
I THINK THAT'S THE GENERAL IDEA, LAMEBRAIN!
I... I SUPPOSE SO...
HEH.
HAHAHAHAHA HAHAHAHA HAHAHAH
WHAT ARE YOU LAUGHIN' AT, YOU CRAZY LITTLE CREEP?! YOU'RE GOIN' BACK TO JAIL, FER CRYIN' OUT LOUD! AN' WITHOUT YER STUPID TOYS!
YES, VITO, BUT THAT'S ALL RIGHT...
...THIS TIME I'LL HAVE YOU TO KEEP ME COMPANY.

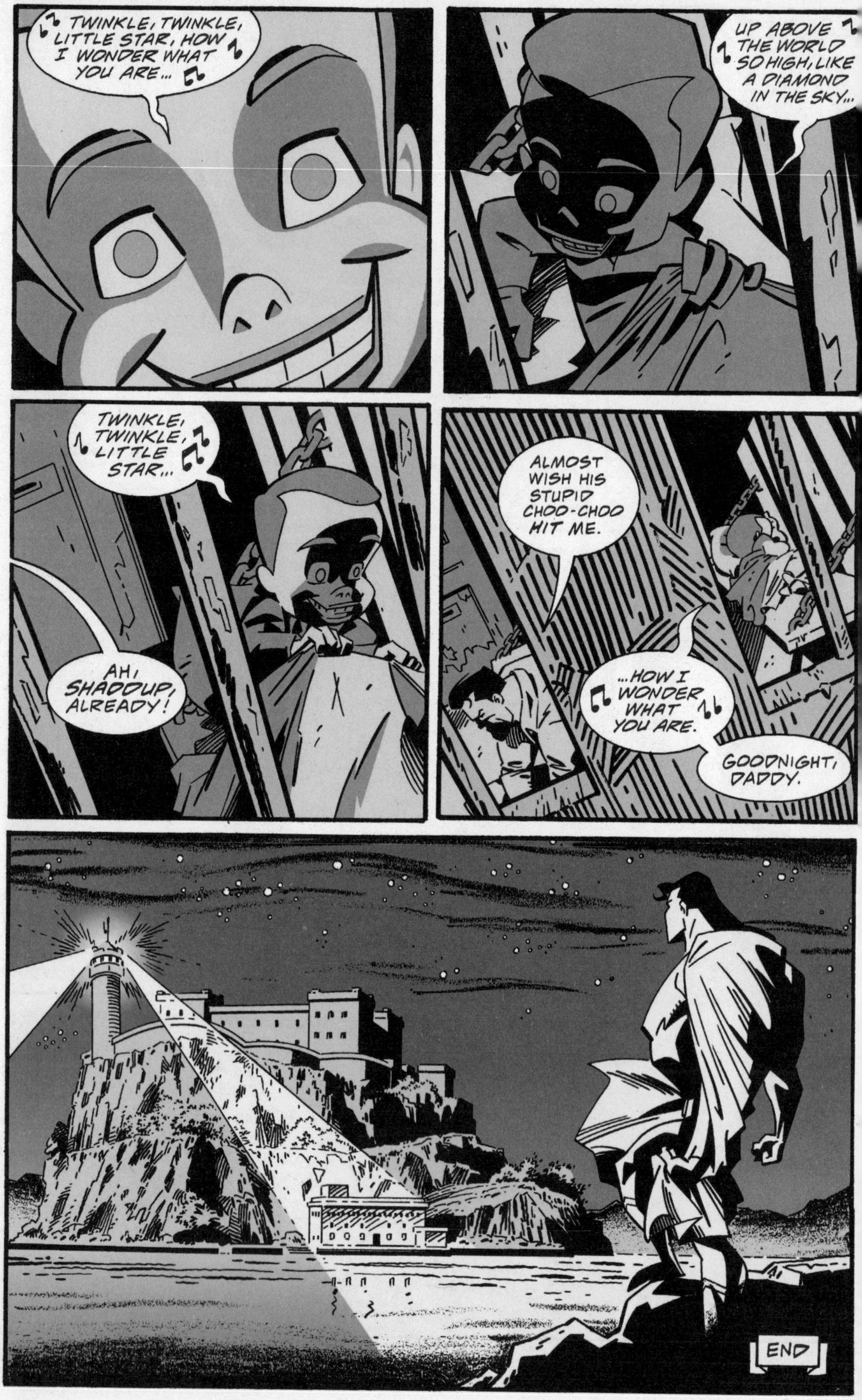
TWINKLE, TWINKLE, LITTLE STAR, HOW I WONDER WHAT YOU ARE...
UP ABOVE THE WORLD SO HIGH, LIKE A DIAMOND IN THE SKY...
TWINKLE, TWINKLE, LITTLE STAR...
AH, SHADDUP, ALREADY!
ALMOST WISH HIS STUPID CHOO-CHOO HIT ME.
...HOW I WONDER WHAT YOU ARE.
GOODNIGHT, DADDY.
END